D1488566

The seemingly inexorable decline of religion in twentieth-century Britain has for long fascinated historians, sociologists and churchmen. They have also been exasperated by their failure to understand its origins or chart its progress adequately. In the light of that failure, a new school of 'revisionists' has arisen to challenge the basic premises of decline and its putative causes. Sceptical both of traditional accounts and of their more recent rejection, S.J.D. Green concentrates scholarly attention for the first time on the 'social history of the chapel' during the crucial years and in a characteristic industrial urban setting. He demonstrates just why so many churches were built in these years, who built them, who went to them, and why. He evaluates the related 'associational ideal' during the years of its greatest success, and explains the causes of its subsequent decline. Finally, he considers the shifting range and altered significance of religious experience, both within and extending beyond religious organisations, at that time. In this way, *Religion in the age of decline* offers a fresh and cogent interpretation of the extent and the implications of the decline of religion in early twentieth-century Britain.

Religion in the age of decline

Religion in the age of decline

*Organisation and experience
in industrial Yorkshire, 1870–1920*

S.J.D. Green

*All Souls College, Oxford and
School of History, University of Leeds*

Published by the Press Syndicate of the University of Cambridge
The Pitt Building, Trumpington Street, Cambridge CB2 1RP
40 West 20th Street, New York, NY 10011–4211, USA
10 Stamford Road, Oakleigh, Melbourne 3166, Australia

First published 1996

Printed in Great Britain at the University Press, Cambridge

A catalogue record for this book is available from the British Library

Library of Congress cataloguing in publication data is available

ISBN 0 521 56153 1 hardback

CE

For
P.W.G. and B.J.G.

Contents

ix

Acknowledgements

This book was conceived, researched and written during my years as a Fellow of All Souls College, Oxford. As such, it is the inadequate repayment for a treasured loan. Asa Briggs was an inspiring supervisor of the D.Phil. thesis on which it is loosely based. Hugh McLeod and John Walsh were sympathetic examiners of the original, and have been helpful critics of later versions. Bryan Wilson served throughout as mentor, advisor and friend. The course of my research was immeasurably aided by two dedicated archivists, Alan Betteridge at Calderdale District Archive and Ian Dewhirst in Keighley Public Library. I am deeply grateful to them both. I also gladly acknowledge the kindness of the Rev. Dr J.N. Rowe of St Paul's, Church of England, Denholme Gate, and of Mr A. Vine of Denholme Baptist Church, for allowing me to conduct research in their own homes, thereby affording access to otherwise unavailable material. Humaira Ahmed, Laura Lamont and Deborah McGovern laboured hard to transform an unintelligible scrawl into an elegant, if not necessarily intelligent, typescript. Richard Fisher was an exemplary editor at Cambridge University Press. The dedication records my oldest, deepest and least requited debt. That to my wife continues and grows.

Parts of chapter 3 previously appeared, in a very different guise, as 'The Death of Pew Rents, the Rise of Bazaars and the End of the Traditional Political Economy of Voluntary Religious Organisations: The Case of the West Riding of Yorkshire, c. 1870–1914', *Northern History*, vol. 27, 1991, 198–235; parts of Chapter 5, similarly primitive, as 'Religion and the Rise of the Common Man: Mutual Improvement Societies, Religious Association and Popular Education in Three Industrial Towns in the West Riding of Yorkshire, c. 1850–1900', in Derek Fraser (ed.), *Cities, Class and Communication: Essays in Honour of Asa Briggs* (Brighton, Harvester, 1990), pp. 25–43, and 'The Religion of the Child in Edwardian Methodism: Institutional Reform and Pedagogical Reappraisal in the West Riding of Yorkshire', *Journal of British Studies*, vol. 30, no. 4, October 1991, 377–98; and parts of Chapter 6, now largely transformed, in 'Spiritual Science and Conversion Experience in Edwardian Methodism: The Example of West Yorkshire', *The Journal of Ecclesiastical History*, vol. 43, no. 3, July 1992, 428–46. I am grateful to the various editors and publishers for permission to republish here.

Tables

Abbreviations

BDA	West Yorkshire Archive Service, Bradford
CB	County Borough
CDA	West Yorkshire Archive Service, Halifax
CDA (HTC)	Horsfall Turner Collection of Books, Pamphlets and Memorabilia for the History of Halifax and the Halifax District, Horsfall Turner Room, Calderdale District Archive
KPL	Archive Room, Keighley Public Library
LBD	Local Board District
LDA	West Yorkshire Archive Service, Leeds
MB	Municipal Borough
PP	Parliamentary Papers
PRO	Public Record Office, Census Search Room
RG	Registrar General
WHQ	West Yorkshire Archive Service, Headquarters, Wakefield
incom. arch. ref.	Incomplete archive reference; the reference cited is provisional, as the archive consulted is currently being recatalogued
unpub. enum. Ms	Unpublished enumerator manuscripts from the Census of England and Wales, 1871
uncat. Ms	Uncatalogued manuscript, held in an archive source
uncat. pub(s).	Uncatalogued publication, held in an archival source, and consulted there
uncat. type	Uncatalogued typescript (unpublished), held in an archival source, and consulted there
n.d	No date of publication known
n.p.	No place of publication known
ASHHPM	*All Soul's, Haley Hill, Parish Magazine*
HDCM	*Halifax and District Congregational Magazine*
HPCM	*Halifax Parish Church Magazine*

KDCM	*Keighley and District Congregational Magazine*
KPCM	*Keighley Parish Church Magazine*
KWMCM	*Keighley Wesleyan Methodist Circuit Magazine*
SPCKCPM	*St Paul's Church, King Cross, Parish Magazine*
THAS	*Transactions of the Halifax Antiquarian Society*

Note: References to parish magazines are frequently followed by the instruction '(no page number)'. This indicates that the magazine in question was not paginated, and therefore no references to a page number can be given in the footnote.

Introduction: Modern religious history, the sociology of religion and the problem of religious decline

Prologue

What follows is a study in the history of religion in late nineteenth- and early twentieth-century Britain. More specifically, it is a case study, presenting an interpretation of some of the characteristic forms of ecclesiastical organisation, liturgical practice and supernatural belief which thrived in three contiguous industrial towns, namely Halifax, Keighley and Denholme, in the West Riding of Yorkshire, between about 1870 and 1920. Self-consciously limited in geographical scope and chronological range, this book is nevertheless concerned with a central problem in the history of religion in the modern world. This is the problem of decline. The recent historical experience of religion, whether in West Yorkshire, in England generally, or indeed in any of the advanced societies, can scarcely be approached without confronting an almost overwhelming sense of decline. That sense is shared both by practitioners and by students of religion, and shared even if their respective explanations for its cause, and of its consequences, are at variance. To both, decline is unquestionably a problem: for the former, a disturbing trend which begs to be reversed; for the latter, a social phenomenon which demands to be explained.

For many, in both camps, an appreciation of decline is often accompanied by an assumption of decline. The evidence of associational membership, attendance at worship, and adherence to supernatural beliefs amongst the population allegedly proves it. Indeed, a proper understanding of the inexorable direction of decline – towards further decline – is presumed to follow from an intelligent appreciation of those facts.[1] The validity of that presumption will be neither immediately

[1] For concise summaries of the statistical evidence, drawn from data throughout the advanced world, see S.S. Acquaviva, *The Decline of the Sacred in Industrial Society*, trans. by Patricia Lipscomb (Oxford, 1979), pp. 49–84; also Bryan Wilson, *Contemporary Transformations of Religion* (Oxford, 1976), pp. 14–26. For the English evidence, presented in tabular form, see Robert Currie, Alan Gilbert and Lee Horsley, *Churches and Churchgoers: Patterns of Church Growth in the British Isles since 1700*

challenged nor wholly corroborated here. But it cannot be ignored because it follows from that presumption that, if the future of religion is so unpromising, and if its past was so glorious (an additional assumption which the prophets of decline are wont to make), then there must have been, at some historical moment, in some historical place, for some historical cause, a moment, a place and a cause of decline. And for most of these modern prophets, whether theologians, sociologists or even historians, that moment, that place, and that cause, can be identified; indeed, they have been identified. The moment was the last two decades of the nineteenth century.[2] The place was the industrial town.[3] The cause was the process of secularisation in modern, industrial urban society.[4]

Yet religion is still alive in the modern world. Decline has not proceeded in an orderly fashion to demise. Even in the West, those 'eloquent and knowing mourners at the wake of Christian culture' who predicted the end of the reign of superstition and unreason have not been entirely vindicated.[5] Elsewhere, their more sceptical successors,

(Oxford, 1977), pp. 128–60; also Adrian Hastings, *A History of English Christianity, 1920–1985* (London, 1986), pp. 602–6. For a different interpretation of the same evidence, see Keith Ward, *The Turn of the Tide: Christian Belief in Britain Today* (London, 1986), pp. 11–20. For the divergent case of the USA, the most reliable modern guide is Wade Clark Roof and William McKinney, *American Mainline Religion: Its Changing Shape and Fortune* (New Brunswick, N.J., 1987), pp. 11–39 and 252–6.

[2] See, for instance, Hugh McLeod, *Religion and the People of Western Europe, 1789–1970* (Oxford, 1981), p. 69; see also similar remarks in Norman Stone, *Europe Transformed, 1878–1919* (London, 1983), p. 392; and in E.R. Wickham, *Church and People in an Industrial City* (London, 1957), p. 166. Statistical corroboration for the British example, drawn from Methodist evidence only, is offered in Currie *et al.*, *Churches and Churchgoers*, pp. 69–70.

[3] For an explicit statement of this view, see Eric Hobsbawm, *Worlds of Labour: Further Studies in the History of Labour* (London, 1984), p. 37. For corroborating evidence, see R.M. Goodridge, 'Nineteenth-Century Urbanisation and Religion: Bristol and Marseille, 1830–1880', *A Sociological Yearbook of Religion in Britain*, 2 (1969), 123–36; or Gabriel le Bras, *Etudes de sociologie religieuse*, vol. I: *Sociologie de la pratique religieuse dans les campagnes françaises* (Paris, 1955), pp. 184–5. For some reasons why, see McLeod, *Religion and the People*, pp. 93–5; or, in a different context, see Kevin J. Christiano, *Religious Diversity and Social Change: American Cities, 1890–1906* (Cambridge, 1988), pp. 19–21 and 71–88. An important, and balanced, appraisal of the arguments and the evidence is found in Hugh McLeod, 'Religion in the City', *Urban History Yearbook, 1978*, 7–22.

[4] See, for example, Jeffrey Cox, *The English Churches in a Secular Society: Lambeth, 1870–1930* (New York, 1982), pp. 3–20, and 265–76, where this issue is sensitively discussed; see also Owen Chadwick, *The Victorian Church: Part II* (London, 1970), ch. 8; Hugh McLeod, *Class and Religion in the Late Victorian City* (London, 1974), ch. 8; Alan D. Gilbert, *Religion and Society in Industrial England: Church, Chapel and Social Change, 1740–1914* (London, 1976), pp. viii, 23–48 and 198–207; and Stephen Yeo, *Religion and Voluntary Organisations in Crisis* (London, 1976), pp. 2–4.

[5] Philip Rieff, *The Triumph of the Therapeutic: Uses of Faith after Freud* (New York, 1966), p. 1. For a full account of the prophecy of secular reason, see Owen Chadwick, *The Secularization of the European Mind in the Nineteenth Century* (Cambridge, 1975), pp. 143–266.

who prophesied no less than the eclipse of the sacred in a world of mundane rationality, have not been proved wholly correct either. Religion thrives along the Pacific rim, in some of the fastest modernising, industrialising and urbanising countries in the world. It is enjoying a massive revival in the Middle East. It is undergoing the most profound transformation and reinvigoration in Latin America.[6] In the wake of such progress, whether to universal enlightenment or to cosmic indifference, some scholars have begun to doubt the received wisdom of sociological and historical orthodoxy. They have suggested that religious belief and practice, so far from being in terminal decline, are now in fact re-emerging from a period of specific, perhaps even of geographically limited, decline. They have also observed that, if this is so, then the *theory* of decline cannot be true or, at the very least, that it cannot be so comprehensively true as was once thought.[7] And finally they have acknowledged that, if the realities of the present and the possibilities of the future do not point unambiguously to demise, then the truth about the past, even in the West, even indeed in Britain – the most apparently dechristianised of all the advanced, industrial societies – must be more complex than historians of religion have traditionally allowed.[8] Some sociologists have, accordingly, begun to envisage a genuine – even a healthy – future for religion in modern society.[9] And some historians have, in turn, begun to look afresh at some of the hitherto neglected

[6] See the remarks by Peter L. Berger in his 'Foreword' to David Martin, *Tongues of Fire: The Explosion of Protestantism in Latin America* (Oxford, 1990), pp. vii–x and chs. 2 and 13; John J. Donohue and John L. Esposito (eds.), *Islam in Transition* (Oxford, 1982), esp. ch. 4; and Geoffrey K. Nelson, *Cults, New Religions and Religious Creativity* (London, 1987), esp. chs. 10–13 for introductions to Protestant revivalism, Islamic resurgence and new religious movements.

[7] See, e.g., Daniel Bell, 'The Return of the Sacred? The Argument on the Future of Religion', *British Journal of Sociology*, 28 (1977), 418–49; Robert Nisbet, *History of the Idea of Progress* (New York, 1980), pp. 356–7; Keith Ward, *The Turn of the Tide*, pp. 9–11. For cautionary remarks on this development, see Bryan Wilson, 'The Return of the Sacred', *Journal for the Scientific Study of Religion*, 18 (1979), 268–80; and Roy Wallis and Steve Bruce, *Sociological Theory, Religion and Collective Action* (Belfast, 1986), pp. 61–71. For an explicit repudiation, see Phillip E. Hammond and Mark A. Shibley, 'When the Sacred Returns: An Empirical Test', in Eileen Barker, James A. Beckford and Karel Dobbelaere (eds.), *Secularization, Rationalism and Sectarianism: Essays in Honour of Bryan R. Wilson* (Oxford, 1993), pp. 37–45. And for a wider view, see James Davison Hunter, *Evangelicalism: The Coming Generation* (Chicago, 1987), ch. 1.

[8] See, e.g., Cox, *English Churches in a Secular Society*, pp. 265–76; also David M. Thompson, 'The Making of the English Religious Classes', *Historical Journal*, 22 (1979), 477–91; and, especially, the remarks of McLeod, 'Religion in the City', p. 19.

[9] Rodney Stark and William Sims Bainbridge, *The Future of Religion: Secularization, Revival and Cult Formation* (Berkeley and Los Angeles, 1985), pp. 1–3 and 429–39. For the suggestion that modernisation may not necessarily be synonymous with secularisation as a *cultural* process, see Peter L. Berger, *Facing Up to Modernity: Excursions in Society, Politics and Religion* (New York, 1977), pp. 78–80; see also the remarks of

ambiguities of the process, or processes, of religious decline in the recent past; even in Britain's religious past.[10]

In what follows, both the reality and the significance of the intellectual symbiosis between that general sociological prognostication and those particular historical investigations will be presumed. To be sure, historians, especially British historians, habitually balk at the very idea of contaminating the pristine autonomy of the past with the poisonous presuppositions of the present. They tend to prefer the comforting illusion that whilst the past (their provenance) may illuminate the present (the provenance of all), the trajectory of that understanding can never be inverted. No doubt this illusion has it uses. But it also has its limitations, both in general and in particular. In general, it cossets historians from an otherwise disagreeable appreciation that the past may only be understood at all through the critical language of the present.[11] In particular, it has protected religious historians from the uncomfortable truth that their subject was largely the creation of another academic discipline, and that its organising concepts have been drawn overwhelmingly from an intellectual heritage other than their own.[12] Of no concept is that debt more explicit and more unambiguous than of the theory of secularisation. Yet it is an academic due which is not only uneasily borne but which was, ironically, most unpropitiously acquired. For just at the moment when most religious historians began to apply the

---

David Martin, 'The Land of the Free to Believe', *Times Literary Supplement* (12–18 February 1988), 170.

[10] McLeod, 'Religion in the City', pp. 19–20; McLeod, 'New Perspectives on Victorian Class Religion: The Oral Evidence', *Oral History*, 14 (1986), 31–49; and Ward, *The Turn of the Tide*, ch. 1; and most importantly of all, Callum G. Brown, 'Did Urbanization Secularize Britain?', *Urban History Yearbook, 1988*, pp. 1–14. The most striking recent effort to bring these arguments, sociological and historical, and the relevant data together can be found in the various essays collected in Steve Bruce (ed.), *Religion and Modernization: Sociologists and Historians Debate the Secularization Thesis* (Oxford, 1992).

[11] It is customary to invoke the authority of Sir Herbert Butterfield against this Whiggish indecency. Yet note what he actually said in *The Whig Interpretation of History* (London, 1931), p. 17: '[T]here may be a sense in which study[ing] the past with reference to the present . . . is unobjectionable . . . and there may be a sense in which it is inescapable.' For a characteristically trenchant dismissal of the very idea of an autonomous 'past-as-it-was', see Maurice Cowling, *Religion and Public Doctrine in Modern England*, vol. II: *Assaults* (Cambridge, 1985), p. xxvii: '[T]he past as it was is unknowable[,] . . . the search for it professionalized to the point of imbecility . . . . [T]he fact [is] that . . . every serious historian ratiocinates the past that he needs.' For a gentler expression of the same view, see Asa Briggs, *Images, Problems, Standpoints, Forecasts: The Collected Essays of Asa Briggs*, vol. II (Brighton, 1985), pp. 272–3: '[W]e cannot write about the past unless we live in the present.'

[12] For some illuminating remarks on this relationship, see Patrick Collinson, 'What Is Religious History?', in Juliet Gardner (ed.), *What Is History Today?* (London, 1988), p. 58; for a more traditional interpretation of that relationship, see Thompson, 'The Making of the English Religious Classes', p. 477.

theory most tellingly to their own research, many sociologists of religion had started to question its validity and applicability, both to modern society and to the future of religion. Hence the simple question arises which the religious historian, much as he might prefer the safety of empirical specificity, cannot avoid: what is the force, and what are the weaknesses, of the theory of secularisation?

The theory of secularisation and its criticism

The theory of secularisation is arguably the most significant, and was unquestionably the most influential, thesis about the form and dynamics of social change in modern societies advanced by the great masters of sociological theory. For Max Weber it was the defining feature of Western civilisation, the very basis of his seminal concepts of rationalisation, bureaucratisation and the disenchantment of the world.[13] Emile Durkheim traced its progress to the most basic structural and organic differentiation of modern society, which made new moral demands upon social institutions – especially the demand for social justice – and which also diminished the place of the mysterious in the processes of social integration.[14] Subsequently, the 'Chicago School' of sociologists identified it as one of the peculiar features of urban life, at once deriving from its mechanistic ethos and critically contributing to its ideological pluralism.[15] More recently, a loosely knit 'British tradition' of sociology has again developed the theory, allying many of the general insights of the sociological masters to the evidence of British, North American and European religious decline to produce a more subtly nuanced and empirically substantiated interpretation of the diminishing significance of religion in the advanced, industrial societies.[16]

[13]   Max Weber, *Economy and Society: An Outline of Interpretative Sociology*, ed. by Guenther Roth and Claus Wittich (Berkeley and Los Angeles, 1978), see esp. pp. 24–6, 85, 476–80 and 576–83; Weber, *General Economic History*, ed. by Ira J. Cohen (New Brunswick, N.J., 1981), pp. 368–9; and esp. Weber, *From Max Weber: Essays in Sociology*, trans. and ed. by H.H. Gerth and C. Wright Mills (London, 1984), p. 155.

[14]   Emile Durkheim, *The Division of Labour in Society*, trans. by W.D. Halls (London, 1984), esp. pp. 118–20; also Durkheim, *The Evolution of Educational Thought: Lectures on the Formation and Development of Secondary Education in France*, trans. by Peter Collins (London, 1977), pp. 30, 210 and 284.

[15]   R.E. Park, E.W. Burgess and R.O. McKenzie, *The City* (Chicago, 1925), pp. 130ff.; L. Wirth, 'Urbanism as a Way of Life', *American Journal of Sociology*, 44 (1938–9), 1–24; Wirth, 'Urban Society and Civilization', *American Journal of Sociology*, 45 (1939–40), 743–55; and Wirth, 'Urban Communities', *American Journal of Sociology*, 47 (1941–2), 829–40.

[16]   See, especially, Bryan Wilson, *Religion in Secular Society: A Sociological Comment* (London, 1966), *passim*; Wilson, *Religion in Sociological Perspective* (Oxford, 1982), pp. 153–9; and David Martin, *A General Theory of Secularization* (Oxford, 1978), pp. 1–11;

Though rooted in subtly different insights about the morphology of modernity, whether they be economic rationalisation, social differentiation or cultural relativism, each of these theories of secularisation was itself grounded in a sociological analysis which identified a profound and irreversible historical transformation, occurring first in the West and then spreading generally across the developing world, from the essentially agricultural, or traditional, to the industrial, or modern, mode of production. This was a transformation of productive technique, in the substitution of machines for human skills, inanimate for animate power and the use of newer and more abundant raw materials. It was also a transformation in the prevailing forms of economic organisation, wrought through the establishment of the 'factory system' of production, a system based upon the application of rational planning and technical procedures, which replaced traditional methods and conventions of manufacture. That economic transformation, so it was argued, simultaneously brought about an unprecedented structural differentiation in the organisation of persons in society, a form of social differentiation which was forged by the principle of the division of labour and justified by an ethic of individual achievement. The effects of structural differentiation, so defined, were naturally manifold. So much so that sociologists generally tended to disagree about them. But on one thing they did agree. Structural differentiation emphasised the fundamental separation of different types of human activity, ensuring that work, family, education, and religion, which had once been intimately bound up with each other in the life of self-sufficient *communities*, evolved into separate activities, staffed by specialised personnel, and discretely practised in complex *societies*.[17]

In these – modern – societies, religion, which had once been the primary socialising agency of mankind, became little more than one amongst many possible outlets, including politics, psychoanalysis and consciousness-altering drugs, for individual satisfaction and release. No longer explaining the mysteries of life to men, because rationally planned life was no longer mysterious; no longer justifying changeless forms of social life, because none remained; and no longer teaching the eternal verities because all truths were now subject to critical revision, religion, so it was contended, became progressively a less pervasive and a less

for the most recent (re)statement of this view, and for a general summary of the 'British School' and its perspective, see Roy Wallis and Steve Bruce, 'Religion: The British Contribution', *The British Journal of Sociology*, 40 (1989), 493–520, esp. pp. 493–9; or Wallis and Bruce, 'Secularization: The Orthodox Model', in Bruce (ed.), *Religion and Modernization*, pp. 8–30.

[17] The classic distinction between 'community' and 'society' is found in Ferdinand Tönnies, *Community and Association*, trans. by Charles P. Loomis (London, 1955).

socially significant form of individual consolation. Once, figuratively speaking, at the 'centre' of society, it moved, inexorably, towards its 'periphery'. Religion, of course, still existed. There were still churches, liturgies and doctrines. And religious faith continued to be important in the lives of many religious persons. But neither as a social institution nor as a body of legitimating beliefs was it, or could it ever be again, socially significant.[18]

Quite apart from its intrinsic merits as a general sociological theory, the attractions of the theory of secularisation to religious historians were many and various. It appeared to explain so many *different* forms of institutional change in the sociological significance of religious belief and practice in modern societies. It accounted not simply for the political emasculation of the Church throughout North America and Western Europe from the end of the eighteenth century, but also for the decline in the socio-economic status of its professional and lay officials in more recent decades.[19] It gave meaning and significance not only to the reduction in the numbers of persons formally affiliated with religious denominations over the last hundred years or so, but also to the diminished frequency with which people attended church and chapel services.[20] It even furnished a plausible interpretation for those gestures towards institutional reform, such as the ecumenical movement, through which so many churches sought not only to obliterate their supposedly harmful doctrinal differences but also to render their administrative structures more efficient, and their organisational profiles more amenable, to the demands of the modern world.[21] Above all, secularisation

---

[18] On the idea of 'centre' and 'periphery' in sociological theory, see Edward Shils, 'Center and Periphery', in Shils, *Center and Periphery: Essays in Macro-Sociology* (Chicago, 1975), pp. 3–16.

[19] See, *inter alia*, B.R. Wilson, 'The Pentecostal Ministers: Role Conflicts and Status Contradictions', *American Journal of Sociology*, 64 (1959), 494–504; J. Brothers, 'Social Change and the Role of the Priest', *Social Compass*, 10 (1963), 477–89; L. Paul, *The Deployment and Payment of the Clergy* (London, 1964), *passim*; A.P.M. Coxon, 'Patterns of Occupational Recruitment: The Anglican Ministry', *Sociology*, 1 (1967), 73–80; R. Towler, 'The Social Status of an Anglican Minister', in R. Robertson (ed.), *Sociology of Religion* (Harmondsworth, 1969), pp. 443–50; F. Absalom, 'The Anglo-Catholic Priest: Aspects of Role Conflict', *A Sociological Yearbook of Religion*, 4 (1971), 46–61: S. Ransom, A. Bryman and B. Hinings, *Clergy, Ministers and Priests* (London, 1977), *passim*; and A.J. Russell, *The Clerical Profession* (London, 1980), *passim*.

[20] See esp. Currie, Gilbert and Horsley, *Churches and Churchgoers*, pp. 127–60; and P. Brierley, 'Religion', in A.H. Halsey (ed.), *Social Trends in Britain since 1900* (London, 1988), pp. 28ff.

[21] See esp. Wilson, *Religion in Secular Society*, pp. 125–76 and 223–6; also Robert Currie, *Methodism Divided: A Study in the Sociology of Ecumenicalism* (London, 1968), pp. 293–316; for a trenchant critique of this interpretation, see David M. Thompson, 'Theological and Sociological Approaches to the Motivation of the Ecumenical Movement', in Derek Baker (ed.), *Religious Motivation: Biographical and Sociological*

theory offered the modern historian an explanation for these otherwise disparate forms of institutional and cultural decline within a general theory of social and economic change which was applicable, given appropriate qualifications, throughout the developed world. Of course, it was acknowledged that the specific causes, and the particular pace of industrialisation, urbanisation and rationalisation in any given society varied. But that these social processes were, together, essential to the modernisation model was widely acknowledged. It was also generally recognised that they were, together, crucial to secularisation theory. Accordingly, so long as modern religious historians adhered to the secularisation thesis, their histories remained wholly compatible with, indeed an integral part of, mainstream modern social and economic history. And that was generally understood to be a good thing.[22]

The theory of secularisation still commands much explanatory power. The narrative which it describes, and the fate which it projects for religious belief, practice and organisation in advanced industrial societies are, together, still highly plausible.[23] But it does not command the general assent within the sociological profession which it enjoyed little more than two decades ago. During the last ten years or so, critics of the secularisation thesis have ceased to conceal their doubts about its validity under the guise of petty theoretical quibbles or minor empirical qualifications. Increasingly, they reject the theory outright. Or, at the very least, they reject the generalised claims of the theory to be as true for belief as for practice and for culture as for social institutions. And, in so doing, they have begun to conceive of a theory of modernisation which neither entails nor requires the corollary of secularisation.[24] Their assault on the secularisation thesis assumes many forms, both theoretical and empirical. Naturally, those forms interrelate and interconnect. But

Problems for the Church Historian, Studies in Church History, 15 (Oxford, 1978), pp. 467–79.

[22] For a particularly striking example of this assumption, and assertion, see Harold Perkin, *The Structured Crowd: Essays in English Social History* (Brighton, 1981), p. 228.

[23] See Wallis and Bruce, 'Religion: The British Contribution', pp. 498–9 for a strident reassertion of its validity against an acknowledged tide of recent criticism, qualification and rejection; and the remarks of Bryan R. Wilson, 'Reflections on a Many-Sided Controversy', in Bruce (ed.), *Religion and Modernization*, pp. 195–210.

[24] See the introduction to Phillip E. Hammond (ed.), *The Sacred in a Secular Age: Toward Revision in the Scientific Study of Religion* (Berkeley and Los Angeles, 1985), for an endorsement of this trend; or, for a reluctant admission of it, see Steve Bruce, *The Rise and Fall of the New Christian Right: Conservative Protestant Politics in America* (Oxford, 1988), p. 192: 'Twenty ... years ago many ... sociologists ... supposed that secularisation ... was an irreversible characteristic of modern societies. Recently the sociological orthodoxy seems to have been running in the opposite direction.' For the most recent, and most controversial, statement of this view, see Callum G. Brown, 'A Revisionist Approach to Religious Change', in Bruce (ed.), *Religion and Modernization*, pp. 31–58.

at some risk of oversimplification, they may be reduced to four types. These may be called respectively: the theory of transformation; the theory of relocation; the theory of divergence; and, finally, the theory of spontaneous renewal.

The theory of religious transformation constitutes the most radical challenge of all to the theory of secularisation. This is because it rejects its underlying principles, *tout court*. Its essential argument contends that the – unquestioned – institutional decline of traditional organised religions actually constitutes the transformation of the 'sacred' from old, acknowledged, elementary forms to new, implicit, complex manifestations as part of the wider shift from ancient order to modern society. Critical to the force of the argument is its definition of what 'religion', properly speaking, is. It rejects the commonsense understanding of religion as 'a set of beliefs and procedures relating to non-empirical ends and supernatural categories'.[25] In its place, it suggests that 'religion', properly defined, is no more nor less than the sacred bond of society, that is, 'a unified system of beliefs and practices relative to sacred things'. Whether or not every society must, by definition, live according to such a system of beliefs and practices is generally left unclear. What is insisted upon is that 'modern society' does. Once that is understood, then it can soon be appreciated how the modern cults of 'moral individualism' and 'democracy' or 'choice', even of the 'sovereign individual', have come to constitute modernity's 'transformed' understanding of the transcendentally significant; more still have actually succeeded in creating a new symbolic community similarly capable of sustaining the sacred bond – or religion – in society.[26]

This argument has some merits. First, it points to ways of identifying important links between the seemingly 'secular' and the unambiguously 'religious' in the complex cultural codes of modern society. Secondly, it provides a means of understanding many of the ostensibly abstract concepts of modern political philosophy within a richer, sociological, and even historical, context. But it is surely vitiated as a critique of secularisation theory more generally by its sheer semantic perversity. After all, it is one thing to observe that modern society tends to invest some of its most treasured political values with a pseudo-sacred

[25] The definition offered in B.R. Wilson, 'The Debate over Secularisation', *Encounter*, 45 (1975), 5–10.

[26] These quotations are directly drawn from Kenneth Thompson, 'Religion: The British Contribution', *The British Journal of Sociology*, 41 (1990), 531–5; the argument is best developed in James Beckford, *Religion and Advanced Industrial Society* (London, 1990), *passim*; its underlying debt to Durkheim may be traced in Emile Durkheim, *Elementary Forms of the Religious Life*, trans. by J.W. Swain (Glencoe, Ill., 1954), esp. pp. 62 and 243.

character; quite another to conclude that it actually presumes them to be the sacred. And the theory is irredeemably flawed through its hopeless empirical obscurity. As normally stated, it can be neither corroborated nor falsified because it consists only in the most amorphous description of quasi-sociological categories. Thus – ultimately – it is not so much an argument which is demonstrably false as a critique which remains beyond investigation. All of which, unfortunately, is another way of saying that it is critically worthless.[27]

A more plausible theory of sacred relocation acknowledges the commonsense definition of religion, but argues that proof of the diminution of the Church, or of the churches, in modern societies is not evidence for the decline of the significance of religious beliefs in these societies. This is because, so the argument goes, such beliefs have *relocated* themselves beyond those traditional, declining, ecclesiastical institutions into new developing, religious and quasi-religious organisations. Hence, in the words of one of its most prominent proponents: 'to concentrate on the church in a discussion of the modern religious situation is misleading, for it is precisely the characteristic of the new situation that religion is no longer the monopoly of any group explicitly labelled religious'.[28]

Why? What happened? And why was this so different from what seemed to happen? In the traditional world, so it is contended, religious beliefs and practice were institutionally focused upon the Church. The Church was the self-appointed and the exclusive guardian and propagator of the sacred in society. The Church was also a significant social institution in many other areas of life – the law, education and welfare. However, the trajectory of organisational change in modern societies – above all the differentiation of particular functions within them – has relocated the provision of those various services which were once the exclusive domain of the Church into other, more specialist, secular and quasi-sacred institutions. As a result, the traditional social significance of churches has diminished. And the authority of those ostensibly sacred bodies has declined, so their ability to secure and retain the institutional loyalty of the vast mass of the population has gradually evaporated. But

[27] The view maintained by Wallis and Bruce in 'Religion: The British Contribution', at pp. 510–13.

[28] Robert Bellah, *Beyond Belief: Essays on Religion in a Post-Traditional World* (New York, 1970), p. 42. Bellah's argument was applied to the modern world in general, especially the USA and Japan, and not simply, or even primarily, to England. Nevertheless, for all its generality, his argument was intended to apply to England similarly. More recent examples of the same argument are found in A.M. Greeley, *The Sociology of the Paranormal: A Reconnaissance* (Beverley Hills, 1975); D. Hay, 'Religious Experience amongst a Group of Postgraduate Students: A Qualitative Study', *Journal for the Scientific Study of Religion*, 18 (1979), 164–82.

religion has not declined. It has 'dispersed' into other public institutions, and even into private life. People remain religious; that is, they retain their religious beliefs. They carry those beliefs with them, not only through their personal relations but also into their secular vocations. Traditional religious institutions decline. But continuing religious beliefs go on mattering.

Take the example of Britain. Fewer than 20 per cent of the population of the United Kingdom today are members of Christian churches;[29] and perhaps fewer than one in twenty regularly attends Christian services.[30] But more than three-quarters of the population still profess to believe in God, nearly one-half believe Jesus to have been His Son, and about one-quarter consider religion to be 'very important' in their lives.[31] Secularisation theorists conclude that these facts – if such they are – point to no more than a residual religious sensibility amongst an otherwise secular people. Relocationists argue that they are real evidence for their continuing religious convictions. And they suggest that this can be shown to be so in so far as research about religion in modern society is directed away from the fortunes of the churches, as institutions, and towards the religious orientation of those modern institutions – political parties, trades unions, welfare organisations and the like – which are generally agreed to have usurped the wider social role of the Church during the twentieth century.

If this latter argument is valid, and if its implications are significant, then it follows that any theory of religious change which identifies the phenomenon of religious decline solely, or even primarily, from the evidence of patterns of church growth and decline, and moreover any theory which does so in the belief that those patterns furnish the best evidence of changes in the social significance of religion over time, must be rendered if not intellectually redundant then at least sociologically denuded. It is a daunting thought. But is the argument valid? If it is to be taken to be so, then its proponents must surely produce concrete evidence of precisely where the sacred has been relocated in modern life, and of the exact extent of this relocation. And they must establish that, in its relocated form, it is at least as significant, and at least as influential, in society as it was in its traditionally situated *locus*. This, to a striking degree, they have so far failed to do. To some extent, of course, that failure is in the nature of the argument itself. The very idea of general

<hr>

[29] Ward, *The Turn of the Tide*, p. 11; this figure is, necessarily, a vague estimate. On the difficulties of constructing such data, see Robin Gill, 'Secularization and Census Data', in Bruce (ed.), *Religion and Modernization*, pp. 90–117, esp. 90–101.
[30] Wilson, *Contemporary Transformations of Religion*, p. 22.
[31] Ward, *The Turn of the Tide*, p. 12.

relocation, after all, implies something of a sociological thinning-out. However, on every occasion where the relocated forms of religion have been explicitly isolated and examined (Robert Bellah's 'civil religion' springs to mind readily), they have proved not merely to be thinner but also to be weaker types too.[32] *That* fact, on careful reconsideration, may come to constitute only a more precise exposition of what the theory of secularisation really means; that is, the relocation of religion actually describes the diminution of its significance. In the churches it was significant. Beyond the churches it has ceased to be significant, no matter how healthily, no matter indeed how much more purely or nebulously, vigorously or implicitly, exclusively or commonly, it now survives.[33]

There is, however, an alternative possibility. This suggests that the theory of relocation may be not so much historically insignificant as sociologically incomplete. That is, whilst it crudely captures the reality of religious change, it fails to appreciate the subtle social and historical context of that alteration. To appreciate this context, so the argument goes, is to acknowledge the theory of 'divergence'. First formulated over thirty years ago by Charles Glock, the theory of divergence asserts that the prevailing sociological model of secularisation, then as now, presumes a 'uni-dimensional model' of religious commitment; that is, it presumes that religious commitment, for any given person, is constituted by his or her membership of a church, attendance at its services, regular financial contributions to its associations, devout adherence to its doctrines, belief in the possibilities of religious experiences, and by a commitment to all these things *together*. That presumption, Glock argued, is false. To be sure, that religious institutions, whether by professed, articulate doctrine, or merely through established convention, have differed and continue to disagree in the emphasis they require of members and adherents in their observation of these different forms of religious commitment has long been known. Indeed, it was, and is, the very stuff of denominational conflict. But Glock and his associates established that, even *within* particular religious organisations, there remained considerable divergence in the extent of the fulfilment of those different dimensions of religious commitment between different individuals.

Accordingly, Glock proposed a 'multi-dimensional model' of religious commitment, affiliation and devotion. First, he identified the five dimensions of that commitment which, he believed, all major religious societies required, to some degree, of their members and adherents:

[32] Robert Bellah, 'Civil Religion in America', *Daedalus*, 96 (1967), 1–21.
[33] For this argument, explicitly stated, see Wilson, *Religion in Sociological Perspective*, pp. 149–50; also the remarks in Wallis and Bruce, 'Religion: The British Contribution', pp. 495 and 498–9.

belief, practice, experience, knowledge and a commitment to the consequences (personal, moral and political) of faith.[34] Then he tested the degree to which different kinds of individuals registered in each of these different dimensions of religious commitment. Naturally enough, some persons registered high in one dimension and low in another. More important, distinct categories of persons seemingly registered high in one dimension and low in another. The clearest example of this form of discrepancy was uncovered in research exploring the relationship between religious commitment and social class.[35] Here, the data consistently demonstrated that the socially elevated (the middle classes and upwards) dominated those aspects of religious commitment which are most nearly represented as aspects of social standing (such as membership, attendance and affiliation); whilst the most socially deprived dominated those realms of commitment most likely to constitute forms of individual consolation (such as prayer and belief).[36] Different kinds of religious commitment, in other words, were (and still are) skewed by disparate cultural values, reflecting diverging social priorities. It follows that different foci of historical and sociological research have always in the past and will always in the future produce different (and perhaps even diverging) results. So, for instance, an increase in religious affiliation traditionally measured need not be synonymous with an intensification of religious belief generally, in any given society; and, correspondingly, the relative decline of participation by some groups in some forms of religious commitment was not necessarily proof of a growing indifference to religion *per se* amongst these groups.

Divergence theory in this way fleshes out the simple insight of relocation theory. Specifically, it allows for the significance of particular social contexts as well as for the importance of general historical change in the fortunes of religious organisations. But, much like each of the various forms of relocation theory, it does not really repudiate secularisation theory so much as to some degree qualify it. Even if it was accepted as substantially true (which has proved far from the case), the 'problem' of the churches and their decline (real or apparent), and the relationship

---

[34]   Charles Glock, 'The Religious Revival in America?' in Jane Zahn (ed.), *Religion and the Face of America* (Berkeley, 1959), pp. 34–63; also Charles Y. Glock and Rodney Stark, *Religion and Society in Tension* (Chicago, 1965), ch. 2.

[35]   See Glock and Stark, *Religion and Society in Tension*, ch. 2; also, Rodney Stark, 'Class, Radicalism and Religious Involvement in Great Britain', *American Sociological Review*, 29 (1964), 698–706.

[36]   Stark, 'Class, Radicalism and Religious Involvement'. See also Rodney Stark and William Sims Bainbridge, 'Towards a Theory of Religion: Religious Commitment', *Journal for the Scientific Study of Religion*, 19 (1980), 114–28.

between that decline and the process of secularisation would still remain. Decline, defined as the decline of popular involvement in religious membership, attendance and affiliation, may indeed be socially skewed. It may also be an aspect of the social history of some groups more than others. And finally it may differ amongst all such groups rather more according to the specific form of commitment isolated than of the general chronology so understood. But it could *still* be general, and of general significance, albeit in a number of different, even diverging, ways. The evidence, after all, suggests precisely that: so far as we can tell, middle-class association has declined more slowly than working-class affiliation, but both have declined; proletarian spirituality has ebbed less dramatically than bourgeois superstition, but neither has flowed. These variations hold for other groups too: for women and for self-styled minorities (in European societies) but none seems to register a really significant, diverging, *increase* in religious sensibilities.[37]

This problem is squarely confronted in yet another theoretical approach to the phenomenon of the decline of religious institutions which argues for an explicitly 'self-restricting' model of secularisation, based upon a 'spontaneous renewal' theory of religious economies. Proponents of this idea contend that secularisation is a specific – and limited – phenomenon: namely the contingent and measurable product of a sufficient degree of institutional accommodation between religious organisations and secular powers, especially between the dominant religious organisations in society and those worldly authorities. In this understanding, the rise of particular religious organisations to political authority and social respectability necessarily involves a series of institutional and doctrinal compromises with worldly power. Inevitably, such compromises render those religious organisations more worldly: that is, more secular. But the culmination of this process is not the end of religion. Nor is it the general secularisation of society. It is merely the inevitability of perennial oscillation in the social and spiritual fortunes of religious organisations, as those which have become too worldly are supplanted by more vigorous and less worldly religions. The *process* of secularisation, it is argued, is self-limiting because it spontaneously induces two countervailing and renewing processes: religious revival and religious innovation. The first results in schism, wrought by disheartened adherents of a particular faith who create a new sect in the name, or

---

[37] For this argument, see Martin, *A General Theory of Secularisation*, ch. 1; and Wallis and Bruce, 'Religion: The British Contribution', pp. 497–8; also the evidence advanced in Sabino Acquaviva, 'Some Reflections on the Parallel Decline of Religious Experience and Religious Practice', in Barker, Beckford and Dobbelaere, *Secularization, Rationalism and Sectarianism*, pp. 48–58.

spirit, of their old beliefs. The second issues in the 'cult' of new beliefs, or novel expressions of belief, professed to both those inside and those outside existing associations, and offered in a spirit of renewal. Secularisation, it is concluded, is as a matter of historical fact a process found in all religious economies. But it is also, similarly as a matter of similar historical fact, restricted through the essentially dynamic character of those economies.

To understand the future of religion, accordingly, is to devote attention to the fringes of that economy, for that is where its future lies. Hence, to concentrate attention upon any particular group of religious organisations at any given time, even over a long period of time, and to equate their decline with the irreversible demise of religion is to misunderstand the phenomenon of religious change; whilst to direct critical analysis solely towards the fate of declining institutions is to neglect half of the religious economy. Take the example of Britain again: the decline of the Anglican Church, of Protestant dissenting denominations, and even of the Roman Catholic Church is a function of *their* secularisation, and not of the secularisation of the society more generally. This is because their decline either has provoked schism and innovation, or soon will do. Religion will live on, in much the same way, and even to much the same extent as it always has, secularisation notwithstanding; with secularisation, indeed, properly accounted for.[38]

This theory constitutes a major challenge to the theory of secularisation both because it at once rejects the central premise of secularisation theory – that religion is in decline in the modern world – and, paradoxically, because it also defines (and limits) the concept of secularisation, robbing it not so much of its actual historical standing as of its peculiar sociological significance. Moreover, in directing attention away from the trials of specific churches and towards the concept of a religious economy, it is both inventive and arresting. Finally, in locating the phenomenon of secularisation throughout history, it is persuasive and important. But in its insistence upon the reality and the significance of a self-adjusting institutional mechanism in that economy, a mechanism that, so it is claimed, works just as efficiently in the advanced as

---

[38]   Stark and Bainbridge, *The Future of Religion*, pp. 1–3. It is, perhaps, of interest that this theory parallels, and perhaps originates in, a much older theory within the sociology of religion, namely the 'cult–sect–church' continuum of institutional change in religious organisations, a theory traceable to Weber but developed in H.R. Niebuhr, *The Social Sources of Denominationalism* (New York, 1925); the force of the argument, of course, lies in its novel assertion that social change in religious organisations along the model of the Weber/Niebuhr continuum does not represent *part* of the process of social change within religious organisations but rather the *whole* of the process of secularisation within the religious economy.

in traditional societies, the theory suffers from a debilitating deficiency of corroborative evidence. In Britain at least, the institutional decline of mainstream churches has since the First World War been very much greater in extent than the rise of new schismatic or cult religious movements. So the critical (and presumably falsifiable) assumption of a balance between the firm evidence of those religious institutions in decline and the naturally precarious information about those in ascent makes no empirical sense in the British case. Indeed, on the basis of the concrete historical evidence, one might actually go further and argue that religious decline in Britain, that is, the imbalance between institutional demise and institutional birth and rebirth in the religious economy of Britain, has been so great since the First World War that it might perversely require something more than simply a general theory of secularisation to explain it.[39]

Taken alone, none of these counter-theories constitutes a decisive refutation of the theory of secularisation. Even taken together, they are something less than entirely persuasive.[40] However, they do point to a theory at the semantic, conceptual and empirical crossroads. So many and such inventive objections to the theory, and to its underlying evidential basis, point not just to a general unease but also to genuine disagreement amongst sociologists about the course of religion in modern, industrial, and even post-industrial, societies. So many and such subtle alternatives to the received understanding also suggest that the presumed and melancholy fate of religion in twentieth-century Britain may turn out to be a contingent exception and not, as was once believed, the exemplifying rule. Whatever the case, no fair-minded observer can deny that the question of secularisation is now open, where once and not so long ago it seemed resolutely closed. And that openness, however minimally, properly extends to the British case too. Certainly, the recent religious history of Britain cannot be written under the simple assumption of its unifying teleology. On the other hand, it might be possible to write a history of religious change in nineteenth- and twentieth-century Britain which was significant in its own right: which was capable, in its own right, of contributing to a newer, fuller and more subtle perspective on the general theory of secularisation. It would definitely be worth trying.

---

[39] Wallis and Bruce, *Sociological Theory, Religion and Collective Action*, pp. 62–3.

[40] This, for instance, is the view of Karel Dobbelaere; see his 'Church Involvement and Secularization: Making Sense of the European Case', in Barker, Beckford and Dobbelaere, *Secularization, Rationalism and Sectarianism*, pp. 19–36.

The ambiguities of decline and the problems of analysis in recent British religious historiography

One thing is clear. It is the anti-secularisation model which has made most of the running in recent British religious historiography. To some extent, this bias may be traceable to the seemingly natural aversion of British historians to sociological theory, *tout court*. But more probably it is the product of their increasing immersion in that theory and, more strikingly still, in some of the more recent developments of that theory, as they have applied to the field of modern religious studies. True, so-called transformation theory has been largely ignored by the historical profession. But under the influence of relocation theory, historians have of late been much less willing to equate the decline of mass membership in mainstream ecclesiastical organisations with a diminution in the social significance of religion in later Victorian and Edwardian Britain; and altogether more inclined to search for evidence of the survival of religious norms and sacred life beyond the boundaries of traditional organised religion.[41] In the light of divergence theory, they have tentatively re-evaluated the apparent indifference of the industrial working classes in late nineteenth- and early twentieth-century manufacturing towns towards the life of regular religious worship; and they have often discovered that a seemingly lackadaisical attitude towards the demands of association only obscured an otherwise profound popular devotion to sacred things.[42] Finally, under the inspiration of the theory of spontaneous renewal, they have begun to investigate the previously unexplored phenomena of self-consciously novel and seemingly marginal religious organisations and practices in the manufacturing towns of urban and industrial Britain; and as they have investigated the evidence of surviving, emerging, even of thriving religion – beliefs, liturgies and institutions – in new churches, beyond the churches, and between the

---

[41] Especially following the example of Cox, *English Churches in a Secular Society*, p. 9, fn. 11, who takes to task Currie et al., *Churches and Churchgoers*, 'where statistics of the decline of church-going ... are confidently cited as evidence for the theory of secularisation, as if the fact of decline is itself evidence in support of a particular theory of decline'. For a rather different argument, challenging orthodox interpretations of the figures themselves, see Gill, 'Secularization and Census Data', pp. 101ff.

[42] See, e.g. Elizabeth Roberts, *Working-Class Barrow and Lancaster, 1890–1930* (Lancaster, 1976), pp. 62ff.; and Roberts, *A Woman's Place: An Oral History of Working-Class Women, 1890–1940* (Oxford, 1984), pp. 4–6, 44–5, 68–70 and 184–5. For remarks on the significance of these and other findings, see McLeod, 'New Perspectives on Victorian Class Religion', pp. 31–49. And for the particular case of 'rites of passage', see Sarah Williams, 'Urban Popular Religion and the Rites of Passage', in Hugh McLeod (ed.), *European Religion in the Great Cities, 1830–1930* (London, 1995), pp. 216–36.

classes, so they have redefined some of the intellectual boundaries of their discipline.[43]

This is true not simply of the content, but also of the context, of much of that recent historiography. Just as the evidence of a surviving, diverging, even of an emerging modern urban and industrial religious ethos has mounted, so the very notions of 'industrialisation', 'urbanisation' or, still more nebulously, 'rationalisation', once uncritically conceived as the general causes of the *decline* of religion in Victorian and Edwardian Britain, have been increasingly either exposed as false presuppositions (that is, they never really happened), or condemned as reified sociological categories (they happened, but not so simply), inadequately describing what was in reality a historically complex and often geographically various process of religious *change* occurring in British society during those years. In this way of thinking, it has become more and more important to emphasise that industrialisation was not quite the same thing in Manchester as in Birmingham;[44] similarly, that urbanisation was rather different in Leeds and in Middlesbrough.[45] Finally, so the argument goes, rationalisation – whatever that might have been – was probably never a similar process in *any* two places.[46]

According to this analysis, the processes of social change varied everywhere in industrialising and urbanising Britain. So too did their relationship vary with the processes of religious change. As a result, industrialisation did not always and everywhere lead to a decline of religious affiliation and belief in Victorian and Edwardian Britain. Nor did the process of urbanisation. Indeed, they may even have had the

[43] See, e.g., Janet Oppenheim, *The Other World: Spiritualism and Psychic Research in England, 1850–1914* (Cambridge, 1985), chs. 2 and 3; Logie Barrow, *Independent Spirits: Spiritualism and English Plebeians, 1850–1910* (London, 1986), chs. 1 and 5; or even Tony Jowett, 'Religion and the Independent Labour Party', in Keith Layburn and David James (eds.), *'The Rising Sun of Socialism': The Independent Labour Party in the Textile District of the West Riding of Yorkshire between 1890 and 1914* (Wakefield, 1991), pp. 121–34.

[44] Which, at one level, is obvious. But in so far as it points to different *types* of industrialisation, in different parts of nineteenth-century Britain, it is far from obvious, and very important. On the 'regional model' more generally, see Pat Hudson, 'The Regional Perspective' in Hudson (ed.), *Religions and Industries* (Cambridge, 1989), ch. 1.

[45] A development which began as early as Asa Briggs, *Victorian Cities* (London, 1963); see his introduction and separate chapters on each of these towns. It is continued in P.J. Waller, *Town, City and Nation: England, 1850–1914* (Oxford, 1983), chs. 3–5. For a summary of the current state of knowledge, see R.J. Morris and Richard Rogers (eds.), *The Victorian City: 1820–1914* (London, 1993), ch. 1.

[46] In so far as the term is employed at all by historians. On the relationship between industrialisation and Victorian culture more generally, see Christopher Harris, Graham Martin and Anson Scharf (eds.), *Industrialisation and Culture, 1830–1914* (London, 1970), *passim*.

opposite effect; at least in some places, at some times, and especially down to 1914.[47] To be sure, the processes of industrialisation and urbanisation invariably caused great problems for organised religion in many parts of England. But they also created new opportunities for it, often at the same time, often in exactly the same parts of the country. For, whatever else they did, industrialisation and urbanisation gave birth to new classes of men and women in search of spiritual solace. They brought forth new technical and organisational means to advance those institutions best capable of providing it. And they provided new social and pedagogical opportunities for those individuals motivated by the overriding belief that what modern man needed most was the gift of God's timeless grace.[48]

So much self-consciously 'revisionist' socio-religious historiography has certainly undermined all the old orthodoxies of the subject.[49] But it has been less noticeably successful in establishing a new synthesis in their place. This is partly because the eclipse of secularisation theory as an explanation of religious change has not been accompanied by the rise of any other conceptual model, and especially any other model of decline, capable of claiming general assent. It is also to some degree traceable to a growing uncertainty amongst religious historians about whether the limits to decline, which they now increasingly identify, are best understood within a framework which emphasises the significance of institutional survival, or according to an analysis which highlights the importance of cultural adaptation. And finally, it is the product of a growing disagreement amongst the most actively concerned scholars in the field about whether such a process of decline or survival or adaptation is still best interpreted through the existing categories of

[47] Patrick Joyce, *Work, Society and Politics: The Culture of the Factory in Later Victorian England* (Brighton, 1980), esp. chs. 2, 3, 5, 7 and 8; Brown, 'Did Urbanization Secularize Britain?', *Urban History Yearbook, 1988, passim.* For general remarks on this, see S.J.D. Green, 'Secularisation by Default? Urbanisation, Suburbanisation and the Strains of Voluntary Religious Organisation in Late-Victorian and Edwardian England', *Hispania Sacra, Revista de Historia Eclesiástica*, separata del volumen 42 (1990), 423–33.

[48] I owe this insight to Dr J.D. Walsh. For an analysis of the empirical evidence, see Callum G. Brown, 'The Mechanism of Religious Growth in Urban Societies: British Cities since the Eighteenth Century', in McLeod (ed.), *European Religion in the Great Cities*, pp. 239–62.

[49] For which, see most recently, and notably, Mark Smith, *Religion in Industrial Society: Oldham and Saddleworth, 1785–1865* (Oxford, 1994). However, much of this work remains, sadly, in unpublished dissertation form; see esp. Gerard Connolly, 'Catholicism in Manchester and Salford', 2 vols. (Ph.D. diss., University of Manchester, 1980); Rosemary Chadwick, 'Church and People in Bradford and District, 1880–1914: The Protestant Churches in an Urban Industrial Environment' (D.Phil. diss., University of Oxford, 1987); and Alan Bartlett, 'The Churches in Bermondsey, 1880–1939' (Ph.D. diss., University of Birmingham, 1987).

social theory, even through the available vehicle of social history *per se*, as was once so readily assumed.[50]

Hence a paradox. As the (partial) inversion of secularisation theory has rendered the causal trajectory of recent social histories of religion increasingly uncertain, so the wholescale complication of recent understanding of nineteenth-century religious life has effectively disengaged much new religious historiography from theoretically informed social history altogether.[51] Now seemingly freed from the suspicion of mindless antiquarianism and all too obviously liberated from the necessity to be socially relevant, the high politics of religion, the internal history of the churches and the history of religious ideas have enjoyed a considerable contemporary renaissance. So much so that, in the words of one of the most distinguished practising social historians of religion, 'the social history boom of the 1960s and 1970s', with its 'crusading commitment to writing history from below, [for] rediscovering the beliefs and experiences of ordinary people and sharing what their religion meant for the day-to-day life' would 'appear to have gone bust'.[52] No doubt this is an exaggeration. But it expresses an important truth, for it suggests that the new social history of religion, like much of the rest of the new social history generally, may initially have claimed too much for its explanatory powers and paradoxically ended up ignoring too much of what remained well worth explaining.[53]

If that is so, then as McLeod rightly puts it, 'the greatest need' now is for work which 'integrates the insights of social history with those of church history and the history of ideas'.[54] And, specifically, the greatest need is for such a unified account which also takes seriously one of the most commonly held sentiments amongst mid-nineteenth-century

---

[50]   The extent to which this dissensus represents a state of affairs peculiar to religious history, or more generally to social history, and even to history, *tout court*, I pass over here. I hope to deal with this topic in the future.

[51]   A point made and lamented by Jeffery Cox; see his 'On the Limits of Social History: Nineteenth-Century Evangelicalism', *Journal of British Studies*, 31 (1992), 198–203, esp. at p. 201; and, again, his 'A Reply to Albion Urdank', *Journal of British Studies*, 32 (1993), pp. 282–4, esp. at p. 282.

[52]   Hugh McLeod, 'Varieties of Victorian Belief', *Journal of Modern History*, 64 (1992), 321–37; there McLeod cites for example, J.P. Parry, *Democracy and Religion: Gladstone and the Liberal Party, 1867–1875* (Cambridge, 1986); Richard Brent, *Liberal Anglican Politics: Whiggery, Religion and Reform, 1830–1841* (Oxford, 1987); Pietro Corsi, *Science and Culture in Victorian Britain* (Bloomington, 1989); G.I.T. Machin, *Politics and the Churches in Great Britain, 1869–1921* (Oxford, 1987); D.W. Bebbington, *Evangelicalism in Modern Britain: A History from the 1730s to the 1980s* (London, 1989), amongst many other recent works.

[53]   I have made this point at greater length in my review of F.M.L. Thompson (ed.), *The Cambridge Social History of Britain, 1750–1950*, in *The Journal of Modern History*, 65 (1993), 398–402, esp. at p. 399.

[54]   McLeod, 'Varieties of Victorian Belief', p. 337.

churchmen, ministers and laity: that, in the new industrial towns, all was not well with God's work, but all was not lost either. That is what this book tries to do. To this end, it describes a social history of religion in one part of nineteenth- and twentieth-century urban, industrial, British society. It also furnishes an account of the response of the major churches to the problems and opportunities confronting them in three of the manufacturing towns of later Victorian and Edwardian England. Finally, it seeks to evaluate the successes and the failures of that response through a detailed analysis of the ideas – principally the religious ideas – which guided churchmen, ministers and laity in their quest to forge from such raw material and through such methods the makings of a truly Christian nation, neither presuming its necessary fate nor supposing any binding connection between its fortune and the changing religious life of the emerging nation.

The approach and method of this study

This makes for an essentially institutional history: a description and an analysis of the ends, activities and fate of religious institutions. No apology is offered for that bias. On the contrary. No other method permits a more integrated understanding. For an institutional history, properly conceived, necessarily comprehends the social history of religion, the history of the churches and the history of religious (and many other) ideas. As such, no other approach better respects the concrete realities of contemporary spiritual life. To be sure, no social history of religion in nineteenth- or twentieth-century Britain would be worth much if, in the words of one historian, it merely 'judged the religion of the masses by the view of the deanery window, seldom [to] require how the deanery appeared from the outside'.[55] Similarly, the social history of religion beyond the churches in nineteenth- and twentieth-century Britain is an important subject, worthy of examination and capable of yielding significant results.[56] But that is not to say that the social history of religion in nineteenth- and twentieth-century Britain

---

[55] Brian Harrison, 'Religion and Recreation in Nineteenth-Century England', *Past and Present*, 38 (1967), p. 98.

[56] See, e.g., John Kent, 'Feelings and Festivals: An Interpretation of Some Working-Class Religious Attitudes', in H.J. Dyos and Michael Wolff (eds.), *The Victorian City: Images and Realities*, vol. II (London, 1973), pp. 855–71; also, Jim Obelkevich, Lyndal Roper and Raphael Samuel (eds.), *Disciplines of Faith: Studies in Religion, Politics and Patriarchy* (London, 1987), esp. chs. 1, 3, 6, 9 and 20–2; and Roberts, *Working-Class Barrow and Lancaster, passim.*; and Roberts, *A Woman's Place*, esp. pp. 4–6 and 44–5. For rural popular religion, see Obelkevich, *Religion and Rural Society: South Lindsey, 1825–1875* (Oxford, 1976), pp. 259–312. The present author, however, retains much sympathy for a view expressed in Cox, *English Churches in a Secular Society*, p. 90: 'the

is best studied in an essentially super-institutional, still less in an exclusively popular, context.

This is because the image of aloof churches and an alienated people in the cities and towns of Victorian and Edwardian Britain is, in fact, largely false. Despite all their apparent weaknesses, Established and voluntary religious organisations were, after the public house and the corner shop, very possibly the most socially accessible institutions in the life of characteristic Victorian and Edwardian cities.[57] As such, they touched each person, from every class, at least during some part of their lives. Virtually everyone went to Sunday school. Many, if not most, adolescents joined the Band of Hope or the Mutual Improvement Society, then usually attached to a church or chapel.[58] The majority of adults attended church occasionally, some just to perform the rites of passage, but others also to mark the passing of the ceremonial year. True, the greater part of the working classes, taken as a whole, probably did not worship regularly. But a very large proportion of working-class women certainly did.[59] And even in those big cities where the preponderant part of the population did not attend church every Sunday, it was often the case that the majority of those who did attend were drawn from the working classes.[60]

None of this, of course, is to claim that urban religious institutions ever assumed the characteristics of a *Volkeskirche*, whether in the West Riding of Yorkshire or anywhere else in later nineteenth-century Britain.[61] It is, however, emphatically to deny the assertion that organised religion was something essentially confined to the middle classes, which is therefore best understood in terms of their aspirations and activities.[62] To be sure, a discernible gap existed between the doctrinal and institutional claims of organised religion and the private

religious views of early-nineteenth-century villagers may be easier to retrieve than those of late-nineteenth-century city-dwellers'.

[57] Yeo, *Religion and Voluntary Organisations in Crisis*, esp. pp. 51–70; note similar remarks in Thompson, 'The Making of the English Religious Classes', p. 485.

[58] See Yeo, *Religion and Voluntary Organisations in Crisis*, pp. 52ff; and McLeod, 'New Perspectives on Victorian Class Religion', pp. 31–5; also Callum G. Brown, *The Social History of Religion in Scotland since 1730* (Cambridge, 1987), pp. 160–4; and Brown, 'Did Urbanization Secularize Britain?', pp. 10–12.

[59] Rosemary Chadwick, 'Church and People in Bradford and District, 1880–1914', pp. 163, 171–3. And see below, ch. 4, esp. pp. 205–9.

[60] Peter Hillis, 'Presbyterians and Social Class in Mid-Nineteenth-Century Glasgow: A Study of Nine Churches', *Journal of Ecclesiastical History*, 32 (1981), 47–64.

[61] On the concept of *Volkeskirche*, see David Luker, 'Revivalism in Theory and Practice: The Case of Cornish Methodism', *Journal of Ecclesiastical History*, 37 (1986), 603–19. For a contemporary example, see David Clark, *Between Pulpit and Pew: Folk Religion in a North Yorkshire Fishing Village* (Cambridge, 1982), esp. chs. 1, 3 and 5.

[62] As, for instance, advanced recently in J.N. Morris, *Religion and Urban Change: Croydon 1840–1914* (Woodbridge, 1992), pp. 12–14, and *passim*.

beliefs and public behaviour of the mass of the people. Contemporaries saw it and many certainly grieved about it. Indeed, it is precisely because there was such a gap that it makes sense to investigate the attempts of those individuals and associations who probably understood it best and lamented it most, to close it. But that gap was not a chasm. It was a matter of degrees, not of absolutes. Because it was a matter of degrees, because the people were not prematurely and irreversibly alienated from the churches, the study of local religious beliefs, practices and institutions through the medium of the records of organised religious societies need not be – is not – a repudiation of history from below, still less an abandonment of the attempt to rediscover and analyse the 'beliefs of ordinary people' and the 'role of religion in their day-to-day lives'. Rather, it demonstrates that any effort to draw a sharp distinction between institutional and non-institutional forms of popular, urban religion soon becomes an impediment to understanding. For much of that so-called non-institutional religion was, in fact, parasitic upon the churches; at least of the churches as they actually were, if not as they wished to be. It was, of course, modified by its subsequent freedom, in many cases. But, equally obviously, it usually prospered best in them, and can for the most part properly be studied through them.

That last observation is important. This is not simply because it justifies the study of popular religion through religious institutions. It is, more importantly, because it points to the peculiar significance of those organisations in the social life of the industrial town, for the churches and chapels of West Yorkshire, as elsewhere in late nineteenth-century Britain, were not only the most generally accessible of all the major voluntary organisations in industrial, urban society. They were also the most particularly ambitious. It was that combination of general accessibility and particular ambition which marked their unambiguous peculiarity among contemporary voluntary organisations. People at the time recognised this. Naturally, they appreciated the obvious similarities between voluntary religious organisations – churches and chapels – and voluntary secular organisations – literary societies, friendly groups, benevolence trusts, and the like. But they were more impressed by the differences. Where secular societies characteristically limited their purposes to specific and stated goals, sacred organisations interpreted salvation in the widest possible institutional framework. Secular societies usually demanded commitment to no more (nor less) than an explicit body of rules, and those rules were rarely institutionally exclusive. Sacred societies, on the other hand, usually imposed both a more nebulous and a more demanding code on their members and adherents. Finally, perhaps most importantly of all, secular societies were, in almost

all cases, open only to those who paid their financial dues. Sacred
societies were, in every case, open to all. Everyone was encouraged to
contribute financially. But there was no entrance fee.

More widely directed, more generally conceived and (ironically) more
precariously financed, sacred societies were, accordingly, altogether
more socially comprehensive and much more socially influential than the
normal run of secular voluntary organisations. Contemporaries understood this. Some recent historians have tended to obscure it, thus
conflating the two and describing their nature, their evolution and even
their decline in strikingly similar terms.[63] There are merits in such a
general and comparative approach, for there were similarities, both in
their form and of their development. But it was the differences between
the two types of organisation which enabled churches and chapels, for
instance, to promote literary studies amongst their members without
degenerating into rarefied bourgeois societies.[64] It was also a distinguishing feature of religious organisations that they might assume
exclusive theological, social and political stances which demanded of
their members that they renounce other, disapproved, associations.[65]
Finally, and most importantly of all, it was of the very essence of every
sacred society, no matter how grand, that it seek to transcend its many
human limitations – especially its social limitations – in the divine work
of evangelical mission. In short, sacred societies were very special types
of voluntary organisation. In what follows, they will be treated as such.[66]

Of course, even to speak of 'organised religion' as if it lived and
worked as one is to run the risk of imposing an anachronistic unity onto
the contemporary realities of institutional pluralism. There was, indeed,

---

[63] See, for instance, Yeo, *Religion and Voluntary Organisations in Crisis*, ch. 1; or, more
generally, Theodore Koditschek, *Class Formation and Urban Industrial Society:
Bradford, 1750–1850* (Cambridge, 1990), chs. 10–11; and R.J. Morris, 'Clubs, Societies
and Associations', in F.M.L. Thompson, *The Cambridge Social History of Britain, 1750–
1950*, vol. III: *Social Agencies and Institutions* (Cambridge, 1990), pp. 395–443; also
Morris, *Class, Sect and Party: The Making of the British Middle Classes: Leeds, 1820–1850*
(Manchester, 1990), *passim*. For the purposes of this discussion, 'Established' religious
organisations are defined as 'voluntary' though of course, strictly speaking, they were
not. The point is this: they shared so many similar characteristics that it makes good
sense, sociologically, to speak of them in this way.
[64] As shown, for instance, in S.J.D. Green, 'Religion and the Rise of the Common Man:
Mutual Improvement Societies, Religious Organisations and Popular Education in
Three West Riding Towns, 1850–1900', in Derek Fraser (ed.), *Cities, Class and
Communication: Essays in Honour of Asa Briggs* (Hemel Hempstead, 1990), pp. 25–43.
[65] For some extremely illuminating remarks on the remarkably exclusive relationship
between religious organisation and political expression, see McLeod, 'The Varieties of
Victorian Belief', pp. 326–8.
[66] A point made at greater length in S.J.D. Green, 'In Search of Bourgeois Civilisation:
Ideals and Institutions amongst the Nineteenth-Century Middle Classes', *Northern
History*, 28 (1992), 228–47.

no acknowledged 'church of the nation' in mid-Victorian West Yorkshire. The division of local Christian society into competing, indeed conflicting, denominations was not an illusion of paranoid churchmen, priests and ministers. It reflected profound doctrinal, liturgical and pastoral disagreements which surfaced even in the simplest forms of lay attention. It also marked overt and covert social distinctions.[67] For one group, the Irish, it highlighted, perhaps it even accentuated, a self-conscious ethnic differentiation.[68] Thus a religious history of these towns during the late nineteenth and early twentieth centuries which did not acknowledge the all too real existence of institutional differentiation and mutual suspicion would simply be a false history. But a religious history faithful to the mental world of those same churchmen, priests and ministers would also appreciate a much more important division of mankind, which they themselves identified. This was the distinction between those who had sought and found 'the glad tidings of the Gospel' and those 'masses of men [outside] the House of God', whose 'minds' were 'unlighted', and whose 'understanding' was 'uninformed'.[69] It was because that distinction actually mattered more to contemporaries than the historical trichotomy of British Christian society, that is, into Anglican, dissenting and Roman Catholic churches, that a respected local churchman could happily presume that 'those who [had] placed themselves under other ministers or attended other places of worship' will 'readily understand our [giving] our whole time to shepherding those who neglect public worship altogether' and who 'especially need our pastoral care'.[70] For those 'who have put themselves under the charge of other religious organisations' were left, to a remarkable extent, to their own devices and to the care of others.[71]

That the number of those who 'did not attend any place of worship' with any degree of approved regularity was large, and that it might easily increase, were dreadful possibilities which every concerned churchman

[67] But for salutary caution about the *social* basis of denominationalism in nineteenth-century England, see David Thompson, 'The Making of the English Religious Classes', p. 490; and in nineteenth-century Yorkshire, see E.D. Steele, 'Class, Religion and Politics', *Northern History*, 21 (1985), 308–19, esp. pp. 310–14. For an important argument that the essential divide in religious practice in nineteenth-century Britain was *within* classes, see Brown, 'Did Urbanization Secularize Britain?', pp. 8–9.

[68] On the Irish in Britain and their religion, see John Archer Jackson, *The Irish in Britain* (London, 1963); on the Irish in the West Riding and East Lancashire, see Joyce, *Work, Society and Politics*, pp. 250–3.

[69] J. Thornton Cox, *A Brief History of the Church and Parish of Holy Trinity, Lawkholme, Keighley* (Keighley, 1932), p. 13.

[70] Frederic Damstini Cremer, 'Vicar's Letter', *KPCM*, vol. 13, no. 1, January 1890 (no page number).

[71] Frederic Damstini Cremer, 'Interdominationalism', *KPCM*, vol. 21, no. 4, April 1898 (no page number).

and minister properly feared. But if they confronted these challenges, for the most part in and through their separate societies, they did so with organisational methods and institutional resources which were nevertheless remarkably similar. Indeed, they were to a considerable degree actually borrowed, and sometimes shamelessly copied, from each other. Hence Francis Pigou, Vicar of Halifax parish church in the 1870s and 1880s, noted acerbically that local 'nonconformity' was 'vigilant, active, [and] not slow to initiate and utilise anything that the Church of England introduces into its churches and parishes'.[72] On the other hand, his neighbour and colleague, Frederic Damstini Cremer, Rector of Keighley, was happy to 'learn from the nonconformists', whenever the opportunity presented itself.[73] So, despite the differences of liturgy, doctrine and even of social status, it is meaningful to speak of 'organised religion' as if it was one, at least in this sense: in its most important mission, and in the means by which it attempted to fulfil that mission, whether its agents willed it or not, it was as one.

Finally, this is a local study. And it is written in the assumption that locality, that is, local variation matters. Hence it follows that no peculiarly significant theoretical status is claimed for these towns. Certainly, they were neither characterised by any peculiar representativeness, nor are they here presented as 'ideal-type' exemplars, whether 'atomistic' or 'paternalistic', large-scale or small-scale. Apart from anything else, they were very different from each other. Halifax, in the late nineteenth century was, or believed itself to be, a city in all but name.[74] Keighley, less than half its size, was on the other hand 'very much a town and not a village or a city'.[75] But Denholme really was a village, emphatically neither a city nor a town, and largely the creation of two worsted manufacturing families.[76] Nor are they posited in laborious comparison with one another. Rather they are analysed alternatively together and in isolation, as a group and through their differences, in the hope of establishing intelligible and meaningfully related conclusions across a range of significantly distinct but minimally integrated urban industrial environments, at once sufficiently extensive to make such generalisations fruitful, and yet sufficiently compact to permit investigation across the full tranche of local religious organisations.

---

[72] Francis Pigou, *Phases in My Life* (London, 1898), p. 346.
[73] Frederic Damstini Cremer, 'The Nonconformists: What May We Learn From Them?', *KPCM*, vol. 13, no. 7, July 1890 (no page number).
[74] Anon., *The Restoration of Halifax Parish Church* (Halifax, 1877), p. 21.
[75] Asa Briggs, 'Plus Ça Change: Back to Keighley: The Largely Forgotten Story of Sir Swire Smith', in Briggs, *The Collected Essays of Asa Briggs*, vol. III: *Serious Pursuits: Communications and Education* (Hemel Hempstead, 1991), at p. 418.
[76] Anon., *Industrial Advantages of Denholme* (London, 1921), *passim*.

At the same time, they have been consciously selected for such study because all, in their different ways, experienced all of the major processes normally associated with the industrial revolution: technological innovation, the establishment of a factory system of production, and a revolution in local communications. Yet, they endured few of the experiences of industrial dislocation, deskilling and casualisation which, for instance, make nineteenth-century London a tricky exemplar for sound generalisations about the characteristic social forms of industrial cities.[77] Each also underwent the major forms of social transformation, especially of structural differentiation through the intensification of the division of labour and of the creation of a recognisable modern class system, generally associated with the rise of the industrial-capitalist mode of production. And each expanded, diversified and industrialised from a recognisable and pre-existing urban base; that is, they were each the *locus* both of a relatively expeditious, and of a relatively mature, process of industrialisation, in which economic growth and social differentiation were sustained by local fertility and local migration. In other words, they were neither created virtually *ex nihilo*, like Manchester, nor were they the product of mass overseas immigration, like Liverpool.[78] On the contrary, they were the natural products of their own economic and demographic, and also of their own cultural and linguistic, resources. They were also large, middle-ranking, and small *towns* – altogether more typical of the industrial revolution in nineteenth-century Britain than the more famous, more cosmopolitan and less characteristic cities, especially Leeds but also Bradford, in their immediate neighbourhood.[79]

Most significantly of all, those general economic and social transformations were effected in a part of West Yorkshire – the Calder and Aire Valleys – long characterised by a vigorous and resilient religious tradition, a tradition which had been established prior to the onset of industrialisation and urbanisation. These localities had long been home to ancient Anglican parishes. But they had become, by the early

[77] On the peculiarities of London, see Asa Briggs, *Victorian Cities* (London, 1963), ch. 8; also Gareth Stedman Jones, *Outcast London: A Study in the Relationship between the Classes* (Oxford, 1971), ch. 1.

[78] On Manchester, see Briggs, *Victorian Cities*, ch. 3, and bibliographical note; on Liverpool, see P.J. Waller, *Sectarianism and Democracy: A Political and Social History of Liverpool, 1868–1939* (Liverpool, 1981), ch. 1.

[79] This point is well made in Alan Dingsdale, 'Yorkshire Mill Town: A Study of the Spatial Patterns and Processes of Urban Industrial Growth and the Evolution of Spatial Structure in Halifax, 1801–1901' (Ph.D. thesis, University of Leeds, 1974), p. 404. '[U]rban-industrial growth in the nineteenth century [characteristically] occurred ... in market towns of varying status in the pre-industrial period ... Few towns were wholly the creation of the Industrial Revolution.'

nineteenth century, major nonconformist strongholds. Then, during the 1840s and 1850s they received (often less than gratefully) some of the earliest 'new' Irish Catholic communities in Britain. The religious life of later nineteenth- and early twentieth-century Halifax, Keighley and Denholme revolved, almost entirely, around this organisational trichotomy. The nature and impact of their response to those demographic, economic and social revolutions which were going on around them will, accordingly, be the subject of this study. The variety of their activities, and the subtle relationship between pressing social imperatives and timeless religious aspirations, are the justifications for studying that response in the context of these three, closely related but significantly different, urban environments.

Plan of the work

The chapters which follow attempt to identify, describe and analyse the most significant aspects of the mission of organised religion to the people of industrial West Yorkshire. Because that mission was essentially institutional in its form, and because it became the expression of increasingly complex institutions in its development, no neat division of the work into simple chronological order has been judged either possible or desirable. Instead, this study is presented as a series of interrelated analytical studies. It is divided into three parts. Part I concentrates upon the provision of the means of worship by religious organisations. Part II devotes its attention to the efforts to draw the people into regular communion with those institutions. Part III evaluates some of the results of these labours. These parts, in turn, are divided into nine chapters. Chapter 1, as a precursor, describes the social and economic background to that mission. It employs some of the intellectual insights in the field of historical geography to place the demographic explosion, industrial revolution and social transformation which occurred in nineteenth-century West Yorkshire into a more adequate conceptual and empirical framework for the social study of religious history. To this end, it exploits spatial analysis to describe precisely the processes by and through which industrial urbanisation assumed its modern pattern in the Calder and Aire Valleys. In the same way, it employs demographic material to illuminate some of the reasons why local society forged some of the characteristic institutional forms for which it eventually became noted. The chapter concludes with a consideration of the social and institutional difficulties which these technical, demographic and spatial revolutions caused for local religious organisations.

Chapter 2 analyses the origins, dynamics and consequences of what became known as church extension; more specifically, the process of building new churches and rebuilding old ones in the urban ecclesiastical plan. This was certainly the most visible and very probably the most significant contemporary *response* of local religious organisations to the various social changes and institutional difficulties which they faced. From the surviving evidence, it considers the questions of who built the churches of Victorian and Edwardian Yorkshire; why they built them, where they built them, and what they built them with. Chapter 3 analyses one of the most important, if the least visible, consequences of so much local building activity: the transformation of the political economy of established and voluntary religious organisations during the last years of the nineteenth century. The consequences of this change – in short, the intrusion of more 'worldly' forms of financial organisation into the political economy of religious associations – are evaluated in the latter half of the chapter where particular attention is given to the way the churches raised the money they had spent (*sic*), and to the forms of institutional order and symbolic life which arose from this financial régime.

Chapter 4 describes the associational impact which church extension and economic liberalisation together wrought. This was the expansive voluntary (or Established) religious organisation. It shows how this was, to a considerable degree, the product of a multi-chapel community, a reflection both of its denominational pluralism and of its social diversity. It demonstrates how this institution, whilst retaining profound, if formal, national and regional links, became, to a considerable degree its own body: effectively self-financed, self-motivated and self-sustaining. And it explores both the ambitious 'greed' with which this institution sought to incorporate all of neighbourhood society within its associational compass, and also the traditional generosity with which it was willing to support many of the most vulnerable in that society, even some of those with only the most tenuous connection to its ideals and purposes. Finally, it considers the significance of this development for the self-image of the later nineteenth-century religious organisation, and the consequences for twentieth-century understanding of its success or failure.

Chapters 5 and 6 explore two crucial aspects of the relationship between church extension, institutional expansion and the attempts of late nineteenth- and early twentieth-century Established and voluntary religious organisations to enlist and keep new recruits, both young and old. Chapter 5 analyses how local religious organisations sought to exploit the long-standing and continuing popularity of Sunday schools in order to provide themselves with a regular and disciplined supply of religious conscripts for their congregations and societies. It describes, first, the pedagogical and institutional innovations which were formulated with the hope of achieving these ends; then why they failed or seemed to fail, and finally why that failure, in turn, provoked a major intellectual reappraisal of the possibilities and limitations of the 'religion of the child' which was characteristic of Edwardian religious organisations. The question of recruitment and its pitfalls is pursued at another level in chapter 6, which considers how far contemporary associations succeeded, and how far they did not succeed, in extending their evangelising mission to adult society in these towns during the late nineteenth and early twentieth century. Specifically, it considers the phenomenon of urban religious revivals, and the degree to which these were transformed into something rather different, that is, self-styled ecumenical religious mission, during the first and second decades of the twentieth century.

In chapter 7, an attempt is made to evaluate the specific and changing devotional and experiential content of contemporary organised religious life, and to interpret its relationship with pre-existing and surviving forms of super-institutional religious belief and activity. To this end, the growth of the doctrine and practice of 'public worship' as the core of organised religion, a development which both displaced and compensated for the loss, or perceived loss, of more informal 'experiential' religion, is analysed at length. The integration of the institutions of public worship into other forms of public order and other techniques of general socialisation is described in chapter 8. So too is the disparity between official conceptions of regular worship and the mundane realities of popular intermittency. Finally, the often tense relationship between official attitudes towards popular religion and popular attitudes to organised faiths is considered. Then in chapter 9, the various strands of local religious life, both in its continuing institutions and of its evolving mission to the people, are brought together in a wider interpretation of the various impacts of popular politics, radical secularism and the First World War upon the organisational realities, as well as upon clerical and lay perceptions of those institutions and of that mission. In conclusion, these developments are analysed, together, as a means to understand a profound paradox: why it was that at the very moment when they achieved the greatest influence they had in British society, the Established and voluntary organisations of industrial and urban Britain perversely concluded that they had failed in their mission to the people.

Part I

Providing the means

1 The environment and its constraints: economic revolution, social transformation and spatial evolution

Introduction: historical geography and the social context of religious history

To the extent of their present boundaries, the County Borough of Halifax and the Metropolitan Districts of Denholme and Keighley are very nearly contiguous. But as recognisable towns, they are separated across about twelve miles of high moorland. Keighley stands at the confluence of the Rivers Aire and Worth, cradled in a stretch of land situated around North Beck and the River Worth. It is just over ten miles north-west of Bradford, and seventeen miles, in a slightly more westerly direction, from Leeds. Five miles almost due south is Denholme. Once little more than an ecclesiastical parish, then a thriving industrial village, it is now a straggling country town and a dormant commuter haven. To a visitor, perhaps the most striking aspect of the town is the fact that it stands out upon a broad shoulder of moorland which reaches up to Ogden and Thornton Moors. The centre of the town is about 900 feet above sea level, rising to 1,200 feet at Upper Bradshaw Head. Running gently downhill, about six miles further south still, lies Halifax. It is located in the Upper Calder Valley, on an extensive piece of low-lying land broken by Hebble Brook, a tributary of the River Calder. It is eight miles west of Bradford; about fifteen west-south-west from Leeds.

Geography accounts for much in this part of the world. The significance of raw impediment and natural facility is still quite striking in a region of England where fabulous artifice and untamed wild confront each other so starkly. Historically, that geography has accounted for even more. The rise of Halifax as a major commercial centre, long pre-dating its industrial transformation during the second half of the nineteenth century, was a simple consequence of its dominant focus in the local settlement hierarchy.[1] That it ceased to be the major

[1] Dingsdale, 'Yorkshire Mill Town', pp. 18–19.

33

cloth market for the region, ceding pre-eminence to Bradford, was also due more than anything else to the accidents of geography; the result in part of Bradford's physical proximity to Leeds, and in part of the relative ease of Bradford's communications to the south and east.[2] The rapid expansion of Keighley in the 1840s and 1850s was also, to a considerable degree, the result of the remarkable geographical position which it commanded at the corner of the Aire Gap, and through which innumerable canals, railways and roads eventually joined together so many of the industrial towns of Lancashire and Yorkshire.[3] In contrast, geographical isolation ensured that Denholme, despite an early start in textile production, soon ceded superiority to its northern, southern and eastern neighbours.[4]

But urban geography neither was nor is merely a record of timeless physical obstructions or unproblematic natural advantages. It was and is an eloquent expression of social order and social change. Just as economic transformation is only another way of describing social change, so social change is only another way of describing spatial evolution. Historical geography is about all three. And the problems and possibilities of religious organisation in late nineteenth- and early twentieth-century Halifax, Keighley and Denholme cannot be understood in ignorance of local historical geography. To acknowledge so much need not be to fall into the error of reducing the complexities of religious belief and religious devotion to their alleged 'foundations' in the social relations of these practices.[5] Nor is it to plunge into the hopeless banality of insisting that whilst religious beliefs may not be reduced to the sociological circumstances of their origins, nevertheless they must be *related* to the society in which they flourish; a truism which actually explains nothing in the pretence of comprehending everything.[6] On the contrary, to consider religious organisation in the same breath as historical geography is to concede no more than the reasonable hypothesis that religious organisation is about organisation as well as about religion; perhaps also to acknowledge that the possibilities of any organisation may be bound by the economic and social circumstances of the organisers as well as those whom they, in turn, wish to organise.

[2]   H.W. Harwood, *Centenary Story, 1848–1948* (Halifax, 1948), p. 19.
[3]   Harry Bancroft, Asa Briggs and Eric Treacy, *One Hundred Years: The Parish of Keighley, 1848–1948* (Keighley, 1948), p. 9.
[4]   Anon., *Industrial Advantages of Denholme* (London, n.d.), pp. 7–9.
[5]   For an excellent summary of the philosophical issues at stake in the debate about social reductionism and religious belief, see D.Z. Phillips, *Through a Darkening Glass: Philosophy, Literature and Cultural Change* (Oxford, 1982), pp. 7–8; or, for a fuller account, see Phillips, *Religion without Explanation* (Oxford, 1981), *passim*.
[6]   This problem is intelligently discussed in Keith Dixon, *The Sociology of Belief: Fallacy and Foundation* (London, 1980), ch. 4.

Whatever else it is, religious belief is a powerful motive for organisation, and a motive which, characteristically, induces the few to seek to organise the many. It is in the very nature of religious organisation that the justification for that motivation is essentially doctrinal *in the first instance*. That there is any organisation at all is the product, first, of an idea, not of an unreflective pleasure in the joys of organisation for its own sake. But it is also in the nature of religious organisations, *qua* organisations, that the boundaries of their organisational competence are dictated by something more than the definition of their doctrinal imperatives alone.[7] There are, in other words, both what are generally called endogenous and what are invariably referred to as exogenous factors in the patterns of church growth.[8] Endogenous factors include soteriological doctrine, recruitment techniques and church-building programmes. Exogenous factors include industrialisation, urbanisation, war, etc. Exogenous factors define, even if they do not strictly determine, the social constituency to which any motivated organisation may – successfully – appeal in order to secure its membership, affiliation and hearing. They define the nature and the extent of that part of wider society apparently susceptible to conversion and to organised religious commitment at a given time and in a given place. Cloudy metaphysical questions about the causal primacy of endogenous and exogenous factors in the historical patterns of modern English church growth need not concern us here.[9] We need only allow that whilst the determinants of historical geography did not define the nature, or the possibilities of individual belief, devotion and commitment – either in late nineteenth- and early twentieth-century West Yorkshire or anywhere else – they did to a much greater extent constitute a strict limitation upon the nature and the extent of religious organisations in those places: on what those organisations could call upon; on what they could turn to; and on what they could reasonably achieve in a world constituted of mundane things and complex persons rather than gracious gifts and angelic messengers.

---

[7]   This is a major theme, possibly indeed the defining insight, of the sociology of religion. Perhaps the most accessible introduction to it may be found in Bryan R. Wilson, *Magic and the Millennium: A Sociological Study of Religious Movements of Protest among Tribal and Third World Peoples* (London, 1973), ch. 1, esp. pp. 11–30. The classic account remains Ernst Troeltsch, *The Social Teaching of the Christian Churches*, trans. by O. Wynn (New York, 1931).

[8]   See Currie *et al.*, *Churches and Churchgoers*, pp. 96–115.

[9]   For the assertion that exogenous factors *are* primary, see *ibid.*, pp. 96ff. On closer inspection, this argument turns out to be little more than a platitude. See, e.g., p. 98: 'However a church fares, it relies for its growth not only upon an internal constituency, but upon an external constituency over the formation of which it exercises little or no control.' This is true, but scarcely revealing.

Economic revolution: the rise of the worsted industry, the diversification of manufacturers and the rewards of labour

During the nineteenth century, Halifax, Keighley and Denholme were transformed. Unprecedented economic growth in the West Riding of Yorkshire during the fifty years after about 1790 galvanised the local worsted wool trade, turning a small-scale, jobbing enterprise into a modern, factory-based industry. The growth of this industry then induced others, especially engineering and machine-tools, to develop locally in its wake. Finally, a mature and diversified manufacturing economy sprouted numerous tertiary services – especially retailing, and to a lesser extent professional, services – to tend to its sophisticated needs. In this way, an erstwhile commercial backwater of England became, in little more than two generations, one of the principal industrial workshops of the world. No contemporary observer doubted that the region had witnessed something little short of a social and economic miracle in a period little longer than a lifetime. In such a scheme, the influence of the Almighty could not be wholly discounted. Some unashamedly invoked His agency in this respect. Keighley's first business historian, writing in 1879, insisted, after making due allowance for the 'energy and enterprise of [its] merchants and manufacturers', upon singling out 'an open Bible' and 'Protestant Christianity' as the truly efficient causes of his town's (and nation's) historic and continuing prosperity.[10]

Whatever the case, the principal evidence of that wealth during the second half of the nineteenth century was the continuing ubiquity and importance of the worsted trade. Worsted wool was 'king' everywhere in the far western tip of the West Riding of Yorkshire, from Bradford to Todmorden. And three of the crown's principal urban representatives there were Halifax, Keighley and Denholme. Legend had it that the first to engage in the worsted wool business in the area were the Horsfell family, who owned estates in Haworth and Denholme in the seventeenth century. If so, then Denholme may have some claim to be the *fons et origo* of the worsted trade.[11] What is clear is that worsteds began to take root in the neighbourhoods of Halifax and Keighley sometime in the early eighteenth century. It was a geographically concentrated industry, much more so than woollen textiles. Its organisational framework was also quite different from the older trade. Whereas wool had many

[10] John Hodgson, *Textile Manufacture and Other Industries in Keighley* (Keighley, 1879), p. 9.
[11] *Ibid.*, p. 16.

producers in an overwhelmingly small-scale industry, the 'small, independent clothier' seemingly never existed in the worsted business. Worsteds were dominated by a small number of merchant manufacturers who controlled production by 'putting-out' wool to 'an army of dependent domestic workers who virtually formed a rural, industrial proletariat'.[12] This was partly the product of historical accident; that is, of the emergence of a newer industry superimposed on an older form. It was also partly the outcome of technological differences between the two trades; worsteds employed a long, stapled wool which was more expensive and less readily available than the traditional type. Finally, it was the result of political preference; the various Worsted Acts from 1770 decisively biased productive relations in favour of the merchant-manufacturer over the producer-labourer.[13]

During the next half-century, each of these characteristic features of the industry became still more pronounced. The geographical concentration of the industry was further intensified, effectively limiting it to a small number of urban centres. Of these, the greatest, from about the accession of Queen Victoria onwards, was Bradford.[14] But Halifax and Keighley remained notable local powerhouses.[15] There, as elsewhere in the industry, a local business aristocracy emerged during the early nineteenth century. John Crossley and Sons began to manufacture carpets in the Hebble Valley district of Halifax in 1803.[16] Jonathan Akroyd built a worsted mill at Bowling Dyke, in the same valley, in 1818. His brother, James, purchased a weaving shed on Haley Hill in 1836, bringing his sons, Henry and Edward, into the business soon afterwards.[17] The Craven and Brigg families, first yeomen farmers at

[12] P. Hudson, 'Proto-Industrialisation: The Case of the West Riding Wool Textile Industry in the Eighteenth and Early-Nineteenth Centuries', *History Workshop* 12 (1981), pp. 34–61; H. Heaton, *The Yorkshire Woollen and Worsted Industries* (Oxford, 1965), p. 297.

[13] Tony Jowett, 'The Retardation of Trade Unionism in the Yorkshire Worsted Textile Industry', in J.A. Jowett and A.J. McIvor (eds.), *Employers and Labour in the English Textile Industries, 1850–1939* (London, 1988), pp. 84–106, at p. 86.

[14] On which, see Koditschek, *Class Formation and Urban Industrial Society*, chs. 2 and 3.

[15] See H.W. Harwood, *Centenary Story*, p. 38: 'The late Sir Henry Whitehead, of Bradford, said a few years ago that Halifax was now spinning one-seventh of the world's worsted yarns.' Or J.M. Brendan, 'John Mackintosh', in J.J. Mulroy (ed.), *The Story of the Town That Bred Us: Halifax, 1848–1948* (Halifax, 1948), p. 70: 'Halifax ... has the largest carpet factories in the world.' On worsteds in Keighley, see William Keighley, *Keighley, Past and Present, or an Historical, Topographical and Statistical Sketch of the Town, Parish and Environs of Keighley* (Keighley, 1879), pp. 115ff.; and for a modern account, see Ian Dewhirst, *A History of Keighley* (Keighley, 1974), pp. 10–11 and 92–3. On the growth of early nineteenth-century Bradford, see Koditschek, *Class Formation and Urban Industrial Society*, chs. 2 and 3.

[16] Dingsdale, 'Yorkshire Mill Town', p. 32.

[17] Harwood, *Centenary Story*, p. 38. On the Crossleys more generally, see Various

Laycock, then cotton traders and partners in the first decade of the nineteenth century, shifted their businesses to (separate) worsted mills in Keighley, in 1822.[18] The Cloughs purchased their first worsted mill, also in Keighley, during the same year.[19] John Butterfield bought his first factory in 1833.[20] The Foster brothers purchased the site for what became known as Denholme Mills in 1838.[21] These families, *in situ* and in business by 1840 at the very latest, dominated the social and political landscape of their respective towns for the rest of the century and beyond.

Of course, neither the presence of small-scale industry nor the ambitions of a few industrialists were synonymous with the process of industrialisation. That was brought about, above all, by the introduction of the power loom into the manufacturing process. James Akroyd was the first to do so in Halifax, this in 1822.[22] Nine years later, William Lund obtained two power looms from Halifax and set them up in his business in Keighley.[23] The Cravens began to use power looms in their factories in 1834.[24] So too the Briggs.[25] Robert Clough followed suit two years later.[26] Francis Crossley extended the technology to carpet weaving in 1850.[27] By mid-century, power-loom technology was common to worsted manufacture in all three towns.[28] This was of enormous significance. The power loom transformed a domestic hand trade into a mechanised factory-industry. It did so in two ways: through technical advance, particularly through the dissemination of those forms of technical progress which rendered previously human processes mechanical, notably combing and weaving (and which, incidentally, made redundant the concomitant human, and especially male-domi-nated, skills);[29] and, more importantly still, through organisational

Writers, *Fortunes Made in Business*, vol. III (London, 1887), pp. 253–312; and R. Bretton, 'Crossleys of Dean Clough', *THAS*, 47 (1950), 1–9; 48 (1950), 71–83; 49 (1952), 49–58; 50 (1953), 1–20, 87–102; 51 (1954), 11–28. On the Akroyds, see Bretton, 'Colonel Edward Akroyd', *THAS*, 45 (1948), 61–100.

[18] Hodgson, *Textile Manufacture*, p. 41.

[19] *Ibid.*, p. 65.

[20] *Ibid.*, p. 104.

[21] Anon., *Industrial Advantages of Denholme*, p. 9.

[22] J.S. Fletcher, *The Story of English Towns: Halifax* (London, 1923), pp. 100–1.

[23] Hodgson, *Textile Manufacture*, p. 58. On the sluggishness of mechanisation in the West Riding worsted industries, see Joyce, *Work, Society and Politics*, pp. 73–4; and Hudson, *Genesis of Industrial Capital*, pp. 42–5.

[24] Hodgson, *Textile Manufacture*, p. 30.

[25] *Ibid.*, p. 42.

[26] *Ibid.*, p. 66.

[27] Various, *Fortunes Made in Business*, vol. III, pp. 269, 270.

[28] For a general account, see Pat Hudson, *The Genesis of Industrial Capital: A Study of the West Riding Wool Textile Industry* (Cambridge, 1988), pp. 43ff.

[29] Jowett, 'The Retardation of Trade Unionism', pp. 86–7.

advance, specifically in the physical concentration of a once domestically scattered labour force into larger workshops, or factories.

The factory system developed most rapidly in this part of West Yorkshire during the years between 1855 and 1865. At mid-century, there were 24 mills in Halifax. Their number more than doubled between 1855 and 1865; 32 additional factory units were built or converted in that time.[30] Progress in Keighley followed a similar pattern. The pioneers set out in the 1820s and the early 1830s. By 1858 there were about 30 worsted mills in the parish.[31] The Foster brothers built their first factory in Denholme during 1838–9. It blew down in a storm the following year. They rebuilt it immediately, enlarged it in 1857, and then again towards the end of the century when, after much investment of both time and money, it became recognisable as 'Denholme Mills', one of the most impressive factory complexes in late-Victorian West Yorkshire.[32]

The proliferation of the factory system in worsted manufacture not only transformed the organisation of labour. It was crucial to the development of the modern business enterprise in later Victorian West Yorkshire. First, it enabled it to grow in size. Early nineteenth-century textile firms in the region were generally very small, employing dozens rather than hundreds of hands. As late as 1851, only the two giant local businesses in Halifax, Akroyd and Son, and Crossley and Sons, in addition to seven other local firms, employed more than 100 workers. Just ten years later, some 30 firms in the same town gave work to more than 100 employees. And some of the big firms became very big. For instance, the Crossleys, who as late as 1837 had employed only 350 workers, increased their labour force by a factor of ten during the next twenty-five years.[33] This 'at a bound' transformed their position from one of 'moderate success' to almost 'unlimited prosperity'.[34] As firms increased in size, so the industry became increasingly concentrated. By 1871, over one-third of the local textile labour force was employed in factory units of more than 100 hands; nearly one-half in workshops of 50 or more. At the turn of the century, a dozen leading firms accounted for about 40 per cent of textile employees in the town.[35] Concentration was slightly less marked, but still important, in Keighley. In 1871, consider-

[30] Dingsdale, 'Yorkshire Mill Town', p. 33.
[31] Keighley, *History of Keighley*, p. 119.
[32] Anon., *Industrial Advantages of Denholme*, pp. 20–1.
[33] J.A. Jowett, 'Copley, Akroyd and West Hill Park: Moral Reform and Social Improvement in Halifax', in Jowett (ed.), *Model Industrial Communities in Mid-Nineteenth Century Yorkshire* (Bradford, 1986), ch. 3, at p. 74.
[34] Various, *Fortunes Made in Business*, vol. III, p. 273.
[35] Dingsdale, 'Yorkshire Mill Town', p. 33; Joyce, *Work, Society and Politics*, p. 160.

ably fewer than one-third of all textile workers in that town was employed in factories of more than 100 hands.[36] And Keighley had its giants too. The Craven family business gave work to more than 2,000 persons in their various enterprises at Walk Mill, Low Mill and Dalton Mill during the 1870s.[37] At much the same time, the Lund family of North Beck Mill employed over 1,000 workers in their own factory.[38] In Denholme, by contrast, numerical concentration was achieved most swiftly and most completely. By the end of the second third of the nineteenth century at the latest, two factories accounted for nearly one-half of the textile working population in the village.[39]

Growth and concentration, in turn, permitted the vertical integration of productive processes which the factory system made possible. Most early nineteenth-century firms, even those working from the early mills, had been not only small, but specialised, undertaking only one part of the highly complicated processes of worsted manufacturing, and 'putting-out' the rest of the work for others to complete.[40] Growth and concentration *within* the factory system reversed this otherwise disintegrative tendency within the industry. In addition to its organisational dynamic, permitting a scale and complexity of manufacture hitherto undreamt of, it was also crucial for the introduction of new techniques, notably of steam-powered manufacture, into the industry.[41] John Baldwin, first Mayor of Halifax in 1848, was also the first to introduce steam-power into a local factory; this at J. and J. Baldwin Ltd in 1830.[42] Its use was universalised during the next thirty years.

The triumph of steam probably gave Halifax, blessed with local coal resources, something of an advantage over Keighley. The businessmen of Keighley certainly thought so. 'Whilst water continued to be the principle [*sic*] element of power, Keighley appears to have taken the lead, but in consequence of Bradford and Halifax being better situated for coal, Keighley was left in the rear,' wrote one. Yet it did not fall too

36 PRO, RG 10. 4315–21, Census of England and Wales, 1871, unpub. enum. MSS for the Local Board District and 'township' of Keighley. The figure was 1,557 of 5,505. NB. All figures for the 1871 Census are based upon the author's own calculations from the evidence of the enum. MSS, unless otherwise stated.
37 Hodgson, *Textile Manufacture*, p. 31.
38 *Ibid.*, p. 63.
39 PRO, RG 10. 4390–1, Census of England and Wales, 1871, unpub. enum. MSS for the Local Board District of Denholme. The figure was 567 out of 1,250.
40 Dingsdale, 'Yorkshire Mill Town', p. 33; Joyce, *Work, Society and Politics*, pp. 74–5; Hudson, *Genesis of Industrial Capital*, p. 45.
41 Joyce, *Work, Society and Politics*, pp. xiii and 53–8; Hudson, *Genesis of Industrial Capital*, pp. 13–14, 45. On the wider issue of the factory system and work discipline, see Sidney Pollard, *The Genesis of Modern Management: A Study of the Industrial Revolution in Great Britain* (London, 1965), pp. 71ff.
42 Harwood, *Centenary Story*, p. 37.

far behind up to the end of the nineteenth century. '[T]his town', declared John Hodgson, 'still maintains its rank as the third manufacturing town in the worsted trade.' William Keighley concurred: 'This town still maintains its rank as the head of the third division of the Yorkshire Worsted District.'[43] The surviving evidence supports their views. As late as 1879, perhaps one-tenth of the mills, one-eighth of the spindles, and one-twelfth of the looms employed in the worsted trade throughout the United Kingdom were accounted for in the seventy mills owned and managed in and around Keighley by Messrs J. and J. Craven, B. and W. Marriner, John Brigg, and William Lund and Sons together.[44]

That was, perhaps, its high point, if not nationally then certainly internationally. For the relative decline of Keighley's textile trade in relation to that of Halifax and, to a greater extent, Bradford, mattered little during the era of general boom in the British, and specifically West Riding, industry which marked the decades from about 1840 to around 1870.[45] Moreover, the years of the Franco-German war actually witnessed a growth in the local trade and an 'enlargement of [local] plant' which was generally believed to be 'unexampled'.[46] But the bubble burst in the 1870s. Peace, tariffs and changes in ladies' fashions together conspired to shift the balance of international manufacturing power away from the West Riding trade (Bradford and Halifax included) towards its emerging German, American and French rivals. Above all, changing fashions, and especially from France, 'mistress of the fashions'.[47] Stiff, mixed, long-standing fibres gave way to soft, pure dress fabrics notably in the critical sector of women's clothing. These required a different manufacturing process and a quite novel organisation of the industry. They would have required West Riding manufacturers to import French combing and drawing machinery, and to replace the cap and frame trestle by the mule in spinning procedures. Some, like Swire Smith, urged Keighley's worsted manufacturers to do just that.[48] Few took up the challenge. Some put their faith in the Countess of Bective's bizarre public crusade for 'home patronage [of] home products', probably the first recorded example of a national 'Buy British'

---

43 Hodgson, *Textile Manufacture*, pp. 240–1. See also Keighley, *History of Keighley*, pp. 118–19. On water- and steam-power, and the worsted industry, see Hudson, *Genesis of Industrial Capital*, pp. 42–3.
44 Dewhirst, *A History of Keighley*, p. 92.
45 Jowett, 'The Retardation of Trade Unionism', p. 94.
46 Keighley Snowdon, *The Master Spinner: A Life of Sir Swire Smith Ll.D., MP* (London, 1921), p. 73.
47 *Ibid.*, p. 129.   48 *Ibid.*, p. 143.

campaign.[49] More realistic, if defeatist, souls turned to new products, notably men's suiting and overcoats, to new markets, especially the empire; and, significantly, to a newly subordinate state, supplying foreign, and especially French, manufacturers with semi-manufactured goods.[50]

Whatever its exact position in national and international worsted manufacturing leagues during the last quarter of the nineteenth century, Keighley remained an important centre of British manufacturing industry generally, at least until the outbreak of the First World War. To a great extent, its survival in this respect was a product of the capacity of its economy to diversify. This occurred fairly quickly. As early as 1879, Hodgson believed Keighley was 'second to none of the same size, for its extensive machine making establishment', adding that 'the greatest part of worsted spinning machinery is made in this town, besides a large quantity of power looms'.[51] William Keighley corroborated this view wholeheartedly. The town, he declared, was notable for 'the making of woolcombing machines, spinning and weaving machinery, slays, and healds [also] for the manufacture of rollers, spindles, flyers and other materials used in spinning, and the making of machinery'.[52] And not just textile machinery either. 'The iron trade, during the last twenty years,' wrote Hodgson, 'has made rapid strides in Keighley in a new direction, such as the making of washing and sewing machines. [B]esides there are several extensive firms which are engaged in making very costly machine engine tools, which are exported to all parts of the world.'[53]

This was more than well-meaning hyperbole. The economy of Keighley did diversify, and markedly, during the 1870s and 1880s. So much so that by the turn of the century the biggest business, and the 'really big employer' in the town, was not a worsted firm at all but the textile-machinery business of Prince Smith.[54] Diversification, both of textile output itself and amongst many different industrial manufacturers, preserved the prosperity of Keighley, certainly for another generation. But a price was paid at least indirectly, for the diversification of the local economy, both between sectors and within the worsted sector itself, was not only a positive response to change. It was also a reflection of the fact that the large mills were most affected by the changing trading situation in the late Victorian economy.[55] And it often

49 Various, *Fortunes Made in Business*, vol. III, p. 49.
50 Jowett, 'The Retardation of Trade Unionism', pp. 94–5.
51 Hodgson, *Textile Manufacture*, p. 241.
52 Keighley, *History of Keighley*, p. 119.
53 Hodgson, *Textile Manufacture*, p. 241.
54 Briggs, 'Plus Ça Change', p. 432.
55 For a case study from the Bradford area, with implications similar and significant for

resulted in the splitting up of previously integrated units, the increased use of specialist 'commission' firms to perform specific tasks, and the growth of a more uncompromisingly competitive environment in which survival was as much a product of an 'essential and continuing logic' towards 'cheapen[ing] the cost of its labour' as of increasing the market penetration of its product.[56] The overall effect was a local economy characterised more by sickly growth than diverse health: at once and paradoxically structurally mature but also organisationally precarious.[57]

Something similar, if rather less drastic, also occurred in Halifax. In fact industrial diversification was, if anything, more marked still in Halifax. There, textiles quickly brought other industries in their wake, many long before the troubles of the 1870s. First came the building trade; then machine-tools and engineering; finally, albeit indirectly, confectionery and other specialist trades. In one sense, of course, the economy of Halifax had always been diverse. For the local textile trade was, itself, highly variegated. While the Crossleys made carpets, the Holdworths made damask, repp and tapestry. Cotton was spun and doubled by William Harrison and Company after 1850, S. Whitley and Son (specialising in Egyptian cotton after 1860), and Bowman Brothers from 1864. Silk was manufactured at Wellington Mill, founded by Lemuel Clayton. The growth of the textile industry in turn stimulated allied trades such as carding and wire-drawing. And it is highly probable that engineering, which by the early twentieth century was second in importance only to textiles, first developed as a direct response to the needs of spinners and weavers for repair and maintenance services.[58] At any rate, industrial diversity proceeded at an impressive rate locally after 1860. The engineering and machine-tool firm of William Asquith was founded at Highroad Well in 1865. A year later, John Stirk began similar works at Ovenden. James Butler (1879), George Snipe (1880) and Frederick Town (1898) followed soon after. Engineering, like textiles, was inherently diverse. Gas-construction engineering began in Halifax as early as 1847; boiler-making and heating-apparatus engineering after 1858; wood-working machinery from 1875.[59]

Further variety was added to the manufacturing base of Halifax's economy by the growth of the confectionery trade at the end of the nineteenth century. The famous Mackintosh firm was established there

Keighley (and Halifax), see E.M. Sigsworth, *Black Dyke Mills: A History* (Liverpool, 1958), esp. pp. 118–24.
[56] Jowett, 'The Retardation of Trade Unionism', p. 94.
[57] *Ibid.*, pp. 94–6; see also Joyce, *Work, Society and Politics*, pp. 74–5.
[58] Harwood, *Centenary Story*, pp. 39–40.
[59] *Ibid.*, p. 39; J.M. Brendan, 'Evolution of the Machine Tool Trade', in Mulroy (ed.), *Town That Bred Us*, p. 39.

in 1890; the firm of Riley Brothers a little later. John Whittaker introduced biscuit-making on a major scale to the town around the turn of the twentieth century.[60] Diversification on this scale and to this degree created, for good or ill, a virtually self-sufficient local economy in the early twentieth century. It also stimulated the growth of a highly sophisticated local retail trade, which transformed an ancient market town into a modern commercial centre. By the outbreak of the Second World War, 3,670 shops and small workshops complemented 1,114 workshops and factories in what had become the principal trading, as well as manufacturing, centre of the extreme western tip of the West Riding conurbation. Put another way, it had become a place where, as its local historian claimed with justifiable pride, '[w]hatever it is, Halifax can make it and can sell it'.[61]

Variety was, however, a quality which the economy of Denholme signally lacked. Its industrial base did not diversify in the later Victorian decades. Indeed, no new industries were attracted to this isolated hamlet throughout the whole of the nineteenth century. Those which remained in 1900 were more the relics of social inertia than the products of economic innovation. Farming, like mining, pre-dated the textile industry. Unlike mining, it also survived the transformation of the town.[62] Brewing remained an important industry under the aegis of the Knowles family at Denholme Gate. But the main local industry, worsted manufacture, was increasingly dominated by one factory, Denholme Mills, owned by one family, the Fosters. This was especially true after about 1860 when the Knowles' connection with the town effectively died away. The firm of Foster and Sons became a private limited company in 1890. This was in some ways an ironic transformation of its legal status, for it had long been, albeit unofficially, something of a public institution, perhaps indeed *the* public institution, in the town.[63] There it had become a perfect example of the paternalistic enterprise in the 'semi-rural industrial colony' which survived in the West Riding worsted industry throughout the nineteenth and much of the twentieth centuries.[64]

---

[60]   Harwood, *Centenary Story*, p. 39; J.M. Brendan, 'John Mackintosh', in Mulroy (ed.), *Town That Bred Us*, p. 70, described Mackintosh's as the 'largest toffee factory in the world', in 1948. George W. Crutchley, *John Mackintosh: A Biography* (London, 1921), pp. 131–43, provides a full account.

[61]   Harwood, *Centenary Story*, p. 40.

[62]   PRO, RG 10. 4490–1, Census of England and Wales, 1871, unpub. enum. MSS, Denholme, lists 59 'farmers'.

[63]   On the Foster family, see Anon., *Industrial Advantages of Denholme*, pp. 20–1.

[64]   Joyce, *Work, Society and Politics*, p. 74. For another, local, example, see Various, *Fortunes Made in Business*, vol. II (London, 1884), pp. 1–56, on the Fosters of Queensbury.

That it survived at all, however, points to the essential crudity of economic development in this part of West Yorkshire. Indeed, for all the glamour of Crossley Carpets, Mackintosh's Toffee and the Halifax Building Society, the final – or at least the early twentieth-century – form of that development was relatively primitive. By comparison with the cotton industry in East Lancashire, West Yorkshire worsted manufacture had been slow to mechanise. Even in its later, mechanised form, it was less sophisticated and less capital-intensive than the cotton industry to the west.[65] To be sure, large factories and large firms were not unknown in West Riding worsted manufacture. But the small firm survived, especially in Halifax and Keighley. The sheer variety of specialist processes in the worsted trade and, just as importantly, the general unwillingness of local business to change ensured its survival. The industry which had begun the eighteenth century relatively concentrated ironically ended the nineteenth relatively diversified, by ownership and in geographical location. Moreover, many of the other industries which developed in this part of West Yorkshire during the late nineteenth and early twentieth centuries also remained structurally and physically diverse, and generally small-scale. Halifax was not called the 'town of a thousand workshops' for nothing.[66] It remained, despite the Crossleys and the Akroyds, and in a later era Mackintosh, essentially a multivarious and multitudinous workshop town. So too did Keighley, both in its heyday and in its later decline.[67] Similarly Denholme.

That left them increasingly vulnerable. The so-called 'agricultural depression' of West Yorkshire worsteds during the 1870s inevitably, if imperceptibly, took its toll.[68] The 'prohibitive tariffs' of American trade subsequently exacted a further and rather more visible penalty.[69] Slowly, the technologically impoverished and culturally regressive West Riding trade began to decline. The speed of its demise should not be exaggerated. Not until after the First World War did it reach crisis proportions.[70] But from the turn of the twentieth century onwards, it began to have an adverse effect upon other local trades. Then, instead of benefiting from the (relative) decline of textiles, as they had done in the 1880s and 1890s, they began to suffer too, as some of their own most

[65] Joyce, *Work, Society and Politics*, pp. 74–5.
[66] Harwood, *Centenary Story*, p. 39.
[67] No figure has survived for Keighley. But there must have been several hundred workshops within its municipal boundaries in 1882. See Hodgson, *Textile Manufacture*, pp. 174–6; and, in general, Various Writers, *Industries of Yorkshire*, 2 vols. (London, 1890).
[68] Various, *Fortunes Made in Business*, vol. II, p. 48.
[69] *Ibid.*, vol. III, p. 292.
[70] Jowett, 'The Retardation of Trade Unionism', p. 103.

Table 1. *Comparison of weekly wage-rates in the major textile trades of the United Kingdom*

	Cotton	Woollen	Worsted	Linen
Men	25s 3d	23s 2d	23s 4d	13s 9d
Lads and boys	9s 4d	8s 6d	6s 6d	6s 3d
Women	15s 3d	13s 3d	11s 11d	8s 11d
Girls	6s 10d	7s 5d	6s 2d	4s 11d

Source: PP, 1889, LXX, c. 5807, *Return of the Rates of Wages in the Principal Textile Trades of the United Kingdom, with Report Thereon.*

lucrative markets withered. Even local engineering and other machine-tool industries stagnated in the early twentieth century.[71] With that, most tellingly of all, local population began to fall. There was an absolute decrease in Keighley after 1901, and in Halifax after 1911.[72] The figures were not large but they were significant. One of the most important contributing factors was net emigration amongst the young. As a contemporary, lamenting the decline of Halifax just after the First World War, put it, 'The ... town ... offers little scope for young people ... and [so] the population tends to decline.'[73]

Not that life had ever been exactly rosy for the majority. Of course, a very few had made very good. In 1847, Edward Akroyd inherited an estate of £1,750,000 in the family business of James Akroyd and Sons.[74] When Crossley Carpets became a limited liability company in 1864, it was worth £1,165,000. And it was soon valued at a good deal more.[75] But these were exceptions, giants of local business which 'probably contributed more than all the other local enterprises combined to make Halifax the prosperous town' it became during the second third of the nineteenth century. Not until the rise of Mackintosh was there anyone, locally, to match them.[76] Common wisdom had it that a few more great 'personal fortunes', both in worsted textiles and machine tools, had been amassed in Keighley, especially during the 1870s.[77] And many others in the professions did well enough, both before and after the mid-Victorian boom. But for most of the rest of the population, the rise of a supposedly

[71] *Ibid.*, p. 93; J.H. Waddington, 'Changes, 1866–1937', in Waddington, *Essays and Addresses* (Halifax, 1938), p. 26; Dewhirst, *A History of Keighley*, p. 108.
[72] Dingsdale, 'Yorkshire Mill Town', p. 21; Dewhirst, *A History of Keighley*, p. 108.
[73] Christopher Teasdale, *Historical Sketch of Booth Congregational Church, Halifax* (Halifax, 1919), p. 19.
[74] R. Bretton, 'Colonel Edward Akroyd', p. 74.
[75] Bretton, 'Crossleys of Dean Clough', *THAS*, 48 (1951), p. 77.
[76] Various, *Fortunes Made in Business*, vol. III, p. 258.
[77] Snowdon, *The Master Spinner*, p. 73.

Table 2. *Comparative wage-bands of worsted and other workers in the United Kingdom, 1886*

	Wage	Worsted (% of workers)	Average[1] (% of workers)
Men	under 10s	–	0.1
	10–15s	11.9	3.9
	15–20s	24.3	25.7
	20–25s	13.0	30.3
	25–30s	37.6	20.5
	30–35s	12.6	11.4
	35–40s	0.4	4.8
	40s +	0.2	3.3
	Average wage	23s 4d	24s 7d
Lads and boys[2]	'Half-times'	37.2	4.1
	under 10s	54.4	59.8
	10–15s	8.4	30.8
	15–20s	–	5.2
	20–25s	–	0.1
	Average wage	6s 3d	8s 11d
Women	under 10	24.2	47.8
	10–15s	75.0	43.0
	15–20s	0.7	7.7
	20–25s	–	1.4
	25–30s	–	0.1
	Average wage	11s 11d	12s 8d
Girls	'Half-times'	36.9	10.4
	under 10s	63.1	84.7
	10–15s	–	4.7
	15–20s	–	0.2
	Average wage	6s 2d	6s 4d

[1] 'Average' for males was calculated from 38 comparable towns; for females from 27.
[2] 'Lads and boys' and 'Girls' was the customary categorisation as observed in factory life. It was not a fixed definition.
Source: PP, 1893–4, LXXXIII, pt 2, c. 6889, *Classes in the United Kingdom with Tables of the Average Rates of Wages and Hours of Labour and Persons Employed in Several of the Principal Trades in 1886 and 1891.*

modern, mechanised worsted industry provided only a very meagre livelihood; meagre by contemporary standards, meagre even by local contemporary standards. This was because the worsted industry paid badly. A Wage Census of 1886 proved that it was one of the poorest paying of the major textile industries (see table 1). And a later report compared it unfavourably with national average wages for all manual workers (see table 2).

Moreover, the susceptibility of the trade to fluctuations of season and flushes of fashion, to variations in the cost of raw materials, and finally to vagaries in the impact of foreign tariffs, ensured that weekly wage-rates seldom accurately reflected the real annual income of worsted employees, for much of their work was, in effect, casual labour. Weavers were generally hired by the piece. In periods of bad trade, they were often kept waiting for the next piece to arrive. The Census of 1886 concluded that they lost at least 10 per cent of their income through 'broken time' caused in this way.[78] Woolcombers, similarly, reported for work each day (or evening). Yet they rarely worked more than four days (or night-shifts) per week. And in years such as 1880, they lost up to twenty weeks' wages per year for want of regular employment.[79] For all these reasons, the 1886 Census calculated an average adult male income of £26 per head in the worsted trade. On that basis, Halifax at £24 per head was below the national average.[80] Keighley, at £29 per head, was slightly above it.[81]

Wages in Halifax were low not only within the worsted trade but across the range of all the major textile trades. Its cotton workers, for instance, earned £36 in 1886; those in Burnley £42; in Preston £40; even in Oldham £38.[82] Its wool workers earned slightly more, at £38 per head, but that figure compared unfavourably with similar labourers in Dewsbury, or indeed those in neighbouring Huddersfield, who were paid £39.[83] What was true for workers generally was particularly true for female workers. This was especially so in the West Riding worsted trades. There, women were paid less than men, somewhere between one-third and one-half of the wages of men.[84] Why? Certainly, the most responsible jobs in the worsted industry, above all that of onlooker, were reserved exclusively for men.[85] Similarly, 'heavy' jobs such as the more burdensome forms of weaving were generally retained as male strongholds, and better paying ones at that.[86] Finally, structural change within the industry itself seems to have counted against the higher rewards of female skills. This was unquestionably one of the consequences of vertical disintegration, and of the rise of so-called commission firms, after about 1880. They paid hourly rates for specific tasks such as mending, an exclusively female skill. And these were invariably low.[87]

---

[78] Jowett, 'The Retardation of Trade Unionism', p. 98.
[79] Joyce, *Work, Society and Politics*, p. 74.
[80] PP, 1889, LXX, *Return of the Rates of Wages*, pp. xviii, xix.
[81] *Ibid.*, p. xxxi.   [82] *Ibid.*, p. viii.   [83] *Ibid.*, p. xiii.
[84] Deirdre Busfield, 'Skill and the Sexual Division of Labour in the West Riding Textile Industry, 1850–1914', in Jowett and McIvor (eds.), *Employers and Labour*, pp. 153–70, at p. 153.
[85] *Ibid.*, p. 154.   [86] *Ibid.*, p. 155.   [87] *Ibid.*, p. 156.

Nevertheless, it is difficult to avoid the conclusion that whilst the processes of mechanisation and concentration increasingly turned the textile trade into a sexually divided industry – in which loosely speaking, men dominated the initial and finishing processes (sorting, winnowing, felting, scouring, milling, raising the nap, shearing, pressing and packing) and women performed the intermediate functions (spinning, doubling, hanking and warping) – the effective causes of that division were actually more closely related to the force of surviving custom, and the impact of contingent negotiation, than to the ineradicable imperative of sexually differentiated skills, or even to the logic of profit maximisation.[88] This conclusion is reinforced by the simple fact that women eventually did undertake most of the tasks previously barred to them during the First World War, under a series of emergency trade agreements which came into force in 1916. Then, and only then, they were also paid men's rates for men's work, or (by agreement) four-fifths of that rate if they proved incapable of matching masculine productivity. During this period women's average earnings in the industry rose to 36s 6d, compared with men's average of 56s. If that was scarcely parity, it was something much closer to equality than women had experienced in living memory.[89]

Yet if it was ingrained social habit rather than strict manufacturing imperatives which kept much of the structure of local wage-rates so rigid and so differentiated, it was market forces, in the shape of inexorable international competition after 1880, which squeezed wages generally and which kept the conditions of labour poor; indeed, which made them in many cases worse. That pressure was rarely direct. For the most part, it was the product of changes in the organisation of production during the last quarter of the nineteenth century. These, at one level, shifted an increasing proportion of workers away from weaving and towards spinning and combing. At another level, they sped the dynamic towards the substitution of unskilled for skilled, female for male, juvenile for adult, labour. Consider the example of spinning. Juveniles made up a disproportionately large number of worsted spinners. That continued to be true even after 1870. This was because local by-laws enabled children to go on working as half-timers well into the twentieth century, thereby avoiding much of the spirit, if not the letter, of the Education Act.[90] And their wages were pitiful. As late as 1906, lads and boys working in the

[88] *Ibid.*, p. 154.
[89] PP, 1919, XXXI, c. 135, *Report of the War Cabinet Committee on Women in Industry*, p. 131.
[90] David Howell, *British Workers and the Independent Labour Party, 1888–1906* (Manchester, 1983), p. 185.

textile trade were paid an average of 15s 2d per week for full-time work, and 3s 8d per week for half-time; girls 9s 3d, and 3s 8d.[91]

Or take the case of woolcombing. This trade was not, for the most part, feminised or converted into a juvenile speciality. But the conditions of combing labour worsened markedly under the structural and mechanical changes of the 1880s. After that time, it was common for night-shift workers to labour from 5.15 p.m. to 6 a.m. the following morning without a proper meal break. During those hours, they invariably put up with temperatures of up to 100°F. For this they were paid about 20s per week in 1880; closer to 10s per week in 1890.[92] And if they experienced most hardship, all textile workers suffered a noticeable deterioration in their conditions of work after 1880. This was because what investigators called 'improved ... machinery' not only exaggerated the general impetus to shift the skill, sex and age basis of labour, but also provoked repeated attempts to increase the speed of machinery, to increase the number of machines operated by each worker, and generally to 'increase [their] output' and the productivity of the labour force.[93] These attempts were generally successful. Coupled with low levels of real technological innovation, and steady raw material costs, they enabled short-term profits to rise during the 1890s.[94]

To compound matters further, wages did not rise with prices during the 1890s. Indeed, there is some evidence that they actually fell at this time.[95] Even when they did grow, during the first decade of the twentieth century, they did so much less slowly than in other, comparable, industries (see table 3). Moreover, if worsteds lagged behind most other textiles, Halifax and Keighley lagged behind most other worsted towns (see table 4).

Thus it was that, in their 'poverty, insecur[ity] and miser[y]', the later Victorian Yorkshire worsted workers reminded the German social investigator, von Schultz-Gaevernite, of 'Lancashire [cotton workers] fifty years [earlier]'.[96] Yet it would be wrong to suggest that such insecurity and misery in this part of England were limited to worsted workers. It seems to have been the common experience of the working classes of late nineteenth-century Halifax, Keighley and Denholme.

[91] PP, 1909, LXXX, c. 4545, *Report of an Inquiry by the Board of Trade into the Earnings and Hours of Labour of Workpeople in the United Kingdom*, pp. xvi, xvii.
[92] Jowett, 'The Retardation of Trade Unionism', p. 95; Joyce, *Work, Society and Politics*, p. 74.
[93] PP, 1909, *Report of an Inquiry by the Board of Trade*, p. xix; also fn. 3, p. 52.
[94] Jowett, 'The Retardation of Trade Unionism', p. 97.
[95] Laybourn, 'The Attitudes of Yorkshire Trade Unions', ch. 9; Joyce, *Work, Society and Politics*, pp. 77–9.
[96] G. von Schultz-Gaevernite, *Social Peace: A Study of the Trade Union Movement in England* (London, 1893), p. 192.

Table 3. *Changing earnings in the textile trades of the United Kingdom, 1886–1906*

	Men			Women		
	1886	1906	% increase in income	1886	1906	% increase in income
Cotton	23s 7d	8s 10d	22	15s	11s 8d	24
Wool and worsted	24s 3d	26s 10d	15	12s 7d	13s 10d	10
General textiles	22s 11d	27s 7d	20	12s 9d	15s 7d	22

Source: PP., 1909, LXXX, *Report of an Inquiry by the Board of Trade*, pp. xxi.

Table 4. *Wool and worsted earnings in the United Kingdom and comparative regions in 1906*

	Men	Lads and boys		Women	Girls		All
		Full-time	Half-time		Full-time	Half-time	
United Kingdom	26s 10d	10s 2d	3s 8d	13s 10d	9s 3d	3s 8d	15s 9d
West Riding of Yorkshire	27s 3d	10s 3d	3s 8d	13s 10d	9s 6d	3s 8d	15s 9d
Halifax	26s	9s 7d	3s 2d	12s 4d	9s	3s 3d	13s
Keighley	26s 2d	10s 3d	3s 10d	13s 6d	10s 2d	4s 1d	14s

Source: PP, 1909, LXXX, *Report of an Inquiry by the Board of Trade*, p. xli.

Certainly, it was normal for a local family to be maintained in food and clothing only through the paid labour of both partners and, where applicable, their children.[97] And this was not just a matter of capitalist expropriation. For instance, a cab driver working for Halifax Corporation earned around 25 shillings per week at this time, his hours a little longer, if his conditions much easier, than a worsted worker.[98] But the poverty of the local population was increasingly attributed to the structure of social relations during the early years of the twentieth century. And not only by visiting intellectuals. That had an increasingly profound impact on how those relations were perceived at the time.

Social transformation: demographic explosion, structural change and the rise of a class society

It all began with something very much more simple. The most dramatic and most far-reaching form of social change in nineteenth-century West

[97] Howell, *British Workers*, pp. 183–6.
[98] Waddington, 'Changes, 1866–1937', p. 25.

Yorkshire was a demographic explosion. The population of Halifax in 1801 was 8,886. It more than doubled, to 19,768 over the next forty years; it almost doubled again, to 37,014, in the twenty years between 1841 and 1861; and then very nearly one more time, to 65,510, in just one decade to 1871. Thereafter it grew steadily, if unspectacularly, to reach a natural high mark of 104,936 in 1901.[99] The pattern of growth in Keighley during the corresponding period was almost exactly similar. Beginning at a base of 5,745 in 1801, the population of the town more than doubled in the forty years to 1841; and almost doubled again during the next twenty years. Then it expanded by about one-third between 1861 and 1871, and by about another one-third between 1871 and 1881. Thereafter, measurable local increases owed as much to the reorganisation of administrative boundaries as to natural demographic pressures. The figure for 1901, at 41,564, represented something of a peak.[100] The growth of Denholme can be described more simply. At the formation of the Ecclesiastical Parish of Denholme in 1846, it was an industrial village of little more than 1,000 persons. The population of the town rose to 3,469 by 1871. Fifty years later, it had fallen slightly, to 2,938. It would be an exaggeration, but a pardonable exaggeration, to conclude that the last figure represented little more than the sum total of the labour force of one mill, Denholme Mill, and the dependent families of mill workers there, plus attendant retail and other services. There was not much else to be accounted for.[101]

The mid-nineteenth-century population explosion in these towns

[99] See Dingsdale, 'Yorkshire Mill Town', p. 21. The figures for 1801 and 1841 are for the Township of Halifax; those for 1861 and 1871 are for the Municipal Borough; that for 1901 for the County Borough. Each represented different geographical areas and administrative units. Halifax became an incorporated Municipal Borough in 1848 and a County Borough in 1888. Further additions were made to the physical and geographical extent of the County Borough in 1892 and 1899, and again in 1902. For a comparative perspective, see C.M. Law, 'The Growth of Urban Population in England and Wales, 1801–1911', Transactions of the Institute of British Geography, 41 (1967), 125–43. On the crucial significance of demography in nineteenth-century urban social change, see J.A. Banks, 'Population Change and the Victorian City', Victorian Studies, 11 (1968), 277–89.

[100] The figure in 1841 was 13,378; in 1861, 21,859; in 1871, 28,059; in 1881, 33,540. The figures for Keighley between 1801 and 1881 are for the Local Board District and the township which were, effectively, coterminous. Keighley became a Municipal Borough in 1882. The rise in population from 36,176 in 1891 to 41,564 in 1901 was due largely to a boundary extension in 1895 which brought Ingrow, Hainsworth, Exley Head and Utley into the borough of Keighley. See Dewhirst, A History of Keighley, pp. 49, 79 and 108.

[101] The figure quoted is for the Local Board District of Denholme. It was coterminous with the Ecclesiastical District (of Bradford). See Census of England and Wales, 1921: Yorkshire (London, HMSO, 1923), p. 28.

Table 5. *Population of Halifax, Keighley, and Denholme in 1871: regional and ethnic origins*

	Halifax	Keighley	Denholme
Total population	65,510	20,242	3,469
Indigenous birth	35,142	10,814	2,088
Migration within 30-mile radius	18,013	5,593	1,169
Migration beyond 30-mile radius	12,355	3,835	212
o/w Irish immigrants	2,620	1,203	–

Source: PRO, RG10, 4388–4402, 4315–21, 4490–1, unpub. enum. MSS, for Halifax MB., Keighley LBD and Denholme LBD (author's calculations).

owed relatively little to immigration. Indeed, by 1871, following three decades of continuous and unprecedented growth, more than half the population of the townships of Halifax and Keighley, and nearly two-thirds of that of Denholme, could boast indigenous birth. A further one-third, in each case, was drawn from other, mainly smaller, centres of population within a 30-mile radius of each town. The remainder had migrated from Ireland, Lancashire, other parts of Yorkshire, and from the rest of England. The Irish constituted the only significant ethnic minority group in any of these towns; in 1871, the Irish community constituted about 4 per cent of the population of Halifax township and 6 per cent in Keighley (see table 5).

In other words, demographic growth in the 1850s and 1860s was a natural growth, a natural response to local economic opportunities. Contemporaries were aware of this. They attributed the population explosion of the 1860s in Keighley to 'the expansion of works connected with the iron, worsted and other trades'; and in Halifax to 'the erection of many new mills and ... the extension of worsteds and other manufactures.'[102] They were less immediately aware of its consequences, but these were of profound significance.

The most important of these consequences, and the most striking feature of the age distribution of the population of these towns in 1871, was the predominance of youth. One-third of those alive in each town or township was aged under 15; four-fifths under 45; and less than one-twentieth over 65 (see table 6).[103]

True, there was nothing especially remarkable about these figures by

[102] *Census of England and Wales, 1871: Population Tables Area, Houses and Inhabitants*, vol. II: *Registration of Union Counties* (London, HMSO, 1872), pp. 436 and 438.
[103] For some of the implications, see ch. 5 below, *passim*.

Table 6. *Population of Halifax, Keighley, and Denholme in 1871: age structure*

	Halifax	Keighley	Denholme
Total population	65,510	20,242	3,469
Aged under 15	21,615	6,761	1,242
Aged 15–44	31,440	9,736	1,623
Aged 45–64	10,162	2,815	502
Aged 65+	2,293	930	102

Source: PRO, RG10, 4388–4402, 4315–21, 4490–1, unpub. enum. MSS, for Halifax MB., Keighley LBD and Denholme LBD (author's calculations).

Table 7. *Population of the West Riding of Yorkshire and England and Wales in 1871: age structure*

	West Riding	England and Wales
Total population	1,874,611	22,712,266
Aged under 15	584,831	8,219,041
Aged 15–44	860,488	9,797,789
Aged 65+	57,945	977,643

Source: *Census of England and Wales, 1871: Population Abstracts: Ages, Civil Condition, Occupations and Birth-Place of the People*, vol. III (London, HMSO, 1872), pp. xii–xv.

contemporary standards. They merely reflected, with a few local variations, both regional and national proportions (see table 7).

In that sense, Halifax, Keighley and Denholme were, in 1871, fairly representative mid-Victorian towns. But they were remarkable by comparison with previous and subsequent experience, there as elsewhere. The principal cause of this noticeably youthful demographic profile was, almost certainly, a historically high birth-rate, reaching, in Halifax at least, a figure of 35.4 per 1,000 between 1875 and 1879. And the principal cause of that relatively high fertility rate seems to have been a high marriage rate.[104] The characteristic form of domestic composition which this pattern of fertility reflected was entirely consistent with the economic and social development of those towns. By furnishing a very considerable, and an apparently expanding supply of semi- and unskilled

[104] Dingsdale, 'Yorkshire Mill Town', pp. 20–3; see also, N.J. Smelser, 'Sociological History: The Industrial Revolution and the British Working-Class Family', in M.W. Flinn and T.C. Smout (eds.), *Essays in Social History* (London, 1974), pp. 23–38.

Table 8. *Population of Halifax, Keighley and Denholme in 1921: age structure*

	Halifax	Keighley	Denholme
Total population	99,027	42,006	2,928
Under 15	21,740	9,761	626
Aged 15–44	47,732	20,732	1,375
Aged 45–64	23,350	9,002	672
Aged 65+	6,205	2,511	255

Source: Census of England and Wales, 1871: Population Abstracts: Ages, Civil Condition, Occupations and Birth-Place of the People, vol. III (London, HMSO, 1872), pp. xii–xv.

manual employment, open to men, women and children, the economic organisation of the textile industry positively encouraged early marriage and extensive family formation amongst adolescent and young adult workers. They, in turn, responded rationally.

Thereafter, the population began fairly quickly to age. Between 1871 and 1921 the change was quite striking. 'Under-15s' declined as a fraction of the local population from about one-third to about one-fifth of the whole. Adolescent and young adults (i.e. those aged between 15 and 44) remained, figuratively speaking, stable. The proportion of those aged 65 and over marginally increased. But really significant growth was concentrated within the middle-aged sector of the population (i.e. those between the age of 45 and 64). Accounting for between one-eighth and one-seventh of their respective populations in 1871, they constituted about one-quarter of the total in each town by 1921 (see table 8).

The fundamental cause of the rise in the average age of the population was a decline in the local birth-rate, well in excess of the national rate; this coupled with a decline in the local death-rate more in keeping with national trends.[105] The gradual decline in fertility was a natural response to a reduction in national and local infant mortality rates – common across all classes – which stimulated more systematic family planning. But it was also, in part, a cultural response to altered local social

---

[105] Dingsdale, 'Yorkshire Mill Town', p. 23, offers graphic evidence for the decline of the birth-rate in Halifax. In 1879, it was 31.6 per 1,000; in 1901, 22.8 per 1,000. Compared with 33 other towns of similar size and social composition in the last quarter of the nineteenth century, the evidence is particularly revealing. Between 1875 and 1879, the average in these 33 towns was 35.9; in Halifax, 35.4. In 1900–3, it was 28.6 in those towns, and 21.6 in Halifax. No comparable evidence exists for Keighley and Denholme, but since their demographic profiles followed exactly the same pattern, it is reasonable to assume, in this instance, that the process of decline was similar. On the evidence for the declining death-rate in late nineteenth-century Halifax, see *ibid.*, pp. 22–3.

Table 9. *Population of Halifax, Keighley and Denholme in 1871: social structure*

	Halifax	Keighley	Denholme
Total population	65,510	20,242	3,469
Labour force[106]	34,936	10,948	2,162
Professional, entrepreneurial[107] and other middle classes	2,378	447	92
Shopkeepers, independent craftsmen and lower middle classes[108]	4,582	1,123	195
Working and labouring classes[109]	27,976	9,378	1,875

Source: PRO, RG 10, 4388–4402, 4315–21 and 4490–1. *Census of England and Wales*, unpub. enum. MSS, Halifax MB, Keighley LBD and Denholme LBD (author's calculations).

circumstances.[110] Alderman Waddington, a Halifax antiquarian of some note, put it this way in 1937: 'In former days, families were generally big – in the latter days they are generally small. I am told that young married people today say "they are not having many children because they cannot afford them." You never heard married people of fifty years ago talking that language.'

Poverty, as Waddington insisted, was relative. In West Yorkshire, as elsewhere, the revolution of rising expectations had taken its toll. And it had wrought a profound demographic effect: 'Adults lead a much fuller life and they in turn must give children greater opportunities. More than anything else it is "fear" for the children's future that deters parents

[106] The 'labour force' was calculated from those *not* categorised from the enum. MSS as 'scholar', 'housewife' or 'retired' or those under five years of age. So-called 'half-timers' (children under the age of twelve, employed 'half-time' and in half-time education) were included in the labour force. It is, therefore, a very rough figure, though it is salutary to note that even today, this figure is, essentially, an approximation.

[107] Made up of: so-designated 'employers of labour', specifically entitled 'managers' in industry and commerce, administrators in local government, doctors, lawyers, school-masters and ministers of religion.

[108] Made up of: shopkeepers and other retailers, employing craftsmen, small dealers and makers, lesser white-collar workers.

[109] Made up of: skilled working men (and women), factory workers, labourers and domestic servants. The concept of 'social class', conceived either analytically or descriptively, whether in relation to the ownership of the means of production, or in relation to the means of consumption, is endlessly contested in social theory. The approach adopted here derives, largely, from Max Weber, *Economy and Society*, Part I, ch. 4, 'Status Groups and Classes'. The translation of occupational categories (however established) into social classes (however defined) is irreducibly complicated by the ambiguities of description in the 1871 Census. Accordingly, the above figures should be regarded as *approximations only*.

[110] Waddington, 'Changes', pp. 26ff.

Table 10. *Population of Halifax, Keighley, and Denholme in 1871: structure of employment*

	Halifax	Keighley	Denholme
Total population	65,510	20,242	3,469
Labour force	35,936	10,948	2,152
Textile industries	14,672	5,502	1,250
Engineering, machine-tool and metal workers	3,567	1,548	–

Source: PRO, RG 10, 4388–4402, 4315–21, 4490–1. *Census of England and Wales*, 1871, unpub. enum. mss., Halifax M.B., Keighley LBD and Denholme LBD (author's calculations).

from having their quiver full.' As a result, 'the birth-rate today is just about half what it was sixty years ago', and, as a corollary, 'the scholars attending Elementary Schools in Halifax today are about half what they were thirty years ago'.[111]

Whatever the changing structure of the family, these were overwhelmingly working-class towns. That is, they were towns in which the great bulk – between 75 and 85 per cent of the active labour force in each place – was made up of persons engaged in manual labour; and, by extension, in which the great majority of the population was constituted of those persons and their dependants (see table 9).

If it was a working and labouring population, it was also, in 1871, very much of a textile working and labouring population. In Halifax, very nearly one-quarter of the total population, and something like two-fifths of the labour force, were employed in the textile industry. The corresponding propositions in Keighley were one-quarter and nearly one-half; in Denholme, one-third and two-thirds. However, the processes of industrial diversification over the next fifty years in turn created a rather more diversified proletariat. From the 1860s onwards, the growth of engineering and machine-tool industries gradually reduced the overwhelming predominance of textiles as an employer of labour. That decline was scarcely dramatic, but it was real enough: in Halifax, from two-fifths to just under one-third of the total in 1921; from about one-half to one-third of the whole in Keighley by the same date. There was little change in Denholme. On the other hand, engineering, machine-tool and other metal workers, constituting about one-tenth of the work-force in Halifax township in 1871, made up about one-seventh of the labouring population there in 1921. Over the same period, the proportion of

[111] *Ibid.*, p. 26.

Table 11. *Population of Halifax, Keighley, and Denholme in 1921: structure of employment*

	Halifax	Keighley	Denholme
Total population	99,227	42,006	2,938
Labour force[112]	51,872	22,010	1,563
Textile industries[113]	16,512	7,678	949
Engineering, machine-tool and metal workers	7,841	5,398	124
Transport and communications	2,857	896	37

Source: *Census of England and Wales, 1921: Yorkshire*, pp. 200–59. Figures are for Halifax CB, Keighley MB and Denholme LBD.

Table 12. *Population of Halifax, Keighley and Denholme in 1871: age structure of labour force*

	Halifax	Keighley	Denholme
Labour force	35,936	10,948	2,162
Labour force under the age of 15	4,128	1,962	414
Labour force over the age of 15	31,808	8,986	1,738

Source: PRO, RG. 10, 4388–4402, 4315–21, 4490–1, *Census of England and Wales, 1871*; unpub. enum. MSS, for Halifax MB, Keighley LBD and Denholme LBD (author's calculations).

workers similarly employed in Keighley rose from about 15 per cent to about one-quarter of the total. Secondary beneficiaries included the transport and communications industries. Albeit relatively slowly, their emergence in the West Riding of Yorkshire at the end of the nineteenth and in the early years of the twentieth century marked the growth of a local uniformed working class. Virtually insignificant in 1871, these occupations employed over 5 per cent of the working population of Halifax in 1921, and just under that figure in Keighley (see tables 10 and 11).

As its relative significance diminished, so the social composition of the textile industry changed in two ways: first, in an increase of child labour; and secondly, by an intensification of the (pre-existing) numerical domination of the labour force by adult females. In 1871, persons aged

[112] The 1921 Census differentiated between: the total population; those 'occupied' aged twelve years and above; and those 'unoccupied' aged twelve years and above (males and females). See *Census of England and Wales, 1921: Yorkshire*, p. xxxv.

[113] Given the extremely wide-ranging nature of this category and the widespread redefinition of occupations in this sector of the economy over a 50-year period, these comparisons must be regarded as approximate. It is not possible to match the sub-categories of the 1921 abstract with the evidence of the 1871 enum. mss. The categorisation of occupations was much cruder in 1871 than in 1921.

Table 13. *Sex and age structure of worsted weaving labour force in Halifax and Keighley, 1886*

	Total	Males	Lads and boys	Women	Girls
Halifax	4,937	545	1,040	1,976	1,376
Keighley	5,996	1,534	942	2,287	1,233

Source: PP., 1889, LXX, *Return of the Rates of Wages*, p. xxxi.

under 15 years constituted nearly one-fifth of the labour force in Keighley and Denholme, and about one-seventh of the working population in Halifax (see table 12).

Examinable figures do not exist for 1921, since the Census abstract compilers considered children under the age of 12 to be a negligible proportion of the labour force.[114] Nor have they survived in comparable detail for earlier periods. However, a breakdown of the worsted industry alone in Halifax and Keighley for 1886 suggests an actual increase in child and adolescent labour (see table 13).

The same figures point unequivocally to an intensification of female numerical domination of the industry. And that calculation *is* substantiated in the 1921 Census Abstract figures:

Table 14. *Population of Halifax, Keighley and Denholme in 1871 and 1921: female labour in the textile industry*

	Halifax	Keighley	Denholme
1871	8,383	3,407	616
1921	10,538	5,346	448

Source: PRO, RG 10, 4388–4402, 4315–21, 4490–1. *Census of England and Wales, 1871*, unpub. enum.MSS, for Halifax MB, Keighley LBD and Denholme LBD (author's calculations); and *Census of England and Wales, 1921: Yorkshire*, pp. 213, 215 and 259.

Why did this happen? Textiles, of course, had always employed female labour.[115] The factory system only relocated it. But it also changed it. Even more than in the comparable cotton and wool textile industries, the twin processes of technical mechanisation and organisa-

[114] See *Census of England and Wales, 1921: Yorkshire*, p. xxxv. No figure was calculated for those in employment under the age of twelve in the Census abstracts. It cannot, of course, be concluded, especially for these towns, that no one under the age of twelve *in fact* was in employment in 1921.
[115] Busfield, 'Skill and the Sexual Division of Labour', p. 153.

tional concentration established a certain logic of deskilling in the industry and facilitated the growth of an overwhelmingly female, and indeed juvenile, labour force.[116] This process started near the onset of industrialisation. Threats to the traditional male bastions of hand-combing and handweaving had led to the notorious Bradford strike of 1825 and fuelled many of the popular protest movements – Factory Reform, Anti-Poor Law agitation, Owenism, trade unionism and Chartism – of the 1830s and 1840s.[117] Keighley, in particular, was a major centre of the so-called 'Ten Hours Movement' at that time.[118] Protest or not, the privileges of male labour were the principal victims of those struggles. The mechanisation of woolcombing processes during the 1850s diminished their hold still further. It also deprived working-class agitation of much of its erstwhile manpower. Woolcombers had provided Keighley with much of its militant working-class leadership in the 1840s. Clough Mills introduced combing machines in 1853. By 1860, there were no handcombers employed at the Mills; and there was relatively little industrial strife either.[119]

In other words, most of the changes which occurred in the local textile industry after 1870 were really no more than extensions of a much longer process of deskilling, feminisation and the increasing employment of juvenile labour which had been going on in the industry for a very long time. Of course, there were limits to deskilling, both organisational and social. However mechanised, the industry always needed *some* skills, often new skills, and some skilled workers were successful in fighting to preserve their traditional (or emerging) status and privileges.[120] More-over, the supply of juvenile labour was, if not cut off, then substantially slowed by the gradual implementation of the 1870 Education Act, with its provision for the full-time education of those under the age of twelve.[121] The effect of these general changes within the textile trade upon local manufacture and local social relations was to forge not merely an increasingly diverse, but also a more sexually segregated

[116] Jowett, 'The Retardation of Trade Unionism', p. 86.
[117] *Ibid.*, p. 87; see also D. James, 'Paternalism in Keighley', in Jowett (ed.), *Model Industrial Communities*, pp. 104–19, at p. 105; and Jowett, 'Copley, Akroydon and West Hill Park', *ibid.*, p. 75.
[118] James, 'Paternalism in Keighley', p. 105.
[119] M. Smith, 'Robert Clough Ltd., Grove Mill, Keighley: A Study in Technological Redundancy', (MA thesis, University of Leeds, 1982), ch. 2.
[120] Jowett, 'The Retardation of Trade Unionism', pp. 84–5, 98–9; Busfield, 'Skill and the Sexual Division of Labour', pp. 160–2; Laybourn, 'The Attitudes of Yorkshire Trade Unions', ch. 3.
[121] Harwood, *Centenary Story*, p. 24; W.A. Davies, 'Local Educational History' in Mulroy (ed.), *Town That Bred Us*, pp. 82–3; Dewhirst, *A History of Keighley*, p. 80; Keighley, *History of Keighley*, pp. 224–5.

industrial proletariat. As first juveniles and then women especially came to dominate the textile industry – in numbers if not in authority – so the adult male population gradually passed into and specifically came to dominate the other, growing, industries of the locality. For instance, in 1901, at a time when something like 65 per cent of the female labour force was working in textiles, only 16 per cent of their male counterparts were similarly employed. Yet around 30 per cent of the male cohort, even at that early date, had found jobs in engineering and its allied trades.[122]

This curious local development was of considerable social significance. The predominance of women and juveniles explained much of the low level of wages in the worsted trade. It also helps to explain the extremely low level of unionisation in the industry, at least until the First World War.[123] Finally, it provides some sort of explanation for the striking absence of any really significant co-operation between textile and other workers in late Victorian and Edwardian West Yorkshire. Indeed, in 1914, two social investigators and committed socialists, G.D.H. Cole and W. Mellor, denounced a textile trades union movement 'still in its infancy ... lamentably ... backward compared with any other industry'.[124] They blamed a 'narrowness of attitude' within the industry for this lamentable fact. They might more profitably have identified an unskilled, poorly paid and sexually demarcated labour force. They might also have observed how little support those few unions which actually existed within the industry had received from other labour organisations during the Bradford strike of 1890–1.[125] Yet in their Olympian condescension they captured a critical truth about the structure of local working-class society: it was divided and differentiated, and as much by age and gender as by skill and disposition.

The same was true, mutatis mutandis, for the local lower middle classes. The number of small commercial employees, especially skilled craftsmen and artisans within their number, declined. Smiths, masons, tailors, coopers and other independent, petit-bourgeois producers and distributors disappeared rapidly.[126] In other words, new wealth and new

[122] James, 'Paternalism in Keighley', p. 106.
[123] C. Johnson, 'The Standard of Living of Worsted Workers in Keighley during the Nineteenth Century', (D.Phil. thesis, University of York, 1978), p. 80; Jowett, 'The Retardation of Trade Unionism', pp. 84, 99–102.
[124] G.D.H. Cole and W. Mellor, 'Sectionalism and Craft Prejudice, Yorkshire's Need for Greater Unionism', Daily Herald, 14 April 1914.
[125] Jowett, 'The Retardation of Trade Unionism', pp. 100–2.
[126] Census of England and Wales, 1921: Yorkshire, pp. 200–45. Since conventional descriptive categories bear little relation to census abstracts, no very reliable figures can be established for the relative fortunes of the old trades in the local economy. However, for a revealing comment on them, see Waddington, 'More Changes, 1838–

sophistication effectively changed the structure of the tertiary sector of the local economy. To take one example: the number of publicans, as a proportion of the population, diminished slightly in this period. More significantly, the nature of the service they provided changed from the provision of shelter to the retail of goods, as the earlier predominance of innkeepers, lodging-house keepers and 'general publicans' amongst this group was gradually undermined by a newer breed of restaurant owners, eating-house keepers, and beer sellers.[127] The growth of specialist shops also hailed the rise of a new retailing class. One, no doubt biased, source claimed for Halifax some of 'the finest shops in the West Riding' in the 1880s.[128] Certainly jewellers, such as J.W. Davis of Old Market, were men of substance who provided only for men and women of similar mould. But Halifax was also justly known for its drapers. John Walker's, at no. 2 Northgate, retained the same name, the same family ownership and the same location for nearly a century.[129]

What of the real middle classes? Their most important, or at least most striking characteristic was, of course, their paucity of numbers. A very loose definition – including employers of labour whether large or small, 'managers' in industry and commerce as defined in the Census abstract, those of unequivocal professional status (e.g. doctors, lawyers, ministers of religion, and schoolmasters), and those in positions of recognised administrative importance (e.g. local government officers) – suggests that about 7 per cent of the working population of Halifax in 1871, about 5 per cent of the working population of Keighley, and perhaps 4 per cent of the working population of Denholme were of 'middle-class' entrepreneurial and professional standing at that time.[130] Of these, administrators in public and private sectors were much the most numerous. Employers of labour followed them. Revealingly, perhaps, the profile of the professions in mid-Victorian Halifax, Keighley and Denholme was, in the words of one notable authority, 'absurdly small by national standards'. In 1871, there were precisely 25 lawyers, 26 schoolmasters and 25 doctors in Halifax. The corresponding figures for Keighley were 6, 5 and 7; for Denholme nought, 3

1938', p. 56: 'Some trades ... that were good in Halifax fifty years ago ... have entirely gone out ... [W]e think of ... Cloggers ... Button-Makers, Cloth-Cap Makers, Straw-Hat Makers, Coopers, Curriers, Saddlers, Straw-Makers, Cases and Gilders, Blacksmiths, Oat Cake Makers, and Makers of Clay Pipes for Smokers.'

[127] PRO, RG 10. 4388–402, 4315–21, 4490–1, Census of England and Wales, 1871, unpub. enum. MSS, Halifax M.B, Keighley LBO, and Denholme LBD (author's calculations); Census of England and Wales, 1921: Yorkshire, pp. 237 and 239. The figures were: Halifax, in 1871, 181; in 1921, 331; Keighley, in 1871, 39; in 1921, 118. Decline was marginal in both cases. Reliable figures for Denholme are unavailable.

[128] Waddington, 'Changes', p. 7.   [129] Ibid., p. 12.

[130] Author's calculations; see table 9.

and 2.[131] So, by default if nothing else, mill-owners and senior industrial managers played a much greater role in the affairs of these towns than in the public life of, for instance, contemporary Leeds.[132]

This is not to say that there was no professional or commercial middle class in this part of mid-Victorian West Yorkshire; only to note that it was very limited in extent, and correspondingly also in influence. The case of Halifax is particularly instructive in this respect. From the late eighteenth century onwards, it supported a recognisable *haute bourgeoisie* of attorneys, bankers and auctioneers, in order to serve its many commercial interests. Demographic expansion and economic diversification in the mid-nineteenth century stimulated the growth of a number of new professional groups: for instance, insurance agents, accountants and stockbrokers. In time, a growing middle class of relatively highly paid professional workers was able to patronise a penumbra of specialised retail trades.[133] Certainly, the growth of commercial and professional services in Halifax during the first half of the nineteenth century was real and significant. In 1810, 78 firms were engaged in 16 different forms of commercial and professional activity in the town; in 1858, that figure had risen to 1,184 firms in 56 different forms of activity.[134] The new professions benefited most from industrial expansion. For instance, there were just 9 different accounting and agency firms in Halifax in 1837; there were 23 in 1858. There were just 12 fire- and life-insurance offices in the town in 1822, but 56 in 1858. Older professions, such as banking and law, also expanded, less spectacularly. In some cases, they actually declined.[135]

The proportion of the population in these towns categorisable as 'middle class', or 'entrepreneurial' or even 'professional' scarcely changed at all during the decades from 1871 to 1921.[136] Perhaps the only really important change was in the rising number of so-designated 'employers and managers' in industry.[137] Changes within the profes-

---

[131] Briggs, 'Plus Ça Change', p. 426; PRO, RG. 10, 4490–1, unpub. enum. MSS for Denholme LBD (author's calculations).

[132] See Morris, *Class, Sect and Party*, ch. 5.

[133] Dingsdale, 'Yorkshire Mill Town', pp. 26–9; Harwood, *Centenary Story*, pp. 39–40; J.H. Waddington, 'Shops and Shopkeepers: Fifty Years Ago and Today', in *Essays and Addresses*, pp. 7–18.

[134] Dingsdale, 'Yorkshire Mill Town', p. 27.

[135] For example, there were 22 attorneys in Halifax in 1837; and the same number of their kind in 1858. The number of bankers actually fell, from 6 to 4 over the same period. See H. King Roth, *The Genesis of Banking in Halifax* (Halifax, 1914), ch. 1 and *passim*.

[136] *Census of England and Wales, 1921: Yorkshire*, pp. 200–45. The figures were: Halifax, 3,926; Keighley, 1,467. No reliable figure for Denholme can be derived from the 1921 Census abstract.

[137] 'Employers and Managers' was a category invented for the Census abstract. It did not differentiate between a purchaser and an administrator of labour. For what they are

sional élite were only of marginal significance, with one important exception: the declining numerical position of the religious ministry within the old 'notability' of clergymen, lawyers, doctors, senior administrators and major employers. The religious ministry, whether Anglican or dissenting, was unquestionably one of the most visible élite groups in these towns during the nineteenth century. It was also fairly numerous. There were considerably more clergymen and ministers in Halifax, in 1871, than the total number of barristers and solicitors combined; and nearly twice the number of physicians and surgeons. The pattern was very similar in Keighley: there were three times as many clergymen and ministers as lawyers and schoolmasters; and twice the number of physicians, surgeons, and local government officers. In Denholme, no section of an admittedly exiguous professional middle class was larger.[138] But by 1921, the numerically pre-eminent standing of the clergy and ministry within the old professional middle class and upper middle class of this locality had been seriously undermined. In Halifax, its number had been virtually equalled by those of senior medical practitioners and lawyers. It had been surpassed by school-masters. In Keighley, the combined number of legal and medical officers of senior rank was greater than that of the ministry; that of schoolmasters probably so.[139] Little, of course, should be inferred from such raw numbers alone. But they do suggest that the religious ministry may have been beginning to lose some of its erstwhile public profile in the years just after the First World War. Less numerous within the professions than it had once been, a little less densely spread on the ground, it was, perhaps, also just a little less socially significant.[140]

So, in general, the figures reveal important – if strictly bounded – changes *within* each of the major social groups in late Victorian and Edwardian urban industrial society. Yet they point to relatively little

worth, the figures were: Halifax, 'Employers and Managers' in 1871, 95; in 1921, 1,347; Keighley, 'Employers and Managers' in 1871, 18; in 1921, 666.

[138] PRO, RG 10. 4388–402, 4315–21, 4490–1, Census of England and Wales, 1871, unpub. enum. MSS, Halifax, Keighley, Denholme. In Halifax, in 1871, there were 121 clergymen, dissenting ministers, Roman Catholic priests, missionaries, scripture readers, and other full-time church and chapel officials, etc.; in Keighley, there were 23; in Denholme, 4.

[139] *Census of England and Wales, 1921: Yorkshire*, pp. 237–8. The figures were: Halifax, men of religion, as defined above, 78; barristers and solicitors, 50; physicians and surgeons, 46; Keighley: men of religion, 30; barristers and solicitors, 15; physicians and surgeons, 16; teachers, 44.

[140] For a study of the clergy in their 'golden age', see Brian Heeney, *A Different Kind of Gentleman: Parish Clergy and Professional Men in Early- and Mid-Victorian England* (Hamden, Conn., 1976). Note also the remarks of Thompson, 'The Making of the English Religious Classes', pp. 483–4. For a later age, see Anthony Russell, *The Clerical Profession* (London, 1980).

change in the balance of social forces *between* them. Put bluntly, the middle classes, the lower middle classes and the working classes formed roughly the same numerical proportions in local society in 1921 as they had in 1871. In this sense, however, the raw data were and are poor guides to the changing nature of social relations in later nineteenth-century West Yorkshire, for the basis of those relations shifted from apparent social consensus to genuine class antagonism during the last decade of the century. This shift was neither complete in its movement nor unambiguous in its direction. Similarly, it was not without earlier precedent or later development. But it was at its most pronounced, locally, during the 1890s. This decade witnessed the collapse of social paternalism and the rise of radical political parties.

Some contemporaries spoke of an 'old paternalism' in the textile towns of mid-Victorian West Yorkshire.[141] Modern observers tend to identify an 'attenuated paternalism', or a form of employer–employee reciprocity which fell far short of the ideals of contemporary model societies – like nearby Saltaire – and which, indeed, fell some way short of the range of mutually informed and concerned relationships between capital and labour which characterised the Lancashire cotton towns to the west; but which, nevertheless, amounted to something more than the brutal 'cash nexus' of Carlyle's nightmare and Marx's prognosis.[142] It consisted of (limited) model village developments, of (extensive) benevolent institutions associated with factory life, and finally of a common commitment, both amongst mill-owners and their more articulate workers, to the political doctrines and political fortunes of the mid-Victorian Liberal Party. It declined as a later generation of mill-owners' sons eased their way out of the towns in which their fathers had made the family fortune, then ceased to take an active part in the affairs of the firm and the activities of the locality, and finally severed the ever weak but hitherto widely perceived connection between successful business and the prosperity of the community in the drive for greater profits and lower wage costs which characterised later nineteenth-century local economic life.[143]

Full-scale 'model village' projects were limited to Halifax. Three stand out: Sir Edward Akroyd built the village of Copley, two miles south-west of Halifax during the 1840s, establishing a new mill there, providing common back-to-back houses for his work-force and furnishing numerous communal institutions, such as schools, libraries, dining

---

141 See Jowett, 'The Retardation of Trade Unionism', p. 96.
142 E.g. Joyce, *Work, Society and Politics*, pp. 341–2.
143 Jowett, 'The Retardation of Trade Unionism', pp. 96–7.

clubs, burial clubs, allotments and banks for their benefit.[144] A little later, he pioneered in Akroydon, the hamlet named after him and situated around the family's main works, a model village conceived in a medieval, Gothic mode and dedicated to the ideal of working-class home-ownership as the 'key to working-class self-improvement'.[145] This scheme was quickly followed by the efforts of Akroyd's arch-rivals, the Crossleys, to create a model mixed community, with church and school provided, at West Hill Park on the emerging western tip of the town.[146]

There were no model villages in Victorian Keighley; nor, self-evidently, in Denholme.[147] In Keighley, this was because no one family exercised sufficient direct power – wealth, landownership, control of a labour force – to forge such an arrangement.[148] In Denholme, it was simply because there was no need. But the resulting differences can easily be overstated. True, the ideals which drove the model village schemes implied an altogether higher degree of business-driven social engineering. So a contemporary history of the Akroyd business happily confessed to the aim of Colonel Akroyd of bringing about 'a kindly feeling between the opposing classes of employer and employed' in the new villages.[149] This was to be done, above all, by forging a residential environment which 'mix[ed] the classes up'.[150] But that was precisely what they failed to do. They were either too far away from the main part of the town to be anything other than semi-isolated colonies, as in the case of Copley; or simply too expensive to develop as anything other than respectable lower middle-class and upper working-class suburbs, as in the examples of Akroydon and West Hill Park. Consequently, as mechanisms of social integration, they were failures for the most part. Only as one of the many vehicles in a wider project of social consensus did they have any significant impact.[151]

Nor were they the most important of these vehicles. If model villages were restricted to Halifax, mutual improvement institutions were

[144] S.J. Daniels, 'Moral Order and the Industrial Environment in the Woollen Textile District of West Yorkshire, 1780–1880' (Ph.D. thesis, University of London, 1980), pp. 167–75.

[145] Jowett, 'Copley, Akroydon and West Hill Park', p. 79; S.M. Gaskell, 'Housing Estate Development, 1848–1919, with particular reference to the Pennine Towns' (Ph.D. thesis, University of Sheffield, 1974), p. 92.

[146] Daniels, 'Moral Order and the Industrial Environment', pp. 222–7; on Akroydon and West Hill Park as architectural achievements, see Derek Linstrum, *West Yorkshire: Architects and Architecture* (London, 1978), pp. 133, and 136–9; and Roger Dixon and Stefan Muthesius, *Victorian Architecture* (London, 1985), pp. 71–2, on the subsequent architectural and aesthetic influence of Akroydon.

[147] James, 'Paternalism in Keighley', p. 104.   [148] *Ibid.*

[149] Anon., *History of the Firm of James Akroyd and Sons* (Leeds, 1874), pp. 15–16.

[150] *The Builder*, vol. 21, no. 1045 (14 Feb. 1863), p. 110.

[151] Jowett, 'Moral Order and the Industrial Environment', pp. 80–4.

common to all three towns. These included public amenities, such as the famous People's Park, established in Halifax in 1857 by Francis Crossley at a personal cost of over £40,000, and dedicated to the ideal (if rarely the reality) of common recreation and agreeable social intercourse.[152] They also included popular societies, such as the Yorkshire Savings Bank, pioneered by Akroyd as a 'means to bridge over the wide chasm intervening between high and low in society without injury to the self-respect of either side'.[153] Finally they included punitive customs, privately imposed to enforce strict social taboos. Hence James Sugden, legendary Methodist manufacturer in Keighley, laid down a code of improving morals for his employees, backed up with the threat of dismissal, which required of them that they 'attend some place of . . . worship every Lord's Day', that they send their children to Sunday school and, *inter alia*, that they refrain from gambling, drinking or the other forms of sin (unless rendered respectable by marriage).[154]

Sugden's was an extreme case, even at the time. Most interfering employers relied on a blend of overt generosity and tacit expectations. But to forge that necessary degree of consensus which the business classes sought, such a strategy had to combine exactly the right degree of coercion and consent. Much the best way to do that was to cloak the extraordinary degree of control which many employers had over the immediate prospects of individual employees with an almost equally extraordinary personal involvement in the lives of their workers which the best, and certainly the most successful, businessmen achieved in the mid-Victorian town. The means of such involvement were rather nebulous, but they were well recognised.[155] In this way Swire Smith 'took the same lunch' as the workers in his mill.[156] It was important that James Ickringhill 'live[d] within a stone's throw' of the place where he served his apprenticeship as an onlooker.[157] Finally, it was significant that John Clough served as a simple 'mill apprentice' in the very factory where his father had made a fortune before he assumed the reins of entrepreneurial responsibility and the privileges of manufacturing authority.[158]

There is no need to romanticise any of these often largely symbolic gestures in order to appreciate their real social significance. That significance was in the degree to which, by a mixture of general provision

---

[152] Various, *Fortunes Made in Business*, vol. III, p. 276.
[153] E. Akroyd, *The Yorkshire Penny Bank* (Leeds, 1872), p. 2.
[154] R. Spence Hardy, *Memorials of Joseph Sugden* (London, 1858), pp. 94–101.
[155] James, 'Paternalism in Keighley', p. 104.
[156] Snowdon, *The Master Spinner*, p. 141.
[157] A. Almond, *Biography of James Ickringhill Esq., Balcony House, Keighley and Sunset House, Heysham, Morecombe* (Keighley, 1919), p. 21.
[158] James, 'Paternalism in Keighley', p. 107.

and individual persuasion, they sustained a régime of personal relations which, however unequal, maintained or seemed to maintain, a sense of mutual commitment. Legend had it that Martha Crossley, wife of the first John Crossley, had vowed in the bowels of Dean Clough Mill that '[i]f the Lord bless us at this place, the poor shall taste of it'.[159] Such fanciful stories aside, it actually was the case that Swire Smith, otherwise unrepentant opponent of trade union organisation, also 'refused to have anything to do with an association of factory occupiers [or] with a national federation of capitalists'.[160] In this way, the reality of his personal relationship with his workers, the fact that 'many of them remained with him for thirty years' and more, that he 'stood by' the 'worthy ones' who 'fell into any special misfortune', and that his firm 'paid half of the fees of any workers who cared to attend evening classes', assumed the appearance of a real partnership, indeed to some degree actually was a partnership, if not of partners, then at least of the similarly engaged.[161]

This was anything but trivial. The reality of personal involvement and the sense of common commitment it engendered really sustained the social consensus that made local political stability possible. Mill-owners were the MPs, the mayors, the chairmen of local boards, school boards and the like. But they were Liberal MPs, mayors and chairmen, dedicated to radical causes such as free trade, elementary education and even disestablishment, holding together in a politics made up as much of urban deference as of radicalism an otherwise formless coalition of industrialists and workers, teetotallers and Irishmen.[162] Hence the Akroyds sat for Halifax until Colonel Edward's insidious Anglicanism and Conservatism (as well as growing poverty) permitted a natural transition of the Crossleys to power, in 1874.[163] Keighley's first MP, elected in 1882 after the town finally gained municipal and parliamentary status, was Sir Isaac Holden, an upstanding businessman, impeccable Liberal and stout nonconformist.[164] He was followed by John Brigg and Swire Smith – similarly so.[165] In addition, the Liberals – or the Cloughs, Briggs and Smiths – held absolute majorities on the local Board and the Borough Council in every year to 1900, except 1896; and on the School Board, for all but three years to the end of the nineteenth century.[166]

[159] Various, *Fortunes Made in Business*, vol. III, p. 266.
[160] Snowdon, *The Master Spinner*, p. 140.   [161] *Ibid.*, pp. 140–1.
[162] James, 'Paternalism in Keighley', p. 113.
[163] Jowett, 'Copley, Akroydon and West Hill Park', pp. 82–3.
[164] Elizabeth Jennings, 'Sir Isaac Holden, 1807–97. The First Comber in Europe. A Critical Appraisal of a Victorian Entrepreneur, with special reference to textiles, politics and religion and their interdependence' (Ph.D. thesis, University of Bradford, 1982).
[165] James, 'Paternalism in Keighley', p. 113.   [166] *Ibid.*

But it was also that reality of personal involvement and that powerful sense of common commitment which dissolved during the later 1880s. To some extent, this was because many of the most ambitious mutual improvement schemes, especially the model villages, had run their own (not always very successful) course by the end of the 1870s. It can also be traced to the death, or simply to the eclipse, of some of the mid-Victorian pioneers. Colonel Akroyd retired to St-Leonard's-on-Sea in much straitened circumstances (he left less than £1,500) before his death in 1887.[167] The younger John Crossley retired to London.[168] Following the death of Francis in 1872, his widow moved to Suffolk. His son became MP for Lowestoft.[169] Even those who did not move far from West Yorkshire seemed to move out of its textile towns, both literally and figuratively. Henry Butterfield built a celestial mansion, Cliffe Castle, on the edge of Keighley between 1877 and 1883.[170] Swire Smith went three miles further to Stretton Manor ten years later.[171] These were gestures, albeit symbolically important gestures. Underlying them, the brutal and simple reality of industrial reorganisation and the increasing pressures on working practices and labour costs finally severed the ties of personal bonding and mutual esteem. The repeated attempts of local employers to feminise production, to increase the speed of machinery and to increase the number of machines per worker at last led to an upsurge in trade union activity and membership in West Yorkshire at the end of the 1880s.

It is important not to exaggerate the extent of the change involved. After all, it scarcely involved massive unionisation. By 1900, just 8,797 wool textile workers *in toto* were unionised, compared with 167,666 cotton workers. And as late as 1911, only 23,102, or 10 per cent of wool textile workers, were members of a trades union.[172] Nor was it a particularly effective form of unionisation. By the outbreak of the First World War, some thirty unions were represented in the wool textile industry generally, many with minuscule memberships, some with little more purpose than to deny their respective trades to female participation.[173] As sectional unions continued, industrial and general unions emerged only very slowly. Some, such as the Amalgamated Society of Dyers, achieved great success – almost 100 per cent membership – by the turn of the century. Others, especially the more ambitious, such as the General Union of Textile Workers, were altogether less successful.

---

[167] Bretton, 'Colonel Edward Akroyd', p. 98.
[168] Jowett, 'Copley, Akroydon and West Hill Park', p. 85.
[169] *Ibid.*   [170] Dewhirst, *A History of Keighley*, p. 89.
[171] Snowdon, *The Master Spinner*, pp. 211–12.
[172] Jowett, 'The Retardation of Trade Unionism', pp. 84–5.   [173] *Ibid.*, p. 102.

And they were notably less effective in worsted towns like Halifax and Keighley by comparison with wool towns like Huddersfield.[174]

Yet it was the very weakness of local trade unionism, paradoxically, which made contemporary radical politics so significant. The failed Bradford strike of 1890–1 and the failure of organised labour to develop a coherent trade unionism in Bradford, Halifax and Keighley, convinced working-class activists in the locality of the need to forge a new, independent, radical working-class political association. This was the Independent Labour Party.[175] Its very existence heralded the end of deferential politics in the West Riding; in 1899, the party won seven council seats in Keighley, and the next year it captured three School Board places.[176] It also paralleled the repudiation of social consensus which was marked by the emergence of a Local Labour Church; also of the socialist Sunday schools, where 'prayers took for granted an equality that did not exist in the homes or streets of the town'.[177] Finally, it fuelled the rejection of paternalism that was marked not only by the Bradford textile strike, but also by the 1889 engineering strike and the 1896 ironworks strike. These were the first disputes in these industries locally for more than a generation; also the most concrete evidence, to locals especially, that an era of social peace had passed.[178] To be sure, the pace of social and political change was relatively tardy. Unionisation still proceeded slowly after 1900. Only after the First World War – during which conflict the General Union of Textile Workers grew from 12,950 to 63,828 – did it become unstoppable.[179] Radicalism, symbolised by the formation of the Independent Labour Party locally in 1893, developed little quicker. And, ironically, its earliest real impact, in splitting the radical vote, was to bring about the election of Keighley's first Conservative MP, in 1919.[180] Three years later, however, the town elected a Labour MP at last. The class struggle had begun for real.[181]

So, curiously, just as industrial maturity made for economic instability, the consolidation of local social structure produced social strife, not social stability, in the West Riding of Yorkshire. It certainly resulted in social change. Not all of this was clear at the time. Contemporaries certainly noticed the passing of the mid-Victorian giants. Some pondered upon the changing nature of the working man. Few looked at the ground. Thus what they missed was that more than the economic organisation of the locality, more certainly than the social

[174] *Ibid.*   [175] *Ibid.*, pp. 100–1; Howell, *British Workers, passim.*
[176] James, 'Paternalism in Keighley', p. 117.
[177] Briggs, 'Plus Ça Change', p. 435.   [178] *Ibid.*
[179] Jowett, 'The Retardation of Trade Unionism', p. 102.
[180] James, 'Paternalism in Keighley', p. 113.
[181] Briggs, 'Plus Ça Change', p. 435.

structure of the region, the face of its major towns had changed during the late nineteenth and early twentieth centuries. Halifax and Keighley (if not Denholme) had become bigger, more sprawling, less immediately recognisable and comprehensible places. They had evolved, as urban landscapes, into something very different from what they had been two generations before. From the point of view not only of the quality of local life, but also in terms of the nature of local social relations, this was not the least important of the changes which had occurred in the late Victorian industrial town.

Spatial evolution: the expansion of the centre, industrial suburbanisation and the growth of residential segregation

Whatever else they did, economic transformation and social change created a new demand for space. Economic transformation brought forth new commodities and forged new methods for their distribution and exchange. Social change wrought new classes of men. Together, they also gave birth to new places – new villages, new hamlets, new streets. The geographical pattern of that change defined the spatial evolution of nineteenth- and twentieth-century Halifax, Keighley and Denholme.[182] In 1801, the built-up area of Halifax amounted to little more than a small cluster of buildings grouped around the ancient parish church at the bottom of Hebble Brook, and a second, even smaller cluster situated at the junction of King Cross Street and West Parade, about one-quarter of a mile to the west of the parish church. Together, they can have constituted an urban site little more than a few hundred acres in expanse. In 1901, the built-up area of Halifax was approximately 4 square miles in extent, and the administrative area of the borough stretched out for no less than 22 square miles.[183] Over roughly the same period of time, Keighley grew from a tiny centre on High Street, Low Street and Church Green, occupying a minimal acreage, into an integrated municipal parliamentary borough of about one mile across.[184] Denholme, of course, never grew to any comparable, or indeed significant, extent.

Spatial evolution, here as elsewhere in nineteenth-century Britain, was – overwhelmingly – the product of innumerable separate decisions taken by innumerable separately, and usually imperfectly, informed individuals, each in pursuit of similarly innumerable, and frequently

[182] The best introduction to 'spatial theory' in historical geography can probably be found in Richard Dennis, *English Industrial Cities in the Nineteenth Century: A Social Geography* (Cambridge, 1984), ch. 7.

[183] Dingsdale, 'Yorkshire Mill Town', abstract, pp. 1–2; Waddington, *Essays and Addresses*, pp. 38–44.

[184] Dewhirst, *A History of Keighley*, pp. 21 and 97.

incompatible, ends. And, whatever the workings of the 'invisible hand' elsewhere in British life, spatial evolution in the West Riding did not conform to a simple logic. The pattern of its eventual progress was anticipated by no one. Certainly, during the most turbulent era of local economic and social expansion, lasting roughly from 1850 to 1880, the pattern of urban growth in these places never followed a wholly rational – that is, a strictly economically determined – course governed by the demand for productive land and the costs of its economic transformation. The explanation for this paradox is quite simple. Halifax, Keighley and Denholme, like most other nineteenth-century industrial towns, were not wholly the product of the industrial revolution. They had been market-towns of varying size and significance in the pre-industrial period.[185] Halifax was a major centre of the cloth trade in the West Riding of Yorkshire throughout the second half of the eighteenth century.[186] Early nineteenth-century Keighley had been 'a considerable market town'.[187] Pre-industrial development in these places had a significant impact upon the course of post-industrial expansion, at once profoundly influencing, and often critically diminishing, the supply of land for building purposes, and especially for new industrial building purposes.

The case of Halifax was, and is, particularly instructive. Immediately to the east of the ancient centre of the town, urban growth was constrained by the sheer physical presence of Beacon Hill. To the north and east, the early discovery of coal deposits enabled the Lister family, the ancient owners of much of the adjacent land, to sink numerous shallow coal mines, to draw a considerable revenue from their sub-surface wealth, and (incidentally) to deny the use of the land to others.[188] To the south was flat land, ideal for building. Yet no manu-facturing mills or workers' cottages ever found their way there. This was because the south of the town was the traditional home of the seigneurial and land-owning classes of 'old Halifax'. Throughout the period of industrialisation, their continuing political cohesion and their surviving wide-ranging economic clout proved sufficient to maintain the 'social value' which they placed upon the integrity of their ancient land and its use. A system of legal covenants, enforced by personal probity and peer-group pressure, controlled and restricted the future use of all the land that any of these individuals alienated. These were the 'social limits' to

---

[185] Dingsdale, 'Yorkshire Mill Town', p. 404.
[186] Ibid., p. 18.
[187] Keighley was so described in Edward Baines' Directory for 1823 (Keighley, 1823), as cited in Dewhirst, A History of Keighley, p. 21.
[188] Dingsdale, 'Yorkshire Mill Town', p. 55.

growth in southern Halifax during the nineteenth century.[189] Under their influence, the mansion-estates of pre-industrial Halifax were eased along a benign path of purely domestic transformation into the upper- and upper middle-class 'leafy suburbs' of early twentieth-century Halifax. The industrial revolution all but passed them by. Modern, productive, building went west. So too did industrial development, suburbanisation and the growth of the modern town.[190]

The social forces driving growth in the western part of the town during the later Victorian years were equally profound, but they were highly variegated. They cannot be reduced to the impact of the personal and political rivalries of the great local entrepreneurs.[191] Still less can they be understood as the physical product of their economic patern-alism. Of course, no geographical account of the development of Halifax can wholly ignore the historical significance of the great model-village experiments planned by the Crossley brothers at West Park Hill, or by Colonel Akroyd at Copley and at Akroydon. And, viewed separately, they were 'the largest building schemes undertaken [in nineteenth-century] Halifax'.[192] But their contribution to the total housing stock of the town was very small. Indeed, it probably amounted to fewer than 500 houses.[193] Consequently, no more than about 4 per cent of those houses for which planning permission was granted in Halifax between 1851 and 1901 were the brainchildren of philanthropic intervention, whether at West Hill Park, Copley, Akroydon, or anywhere else in the town. The remaining 96 per cent were the cruder products of private profit-making initiatives.[194]

Moreover, that initiative generally came from beyond the millocracy. Only eleven of Halifax's mid-Victorian entrepreneurial élite actually owned houses in the vicinity of their factories.[195] In Keighley there is

---

[189] I owe this term, and the concept it expresses to Fred Hirsch, *Social Limits to Growth* (Cambridge, Mass., 1981), esp. ch. 3. There Hirsch distinguishes between *market* goods which are 'receptive to mechanization or technological innovation without determination in quality as it appears to the consumer'; and *positional* goods which are either '(1) scarce in some absolute or socially imposed sense, or (2) subject to congestion or crowding through more extensive use', p. 27. Building land in the southern districts of late nineteenth-century Halifax was in this sense a 'positional' good, and part of the *positional economy* of the locality.

[190] Dingsdale, 'Yorkshire Mill Town', pp. 53, 55, 82–3 and 344–7.

[191] For this argument, see D.I. Scargill, 'The Factors Affecting the Location of Industry: The Example of Halifax', *Geography*, 48 (1963), 166–74.

[192] Dingsdale, 'Yorkshire Mill Town', p. 114.

[193] Jowett, 'Copley, Akroydon and West Hill Park', pp. 76–84.

[194] Dingsdale, 'Yorkshire Mill Town', p. 88. Compare this with the example of Saltaire; see Jack Reynolds, *The Great Paternalist: Titus Salt and the Growth of Nineteenth-Century Bradford* (London, 1983), pp. 256ff.

[195] Dingsdale, 'Yorkshire Mill Town', p. 88. For a general discussion of the issue of employer housing, see Dennis, *English Industrial Cities*, pp. 176–80.

some evidence, at least until around mid-century, of employers building houses for their work-forces. But this practice seems to have largely ceased after about 1860.[196] In fact, nothing so exposed the profound social limits to paternalism in this part of the West Riding as the meagre contribution of the great manufacturing capitalists of the region to the *general* provision of housing stock for a growing working population. To be sure, if private paternalism contributed very little, local municipal authorities contributed virtually nothing to the local housing stock.[197] Residential accommodation in Halifax, Keighley and Denholme at the turn of the century was, overwhelmingly, the product of small-scale, profit-seeking speculation. Built in small lots, poorly designed and constructed, and grossly undercapitalised for the most part, it represented not only a myopic but also a mean legacy bequeathed by one generation to the next.[198]

There was another peculiar local factor. In many Victorian towns of similar size and comparable patterns of urban development, local municipal authorities did contribute significantly to the ends and means of urban spatial evolution because, whilst they contributed relatively little to the domestic amenities of its population, more than any other single body they planned for, and even provided for, the development of intra-urban transport facilities. But this was not the case in either later nineteenth-century Halifax or Keighley. Indeed, the urban 'transport revolution', which proved so crucial to the pattern of growth elsewhere, and which afforded (in theory) the only legitimate occasion for the general exercise of public authority over private interest, proved to be relatively unimportant, at least if viewed from a spatial perspective, to the physical development of either town. And it was wholly irrelevant to the final form of modern Denholme.[199]

For a town of its size and economic importance, the town was relatively late in acquiring efficient external communications. The railways first made their way down the Calder Valley from the west in

---

[196] See Hodgson, *Textile Manufacture*, pp. 44–51, and Joyce, *Work, Society and Politics*, p. 121. See also J.D. Marshall, 'Colonisation as a Factor in the Planting of Towns in North-West England', in H.J. Dyos (ed.), *The Study of Urban History* (London, 1968), pp. 215–30.

[197] Waddington, 'Changes', p. 30.

[198] Dingsdale, 'Yorkshire Mill Town', pp. 126–30. See also the remarks in Linstrum, *West Yorkshire*, p. 132.

[199] On the transport revolution and Victorian urban development, see Asa Briggs, *Victorian Cities* (London, 1963), pp. 14–16; also Dennis, *English Industrial Cities*, pp. 110–16. On the theme of public intervention, see A. Sutcliffe, 'The Growth of Public Intervention in the British Urban Environment during the Nineteenth Century: A Structural Approach', in J.H. Johnson and C.G. Pooley (eds.), *The Structure of Nineteenth Century Cities* (London, 1982), pp. 107–24.

1839–40, but got no further than Sowerby Bridge, several miles away. A branch line was established at Shaw Syke, just outside the town, in June 1844, but not until June 1855 was the Old Station in central Halifax finally opened. A line from Beacon Hill to Bradford was opened in 1850, and another to Holmfield and beyond in 1878, but Halifax was consistently frustrated in its attempts to secure a main-line connection. Negotiations for a projected extension of the Midland Railway through Halifax began in 1864, were resumed in 1874, 1897, 1899, and 1902, and were finally abandoned in 1915.[200] Only the construction of modern road communications finally put an end to the geographical isolation of Halifax. For the most part, Victorian Halifax was connected to the outside world by a system of turnpike roads which remained essentially unchanged from their eighteenth-century state.[201] The essential features of its intra-urban road network were also long established before industrialisation. The great roads which ran westward up Mount Pellon from the central lowland – Pellon Lane, Hanson Lane, Gibbet Street and King Cross Street – were largely in place by the end of the 1770s.[202] Only one major new road was constructed during the nineteenth century. Running from King Cross Road in the south, to Pellon Lane in the north, Queen's Road was the first north–south link road to be laid in western Halifax. Cut after the town corporation had secured compulsory public orders against eleven land-owners in 1861, it was also the sole example of a major transformation of the urban landscape forged by local authority initiative in Halifax throughout the entire period of its major economic development.[203] A scheme to develop a Halifax and District Tramway Company in 1882 failed. No tram ran in Halifax until 1898.[204] Consequently, for its working classes, and for all those unable to finance their daily journeys to and from work by hackney-carriage or by horse omnibus, Halifax remained an essentially pedestrian town until the turn of the twentieth century. The social significance of this public anomaly extended far beyond any nebulous sense of relative urban deprivation. It effectively precluded the opening of the suburbs for

---

[200] Harwood, *Centenary Story*, pp. 19–21. See Waddington, 'More Changes', p. 48: 'It is often said that Halifax is on a "siding".' For what might have been, see J.R. Kellett, *The Impact of Railways on Victorian Cities* (London, 1969).

[201] Dingsdale, 'Yorkshire Mill Town', p. 162.

[202] *Ibid.*, p. 162. T.W. Hanson, *In Search of Halifax, No. 1, Halifax Street Lore* (Halifax, 1932), p. 30, describes those 'western lanes' as 'like the palm of a hand [with] lanes running off it like fingers'. It is a beautifully apt analogy.

[203] Dingsdale, 'Yorkshire Mill Town', pp. 68–9.

[204] *Ibid.*, pp. 168–9; Harwood, 'The Making of Our Municipality', in Mulroy (ed.), *Town That Bred Us*, p. 33. On the history of tramways and urban development, see Dennis, *English Industrial Cities*, pp. 119–25.

working-class residential purposes. In so doing, it profoundly restricted the spatial flexibility of the town far into the twentieth century.[205]

The local 'transport revolution' in Keighley was similarly unspectacular. And its impact upon the spatial evolution of the town was also restricted. The development of a railway system in and through the town was begun early, but abandoned incomplete. An extension of the Leeds–Bradford line reached Keighley in 1847. Links to East Lancashire, through Colne to Manchester and Liverpool were established two years later. In 1867, the Keighley and Worth Valley Railway Company opened its line from Oxenhope to join the Midland Railway at Keighley. But the Great Northern Railway did not come to Keighley until 1884. A projected line to Halifax was never started.[206] Nor did the development of local transport facilities – such as they were – have much of an impact on the evolution of the urban landscape. The principal roads of the town were left unchanged by the industrial revolution. Public transport within the borough was limited to a few private omnibuses and hackney-cabs until 1889, when the Keighley Tramways Company laid rails between Ingrow, in the south of the town, to Utley in the north. But they ran on well-established roads between the two villages via South Street, Church Green, North Street and Skipton Road, and never really provided a comprehensive intra-urban service. The service they provided was quite insufficient to permit any significant change in popular residential patterns. In 1901, having consistently failed to make a profit, the company sold out to Keighley Corporation. The Corporation electrified the system in 1904, but did not greatly extend its capacity or range.[207]

The anarchy of housing provision, together with the relative insignificance of transport amenities, ensured that those little-conscious forms of urban landscaping which did occur in the latter half of the nineteenth century, notably the dedication of public parks from private property, had remarkably few lasting spatial or social consequences locally. To be sure, this was not for the want of trying. Crossley's 'People's' Park in Halifax was soon followed by 'Saville' (1866) after Captain Saville, and two Akroyd donations, 'Shroggs' and 'Akroyd', both in 1877.[208] Even Keighley's wealthy families finally got into the spirit, with 'Devonshire' Park in 1887, presented by the eponymous Duke, and 'Victoria' Park a

[205] Dingsdale, 'Yorkshire Mill Town', p. 172; Dennis, *English Industrial Cities*, pp. 132–4 and 138–9.
[206] Dewhirst, *A History of Keighley*, pp. 74–6.
[207] *Ibid.*, pp. 99–100; Briggs, 'Plus Ça Change', p. 418. On intra-urban transport in general, see J.P. McKay, *Tramways and Trolleys: The Rise of Urban Mass Transport in Europe* (Princeton, N.J., 1976).
[208] Hodgson, *Textile Manufacture*, pp. 99–100.

few years later.[209] But these gifts, admirable though they were in their own way, had the effect neither of drawing the classes together nor of significantly changing the more important forms of the local landscape. By definition, they rendered public what had once been private. But they did so, in every case, in a manner in tune with the natural evolution of the specific neighbourhood which they served. Hence Devonshire Park, situated in the emerging respectable district of the town, became its middle-class park; and Victoria Park, stranded in a working-class district, assumed the role of a less desirable, plebeian amenity.[210] In sum, spatial evolution reaped the benefits neither of rational authority nor of efficient allocation. The result was something of a mess. It can be reduced to three significant spatial consequences: central extension, industrial relocation and residential segregation.

Although both towns expanded naturally from their traditional central nuclei, they eventually stretched out so far beyond their ancient anchorages that the centre of gravity of their respective urban communities shifted quite noticeably. The extension of the central area of Halifax began in the 1820s, springing from a small cluster of buildings at the junction of Northgate, Woolshops, Market Street and the Market Cross near the parish church. It moved continually westwards during the next two or three decades, passing along an axis formed by Old Market, Corn Street and Silver Street, and running, by the mid-1870s, about a quarter of a mile up the gentler western slopes of the town. In subsequent years, it moved further west still, this time reaching up to Bull Close and beyond, perhaps half a mile from the ancient centre.[211] At the same time, the east central district of the town began to decline. So, by the early 1890s, some of the worst slum ghettos of the borough were concentrated around St John the Baptist Church, and on the old roads leading east, in and around the old centre of the town.[212]

The central nucleus of Keighley began to expand in the 1830s. The opening of a new market-place, situated to the east of the parish church, in 1833 shifted the trading centre of the town out of Church Green for the first time in five centuries. During the next ten years, substantial new civic and commercial building began to stretch north along the appropriately named North Street. A mechanics institute was built there in 1825 (and rebuilt on the same spot in 1870); a courthouse was erected

---

[209] On private benefaction for public purposes in Keighley, see Dewhirst, *A History of Keighley*, pp. 100–4. On paternalism and deference in Keighley's factories, see Joyce, *Work, Society and Politics*, pp. 163–5, 175–6, 322.

[210] Briggs, 'Plus Ça Change', p. 435.

[211] Dingsdale, 'Yorkshire Mill Town', pp. 253–6; also Hanson, *The Story of Old Halifax*, p. 260.

[212] Dingsdale, 'Yorkshire Mill Town', pp. 349 and 354.

in 1831; then St Anne's Roman Catholic Church, a minor masterpiece designed by Pugin, was opened for worship in 1840.[213] Gradually, the centre of gravity of the central district moved further north, shifting from the old High Street, near the parish church, towards what became the new Town Hall Square. By the turn of the century, the parish church and Church Green were, emphatically, 'not the centre[s] of [either] the social or the spiritual life of the town'.[214] That privilege was reserved for the new Town Hall Square. It was not, initially at least, a particularly beautiful town centre. As late as 1900 its most noticeable feature was a corporation rubbish dump.[215] Eventually, if somewhat cruelly, it was dignified by a war memorial, commemorating the deaths of some 900 Keighley men during the First World War.[216] More importantly, if less poignantly, this site mirrored the general physical growth of the town.[217]

As their respective centres moved out, so the dynamics of industrial evolution extended towards the suburbs too. This was important, for nineteenth-century industrial development rarely began in the suburbs.[218] Traditional constraints upon the location of manufacturing plant, particularly upon the availability of flat land and cheap premises, the additional costs of assembling equipment and raw materials, further problems of access to fuel, intractable difficulties with the supply of labour, and the paucity of similarly engaged firms, each separately and all together placed a very heavy premium upon central, traditional river valley sites. Halifax was no exception to this rule. In the 1820s, industrial development, such as it existed there, was concentrated upon three focal points along Hebble Brook: Dean Clough, Bank Bottom and Swan Bank.[219] By the mid-1850s, and after the first major boom in factory building, the whole stretch of river along both banks, from Lee Bank to Shaw Syke, was littered with manufacturing plant. Away from the river, industrial sites in the town were few and isolated. With the second and third waves of factory concentration both banks filled up, so much so that by the 1890s virtually all possible sites for the erection of mills in the valley had been occupied. Gradually fringe locations became more attractive.[220]

The eclipse of the Hebble Valley as the exclusive location for

[213] For more on St Anne's and its genesis, see ch. 2, below, pp. 97–8.
[214] Briggs, 'Plus Ça Change', p. 418.
[215] Ibid., p. 426.   [216] Ibid., pp. 436, 437.
[217] Dewhirst, A History of Keighley, pp. 44 and 108. Dingsdale, 'Yorkshire Mill Town', p. 55.
[218] Dingsdale, 'Yorkshire Mill Town', p. 232. For comparative evidence, see Dennis, English Industrial Cities, pp. 237–8.
[219] Dingsdale, 'Yorkshire Mill Town', pp. 294–6. See Hudson, The Genesis of Industrial Capital, pp. 33–7, for comparative remarks.
[220] Dingsdale, 'Yorkshire Mill Town', pp. 355–6.

industrial premises was not solely the result of the exhaustion of space. The construction of a high-level railway on the very western edge of the built-up zone between 1885 and 1889 eased some of the problems of communications in that area.[221] Just as importantly, fundamental changes in the nature of industrial manufacturing processes diminished some of the advantages of river valley locations and enhanced some of the benefits of large-scale production on vast expanses of previously underused land. Widespread adoption of steam-driven machinery in mills, coupled with a general increase in the scale of operations and a preference for vertical integration within the organisation of textile firms, gradually tipped the economic balance in favour of the western fringes. Even the later structural disintegration of the worsted trade during the 1880s did not entirely outweigh these new-found and hard-won benefits. Significant parts of the industry therefore moved to the north-west around Hopwood Lane, Queen's Road and the valley of Upper Hebble Brook, and out to the western fringes, consolidating its presence on older sites such as in the environs of Pellon Lane, or establishing itself anew in some of the outlying villages, such as King Cross and Siddal.[222]

These, in themselves relatively modest, economic initiatives had profound spatial and social consequences for the town. Because manufacturing industry itself, rather than just a dormant working-class population, was to that extent *suburbanised* in Halifax during the last three decades of the nineteenth century, it followed that new 'industrial' subdistricts or subnuclei sprang up quickly, indeed almost unannounced, on many of the urban fringes of the town. These had been up to then no more than outlying villages, districts beyond the organisational competence, or even the organisational concern, of the major institutions of erstwhile urban society. Their overwhelmingly industrial working-class populations accordingly lived and worked in what were, especially during the early years of their development, effectively self-sufficient residential suburbs, which were also – as manufacturing districts – in constant communication with the centre of the town. What had once been yonder regions, fit only for salutary neglect, suddenly became the 'new' districts of a burgeoning whole. So the spatial significance of 'industrial' Halifax continued to expand, even as its purely economic standing began to contract. Hence there was no visible, nor indeed necessarily any underlying incompatibility between the contemporary perception of a growing town and the deeper reality of a declining economy. Both were true.[223]

---

[221] *Ibid.*, p. 316. Harwood, *Centenary Story*, p. 21.
[222] Dingsdale, 'Yorkshire Mill Town', pp. 308–9.
[223] *Ibid.*, p. 323; Dennis, *English Industrial Cities*, pp. 237–8.

A similar process occurred in nineteenth-century Keighley, beginning if anything a little earlier. The first industrial developments there were sited around Low Bridge, South Street and Greengate in the south-central core of the town. Subsequently, the famous Dalton Lane Mills, owned by the Robinson family, became a focus of manufacturing concerns in the same district. Finally, Prince Smith's Burlington Sheds were erected 'near the heart of Keighley, alongside the main railway line and behind . . . its leading shopping street, Cavendish Street'.[224] But the geographical concentration of industry in Keighley was fairly short-lived. As early as the 1830s, the Butterfields branched out onto the Halifax Road, to the south. The Haggas brothers purchased Ingrow Mill in 1860, and effectively sucked that small, and similarly southerly, village into the economic orbit of the town. Later developments by other local industrialists then brought Fell Lane, Exley Head, Thwaites, and Utley to the north, all of which had generally been considered to be separate hamlets during the first half of the nineteenth century, into the institutional and administrative competence of the later Victorian town. As in Halifax, they were, and remained, suburbs, but they were no longer dormant suburbs. Like their Halifax counterparts, they had become productive outer districts, integral parts of an increasingly intricate whole, concrete expressions of growth in an industrial town which was, in other respects, imperceptibly declining.[225]

Nothing, however, changed more than housing. The sheer extent of the exclusively residential area of both Halifax and Keighley developed rapidly in the second half of the nineteenth century under the pressure of demographic increase, and with increases in scale came a fundamental change of nature. The new urban middle classes became aware as never before of the *quality* of their domestic environment. This, in turn, led to a reordering of the housing priorities between different socio-economic groups which assumed a profoundly significant spatial expression in the emergence of socially segregated residential districts during the last years of the nineteenth century.[226] To be sure, residential segregation emerged slowly and fitfully from nearly a century of haphazard social development and economic change. Indeed, not until the 1890s was the population of Halifax sufficiently large, or the sheer physical expanse of the town sufficiently great, for the *fact* of socially distinct residential

---

[224] Briggs, 'Plus Ça Change', p. 433.

[225] Hodgson, *Textile Manufacture*, pp. 31, 50 and 104; Dewhirst, *A History of Keighley*, p. 108.

[226] Dingsdale, 'Yorkshire Mill Town', p. 325. For a comparative discussion, see Dennis, *English Industrial Cities*, pp. 211–21; also David Cannadine, 'Residential Differentiation in the Nineteenth-Century English Town: From Shapes on the Ground to Shapes in Society', in Johnson and Pooley (eds.), *The Structure of Nineteenth Century Cities*, pp. 235–51.

districts to be readily discernible to those who lived in them. In Keighley, it probably was never fully so acknowledged. And only in the areas of highest and lowest social status in either town did social segregation ever approach exclusive social homogeneity. Moreover, in neither place was it planned; certainly not anyway in the form which it eventually assumed. Some districts retained much of the same social ambience and status as they had enjoyed, or endured, before industrialisation and urban evolution, partly by design and partly by good or ill fortune. Many districts were transformed for good or ill by growth. Most simply arose anew. Of these, some changed in a way quite contrary to the earliest expectations or aspirations of their progenitors and first residents. A few, in both towns, sank slowly and irretrievably into decay and squalor, becoming, by the end of the nineteenth century, something they had never quite been before: the sole preserve of the hopelessly poor, the urban residuum, the ghettos.

In 1900, the southern outskirts of Halifax and the northern fringes of Keighley housed the rich (new and old) and the famous (such as they were) of their respective towns. However, their historical routes to grandeur differed markedly. One was a historical legacy. The other was an urban development. The old gentry and élite landowners of southern Halifax had laboured, for the most part successfully, to retain the cultural ambience and social status of their traditional estates in the face of the changes going on around them. Moreover, some of those changes actually worked in time to their benefit. Developments during the 1850s and 1860s, particularly around People's Park and the West Hill Park district of the town, initiated by the Crossley brothers at the height of their local prosperity and prestige, created a new and highly fashionable residential district in the west of the town, which, as late as 1870, might have superseded the ascendancy of the old southern districts. That it failed to do so was, to a considerable degree, the result of the suburbanisation of industry onto the western fringe of the town during the 1870s and 1880s, and the consequent development in those areas of artisan and working-class housing districts.[227]

Ironically, the original embourgeoisement of the lower western slopes around West Hill Park and Park Road in mid-century was in itself an eloquent tribute to the strictly limited powers of paternalistic planning in an unregulated urban environment. For West Hill Park had, of course, been conceived and erected as a model village by the Crossley brothers in order to house the workers from their factories at Dean Clough, less than one mile away. Two hundred and three houses were indeed built.

[227] Dingsdale, 'Yorkshire Mill Town', pp. 345–7.

But it never fulfilled the purpose of paternalistic provision and for the simplest of reasons. The prices of the houses (between *c*. £120 and *c*. £450 in the 1860s) were too steep for the local proletariat to buy them, even on the advantageous terms which the family offered to its employees.[228] Only the middle and lower middle classes could afford them, and so they settled in the area of the park – ironically named People's Park – and its environs. Plans for a village school and church were summarily abandoned. Thus a scheme whose acknowledged object was the pursuit of social integration became an integral part of the process of social segregation in the town. Not even the impact of industrial suburbanisation some twenty years later wholly succeeded in reversing this most ironic of all possible outcomes. Indeed, to some degree it consolidated that development. West Hill Park never became a patrician suburb. Nor did it decline into proletarian indecency. Rather, it remained solidly middle class.[229]

Patrician Keighley was, at least in the early nineteenth century, probably better defined by a roll-call of dynastic sees spread around the suburbs of a fitfully growing town than through the identification of a recognisable upper-class residential district. The Sugdens at Eastwood House, the Briggs at Guard House, the Greenwoods at the Knowle, the Butterfields at Cliffe Hall, the Haggas at Oakworth Hall and the Claphams at Aireworth House certainly lived well during the years, if relatively modestly by the standards of later Victorian magnates. They intermarried. They forged a social and cultural unity. But they did not, at least before mid-century, retreat into a spatially defined social ghetto. It was the redevelopment of Cliffe Hall, subsequently honoured with the title Cliffe Castle, by Henry Isaac Butterfield between 1875 and 1883, which so galvanised the energies of the Keighley élite, and led them down the path of physical segregation. Whether or not the mock-Elizabethan family home of the Butterfields, suitably adorned with castellated turrets, towers and marble fountains, really was 'one of the finest residences [to] have been constructed in Yorkshire, or even the whole kingdom, during the last decade', must remain a question for aesthetic debate.[230] What was unquestionable was its power, as if by magnetic attraction, to draw upper- and upper middle-class villadom down the Skipton Road to the north and north-west of the town where, by the late 1880s, it rested solidly and securely. Respectable middle-class

[228] Jowett, 'Copley, Akroydon and West Hill Park', p. 84.
[229] Dingsdale, 'Yorkshire Mill Town', pp. 340–3; Derek Linstrum, *West Yorkshire: Architects and Architecture* (London, 1978), p. 138.
[230] Source unknown. Cited in Dewhirst, *A History of Keighley*, p. 89; see also Linstrum, *West Yorkshire*, pp. 85–7.

Keighley slowly followed it. Creeping along North Street in the second half of the nineteenth century, to Devonshire Street and its 'influential Congregational Church' and beyond – through rows of solid residential streets named after Whig-Liberal politicians – Argyll, Granville, Spencer, Campbell and Russell – it also edged gradually uphill across former nursery gardens to the west of North Street.[231] True, it never quite detached itself from the life of the town in the manner of southern Halifax. It was, after all, a product of the town's growth. But it was a different product, and everyone knew it.

Possibly the most significant and certainly the most characteristic creation of the late nineteenth-century industrial town was the 'improving' artisan and working-class residential district. Examples of this form emerged relatively quickly in Halifax, especially between 1860 and 1890, on the western fringe at King Cross, along the Queen's Road, also towards the north-west of the town on Lee Bank and Lee Mount, and on the higher part of Claremont.[232] They arose too in Keighley, particularly in the 1870s and 1880s, in new housing developments hugging the Halifax Road.[233] So-called 'improving districts', as they were often known, were a necessary response to demographic increase, and, to a lesser extent, to the suburbanisation of industry. But they were also the increasingly characteristic expression of local working-class respectability, home of the skilled and semi-skilled industrial working classes, physically segregated – indeed almost a world apart – from the vice and depravity of the 'slum'.

In Halifax, the slum ghettos were concentrated, by the end of the nineteenth century, around the parish church, on the old roads leading east, at Cross Field and Chapeltown on the western edge of the commercial district, and on Foundry Street and at the junction of West Parade and King Street. Away from the blighted central-eastern district of the town, slum ghettos also emerged in Northowram and Charlestown, and in those areas of Haley Hill (in the north-east) which had not been incorporated into the model village of Akroydon.[234] Keighley's poverty was also concentrated in the old town centre, particularly in the Irish settlement – Deanside and the Pinfold, the Ginnel and Baptist Square. Other districts, such as Carrodus Square at Upper Green,

---

[231] Dewhirst, *A History of Keighley*, p. 92. On residential propinquity between manufacturing masters and their work-force in mid-nineteenth-century Keighley, see Joyce, *Work, Society and Politics*, pp. 26–7. This social phenomenon declined, though it never wholly disappeared, after 1900.

[232] Dingsdale, 'Yorkshire Mill Town', pp. 373–4.

[233] See the *Keighley Year Book, 1907* (Keighley, 1907), p. 139. This area is referred to as a 'working-class parish'.

[234] Dingsdale, 'Yorkshire Mill Town', p. 349.

South Street along to Nelson Street and King Street, were also notorious
by mid-century, home to an 'idle riff-raff ... who alarmed the towns-
folk'.[235] Church Green and Westgate, in the vicinity of the parish
church, deteriorated noticeably in the second half of the nineteenth
century. The ghettos of both towns were home to a population made up
of casual labourers, the unemployed, and a variegated underclass of
strays, prostitutes and the down-and-out. Disproportionately Irish, the
very epitome of unrespectability and of moral and spiritual hopelessness,
they constituted a recognisable niche in society all but lost to the
missionary work of the Protestant churches by the turn of the twentieth
century. The ghetto Irish were loyal to the Catholic Church in their own
way; for the rest, the very idea of religious participation and commitment
was all but inconceivable.[236]

The task of religious organisation: the mission to the people and trials of Christian proselytisation in the industrial town

Economic revolution and the miserable insecurities of daily life; social
transformation and the rise of antagonistic political consciousness;
spatial evolution and the division of domestic existence: these were the
urgent contingencies of urban society which religious institutions
confronted in this part of West Yorkshire during the last third of the
nineteenth century. Moreover, as the era of economic growth, to 1870,
passed into an age of apparent consolidation, to the turn of the century,
and then one of decline, especially after the First World War, the
structure of local society changed continually and the face of the local
landscape evolved continuously. Hence the task of religious organisation
and the mission to the people it implied was carried on in a
fundamentally uncertain urban environment which, literally as well as
figuratively, never stopped moving. And even its literal movements were
far from predictable. Urging his congregation to give willingly and
generously for the establishment of a new mission church in Knowle
Park, a new district of the town, Edward Pringle, Pastor of Devonshire
Street Congregational Chapel, Keighley, noted that: 'For some time past
houses have been building [sic] at the rate of four hundred a year.

---

[235] Quoted in Briggs, 'Plus Ça Change', p. 428.
[236] Dewhirst, *A History of Keighley*, pp. 49–52. Berry, *Keighley Catholic Church: One Hundred and Fifty Years. Anniversary Celebrations, 1835–1985* (Keighley, 1985), pp. 3–13; on slum religion, especially Irish slum religion, see Sheridan Gilley, 'The Catholic Faith of the Irish Slum', in Dyos and Wolff (eds.), *The Victorian City*, vol. II, pp. 837–53.

Should the town keep on increasing at this rate, another century will show a Keighley equal in population to the Leeds or Bradford of today.'

In that prognostication he turned out to be very wrong. Perhaps his analysis of the real needs of Knowle Park district was wrong too. But Pringle was not stupid. Nor was he ignorant. And he was anything but blind. That late Victorian Keighley was moving out into new or neglected pastures was all too obvious to him, and to others too. Where it was moving to and why it was moving there, they did not know. How far it would eventually move, they had not the slightest clue. But that they were obliged to *respond* to its movements, however eccentric and however unpredictable those movements might be, they knew well enough. In Pringle's own words: 'Surely we cannot be content to see the town increasing all around us and ourselves making no attempt to spread the principles we believe in.'[237]

It was that continuing sense of a comprehensive social obligation, itself confronted with the continued reality of social unpredictability, which truly defined the scale of the mission faced by organised religion in its task to evangelise the industrial towns of the far West Riding of Yorkshire. Those difficulties were not, of course, limited merely to the exigencies of unplanned urban evolution. Organised religion in nineteenth-century Britain worked in and through a society divided into distinct socio-economic classes; many of its institutions reflected those divisions, and all were informed by them. But religious organisations were, or at least believed themselves to be, something more than just one amongst the many local voluntary organisations, thus equally committed and similarly vulnerable to an amorphous sense of social solidarity. They appealed, by their very nature, to the mortal soul of every human being, an appeal which they believed – of its very nature – rendered all other differences amongst men unimportant. The extent of their success was, to some degree, measurable by the degree to which they succeeded in persuading individuals, of all districts and from all classes, that their appeal really did transcend the increasing divisiveness of developing social differentiation. The extent of their problem was, to a still greater degree, definable by the fact that while their appeal was of its very nature self-consciously timeless and immutable, local society was at that time fast changing and becoming more differentiated, more divided, indeed simply more disputatious.

To a greater degree, but not entirely; for whilst it can scarcely be denied that in such a socially differentiated community the souls of some were rather more officiously attended to than others – if for no

[237] Edward Pringle, 'Pastor's Address', *Devonshire Congregational Church, Keighley, Church Manual, 1900* (Keighley, 1900), p. 14.

other reason than that they had not simply more money but also more time at their disposal – it did not follow either that the churches were wholly unable to compensate for these brutal facts of contemporary social life, nor that they were entirely unwilling to make proper, and fruitful, allowances for them. There is no need to romanticise the social vision of Victorian and Edwardian religious institutions to appreciate the force of this argument. The most elementary appreciation of local social structure was (and is) sufficient for this purpose. The mission of the Church in those towns was, as its ministry well knew, to an overwhelmingly *working-class society*. Consequently, its needs, its aspirations, more still its limitations, both of income and of leisure, were necessarily at the forefront of contemporary ecclesiastical social thinking. It could not have been otherwise for institutions which had the slightest pretensions towards social – and thereby spiritual – comprehension. Nor did they despair at that fact. Confronted with an unpredictable, shifting urban landscape, left to cope with an increasingly divided and antagonistic society, forced to mount their crusade amongst an inexorably poor, insecure and unleisured population, the religious institutions of West Yorkshire took to their task undaunted. Of course, they brought a solid faith to their work. Naturally, they preached the word to rich and poor alike. Unquestioningly, they bore Christian witness amongst those who rudely rejected them as well as those who openly accepted them. But to bring their message, to stand their ground and to comprehend their obligations in a world they never made, they now used one method of evangelical response more than any other. They built more churches – many, many more churches – than they had ever built before.

2 The many houses of God: churches, church building and church extension in the industrial town

Introduction: the modern ecclesiastical landscape and the Victorian church-building boom

Any visitor travelling to Halifax, Keighley and Denholme today cannot but be struck by the number and grandeur of their churches. There are probably more than one hundred standing scattered around these three towns. And many of them are magnificent sights. No modern secular building, no factory, certainly no rail or road terminal can match the ornate splendour of All Souls', Haley Hill, in the north-east of Halifax. Closer into town, Ebenezer Primitive Methodist Church still dominates the new, western, centre just as St John the Baptist Parish Church presides over the old valley bottom. Watching over them all, perched seemingly precariously near the moorland on the hills to the east, sits St Thomas's, Claremount. Driving north towards Keighley, the same traveller will inevitably come across the isolated glory of St Peter's Church of England, Denholme, stuck out on its own half a mile from the main residential part of the village, and towering above everything else in an otherwise colourless local landscape. Finally, entering Keighley from the south, he will pass by the dignified serenity of St Andrew's Parish Church, then make his journey down North Street to St Anne's Roman Catholic Church. On his way, he will surely notice, just up the slopes to the west is Devonshire Street United Reform Church. As he leaves, he may observe, on his right, the Friends' Meeting House.

These are not just isolated sacred spots in an otherwise profane landscape. In fact, to follow each of those towns into their suburbs is to continue to be impressed by the sheer physical extent, as well as the considerable aesthetic quality, of their surviving ecclesiastical plan. Hence to trace the development of Halifax to the west is, immediately, to confront St Paul's, King Cross, amongst many other fine churches; and, today, mosques. Or, to pursue the residential tentacles of Keighley into its northern, eastern and western extremes is to discover, *inter alia*, the plan of its Methodist Connexion, whether in Utley, Long Lee or

Hermit Hole. In Denholme, it is to discover the nonconformist heart of an apparently Anglican town, amongst Baptist, Methodist and United Reformed churches. In short, churches and chapels are still to be found almost everywhere in this part of urban West Yorkshire. To be sure, their very ubiquity now often seems anachronistic, almost an encumbrance, the evidence of so much material and spiritual wealth once unwisely invested and now ungainfully employed. And, in their embarrassment, modern ecclesiastical authorities tend to distance themselves from the real significance of that now underused erstwhile richness. 'Buildings alone are not Methodism,' declares a recent history of the Halifax Methodist Circuit.[1] A few years earlier, three historians of the Keighley Methodist Circuit came to much the same conclusion. 'We have not forgotten', they proclaimed, 'that a church is more than a building.'[2]

The point, such as it is, was not, in fact, lost upon their Victorian forebears. Indeed, purer Protestant souls were willing, even then, to take the argument much further: '[A] house of prayer is not essential to Christianity, nor even one and the same definite place of prayer,' declared one Dr Mellor in the Halifax Congregational magazine for May 1886.[3] But what the Victorians understood well enough, they nevertheless interpreted rather differently. This was certainly true of Dr Mellor himself. In his own words: 'A [church] building [is] some sort of symbol of our religious faith; by which I mean it is ... a silent, but significant witness to the fact that, in our judgement, the highest relation which a man sustains is that which connects him with the God that made him.'[4] Symbolic of what was most important, it was also a place to do what was most significant in and for that faith. Indeed, according to Mellor's colleague, the Reverend A. Galbraith, it was the best place man had yet invented 'for Christian fellowship, edification and worship, the observance of Christ's laws and ordinances, and the extension of His truth in the world'.[5] It was, in other words, the best place known to Christians in which to worship; at which to join others in the fellowship of worship, and from which to mount a righteous mission to extend the possibilities of worship to all.

As symbol and as facility together, late Victorian church buildings

---

[1]   Eve Chapman, *Two Hundred Years of the Halifax Methodist Circuit, 1785–1985* (Halifax, 1985), p. 19.
[2]   John Coulson, T.M. Farrington and H. Feather, *Centenary of the Methodist Cause at Wesley Place, Keighley, 1840–1940* (Keighley, 1946), p. 14.
[3]   Dr Mellor, 'Congregational Principles', *HDCM*, vol. 4, no. 5, May 1886, p. 102.
[4]   *Ibid.*, p. 99.
[5]   Rev. A. Galbraith, 'Congregational Life and Polity', *HDCM*, vol. 1, no. 12, February 1884, p. 279.

were neither an anachronism nor an embarrassment to contemporary churchmen and ministers. On the contrary. They were something to celebrate. More: they were something through which to plot the growth of Christ's mission on earth. Thus, evaluating the 'progress' made by his own church during the nineteenth century, Edward Pringle, Pastor of Devonshire Street Congregational Chapel, Keighley, identified first not the evidence of an increased society membership roll (though it had increased), nor even his sense of an enhanced collective spiritual life (though he was convinced of that too), but the simple, almost mundane, fact that '[a]t its beginning [i.e. at the beginning of the nineteenth century] the Congregationalists [in Keighley] possessed one small incommodious building, whereas they now have six buildings in which public worship is maintained and religious instruction is imparted'.[6] Just six years later, at a service held at Temple Street Wesleyan Methodist Church, Keighley, in order to honour 'sixty years ... of work done at Temple Street since its foundation', a certain J.W. Laycock remarked that: 'a new chapel has been built in every place in the circuit [Temple Street was the "mother-church" of Keighley Wesleyan Methodist Circuit], eight new schools have been erected and four ministers' houses built'.[7] It would be possible to multiply such examples almost endlessly. It is more important to appreciate how they bear witness to a particular confidence, now also to a faded sensibility: that is, to the Victorian notion of sacred progress measured in ecclesiastical bricks and mortar.

This may now seem a curious concept. Indeed, it might appear to be an odd conflation of categories, the illegitimate elision of the spiritual into the material, long since rightly repudiated. As such, its physical remains might look like the modern residue of a profound error of historical judgement, that is, the false assumption that church building was no more (nor less) than an appropriate institutional response to natural population growth, the simple provision of more symbols and more facilities for more people who needed them in greater numbers still. More damningly still, it could be judged as the malignant product of an erroneous belief that the provision of so many more such symbols and such facilities would, in itself, stimulate an otherwise indifferent or lapsed nation to resume its proper religious obligations. These, critical, contemporary arguments are well known. They are supported by voluminous surviving evidence for the extent of Victorian church-building activity, a phenomenon common across all denominations and continuing in excess of the rate of growth of the national population, especially during the second half of the nineteenth century; and by an all

[6] Pringle, 'Pastor's Address', pp. 13–14.
[7] *Keighley News*, 27 April 1906.

too conspicuous lack of proof that such efforts produced any significant increase in the absolute or relative number of persons who attended regular worship as a result.[8]

They are also – apparently – corroborated by the local evidence. Certainly, this points to a Victorian building boom, pushed far beyond the extent of local demographic increase. Consider the raw data. In 1801, there were just seven churches and chapels standing in the urban 'township' of Halifax. Two were of the Church of England: St John the Baptist, the parish church, founded in the early twelfth century, and Holy Trinity, founded in 1798. The oldest dissenting place of worship in the town, Northgate End Unitarian Chapel, dated from the late seventeenth century. Subsequently, Wesleyan Methodist (1763), Baptist (1763), Congregational (1764), and Methodist New Connexion (1797–1800) churches were added to their number. By 1851, there were 25 churches and chapels serving the recently incorporated Municipal Borough of Halifax. Yet at the turn of the twentieth century, there were probably 99 churches and chapels scattered about the County Borough of Halifax.[9] That figure rose to 104 just after the end of the First World War.[10]

This pattern of growth was repeated in Keighley. Three places of worship, one Anglican church (the parish church of twelfth-century foundation), one Quaker meeting house, dating from the seventeenth century, and one Congregational chapel, built in 1760, served the town in 1801. Fifty years later, nine sufficed. Two more Anglican churches had been built in the interim, plus five new premises, one each respectively for the Baptists, Wesleyan Methodists, Primitive Methodists, Roman Catholics and Swedenborgians. Yet, by 1900, there were some 46 churches, chapels and mission halls standing in the Municipal Borough of Keighley.[11] That figure rose to 50 by the time of the First World War.[12] The pace of church building in Denholme naturally was less remarkable. In 1801, there was just one church, a Methodist chapel,

---

8   Brown, 'Did Urbanization Secularize Britain?', pp. 10–14; Chadwick, *The Victorian Church, Part II*, pp. 227–8 and 232; Gilbert, *Religion and Industrial Society*, p. 130; Parry, *Democracy and Religion*, pp. 6–7; see also the remarks of Jeffrey Cox, Review of Donald M. Lewis, *Lighten Their Darkness: The Evangelical Mission to Working Class London, 1828–1860* (Westport, Conn., 1986), *American Historical Review*, 93 (1988), 702. The wider significance of this development is considered in Gill, 'Secularization and Census Data', esp. pp. 99–108.

9   Author's calculations. Paradoxically, it is virtually impossible to establish an exact figure for the number of places of worship in a major town at any given time, since the division (or demarcation) between a room, a hall and a chapel was a matter more of convention than of legal status (the practice of consecration notwithstanding).

10   *Census of England and Wales, 1921: Yorkshire*, p. 77.

11   *Keighley Yearbook, 1900* (Keighley, 1900), pp. 137ff.

12   *Keighley Yearbook, 1914* (Keighley, 1914), pp. 116ff.

standing in the village. By 1851, there were four: St Paul's Church of England was constructed to serve the Ecclesiastical District of Denholme in 1846. A Primitive Methodist chapel at Denholme Gate preceded it by twelve years. An Independent chapel was built in the centre of the village in 1844. In 1901, the total had risen to seven. No major religious building was undertaken in Denholme after 1869.[13]

In fact, local patterns diverged from natural trends in one important respect. Those trends pointed to a figurative orgy of construction around mid-century, slowing down to a gentler flow towards its end. The local evidence suggests something like the opposite. It is not as if there was no mid-century boom in West Yorkshire. There was. So much so that one local antiquarian noted a 'church-building explosion [in] the mid-nineteenth century'.[14] And many of the most prominent, and certainly almost all of the most famous, local churches date from that time. One of the most notable of these was All Souls' Church of England, Haley Hill. But more Anglican churches and mission churches were built in Halifax in the twenty-five years *after* 1865 than in the preceding quarter of a century.[15] Nor was this pattern confined to the Established Church. Rather, it seems to have been loosely reproduced amongst the major nonconformist denominations. For instance, Temple Street Wesleyan Methodist Church, Keighley, was also of early Victorian vintage. Yet the Wesleyan Methodist Connexion in Keighley grew faster – in terms of churches built – during the decade after 1870 than at any other time in its previous or its subsequent history.[16] And there were other examples too. Square Church, Halifax, dates from 1856; Devonshire Street, Keighley, from the same year. However, the number of Congregational churches doubled in Halifax, and sextupled in Keighley, during the last third of the nineteenth century.[17] In fact, the local evidence suggests that, whilst the most prestigious projects were concentrated around mid-century, probably two-thirds of all those churches, chapels and mission-churches *ever built* in Halifax and Keighley were constructed between the passing of the Second Reform Act and the death of Queen Victoria.[18]

Of course, this contemporary development only compounds the

[13] See Anon., *Industrial Advantages of Denholme*, pp. 11–13.
[14] Anon., *Church of St John the Evangelist, Warley, Centenary, 1878–1978* (Todmorden, 1978), p. 8.
[15] A. Goodwin, 'How the Ancient Parish of Halifax Was Divided', *THAS*, 57 (1961), 23–36.
[16] *Keighley Yearbook, 1880* (Keighley, 1880), p. 76.
[17] CDA, unpub. TS, (?) Biggs, 'Congregationalism: Its Growth and Development in Halifax' (n.d.), p. 22; Pringle, 'Pastor's Address', pp. 13–14.
[18] Author's calculations; cf. Brown, 'Did Urbanization Secularize Britain?', p. 10; also Gill, 'Secularization and Census Data', pp. 99–101.

problem of subsequent comprehension, for such local variations, seen in this light, suggest that whilst the comparative rate of church increase in this part of West Yorkshire actually fell slightly behind the national and regional rate of population growth between 1800 and 1850, it moved even more markedly ahead of either during the next half-century. Put another way, the number of church buildings standing in Halifax and Keighley more than doubled during the last third of the nineteenth century during a period in which the demographic growth of each town was less than 50 per cent. That divergence may have represented nothing more remarkable than a local 'construction time-lag'. If so, it remains curious – why West Yorkshire? And it is also difficult to square with further evidence, similarly calculated, that more churches continued to be built in both towns even after their local populations had actually begun to decline. Moreover, neither piece of information sits easily with the very different patterns of construction observable in Denholme, where church-building projects effectively ceased *before* the town's population had peaked, and long prior to its decline.[19]

The unquestionably anomalous impact of all this activity emerges even more clearly still when it is represented in terms of the potential number of seats in church or chapel available for worship, in relation to the population, at any given time. Here, sufficient and reliable data have survived only for Keighley, but there is no reason to believe that they tell a tale inapplicable to Halifax. Indeed, there is every reason to believe from parallel church-building patterns that the similarities would have been very strong. This evidence suggests that, in 1801, Keighley's 5,745 citizens probably enjoyed access to no more than 1,000 church and chapel seats. By 1851, a population of some 17,000 there was served by perhaps 6,000 seats, a ratio of around 3 to 1. Twenty years later, about 28,000 were provided with a choice from amongst something close to 13,000 seats, a ratio now down to little more than 2 to 1. And that was when the most intensive phase of local ecclesiastical building *began*. Hence the provision of about 25,000 seats, for just over 40,000 persons around the turn of the century. In 1917, the last date for which reliable figures have survived, that supply had risen to something like 27,500 for 40,000, a ratio of less than 1.5 to 1.[20]

In other words, the rate of the additional provision of seats for worship almost certainly exceeded the rate of increase in the local population throughout the nineteenth century. More importantly, it went on increasing as that population growth first stalled and then actually

[19]   Author's calculations; cf. ch. 1, pp. 52–5.
[20]   Author's calculations; see *Keighley Yearbook, 1917*, pp. 151ff. For wider reference, see Gill, 'Secularization and Census Data', pp. 103–4 and 109.

reversed. One further point should be noted. With the sole exception of St Anne's Roman Catholic Church, there is no evidence of any church in Keighley being built, rebuilt or even enlarged *directly* as a consequence of congregational pressure on available seating space. To be sure, there is a superabundance of anecdotal material justifying such building in terms of congregational or even associational need, but at St Anne's alone was a contemporary building actually declared 'inadequate in dimension for worshippers' (i.e. for the actual number of persons seeking to worship there).[21] And, more pointedly still, at St Anne's alone were services held more than once on a Sunday morning (four times in fact) solely 'on account of ... deficiency of room'.[22] Put bluntly, whilst there is little contemporary evidence of pressure on congregational space, there was a vast increase in provision. All of which strongly suggests that not only did local religious organisations continue to build churches and chapels after their respective populations had begun to decline, but also long after those (rising or falling) populations had conclusively proved their inability, or unwillingness, to fill such buildings as had already been provided for them. Finally, just to deepen the mystery, these organisations actually congratulated themselves for doing so, even indeed measured part of the success of their spiritual labour by these seemingly self-defeating efforts. Why?

Part of the explanation lies in the inherent complexity of motives surrounding church-building activity itself. There never was just one motive for any church-building effort, whether as simple response to demographic growth or as naive anticipation of pious revival. And if this was true generally, it was especially so in the context of the later-nineteenth-century industrial town. For there, particularly, the church-building boom did not arise *ex nihilo*. Certainly, it did not proceed unaffected by its surrounding environment. Rather it emerged, developed – and even changed – in the midst of an ever expanding and fast transforming urban environment, a continuously evolving economic and social milieu which often radically altered its earlier goals and purposes. Secondly, it was a question of authority, or rather of the plurality of authority; put another way, of the absence of any clear lines of authority in the midst of complex motives and changing contexts, which ensured that every church-building project in late Victorian and Edwardian West Yorkshire was subject to the ends and means of several authorities: national, regional, local, at times purely individual. Consequently, a proper understanding of why so many churches and chapels were built, when they were built and where they were built will depend upon an

[21]   *Keighley Yearbook, 1887*, p. 109.
[22]   *Keighley Yearbook, 1890*, p. 113.

equally clear appreciation of how so many authorities worked, often unconsciously but occasionally quite explicitly, as much against as for each other, for all this effort occurred in a context which was not only changing, sometimes in ways they never knew, but always amongst a plethora of ideals which each only partially understood and none could wholly control.

Contesting the commanding ground: the expansion of the centre, the rise of ecclesiology and the impact of inter-denominational competition

It is unremarkable to observe but, none the less, important to remember that there were at least sixteen separate denominational organisations – the Church of England, the Roman Catholic Church, the Wesleyan Methodist Church, the Methodist New Connexion, the Primitive Methodists, the United Methodist Free Church, the Wesleyan Reform Church, the Congregationalists, the Baptist Church, the Unitarians, the Catholic Apostolic Church, the Christadelphian Ecclesia, the Christian Brotherhood, the Spiritualists, the Progressive Spiritualists, and finally the Salvation Army – represented in early Edwardian Halifax. And there were only two fewer thriving in Keighley at much the same time: the Church of England, the Roman Catholic Church, the Wesleyan Methodists, the United Methodist Free Church, the Primitive Methodists, the Congregationalists, the Baptists, the Quakers, the Swedenborgians, the Spiritualists, the Catholic Apostolic Church, the Christadelphians, the Salvation Army and the Latter-Day Saints. Even in Denholme, six different religious associations flourished at the turn of the century: the Church of England, the Wesleyan Methodists, the Wesleyan Reformers, the Primitive Methodists, the Independents and the Baptists.

During the course of the nineteenth century some of those organisations built more churches than others. The Church of England built perhaps twenty-five, and the Wesleyan Methodists nineteen in Halifax, between them accounting for nearly one-third and one-fifth, respectively, of the total number of religious buildings standing in that town at the turn of the twentieth century.[23] Other Methodist organisations (Primitive, New Connexion, and the United Free Church) together built another twenty.[24] Then the Congregationalists and Baptists

---

[23]   E. Robinson, *Commercial and General Directory of Halifax* (Halifax, 1906), *passim.* Robinson lists 27 Anglican and 17 Wesleyan Methodist churches and chapels (of a total of 99) in 1906. The Anglican figure is probably a slight underestimate, excluding a small number of mission-churches.

[24]   *Ibid.* Robinson lists 9 Primitive Methodist, 7 New Connexion and 4 United Methodist Free Churches and chapels, a total of 20.

contributed just over, and just under, one-tenth of the total respectively.[25] In other words, the seven leading denominations were responsible for nearly 90 per cent of the total number of religious buildings in this town at the turn of the twentieth century.[26] The distribution of places of worship between these groups was similar in early Edwardian Keighley. The Church of England claimed one-fifth of the total; Wesleyan Methodists about the same; the Primitive Methodists accounted for nearly one-seventh; Congregationalists for one-tenth; Baptists for a little more than one-twentieth of that sum.[27]

To be sure, simple numerical advantage – the number of churches on the ground – was not necessarily synonymous with greater social significance. For instance, the Irish Catholic presence in both towns was considerable. Yet there were only two Roman Catholic churches worthy of the name in late Victorian Halifax, and just one in Keighley.[28] Similarly, a solitary Unitarian chapel in Halifax, Northgate End, wielded a local social and political influence far beyond its isolated institutional status. And the Congregationalists, though they built relatively few churches and chapels in either town, built them well. But whatever the significance of numerical presence, and whatever the implications of aesthetic gesture, one simple fact remains. In late nineteenth- and early twentieth-century Halifax there were possibly a dozen, in Keighley perhaps ten, and in Denholme probably six, discrete denominational authorities, actively seeking the opportunity to provide places of worship, and seats in order to worship, for as many persons as they could severally persuade to patronise their separate and exclusive services. Moreover, they were competing amongst themselves for that opportunity; for Victorian churches and chapels were not just social amenities, whose geographical distribution was rationally determined as a matter of public policy, comparable to the provision of elementary schools. By their very existence, they proclaimed a particular spiritual truth and a presumed moral righteousness which observed few of the rational proprieties of social resource allocation.

Churches and buildings were, after all, the most obvious symbols of their respective denominations. Metaphorically speaking, they voiced its

25 *Ibid.* Congregational, 10; Baptist, 7.
26 That is, 81 out of 99.
27 *Keighley Yearbook, 1900*, pp. 137ff. Church of England, 10; Wesleyan Methodist, 10; United Methodist Free Church, 4; Primitive Methodist, 7; Congregationalist, 6; and Baptist, 3. The Wesleyan Methodist figure excludes those stations which were part of the Keighley Wesleyan Methodist Circuit, post-1871, but not within the borders of the Municipal Borough.
28 St Mary's Church, Gibbet Street, and the Church of the Sacred Heart and St Bernard, Range Lane, Halifax; and St Anne's Church, North Street, Keighley.

beliefs, they bore witness to its taste and made public its resources. Or, as the worldly Dr Mellor put it, they expressed '[partly] in substance and partly in form' the 'nature of the church' in question and 'the pecuniary [wealth] at [its] command'.[29] Above all, they expressed its ambition: its denominational ambition and its associational ambition. And that, in mid-nineteenth-century West Yorkshire was a competitive ambition. Naturally, the force of this 'competitive principle' varied from denomination to denomination, from church to church, and even from person to person. It also varied over time. Some took virtually no part at all in the contest. Local Roman Catholic priests and missionaries, for instance, generally built for and tended to their own, predominantly Irish flock, both in Halifax and in Keighley. In this sense, theirs was as much a mission to ethnicity as to creed, and though they denied that salutary truth in public words and deeds, most contemporary Roman Catholic officials understood it well enough.[30] Others, however, took the competitive game very seriously. In this way, one of the most important motives underlying the building projects pursued by the major nonconformist organisations during the middle years of the nineteenth century was their very specific ambition to challenge, publicly and directly, the traditional assumption of the Church of England that it fully represented the spiritual needs of the nation, and to prove 'that the Nonconformist Churches as a whole are capable of asserting ... their claim to be considered ... a national church'.[31]

In the manufacturing towns of early Victorian West Yorkshire, this challenge was anything but an idle threat. Nonconformist organisations locally were numerous. They were represented by eight different denominations in Halifax as early as mid-century; six in Keighley; five even in Denholme. They were popular. So much so that the Vicar of Halifax described the early Victorian borough as a 'Nonconformist ... stronghold'.[32] Even Keighley was acknowledged as a 'pioneer ... Methodist ... town'.[33] Finally, they were wealthy. There was Congregational money amongst the Crossleys in Halifax, and the Briggs in Keighley; and Methodist money in the early days from Sugden in Keighley, then later Mackintosh in Halifax. To be sure, they enjoyed no

29   Mellor, 'Congregational Principles', pp. 101–2.
30   See J.J. Mulroy, *Upon This Rock: The Story of the Church in Halifax* (Halifax, 1952), pp. 34ff; also Berry, *Keighley Catholic Church*, pp. 4–7 and 26.
31   J.R. Bailey, *Progressive Congregationalism: An Address Delivered at the Annual Meeting of the Yorkshire Congregational Union and Home Missionary Society Held at Keighley, 5th April 1892* (Keighley, 1892), pp. 21–2.
32   Pigou, *Phases in My Life*, p. 300.
33   Keighley, *Keighley, Past and Present*, p. 174.

peculiar advantages in this last respect. Indeed, they actually endured some notable disadvantages. The Church, at least initially, had access to public funds. They did not.[34] Also, the Church, again at least initially, had access not only to new local money, from Colonel Akroyd amongst others in Halifax, but to old landed influence, from the Cavendish family in Keighley. Moreover, prime building land was not made more easily available to dissenters than to the Church; indeed rather less so. Nor were the best building materials.[35] But that was not the point. Comparatively disadvantaged or not, they had the resources to compete. In time, they gained the opportunity to compete. And finally they acknowledged a style with which to compete.

Resources meant money; not simply, or even primarily the money of the very rich, but the money of a dedicated community, committed to the voluntary principle.[36] Opportunity meant space; not only the space which contemporary economic developments had, quite literally, created, but also the space which nonconformists were now eager to fill. In the words of one contemporary Congregationalist historian, J.G. Miall: 'Nonconformists now came boldly out of the corners in to which they had crept for security and privacy, and placed their buildings in commanding positions. The movement once begun extended rapidly.' Style meant a new style; specifically, a revived style, and more especially still a first narrowly revived but then much more widely disseminated style. Miall again: 'The chapels of the Nonconformists had been hitherto characterized by few architectural pretensions ... But about 1835, a more advanced style of building was attempted.'[37] That 'advanced style' was otherwise known as 'dissenting Gothic'.[38] A product of mid-century, this was a self-conscious development in nonconformist building style, an attempt to replace the traditional, and strictly functional, preaching-house with an 'attractive form, agreeable to the eye'.[39] Ironically, it originated in the revival of the Perpendicular, or pointed, style associated with contemporary Anglo-Catholicism. The ecclesiology which it implied was first formulated by the Cambridge Camden Society. Subsequently it was much associated with the Oxford Tractarians.[40] It found its finest local exponent (and national champion)

[34] On which, see G.F.A. Best, *Temporal Pillars: Queen Anne's Bounty, The Ecclesiastical Commissioners and the Church of England* (Cambridge, 1964), chs. 7 and 9.
[35] A point made particularly well in Binfield, *So Down to Prayers*, pp. 147ff.
[36] *Ibid.*, pp. 151ff.
[37] James G. Miall, *Congregationalism in Yorkshire* (London, 1868), pp. 199–200.
[38] Binfield, *So Down to Prayers*, p. 145; I owe this term to Binfield.
[39] *Congregational Year Book, 1847* (London, 1847); cited in Binfield, *So Down to Prayers*, p. 148.
[40] On nineteenth-century ecclesiological doctrine, see Nigel Yates, *Buildings, Faith and Worship: Liturgical Arrangement of Anglican Churches, 1600–1900* (Oxford, 1991),

in A.W.N. Pugin.[41] His masterly Roman Catholic Church at St Anne's, Keighley, built in 1840, was an especially fine example of the early genre.[42] From these distinctly dubious origins, the Gothic revival nevertheless found its way, or at least part of its way, into contemporary nonconformist building style. This was partly because it spoke so clearly to the imperatives of individual ambition: to rich dissenters who wished to place their mark on the emerging ecclesiastical landscape. It was also because it addressed the growing need to ally a newly self-conscious taste with that presumed utility which defined much of the drive towards collective respectability in the early Victorian puritan sensibility.[43] Put another way, it demonstrated that nonconformist money might increasingly be put not simply to good, but also to civilised, purposes.

Naturally, there were doubters within the fold. One, to a limited degree anyway, was Miall himself. He, at least, remained unimpressed by the emergence of a new generation of buildings which spawned 'arches which no processions are intended to traverse ... huge pillars which serve only to obstruct the hearer's view [and] high roofs which defy every principle of acoustics' and, still worse, by the coming prospect of 'ecclesiastical adornments which present windows in the form of mitres, brackets suggestive of the Trinity [and] traditionally Romanistic demons which fly from the face of the consecrated host [and] which can never find in nonconformity a congenial home'.[44]

But to a remarkable degree they could and did. Of course, there were limits. Not all of the characteristic innovations of contemporary ecclesiological doctrine found their way into dissenting Gothic. There were no raised altars, no separated chancels, no situated fonts within its midst. But it is perhaps rather more significant that there were many early English spires, stone façades and varnished pews amongst its examples.[45] And in that way, certainly to an extent which would have struck an earlier generation as unthinkable, Camden dogma and dissenting convenience increasingly dedicated themselves to remarkably similar physical products, albeit still to diverging theological interpretation.[46] In that way too, the triumph of such nebulous but widespread ecclesiological principles generally ensured that a certain type of church

pp. 133ff.; and, for a wider context, Roger Dixon and Stefan Muthesius, *Victorian Architecture* (London, 1978), esp. pp. 192–4.

[41] On whom, see David Watkin, *A History of Western Architecture* (London, 1986), pp. 404–6; and Dixon and Muthesius, *Victorian Architecture*, pp. 182–8.

[42] Linstrum, *West Yorkshire*, p. 221.

[43] Binfield, *So Down to Prayers*, p. 147.

[44] Miall, *Congregationalism in Yorkshire*, pp. 199–200.

[45] Binfield, *So Down to Prayers*, p. 146.

[46] Yates, *Buildings, Faith and Worship*, p. 159; Binfield, *So Down to Prayers*, pp. 147, 154.

– a characteristically nineteenth-century English Gothic church –
increasingly filled the central spaces of many developing industrial towns
in later Victorian Britain. Moreover, this similarity of style reflected a
deeper similarity – if profound incompatibility – of ecclesiastical
purposes. This was true in the country generally. And it was particularly
true of this part of the West Riding of Yorkshire.

Between the mid 1840s and the late 1870s, Anglicans and nonconformists built numerous, and notably similar, churches and chapels in
Halifax, Keighley and Denholme to contest the commanding ground –
physical, social and spiritual – in their respective towns.[47] Allying the
aesthetic properties of a revived architectural style to the economic
resources of new manufacturing wealth, they first laid claim to and then
gradually transformed the open spaces – physical, social and spiritual
open spaces – of their hitherto underdeveloped inner urban environments.[48] Their individual purposes were, of course, mutually exclusive.
They aimed, separately, to win institutional supremacy for their own
denominations in this effort. But the effect was, paradoxically, socially
unifying, for the very act of such widespread ecclesiastical competition,
so driven, so expressed and so located, also served to reinforce the
prevailing conception of churches, and particularly of church buildings,
as especially attractive social institutions, thus playing their 'part in the
Christian education of the people' by their seemingly unique capacity to
draw the faithful, literally as well as figuratively, into 'the town centre',
there to bear witness to their different faiths but also, incidentally, to
affirm at least a nebulous sense of a developing urban unity.[49]

To be sure, neither denominational competition nor social integration
exhausted either the narrower aims or the wider possibilities of early
Victorian, inner urban, church-building activity. There were other
motives: individual vanity played its part, particularly in new towns with
new and aggressive leaders. Intra-associational strife was often significant too, between romantics and radicals in the Church, progressives
and traditionalists in dissent, ultramontanists and moderates in Catholicism. Even the impulse of ingenuous social philanthropy cannot be
entirely discounted. Similarly, there were other consequences. Not all of
them contributed to the growing integrity of Victorian town centres.
But, increasingly, each of these disparate goals and uncertain effects was
subsumed under the wider social rubric of institutional rivalry and social

---

[47] Miall, *Congregationalism in Yorkshire*, pp. 199–200; corroborated in Linstrum, *West Yorkshire*, pp. 209ff.

[48] Linstrum, *West Yorkshire*, pp. 224ff; also Dixon and Muthesius, *Victorian Architecture*, pp. 188–200 and 229–33.

[49] Biggs, 'Congregationalism', p. 22.

comprehension. At the very least, the organisational significance of such competitive principles, and their paradoxically unifying purposes, was more explicitly defined and more assiduously practised during these middling decades than at any time before or since. This was the product, above all, of the sheer extent of building; also of the size of building; and finally of the cost of building.

Examples abound. In 1844, the Independents (as they were then called) built a handsome chapel (their first) in the centre of what was then the new ecclesiastical district of Denholme, at a cost of £1,000.[50] But their efforts were – not surprisingly perhaps – quickly matched and then surpassed by the Church of England. St Paul's, Church of England, Denholme Gate was completed in 1846. It cost £4,000, much of it furnished from the local Knowles and Foster manufacturing fortunes. Early English in style, finished with a beautifully proportioned Gothic spire, it was immediately described as 'The Minster in the Hills'. This was only just an exaggeration. Constructed on 'an imposing position on the brow of a hill half a mile from the village', and erected quite explicitly with the purpose of commanding the high ground 'midway between the two communities' of Denholme Clough, then 'a thriving industrial district', and Denholme Gate, the expectation was that it would eventually fill the centre of the major industrial town which the developing site of Denholme was expected to become. But Denholme, of course, never quite developed in this way. Hence St Paul's remained, and remains to this day, physically removed from the centre of local population, gloriously (if quite dysfunctionally) isolated from it and them.[51]

Others were luckier, at least in this respect. In 1846, Keighley's Wesleyan Methodists deliberately relocated the 'mother church' of their circuit to Temple Street, in the very hub of the developing industrial town. Their investment was massive. The new church was designed to seat 1,655 persons, equivalent to about one-fifth of the entire adult population of the town at that time. And the building cost £14,000, a price higher than any paid in Keighley throughout the nineteenth century.[52] Yet it was not wasted money. Keighley did grow, and around Temple Street. So too did its Wesleyan Methodist Connexion. It was, however, a fully contested bid for local dominion. Certainly, the Establishment responded immediately. St Andrew's Parish Church was

50 Anon., *Denholme Independent Chapel: Jubilee Celebration, March 24 and 25, 1894* (Denholme, 1894), p. 6.
51 Anon., *The Church of St Paul in Denholme Gate, 1846–1946* (Denholme, 1946), p. 1; also Linstrum, *West Yorkshire*, pp. 374 and 384.
52 *Keighley Yearbook, 1900* (Keighley, 1900), p. 137.

wholly rebuilt during the following two years. The new building was conceived in the newly fashionable 'Perpendicular ... English style'. Seating space was extended to accommodate 1,000 persons. It cost a lot: £7,000. But it was sponsored at a time which local churchmen understood to be 'a critical [historical] juncture', and by an 'Episcopalian Party ... alive to the responsibilities of wealth [and] the merits of a rapidly rising population'.[53] In this, at least, they were not alone. Ten years later, the Congregationalists established a new permanent home at Devonshire Street, also towards the centre of the new town, in a 'general arrangement of buildings', this time executed in the 'Italian style', with seating for 1,036 faithful.[54] It cost £4,000.[55] Donations of £1,000 by the Craven brothers and £500 from John Brigg 'indicated both the prosperity and generosity of supporters of Independency at the time'.[56] They also demonstrated the willingness of its leaders to pay for the competitive significance of Congregationalism in the emerging industrial society of early Victorian Keighley.

But the 'competitive principle' in inner urban church building found its most extravagant local expression in Halifax. There, in 1857, the squat and austere eighteenth-century chapel, which had served as the historic home for Square Congregational Church, was discreetly converted into a Sunday school. It was replaced by a majestic Gothic building, a new church little less in substance than a small cathedral, costing £15,000, seating 1,500 persons, and featuring a nave with a cloister at each side, north and south transepts, and finally a tower and bowed spire at the side of the west front, all standing 235 feet high. It was at once described as 'a most conspicuous object [which] will always be looked upon as one of the greatest ornaments of the town'.[57] It certainly was conspicuous. It soared above the Piece Hall, Georgian symbol of Halifax's manufacturing wealth. It looked down upon its new fledgling railway station. And it dwarfed its old, Established parish church. It was definitely ornamental. Architect Joseph James adapted the design of the east window of Selby Abbey for the 'west front' of the church, and put rose windows in the transepts. Inside, he carved the figures of musical angels to form the corbels of the roof, while at the 'east end' he placed an octagonal case stone pulpit, decorated by the emblems of the Passion, in front of a large organ case. As a parting touch, Gothic tracery panels were incorporated into the pews in the

[53]   Keighley, *History of Keighley*, pp. 142–3.
[54]   Keighley, *History of Keighley*, p. 165.
[55]   *Ibid.*, p. 164.
[56]   W. Reid Marchbank, *One Hundred Years of Progress: An Account of the Expansion of Congregationalism in Keighley* (Keighley, 1956), p. 23.
[57]   *Builder*, 15 (1857), p. 482.

nave.[58] Finally, it was self-evidently significant, for it was the gift, almost entirely, of the Crossley brothers. Vast in expense, ingenious in design, costly in production it stood awesomely and unambiguously as a monument to civic pride, to commercial prosperity and as an expression of the strength of local Congregationalism in general, and of one pre-eminent Congregationalist family in particular. In that way, it represented a clear challenge to the cultural and spiritual supremacy of the Established Church in Halifax.

That challenge was soon met. It took the form of All Souls' Church of England, Haley Hill, erected between 1856 and 1859. Its architect was the legendary George Gilbert Scott. It was one of seven churches he designed in the region. And it was, he believed, 'on the whole, my best church'.[59] Its benefactor was Sir Edward Akroyd, local Anglican dignitary, scion of the legendary manufacturing family, and chief rival to the Crossleys. Akroyd spent up to £100,000 on All Souls'.[60] He intended it to dominate the landscape of central Halifax. It did and it still does. Erected on a commanding site overlooking the industrial heart of the town from the north-east, it stands 236 feet high. It was executed in an exquisite Anglo-French Gothic. The west front was faced with diapered patterned stone and canopied saints and prophets. The ceiling was geometrically patterned in pale and dark blues, white, black and gold. The chancel walls were decorated with painted medallions. Only the finest artists and craftsmen were employed upon the more intricate details of Scott's masterpiece, all at Akroyd's expense. Francis Skidmore made the wrought-iron screen and gates. Clayton and Bell, William Waites and John Hardman designed and produced the glass. Hardman's west window, an image of the Last Judgement inspired by Blake, was immediately recognised as a notable artistic achievement of great beauty and drama. Almost as an afterthought, seating was provided for around 1,000 persons.[61]

But All Souls' was, from the beginning, 'more than just a beautiful building'.[62] It embodied Akroyd's hopes for reviving the faltering Anglican cause in Halifax. It also represented the most obvious attempt to reassert his family's flagging social dominance within the town. And, uniting those twin ambitions, it constituted the most significant single effort ever made to bring all the social classes of the borough together, under one roof, and for the worship of the only God. To that end,

---

[58] Linstrum, *West Yorkshire*, p. 225.
[59] G.G. Scott, *Personal and Professional Recollections* (London, 1879), p. 176.
[60] Bretton, 'Colonel Edward Akroyd', *THAS*, 45 (1948), p. 87.
[61] *Builder*, 17 (1859), pp. 727ff., contains the most detailed description of the building and its decorations. See also, Linstrum, *West Yorkshire*, pp. 227–8.
[62] Jowett, 'Copley, Akroydon and West Hill Park', pp. 80–1.

Akroyd built All Souls' big as well as grand. More pointedly still, he situated it close to his own home, Bankfield, facing his own model village, Akroydon, and overlooking his own manufacturing plant, the weaving works of James Akroyd and Son. In this way, he fulfilled a vision, formed many years earlier, of 'keeping up the old notion of a village' within the evolving industrial town, by reinforcing – through simple will power and complex planning – the hierarchical society of landlord and labourer, united in the faith.[63] As if to underline that point for those few who can have failed to realise it, Akroyd commissioned Birnie Phillips to sculpt a statue of himself, standing between church and village and holding a map of the whole town. It was unveiled in 1875.[64]

By that time, however, the whole project of which All Souls' was a part was already little more than a gigantic exercise in self-delusion. To have believed that the evolution of so complex and variegated an urban environment could be fundamentally redirected by the thoughts and efforts of one man was optimistic, even in the 1850s.[65] To have continued in that belief, particularly given the precarious state of Akroyd's own personal finances, right through into the mid-1870s, was simply nonsensical.[66] But Akroyd's poignant delusion proved the Church's simple gain. His pointless megalomania bolstered its precarious competitiveness. What was more, they had reason to be grateful to him again soon afterwards, for the nonconformist challenge to Anglican church-building supremacy did not go away with construction of All Soul's. Indeed, in some ways it intensified. In this respect, the refurbishment and improvement of Northgate End Unitarian Chapel in 1872–3 was widely acknowledged to be a reflection of an ecclesiastical battle still drawn. Situated right in the centre of the town, a noted bastion of both enlightened and popular opposition to Anglican hegemony, its structural renovation and above all its architectural redefinition as a fine, even ornate, 'churchy' building, was widely interpreted as being yet another direct assault upon the local Anglican Establishment.[67] This was certainly the Anglican view. Thus, on assuming the incumbency of St John the Baptist, Halifax, in 1875, the Reverend Francis Pigou immediately denounced the 'overpowering' nonconformist presence in his midst, and then set about confronting that threat in what was, by then, a very well-tried fashion: by rebuilding

---

[63] *Builder*, 21 (1863), p. 110. See also the remarks in Linstrum, *West Yorkshire*, pp. 136–7.
[64] Linstrum, *West Yorkshire*, p. 228.
[65] Dingsdale, *Yorkshire Mill Town*, pp. 98 and 113–120.
[66] On Akroyd's finances by the 1870s, see Bretton, 'Colonel Edward Akroyd', p. 94.
[67] Robert and Clarissa Eccles and A. Elliott Peaston, *The History of Northgate End Chapel, Halifax, 1696–1946* (Halifax, 1946), pp. 2–3.

and renewal.[68] Almost entirely at his insistence, though very much not at his expense, St John the Baptist was restored and refurbished between 1877 and 1879. Pigou's proclaimed object was 'to increase the accommodation in the body of the church for the congregation, to allow the service to be more efficiently performed, and to render the interior more worthy of the parish to which it belonged'.[69] In this way, he hoped to make 'their church ... second to none in its decorous arrangement and its facilities for reverent worship'.[70] To that end, Pigou proposed 'to raise a sum of not less than £10,000'.[71] In the event, he succeeded in raising more than half that sum again.[72] First, he sought and won the patronage of Colonel Akroyd.[73] The Colonel, along with thirteen other major subscribers, contributed £5,000 to the scheme.[74] Then Pigou sought to extend 'this movement ... throughout the Parish'.[75] And he succeeded. Some 245 individual contributors eventually subscribed another £12,000 over the next five years.[76] To cap his good fortune, he also succeeded in acquiring the services of Akroyd's favourite architect, George Gilbert Scott.[77] Despite local misgivings, and despite contemporary criticisms of the very *idea* of restoration, criticism directed especially at Pigou, a noted High Churchman and militant ecclesiologist, but even against Scott himself, the result was a notably beautiful amalgam of fifteenth-century inspiration and nineteenth-century improvement.[78] What stands today, virtually unchanged from its nineteenth-century restoration, is generally acknowledged to be one of finest churches in West Yorkshire.[79]

[68] Pigou, *Phases in My Life*, p. 300.
[69] Anon., *The Restoration of the Halifax Parish Church* (Halifax, 1877), p. 8.
[70] *Ibid.*, p. 3.
[71] *Ibid.*, p. 8.
[72] WHQ, D/53, incom. arch. ref., Halifax, St John the Baptist Parish Church Restoration, Account Book, 1877–80. In July 1883 £16,957 17s 8d had been deposited in the bank and £4,726 18s 3d remained in uncollected subscriptions from the Restoration Fund. The Fund was closed in that month though the Account Book was kept beyond 1880, despite its title.
[73] Anon, *The Restoration of Halifax Parish Church*, p. 3.
[74] *Ibid.*, p. 5.
[75] *Ibid.*
[76] WHQ, D/53, incom. arch. ref., Halifax, St John the Baptist, Parish Church Restoration, Account Book, 1877–80. In 1878, 78 subscribers; in 1879, 77; in 1880, 66; in 1881, 24. Those are listed in the Account Book as 'individual subscribers'. No doubt there were repetitions.
[77] Anon., *The Restoration of Halifax Parish Church*, pp. 3 and 7.
[78] Linstrum, *West Yorkshire*, p. 179.
[79] Alec Clifton-Taylor, *English Parish Churches as Works of Art*, 2nd. rev. edn (London, 1985), p. 241.

The flight to the suburbs: spatial evolution, urban differentiation and the impact of the church extension movement

The restoration of Halifax parish church was also in many ways the last great ecclesiastical building project to grace the centre of Victorian Halifax. Nor was Halifax peculiar in this respect. After the refurbishment of Upper Green Congregational Chapel, in 1874, very little significant religious building was undertaken in the centre of Keighley until the refurbishment of St Anne's Roman Catholic Church in 1907.[80] And no important new church building disturbed the centre of Denholme village at all during the last third of the nineteenth century. But if the church-building explosion simply fizzled out in Denholme, its flames still burned brightly, indeed more brightly still, to the north and south. Building priorities changed, but building activity if anything intensified. The battle for the high ground moved to the geographical peripheries of these fast-developing towns. To some extent, this was a simple matter of moving on from satiated central sites, as manufacturing industry was doing at much the same time. But it was about something more than that. Churches, after all, were more than just religious factories. Rather, it was a function both of diminishing space and of reordered priorities. For as the physical location of church-building activity shifted, so the principal ends of church-building effort subtly altered. As it ceased, quite literally, to be centred upon the physical urban core, so its specifically integrative ends shed much of their aspect of centripetal attraction and developed something like a notion of centrifugal comprehension.

At one level, this meant that church building became a means – perhaps indeed the most important means – through which organised religion responded to the physical movement of the population within the industrialising town. At another level, it represented the recognition of a subtle but profound redistribution of local social authority, of a shift of local economic power away from the pioneering giants and towards a larger, more amorphous bourgeoisie, itself increasingly located in the suburbs and more and more confident of asserting its right to claw the best sacred trade away from the now unfashionable town centres. Finally, it acknowledged the emergence of a greater institutional diversity within religious organisations themselves, of the development of a system of organisations made up of many, and often quite different, types of societies, that is, of associations quite willing to compete with

---

[80] Berry, *Keighley Catholic Church*, pp. 21–3.

one another in their quest for scarce ecclesiastical resources, even as they ostensibly co-operated against their professed denominational rivals. In that way, not only did the flight to the suburbs recognise a change in the characteristic forms of local ecclesiastical integration, but it also acknowledged a significant alteration in the rules of inter- (and intra-)denominational competition, as the typical norms of associational rivalry developed from the crude zero-sum game of mid-century antagonism into a rather more complicated, negotiated compromise between pluralistically motivated partners in the Edwardian town.

These changes were of essentially local origin. They may be traced to the suburbanisation of industry and population which marked the evolution of Halifax and Keighley during the last third of the nineteenth century. In that sense, they represented no more than a rational response to what the Archdeacon of Halifax called in 1896, 'our shifting and growing population'.[81] Certainly, rapid contemporary economic and social change was accompanied, as the Archdeacon lamented, by the emergence of 'large populations which have grown up in places more or less remote from their Parish Churches [in] numerous hamlets or villages, with populations varying from 300 to 2000 which ... through lack of men and means, the Church has too long neglected ... and in many of which the Church has little or no hold'.[82]

Moreover, spatial evolution and demographic displacement were facts of urban life which observed no denominational boundaries. So a history of Rhodes Street Wesleyan Methodist Church, Halifax, written in 1917, observed that:

The progress of Halifax in the fourth, fifth and sixth decades of the last century ... was steady ... the population moved west and north-west ... [L]ittle effort appears to have been made to provide for the religious needs of this section of the population. The church of which we are celebrating the jubilee was the first to be erected in a part of the town as yet much in want of religious edifices.[83]

And the town kept on moving to the west and to the north-west in the seventh, eighth and ninth decades of the nineteenth century.[84] So, only twenty years after the foundation of Rhodes Street Chapel, its trustees were confronted by what was, in effect, a repetition of the very same problem which had brought their own society into existence. Thus, in 1887, they were urged of the 'necessity of having a place of worship on

[81] *A Charge Delivered on Wednesday, 22nd April 1896, by the Venerable Archdeacon of Halifax* (Halifax, 1896), pp. 4–5.
[82] 'Archdeacon's Charges', *HPCM*, vol. 15, no. 6, June 1890 (no page number).
[83] Anon., *Rhodes Street Wesleyan Chapel, Halifax, Jubilee Celebration, 1867–1917* (Halifax, 1917), p. 4.
[84] Dingsdale, 'Yorkshire Mill Town', pp. 201–2.

Queen's Road, near Parkinson Lane', a quarter of a mile or so from their own building.[85] This was because 'the town was rapidly moving in that direction'[86] and there was a 'large and increasing population [in] the neighbourhood'.[87]

Yet the simple growth of the town was not a binding reason to build more churches. Nor was it a definitive proof of previous ecclesiastical neglect. For the inner urban cathedrals had been *deliberately* built too big. This was partly to cater for possible future demand. It was more to attract the faithful from the outlying suburbs and villages. And if the faithful and faithless were, by 1896, spread further out still, few if any actually lived much more than a mile from a big, impressive and half-empty church. What the Archdeacon and the anonymous historian were really talking about was less a question of demographic dispersion and more a matter of complex social differentiation. What they were addressing was a population which was not merely increasingly spread out but much more clearly divided into sociologically distinct neighbourhoods. And what they were really concerned about was a town which was not simply getting larger but becoming progressively separated into discrete industrial urban communities. Together, these changes pointed to the awful possibility of populations not merely effectively removed from, that is, not actually participating in, but also apparently deprived of the very possibility of religious worship; of a people over which 'the church [has] no hold', and for whose 'needs' no 'effort' had 'been made'. Both charges were, strictly speaking, false. Neither local demography nor ecclesiastical geography bore them out. But the character of local relations seemingly did. And it was to that, apparently malignant and unquestionably novel, feature of urban life that churchmen and ministers necessarily now turned their attention.

Their solution to this problem was to promote a system of so-called 'church extension': that is, to encourage the construction of new churches, chapels and mission halls in new urban districts, as those districts emerged on the urban plan. The underlying idea was not new. It can be traced back at least as far as the New Parishes Act of 1843, which had envisaged the provision of new (though only Anglican) endowments in previously neglected industrial outposts. Halifax had been assigned five such districts and Keighley one. The parish of Denholme was itself wholly a product of that initiative.[88] But later

---

[85] CDA, MR/144. Providence, Queen's Road, Wesleyan Methodist Chapel, Trustees' Meeting Minute Book, 1887–1942; unpub. MS, 'A History of Providence Wesleyan Methodist Chapel', p. 2.

[86] 'History of Providence Wesleyan Methodist Chapel', p. 6.

[87] *Ibid.*, p. 5.

[88] Best, *Temporal Pillars*, pp. 335–9.

Victorian church extension, or the church extension movement, was rather a different affair. For one thing, it was emphatically multi-denominational. Secondly, it was a continuous, living institution, not a periodic, parliamentary event. Finally, and as a consequence both of its diversity and its informality, it became a self-conscious mechanism which enabled local authorities to transcend the traditional 'parochialism' of their own various organisations in pursuit of their now seemingly urgent duty, a duty defined in the words of the progenitors of Keighley's Church-Extension Scheme for 1874, to 'meet the pressing needs of the Parish'.[89]

To do this, church-extension committees increasingly set their sights on what they pointedly identified as 'the whole' of their local evolving urban landscape.[90] On occasion, that actually meant 'canvassing the [whole] of the ... town' in order to seek support for their schemes.[91] And this was rather more of a departure from historic practices than it might first appear, for it represented a shift of authority from formal and regional to more informal, and specifically urban, forms of ecclesiastical organisation. That alteration, in turn, reflected the frequently changing basis of local institutional finance.[92] Hence a Congregational Chapel Building Association, founded in Halifax in 1866, was charged with the object of 'assisting ... local efforts in populous districts for the building of chapels', and left with the responsibility of raising the 'necessary conditional grants and loans itself'.[93] Nor was this devolution of concern (and burden) limited to the Independents. In the words of the ubiquitous Archdeacon of Halifax,

when in times past the Ecclesiastical Commissioners ... were able to endow a district containing a certain population with £200 year for his [sic] incumbent, there was naturally a strong stimulus given to the building of churches, and the separation of districts that were qualified to receive this bounty. Now an endowment must be provided, in part, from other sources ... the Ecclesiastical Commissioners have ceased to endow the New Parishes on the grounds of population.[94]

Naturally, church extension, whether in late Victorian Halifax or anywhere else, was about more than just money. It was also about the

---

[89] Cited in Keighley, *History of Keighley*, p. 160.
[90] *A Charge Delivered*, p. 5.
[91] KPL, 105D77/1/3/2/1, Keighley Wesleyan Methodist Circuit, Quarterly Meeting Minute Book, 22 December 1873.
[92] David M. Thompson, 'Church Extension in Town and Countryside in Later-Nineteenth-Century Leicestershire', in Derek Baker (ed.), *The Church in Town and Countryside*, Studies in Church History, 16 (Oxford, 1979), p. 440.
[93] Biggs, 'Congregationalism', p. 9.
[94] 'Archdeacon's Charges'.

quality of local organisation. To this end, Halifax's Congregational Association was also charged with authority to 'give to all who apply, practical information on the details of chapel building'. And finally, it was about the provision of ecclesiastical local mission. So the association was allocated the task of 'the gathering of new congregations and also ... of giv[ing] attention to the claims of the working classes'.[95]

Yet if church extension constituted a co-ordinated institutional response to changing local circumstances, it represented something less than a coherent plan for church growth. There were three reasons for this. First, all church-extension schemes were purely voluntary, and support for them was always grounded in personal commitments. This meant they had to be directed in such a way as to be acceptable to their many individual subscribers. And that implied catering for selfish as well as altruistic motives.[96] More exactly, it presumed the pursuit of charitable efforts more geared to the needs of local societies than of national organisations; even of particular communities at the expense of the town as a whole. Yet at the same time, despite their often ambitious ends and their continuous existence, church-extension schemes were necessarily limited institutions. This was because they were not only dependent upon the benevolent (or other) motives of individual contributors, but also because they were subject to the varying fortunes of collective resources. So, crucial as such plans and funds were for the building of new churches and chapels in these towns after 1870, only very rarely did they actually bring them into the world *on their own*.[97] That limiting dimension mattered, because it determined the institutional context in which church extension actually took place.

To acknowledge that context is to appreciate how, as David Thompson has remarked, 'the socio-religious context of a multiple chapel community differed markedly, and came to differ still more markedly towards the end of the nineteenth century, from that of a church-and-chapel community or a single-church village'.[98] It differed because the terms of denominational competition were much more complex in the multi-chapel religious community. This was because the construction of so many new churches allowed for the significant intrusion of intra-denominational tensions into the evolution of the urban ecclesiastical plan. As the urban landscape evolved, those tensions and their concomitant complexities were, almost imperceptibly, imposed upon the churches, chapels and missions which traced the path

[95] Biggs, 'Congregationalism', p. 9.
[96] Thompson, 'Church Extension', p. 440.
[97] See esp. the remarks in Keighley, *History of Keighley*, pp. 160–1.
[98] Thompson, 'Making of the English Religious Classes', p. 490.

of its progress. And in these complexities lay the germs of so many intra-denominational divisions: the divisions of the poor against the rich, of the new against the old, and of the urban periphery against the rural hinterland.

It is a moot point whether the town ever significantly influenced, still less benefited, the religious life of village and shire in nineteenth-century England.[99] What is clear is that even in so far as either may have been the case in the earlier part of the century, and even in so far as this may have been more true of the Wesleyan Methodist Connexion than of other denominations, it ceased to be true, whether of the Wesleyan Methodists, or of any other denomination, in the late Victorian town. Consider the following example. On 21 March 1871, the Keighley Wesleyan Methodist Circuit blandly announced its recommendation

that this circuit be made into two circuits, the one to include Keighley [i.e. Temple Street], Morton Banks, Steeton, Laycock, Wesley Place, Hermit Hole, Hainworth, Exley Head, Eastwood, Thwaites, Utley Village, Long Lee and Street ... [T]he other to include ... Haworth, Lower Town, Oakworth, Scartop, Stanbury, Pickles Hill, Marsh, Sawood and Lees, and that the latter be called 'Haworth and Oakworth Circuit'.[100]

This was not an arbitrary division of stations. It was an act of reorganisation which exquisitely expressed the shifting balance of authority and influence in the mid-Victorian circuit, for it described the power and the ambition of the urban church. Division was agreed, reluctantly, by the representatives of the new Haworth and Oakworth Circuit. Their reluctance was understandable. The new 'Keighley Circuit' included almost all of the most important and prestigious urban chapels in the old circuit. And the new arrangement absolved these wealthier, town churches, on payment of £100 per annum for three years, from any further responsibilities towards their poorer rural and semi-rural brethren.[101] Within months of the final promulgation of this division, the new Keighley Circuit began the most extensive and most ambitious programme of chapel building in its history. In one decade, no fewer than eight chapels were either built, or substantially rebuilt, under circuit auspices.[102] This juxtaposition of events was not entirely

---

[99] Thompson, 'Church Extension', pp. 440ff.

[100] KPL, 105D77/1/3/2/9, Keighley Wesleyan Methodist Circuit, Quarterly Meeting Minute Book, 21 March 1871.

[101] *Keighley News*, 27 April 1907, quoted a figure of £1,000 as a severance payment. No independent documentary evidence has survived to corroborate or repudiate either figure.

[102] The chapels were: Heber Street (1872); Sun Street (1873); Hermit Hole (1874); Worth (1875); Devonshire Park (1877); Fell Lane (1878); Long Lane (1880); and Utley (1880).

coincidental. Nor was it unique to the Wesleyan Methodist Circuit. When Keighley Primitive Methodist Circuit split, acrimoniously, in 1874, one of its principal victims was Denholme Clough Primitive Methodist Chapel. Though situated six miles outside the conventional boundaries of the old township, Denholme Clough Chapel had been a station in the Keighley Primitive Methodist Circuit from the time of its construction in 1834. When that circuit divided, some forty years later, the chapel was spurned by both of the new circuits. It was thereby denied, albeit temporarily, any official connexional status at all. It passed first to Bingley Circuit, then, at the turn of the twentieth century, to Halifax (Ebenezer) Primitive Methodist Circuit. It celebrated its centenary, in 1934, as a place according to its own account in 'a solitary situation ... disposed ... to an insular outlook'.[103]

As the conventional boundaries of the urban landscape moved outwards, both in Halifax and in Keighley, so the associational priorities of local voluntary religious organisations turned inwards. But the concentration of associational initiative to peculiarly urban ends rarely presumed, and still less frequently actually resulted in a subsequent harmonisation of urban interests. Indeed there is reason to believe that, particularly after about 1875, it often had the opposite effect. Here lies a paradox. To have directed so much attention – indeed very nearly exclusive attention – towards the needs of the town, and of its growing and shifting population, may have seemed no more than an exercise in applied common sense. But it soon became something of an excuse for the pursuit of bitter intra-denominational, and inter-associational rivalry. For to concentrate on the 'needs of the town', so called, was to be made all too painfully aware that even *within* denominations those needs were increasingly plural and the aspirations of their associational representatives ever more incompatible.

Consider the case of Providence Wesleyan Methodist Chapel, Queen's Road, Halifax. It was built in 1887, to serve a 'large and increasing population', in an 'expanding' part of the western fringe of a westwards-growing town. According to contemporary accounts, this was precisely one of those fringes which, up to that time, had been 'denied' local spiritual sustenance. Providence was, nevertheless, established in the teeth of official opposition; and official opposition not from rival organisations, and not from afar, but from within Halifax Wesley Circuit, of which it would eventually become part.[104] To its proponents, mainly trustees at the nearby Rhodes Street Chapel, the Providence

---

[103] Anon., *Denholme Chapel Primitive Methodist Chapel, 1834–1934* (Halifax, 1934), no page number.
[104] *History of Providence Chapel*, pp. 5–6.

scheme was straightforward. As the urban fringe shifted inexorably westwards so, they argued, the circuit should follow it. But theirs was an argument perceived solely from the point of view of the town. And Wesley Circuit, like so many Methodist connexions in this part of mid-Victorian West Yorkshire, was not, and never had been, just an urban circuit. Several stations on the circuit were attached to small rural villages and hamlets in the open dale country beyond the urban fringe. To the faithful in those rural stations, the westward shift of the town, and the spatial extension of late nineteenth-century Halifax, represented a shift in the balance of forces *within* Wesley Circuit; moreover, a shift away from the rural hinterland and towards its ever-encroaching urban fringe and the ever-assertive urban stations. So they subtly opposed the construction of Providence. When the issue was raised, they challenged not the necessity of a new chapel *per se*, but the order of circuit priorities which the projected scheme implied. And they won the argument. At a Circuit Building Committee meeting, convened to discuss the matter on 1 April 1887, it was determined that 'subscriptions should be opened [throughout the whole circuit] called the Jubilee Fund ... for assisting the country places and that for the moment the Parkinson Lane Scheme should remain over'.[105] This was, of course, a great disappointment for the advocates of Providence. But they did not leave the matter there. One month later, they decided, 'unanimously', to purchase 'a plot of land on the south side of Parkinson Lane.'[106] A trust deed was established in their names alone. Then they raised £1,650 in order to finance the erection of a new chapel.[107]

Not everyone in the Wesley Circuit itself was willing to accept this *fait accompli*. Most striking of all, not everyone even within the town was willing to accept it. Before the foundation stone of Providence Chapel had been laid, the new trustees received a letter from the Reverend J.B. Every expressing 'the regret of the friends of King Cross [Wesleyan Methodist Chapel, Wesley Circuit] that we had selected a site so near them', since 'it [i.e. Providence Chapel] would be detrimental to their success'. The new trustees of Providence responded cautiously. 'The scheme', they assured their friends of King Cross, 'is not proposed in any spirit of competition.' Providence, they argued, was situated 'south of King Cross Street ... in Parkinson Lane', which had been built 'within the last three years'. Moreover, this street and 'the whole of the adjoining land which will shortly be built on ... might be described [as] their district [i.e. the district of Providence Chapel]'. In any case, it was 'imperative that work should proceed' there. Their apologia concluded

---

[105] *Ibid.*, p. 8.   [106] *Ibid.*, p. 9.   [107] *Ibid.*, pp. 12–14.

with the following words: 'should the branching out at Parkinson Lane bring about a division of Wesley Circuit, Parkinson Lane Trustees would consider favourably the inclusion of King Cross in the new Halifax Circuit'.[108] This was gambling for high stakes. What it meant was that the trustees of the new Providence Chapel were willing to risk the dissolution of the old Wesley Circuit, with which they had long been otherwise associated, in order to get their own way over this one issue. They were also willing, notwithstanding a few sugary words to the contrary, to force their own ambitions upon another station, offering only the possibility of 'favourable consideration' towards the plight of King Cross, should their institutional brinkmanship prove destructive. And it did prove destructive. Shortly afterwards, old Wesley Circuit was broken up into two 'new' circuits. But whilst Providence became part of the exclusively urban Rhodes Street Circuit, King Cross was shunted off into the semi-rural Wesley Circuit. 'Favourable consideration', whether sincerely offered or not, proved insufficient to preserve the ancient standing of King Cross station.[109]

Providence was an extreme case. Yet it highlighted a common theme, for the divergence of intra-denominational interests identified in this particular example of church extension was by no means confined to the dichotomy of town and country. Indeed, as the towns themselves expanded, it became rather more of a specifically urban problem. This was especially true of ecclesiastical developments in the new suburbs of these towns. The early history of Park Congregational Church, Halifax, admirably illustrates the workings of this ambiguous principle. Park was built to serve the West Hill Park housing estate in 1869. To a later generation, this must have seemed reasonable enough. At the time, it was distinctly controversial. This was because of the challenge it represented to the hegemony of the Crossley brothers, and to the pre-eminence of Square Church, in the Congregational ecclesiastical plan. The development of West Hill, of course, had gone wrong once before. The workers' haven of Crossley family dreams in the 1850s had actually become the middle-class suburb of the 1860s. As such, it now lacked only one amenity to secure its unimpeachable respectability: a local church. Ironically, a chapel had been envisaged for the mixed community which the brothers had planned. It had been abandoned only after the unanticipated social evolution of the district overtook their earlier schemes.[110] All too willing to provide for a deserving work-force, the

---

[108] *Ibid.*, p. 14.
[109] CDA, MR/70, Halifax (Rhodes Street) Wesleyan Methodist Circuit, Local Preachers' Meeting Minute Book, 16 December 1895.
[110] Jowett, 'Copley, Akroydon and West Hill Park', p. 84.

brothers naturally shied away from subsidising an unattached bourgeois neighbourhood. Instead, they put their hopes in the continuing predominance of Square Church, trusting that it would continue to attract worshippers from both Dean Clough and West Hill Park.

These hopes were dashed during the next decade. The impetus to build a chapel in the West Hill area finally proved irresistible. In August 1864 a requisition signed by representatives of three local congregations, and submitted to the ministers and deacons of Harrison Road Chapel (the Congregational mother church), expressed 'the opinion [that] the condition of Independency and the great increase of the population in the Upper Part of the town require the erection of another Congregational place of worship'.[111] The progenitors of the scheme then sought and secured 'the full approval of the existing [Congregational] churches of the town'.[112] They also persuaded a reluctant John Crossley, who icily acknowledged 'a plan for church work', which 'the majority [had] see[n] good to adopt'.[113] Even more reluctantly, the Crossley brothers eventually contributed £1,500 of the total cost. But the church was financed 'in the main by small public subscriptions'.[114] Some seventy-three sponsors contributed £6,000 towards the cost of construction within the first twelve months of appeals.[115] The remainder was easily raised during the following three years. By the time of its official opening in 1869, 779 of a possible 922 sittings in the church had been appropriated and financed through the traditional mechanism of individual 'pew-renting'.[116]

Put less politely, West Hill Park had served itself: built its own church, rejected traditional authority, and ignored the claims of other local institutions. The neighbourhood church had arrived. Its example would be multiplied many times over in the years that followed. It would be multiplied by the growth of new, respectable, self-serving neighbourhoods like West Hill Park. And paradoxically, it would be multiplied by the emergence of new, unrespectable, neglectful neighbourhoods too. If the neighbourhood principle was, almost by definition, an institutional imperative of differentiated social respectability, it did not follow that, in the context of such rapidly developing and changing urban environments, the question of appropriate ecclesiastical provision – even when strictly determined by such precise measures of class distinction – was

[111] Anon., *Historical Record of Park Congregational Church Brought down to the Year 1869* (Halifax, 1869), p. 3.
[112] *Ibid.*, pp. 3–4.
[113] Anon., *Fortunes Made in Business*, vol. III, p. 203.
[114] Biggs, 'Congregationalism in Halifax', p. 19.
[115] Anon., *Historical Record of Park Congregational Church*, p. 4.
[116] *Ibid.*, p. 8.

ever definitely settled. Not all neighbourhoods prospered. Some neighbourhoods, after all, declined: even once respectable neighbourhoods. Under those circumstances, the principle of wealth, often as not, pitted itself against the fact of physical location. Put another way, some congregations were prepared to build again, that is, literally to remove a church from a declining district in order to reconstitute their respectable chapel 'constituency' in another place.

Consider the following example. In 1890, the Wesleyan Methodist Chapel of Eastwood, Keighley, celebrated its twenty-fifth anniversary.[117] And it enjoyed its long standing as a numerically healthy society, made up of 88 members and 20 junior members. In addition, an average of 200 'hearers' attended its weekly services.[118] But it was not a happy place. Following a chapel meeting in the spring of that year, some 70 members and friends signed and forwarded to the trustees a petition that 'we wish you to take immediate steps, if possible, toward the building of ... a new chapel for Eastwood'. To justify that petition, they claimed that 'the disadvantages of the old chapel are many and grievous'. Interestingly, those disadvantages did not include overcrowding. Even according to their own figures, the chapel was rarely more than half full.[119] Nor was it a geographically isolated building. On the contrary. In the intervening quarter of a century since its foundation, there had been an 'increase of population in the neighbourhood.'[120] The problem was its 'background and obscure situation', and its close proximity to a 'Public House' which made it 'repulsive and uninviting ... often disagreeable – even dangerous – especially for females'. The result, so the petitioners argued, was that 'the congregation seems gradually to decrease and we attribute [this] very largely to the above mentioned state of things'. To reverse that trend, and to 'attract the inhabitants [of the area] in far greater numbers' there was, they contended, only one solution: 'a new chapel in a more inviting situation'.[121] Far from rebuking so lame a failure of the missionary spirit amongst their flock,

---

[117] Keighley, *History of Keighley*, pp. 191–3; a mission and school had operated there from 1855.

[118] KPL, uncat. MS, Keighley Wesleyan Circuit, 'Form of Application to the Wesleyan Chapel Committee for Permission to Sell Trust Property' (no date).

[119] *Keighley Yearbook, 1878*, p. 143, records that Eastwood Wesleyan Methodist Chapel (1866) had a seating capacity of 460.

[120] Keighley, *History of Keighley*, p. 192, describes the neighbourhood as 'populous' and suggests that the chapel had been built in 1866 *because* the original mission-school room was overcrowded at that date.

[121] KPL, uncat. MS, 'Petition to the Trustees of Eastwood Wesleyan Chapel': 'we the members and friends of the Eastwood Wesley Chapel wish you to undertake immediate steps if possible towards the building ... of a new chapel for Eastwood' (70 signatures appended).

the trustees of Eastwood Chapel promptly pursued the matter with the regional Wesleyan Chapel Committee in Manchester.[122] On 24 March 1891, they applied for a licence from that authority to sell the site and property of Eastwood Chapel, and for permission to relocate (and reconstruct) their society in a different place.[123] They were asked: 'What circumstances render it necessary, in your opinion, to sell the property?'. They responded, candidly: 'Deterioration of the locality.'[124] Licence and permission were duly granted on 19 May 1891. A 'much better site' in the midst of an 'artisan population' was acquired; Eastwood New Chapel was erected there in the same year.[125] Eight years later it changed its name to Victoria Park Methodist Church.[126]

The sheer pace of social change in this part of West Yorkshire during the second half of the nineteenth century ensured that in some of the newer and more marginal districts of Halifax and Keighley decisions of this sort sometimes had to be taken more than once during the lifetime of a church. However, the outcome of such a decision was not always entirely predictable. So, in a gesture much like that of Eastwood Wesleyan Methodist Chapel, the fellowship of North Parade Baptist Chapel, Halifax, resolved in 1854 to move away from their erstwhile home in the slums of Haley Hill to the north-east of the borough, in order to relocate their society in 'a more favourable part of the town', this time in the new 'artisan suburbs of North Parade', to the north-west.[127] Unfortunately, within thirty years of its relocation, these new surroundings themselves had dramatically changed and thus the church was left stranded – once again – in what had become one of the poorest quarters of the town. But 'the fellowship', on this occasion, 'saw in these conditions an opportunity and a challenge, [and] excellent social work, which brought much blessing to the poor ... of the surrounding district

---

[122] KPL, uncat. MS, 'Application to the Wesleyan Chapel Committee to Sell Trust Property'.

[123] KPL, uncat. MS, 'Form of Application to the Wesleyan Chapel Committee for Permission to Erect a Chapel at Eastwood in the Keighley Circuit', 24 March 1891. This second form incorporated both the question and the answer to the first form, in addition to the further request to purchase a new site and to build a new trust property upon it.

[124] KPL, uncat. MS, 'Application to the Wesleyan Chapel Committee to Sell Trust Property', p. 1.

[125] KPL, uncat. MS, 'Form of Application to Erect a Chapel at Eastwood', p. 1. The chapel was known, officially, as Eastwood New Chapel for a number of years after the relocation of its site and rebuilding.

[126] *Keighley Yearbook, 1899* (Keighley, 1899), p. 201. The change of name was first recorded in the *Keighley Yearbook* for this year. Significantly the seating capacity of Victoria Park at *c.* 250 was barely *half* that of Eastwood Old Chapel.

[127] Anon., *Origins of Baptist Churches in the Halifax and Calder Valley District* (Halifax, n.d.), p. 41.

... was undertaken'.[128] Precisely why remains unclear. What is certain is that a church which had once been dedicated to a particular social constituency, and hostile to its immediate locality, seemingly overnight became a society dedicated to its locality and indifferent to constituency. In that way, the church *itself* had changed.

Filling in the gaps: providing for the poor and the institutional imperatives of urban church mission

Conceived in this way, North Parade was but a bizarre example of what would become a fairly common later nineteenth-century phenomenon: the mission-church. These were ecclesiastical developments which explicitly inverted the neighbourhood principle. They were built in neighbourhoods, but they were not of, or even from, those particular neighbourhoods. On the contrary. They were specifically provided for poor neighbourhoods by richer and distant urban, district, regional or even national organisations. As such, they were institutional acts of charity. More pointedly, they were concrete forms of Christian evangelical effort. And they were very numerous in later Victorian West Yorkshire. The Archdeacon of Halifax identified twenty-two Anglican mission-churches or rooms in the parish in 1896, of which 'a considerable majority' had been 'provided since 1880'.[129] Other denominations seem to have followed suit, in similar proportions and following much the same time scale.[130] These institutions were constructed, overwhelmingly, in the new working-class suburbs and in the old declining centres of their respective towns. And their purposes, ostensibly at least, were clear enough. They were provided, so the Rector of Keighley argued in 1897, 'chiefly for those who are ill supplied with the good things in life and are shy about entering ordinary places of worship, [and] for those who lack Sunday clothes and are short of education'.[131]

As a consequence, they were normally rather simple buildings, which

---

[128] *Ibid.*, pp. 3–4.

[129] *A Charge Delivered*, pp. 4–5. This figure should be treated with caution. It probably refers to the ancient parish of Halifax, which was much larger either than the parish of St John the Baptist or the County Borough of Halifax in 1896.

[130] It is almost impossible to quote an exact figure of how many 'mission' churches and mission halls each denomination maintained at any given time, since the life of a mission was often very short, and the status of a mission was equally often insecure. Nevertheless, it is quite clear that 'mission' churches, chapels and rooms were, in this part of England, a *particular* feature of the church extension movement, arising with it, and falling into abeyance after its eclipse, in the early twentieth century.

[131] Frederic Damstini Cremer, 'Rector's Address', *KPCM*, vol. 20, no. 3, March 1897 (no page number).

did not 'risk ... money on ornamentation'.[132] Yet at the same time, they were places proud to boast attractive facilities such as '[r]ecreation rooms [and] a billiard table', specifically furnished in order to lure the young – and the not so young – into their benevolent orbit.[133] More significantly, they generally maintained a working Sunday school and encouraged a thriving Sunday service. Both were usually geared towards a specifically evangelical and missionary bent. Neither tended to place much emphasis upon liturgical discipline. Hearty singing and fervent prayer were the norm. In so doing, mission-churches provided religious services, and the possibilities of religious experience, in parts of Halifax and Keighley and Denholme which might otherwise never have enjoyed that benefit. And, if the spirit they imbued was often more emotionally charged, or the faith they propagated often more enthusiastic than in their mother churches, then these maternal authorities were generally willing to tolerate a necessary degree of doctrinal and psychological latitude, at least for 'as long as the brethren [in these places] labour[ed] in the spirit of Christ'.[134]

But there were limits to such tolerance, for the righteous spirit sometimes comprehended ulterior motives, even latent fears. This was especially true if, as occasionally was the case, a mission-church was *not* the product of a mother church's benevolence. Consider the following example. During the mid-1870s a 'series of college prayer-meetings' began at no. 50 Marlborough Street, Keighley. Thus, very humbly, began a new offshoot of Congregationalism in a part of the town, towards its northern ridge, which was 'rapidly growing', and where 'houses were springing up', but which at that date had 'neither school nor chapel'. The future Marlborough Street Congregational Church was not the product, however, of judicious planning in the highest offices of Keighley Congregationalism. It was the individual brainchild of one Mr Ramsden, a draper in Low Street, who 'commenced the meetings on his own initiative, without being requested to undertake the work either by the Mother-Church at Devonshire Street, or by his own Church at Upper Green'.[135] In itself, this gesture was not so very remarkable. Many of the churches and chapels which sprang up in late nineteenth-century Halifax and Keighley, whether Congregational, Methodist, or even Anglican, were, initially at least, the result of heroic individual initiatives. Characteristically they began life in a room, or in a cottage,

---

[132] *Halifax Courier*, 11 September 1886.
[133] Anon., unmarked article, *SPCKCPM*, vol. 16, no. 7, July 1907 (no page number).
[134] *Devonshire Street Congregational Church, Keighley, Church Manual, 1883* (Keighley, 1883), p. 57.
[135] Reid Marchbank, *One Hundred Years of Progress*, p. 28.

even in a barn, supported so it seemed by no one and nothing, and dependent upon personal sacrifice and communal goodwill for their continuing survival. At first sight, Marlborough Street was merely an extreme example of the type. It endured an unimpressive beginning. It was kept going by one man's vision and efforts. And, 'in spite of accidents and prognostications of its utter collapse', Marlborough Street survived.[136] Indeed, it was one of Pastor Pringle's pantheon of 'six buildings' actively imparting the faith in 1900.

That it survived, however, had very little to do with the benevolence, and nothing to do with the foresight, of Devonshire Street mother church. For nearly a decade of precarious existence, supporting a Sunday school of more than sixty and a congregation of more than forty, Marlborough Street received almost no financial help from any local Congregationalist source. Then, in 1882, quite fortuitously Marlborough Street won the attention and sympathy of Sir John Brigg. With his financial backing, a proper church was eventually built at Marlborough Street.[137] Thus, Mr Ramsden's initiative was finally rewarded. But it is clear that officials in Devonshire Street were less than wholly gladdened by this development. They had not planned the birth of Marlborough Street. They did not contribute towards its construction. And they contributed virtually nothing to its subsequent maintenance. True, the Pastor of Devonshire Street paid polite tribute to the 'generosity of one family' which had made possible the new church building, but he pointedly refrained from promising any further, associational, aid.[138] Why? Marlborough Street was not a peculiarly offensive institution. Its pastors preached no false doctrines. Its congregations projected no proletarian crudities that might have offended respectable sensibilities. But it was an organisational complication, a potential diversion for local patronage, effort and success. It was a rival. And it was treated as such.

Such rivalry could rear its ugly head even between a mother church and its erstwhile dependants. On these occasions, tensions centred less around matters of organisational propriety and more on questions of evangelical purpose. Consider the case of the parish church of Keighley. In 1891, there were four mission-churches in the parish of Keighley. Of these, two, at Newsholme and Braithwaite, were established shortly after the renovation of the parish church, in 1846. Two others, Highfield and Utley, were of recent origin. Highfield was founded in 1878.[139] And Utley began life in 1883 as no more than a 'mission ... in a cottage'

---

[136] *Devonshire Street Church Manual, 1883*, p. 66.
[137] Reid Marchbank, *One Hundred Years of Progress*, p. 28.
[138] *Devonshire Street Church Manual, 1883*, p. 57.
[139] *Keighley Yearbook, 1879* (Keighley, 1871), p. 141.

which maintained a Sunday school and held services twice a week.[140] It did not even acquire the more dignified status of mission-church until five years later.[141] Yet by 1896, all four had assumed the title of 'chapels-of-ease'.[142] And the change of appellation in each case had been made against the will of the Rector; the change of function which that implied, similarly so.[143] As he put it, in 1891, '[T]he happiest time in the life of ... mission churches, is the time during which their filial relations with the mother church of the whole parish are proudly ... maintained.'[144]

And, as he observed, in 1897, 'a mission [church] always has a tendency to develop into an ordinary church, as those who attend it get on in the world and rise in the social scale'. His point being that

[t]he right thing is to keep passing on those who we have taught into an ordinary service to the mother-church of his parish, and to be always going out afresh after the hindmost in life's race wherewith to fill their vacant places. Thus the work keeps on the right lines and supplies what no parish should be without – a real mission work.[145]

These remarks expressed, with exquisite preciousness, what might be called the doctrine of differentiation. This was the presumption that, in an increasingly pluralistic society, the provision of the Church to the world was, of necessity, differentiated. This was because the spiritual needs of some of God's flock were, *de facto*, quite different from the needs of others. Hence the need for mother churches and for mission-churches, similarly for normal worship and for evangelical services. Accordingly, the best way to sustain 'real mission', thus defined, was for central authority (in this case the parish church) to establish outreaches, or offshoots, which it maintained *as* outreaches, pursuing mission work in mission-churches. In this understanding, the principal threat to that provision was, ironically, the ambition – religious, ecclesiastical and social – of the missionaries. By seeking to establish the autonomy of their institutions, they only succeeded in perverting the proper purpose of their establishment. That was no abstract threat, as the Rector of Keighley knew well enough, for the window of his perception had been the bitter experience of organisational defeat.

[140] *Keighley Yearbook, 1887*, pp. 104–5.
[141] *Keighley Yearbook, 1890*, p. 109.
[142] *Keighley Yearbook, 1897*, pp. 172–5.
[143] Cremer, 'Rector's Address', March 1897.
[144] Frederic Damstini Cremer, 'Rector's Address', *KPCM*, vol. 14, no. 2, February 1891 (no page number).
[145] Frederic Damstini Cremer, 'Rector's Address', *KPCM*, vol. 20, no. 3, March 1897 (no page number).

The costs of proliferation: church-building, the limits of benevolence and the burden of debt

Between 1870 and 1920 literally scores of churches and chapels were built in Halifax and Keighley: some in response to general population growth, and others according to the particular demands of tiny communities; some in the hope of generally stimulating more frequent public worship, and others in the certain knowledge that no such consequences would follow. They were constructed in town centres with the hope of attracting a wider social constituency, and then flung out into the suburbs to cater for the desires of narrower urban cliques. They were built often enough simply to serve the self-consciously respectable; and then, on occasion, they were provided for the needs of the undeniably poor. They were furnished sometimes by national authority, but they were the more frequent products of local initiative. They reflected inter-denominational competition, but they also acknowledged the realities of intra-associational strife. They were often forged big and grand, but they were sometimes left small and simple. In other words, there simply was no typical church (or chapel) in the later Victorian and Edwardian ecclesiastical plan, nor was there any characteristic reason for its being there. Motives for building were manifold, implications various, consequences numerous and often unanticipated. In this sense, the Victorian measure of ecclesiastical progress in the proliferation of buildings was an open acknowledgement of its own, increasingly pluralistic, purposes. Indeed, apart from a vague sense of Christian co-operation, perhaps the only thing those efforts truly had in common was that they cost money.

That was more significant than it might at first appear. New churches, relocated chapels and mission rooms, after all, had to be paid for. Yet, by 1890 at the latest, state subsidies to the Established Church – at least for Halifax, Keighley and Denholme – were negligible.[146] And the local evidence suggests that what was true of the national Church was increasingly the case for its nonconformist rivals as well. Remarking upon the fact that 'there are many cases – and the number appears to be increasing ... of building operations [which] have been commenced and building debts contracted without the efforts to raise money that should have been preceded in any erection [*sic*]', the Manchester Wesleyan Methodist Chapel Committee resolved, in 1897, to impose upon its subordinate regional circuits and district stations a scheme for a deposit of funds, 'to facilitate the collection and to provide for the safe custody

---

[146] For the evidence of neighbouring Bradford, see Chadwick, 'Church and People', pp. 182–6.

of small sums contributed to circuits for the erection of new chapels'. To this end, it 'urged the trustees of *all* our chapels to subscribe annually to the fund', adding pointedly that 'the committee cannot justly be expected to assist with oversight and advice [for] non-subscribing Trusts'. In return, it offered to accept funds from each of its associated chapels for safe-keeping, but only on the condition that these sums were the product of 'local collections made for the purpose of erecting some [sic] chapels', and only if 'some time elapse[d] between the commencement of effort to raise the funds, and the commencement of building operations', or if 'proceeds from the sale of chapels [undertaken with connexional comment] have been disposed of before it has been found possible to acquire a site for the new erection, or in cases which ... it may be found impossible to proceed with the erection of the new building simultaneously with the old one [sic]'.

The message thus conveyed was clear. Too much unauthorised church and chapel building had been undertaken in recent years. And too little of it had been adequately financed. Finally, too much of the burden had been shifted to regional and national authorities. Moreover, this was all going to have to stop. Certainly, the Committee was determined to see it end. So it had resolved to establish a regional scheme for the disposal of local funds, a neat inversion of the hitherto existing state of affairs. That meant regulating – and thereby limiting – all future building projects other than those financed in the new, prescribed manner. Specifically, it meant laying down a régime of planning and construction which permitted 'no debt ... upon the existing Trust Estate', unless 'responsible persons', acting in 'harmony with the Superintendent of the Circuit', demonstrated themselves to be 'willing to purchase sites in new neighbourhoods' by 'borrow[ing] on their personal security'.[147]

But the implications were clearer still. According to the Committee, a whole generation of buildings had been constructed on shaky ecclesiastical finances. This had left a new cohort of, in this case Wesleyan, societies shackled by the burden of associational debt. Why had it happened? The Committee blamed a lack of foresight, or a failure of the prudential virtues generally. Others pointed to the passing of traditional, heroic local benevolence, noting the gradual eclipse of the 'old brigade', or a 'type of manufacturer' dedicated to town and region, giving way to a 'young' generation uninterested in rendering such concrete public 'service'.[148] This latter view has found some credence – if considerable

---

[147] KPL, uncat. MS, Keighley Wesleyan Methodist Connexion, Keighley, Wesleyan Chapel Committee, 'Scheme for the Deposit of Funds', 1 January 1897.
[148] See Snowdon, *The Master Spinner*, pp. 269 and 346–7.

interpretative redefinition – in the views of modern historians. They have identified the passing of a paternalistic mode of social engagement by the local manufacturing plutocracy after 1870, and the rise of a more distant – literal as well as figurative – relationship between capital and labour during the latter years of the nineteenth century as increasingly antagonistic industrial relations first undermined and then finally destroyed the old, mutually respectful attitudes of masters and men.[149] Such judgements similarly pointed, and point, to the seeming disappearance of those locally forged 'responsible persons' whom the Wesleyan regional committee sought, belatedly, to encourage. But did they really disappear? Had they, in fact, ever existed?

At one level, they clearly had. Business and manufacturing plutocrats, whether heroic or paternalist, had been critical agents in the financing of the mid-nineteenth-century local ecclesiastical plan. The evidence of All Souls', Haley Hill, of Square Church, Halifax, and Temple Street, Keighley, even of St Paul's, Denholme, makes that clear enough. There need be no mystery about this. Benevolent patronage of this nature made good economic and social sense if the number of churches involved was relatively small, where the physical location of those buildings was so prominent and when the overt and covert rewards for such involvement were so considerable. And it continued to make sense late into the nineteenth century in such places as conformed sociologically to what Patrick Joyce has called the characteristics of 'factory society'. In these places 'employers' really 'built and supported the churches and chapels'. There, indeed, they constructed them near their own factories and they 'expected their work-people to attend them'. In that environment, for sure, 'organized religion' acted as a source of 'notions of partnership and community', or as one of 'the elements nurturing the sense of commitment to the employer and his territory', thereby working as 'a principal support for employer hegemony'. For instance, 'the Oakworth district of Keighley was dominated by the Haggas and Clough factories and Oakworth split with geographical precision into church and chapel, Tory and Liberal, Haggas and Clough'.[150]

But these were small places. They did not include the westward-moving heart of Halifax, nor the expanding central core of Keighley; and certainly not the fast-growing suburbs of either town. And in these new, growing areas, employers built relatively few churches and chapels, dictated little of the local denominational balance and determined few of the related political affiliations. It was not that manufacturing benevolence died out in these larger enclaves. Indeed, it frequently held up

[149] Jowett, 'Akroydon, Copley and West Hill Park', pp. 84ff.
[150] Joyce, *Work, Society and Politics*, pp. 176–8.

well. But it simply became less important. This was because the relative contribution of big money diminished as the urban landscape extended, and as the local ecclesiastical plan expanded. Manufacturing money, however heroically employed, just could not provide for the aspirations of so many new societies. Nor did it always wish to do so, for their needs did not always entirely accord with its purposes. And anyway, its relatively simple ends were increasingly lost in their more ambiguous legacies. In this way, the simple imperative of rising church numbers coupled with the complex reality of changing social relations together ensured that business benevolence played less of a part in the ecclesiastical plan of the mature industrial town than it had done in the emergence of its earlier form. Moreover, they also determined that, as it became less significant, so too – curiously enough – it became less exclusive.

There was one other factor. This may be called the 'traditional' dimension. The fact was that the greatest private benefactor of organised religion in nineteenth-century Keighley, the man who gave most land, more cash and other help to the religious institutions of the town, was not an industrialist at all. He was the Duke of Devonshire. No map of the urban ecclesiastical plan in Keighley can ignore the division of the Duke's land-holdings and land grants in the town. Moreover, his contribution to that plan did not especially encourage sectarian interests. Despite firm Anglican beliefs, he regularly gave substantial donations, both of land and of money, to the nonconformist cause in Keighley. Albert Street Baptist Chapel, opened in 1865, was built upon a site 'obtained from the Duke of Devonshire, who generously charged only half the price he would have required, had the ground been purchased for private use'.[151] This became his standard practice. Subsequent beneficiaries included West Lane Primitive Methodist Chapel and Schools in 1887, and Knowle Park Congregational Church in 1892.[152] Naturally, the Duke also patronised the Church of England. The site of Holy Trinity, Lawkholme Lane (opened in 1882), was donated from Cavendish property in 1878.[153] And he made a personal donation of £1,000 to the Chapel Building Committee of St Peter's Church, in 1881.[154]

[151] Craven (ed.), *Commercial Directory of Keighley*, p. 33.
[152] Rev. Frank Baker, *Side-Lights on Sixty Years: Being Contributions to the History of West Lane Methodist Church, Keighley* (Keighley, 1940), p. 9; John Sugden, *History of Knowle Park Congregational Church, 1873–1949: With Notes on the Development of Congregationalism in Keighley* (Keighley, 1930), pp. 7–8.
[153] J. Thornton Cox, *A Brief History of the Church and Parish of Holy Trinity, Lawkholme, Keighley* (Keighley, 1932), p. 9.
[154] WHQ, 74D83/6/6/1, St Peter's, Mission Church, Keighley, Church Building Committee Minute Book, 3 June 1881.

The sheer extent of the Duke's benevolence was, of course, wholly atypical. But the eclecticism of his benevolence was not unique, and in fact became more common after mid-century. Even *parvenu* industrialists occasionally spread their generosity across denominational boundaries. The family of B. and W. Marriner of West Greengate Mill, Keighley, were, so Hodgson recorded, 'churchmen of a very liberal type, ever ready to give the right hand of fellowship to other denominations'. So, '[w]hen a Methodist Sunday school was commenced not far from their works, the elder member of the firm ... attended the anniversaries when the school was struggling ... and always replenished the school funds with a liberal contribution'.[155] Similarly in Halifax. If Edward Akroyd devoted his time and money solely to the Church of England, not every man of property followed suit. John Mackintosh, far instance, did not. His biography records that, though 'his first work was naturally at Queen's Road [Wesleyan Methodist] ... he speedily extended his sympathies to other churches with utter disregard for denominational distinction'.[156]

But if their generosity was characteristically more wide-ranging in its object, it was not necessarily more generally significant in its impact. For that reason, it is important not to exaggerate the financial extent of the entrepreneurial contribution to the local late Victorian and early Edwardian ecclesiastical plan. This is not easy, because contemporary observers frequently did. Remarking upon the 'almost unbounded liberality' of the Clough family towards the 'spread of religion and education in the locality' of Keighley, Hodgson insisted that '[t]hey have been the principal means of building the beautiful Methodist Chapel and schools at Paper Mill Bridge, and, more recently, in promoting the extension fund for building several additional Methodist chapels in the Keighley Circuit'.[157] In fact, no reliable evidence has survived about the financial genesis of Paper Mill Bridge School and Chapel. But it is clear that, whatever it was for Paper Mill Bridge, the Clough family was not the principal means of financial provision for Methodist chapels and schools anywhere else. In 1873, Robert Clough secured and paid for a site for a new chapel in Devonshire Park at a price of £500. However, the completed building cost a total of £8,000. Of this figure, more than £6,000 was raised from small private subscriptions (i.e. £100 and under), and from collections taken at the opening services.[158] And at Wesley Place Chapel, the society with which their 'names will ever be

155 Hodgson, *Textile Manufacture*, p. 55.
156 Crutchley, *John Mackintosh*, p. 143.
157 Hodgson, *Textile Manufacture*, p. 67.
158 Keighley, *History of Keighley*, p. 67.

associated',[159] the family actually contributed rather more of their time than of their money. The foundation stone of the second Wesley Place, put down in 1862, was laid by Robert Clough, who subsequently became both a class leader and society steward at that place. His daughter laid the foundation stone for the third Wesley Chapel, built soon afterwards, in 1867. But very little of the £2,312 required to build the second Wesley Place, or of the additional £2,000 needed to construct the third, was subscribed by the Clough family.[160]

This was a fairly common pattern. Hodgson, ever the apologist for business paternalists, remarked that John Brigg, of J. and B. Brigg and Son at Bow End and Calversyke Mills, had been, in 1856, 'one of the principal contributors ... of ... the new Independent Chapel and minister's home ... in Devonshire Street ... and ... that ... through [his] ... influence ... the beautiful Congregational Chapel at Utley ... was built ... and the ministry supported'.[161] For Devonshire Street that was probably true. At Utley, however, the informal influence of John Brigg may have been more decisive than his financial generosity. Of a total bill of £2,300 for the completed chapel in 1872, only £600 (by no means all from the Brigg family) was collected before the opening ceremony. For the Knowle Park Mission, established as a second offshoot from Devonshire Street in 1892, he contributed a loan of £500, free of interest, for five years, but no more.[162]

Moreover, if it is wrong to overestimate the pecuniary significance of manufacturing paternalism in the evolution of the later nineteenth-century ecclesiastical plan either of Halifax or Keighley (or, to a lesser extent, in Denholme), it is also a mistake to assume a direct relationship between financial generosity and institutional or spatial priority in the development of that plan, for this 'financial generosity' was often less the result of entrepreneurial initiative and rather more the consequence of a belated response by wealthy men towards building schemes which were already well under way. Moreover, such appeals in these far from unusual circumstances were often successful because, whilst there was much to be gained in prestige and authority from generous donations to a good cause, there was much more to be lost by *refusing* to contribute to worthy ecclesiastical efforts once a request had been made. Few, even amongst the very wealthy, took that risk too often. The case of St Peter's Church of England, Keighley, is instructive in this respect. First established, in 1872, as a temporary 'iron-church' (i.e. a church

[159] Farrington and Feather, *Centenary at Wesley Place*, p. 7.
[160] Keighley, *History of Keighley*, p. 191.
[161] Hodgson, *Textile Manufacture*, p. 43.
[162] Sugden, *History of Knowle Park Church*, p. 10.

prefabricated primarily out of iron), in a new improving working-class district of the town hugging the Halifax Road, it was finally completed ten years later, and consecrated on 25 January 1882. The finished product was a fine building, 'an ornament to the [town]',[163] of lofty proportions, with chancel and tower, conceived in English Gothic, and capable of accommodating about 850 worshippers. During the decade that it took to build, St Peter's attracted the attention, even the active concern, of numerous authorities and many individuals. As early as 1872, the Building Committee of St Peter's sought, and was permitted, access to the 'St Andrew's Parish Sick Club', in order to draw a local loan at reduced rates of interest.[164] The Rector then interceded (unsuccessfully) with the Ecclesiastical Commissioners and (successfully) with Ripon Diocesan Building Authorities on its behalf, raising over £500 from extra-regional sources.[165] Finally, in 1878, its Building Committee was amalgamated with the 'General Committee for Church Extension' in Keighley, in a co-ordinated 'Keighley and St Peter's Church Building Committee', a manoeuvre which established the priority of St Peter's in local church-building plans, and set a nominal maximum sum of money to be allocated for its construction. That figure, put at £4,000, proved wildly inadequate.[166] So the Joint Building Committee, as a last resort, approached local men of property and Anglican sympathies, in the hope of raising the necessary additional funds. They responded. The Duke of Devonshire gave £1,000, and W.L. Marriner £500. Three years later, when the physical form of the new St Peter's began to take shape, the Joint Committee, taking note of a widespread 'feeling [that] the church [should] be complete[d] by the erection of a tower', something which was not part of the original design, approached the Duke of Devonshire again. Belatedly, he agreed to furnish the entire sum, a further £1,000, from his own pocket.[167]

Yet, despite the active (and material) support of another diocesan authority, of the Church Extension Committee of the whole town, of the Rector of St Andrew's, of the Duke of Devonshire, and of one of the richest Anglican industrialists in the town, W.L. Marriner, St Peter's Church of England, Keighley, came into the world encumbered with

---

[163] Craven, *Keighley Directory, 1884*, p. 31.
[164] WHQ, 74D83/6/6/1, St Peter's Mission Church, Minute Book of the [Building] Committee, 8 April 1872.
[165] Thomas Handley, *Church of St Peter, Keighley, Jubilee Handbook, 1882–1932* (Keighley, 1932), p. 17.
[166] WHQ, 74D83/6/6/1, St Peter's Mission Church, Minute Book of the [Building] Committee, 15 May 1878.
[167] *Ibid.*, 3 June 1881.

debts. Expenses eventually amounted to £6,475 10s 7d.[168] The Joint Building Committee reported a deficit of £2,500 'on the completion of the whole structure'.[169] These debts were paid off – slowly – by its congregation, over the next decade or so.[170] That, in itself, was quite an eloquent comment on the strict limitations of institutional largesse or individual generosity as means for providing the wherewithal of worship in the late Victorian industrial town. And most new religious foundations, especially those built in the suburbs after 1870, were cast into the world with far fewer influential or wealthy friends than St Peter's, Keighley. For them, a project for a new church or chapel meant the devotion of months of patient work in search of a suitable, and an available, site. Once a property had been secured or promised, tenders for construction were invited from local builders. The best offer – usually the cheapest – secured the contract. In order to compete in such a market, and at a time when the claims upon the construction industry were so various – from manufacturing and private housing concerns and the like – religious organisations were invariably obliged to acquire suitable sites and the appropriate raw materials on the promise of future funding, and only very rarely with sufficient cash in the bank. In those circumstances, specific local knowledge, good local contacts and efficient local organisation were crucial advantages for new associations in search of a site and with their hearts set upon a new building. Above all, however, a new society relied upon its access to a congregation willing and able to put up the money and to bear the debt of the new foundation; either that, or upon the willingness of *another* congregation to do the same for them. Nothing else was sufficient. But how 'sufficient' was that?

It is impossible to say. All that can be concluded with certainty is that most new churches and chapels that came into being in Halifax and Keighley during the last third of the nineteenth century were born into debt. For instance, when Albert Street Baptist Church was opened in the town seventeen years earlier, little more than 'half of the total cost of £3,800 on the building had been accounted for'.[171] And most stayed in debt for years, even for decades, after their construction. So Worth

---

[168] WHQ, 73D83/6/6/2, St Peter's Church, Keighley, Vestry and Churchwarden's and Church Council Minute Book, 26 November 1882.

[169] WHQ, 74D83/6/6/1, St Peter's Mission Church, Minute Book of the [Building] Committee, 10 June 1881.

[170] Apparently at the expense of its new Sunday school, the old 'iron-church' (or temporary church for St Peter's, 1872–82), which fell down for want of restoration funds during that time.

[171] Joseph Rhodes, *A Century of Keighley Baptist History, 1810–1910* (Keighley, 1910), pp. 61–3.

Village Primitive Methodist Church, Keighley, erected in 1874, was freed from debt on its *original* property only some thirty years later.[172] This was true even of those that, like St Peter's, received denominational support in their early foundation. Hence the construction of Pye Nest Primitive Methodist Church in Halifax, in 1902, at the (very reasonable) cost of £3,120, left this society £1,730 in debt. A church-extension fund secured a loan of £1,000 from the Chapel Aid Association of the Primitive Methodist Connexion. But the chapel was still left more than £700 in arrears.[173] And it was even the case for a few which, like St Peter's again, had the support of wealthy patrons. That 'beautiful new' Congregational chapel at Utley, Keighley, built in 1872, may have won the patronage of the Brigg family, but it came into the world with little more than half of its total arrears paid for.[174]

What really was significant, at St Peter's as elsewhere, was the debt itself: its extent, its longevity and its impact. Associational debt was more than a troublesome burden in the voluntary (and Established) religious organisations of later Victorian West Yorkshire. It was a transforming influence. It changed something of the very nature of local religious association. It did this by so altering the terms of its political economy as to redefine many of the traditional purposes and future possibilities of the organised religious life, effectively redrawing the institutional boundaries of each and every religious society in a way, and with an effect, which was at least as profound and similarly as important as the largely unplanned, unintended and almost uncontrolled evolution of the urban ecclesiastical plan itself.

[172] *Keighley Yearbook, 1904* (Keighley, 1904), p. 167.
[173] John Brearley, *A History of Pye Nest Primitive Methodist Church, Halifax, 1902–1932* (Halifax, 1932), p. 11.
[174] *Keighley Yearbook, 1877* (Keighley, 1877), p. 119.

3 The burden shared: the changing political economy of religious organisations

Introduction: the idea of a political economy of religious organisations

The very idea of a *political economy* of religious organisations smells of the worst kind of historical reductionism. For whatever else they were, late nineteenth- and early twentieth-century religious societies were not commercial enterprises in disguise. They did not produce, distribute and exchange sacred, or any other, goods and services in order to maximise private profit. This was because they sought no corporate gain for themselves and presumed no calculating motive on behalf of their customers. Similarly, they eschewed the precise calculation of needs and the exact planning of provision characteristic of the science of bureaucratic organisation, for they trusted that such needs had no bounds and believed that their own efforts should set no proper limits.[1] Yet if so, the foul odour hides a fine fruit. This was because there was a recognisable political economy of religious organisations in later Victorian and Edwardian West Yorkshire. True, its churches and chapels had no commodities to exchange, or goods to distribute. But they did raise and spend money. They had to. The work of the Church and its witness to the Word demanded the survival, indeed the prosperity, of its institutions in the world. To survive, those institutions needed money. To thrive, they needed to use it wisely. How they raised it and how they spent it was of enormous significance for the changing forms, and for the contemporary health, of local religious life.

[1] This is not to say that significant implications cannot be drawn about the economic *consequences* of religious organisation, action and belief; see, above all, Weber, *Economy and Society*, vol. II, chs. 12, 13 and 15; and Weber, *The Protestant Ethic and the Spirit of Capitalism*, trans. by Talcott Parsons (London, 1976), esp. chs. 1, 4 and 5; also Weber, *From Max Weber*, chs. 12, and 13. For a modern discussion, see Gordon Marshall, *In Search of the Spirit of Capitalism: An Essay on Max Weber's Protestant Ethic Thesis* (London, 1982), esp. chs. 4 and 5. And, for a completely different approach, not directly concerned with religion but capable of generating an economic interpretation of religious behaviour, individual or collective, see Gary S. Becker, *The Economic Approach to Human Behavior* (Chicago, 1976), esp. chs. 1, 12 and 13.

To be sure, it was a rather peculiar political economy. This is because it was both self-consciously voluntary and self-evidently purposive. Participation in it was an (almost) entirely voluntary act, intended to be engaged in freely both by those who supplied the goods of religious organisation and those who demanded them.[2] In theory at least, either the producer or the consumer could have withdrawn his or her participation at any time. Certainly, both were engaged in the economy of religious goods and services solely because they wished to be. It was not a matter of life and death, or a question of public or private coercion. Moreover, voluntary participation from both parties was directed towards a specific end. And, again theoretically at least, that was the same end in both cases. So the political economy of religious organisations was differentiated both from the profit motive of private commodity exchange, and from the bureaucratic doctrine of public resource allocation, through its thoroughgoing repudiation of any meaningful differentiation between principal and agent in the characteristic method producing religious goods and services; similarly, in its rejection of any meaningful distinction between the ends and means of voluntary religious association. Put simply, it presumed that both the churches and the faithful were engaged in the same work, and that their engagement in it demanded that this work be righteous, both in how it was done and in its consequences.

So complex a set of demands for general economic organisation required a suitably subtle model both for the raising of religious revenues and for the expenditure of religious resources. This was the doctrine of voluntary beneficence.

The doctrine of voluntary beneficence and the hierarchy of organisational forms

Before any money was spent, it had to be raised. Christian dogma and common sense demanded that it be raised in an ethically appropriate and in an institutionally efficient manner. Of the two, religious apologetics naturally placed rather more emphasis on ethical appropriateness – on how it was raised – than on organisational efficiency – on how much was raised. And, between the two, religious apologetics generally prevailed. This was not just an assertion of unworldly idealism. It was precisely through the discipline of a self-consciously voluntary *and*

---

[2] It has proved virtually impossible to discover anything about the economic organisation of either Halifax's or Keighley's Roman Catholic churches. The discussion below, accordingly, is confined to the experience of the major Protestant churches of the locality. The degree to which the political economy of the contemporary Church of England was, or was not, entirely voluntary is discussed below. See pp. 136–9.

self-evidently righteous economy that pious churchmen and ministers sought to maximise the commitment of each person associated with a religious organisation to the proper purposes of those institutions. To that end they attempted to impose a rigid political ideal upon the organisation and management of that economy. This ideal may be called the 'political economy of voluntary beneficence'.[3] It was a theory of organisational finance rooted in the Christian duty of self-sacrifice. Its practical demands, conceived from the point of view of the donor, were remarkably simple. It required that each person should give as much as he or she could give, and as frequently as he or she could give, so that, through the sum of individual donations so given the work of God's Church on earth could proceed.

That this ethic was divinely justified, and that the duties it imposed upon the individual believer were real and righteous, no contemporary churchman or minister doubted. This was because the act of giving was invariably conceived also as an act of worship. 'I shall [endeavour] ... to accustom my congregation to regard giving as part of [the] worship of God [and] to raise the tone of feeling in connection with so important an element of Christian duty,' wrote Francis Pigou, Rector of St John the Baptist Church of England, Halifax, in 1877.[4] Moreover, as an act of worship, it was widely interpreted as a form of personal sacrifice. Observing, in 1899, that 'on all sides the cry is for more money for the Church's work', Frederic Cooper, Vicar of St Paul's, Church of England, King Cross, Halifax, remarked: 'I am not sorry that it should be so, and that we should not be allowed to settle down into a comfortable easy going religion without any sacrifice. Until our giving reaches the point at which we really feel the loss, and perhaps have to give up a good deal in consequence, it has not got much moral value.' And to be really valuable it 'must be done *willingly* ... by ... those ... whose hearts are moved for money ... gained from people [who] feel that they can't get out of it ... is better thrown away'.[5]

3   For further discussion and a slightly fuller elucidation, see S.J.D. Green, 'The Death of Pew-Rents, the Rise of Bazaars and the End of the Traditional Political Economy of Voluntary Religious Organisations: The Case of the West Riding of Yorkshire, c. 1870–1914', *Northern History*, 27 (1991) 198–235. For a detailed treatment of the theological and doctrinal justification of the related idea of 'systematic beneficence', and for its exposition in contemporary Protestant culture, see E.J. Garnett, 'Aspects of the Relationship between Protestant Ethics and Economic Activity in Mid-Victorian England' (D.Phil. thesis, University of Oxford, 1986), ch. 5; and Garnett, '"Gold and Gospel": Systematic Beneficience in Mid-Victorian England', in W.J. Sheils and Diana Wood (eds.), *The Church and Wealth*, Studies in Church History, 24 (Oxford, 1987), pp. 347–58.

4   Francis Pigou, 'A Pastoral Letter to His Parishioners', p. 9.

5   Frederic W. Cooper, 'The Vicar's Letter', *SPCKCPM*, vol. 8, no. 4, April 1899 (no page number).

But willing, worshipful sacrifice was also a systematic institutional obligation. So much so that in *Church Membership: Its Basis, Its Claims, Its Obligations. An Exposition and an Appeal*,[6] a Congregationalist minister, the Reverend Francis Wrigley, argued that the 'third duty' of church membership 'relates to finance', since, 'to be a church member very properly carries with it a financial responsibility'. And, he added, '[n]o-one who really believes in religion or sincerely loves the Church will wish to escape this obligation'. Indeed, 'a truly educated Christian is one who will deem it not a burden but a privilege to share in the cost of the kingdom of God. He will make it a point of honour ... to uphold the work of the Christian church.' Furthermore, since 'the Church needs funds for the carrying on of its work' he (i.e. the truly educated Christian) will 'give willingly ... sacrificially and ... systematically'. So '[n]othing will so deepen our interest in the Church as the sacrifice we make for its support'.[7] For it alone would ensure that 'our Church membership will stand for something real, something tangible, and something practical'.[8]

Yet, conceived from the point of view of the donee, what was in fact all too real, tangible and practical in the economic organisation of voluntary religious associations in mid- (and indeed late) Victorian West Yorkshire was less the certainty with which such arcane ecclesiastical doctrines were generally acknowledged than the extraordinary variety of institutional means through which churches were actually obliged to raise their revenues. These included national and regional ecclesiastical authorities (both Established and voluntary); wealthy private patrons (direct and indirect); individual society members and associational adherents (in the form of pew-rents, free-will offerings and subscriptions); 'class' members (in Methodist services); ticket-holders (at sacramental services); congregations, especially at collections (anniversary, quarterly, monthly, weekly and other); friends and acquaintances, usually at 'special efforts' ('bazaars', 'sales of work', and 'at homes'); Sunday school scholars (at collections and anniversaries); even, on occasion, from other churches and chapels, in the form of cross-subsidies, made by richer societies to their poorer brethren.

The reason for such variety was simple. The needs of voluntary religious organisations were universal and constant. Yet the means of religious persons were various and fickle. Many highly committed

---

[6] Rev. Francis Wrigley, *Church Membership: Its Basis, Its Claims, Its Obligations. An Exposition and an Appeal* (London, 1900).

[7] *Ibid.*, pp. 7–8; the other duties were: (1) 'faithful attendance at public worship', pp. 6–7; and (2) 'attendance at the special meetings of the church', p. 7.

[8] Wrigley, *Church Membership*, p. 11.

individuals gave regularly in several capacities (e.g. as society members, as communicants, or as parents of a scholar), and on many different occasions. Others gave only rarely, and in very particular circumstances (e.g. on Sunday school anniversaries). Some never gave anything at all. The seeming complexity of financial institutions which marked even the most primitive voluntary religious organisation in mid-Victorian West Yorkshire was thus no more than a necessary organisational response to the vast range and frequent uncertainty of personal motivation and individual competence. In its intricacy, it succeeded in tapping resources precisely where and when such goods became available. In its nebulous-ness, it was capable of inventing new justifications, and even of fabricating old 'traditions', in order to legitimise its many demands upon its several devotional constituencies. But in so doing, it did not abandon the moral (and theological) imperatives of the doctrine of 'voluntary beneficence'. On the contrary. From this apparently multifarious mass of overlapping bodies, churchmen and ministers generally succeeded in imposing a hierarchical order of institutional forms which at once preserved the essential features of the voluntary doctrine – worship, sacrifice and regularity – and which also distinguished the differential moral purpose of different forms of revenue. They did this by dividing the characteristic means of organisational finance – revenue and spending – into specifically designated 'contributions', 'collections' and 'receipts'.

The example of Keighley Congregational Church, Devonshire Street, will serve as a model in this respect. There, 'contributions' were defined as sums of money openly pledged by individual members or affiliates, whether as pew-rents, class monies, or ticket funds. 'Collections' were identified as revenues secured from the whole congregation, whether yearly, monthly, or, later, weekly. 'Receipts' were acknowledged as funds more broadly drawn from a wider, associated community, occasionally in return for specific goods and services and usually on 'special' church or chapel occasions. These formal distinctions of income reflected a moral division of responsibilities. Contributions were the responsibility of an individual. Collections were the responsibility of a particular group of individuals. Receipts were the responsibility of a nebulous community of affiliated persons. And those divisions of responsibility, in turn, expressed a practical difference in the proper purposes of the varying forms of associational revenue. Individual contributions were conceived of as the life-blood of a society of support. They were supposed to keep it in existence. They paid for the minister's salary (in nonconformist societies), and covered essential church and chapel expenses. Congregational collections were understood to be an expression of its wider purposes. They funded evangelical missions, raised alms for the poor, and provided aid to the sick. Associational receipts were taken to be an acknowledgement of its necessary – and additional – means. They restored its fortunes, built and rebuilt its fabric and improved its worldly facilities.[9]

These distinctions were not rigidly imposed at Devonshire Street. Nor were they in any other local society, whether dissenting or Established. But they were well understood in all of them. Accordingly, it was generally recognised at Devonshire Street, as elsewhere, that whilst every penny counted in the pursuit of God's earthly work, contributions mattered more than collections, and collections mattered more than receipts. It is difficult to establish any typical proportion for this preferred or actual distribution. The precise relationship between contributions, collections and receipts varied from society to society. More importantly, it oscillated *within* societies from year to year. But the case of Keighley Congregational was probably not entirely untypical. Its contribution revenues rarely seem to have counted for less than half, and often appear to have constituted something more like two-thirds of total society funds, during the twenty years between 1872 and 1892. Collections never amounted to more than one-third of the whole, often less, at this time. Receipts made up the rest.[10] Hence contributions paid for the Reverend A.B. Morris's not inconsiderable (£300) salary, and for a chapel keeper, at nearly £50, in addition to the wear and tear on the building, in 1872. Collections subsidised church alms, its London Missionary Society and, above all, the daily maintenance of its Sunday school. Receipts served a few minor and residual purposes; very minor, it seems, since the chapel actually incurred a debt of £77 7s 5$\frac{1}{2}$d that year.[11]

Naturally the norm varied, both from society to society and from denomination to denomination. Devonshire Street was, after all, a rich

---

[9]   Anon., *Keighley Congregational Church Manual 1873* (Keighley, 1873), pp. 6–7; this division of financial labour in the economic organisation of Devonshire Street Church was written into the rule book of the society.

[10] *Keighley Congregational Church Manuals, 1872–1892* (Keighley, 1873–1893), *passim*; author's estimates. It is virtually impossible to calculate the total wealth and total income of this, and most other, churches and chapels from surviving records. This is because the propertied wealth of individual churches and chapels was usually recorded separately from their ordinary and extraordinary incomes; and partly because, at least until after the First World War, few churches or chapels calculated even their annual incomes in aggregate terms, preferring to record the incomes of different institutions within their associations (e.g. trust, society, Sunday school, auxiliaries) separately. In most cases, some of these separately calculated sources have been lost; therefore, no *overall* figure can be calculated. Figures quoted in subsequent sections of this chapter must therefore be regarded as approximations based on the surviving evidence.

[11] *Keighley Congregational Church Manual, 1873*, pp. 28–31.

association at the time. It was also an 'Independent Church', well versed in the 'philosophy' that a 'congregation ought to be able to meet its own expenses'.[12] But there were limits to the generally acceptable level of such variations. Certainly, there were occasions when unusual divergence from them provoked widespread opprobrium. Here lay a paradox. The ideal of 'voluntary beneficence' described a moral independence which every church and chapel, of whatever denomination, actively sought. Yet its reality implied a self-sufficiency which by no means all of them could sustain, and which some of them actively avoided. For dependency, in the scheme of things, also meant subsidy. And few were willing to turn down any form of subsidy. The characteristic forms of these associational subsidies can be reduced to three essential types: the diverging (if generally tolerated) impact of private patronage; the distinctive (and often confusing) varieties of intra-denominational co-operation; and finally, the dichotomous (and ever resented) pattern of Established privilege and dissenting exclusion.

The diversity of denominational privileges and the myth of Anglican advantage

One matter of institutional variety regularly raised the local religious temperature. This was the question of Establishment. Victorian non-conformist sensibilities were continually, almost formulaically, offended by the privileges of the Church of England. This was especially true of its fiscal and other financial advantages. That the Church had a legal right, or seemed to have such a right, to benefit from the property and labour of non-churchmen, to employ for its own purposes resources which were the product neither of the generosity nor of the sacrifice of its own congregations, condemned Anglicanism for most nonconformists (and even many Roman Catholics) as no more than a vehicle of moral iniquity, and identified the Anglican Church as an unethical institution, worthy only of righteous attack.[13] There was, of course, an alternative view, and one expressed with disarming simplicity of purpose by a local church historian: 'It was always assumed that the church [i.e. the Church of England] was the property and the responsibility of the whole community, and a Church Rate was collected for the upkeep of the Church, just as the Highway Rate was collected for the repair of the roads, and a Poor Rate for the relief of the poor'.[14] That assumption did

12 Reid Marchbank, *One Hundred Years of Progress*, p. 48.
13 See, esp., E.R. Norman, *Church and Society in England, 1770–1970: A Historical Study* (Oxford, 1976), pp. 190–202.
14 Anon., *St John the Evangelist, Warley*, p. 20.

not survive the latter years of the nineteenth century. Compulsory church rates were abolished nationally in 1868.[15] Further local blows soon followed. In 1877, 'Vicar's Rate', a tax levied on private residences in lieu of Easter dues to maintain the parsonage, was effectively bought out by Halifax's nonconformist community.[16] And in 1890, 'Burial Dues', a payment made to the incumbent minister of the Church of St Andrew's by its dissenters in order to exercise a right to inter their dead in the 'Church's portion of the parish cemetery', was ceded in the face of the 'predominance of nonconformity in Keighley'.[17] The cumulative effect was seriously to undermine the subsidised Church. Certainly, the Vicar of St Paul's, King Cross, was keen to point out, in 1894, that: 'It cannot be too emphatically stated that our Churches receive *not a penny* from the State ... [T]he expenses of the Assistant Curate, choir, lighting, heating, cleaning, repairs, etc. etc. in a church like our own are ... raised ... from Offertories ... alone [emphasis in original].'[18] One result, as the Rector of St Andrew's, Keighley, observed in 1901 was that: 'the Clergy are miserably remunerated and that their ranks are gradually becoming thinned'.[19]

In fact, one form of Church privilege, long available both in West Yorkshire and elsewhere, remained immune to the vagaries of either national or local ecclesiastical politics. Queen Anne's Bounty and the Ecclesiastical Commissioners created new parishes, endowed existing benefices, and refurbished old church buildings throughout this period. And some local Anglican establishments benefited considerably from their generosity. One was Holy Trinity, Lawkholme, Keighley. Begun in 1878, the church opened its doors for public worship on 19 July 1883. But that was about all it opened: it had no endowment, no vicarage and no school at that time. Two years later, the Ecclesiastical Commissioners intervened, furnishing the Vicar of Holy Trinity with an annual income of £200 per annum from public funds.[20] Most local churches were not quite so fortunate. More typical, perhaps, was the experience of St John,

---

[15] For details, see Olive Anderson, 'Gladstone's Abolition of Compulsory Church Rates: A Minor Political Myth and Its Historiographical Career', *Journal of Ecclesiastical History*, 25 (1974), 185–98; on Gladstone's motives, see, H.C.G. Matthew, *Gladstone, 1809–1874* (Oxford, 1986), pp. 141–2. On the wider implications for the Church of England, see Chadwick, *The Victorian Church, Part II*, pp. 194–6.

[16] Pigou, *Phases in My Life*, pp. 300–1.

[17] Frederic Damstini Cremer, 'The Vicar's Letter', KPCM, vol. 14, no. 3, March 1891 (no page number).

[18] Frederic W. Cooper, 'The Vicar's Letter', SPCKCPM, vol. 3, no. 7, July 1894 (no page number).

[19] Frederic Damstini Cremer, 'The Vicar's Letter', KPCM, vol. 24, no. 5, May 1901 (no page number).

[20] Thornton Cox, *Holy Trinity, Keighley*, p. 15.

Warley, Halifax. Though ostensibly a creation of the New Parishes Act
of 1843, this church was not, in fact, built until 1878. And even then its
construction was the product almost entirely of local private initiative.
Thirty years' concentrated effort raised a sum of £5,000 from subscriptions and donations. Of this amount, £4,000 was devoted to the fabric
of the building itself. The remaining £1,000 was invested in Midland
Railway stock. The annual dividend of £40 was made over to fund the
new vicar's stipend. To match that figure, the Ecclesiastical Commissioners made a grant of £36 per annum to the incumbent. Monies
received from other charities raised a further £27, making a total of
£103; enough to live on, if scarcely a generous salary, even in 1880.[21]
Finally, in some cases, the Ecclesiastical Commissioners distributed
what was not strictly speaking 'public money' at all. In 1905, Miss
Elizabeth Porter bequeathed £3,000 to the Vicar and churchwardens of
St Jude's Church of England, Halifax. They, in turn, resolved to devote
this benefaction to the increase of the Vicar's stipend. To that end, they
made over the entire sum to the Ecclesiastical Commissioners, who
invested the money on their behalf. Eventually, it secured an annual
income of £100, which the Commissioners then reallocated to the Vicar
and churchwardens of St Jude's annually. The services of the Commissioners were provided free of charge. But in no other respect did they
make any financial provision to the church, either from their own or
from anyone else's account.[22]

So how much did the local Church benefit – financially – from the
national Establishment? We simply do not know. No figure can be
calculated, or any proportion reasonably estimated, of this amount. The
surviving evidence is simply too sketchy to permit such an exercise.
Morever, even if it were possible to do so, neither the calculation nor the
estimation would be very illuminating, for the Commissioners judged
every case on its individual merits. And every case was different. The
example of Holy Trinity Church, Halifax, may not, however, have been
wholly untypical. A 'Statistical Return of Parochial Work',[23] drawn up
there for the years between 1909 to 1919, reveals that during this decade
at least, incumbent income at Holy Trinity varied between £253 9s and
£310 9s 10d per annum. Down to 1913, the Ecclesiastical Commissioners seem to have contributed £130 each year of that sum; thereafter,
£139 10s. Queen Anne's Bounty accounted for a further £25 per

[21] Anon., *St. John the Evangelist, Warley*, p. 17.
[22] Anon., *St. Jude's Church, Halifax, 1890–1940, Jubilee Souvenir* (Halifax, 1940), (no page
       number).
[23] WHQ, D109/36, incom. arch. ref. Halifax, Holy Trinity Church, Statistical Return of
       Parochial Work, 1909–1919 (no page numbers).

annum, again until 1913; thereafter, £40 19s 10d. Pew-rents, Easter offerings and other fees made up the remainder.[24] But if public funds contributed about one-half of the total income of the incumbent minister during these years, all other major institutional and associational expenditures, that is, for the assistant clergy, at between £150 and £170 per annum, on church outgoings, at between £200 and £300, to the school fund at £60, and towards the sick and poor fund at £30, were borne entirely by voluntary contributions raised from the congregation. Together, they added up to a figure of between £800 and £1,000 per annum during those years. In other words, much less than one-fifth of total society income at Holy Trinity was derived from central sources.[25] And, of course, that money was directed towards a very specific end: the support of a ministry. The contribution of the Commissioners towards the discretionary income of Holy Trinity, to its daily life and work, was negligible.

The vagaries of institutional equality and the boundaries of associational fraternity

To be sure, most local religious societies received nothing at all from the state. But they were not necessarily poor as a result. Indeed, no caricature of contemporary ecclesiastical life could be more misleading than to conceive of an institutional dichotomy between a small number of over-privileged Established churches and a large majority of under-endowed dissenting chapels. True, there were rich Anglican churches in late Victorian West Yorkshire. But the fact that they were rich, in every case, owed very little to their external fiscal privileges. Similarly, there were poor dissenting chapels in this region at this time. But the fact that they were poor was only marginally related to their characteristic exclusion from the largesse of the state. It was much more the product of their own innate poverty. Again, it is impossible to give precise figures for this. Yet it is clear, for instance, that the annual income of Temple Street Wesleyan Methodist Church, Keighley, cannot have been much less, during the 1870s, than about £1,000.[26] This was nearly twice the income enjoyed by St Andrew's Parish Church, Keighley, at much the same time.[27] It was also at least ten times, perhaps even twenty times, the size of the income enjoyed by some of the chapel

---

[24] *Ibid.* (no page number).   [25] *Ibid.* (no page number); author's calculations.
[26] KPL, 105D77/2/21/146, Temple Street Trust Account Book, 1878–1914 (author's estimate).
[27] BDA, 74093/1/6/3a, St Andrews Church of England, Keighley, Ledger Book, 1888–1903 (author's estimate).

stations which were members of its own, Keighley Wesleyan Methodist Circuit.[28]

Put simply, some nonconformist societies within the same denomination, even indeed within the same connexion, were much richer than others. Yet such fortunate beneficiaries were not, as a rule, very keen on sharing that wealth with their less privileged brethren. And that held true even of the Wesleyan Methodist Connexion, where the very interconnectedness of chapel stations might otherwise have encouraged more fraternal behaviour. Hence, only two examples of inter-associational cross-subsidy from the Wesleyan Methodist Circuit in Keighley have survived. On 15 September 1882, the trustees of Temple Street Chapel resolved to pay over to the trustees of Fell Lane Chapel, at that time a new station barely two years old, the sum of £50 in the following quarter (September–December 1882) 'on the condition that the said trustees raise in the same time a similar amount'.[29] Nine years later, the same Temple Street trustees determined to *lend* the trustees of Utley New Chapel, Keighley, another recent addition to the circuit, '£100 at 4% interest subject to three months' notice on either side'.[30] These were scarcely generous gestures. Yet these societies were, and remained, 'fraternal' members of the same circuit. All of which proved that the economic limits of fraternity in Keighley's Wesleyan Methodist Circuit were pretty strict.[31]

There seems to have been nothing peculiar about Keighley in this respect. Indeed, examples of inter-associational generosity were, if anything, even more conspicuous by their absence in the Methodist circuits of Halifax. Hard evidence of only one – itself a highly ambiguous case – has survived. On 15 June 1903, the trustees of Queen's Road Primitive Methodist Chapel received a communication from the Primitive Methodist Conference in Newcastle expressing its 'hearty thanks for the gift [from Queen's Road] of £200 ... to the Pye Nest

---

28   See, e.g. fn. 31 below.
29   KPL, 105D77/2/21/15/b, Temple Street Methodist Church, Trust Minute Book, 15 September 1882.
30   *Ibid.*, 15 May 1891.
31   KPL, 105D77/2/21/14/b, and 105D77/2/6/4/a, Temple Street, Trust Account Book, 1878–1914; trust income, 1882, £415 2s 15d; in 1891, £1,527 0s 8d; Fell Lane Wesleyan Methodist Church Trust Minutes, 1877–1957, trust income, 1887, £46 9s 8d. No figure survives for the annual trust income of Utley New Chapel in this period, but circumstantial evidence suggests that it was unlikely that it was much greater than that of Fell Lane. As with Devonshire Street Congregational Church, no wholly reliable figure can be calculated for *total* society income at any of these chapels during the late nineteenth century; nevertheless, it is reasonable to assume that the degree of *difference* between Temple Street on the one hand and the Utley and Fell Lane Chapels on the other, is reasonably described by a comparison of their annual trust incomes.

[Halifax] Church'. For this gift represented, so Conference remarked, 'an assurance of your loyal devotion to the connexion, and your recognition of the claims of the almighty God on your resources'.[32] To be sure, £200 was a considerable sum. But the gesture was not quite what it seemed. Queen's Road and Pye Nest were closely affiliated societies in 1903. In fact, Pye Nest had been founded as an offshoot of Queen's Road, very probably as an attached mission-church. As late as 1903, the two stations actually still submitted a joint report of stations to the Fairfield Circuit, with which both were connected.[33] The so-called gift of £200 in that year actually seems, in retrospect, to have been something much more like a parting pittance than a generous subsidy. Pye Nest 'achieved' independence from Queen's Road immediately after this gesture. It never received another subsidy from its erstwhile 'mother church'. At the time of parting, its annual income was £100. Its debts amounted to £1,500. A present of £200, no matter how welcome, did not make very much difference to that. It did, however, make a fairly considerable difference, subsequently interpreted and understood, to the financial health – and independence – of Queen's Road Church.[34]

Yet the seemingly miserly behaviour of Queen's Road was probably no more than typical. Certainly, the local evidence suggests precious few instances of long-standing schemes to distribute funds between the various different branches of urban religious organisations, or of specific devices to maintain something like an equality of affiliated institutional incomes. In fact, only one example has survived, from one denomination (the Primitive Methodists), in one town (Keighley), and on one occasion (in 1870). Then, at its September quarterly meeting, the Keighley Primitive Methodist Circuit passed a resolution, '[t]hat we approve the principle of an equalisation of funds for this district'.[35] Exactly what this equalisation was meant to establish is uncertain. Whether it would really have brought about an effective equalisation of circuit funds, or (still more radically) an equalisation of society funds within the circuit, remains unclear. What is clear is that nothing significant ever became of it. There was no subsequent equalisation of funds in this district, whatever the principle seemingly then approved. Even amongst the

[32] CDA, Misc. 287:3, Queen's Road Primitive Methodist Chapel, Halifax, Trustees' Minute Book, 15 June 1903.
[33] CDA, uncat. MS, 'Report of the Second Station to the Primitive Methodist Connexion, Fairfield Circuit, Halifax, at the District Meeting, 1903' (no page number).
[34] *Ibid.*
[35] KPL, 105D77/1/1/1/f, Keighley Primitive Methodist Circuit, General Quarterly Meeting Minute Book, 12 September 1870.

Primitive Methodists, so it turned out, some chapels remained very much more equal than others.

Institutional paternalism and the limits of private patronage

Private, individual patronage could, and sometimes did, make a real difference to the long-term income of an individual church or chapel. In this way, it also indirectly affected distribution of incomes amongst local churches and chapels; even the balance of financial power between the major local denominations. Naturally, the forms of this patronage varied. But three 'types' seem to have been present locally: blanket institutional coverage; continual, visible support; and occasional, invisible subsidy. Of the first type, the best example, perhaps the *only* real example, was that of Edward Akroyd's beneficent treatment of All Souls', Haley Hill, during his lifetime. Akroyd built Haley Hill. He endowed it. And then continually subsidised it. To take one example, quoted almost at random from its vestry account: on 27 April 1872, the vestry meeting recorded 'its grateful thanks to the Parochial Church-warden, Colonel Akroyd M.P., for his generosity in discharging the debt upon the church for the three years 1869–70–1 ... and also for his very handsome support of the church during the past year'. Debt on the church during those three years had amounted to £191 9s 5½d. Akroyd's 'handsome support' had included a sum of £278 5s 7½d, paid into church accounts; an *ex gratia* donation of £50 and further expenses of £50 12s 2d: a total of £378 17s 9½d.[36] Nor was this an unusual gesture. The very next April, the same vestry meeting happily acknowledged 'its great obligation to Colonel Akroyd M.P., the People's Warden, for the liberal pecuniary assistance he has rendered the church during the past year'.[37] No figures were mentioned on this occasion. But it is unlikely that they were insignificant.

Only slightly less publicly intrusive (and effective) was the influence and benefaction wielded on behalf of St Paul's Church of England, Denholme, by the Foster family. True, they did not build the church. It was there before them. They did not endow it either. As a parliamentary church, it was well provided for from public funds. But they offered it, and it gratefully accepted, their continual, visible support. They donated most of its contents. The majority of the stained-glass windows in the nave were presented by various members of the family, at various times,

[36]   WHQ, D/78. incom. arch. ref., Halifax, All Souls' Church, Haley Hill, Vestry Meeting Minute Book, 26 April 1872.
[37]   *Ibid.*, 14 April 1873.

in honour of various other members of their family. The altar table was a gift of William Foster. And manorial mural tablets were presented to the church by the family of Mr Henry Foster.[38] What was already there they maintained in later years. In 1886, the building was redecorated at the expense of Mrs Henry Foster. From 1911 onwards, the church bells were restored through a legacy left by Mrs Eli Foster.[39] In 1925, and again in 1936, W. Garnett Foster refurbished, from his own pocket, the imposing vicarage.[40] The following year (1937), he defrayed the entire cost incurred upon building a wall around a new burial ground adjacent to the church.[41]

A rather less visible, and much less frequent, incursion into the affairs of their favourite society characterised the patronage of the Crossley family towards Square Church; and even more, perhaps, that of John Mackintosh towards Queen's Road Methodist New Connexion. Yet his biographer recorded that when

Mr Mackintosh ... became treasurer of Queen's Road [in 1909] he discover[ed] ... that the trustees had paid [in] interest on [the] debt more money than the entire cost of the premises. [So] he ... resolve[d] to put an end to such a perpetual drain on the financial resources of the church ... ironing out all the debts and creating a small endowment fund.[42]

And so he did. Then, in 1918, he

undertook to collect £950, the amount of the mortgage still on the Queen's Road Estate, from personal friends of his; then when the church was free of debt he would invest the sum of £1,000 in the name of the trustees, the interest of which would be available for church finance ... So the church was freed from debt, and its finances were put in a healthy condition.[43]

Institutional paternalism of this kind was not entirely confined to the ranks of the manufacturing plutocracy. The parish of St John, Warley, for instance, was able to rely upon 'the substantial support of Mr H.C. McCrea and Miss E. Farrier', two wholly respectable but essentially obscure local annuitants, 'through the first twenty years of its existence ... [w]hether it [be] ... for the heavy expense of church alterations or school extensions, or smaller items such as choir outings, Sunday school festivals, or even flowers for Harvest Festival and greenery for

38 Anon., *St. Paul's Denholme Gate*, pp. 13–14.
39 'Records of St Paul's Church, Denholme', unpub. MS, in the private possession of Rev. Dr J.N. Rowe (no date, no page number).
40 St Paul's Church, Denholme, Parochial Church Circuit Meeting Minute Book, 3 August 1925; uncat. MS in the private possession of Rev. Dr J.N. Rowe; 'Records of St Paul's Church', May 1936 (no page number).
41 *St. Paul's, Denholme Gate*, p. 13.
42 Crutchley, *John Mackintosh*, p. 131.   43 *Ibid.*, p. 137.

Christmas'. And their benevolent influence survived beyond the grave. Miss Farrier, who died in 1897, endowed a trust fund to augment the Vicar of Warley's stipend by £50 per annum in perpetuity. In addition, she left bequests to the Sunday school, and to the 'poor of the parish'. Mr McCrea, on the other hand, left a son who continued his work. 'Hardly a year passed', records St John's loyal historian, 'without some special provision being made by Mr McCrea [Jr] in addition to his annual subscription.' When he died, in 1945, he 'remembered the church in his will', leaving the sum of £1,000 to the Parochial Church Council of St John's Church, Warley, for the 'maintenance of the fabric of the said church and vicarage'.[44]

None the less, private patronage was probably the least significant aspect of the political economy of local religious organisations. Certainly, it was not and it could never have been, the norm of associational life in late Victorian Halifax, Keighley and Denholme. Of about 150 churches, chapels and independent missions standing in Halifax, Keighley and Denholme in 1900, only a very small minority, possibly fewer than a dozen, actually received a significant and regular proportion of their ordinary income from sources beyond their immediate membership, affiliation and congregation, over any extended period of time.[45] A few more probably enjoyed the benefits of occasional patronage from wealthy supporters within their own ranks, but for rather shorter spells.[46] The simple fact remains that the overwhelming majority almost certainly went without the benefit of long-term or short-term, large-scale external generosity, or even of major internal benevolence, for their daily sustenance. Why? For a few, it was an example of financial paradise lost. Ironically, the most famous case of such peculiar misfortune was the fate of All Souls', Haley Hill. Colonel Akroyd died in 1879. He made little posthumous provision for his favoured church. This was scarcely surprising. He only left £1,234 1s 10d net.[47] All Souls' felt the pinch very soon afterwards. Indeed, at a bazaar staged in 1889, in order to raise funds for the restoration of dilapidated fabric, the friends

---

[44] Anon., St. John the Evangelist, Warley, p. 10.

[45] Author's estimate; here, I take a 'significant proportion' to be 10 per cent of ordinary income, and a 'regular proportion' as more than five years in any ten. On the basis of examining the financial records of some fifty churches and chapels in this region, I have found only four examples (those cited above) which fit this description; there may have been more, but I have not found them.

[46] Unfortunately, no reliable figure can be calculated, either for the number of local churches which enjoyed this form of occasional beneficence, or for the amounts of money they derived from those occasional services; the surviving financial records are simply inadequate to permit such a calculation. A guesstimate of about two dozen might not, however, be too far from the truth.

[47] Bretton, 'Colonel Edward Akroyd', p. 99.

of the church actually made a point of publicly proclaiming that they had 'not the means of former days'.[48] This complaint was reiterated at a vestry meeting just five years later, when it was lamented that the means of the congregation were 'more limited ... than ... before'.[49] They probably were. Certainly, churchwardens' accounts for 1901 recorded an absolute decline in church income.[50]

For more still, there simply never had been such a moment, still less a generation, of financial bliss. And this was true even for some of those societies which had been founded and patronised by local businessmen, for men of wealth did not always smother their favourite churches with gifts. The Brigg family of Keighley may have been the 'principal contributors' towards the construction of Devonshire Street Church, and to 'a considerable extent' responsible for Utley Church.[51] They were unquestionably the benefactors of Marlborough Street Chapel.[52] And John Brigg was certainly a deacon and treasurer of Devonshire Street.[53] But they never gave any money either individually or as a family to any of those foundations for the purposes of ordinary chapel expenditure. What is more, the account books of Devonshire Street reveal that, between 1873 and 1923, no one else did either. The regular income of that society during those years was made up almost entirely of rents, offertories and collections, continuously drawn from the membership and congregation.[54] No external source of endowment income appears in these accounts until 1922. This, the first sign of any associational 'unearned income' at Devonshire Street, was a legacy drawn from one Hartley Whitaker, which yielded £30 in annual interest, or about 4 per cent of society income for that year.[55]

But for most religious associations in these towns such questions, whether of historical misfortune or of the later vagaries of self-denying family ordinances, just never arose. And this was for the most simple of reasons. There were no wealthy businessmen, annuitants, or spinsters of private means amongst their members, congregation and supporters. Some openly admitted this fact. South Gate Baptist Church, Denholme,

---

[48]   Anon., *All Souls' Church, Halifax, Official Handbook of the Grand Eastern Bazaar* (Halifax, 1889), p. 5.

[49]   WHQ, D/78, incom. arch. ref., Halifax, All Soul's Church, Haley Hill, Vestry Meeting Minute Book, 30 March 1884.

[50]   *Ibid.*, 15 April 1901.   [51]   Hodgson, *Textile Manufacture*, p. 43.

[52]   Reid Marchbank, *One Hundred Years of Progress*, p. 28.

[53]   Hodgson, *Textile Manufacture*, p. 43.

[54]   *Devonshire Street Congregational Church, Keighley, Church Manuals, 1873–1926* (Keighley, 1873–1926). Cash accounts were recorded by the Honorary Treasurer in the Church Manual each year.

[55]   *Devonshire Street Congregational Church, Keighley, Church Manual, 1923* (Keighley, 1923), p. 7.

cheerfully proclaimed that its 'regular patrons were poor'.[56] Others, like Lee Mount Baptists in Halifax, actually made a virtue out of their poverty. A history of this church declared that, for more than seventy years, its premises had been 'a scene of grand devoted sacrifice by men and women ... of lowly origin ... endowed with what was of higher worth: possessing blessed souls' and 'belong[ing] to the true nobility of this world'.[57] Most attributed it to more general denominational characteristics. West Lane Primitive Methodists, Keighley, noted that, as 'Primitive Methodists', they did 'not lay claim to being a fashionable body of religionists' and, correspondingly, neither did 'they number within their pale many wealthy men'.[58] Such evidence as survives bears much of this self-perception out. For instance, a trust cash book for Alice Street Primitive Methodist Chapel, Keighley, maintained between 1892 and 1952, reveals no example of any significant endowment income, or even of irregular grants, made to the chapel for the whole period from 1890 to 1950.[59]

But there was actually nothing peculiar about local Primitive Methodists in this respect. What was true for them was true for most other local churches and chapels too. Certainly, the cash book for St John's Wesleyan Methodist Chapel, Prescott Street, Halifax, complete for the years 1888–1925, tells a very similar story. There, with the exception of a 'Special Fund for the Extinction of Chapel Debt', raised in 1890, which attracted one donation of £250 and another of £100,[60] and a second, undated, 'Subscription towards the Trust Debt', which was graced with one gift of £100 and a second of £50,[61] there is no evidence of any substantial individual donations made to the current account, or even for other extraordinary purposes, over the entire period. Similarly, there is no evidence of continuing endowment income derived from earlier benefactions. Indeed, there is nothing in the accounts of St John's to suggest that benefactions or endowments *ever* amounted to anything above 5 per cent of total annual income, both ordinary and extraordinary; and usually to something much less.[62]

---

[56]   South Gate Baptist Church Regular Church, Meeting Minute Book, 1895–1917, Preface (no date); uncat. MS in the private possession of Mr A. Vine.

[57]   H.J. Carr and Arthur Wilson, *Jubilee and Memorial, Lee Mount Baptist: History of the Church and Sunday School, 1872–1922* (Halifax, 1922), p. 15.

[58]   Feather, *Fifty Years of West Lane*, p. 14.

[59]   KPL, 105D77/2/1/2/a, Alice Street Primitive Methodist Chapel, Trust Cash Book, 1892–1952 (no page numbers).

[60]   CDA, Misc. 152/4, St John's Wesleyan Methodist Chapel, Prescott Street, Halifax. Cash Book, 1888–1925: 'Special Fund for the Extenuation of Chapel Debt' (no date; no page number).

[61]   *Ibid.*; 'Subscription towards the Trust Debt' (no date; no page number).

[62]   *Ibid.*, author's calculations.

The institution of pew-rents and the mid-Victorian system of political economy

Hence the simple truth of the matter. Most local societies really did raise their revenues from contributions, collections and receipts. The theory of 'voluntary beneficence' really did describe the reality of the political economy of local religious organisations, albeit as much by default as by design. Consequently, in the typical local church or chapel, it really was the case that the most important, that is, the most dignified and the most efficient source of regular society income was the periodic contributions made by individual members, associates or affiliates to their respective associations. And the most important contemporary component of such contributions was the pew-rent.

A pew-rent was exactly what its name suggested. It was a sum of money payable, normally quarterly (though occasionally just twice a year), by an individual or a group of individuals, which secured for that payee exclusive access to one or more seats in church or chapel during divine worship. Payment was usually made to a society steward appointed specifically for that purpose. Seats were commonly allocated by number. Occasionally, they were also designated by name. Every society, bar one, in this locality exacted a pew-rent from at least some of its members and associates in 1870. And most of the seats in most of the churches and chapels in the locality at that time were allocated among members of their respective congregations in this way. To be sure, it was not the only form of financial contribution which members, adherents and affiliates made to the political economy of their various societies. Methodists still collected 'class money' from members before class meetings.[63] Other denominations collected 'ticket-monies' from designated holders at specific sacramental services. But, because of its ubiquity, because of its comprehensiveness, and because of its regularity, no single institution raised more money for more contemporary religious organisations.

'The principal source of income is from pew rents,' declared the Treasurer of Devonshire Street Congregational Church, Keighley.[64] And that was true. In 1872, pew-rents accounted for £281 10s 4d. This was something like 80 per cent of what was called the 'Cash Account' income of the church; and very probably more than half of its total income.[65] Ten years later, it was £262 13s 2d, a little down, perhaps,

---

[63] Though, on the decline of the class in late Victorian Methodism, see Currie, *Methodism Divided*, pp. 125–38.

[64] *Devonshire Street Congregational Church Manual, 1897* (Keighley, 1897), p. 40.

[65] *Keighley Congregational Church Manual, 1873*, p. 28.

but again scarcely less than 50 per cent of the whole.[66] And ten years after that, it was still holding up pretty well, at £270 13s 6d, or between one-third and two-fifths of the total sum.[67] Were the Congregationalists unusual in this respect? The record suggests not. Between 1870 and 1900 pew-rent income seems to have made up more than two-thirds of trust income (certainly) and between one-third and two-fifths of total income (probably) at Temple Street Wesleyan Methodist Church, in all but a very few years.[68] Was it, then, an essentially nonconformist institution? Again, the evidence indicates otherwise. At St Paul's Church of England, King Cross, Halifax, in 1896, 'pew contributions' amounted to £155 16s 6d of a probable total church income of £501 10s 2d, or just under one-third of the total.[69] And a 'pew-rent book' for Holy Trinity, Halifax, reveals that between 1870 and 1884 pew-rents yielded between £134 14s and £157 14s per annum.[70] Unfortunately, no reliable figure for total church income there has survived. But comparison with other Anglican churches in Halifax at the time suggests that it is very unlikely to have been more than £500 per annum. If so, then pew-rents probably accounted for about one-third of total, and closer to one-half of discretionary and disposable total income at Holy Trinity.[71]

But it was not just a question of money. Or, at least, it was not just a question of the quantities of money involved. This was because pew-rent, as an institution, succeeded in combining financial efficiency with social flexibility in a way which marked it out as the most ethically appropriate – that is, both the most demanding and at the same time the most generous – of contemporary financial institutions in the political economy of voluntary religious organisations. By drawing an ostensibly pre-paid (in fact more commonly pre-promised) quarterly rent from members and affiliates, it ensured a regular and (to some extent) guaranteed income for each society which it could have secured by no other means. By staggering the price of those seats (a universal practice),

---

[66] *Devonshire Street Church Manual, 1883*, p. 48.

[67] *Devonshire Street Congregational Church Manual, 1893* (Keighley, 1893), p. 30.

[68] KPL, 105D77/2/21/14/a–b Temple Street Trust Accounts, 1834–78; and Account Book, 1878–1914 (no page numbers). The years were: 1881, 1889, 1890, 1891, 1896, 1897. Author's calculations; like so many societies before the First World War, Temple Street kept no *overall* financial account of its income or expenditure; those, like Devonshire Street Congregational Church, Keighley, which did, were relatively rare.

[69] WHQ, D72/99, incom. arch. ref., St Paul's Church, King Cross, Churchwardens' Minutes and Accounts, 29 April 1896.

[70] WHQ, D109/66, incom. arch. ref., Halifax, Holy Trinity, Pew-Rent Valuation (no date, no page numbers).

[71] Author's calculations; discretionary income, in this context, is defined as that church income which was not drawn from central funds and not directed to specific, beneficiary and endowment purposes.

it succeeded in differentiating what might otherwise have been a homogeneous good into multiform product. In this way, it furnished the members and affiliates of each society with what was, in effect, a practical means by which they could match their own personal resources to wider organisational needs. In some societies, the range of available rates was actually very wide. For instance, at Rhodes Street Wesleyan Methodist Chapel, Halifax, prices started high. Of 171 seat-holders registered there in 1874, 57 persons paid £1 or more, per half (not quarter), for their seats; 43 between 10s. and £1; 17 between 6s and 9s; 37 exactly 5s, and another 17 a 'mere' 4s for the privilege of an appropriated seat. The highest rent charged in that year, at £1 16s per half per seat, was exactly nine times greater than that of the lowest, at 4s.[72] By contrast, at Northowram (Halifax) Wesleyan Methodist Chapel in 1894, there were just three rates only, and the most expensive, at 1s 3d per quarter, was priced at less than twice the amount of the cheapest, at 9d per quarter.[73]

These were extreme cases. But they reflected a more general pattern. Rich societies charged high rents. Poor societies exacted low rents. That was obvious. Socially mixed societies charged a variety of rents. This was perhaps less so. But, most important of all, virtually every society charged at least one rent (more usually several different rents) and most of their members and associates paid one (though not necessarily, of course, the same rent). In other words, the phenomenon of pew-rents themselves, and of regular payment itself, had very little to do with comparative degrees of wealth or poverty, either of societies generally or between people particularly. Relatively poor people paid pew-rents as well as unquestionably rich people. Moreover, that they paid and paid regularly, however small the amount, was probably more important to the financial viability of a poor society than to a rich one.[74] This was certainly true for one of the very poorest societies in the whole region. South Gate Baptist Church, Denholme, maintained an elaborate pew-rent system until 1909, much longer than many local churches of greater fortune and blessed with a more prosperous membership.[75] Rents at Southgate were relatively cheap, but not peculiarly so. In 1895, the most expensive seats were priced at 2s a quarter. The cheapest cost 10d. The

---

[72] CDA, Misc. 57/15/1, Rhodes Street Wesleyan Chapel, Halifax, Pew-Receipt Book, 1874 (no page number).

[73] CDA, Misc. 207/4, Wesleyan Methodist Chapel, Northowram, St John's Circuit, Pew-Rent Book, October 1893–July 1894 (no page numbers).

[74] For similar remarks and similar observations on this matter, see Yeo, *Religion and Voluntary Organisations in Crisis*, p. 80.

[75] Southgate Baptist Church, Regular Church Meeting Minute Book, 4 August 1909; uncat. MS. in the private possession of Mr A. Vine.

majority were priced at between 1s and 1s 6d.[76] A total of 146 sittings were occupied and paid for. They yielded £39 9s 6d in quarterly payments. That sum represented more than two-thirds of the total income of the chapel.[77]

What of those who still could not afford to pay the published prices? In certain circumstances, they were offered a specifically reduced price. This was often done, for instance, for the young, and particularly for Sunday school scholars. Keighley Baptists resolved to 'reduce the price of sittings for [all] children' in their chapels during 1889.[78] Queen's Road Methodist New Connexion Chapel passed a similar concession in 1890.[79] A trustees' meeting of St Thomas's Primitive Methodist Chapel, in 1902, determined that 'seats in the chapel be let to scholars from 14 to 21 years of age at 6d. per quarter'.[80] One year later, the annual trustees' meeting of Queen's Road Primitive Methodists resolved that 'scholars and apprentices under 21 years of age be allowed to have sittings in church at half price'.[81] Others were afforded temporary relief. One 'party' who had accumulated 'arrears of 24/6 [on his rent] was reported to the Trustees' Meeting at Queen's Road but spared any further embarrassment after the society steward responsible 'advised the trustees to cancel the arrears seeing [that this] person had been very unfortunate with regard to work and other matters'. This they did.[82] A few were granted something more permanent. Nine years later, in a quite unrelated measure, the trustees of Temple Street, Keighley, 'empower-[ed] their stewards to let twelve sittings free of charge to deserving persons who, in their opinion, should not be expected to pay a pew-rent'.[83]

Naturally, these were a minority. And the 'subsidised poor' were usually associated old hands, especially widows, occasionally the unemployed, recently fallen on hard times. To genuine outsiders and apparent strangers, most local religious societies were rarely quite so accommodating. But the unsubsidised poor were not excluded from

[76] Southgate Baptist Church, Pew-Rent Book, 1894–5; Uncat. MS in the private possession of Mr A. Vine (no page number).
[77] Ibid.
[78] Rhodes, Keighley Baptist History, p. 82.
[79] CDA, Misc. 287/40, Queen's Road, Methodist New Connexion Church, Sunday School Minute Book, 2 April 1890.
[80] CDA, Misc. 57/30, St Thomas Street Primitive Methodist Chapel, Claremount, Northowram, Trustees' Meeting Minute Book, 3 February 1902.
[81] CDA, Misc. 287/3, Queen's Road Primitive Methodist Chapel, Halifax, Trustees' Meeting Minute Book, 28 February 1903.
[82] Ibid., 24th August 1904.
[83] KPL, 105D77/2/21/15/c, Temple Street Methodist Church, Trust Minute Book, 7 March 1913.

their local churches and chapels. Every society which charged a pew-rent also maintained a fixed number of free seats, usually between one-quarter and one-half of the total, which were at all times unappropriated, and which were characteristically made available for the 'use and benefit ... of the poor'.[84] Nor, in fact, were the poor necessarily even confined to that set-aside place in the congregation, for many churches and chapels locally operated what became known as a 'five-minute convention'.[85] This rule empowered society stewards to declare 'free and open' all formally secured seats which had not – in fact – been occupied by their tenants five minutes before the beginning of worship. Part of the thinking behind this practice was, of course, to induce seat-holders to turn up in good time for service. But one of the results of its implementation was, almost as commonly, to render a church *practically ... free and open ... for all who came 5 minutes before the service begins'.*[86] And for those still confined to the poor seats? There were advantages. They really *were* free. And their occupants really did enjoy the benefits of a religious service at no cost. So much so that they occasionally drew not the sympathy but the ire of the churches which served them. Hence a church meeting of St Paul's Church of England, Halifax, resolved on 3 October 1901 to draw up a 'list of regular worshippers in the church who do not contribute towards sittings in the church ... and that a committee ... wait upon those whose names appear ... and ask them if they will in future contribute towards ... church expenses'.[87] Sadly, no record of the committee's subsequent success or failure survives.

In this way, the institution of pew-rent was both something less, and something more, than an entrance fee, payable by individuals for the use of a public amenity. It was something less because it was not compulsory. Not everyone paid it. And non-payment did not result in the immediate withdrawal of those services. It was something more because the act (or the promise) of payment represented something greater than simply the exchange of financial tokens for the supply of religious services. It constituted a statement of allegiance by an individual to a society: and the poorer the society – perhaps even the poorer the individual – so, very often, the more important was the gesture. At the same time, it implied a degree of standing for an individual in a society,

---

[84] KPL, 105D77/2/21/15/b, Temple Street Methodist Church, Trust Minute Book, 28 February 1873.

[85] Frederic W. Cooper, 'Vicar's Notes', *SPKCPM*, vol. 15, no. 3, March 1892 (no page number).

[86] *Ibid.*; vol. 20, no. 1, January 1897 (no page number).

[87] WHQ, D72/101, incom. arch. ref., St Paul's Church, King Cross, Halifax, Meeting of the Church Council (Minutes), 3 October 1901.

not merely according to his (or her) ability to pay, but rather in its provision of something so concrete for him (or her). It was, accordingly, a highly complex institution. It operated in what was, at one level, a recognisable commodity market, but it did not strictly follow the rules of economic exchange. It redefined those rules in a way which, to some extent at least, paid heed to the differential resources at the disposal of individuals, whilst at the same time it sought to reflect the ever-pressing needs of institutions. This made it a much more socially inclusive institution than the mere imperatives of the supply and demand of religious services alone would have permitted. It also, curiously, made it a much more economically comprehensive device than a simple entrance fee would have been. Hence it conformed admirably to the ethical and organisational demands of the doctrine of voluntary beneficence. It truly was, at one and the same time, both righteous and efficient.[88]

The burden of debt and the late Victorian crisis of political economy

Yet one fact remains. In 1870, virtually every church and chapel in Halifax, Keighley and Denholme charged a pew-rent. By 1920, virtually none did. The institution of pew-rents collapsed, locally, during the last decade of the nineteenth century. So much was this so that, by the second decade of the twentieth century at the latest, pew-rents constituted a negligible proportion of church and chapel income in most local societies. And by no means everyone lamented its passing. Indeed, some contemporaries, churchmen, ministers and laity, positively celebrated its demise. More: they advocated it, they hastened it, and then they rejoiced in it. Why?

In a message to his flock in 1896, the Vicar of St Paul's, King Cross, declared that,

if any two systems were the result of diabolical suggestion to keep souls away from Him, they are:
(1) The Pew-System
(2) The Sunday Clothes System.[89]

This was not an isolated outburst. Nor was it a sentiment confined to

---

[88] For a recent alternative, and more market-orientated, interpretation based upon rather different (Scottish) evidence, see Callum G. Brown, 'The Costs of Pew-Renting: Church-Management, Church-Going and Social Class in Nineteenth Century Glasgow', *Journal of Ecclesiastical History*, 38 (1987), 347–61; and Brown, *The Social History of Religion in Scotland*, pp. 155–6.

[89] WHQ, D72/134, incom. arch. ref., Frederic W. Cooper, 'Vicar's Letter', in *SPCKCPM*, vol. 5, no. 12, December 1896 (no page number).

the Church of England. Four years earlier, the Congregationalist
Minister of Park Church, Halifax, preaching in Keighley, expressed
himself in remarkably similar terms. 'I wish to Heaven that the whole
pew-system were done away with as an invention of the enemy for the
handling of the progress of Christ's kingdom, that pew-rents, pew-doors
and pews themselves were as extinct as the dodo'.[90]

The reasoning behind these remarks was, in both cases, fairly simple.
Pew-rents, so the argument went, were the work of the devil because
they were an impediment to the propagation of the Gospel amongst the
mass of the population. This was because they imposed a physical
separation of persons within the body of every place of worship: the best
seats were reserved for the richest, and the worst for the poorest of them.
By demarcating the poor, they stigmatised the poor. By stigmatising
them, they effectively excluded them. By excluding the poor from the
churches of God, they acted as an instrument of the enemy. Far from
being inclusive and comprehensive they were, quite on the contrary,
exclusive and destructive. Moreover, this line of argument extended far
beyond West Yorkshire. And it long survived the last decade of the
nineteenth century. Indeed, it anticipates the reasoning of most modern
religious historians. For them, it has become axiomatic that pew-rent,
long before (and even after) 1890, and far beyond West Yorkshire
(beyond even Britain), was indeed a socially exclusive, morally repug-
nant and institutionally disruptive mechanism, one which shamed
Victorian religious institutions, and one which does much to explain
their subsequent decline.[91]

These conclusions cannot be entirely without weight. And the
thinking behind them cannot have been wholly invalid. But, as
judgements, they fail to explain why the disappearance of pew-rent in
virtually all West Riding religious institutions after 1900 had little or no
impact on the social bases of local religious participation. After all, the
'poor' did not rush back to the church or chapels in any great numbers
after abolition. And, as explanations, they tend to obscure, even to
neglect the essentially partisan origin of the argument against pew-rents.
This dated back to the 1830s. And it was, in the beginning, a High

---

[90] CDA (HTC), Rev. J. R. Bailey, *Progressive Congregationalism: An Address Delivered at
the Annual Meeting of the Yorkshire Congregational Union and Home Missionary Society,
Held at Keighley, April 5th 1892* (Halifax, 1892), p. 14.

[91] See, *inter alia*, K.S. Inglis, *Churches and the Working Classes in Victorian England*
(London, 1963), pp. 48–57, 106–8, and 129–30; Wickham, *Church and People*,
pp. 42–3, 47–9, 57–8, 72–3, 114–15, 142–3 and Appendix II; and, most recently, Paul
T. Phillips, *The Sectarian Spirit: Sectarianism, Society and Politics in Victorian Cotton
Towns* (Toronto, 1982), p. 80; for a more sceptical view, anticipating some of the
reasoning and arguments presented below, see Yeo, *Religion and Voluntary Organisations*, pp. 79–82.

Church thesis. Moreover, it drew much of its early force more from a particular, essentially Tractarian, interpretation of the true nature of God's house, and of the layman's proper place within it, rather than from a general ecumenical concern about the needs of the poor for worship. It was inspired rather more by a sense of disgust at the 'intrusion of human pride' into the citadels of highest divinity than from outrage at the absence of impoverished human bodies within its stalls.[92] That was why, or at least it was one of the reasons why, the first so-called 'free and unappropriated churches' in Halifax, Keighley and Denholme were (High) Anglican churches. It was also why nonconformist, and indeed many (Low) churchmen, ministers and laymen tended to reject the underlying argument behind abolition; and, more forcibly still, to doubt the necessity, even the desirability, of the organisational reforms it implied. Certainly, there is no evidence to suggest that they were any more indifferent to the supposed needs of the poor than their (High) Anglican brethren. What is clear was that until about 1890, most of them drew rather different conclusions about how best to fulfil those requirements.

The first church to adopt a 'free and unappropriated' system in Halifax was All Souls', Haley Hill, in 1859.[93] No local dissenting chapel copied it for more than a decade. Then, on 6 February 1873, '[t]he Congregation [of Northgate End Unitarian Chapel] resolved to adopt the 'Open-Church' system i.e. ... that no seats be appropriated in the New Chapel ... and that instead of Pew-Rent an offertory be collected'.[94] Queen's Road Primitive Methodist Chapel followed suit soon after, probably in 1876.[95] But no other Halifax society did at that time. The pattern in Keighley was very similar. The first church there to offer 'free and unappropriated' seating was, so it seems, St Peter's Church of England, in 1872.[96] Once again, its pioneering gesture was neither quickly nor widely emulated. During the next decade, probably only four local churches or chapels followed suit: Upper Green Congregational Church, in 1874; Worth Baptist Chapel, during the same year;[97] All Saints Church of England, in 1878;[98] and finally St Andrew's Church of England, the parish church of Keighley, in

[92] Yates, *Buildings, Faith and Worship*, pp. 158–9.
[93] I owe this information to Dr J.A. Hargreaves.
[94] CDA, NEC 2, Northgate End Unitarian Chapel, Halifax, Chapel Minutes, 6 February 1873.
[95] CDA, uncat. MS, 'Report of the Second Station to the Fairfield Circuit Primitive Methodist Convention, 1877' (no page number); 'all sittings free' (1876).
[96] *Keighley Yearbook, 1877*, p. 111.
[97] Ibid., pp. 117–18 and 121.   [98] *Craven's Directory*, p. 30.

1882.[99] Nor was this just a question of indifference or inertia. An attempt to abolish pew-rents at St John the Baptist Church of England, Halifax, in 1877 actually failed.[100] So too did a similar effort at Queen's Road Primitive Methodist Chapel, in the same town, during the same year.[101]

So why did the trickle of abolitionism in the 1870s become a veritable flood in the 1890s? Strangely, this is a question few modern historians have asked. The answer has always seemed so obvious. Pew-rent, so the argument goes, was abolished because pew-rent was a bad thing, just as the Vicar of St Paul's and the Pastor of Park said it was. In truth, this answer is weak; as weak, in fact, as the presumption of unreformed infamy is poor as an explanation of why pew-rents existed in the first place. It does not explain why pew-rents were abolished *when* they were abolished. And it does not even consider the question of *how* they were abolished. Answers to both of these questions are vital to a historical understanding of how so significant an institution in the political economy of the late Victorian voluntary religious organisation became so insignificant a financial device for its Edwardian successor. Above all, it is important to acknowledge the specifically institutional context in which the rights and wrongs of the pew-system were debated. Only in that way does it become possible to understand how the balance of moral arguments which persuaded so few in 1870 curiously convinced so many just twenty or so years later.

One fact stands out. The critical debate about the ethics of the pew-system was conducted at the very moment – and often by exactly the same protagonists – as a concurrent debate, equally powerfully engaged locally, about the *efficiency* of pew-rents, in both cases conceived as the most important component of the principal means of ecclesiastical finance. And the institutional context of those two parallel debates, was a managerial crisis of political economy in the religious organisations of late Victorian West Yorkshire. Moreover, in most cases, and especially in those instances which were actually resolved one way or the other during the 1890s, it was the exigencies of economic organisation rather than the imperatives of moral logic which proved to be the real catalysts of institutional change.

The crisis of political economy in the voluntary religious organisations of Halifax, Keighley and Denholme during the last decade of the nineteenth century was a crisis of debt management. There were many

[99] *Keighley Yearbook, 1882* (Keighley, 1882), p. 48.
[100] *Restoration of the Halifax Parish Church*, Appendix, pp. 1–2.
[101] CDA, Misc. 287/2, Gibbet Road/Queen's Road Primitive Methodist Chapel, Halifax, Trustees' Meeting Minute Book, 14 September 1877.

contributory factors. First, the great business depression of the 1880s significantly diminished the general levels of discretionary income available for voluntary and religious work amongst the vast bulk of the local population.[102] Secondly, the missionary ambitions of contemporary churches probably overstretched remaining resources. Certainly, much of the missionary work done locally in the 1880s and 1890s was incompatible with organisational cost-cutting.[103] But no cause was more important than the financial impact of the mid-Victorian church-building boom in the new suburbs and outer districts of these towns. So much credit-financed new building, all in so short a period of time, left too many churches hopelessly in debt. Those societies which had merely rebuilt or refurbished their accommodation in order to compete with their new rivals were scarcely less burdened. Moreover, every society, old or new, refurbished or preserved, was increasingly confronted by the brutal reality of a more open competition for resources – resources of money, people and time – in a straitening ecclesiastical market, in which supply of the final (religious) product was increasingly outstripping the popular demand for it.

The simple truth was that more and more churches were being built at a time when there was less and less hard evidence that there were congregations willing and able to bear the burden of their expense. In this way, what had long been a chronic problem – churches, after all, had always been indebted – suddenly became a matter of acute distress. The extent and significance of those debts varied – very considerably – from society to society, amongst circuits and districts, even between denominations. But two solid generalisations can be made: first, that these burdens weighed down particularly upon those churches which had been built during the 1870s; secondly, they were generally acknowledged to have become intolerable on such churches during the 1890s.

The first of these propositions can be illustrated by the example of Salem (North) Circuit, Methodist New Connexion, Halifax. Salem Circuit was of fairly ancient lineage, founded in 1797. It stretched beyond the boundaries of the Municipal Borough, including stations in Midgley, Queensbury and Ambler Thorn. But most (six of the nine) of the stations in the circuit were situated within the limits of the town. Some, such as Salem Chapel itself, were as old as the circuit, but many had undergone major refurbishment in the 1870s. Salem mother church was a good example of this; it was entirely rebuilt in 1872. Others, such as Queen's Road Chapel, erected in 1877, were wholly new products of

[102] See Howell, British Workers, pp. 177–8; and Joyce, Work, Society and Politics, p. 77.
[103] See below, ch. 6, passim.

the mid-Victorian boom.[104] These efforts were not quickly repeated. Indeed, there were no major construction programmes in the circuit during the next decade; or in the decade after that. A glance at the financial records of the circuit for the period suggests why. A memo, presented to its quarterly meeting in July 1885, revealed a very sorry state of financial affairs. In the circuit as a whole, total debts on society properties constituted more than one-third of total assets. More immediately, they exceeded total income at all stations *combined*, by a factor of ten. And, most disturbingly of all, they were six times greater than the sums paid off that year.[105] This was bad. On that everyone was agreed. Everyone also hoped that, given a period of reasonable retrenchment (i.e. a decade of no church building), things would improve. But they did not. Indeed, a similar memo presented to the same quarterly meeting more than a decade later revealed a sorrier story still. Total debt remained about one-third of total assets. However, remaining debts exceeded the sums paid off during the year by a factor of something closer to 60. And the total sum of debts paid off barely outweighed the sum of *additional* arrears contracted by just two stations. Not one society had succeeded in paying off a significant proportion of its debts during the intervening ten years. No society was out of debt. And none showed any sign of getting out of it. Indeed, as total expenditures outstripped total income throughout the circuit in the financial year 1895–6 there seemed every chance that debt, supposedly incurred in the short term twenty years earlier, would if anything increase as the century neared its close.[106]

The trials of Salem Circuit were not unique to Halifax's Methodist New Connexion. On the contrary, they were all too general to the mainstream of local religious organisations. Their consequences are graphically illustrated in the experiences of Queen's Road Primitive Methodist Chapel, Halifax, a society for which unusually full financial records survive. Queen's Road was yet another product of the church-building explosion of the 1870s, and one of many new churches and chapels to emerge from the westward development of the town. The first Primitive Methodist Chapel there was built in 1873. It cost £3,200.[107]

---

104 Chapman, *Two Hundred Years of the Halifax Methodist Circuit*, p. 16.
105 CDA, MR/77, Halifax Methodist New Connexion, Salem Circuit Quarterly Meeting Minute Book, 8 January 1885; the figures were: value of trust, £27,980; debt, £9,456; income £990 7s 1d; expenditure, £927 15s 5d; debts paid off, £1,537 10s; new debts incurred, £26 14s 1d.
106 *Ibid.*, 16 April 1896; the figures were: value of trust, £28,040; debt, £9,398 7s 8d; income, £995 9s 7d; expenditure, £1,013 10s 3d; debt paid off £176; debts incurred, £153.
107 CDA, uncat. MS, 'Report of the Second Station to the Fairfield Circuit Primitive Methodist Connexion, 1877' (no page number).

That building was actually replaced less than twenty years later, during 1890–1, and at twice the original price, or £6,275.[108] Yet there were, at least on the surface of things, good reasons for this otherwise seemingly reckless decision. Created, almost *ex nihilo*, in 1873, Queen's Road had grown steadily over the next twenty-five years. It claimed 75 members in 1877.[109] This figure had risen to 125 in 1900.[110] Moreover, its Sunday school provided for the religious education of between 200 and 300 scholars during those years and the numbers seem continually to have been rising.[111] It was not a rich society; like the majority of new religious associations created in the latter years of the nineteenth century, its principal assets were its buildings. Yet it was not a poor chapel, either, not at least by local standards. In fact, the accounts for 1877 refer to a modest 'financial prosperity'.[112] Whatever that meant, total chapel income at Queen's Road in fact averaged *c.* £630 per annum during the decade from 1877 to 1886; a little less, at about £600 per annum, from 1887 to 1896; and then considerably more, at nearly £850 per annum, from 1897 to 1906.[113]

Now consider the levels of debt which this chapel endured over the same period. Between 1877 and 1900 the trust declared itself debt-free in only five years: 1887, 1888, 1889, 1890 and 1891. During the other nineteen years for which records survive, the trust was – very substantially – in debt. Indeed, an outstanding debt of £500 or more was recorded in more than half of its annual reports. The relevant years were: 1877–87 inclusive; and 1893–8, also inclusive.[114] Over the whole period, from 1877 to 1900, the average debt incumbent upon the society at any given time was £523.[115] But it bit hardest in the early and mid-1890s. Between 1893 and 1896, debt amounted to £1,500 annually, or to one-quarter of the total assets of the society.[116] No doubt this was in part a product of the costs of reconstruction, following the renovation of the chapel in 1890–1. Yet similar building costs had proved manageable during the 1870s. Now they were seemingly unbearable. Somehow the traditional method for ridding the society of its incumbent burdens – simply sharing the costs out amongst members and friends – was no longer adequate.

What could they do? Appeal to the circuit? They did. In 1894, chapel trustees sought and secured a loan of £200 from the Connexional 'General Chapel Fund', a sum free of interest and repayable over ten

---

[108] 'Report, 1892' (no page number).   [109] 'Report, 1877' (no page number).
[110] 'Report, 1900' (no page number).
[111] 'Reports, 1877, 1900 and 1925' (no page numbers).
[112] 'Report, 1877' (no page number).   [113] 'Reports, 1877–1906' (no page numbers).
[114] 'Reports, 1873–1900' (no page numbers).   [115] *Ibid.*; author's calculations.
[116] 'Reports, 1893–1896' (no page numbers).

years.[117] This was a help. But it was insufficient. Conventional wisdom – and the doctrine of 'voluntary beneficence' – suggested a special event in order to raise substantial 'receipts'. They did that too.[118] But it was still not enough. In truth, they could no longer provide for themselves. The following year they admitted as much when they announced, somewhat disingenuously, that 'the time has arrived when a combined effort of Trust and Circuit be made to reduce the debt on our premises'.[119] The circuit had, however, already given as much as it could, or at least would. The only 'solution' was for the station to begin to give less to the circuit. In 1897, Queen's Road halved its circuit contribution to £20 per annum. The following year it halved it again.[120] Thus debt was not simply crippling the church. It was slowly destroying the circuit principle. Queen's Road was not simply ceasing to be a viable, independent church. It was also, and almost as quickly, becoming less and less of a Methodist, and certainly less of a connexional, chapel. The implications were clear. If either was to prosper during the next century new, or at least significantly altered, methods of church finance would have to be forged – and quickly.

From contributions to collections: the failure of piecemeal reform

In 1892, Devonshire Street Congregational Church, Keighley, found itself in debt for the third year running. Concern was so great that the deacons appointed a Finance Sub-Committee to investigate the matter. Its report (published in the same year) concluded magisterially that, 'the "old system" [of chapel finance] has had a fair trial and has failed'.[121] By this, the committee meant the 'old system' of pew-rents, periodical collections and occasional receipts was no longer adequate and should be replaced. In its place, it recommended that the chapel adopt a new, or what was called an 'envelope', system of chapel finance. The centrepiece of this new arrangement was to be an ingenious mechanism of voluntary financial self-assessment which would enable regular seat-holders in the church to declare, in advance, their intention to contribute a stated amount of money each week towards society expenses. This sum was, so the committee envisaged, to be given in addition to their quarterly seat rent, and as a substitute for periodical collections. Other

---

[117] CDA, Misc. 287/3, Queen's Road Primitive Methodist Chapel, Halifax, Trustees' Meeting Minute Book, 2 July 1894.
[118] *Ibid.*, 14 October 1895.   [119] *Ibid.*, 25 January 1896.
[120] *Ibid.*, 1 March 1897.
[121] *Devonshire Street Congregational Church Manual, 1892* (Keighley, 1892), p. 33.

fundraising mechanisms were to be left untouched. Participants in this scheme were to be allocated fifty-two envelopes by the society steward which they were required to return each week, either before or immediately after service. The envelopes were, in other words, returnable whether or not the individual in fact attended service, since they were assigned to a particular date and payable on, or immediately after, that day. The reasons for recommending this departure were simple and, as far as the committee was concerned, virtually self-explanatory: 'It is quite as voluntary as the old system ... Quite as free as far as conscience is concerned [and] it tends to regularity in giving and church attendance'.[122] Put another way, its ethics were as secure as its efficiency was presumed. More: its greater efficiency, specifically its greater regularity, defined its superior morality. In the words of its most vociferous proponent, the Reverend Edward Pringle, 'weekly free-will offering' of this sort, 'determined by conscience', would, in fact, be 'a better training in Christian giving than quarterly pew-rents and periodical collection'. Not that the moral standing of either of those institutions, *qua* institutions, was at stake. On this, Pringle was insistent. The new system, he declared, was not 'incompatible with the appropriation of sittings'.[123]

Others saw different advantages. It was the attraction not simply of individual regularity, but also of greater social comprehension which especially appealed to the trustees of Prescott Street Wesleyan Methodist Chapel when, in 1891, they inaugurated a 'weekly offertory' system into their chapel services. This, similarly novel, financial mechanism was also introduced initially as a supplement to the old system. Again, the trustees made it clear that they had no ethical objection to the institution of pew-rent, still less to the lay appropriation of seats in church. In fact, the new offertory was quite specifically introduced to replace declining class and ticket-money contributions, and the inefficient practice of occasional collections. To justify this change, the trustees of Prescott argued that a regular offertory, collected in this way, was if anything better grounded in scripture: 'The most simple and scriptural method of raising funds for Christian work [is] setting apart of a definite proportion of income for religious and charitable purposes, and lifts [*sic*] what is in danger of becoming a fitful, spasmodic act, into a sacred position as part of the regular worship of God. I. COR XVI.2.' Secondly, it would be fairer. This was because it would reflect 'a more equitable adjustment of financial obligations between ... society and the congregation ... [T]he ... advantages accruing to members and non-members from the services

---

[122] *Ibid.*   [123] *Ibid.*

of the ministry are almost equal, but the method of contributing to the maintenance of the ministry ... is ... unequal ... Members ... in classes ... and in public collections ... Non-members [in] quarterly collections only ...' And, as a result, it would be more efficient, for the 'offertory system does not tend to diminish congregations, nor to affect unfavourably other sources of income, ... nor need it press heavily upon the poor [who] can give more frequently in smaller portions'.[124] In other words, for the trustees of Prescott Street the advantages of a weekly offertory were as much about securing regular collections from those who had previously given little as they were about achieving more frequent donations from those who traditionally gave much. And theirs was by no means an unusual view. Indeed, it soon found its way into other local ecclesiastical circles. For instance, the Vicar of Holy Trinity, Halifax, arguing the very next year for the virtues of a 'weekly offertory' – unequivocally once again to *supplement* pew-rents – insisted that, theologically speaking, 'The principal [*sic*] ... of ... weekly offertory at all services ... is the right one [since] prayer and almsgiving go together.' Then he suggested that it was only right for the '[whole] congregation ... to maintain the services and expenses in connection with the church'. Finally, he insisted that if they adopted his scheme the funds raised 'ought to be sufficient for the society's needs'.[125] This became the common pattern. In the same year, the deacons of Harrison Road arranged for a system of what they called 'weekly offerings', to enable 'friends' of the chapel to 'supplement the[ir] pew rents' and (just as importantly) to permit 'the congregation' to give 'free will offerings', all to be placed in '[b]oxes ... [situated] ... at the chapel doors'.[126]

It should go without saying that the specific forms of these changes varied subtly from society to society. The envelope system adopted at Devonshire Street was not strictly analogous to the 'weekly offertory' introduced at Prescott Street. The 'free-will' offerings at Harrison Road did not have quite the same significance as the weekly system of 'alms-giving' at Holy Trinity. But the impetus towards, and the reasoning behind, them was the same. Put simply, the 'old system' was not raising

---

[124] CDA, Misc. 481/18, South Parade [Prescott Street] Wesleyan Methodist Chapel, Trustees' Meeting (Minutes), 3 April 1891. The almost excessive length to which this Methodist society went to justify so apparently simple a change in its financial arrangements can, perhaps, be explained by the fact that the Wesleyan Methodist Conference had only sanctioned the institution of the offertory at all, a mechanism which it previously deplored for its alleged popish connotations, as recently as 1889. For further details, see Garnett, 'Gold and the Gospel', p. 352.

[125] H.A. Douglas Hamilton, *Holy Trinity, Halifax, Parish Accounts for 1892* (Halifax, 1893), pp. 1–2.

[126] CDA, CUR 1:13, Harrison Road Congregational Chapel, Halifax, Church and Deacons' Book (Minutes), 2nd March 1892.

enough money. This was partly because those who gave were not giving enough or regularly enough, but mainly because too many were not giving at all, or were giving too little and too rarely. In other words, what was really wrong with the old system was not so much that it stigmatised – and thereby excluded – the poor from the act of worship, but rather that it divided a society's worshippers too strictly – and all too effectively – between those who did, and those who did not, give regularly towards the financial welfare of the whole body. This was because it placed far too great an emphasis not only upon the moral, but also upon the efficient, distinction of economic labour between most favoured contributions, less preferred collections, and least lauded receipts in the political economy of religious organisation. Hence the primary purpose of reform within the new system was to raise the institutional and, if necessary, the ethical standing of weekly collections within the moral order of the political economy of religious organisation. This, it was hoped, would extend both the ethical and the social constituency of the donating worshippers within each society, increasing the numbers of those who gave regularly, and raising the yield of their donations through intensifying the regularity of their giving.

It was an ingenious idea. Did it work? The evidence suggests that it did not. The case of Devonshire Street is highly instructive in this respect. Initial reactions to the proposed organisational change there were highly favourable. The new system was adopted almost immediately. And the next report of the Financial Sub-Committee published in 1893, declared that:

The figures speak for themselves. At the beginning of the year 232 sets of envelopes were distributed amongst the seat-holders – 86 of whom have adopted the new method ... A glance at the Treasurer's balance-sheet will show the amount contributed by those 86 seat-holders to be £149–11s-0d, while the total contributions of the 146 who prefer to continue in the old way is £125–15s-4d.[127]

But the committee spoke too soon, for when the scheme was extended to the congregation *beyond* the old seat-holders, that is, to the free-riding faithful at whom it was in reality rather more pointedly directed, something curious happened. They gave more than before. But chapel income did not really increase. In fact, it was little more than £20 greater in 1896 than it had been in 1892, and well down from 1893.[128] Why? Because pew-rents declined. In 1891, the last full year of the old system, pew-rents had raised £257 1s 10d, from a chapel account income of £408 7s 5d. In 1896, they amounted to a mere £219 3s 7d of

[127] *Devonshire Street Church Manual, 1893*, p. 31.
[128] *Devonshire Street Church Manual, 1897*, p. 44.

a total of £494 9s 9d.[129] Thereafter they continued to decline, both relatively and absolutely, as a constituent part of church income. By 1912, they made up about one-third of chapel account revenues;[130] by 1922 less than one-quarter.[131] The 'supplementary' tactic had failed. More seemingly gave, but each apparently gave less.

The experience of Harrison Road Congregational Chapel, Halifax, revealed a strikingly similar story. In 1891, the year before the fateful deacons' meeting, pew-rents amounted to £303 17s 9d, or very nearly four-fifths of a total chapel account income of £384 8s 3d.[132] As at Devonshire Street, pew-rent then fell, both absolutely and as a proportion of chapel account income, immediately afterwards. In 1892, it was £300 6s 8d, or 63.5 per cent of a total of £461 8s 9d; in 1902, it was £256 4s, or 58 per cent of £444 10s 8d; in 1912, £203 3s, or 57 per cent of £356 13s 1d.[133] And, as at Devonshire Street, total chapel account income rose only very briefly before it began to fall again.[134] By 1901, it was barely greater than it had been in 1891.[135] Finally, the history of Holy Trinity provides pathetic corroboration for the failure of reform. This wretched society did not even enjoy a single illusory year of success. As the Vicar, Douglas Hamilton, was forced to concede in his parish accounts for 1893, 'the [new] voluntary system of church expenses' had been 'a failure'. In fact, it had raised £60 less than the 'old method'.[136]

No doubt the 'new system' was vulnerable to precisely the same iron laws of economic limitation which had bounded the financial affairs of the religious organisations of the region from the very start. There was, after all, only so much discretionary income available in the economies of late nineteenth-century Halifax, Keighley and Denholme and no mere institutional device, no matter how ingenious, could substantially increase it. Yet it is difficult not to conclude that it failed precisely because it diminished the moral order of the traditional understanding of 'voluntary beneficence' without substantially altering the economic basis of the system; that is, whilst it remained, or sought to remain, a

---

[129] *Devonshire Street Church Manual, 1892*, p. 32; *Devonshire Street Church Manual, 1897*, pp. 42–4.

[130] *Devonshire Street Congregational Church Manual, 1913* (Keighley, 1913), p. 38.

[131] *Devonshire Street Church Manual, 1923*, p. 12.

[132] CDA, uncat. MS, Harrison Road Congregational Church, Halifax, Pew-Rent Book, 1870–1918 (no page number); all the figures below are drawn from this source.

[133] *Ibid.*

[134] *Ibid.*; in fact, it rose consistently for six years, up to £468 7s 11d, in 1897, and then fell consistently for four years, down to £389 8s, in 1901.

[135] *Ibid.*, i.e. £389 8s as opposed to £384 8 3d.

[136] H.A. Douglas Hamilton, *Holy Trinity, Halifax, Parish Accounts, for 1893* (Halifax, 1894), pp. 1–2.

system of purely voluntary donation yet it also vitiated, or appeared to diminish, the very kinds of ethical discrimination – assuredly a discrimination between persons as well as donations – which had sustained much of the standing, and much of the sense of purpose, and therefore much of the value, of that system. It demanded sacrifice, but it did not reward it. Indeed, it now seemed scarcely to notice it. It projected the virtues of collective existence but it diminished the sense of social belonging. It made giving less valuable to those who were doing it.

In this respect, it is well worth noting that very few societies actually abolished the institution of pew-rent, or declared themselves 'free and open', before the turn of the twentieth century.[137] Most, in fact, nervously adopted the 'supplementary' tactic, dutifully invoked the communal rhetoric it implied, and then let institutional fate run its all too predictable course. For almost every case, what this actually meant was that 'contributions' generally, and pew-rents particularly, lost much, if not all, of their erstwhile organisational and ethical distinction. In their place, weekly 'collections' assumed principal place in the order of voluntary beneficence. Or rather, the old moral and practical distinction between the two was first blurred and then finally dissolved as weekly offertories of one sort or another became the characteristic form of voluntary financial contribution.

But revenues did not rise. The new system did not prove more efficient. Consequently, it did not establish its moral superiority either. The failure of reform posed immediate practical as well as long-term ethical problems for the political economy of local voluntary organisations. There was no possibility of restoring the old ways, precisely because they had failed practically, far more in fact than they had been discredited morally. But there could be no sticking with the new system either. Whatever its moral basis, it was not a serious alternative. It was for that reason that institutional reform now assumed a second, and far more radical, guise, shifting the balance of the political economy of religious organisations not simply away from contributions but even beyond collections, to receipts. And that eventually amounted to something very much more than a simple extension of the acceptable boundaries of voluntary beneficence. In the eyes of its critics at least, it eventually constituted so great a shift in the economic basis of the system as to destroy the moral order which had given that system a truly religious purpose.

[137] Those who did, in addition to the seven named above, included Holy Trinity Church, Keighley, from 1888, at the latest; Utley School-Church, Keighley, from 1889 at the latest; Braithwaite Church of England, Keighley, from 1893; Newsholme Church of England, also from 1893; there may have been more, but they were, as far as the surviving evidence can be trusted, in a small minority in 1900.

From collections to receipts: the reinterpretation of voluntary beneficence

'[T]here is perhaps no pleasanter way of raising money for religious purposes than the holding of a bazaar ... with its good articles, attractive surroundings [and] persuasive saleswomen.' So observed a reporter on the *Halifax Courier*, describing a church bazaar at Hanover Street Methodist New Connexion Chapel in 1876. But he noted something else too. Bazaars performed an important financial function. In his own words, 'there is no doubt that so long as members ... manifest an enthusiasm for contributing ... handiwork which can so easily be turned into money, bazaars will continue to exist as an important feature of liquidation of debt upon any religious building'. Moreover, he continued, 'by means of bazaars there may be enlisted in the accomplishment of the object in view, the cooperation of those unable to give money, but who can turn their hand to the production of something useful which ... could realize a handsome account'. Thus, he concluded, 'the objections which many people express to such methods of raising money may be easily and comfortably met, and the congregation at Hanover may rest content that not only have they taken the same course as companion bodies in the work of the Gospel, to reduce the debt on their [church] but, perhaps, with manifestly more success'.[138]

Bazaars were, indeed, popular features in the organisational life of religious associations during the second half of the nineteenth century. Their popularity has been variously attributed to rising standards of living and enhanced consumer expectations, to the availability of new technology for purposes of communal amusement, even to a decline of puritan sensibilities in contemporary nonconformist manners and mores; in other words, to the rise of 'religion and a good time'.[139] But this is to confuse the context for the cause. To be sure, bazaars certainly did appeal to a consumer culture. They invariably employed modern recreational technology. And their success often depended upon a relaxation of puritanical ideals, if for no other reason than that they were, self-consciously, festive events. Their true purpose, however, was to raise money.

The Hanover Street bazaar of 1876 was remarkably representative in this respect. True, it was not a public entertainment. Admission was by ticket alone. This, however, was on fairly generous terms, and extended to members, adherents, congregation, Sunday school scholars, friends and acquaintances. Similarly, the Bazaar Committee resolved that 'no

---

[138] *Halifax Courier*, 4 March 1876.
[139] I owe this phrase to Currie, *Methodism Divided*, p. 140.

intoxicating liquors be sold ... and ... no lotteries ... be allowed'.[140] But the bazaar was, and was supposed to be, an enjoyable affair. And it certainly employed a good deal of 'modern', recreational, technology. Attractions included musical boxes, a 'spelling bee', magic lantern views, microscopes, stereoscopes, kaleidoscopes and a pianoforte recital.[141] Finally, something of a contemporary consumer culture may be found in the words of the reporter for the *Halifax Courier*, who described a 'room ... thronged with a brilliant and fashionable company', in the midst of which 'the superb decorations, the bright colours and scores of banners, flags and shields, the richly-laden stalls, and the gaily dressed visitors, formed a scene of unusual beauty and interest'.[142] Yet in such a welter of congratulatory patter and self-indulgence, it is important not to lose sight of the real significance of this event. Its object was to extinguish a debt of over £2,000 which remained upon a school building at Hanover Street. The Bazaar Committee hoped that, through ticket sales and receipts, 'the total proceeds [will] exceed £1,000'.[143] In fact, they succeeded in raising £1,120 9s over four days.[144] Compare that figure with the *annual* income of the Sunday school at that time, at between £30 and £60; of the chapel society, at perhaps £150; of the trust estate, somewhere between £200 and £300;[145] and, indeed, of the entire association, including all its various auxiliary institutions, at something less than £600.[146]

Others were more open about the matter. In 1881, a new Congregational chapel was opened at Stannary, in Halifax. Four years later, a debt of some £7,750 remained on the building. Stannary's authorities blamed their tardy progress in this respect on a 'great trade depression', which had 'prevent[ed] any further effort for reduction'. So much so that merely 'the raising of the yearly interest, in addition to the ordinary expenses of the place, [had] proved a heavy tax upon the resources of the Church, and greatly hindered its usefulness'. Accordingly, in 1882, a 'special effort' to clear off the debt was planned. It was a bazaar. The reporter in the *Halifax and District Congregational Magazine* described the event thus:

[After] a brief speech ... by the Mayor of Halifax, ... 'business' commenced. Soon all the stall keepers were 'hard at it' doing their best to dispose of the various articles that had been got together. Nor were the public behind hand in doing their utmost to relieve the friends of their goods and themselves of the 'cash' they had taken with them. This kind of 'mutual exchange' was continued

---

[140] *Halifax Guardian*, 6 February 1873.   [141] *Ibid.*, 29 February 1876.
[142] *Halifax Courier*, 4 March 1876.   [143] *Ibid.*, 4 March 1876.
[144] *Ibid.*, 11 March 1876.   [145] *Hanover Street Yearly Handbook, 1871*, pp. 5off.
[146] *Ibid.*; author's calculations.

in a very successful manner ... The result was that at the close of the Bazaar ...
total receipts were £825.

There was no mention of aimless entertainment in this account.[147]

That strictly pragmatic attitude, both to associational finance generally, and to bazaars particularly, found its finest local exponent in John
Mackintosh.[148] Part of Mackintosh was, of course, a conventional
patron of Queen's Road Methodist New Connexion Chapel. But
another part of him, and perhaps the greater part, was an entrepreneur
determined to 'consecrate ... his great business gifts to the service of the
church'.[149] As such, he resolved to extend at least some of the financial
discipline of commercial manufacture into the life not simply of Queen's
Road but of all the Methodist churches in the locality. And, to a
remarkable extent, he succeeded.[150] The vehicle which he used was the
bazaar. As his biographer writes, 'Mr Mackintosh's organising genius
naturally fitted him to be a "bazaar expert", and he was recognised as
such.'[151] He became, in fact, something approaching a local authority in
the genre. First, he insisted that they be entertaining. To that end, he
'advised [bazaar] workers to ... arouse curiosity by hinting at something
that would take place, but not making it clear what it would be except
that it would be in the nature of a surprise'. Second, he insisted that they
be profitable. 'You know the old-style of working for a bazaar,' he once
remarked:

the ladies ... band themselves together and begin to sew, making pillow-strips
... selling what they have made for a profit of 4d on each article ... [W]ell ... I
meet a friend in the street. I... say 'we are going to have a bazaar ... will you
give me something for my wife's stall?' ... Everyone should be asked for an
article ... the butcher, the baker, the candlestick-maker, the milkman, the
grocer, personal friends and acquaintances.[152]

Finally, he insisted that they should be defended against their critics.
That was no small part of his contribution. In his own time, bazaars
were bitterly 'condemned' and their promoters frequently came 'in for
severe criticism'. To counter such opprobrium, Mackintosh insisted that
'in justice it must be admitted that there has never yet been devised
anything to equal them as a means of raising money'. On these grounds

---

[147] Anon., 'Stannary Bazaar', *HDCM*, vol. 2, no. 11, January 1855 (Halifax, 1885),
pp. 261–2.
[148] For a modern account of Mackintosh's career in ecclesiastical finance, and for an
excellent assessment of its wider implications, see David J. Jeremy, 'Chapel in a
Business Career: The Case of John Mackintosh, 1868–1920', in Jeremy (ed.), *Business
and Religion in Britain* (London, 1988), pp. 95–117.
[149] Crutchley, *John Mackintosh*, p. 135.
[150] *Ibid.*, pp. 132–40. See also, Jeremy, 'Chapel in a Business Career', pp. 95ff.
[151] Crutchley, *John Mackintosh*, p. 152.   [152] *Ibid.*, pp. 152–5.

alone, he maintained that they should be patronised whenever possible, and he did so whenever and wherever he could. It was once suggested that he opened more bazaars during his lifetime than any of his fellow townsmen. He took the remark as a compliment, and turned the jibe on his opponents: 'Some say [that] I make a hobby of bazaar opening ... some make a hobby of refusing.'[153]

The views of one businessman, no matter how committed, would have counted for relatively little had they not struck a similarly powerful chord in the minds of many contemporary churchmen and ministers. However, they did. Consider the remarks of the Vicar of St Paul's, King Cross, offered as 'a little moralising' to his flock, in 1899:

Most of us have heard serious objections raised against Bazaars, even under the name of 'Sales of Work' in connection with the church ... I have tried to think the matter out, and this is the conclusion I have come to ... A Sale of Work is very objectionable if the goods are not sold at honest prices. The sale should be a purely business transaction and no attempt should be made to get more money for anything than what may be considered its market value ... It is quite a mistake to suppose that 'patronising' a bazaar is an act of charity. It is not. It is simply a matter of business. The buyer gets, or ought to get, a complete equivalent for all that is paid. The charity is wholly with those who provide the goods, and sell them. They get no return whatever, except the sense of having done some work for God and the Church ... for most people come with an idea of picking up something nice at a low price, and very generally they succeed. It is quite right that they should.[154]

It is of course important not to exaggerate the element of the purely business dimension to bazaars. In most cases, the financial imperatives which increasingly drove them were grafted on to older traditions of communality and conviviality. Indeed, the same author, writing in the same journal, just two years later, about the 'at homes' at his church in 1901, acknowledging 'the first object' of that occasion had been 'to reduce the debt on Church expenses', also insisted that the occasion served a second 'and to our minds, a not less important purpose than the first, viz: gathering together members of the Parish and Congregation in a Social way [as a] renewing of old acquaintance and a making of new'; and reminded his audience that, thirdly, 'such gatherings would not take place unless some attractions were provided in the shape of Entertainments, Refreshments, etc.'.[155] It is also important not to exaggerate the actual novelty of these events. Bazaars, sales of work, and at homes were not a late Victorian invention. They were well known in the West Riding of Yorkshire long before 1870. There was nothing very

[153] *Ibid.*, p. 181.
[154] Frederic W. Cooper, 'The Vicar's Letter', *SPCKCPM*, July 1899 (no page number).
[155] Frederic W. Cooper, 'The Vicar's Letter', *SPCKCPM*, March 1901 (no page number).

new or very remarkable, in itself, about the Hanover Street Methodist New Connexion Chapel Bazaar; nor even the Stannary Special Effort. The citizens of Halifax, and the Protestant societies of Halifax, had seen its like before. And they were to see a lot like it again.

Nevertheless, something significant did happen at Hanover Street, at Stannary, and indeed at St Paul's, King Cross, and at many other churches in the years after 1876, and especially during the years after 1890. Bazaars became *significant*; sales of work, and at homes, too. That is, bazaars became institutionally significant to a degree which they had never been before in the political economy of voluntary religious associations. Once periodic occasions, they became regular events. Once justified only by occasional needs, they became regular sources of ordinary income. Infused with a novel – or a more intense – entrepreneurial ethos, and directed towards the support of a flagging system of ecclesiastical finance, they now assumed an organisational significance which they had never enjoyed before, and which their appearance often, indeed, continued to belie. They continued to be enjoyable, even apparently frivolous, events. But they were no longer occasions either for innocent amusement, or even simply for worldly replenishment. They had become essential to the very existence of many religious organisations. As such, they became a defining part of their existence. More: they became a critical element in what it was to be an early twentieth-century religious association.[156]

It was, for instance, more frequent bazaars and not that much-heralded new 'training in Christian giving' which saved Devonshire Street Congregational Church, Keighley, from its apparently inexorable financial decline. In 1896, a bazaar raised nearly one-third of total revenues there.[157] In 1902, it accounted for nearly one-fifth.[158] And it was the impact of special efforts, certainly not the pursuit of regular, weekly, voluntary giving which turned the tide at Queen's Road Primitive Methodist Chapel, Halifax. Trust income there, which had actually *decreased* between 1887 and 1896, increased by nearly 50 per cent between 1897 and 1905. That was due entirely to the revenues from annual special efforts during those years.[159] Much the same was true at Harrison Road. There, the significance of the change was openly acknowledged. In 1903, some ten years after introducing weekly 'free will offerings' and suffering the deleterious consequences, the deacons

---

[156] Cf. Currie, *Methodism Divided*, pp. 136–8.
[157] *Devonshire Street Church Manual, 1897*, p. 44.
[158] *Devonshire Street Church Manual, 1903*, p. 24.
[159] Queen's Road, 'Reports 1897–1905' (no page numbers). Average income at Queen's Road between 1897 and 1905 was *c.* £850 per annum; author's calculations.

voted to 'hold a [triennial] "Sale of Work" to supplement the ordinary income [of the Church]'.[160] This departure was not confined to dissenting societies. At much the same time, St Paul's Church of England, Halifax, began to hold a 'sale of work' as an 'annual institution'.[161] That was what the Vicar was talking about in his 'little' effort at 'moralising' to his flock. Eventually, the authorities there even graced the occasion with the appropriate title – 'the Annual Sale of Work' – in belated confirmation of what had long, in fact, been the case.[162]

For most churches and chapels, the altered burdens of early twentieth-century associational life necessitated a frequency of special efforts somewhere between the triennial arrangements at Harrison Road and the annual event of St Paul's. But one thing was common between them: 'special efforts' and not contributions, not even collections, came to constitute the single most important source of associational income; moreover, not merely in the particular year in which the effort was staged but as part of a running society account. This novel fact of institutional life often quite bemused contemporaries. But it certainly did not escape their attention. As the Rector of Keighley complained in 1901, 'In a parish that could raise £1400 by a bazaar it ought to be possible to obtain £150 in [voluntary] subscriptions for the support of the clergy.'[163] Increasingly, however, it was *not* possible to do precisely that. And the implications of this change were considerable. Receipts from special events, traditionally the least important formal aspect of voluntary associational finance, became, in practice, the most important constituent part of its organisation in many, if not in most, local societies. That hiatus between theory and practice in the political economy of voluntary religious organisations continued to confound local clergymen and ministers well into the twentieth century. 'I am all in favour of "Sales of Work",' argued a (different) Vicar of St Paul's, Halifax, in 1916, 'but', he insisted, 'they should be for capital or extraordinary expenditure ... [W]e ought not to rely on special efforts ... for the ordinary running expenses of the Parish.' But that was exactly what they did. In his own words: 'every penny from our ... Sales has had

---

[160] *Harrison Road Congregational Church, Halifax, Yearbook, 1910* (Halifax, 1910), p. 4. 'It was decided in 1903 to have a "Sale of Work" every three years to supplement the ordinary income [of] the church.'

[161] Frederic W. Cooper, 'The Vicar's Letter', *SPCKCPM*, vol. 8, no. 7, July 1899 (no page number).

[162] WHQ, D72/103, incom. arch. ref., St Paul's Church, King Cross, Halifax, Church Council Minute Book, 20 May 1924.

[163] Frederic Damstini Cremer, 'The Vicar's Letter', *KPCM*, vol. 24, no. 10, October 1901 (no page number).

to go to make up deficiencies in the General Purposes Fund, deficiencies which would not have occurred if St Paul's people as a whole had supported the G.P.F.'.[164] Moreover, 'the people' had not sufficiently 'supported the G.P.F.' for over twenty years. In this sense, the Vicar's traditional distinction between proper (extraordinary) and improper (ordinary) uses of revenues derived from sales of work was no more than an institutional anachronism. It still sounded plausible in principle, no doubt. But it had long since ceased to be viable in practice.

It is only in the light of their transformed significance, increasingly conceived as integral components of the financial organisation of a church or chapel, that the vigour and tenacity of much contemporary opposition to bazaars – precisely what the 'old' Vicar of St Paul's, King Cross, was arguing so carefully against in 1899 – becomes fully comprehensible. That opposition extended across all the major denominational and theological boundaries. Remember, Mackintosh had encountered it in the Methodist churches of his time. Battle was joined as early as the 1870s. But the lines of fire were most clearly drawn, and the issues contested most vehemently, during the two decades between 1890 and 1910. This was, of course, at precisely the same moment – indeed the debate was often conducted by the same protagonists – as the dispute about the ethical and efficient consequences of the pew-system and its alternatives was at its own polemical and organisational apex. That was scarcely a coincidence. Indeed, it is no exaggeration to say that the battle of the bazaars was, if anything, more important than the fight for the pews. For, potentially at least, more was at stake. To some, and they were not a small minority, the very definition of the theory of voluntary beneficence was at stake. This was because the very responsibilities implied in, and required of, membership of or affiliation with a religious association were at issue. In effect, the *difference* between religious life and secular life, and between the political economy of religious organisations and the financial organisation of other voluntary institutions, was being placed in the balance. Why?

Bazaars, sales of work, and at homes, promoted as entertainments, directed towards financial gain and infused with the entrepreneurial ethos, were, as even their more cautious apologists were forced to admit, an intrusion of 'the world, the flesh and [even] the devil ... attempt[ing] to insinuate ... [himself] into every part of our lives'.[165] And if voluntary religious organisations stood for anything, it was as self-conscious

---

[164] Hugh Bright, 'Vicar's Notes', *St. Paul's Church of England, King Cross, Halifax, Yearbook, 1916* (Halifax, 1916), p. 2.

[165] Frederic Damstini Cremer, 'The Vicar's Letter', *KPCM*, vol. 20, no. 11, November 1897 (no page number).

beacons of light, as places where greed, depravity and vice did not rule, but where, on the contrary, the spirit of God governed all. To their critics, the intrusion of such institutions, and of the entrepreneurial ethos which drove them, into the life of the churches threatened to dim the glare of that light and the vigour of that spirit. It was in these terms that H.T. Longsdon, the then Rector of Keighley, warned his flock of their danger when he observed that, though

[b]azaars ... lead ... so many persons to give time, trouble and thought to work for the church [they] also ... have [their] disadvantages [for] in the bustle of the secular side of the work, there is a danger of neglecting our own spiritual needs and of forgetting[,] in our eagerness to gain money[,] the inner meaning of God's words 'Man cannot live by bread alone'.[166]

One solution to this dilemma was strict regulation. Longsdon's successor as Rector of Keighley, Frederic Damstini Cremer, argued as much when he suggested that

where snobbery and exaggeration are avoided in advertisement ... where intoxicants, fortune-telling and raffles are excluded ... where the character of the workers is a guarantee that there will be no unladylike forwardness nor unchristian bickerings and jealousies; and where the choice of entertainments has been carefully supervised; we are in a position to say that an occasional bazaar is a thoroughly useful and even commendable part of our church life.[167]

But neither strict limitations upon the frequency, nor precise regulations about the content of their accompanying entertainments satisfied the objections of traditionalists and purists to the very idea of raising the necessary funds for God's work in so dubious a manner, and from so nebulous a source. Bazaars and their like, conceived not simply as a regular but actually as the principal component of ordinary chapel income constituted, so these critics believed, a fundamental threat to the essential bases of a specifically *religious* political economy. As fund-raising entertainments, they severed the vital link between devotion and sacrifice, wrenching the one from the other, detaching the moment of worship from the gesture of giving. As institutions of mutual exchange, they irrevocably compromised the idea of personal sacrifice. Finally, as trivial amusements, they violated the complex unity of faith and generosity.

It was a real contest, vigorously joined. At the very moment when the *Halifax Courier* was commending the values of the institution to its readers, the Vicar of Halifax was denouncing bazaars to his congrega-

[166] *Ibid.*; H.T. Longsdon, 'The Vicar's Letter', June 1878 (no page number).
[167] Cremer, 'The Vicar's Letter', November 1897 (no page number).

tion. 'Were the good old Bible rule observed and a portion of every man's income religiously devoted to God,' he lamented,

we should not stand in need of special appeals, still less should we countenance or encourage anyone of the unhealthy and spurious incitements which characterise modern [fund-raising] in the form of bazaars. If an object be good and right in itself then I should 'give hoping for nothing gain' ... and not require those unhealthy provocations to induce one to do what in itself is right.[168]

Ironically, views such as these – for all their apparent irreducibility – were often held on a metaphorical knife-edge, balanced precariously between the claims of doctrinal purity and the pressing realities of institutional life. Consider the following remarks: 'it is deplorable that so many people who have money should be willing to part with it [only] in return for a certain amount of pleasurable excitement, or an actual equivalent in shop goods, instead of freely laying it down as the proportion of their income they cheerfully and deliberately devote to doing good in the master's name'.[169] Their substance was surely clear enough. Oddly, however, their author was the very same Frederic Damstini Cremer, who in the very same journal (*The Keighley Parish Church Magazine*), just fifteen months later, would declare himself 'an out-and-out champion of well-conducted Bazaars'.[170]

It might be tempting to conclude that this particular Rector of Keighley was, at best, a man who changed his mind quickly, and at worst, something of an intellectual schizophrenic. Yet that would be glib, for it would be to ignore the real significance of the financial crisis of the 1890s, a genuinely cataclysmic event or series of events, which transformed many a traditionalist and a purist, like Cremer in 1896, into a pragmatist, like Cremer in 1897. Of course, it rarely happened quite so dramatically as in this case. And the stigma of bazaars did not fade away entirely during the last decade of Victoria's reign. In many instances, those who *could* continue to resist their intrusion into church life pointedly did so. For instance, on 25 June 1894, Keighley Baptists, meeting as a united denomination in joint session, determined 'to raise [the funds necessary for a major building project] by means *rather* than a bazaar'.[171] And as late as 1913, Devonshire Street Congregational Church, Keighley, debated, at length, whether to 'raise the funds required ... for alteration to [their] Sunday school ... rely[ing] ... upon ... donations and subscriptions instead of a bazaar'. After much soul-

[168] Pigou, 'Pastoral Letter to His Parishioners', pp. 8–9.
[169] Frederic Damstini Cremer, 'The Vicar's Letter', *KPCM*, vol. 19, no. 8, August 1896 (no page number).
[170] Cremer, 'The Vicar's Letter', November 1897 (no page number).
[171] Rhodes, *Keighley Baptist History*, p. 88.

searching, they voted 'that we rely upon raising the necessary funds by way of donations and subscriptions for the present'. Anachronistic heroism? Sadly not. They did not fulfil their pledge.[172] Hypocrisy? Perhaps. But there was a Sunday school to think about.

In this war, the traditionalists and the purists were painfully aware that they were fighting on several losing fronts. Their sense of defeatism and despair was powerfully evoked by Thomas Keyworth, writing in a history of Harrison Road Congregational Church, Halifax, published in 1894.[173] Referring to 'our heroic age' emphatically in the past tense, he starkly contrasted the ethical and organisational flabbiness of the late nineteenth-century church with the moral rectitude and communal intimacy of mid-Victorian Harrison Road. In this respect, he argued, nothing was more striking than the transformation of associational finance since the 1860s and 1870s. '[I]n those days', he recalled, speaking of the 1860s and 1870s, 'there was no bazaar ... and no sale of work. The money given year after year was "naked" money, no entertainments to spice the task and make it less irksome. A good preacher and a large collection were the order of the day.'[174] A few years after he wrote these words, Harrison Road voted, at a church meeting, to stage annual sales of work in order to balance ordinary income against ordinary expenditures, 'and pay its way' as a 'businesslike church'.[175] Old Harrison Road, it must have seemed, was no more.

This was not just a matter of nostalgia. Keyworth, like others, feared that in the contamination of a very special ideal of individual and voluntary obligation lay the germs of a still more pernicious disease which would eat away the vital health of collective and devoted religious identity. The ethic of individual generosity and the duty of personal sacrifice had ensured, so old hands believed, not only that the necessary funds for the work of the Church were given in a certain way, but also that, for the most part, they were given by a certain type of person: a specifically committed person. Of course, every person in any way connected with any voluntary religious organisation was a proper donor, from whom regular contributions to its associational life were both sought and expected. Indeed, to the advocates of bazaars and their like, the less frequently stated but often residually implied *ethical* attractiveness of special efforts lay precisely in their ability to take this principled possibility seriously; to take it, in effect, beyond the social and economic

---

[172] KPL, uncat. MS, Devonshire Street Congregational Church, Keighley, Church Meeting Minute Book, 30 September 1913.

[173] Thomas Keyworth, *Old Harrison Road: A Study in Origins* (Halifax, 1894).

[174] *Ibid.*, pp. 47–8.

[175] *Harrison Road, Church Manual, 1910*, p. 4.

limitations of the 'contributory' and the 'collective' models of individual participation, so that, in this way, '[t]hose who have the wherewithal are invited to do their part beforehand by laying down their money freely. Others who have but little money are invited to give its equivalent in time and labour; and thus all take their share of the work.'[176]

Disagreement between purists and progressives centred upon a contested definition of what exactly was *an appropriate share* for each. This was because the concept of an appropriate share of collective burdens, as most contemporary Protestant societies and particularly as most contemporary nonconformists understood it, was something rather more subtle than 'a goodly proportion of what God had prospered' each person. Whilst every person connected with a religious association was properly expected to contribute towards its material welfare, those most intimately connected with its society were, according to a long-standing tradition in Protestant sensibilities, expected to contribute most. So in shifting so much of that burden away from the regular sacrifices of those intimately connected with each society, and towards the occasional efforts of many persons peripherally concerned with religious organisations, this new system of voluntary finance actually threatened to invert the most respected proprieties of traditional associational relationships. This was because it disturbed, so the die-hards believed, a delicate balance between associational responsibilities, in which those who had attested most seriously to God and had committed more of their lives to His work, were also expected to commit more of their personal resources – money, time, whatever – to His mission. That view was expressed with exquisite subtlety – even a slight disingenuousness – by the editor of *Keighley Wesleyan Methodist Circuit Magazine* when he observed that,

of course, it is the proper way to look to our members to help steadily [since] the real foundation of their [i.e. religious organisations'] finance [is] the steady contribution of the members[, and] reliance [is] placed first and foremost on that ... One cannot but be grateful for all the energy displayed over 'At Homes' – probably not less than £900 has been raised by such means in the Keighley Circuit since last November [i.e. since November 1922] – but we ought not to shift our base of supply and cease to depend on our members.[177]

But that is exactly what they had done. They had shifted their base of supply. They had ceased to depend on their members, at least as the real foundation of their financial organisation. As such, the editor's observation that 'on the class books there is a column space opposite every name, and we earnestly desire that it may be filled up with a *regular gift*

---

[176] Cremer, 'The Vicar's Letter', November 1897 (no page number).
[177] Rev. F.T. Harvey, 'Pastoral', *KWMCM*, no. 169, June 1923 (no page number).

given in principle for the love of the Master's work and kingdom'[178] was little more than a lament for the old days. It may be compared with the elegiac words of the Vicar of St Paul's Church of England, Halifax, uttered in 1916, or with the legalistic dogma of Pastor Wrigley as expressed in *Church Membership* in 1900; even, indeed, with the scalding observations of Thomas Keyworth. They were all describing a sacrificial, a committed, and, above all else, a hierarchically ordered associational world which simply no longer existed.

A precarious legacy: the voluntary system and the extended political economy of religious organisations

Remarking upon the three most significant features of Victorian church life, Keighley's post-war Congregational historian observed that an 'attempt to replace pew-rent by offertories, as the basis of the Church's finance'[179] was of central importance to the development of the modern church. Fifty years on, he neglected to mention something which contemporaries freely acknowledged. It had failed. True, pew-rent slowly declined at Devonshire Street Congregational Chapel. And offertories, once an insignificant feature of chapel finance, became of greater importance to its management by the beginning of the twentieth century. But the basis of church finance at Edwardian Devonshire Street shifted as much, if not more, towards periodic special efforts as regular (that is, weekly) offertories. The replacement of pew-rents by offertories reallocated some of the burden of associational finance from the regular to the occasional worshipper. It did not effect an overall increase in the level of giving. The intensification of the frequency, and of the seriousness, of special efforts did. And that was not quite the same thing.

In the moral scale of the mid-Victorian ideal, receipts had been a lower form of religious revenue. They were the product of a lesser gift, the act of mutual exchange. They were drawn from a lesser donor, the amorphous crowd of church and chapel acquaintances. And they were directed to a lesser purpose, the refurbishment of building fabric and the provision of multifarious religious hardware. In later Victorian reality, the emergence of regular special efforts as the critical source of associational income blurred the administrative division between the uses of different means of ecclesiastical finance. It also obscured the

---

[178] *Ibid.* (emphasis in original).
[179] Reid Marchbank, *One Hundred Years of Progress*, p. 45; the other two were: the attempts (a) 'to integrate the church and the Sunday school more closely'; and, (b) 'to deepen the loyalty of the adherents to the society'. It is no coincidence that these matters form the basis of chapters 5 and 6 below.

moral distinctions between different forms of sacred donation. This was important, for to blur that division and to obscure those distinctions was, inevitably, to confound the traditional interpretation of the principle of voluntary beneficence. To shift the efficient organisation of the political economy of religious association from the fruits of individual generosity to the product of common enterprise, and also to transfer it from the moment of the devotion to the hour of specialised fund-raising, was not merely to dabble with the symbolic peripheries of voluntary beneficence. It was systematically to redefine the 'price of faith', for it redefined *who* gave; and it redefined *how* they gave. Necessarily, it also redefined *what* they were giving; even, though few fully acknowledged it at the time, the sorts of institutions they were giving it to.

That redefinition had practical as well as symbolic consequences. Certainly, the editor of the *Keighley Wesleyan Methodist Magazine* affected something more than just nostalgia for the 'old ways' when he pointed to the dangers for religious associations of ceasing to depend upon the financial contributions of their membership in order to sustain the collective forms of their associational life. This was because membership, whether formally or informally defined, was for most associations the highest ideal of association. It implied a certain personal status, but it also embodied certain personal responsibilities. Because of that status and because of those responsibilities, it also established a vital bond between members which was critical to the life of a religious society. That bond highlighted not merely an individual, but also a collective, ideal of association, an ideal not simply of collective social standing, but also about collective spiritual purpose: the purpose of devotion to God's work; of each to each other; and of everyone to future generations. And in the decline of one of the most prominent responsibilities of associational membership lay the seeds of the demise of the wider ideal.

The effect of these changes, taken in the round, was to extend not only the bonds of associational affiliation but also their burden. But it was to extend them in both senses of the word: that is, to make them both broader and shallower. They brought – on occasion – more people within the orbit of ecclesiastical organisations than before, but they also demanded less of each person on these, and on other, occasions: less generosity, less sacrifice and less devotion. More individuals attended annual bazaars than the weekly sacrament. More money was raised at one sale of work than at fifty-two weekly collections. But the commitment of the people to the churches was not greater thereby. It was less. So the churches paid a heavy price for their extension. To capitulate before the forces of modernity, and to acknowledge the corrupting influences of the world (especially the business ethos), was a high price to pay for institutional buoyancy. When Edwardian churchmen, ministers and laymen berated popular religious observance for its intermittency, for its inconsistency and for its fickleness, they might perhaps have pondered that the financial and organisational *basis* of contemporary religious associations implicitly encouraged – in a way that it had never done before – the very forms of behaviour which they now publicly deplored. Or, to put it another way, they might possibly have pondered upon the incongruity between the increasingly personal and individual methods by which they were attempting to recruit so many new persons to their societies, and the increasingly impersonal and even instrumental institutions which they were actually inviting them to join.

Part II

Drawing in the people

4 The unfolding of the associational ideal: auxiliary organisations and ambitious societies

Introduction: the associational ideal defined and extended

So disparate a body of religious institutions, precariously financed and nebulously sustained, positively demanded a defining principle for their future prosperity. This was the associational ideal. At one level, it was a very simple ideal. It insisted that the Christian faith was sustained in and through the Christian Church. Hence it placed the highest premium upon the maximisation of the Church's membership. But it was not thereby a shallow ideal, for it did not presume that every person was immediately fit to be a member of the Church. It held only that every adult could become fit for that end. To that end, it extolled the virtuous means of common association; more specifically, of a common association through which men and women might be taught the rudiments of the faith; by which they might be induced to join societies dedicated to the faith, and finally from which they might be emboldened to spread that faith through mission, bands and tracts.

To be sure, it was not an ingenuous ideal. Denominational organisations emphasised its primacy as part of their competitive purposes. Nor did it exhaust the Christian virtues. Even the most devoted partisan still recognised the significance of private prayer. So much was, and is, obvious. Less so was the degree to which it became a way of organisational life increasingly determined, in its characteristic forms, by the urban and industrial environment in which it matured. In that environment Christian mission and the associational ideal developed in a way that was at once orthodox in inspiration yet highly pragmatic in execution, creating in effect a novel or at least a very particular understanding of that ideal. This was the ideal of the 'ambitious society', revealed in the instrument of the auxiliary organisation. It should not be dismissed as a perversion of the Christian ethic. It was not. Nor may it legitimately be derided as the cynical expression of organisational interest. It was always something more than that, for in its sheer comprehensiveness, in the declared aim of securing by every institutional means the most extensive inclusion of all of God's people in Christ's various acknowledged churches, it offered ordinary men and women the real attractions of a divine social activity, the genuine possibility of meaningful self-improvement and the ultimate sacred goal of personal salvation. In so doing, it transformed many individual lives. Almost as a by-product, it altered – out of all recognition – each and every local, established and voluntary, religious organisation.

The multi-chapel community and the development of complex ecclesiastical institutions

It should go without saying that the ideal of association, even so defined, was not of itself new to the later Victorian religious organisation. After all, it was, and is, implied in the very notion of Christian fellowship. Similarly, the goal of efficient organisation was scarcely novel to the sacred societies of these industrial towns. It was, and is, implied in the very notion of Establishment; and in most forms of voluntarism too. What was truly innovative about late Victorian ecclesiastical association, thus understood, was its specific application, for it was an ideal applied within the multi-chapel community and through its multiple churches and chapels. More: it was a form of organised religious life which came out of the new churches and chapels themselves rather than one which emerged from the older structures of particular denominational organisations. This development made each church and chapel into a complex ecclesiastical institution. And it made their separate development the most important fact about all these organisations.

None of this rendered traditional ecclesiastical organisations – national structures, regional institutions, even local plans – irrelevant. On the contrary. They remained vitally important. Nothing, after all, so defined denominational difference as organisational variation. The parochial system remained very different from the circuit mechanism or the associational union. But just as urban growth compromised existing forms so institutional sophistication altered their significant aspects still further. Urban growth, of course, underlay the proliferation of churches. Their number, locale and aspirations, in turn, redefined parochial boundaries, redrew circuit maps and reordered district associations. At one level, that meant an impressive growth of local ecclesiastical organisation. The ancient parish of Halifax spawned no fewer than ten further parishes by 1914, eight of these created after 1840.[1] Prior to

---

[1]   Goodwin, 'How the Ancient Parish of Halifax was Divided', Appendix, pp. 33–6.

amalgamation, it gave life to three Wesleyan Methodist circuits, three Primitives, two New Connexion and one United Methodist Free Church circuit.[2] Even its Congregationalist churches began to form a loose confederation after 1870.[3]

A similar, if slightly less impressive, story might be told for Keighley.[4] Neither tale would have commanded much contemporary interest, for what contemporaries more readily perceived was the growth not so much of specific, urban, organisation (though that did happen) as of particular, associational autonomy. To be sure, the two developments were not entirely incompatible. Indeed, in many ways, each acted as effective bulwarks against national invasions into local affairs. So Keighley's First Primitive Methodist Circuit successfully resisted 'the Conferential [sic] Committee's' proposal for a 'distinct order of Evangelists' by invoking the continuing efforts of the 'Circuit and District Missionary Committee' and (more importantly) by asserting the transcendental value of 'freedom of local action'.[5] Yet what these self-consciously 'divided circuits' eventually sustained, in 'large towns' such as Halifax anyway, were 'pastorates' – separate societies retaining their own ministers over many years – and in a way quite contrary to traditional, peripatetic Methodist practice.[6]

This development was not limited to Methodism. On the contrary. Its basic form was virtually replicated in the Reverend Pigou's observation that 'there is now-a-days a tendency to congregationalism in our different parishes'. That was in 1877.[7] If Pigou was not altogether happy about this departure, deeming it 'prejudicial to . . . unity of action' at that early stage, then the Primitive Methodists of his own town eventually reconciled themselves to it, citing the 'extend[ed] and improv[ed] work' it had wrought.[8] How? Above all, in the extended and improved labours of individual associations, increasingly now recast as complex ecclesiastical institutions as, in the words of the anonymous church historian at Northgate End, Unitarian, Halifax: 'to the original purposes of the Chapel have been added . . . of late, various arrangements for society and

---

[2] Anon., *The Halifax Methodist Circuit*, pp. 10–15.
[3] Biggs, *Congregationalism*, pp. 13/14.
[4] Denholme remained too small and too much of a one-church/chapel per denomination town for any of the above to apply.
[5] KPL, 105077/1/1/1/9, Keighley Primitive Methodist, First Circuit Quarterly Meeting Minute Book, 3 March 1890.
[6] CDA, uncat. MSS, Halifax, Primitive Methodist Connexion, Second Circuit, Minutes of the Quarterly Meeting and Circuit Committees, 4 March 1895.
[7] Pigou, 'A Pastoral Letter to his Parishioners', in Pigou, *Sermons and Addresses*, p. 13.
[8] CDA, uncat. MSS, Halifax, Primitive Methodist Connexion, Second Circuit, Minutes of the Quarterly Meetings and Circuit Committees, 4 March 1895.

amusement, making it a church-home not for Sunday only, but for the whole week'.[9]

These 'various arrangements' were otherwise known as 'auxiliary organisations'.[10] As the name implies, these institutions were attached to a church and charged with specific religious, or quasi-religious, responsibilities within the church, but permitted a social and cultural scope by the church beyond its strictly spiritual mission. Hence their frequent meetings. And hence its increasingly accommodating role in the local community. At Northgate, as elsewhere, auxiliary organisations were overwhelmingly a product of the second half, more strictly indeed the last third, of the nineteenth century. They were a critical contemporary development. For if the simple proliferation of churches delineated the 'neighbourhood principle' in urban ecclesiastical provision, then the concurrent growth of auxiliary organisations reordered these (many) churches into complex religious institutions, societies in which the associational ideal not only made the most obvious sense but, in a new and exciting way, seemed to offer a genuinely profitable way forward.

That sense was eloquently expressed in an article published in the *Halifax and District Congregational Magazine* at much the same time. There, the 'various arrangements' of auxiliary organisation were described in a broader contemporary context. Working from the assumption that the Church (indeed any church) was not 'a private club established and maintained for the benefit of its members alone', this anonymous author first insisted that, in order to serve its 'larger purposes', it must make 'institutional ... arrangements' beyond those simply geared 'to the taste ... or ... interests' of its immediate servants. No doubt this observation reflected little more than the conventional good sense of the time. But then he went on to argue that, secondly, such arrangements would, now and in the future, increasingly assume 'multipl[e] ... and var[ious] ... forms', as the more 'manifold needs of our fellow men' become progressively 'apparent to the Christian Church'.[11] This message could scarcely have been starker or simpler: it suggested that the very future of the church, and certainly its future growth, depended upon its capacity to evolve into a more varied, and even into a more attractive, institutional form. The associational ideal in effect now recognised that imperative. And auxiliary organisations now provided for it. Or so the theory went.

[9]   Anon., 'Information for Strangers', *Northgate End Unitarian Chapel, Halifax, Church Manual for 1890* (Halifax, 1890), p. 3.
[10] *Ibid.*, p. 6.
[11] A.O., 'Church Membership II: Its Duties: Promoting the Undertakings of the Church', *HDCM*, vol. 4, no. 12, December 1886, p. 268.

In practice, ecclesiastical auxiliary organisations tended to fulfil two, rather different, associational functions. At one level, they permitted a tighter, because a more specific, organisation of the contemporary core of each society. At another, they aspired to a looser, but more significant, affiliation of the outer husk of every contemporary association. As a result, there were usually numerous such organisations in any given society: so much so that many committed laymen served in several different auxiliaries. And they were invariably variously directed: as various, in this sense, as men's manifold needs were increasingly seen to be. But, at the risk of oversimplification, they can be reduced to three types: the organisationally ambitious, or auxiliaries essentially designed to demonstrate the vigour, colour and even prestige of a society, thereby to attract new members and affiliates, sometimes in competition against other societies; the institutionally inclusive, or auxiliaries specially forged to bring more people more fully into the fold of church and chapel life, especially those who were known to be on its fringe; and, finally, the associationally supportive, or auxiliaries specifically established to validate the charitable imperative of Christian organisation in particular acts of individual generosity. It should go without saying that many auxiliaries fulfilled more than one of those purposes. It is, perhaps, worth restating that some, seemingly, performed none at all. But for analytical purposes they are best illustrated separately.

The organisation of congregational ambition: the example of church choirs

Nothing, perhaps, expressed the organisational ambition of *individual* churches and chapels so much as the development of church and chapel choirs during the last third of the nineteenth century. To be sure, the thing in itself was scarcely novel to the later Victorian age. What was new was that it became universal at that time. A society without a choir was not unknown in 1870. It was by 1900. And choirs became important institutions in themselves. Indeed, they may very possibly have become more generally important during these decades than at any time before or since. Contemporary anecdotal evidence certainly supports this view. An anonymous contributor to Keighley's *Congregational Magazine* identified the 1870s and early 1880s as the period 'during which ... our Church Choir seemed to ... reach ... the zenith of its strength and efficiency'.[12] And the harsher test of comparative financial provision gives some credence to this argument. For instance, Temple Street's

---

[12] Anon., 'Mr Craven Laycock and the Juvenile Concerts', *KDCM*, vol. 9, no. 5, May 1920 (no page number).

'organ and choir expenses' seem to have risen gradually after 1870, peaking in 1901, at a figure of £88 per annum. Thereafter they fell, gradually, to a sum of £67 18s 10d in 1915.[13]

If so, why? The impact of physical alteration, associated with the rise of 'dissenting Gothic', certainly had something to do with it. Choir stalls fitted more comfortably into Perpendicular churches than square-boxed preaching-houses. But ecclesiological determinism is scarcely a sufficient explanation. Nor is it consistent with all the facts of contemporary church progress. For instance, Temple Street choir was obliged to lobby its trustees for 'one pew [more] on each side of the present orchestra' as late as 1880, over thirty years after the construction of the new chapel there.[14] The intrusion of wind and pipe organs into church interiors (and by definition into church services) also contributed to the process. Long subject to doctrinal and liturgical, also simply to customary resistance – especially in nonconformist circles – these became fairly common locally after 1870.[15] And it was during the years which immediately followed that they established their claim 'to lead worship'.[16]

Above all, it was the product of that widespread liturgical change and common institutional ambition which characterised later nineteenth-century local ecclesiastical society. Liturgical change, of course, entailed many different things. Specifically, in this instance, it implied an enhanced role for music in public worship. That meant a greater incursion of the emotional and sensual into what had once been more strictly confined to the doctrinal and conceptual. This was a common development, true for religious organisations generally at this time. It was, however, most especially the case – for being more acutely novel – amongst the traditionally nonconformist denominations.[17] It also provided dissenting choirmasters, organists and singers with an unprece-dented opportunity to flex their institutional muscles: to demand a greater role in the collective performance of worship; to exact a greater proportion of associational resources in order to do it; and finally, to

[13]   KPL, 105D77/2/21/14/a/b/c, Temple Street, Trust Accounts, 1878–1934; Appendix: Expenses on Organ and Choir, 1870–1925.

[14]   KPL, 105D77/2/15/b, Temple Street Methodist Church, Trust Minute Book, 21 February 1880.

[15]   See ch. 7, below, pp. 298–9.

[16]   Anon., *Wesleyan Chapel, Hermit Hole, Keighley: Souvenir of the Unveiling of Stained Glass Windows, with a Short History of the Society from Its Beginning* (Keighley, 1917), p. 8.

[17]   This subject is treated at greater length in chapter 7, where the origins, forms and consequences of liturgical change, within and between later nineteenth-century (Protestant) denominations, is considered in detail. Suffice it to say here that it happened, and that it had social consequences for choirs specifically and religious organisations generally, at that time.

assert the significance of choral religion and, by definition, of choirs in the public profile of organised religious life. By way of a return, they offered the distant possibility of denominational priority amongst religious organisations, and the immediate reality of greater popular participation within them.

So choirs got bigger. At its peak, Keighley's Devonshire Street Congregational Church Senior Choir seems to have had fifty-seven members, and its Juvenile Choir perhaps as many as nine times that figure. They may also have got better. Certainly, Keighley's memorialist thought so, fondly recalling the 'very high standard' attained by both of its choirs at that time.[18] They undoubtedly got more expensive. Annual costs at Temple Street Wesleyan Methodist, for instance, rose by very nearly 50 per cent – from £62 12s 0d to £88 2s 0d, for the maintenance of its Senior Choir alone during just one decade, from 1891 to 1901.[19] Indeed, so outlandishly costly do they appear to have become at this time that some local societies eventually found that they could no longer afford them. That was the fate, anyway, of Holy Trinity, Halifax, which, at the beginning of the twentieth century declared that it had become 'impossible' any longer to afford 'the luxury of a ... choir'.[20]

This was because, at Holy Trinity as elsewhere, choirs were increasingly professional, or at least semi-professional. To be sure, this was not true in every case. Some remained determinedly amateur. St Peter's Church of England, Keighley, for instance, maintained a 'wholly voluntary' choir from the moment of its inception.[21] But that was something of a rarity after 1870. More common was Harrison Road Congregational Church, Halifax, which resolved to 'secure' an 'efficient choir leader', at £10 per annum, in 1872.[22] Most elaborately organised of all in this respect seems to have been Northgate End Unitarian Church, Halifax, which shortly afterwards determined to 'engage' a 'leader of the choir', then 'leading singers' for 'each department of music', and finally a 'leader of music', specifically to coach 'one hour a week for a period of twelve months' the 'voluntary portion of the choir'. His reward was 2s 10d per week.[23]

True, not everyone in the choir was paid, at least not usually so. But

18 Anon., 'Mr Craven Laycock'.
19 KPL, 105D77/2/21/14/a/b/c Temple Street, Trust Accounts 1878–1934; Appendix: Expenses on Organ and Choir, 1870–1925.
20 WHQ, D109/75, Holy Trinity Church, Halifax, Parochial Church Council Minute Book, 26 January 1906.
21 Keighley Yearbook, 1877, p. 111.
22 CDA, CUR 1:13, Harrison Road Congregational Church, Halifax, Church and Deacons' Book, 1 March 1872.
23 CDA, NEC 202, Northgate End Unitarian Chapel, Halifax, Minute Book of the Singing Choir, 16 February 1877.

even the ostensibly voluntary members of successful choirs were occasionally rewarded. Hence Northgate Committee's recommendation 'that the Chapel Wardens give £2 to the unpaid members of the choir', in 1883.[24] And payment, on occasion, went down as far as the juniors too. The same society, the very next year, was so determined to 'increase ... the efficiency of the choir' that it resolved to 'draft ... boys out of our Sunday School' and to 'pay ... them for their services'.[25] With money at stake, good performances were expected and the results were carefully evaluated. New members of Northgate's choir sang in it, on trial, for four Sundays. If they proved to be good enough they were retained. If not, they were removed. Such was the fate, similarly, for 'anyone absent from weekly practice, except for good reason'.[26]

With performance-related pay came formal institutional organisation. At Northgate End, the link was explicit and immediate. Its professional choir was guided, from the start, by a committee of six, the appropriately entitled 'Committee of the Singing Choir'.[27] Elsewhere, joint control by choirmaster and organist seems to have guided the practice of paid choirs.[28] With formal institutions came standardised rules of conduct. Thus the 'Choir Committee' at Victoria Park Wesleyan Methodist Chapel, Keighley, was formally requested to draw up an appropriate 'code of rules', in 1902.[29] The most significant of these rules were the increasingly widely acknowledged terms of legitimate inter-associational competition, for the real point of each of these organisations was to secure for its favoured society the *best* local singers. Northgate End Committee, for instance, quite openly advertised in local newspapers for 'treble and contralto singers'.[30] The inevitable result was the phenomenon of choirs recruited from beyond the body of church or chapel members; even, strictly speaking, beyond the wider constituency of adherents or affiliates.

Some tried to legislate for this problem, so minimising its deleterious effects. Hence West Lane Primitive Methodist insisted that such outsiders 'be persons of strict moral character'.[31] Others simply apologised for the fact that not all their 'artistes' were 'drawn from their

---

[24]   *Ibid.*, 24 September 1883.
[25]   *Ibid.*, 11 May 1884.
[26]   *Ibid.*
[27]   *Ibid.*, 16 February 1877.
[28]   Davis, *St Paul's, Denholme Gate* (no page number).
[29]   KPL, 105D77/2/22/4/a, Victoria Park, Methodist Church, Trust Minute Book, 12 December 1902.
[30]   CDA, NEC 202, Northgate End Unitarian Chapel, Halifax, Minute Book of the Singing Choir, 28 May 1890.
[31]   W. Feather, *Fifty Years' History of West Lane Primitive Methodist Church, Keighley* (Keighley, 1929), p. 50.

own ... ranks'.[32] But such measures, and the rationalisations which they invoked, at least in the breach, are best taken with a considerable pinch of salt. The point of choirs was the assertion of standing. A measure of their success was their capacity to draw talent from other associations. But the most potent gauge of all was their ability, proven or otherwise, 'materially to increase the prosperity' of their mother organisations. One local society, anyway, paid its organist solely by bonus, and on that basis.[33] To some degree, at least, it seems to have succeeded. Or at least it explains the Juvenile Concerts of famous memory at Devonshire Street Congregational which, during the 1880s and after, 'drew people ... from near and far', were 'recognised throughout the county', and, for that moment anyway, 'linked ... all at Devonshire Street' with the 'general public' which surrounded them.[34]

The pursuit of general inclusion: towards a taming of the stranger

Such moments were, necessarily, fleeting. However, they often resulted in the intrusion of 'strangers' into subsequent, regular church services. 'Strangers' were what their name implies: people unfamiliar with, and not previously inducted into, associational church and chapel worship. They were a widely acknowledged phenomenon. As such, their very existence and, still more strikingly, the common perception of them reflected the curious ambivalence of all religious organisations towards the irregular population: they wanted such patronage, but also they wanted it on their own terms; above all, they wanted it to be amenable to their peculiar ways. In that way, they treated it with a welcoming circumspection, glad of its company but immediately intent upon altering its (religious) manners.

This ambiguous sensibility was probably at its strongest amongst the more rigorous contemporary Protestant denominations. But it was in no sense exclusive to them. On the contrary. It was common across local religious organisations at this time. It was even present within the one denomination – the Church of England – which formally presumed the allegiance of every subject. Churchmen openly referred to 'strangers' in precisely the same way as their dissenting, or indeed Roman Catholic, counterparts. Ironically, they often had more opportunities, even a greater need, to do so. This was partly because, given its very nature, the

---

[32]   Anon., 'Mr Craven Laycock'.
[33]   KPL, uncat. MSS, Devonshire Street Congregational Church, Keighley, Deacons' Meeting Book Minutes, 17 December 1919.
[34]   Anon., 'Mr Craven Laycock'.

Established Church tended to attract so-called 'strangers' more frequently and possibly also in greater proportions. Certainly, that is what locals believed. One of them, at a symbolically significant moment, remarked that Halifax parish church, for instance, had 'for many years past' (this in 1877) 'largely been filled in an evening by . . . strangers'.[35]

It was also, at least in part, because the parish church, for all its professed inclusiveness, was often a place of very particular habitation; specifically a place which all too eloquently expressed the preference of individuals, and families, to occupy the same seats over very long periods of time. The abolition of pew-rents, initially anyway, made very little difference to this widely acknowledged system of social allocation. But the very existence, still more the occasional presence, of 'strangers' continually threatened it. Indeed, there is some evidence to suggest that the passing of pew-rent actually made this problem more acute still. That, anyway, was the experience of Keighley parish church. There, its Vicar, specifically reminding his flock that 'no-one had a *legal right* . . . to a fixed seat . . . in Parish Church', shortly after the abolition of pew-rent at St Andrew's in 1892, further admonished the old appropriators amongst them that whilst 'regular worshippers' might 'kindly' continue to show them this 'respectful consideration', they could no longer 'expect strangers always to do the same'.

He concluded:

Parishioners, who are not regular worshippers with us, but know what the law is about in a parish Church, sometimes do not wait for the guidance of the Verger but walk into any seats they see vacant even before the commencement of the services . . . Though they may appear to you to show a lack of consideration . . . do not, I beseech you, make them uncomfortable . . . Do as you would be done by . . . remember . . . that . . . people are extraordinarily sensitive in such cases . . . If they are made to feel uncomfortable . . . they . . . may . . . give . . . up coming to Church altogether . . . That person you find in your accustomed seat may perhaps be not only a stranger to this House of Prayer, but to any House of Prayer. A little self-denial on your part may lead to his receiving impressions and even forming habits of the utmost importance to his future life . . . and . . . will be a sacrifice of a sweet savour in the sight of God.[36]

And so the matter rested.

But elsewhere, neither fine words nor stern warnings were deemed sufficient to cope with such a delicate, and seemingly ripening, problem. Other societies turned to institutional solutions. As early as 1871, Brunswick Methodists specifically 'appointed . . . eight persons . . . to assist the

---

[35]   Mr Hutchinson, *The Restoration of Halifax Parish Church*, p. 14.
[36]   Frederic Damstini Cremer, 'Subscriptions to the Wardens' Fund', *KPCM*, vol. 15, no. 1, January 1892 (no page number).

chapel keeper in taking strangers to seats in the chapel'; and, incidentally, charged them with the responsibility of giving 'such [persons] a hearty welcome'. Just for good measure, they also 'empowered ... the Leaders' Meeting ... to provide hymn books for the use of strangers'.[37] Others, perhaps not quite so preoccupied about precisely what should be provided on these occasions, were even more concerned about exactly who should do the providing. So Keighley's Albert Street Baptist Church established a self-styled 'Entrance Committee' for the 'reception and welcome of strangers' at its services, in 1887.[38] Exactly how they should receive and welcome them was, however, never made clear.

These were not trivial innovations. Indeed, Halifax's Primitive Methodists took them so seriously that they addressed the matter at circuit level. They solved it there too. Its second circuit formed a 'band' specifically funded and specifically charged with the task of overseeing the welcome and socialisation of strangers 'at public services'.[39] More-over, even those who rigorously maintained the strictly associational dimension of such bodies were often willing gradually to increase the scope of their work. So Hanover Street New Connexion Methodists in Halifax empowered their Strangers' Committee to 'speak to' and 'invite' such persons 'to become connected with the church'.[40] And if logic, perhaps even justice, demanded that such persons be given the right to speak back in return, then that right too was eventually granted. At least this was so at Halifax parish church. Its parochial church council, 'welcoming new people attending the church', in 1920, decided that 'slips be placed in a box in the church porch together with a notice requesting such persons who desired the clergy to call on them to insert their names and addresses on such slips.[41] By which time, perhaps, the 'strangers' had, in their own way, tamed the churches.

The performance of charitable duty: or the evolution of the associational Poor Fund

Victorian and Edwardian churches understood a traditional Christian obligation towards the poor. This was true across the denominational

[37]   CDA, Misc. 57/10, Brunswick United Methodist Free Church, Church Meeting Minute Book, 5 June 1871.
[38]   KPL, uncat. MSS, Albert Street, Baptist Chapel, Keighley, Church Meeting, Minute Book, 27 February 1887.
[39]   CDA, uncat. MSS, Primitive Methodist Connexion, Halifax, Second Circuit, Minutes of the Quarterly Meetings and Circuit Committees, 4 March 1889.
[40]   CDA, Misc. 257/26, Hanover Street, Methodist New Connexion, Leaders' Meeting Minute Book, 5 February 1877.
[41]   WHQ, D/53, Halifax Parish Church, St John the Baptist, Parochial Church Council Minute Book, 4 March 1920.

divide. It was the obligation of charity, a 'duty' which 'devolve[d] upon the rich in relation with the poor'. And that obligation properly understood, that is, 'worthily motivated and directed towards a good end', or inspired not for 'the benefit' of oneself, still less by the thought of 'a future reward', but solely and wholly 'for the sake of those to whom our charity is extended', constituted nothing less than 'a state of grace'.[42] It was also an *inherently* complex ideal, for it demanded a degree of selflessness that few easily attained. Moreover, in its late Victorian, industrial, urban context it assumed another, more sociologically inspired, dimension which in turn imposed a second, even more limiting, aspect. This was the theory and practice of efficient benevolence; more specifically, the pursuit of a form of charity which did not deleteriously affect those who were its intended beneficiaries. Together, those powerful qualifications made the whole question of almsgiving inherently problematic, one which the Vicar of Halifax called quite simply 'the most difficult problem in pastoral work'. This was the dilemma of 'how to relieve our poor without pauperising them, or without encouraging them in posture and deceit'.[43]

It is easy to see all this, in retrospect, as yet another form of respectable condescension towards the continuous and ubiquitous trials of the underprivileged. But it is important to remember that, right across the Protestant spectrum, the characteristic concern of churchmen and ministers was almost as much about the inadequacy of the typical motives and means of giving as of the supposed malignancy in its effect on some of those who might receive. Pigou himself was quite explicit about this, openly condemning the 'unhealthy and spurious incitements' which characterised so much 'modern almsgiving', in 1877, such as 'bills, entertainments, etc. etc.' and reminding his flock that the proper, 'good, old, Bible rule' suggested that 'a portion of each man's income' should be 'religiously devoted' for this purpose. He also insisted that donations be made through 'the legitimate channel' of 'remembrance' at 'Holy Communion', rather than in the 'vicious' institution of 'special appeals', spiced up by sensuous pleasures.[44]

Secondly, it is vital to appreciate that such a particularly Christian form of charity, though ideally selfless in its distribution and benevolent in its impact, was geared above all to a *religious* understanding of the proper purpose of the relief of poverty. Specifically, it was designed to

[42] Anon., 'Editorial', *Northgate Unitarian Chapel, Halifax, Church Manual for 1915* (Halifax, 1915), p. 5.
[43] Pigou, 'A Pastoral Letter to His Parishioners', in Pigou, *Sermons and Addresses*, p. 5.
[44] *Ibid.*, pp. 5–8.

enable the poor to live; but also to worship. Some grants were made especially with this second aim in mind. So Harrison Road Deacons' Meeting voted a sum of 2s 6d per month from 'ordinance monies' to one Florence Bailey that she might 'meet the expenses of public worship'.[45] Others treated the issue more subtly. Hence Northgate End's acclamation for one Abel Wordsworth whose provident dispensation of 'church charity' did the 'invaluable service' of 'attracting many poor people into the congregation'.[46] But the effect was much the same.

In this scheme of things, the true end of organised religious relief was a charitable provision which would justify the rich and elevate the poor; that is, one which would do so by bringing them – and just as important by keeping them – together in one, socially integrated, worshipping community. In such a society, so established and sustained, 'the poor' had 'as much to give the rich', as vice versa. Their understanding of 'the stern realities of life' and the 'absolute necessity of independence' from 'outward circumstances' would protect a fully religious association from the 'misfortune' of 'selective ... respectability'.[47] And in such an environment, everyone so organised and so motivated would be endowed with 'the luxury of doing good'; a gift, if properly understood 'within the reach of all, even the poorest and the humblest'.[48]

If that was fantasy, the institutional forms which it produced were real enough. Certainly, it was on this understanding of Christian duty, responsibly interpreted, and of associational aspiration, realistically understood, that most local societies established and subsequently maintained their designated 'Poor Funds' during the later nineteenth and early twentieth centuries. The result was often something quite complex and wide-ranging. For instance, Rhodes Street Wesleyan Chapel, Halifax, raised and spent just under £40 on poor relief in 1867, collecting monies on fifteen different occasions during the year, and distributing them some twenty-five times. A total of sixty-nine individuals benefited during the year from such charity there. Most received just one donation of around 8s 6d each. But at least seven individuals were helped each quarter, with total benefits adding up to £1 in some cases. Many others received payments on three, or on two, occasions during the year, often to comparable degree. Not surprisingly, perhaps,

---

45 CDA, CUR 1:13, Harrison Road, Congregational Church, Halifax, Church and Deacons' Book, 23 March 1910.
46 Anon., *Northgate End Victorian Chapel, Halifax, Bicentenary, 1896* (Halifax, 1896), p. 3.
47 Pigou, 'The Motive of True Benevolence', in Pigou, *Sermons and Addresses*, p. 24; Anon., *Northgate End Bicentenary, 1896*, p. 3.
48 Pigou, 'The Cigar He Did Not Smoke', in Pigou, *Sermons and Addresses*, pp. 54–5.

widows formed the bulk of the recipients: 42. And they were also in the majority amongst the regular beneficiaries: 5.[49]

But Poor Funds were not just widows' charities. Brunswick Methodists made a specific appeal through their fund for the children of the local unemployed, in 1922.[50] The same year, they extended the provision for the sick.[51] To be sure, these were for the jobless and convalescing associated with the church at that time. Yet if such benefit was concentrated amongst these specifically attached individuals in most places, it was seldom exclusively limited to those lucky few. For instance, Victoria Park Methodists, in Keighley, empowered their Poor Steward to distribute 'the balance of [their] Fund', a sum of 15s 6d, 'to any needy cases he might find', in 1911.[52] Rhodes Street Wesleyans themselves made at least seven distributions 'to the poor generally', in 1867.[53] Perhaps the only fixed rule was that enunciated by Temple Street's Leader, in 1917, that 'our contributions' should never be regarded as 'a permanent source of income' by anyone.[54] And the reason for this was simple. At Temple Street, as elsewhere, the primary function of the Poor Fund was to sustain the breadth of the worshipping population. It was only secondarily a means for alleviating the worst distresses of the needy and unfortunate.

The effect (1): the ideal of the committed religious individual

Auxiliary organisations were also numerous. By the turn of the century, many societies boasted ten or more such institutions as part of their wider association. This was certainly true at Northgate End. By 1890, in addition to its choir, Strangers' Committee and Poor Fund, it also boasted a Sunday school, with 321 scholars and 27 teachers; a Band of Hope, of 224 members; a Penny Bank, financed by 84 subscribers; an Elocution Society, sustained by 16 'attending members'; a Guild of St Christopher, pledged to do 'useful work for the congregation and their neighbours', and with 36 members to do it; a Rambling Society, of

---

[49] CDA, 57/14, Rhodes Street Wesleyan Chapel, Halifax, Poor Stewards' Book, 5 January 1868.
[50] CDA, 57/12, Brunswick United Methodist Church, Leaders' Meeting Minute Book, 20 June 1922.
[51] Ibid., 21 November 1922.
[52] KPL, 105D77/2/22/2/a, Victoria Park, Leaders' Meeting Minute Book, 11 December 1911.
[53] CDA, 57/114, Rhodes Street Wesleyan Chapel, Halifax, Poor Stewards' Book, 5 January 1868.
[54] KPL, 105D77/2/21/7/c, Temple Street Wesleyan Society, Leaders' Minute Book, 19 October 1917.

indeterminate membership, and finally an additional Orchestral Society, numbering 35 members.[55] All of this at a time when the number of registered members of the society stood at 286.[56] Many of those 286 registered members at Northgate End were also members of one or more of its auxiliaries. Some were not. And some of the members of its auxiliaries were not registered members of the church. Membership of church, congregation and auxiliaries overlapped. That was common enough. Fairly typical too was the associational understanding that such multiple (and often minimal) affiliation was, in general, healthy provided that it tended, in the fullness of time, towards the greatest degree of integrated church membership. That projection, in turn, presumed an ideal sort of church member. This was the man (or woman) of many ecclesiastical parts, the tireless church worker, the totally committed individual. For it was he (or she) who realised the highest form of church membership, of him (or her) self and for everyone else: the person who, by unceasing effort, forged out of the sheer diversity of church institutions that longed-for unity of Christian association.

Few, naturally enough, matched up to this ideal. But some, equally clearly, did. More significantly still, amongst their number were laymen as well as professionals, women as well as men, the young as well as the old, for the very essence of the ideal was found in an appeal to what was extraordinary in otherwise ordinary people. Hence the search for remarkable qualities and peculiar achievements, amongst those who might otherwise have been dismissed as no more than representative nonentities amongst the mass of the population. To many nonconformists, of course, that was something of a dissenting article of the faith in itself; a partisan assertion of the essential equality and potentially transforming capacity of each and every priest and man, male and female, even (under certain circumstances) adult and juvenile. This explains Keighley *Congregational Magazine*'s eloquent tribute to one of its finest sons, the (Reverend) Edward Pringle, published in 1917, which made a particular point of elaborating his humanity before his ministry, praising a 'right man' before acknowledging a 'pastor', similarly highlighting his 'true ... enthusias[m]' before it concentrated on his spiritual gifts, and finally commending a personal dedication to the 'common good' as the highest achievement of one who was, at one level, no more

---

[55] Anon., 'Information for Strangers', *Northgate End Unitarian Chapel, Halifax, Chapel Manual 1890* (Halifax 1890), pp. 6/7; on Sunday school as an auxiliary organisation, see ch. 5, below, *passim*.

[56] CDA, NEC 11, Northgate End, Unitarian Chapel, Halifax, List of Registered Members, 1872–1950.

than a 'fellow worker' and yet who became nothing short of a 'public friend'.[57]

That was, of course, an extreme example. But it pointed to a common sensibility. This was the notion of a 'godly man'. More specifically, it was about the personal qualities and potential impact of such a person.[58] And it was an idea perfectly compatible with 'higher' concepts of the 'priesthood', for it combined the impeccably traditional understanding of the 'priesthood of the laity' with a peculiar contemporary interpretation of the obligations of godliness.[59] This revised form combined public commitment, or 'the promotion of our associations' together with private virtue, or 'law-abiding ... honesty' in order to effect 'one another's real welfare'.[60] The point of such commitments was that they were 'voluntary ... self-deny[ing]', and undertaken '*as a point of honour*'.[61] The significance of this virtue was that it made these commitments possible. The goal was the collective prosperity of religious organisations.

For men, specifically, that meant financial responsibilities. And responsibilities beyond simply giving: notably of keeping or trusting, and especially of trusteeship. Hence society trustees were never restricted to the rich in any association. On the contrary. Some, like West Lane Primitive Methodists in Keighley, positively prided themselves on sustaining an appropriate body of 'plain men', privileged by 'no great individual or collective wealth'.[62] It also involved administrative burdens. Deacons, most of all, were expected to undertake 'numerous ... and varied ... duties'.[63] And that despite the 'humble ... station' which many of them, or in some cases 'most of them ... filled'.[64] Finally, there were teaching chores. These were especially the task of 'competent males' and equally unrelated, at least in theory, to 'personal income or social standing'.[65]

Yet it cannot be emphasised too strongly – indeed it distinguished the later nineteenth-century ideal so markedly – that such obligations were

[57]   The Rev. H.H. Oakley, 'Sermon', *KDCM*, vol. 6, no. 1, January 1917 (no page number).

[58]   The Rev. Francis Pigou, 'A Sermon to Friendly and Trades Societies, May 20 1877', in Pigou, *Sermon and Addresses*, pp. 14–15.

[59]   Frederic Damstini Cremer, 'Vicar's Notes', *HSPKCMP*, vol. 6, no. 4, April 1877 (no page number).

[60]   Pigou, 'A Sermon to Friendly and Trades Societies', pp. 14–15.

[61]   Cremer, 'Vicar's Notes', April 1877.

[62]   Feather, *Fifty Years*, pp. 5/6.

[63]   The Rev. A. Craven Wyke, 'The Duties of the Officers and Members of Our Churches', *HDCM*, vol. 1, no. 9, November 1883, p. 193.

[64]   Rhodes, *Keighley Baptist History*, p. 92.

[65]   Cremer, 'Vicar's Notes', *HSPKCMP*, vol. 6, no. 4, April 1897 (no page number).

not limited to men. The understanding of godly commitment extended to women also; not, to be sure, in quite the same way. There were no women priests. Even deaconesses came late, though Northgate End, Halifax, proudly proclaimed that it offered women 'an equal voice in the management of congregational affairs' from the early 1890s.[66] Certainly, both the spirit and the exigencies of 'committed membership' demanded active female participation in church life. Sometimes this took the form of special (i.e. women's) associations. Halifax's Second Primitive Methodist Connexion went as far as establishing a whole system of 'ladies' auxiliaries', in 1904.[67] More often it involved particular female duties. Perhaps the most onerous of these were the various visitation schemes which societies formulated around this time. Devonshire Street Congregationalists 'divided the ... whole ... town' into specific 'geographical areas' and 'assigned ... lady visitors ... to each', in 1892.[68] Less burdensome, but no less significant in some ways, were the various Mothers' Meetings and Unions which sprang up in the later years of the nineteenth century. St Paul's, Denholme, curiously, boasted one of the earliest founded locally by one Mary Sumner, in 1876.[69]

Most striking of all, however, was the sheer extent, and the institutional variety, of financial responsibilities – especially fund-raising responsibilities – which women were increasingly able to assume in later Victorian religious organisations. Such authority was sometimes reluctantly bestowed upon them. The Vicar of St Thomas's, Halifax, was particularly incensed that almost all the financial burdens of church restoration there, in 1910, seemed to be borne by 'mothers' and 'not men'.[70] But others just gratefully acknowledged the sheer 'utility' of the 'female section' of their respective societies which these sorts of efforts invariably demonstrated.[71] Moreover, such activity often served other purposes too. Sometimes it made formal and continuous what had once been informal and *ad hoc*. Hence Northgate End extended the life of its 1888 'Sewing Society' indefinitely from 1890, specifically with the purpose of 'bringing the ladies of the congregation more into contact

[66] F.E. Millson, *Two Hundred Years of Northgate End: A Sketch* (Halifax, 1896), p. 20.
[67] CDA, uncat. MSS, Halifax Second Circuit, Primitive Methodist Connexion, Circuit Committee Quarterly Meeting, 2 June 1904.
[68] Reid Marchbank, *One Hundred Years of Progress*, p. 43.
[69] Davis, *Church of St Paul's, Denholme Gate* (no page number).
[70] WHQ, D 33/25, St Thomas's Church, Charlestown, Halifax, Minutes of the Annual Vestry Meetings, 31 March 1910.
[71] Anon., 'Lund Park Wesleyan Chapel: Opening of the New Organ', *Keighley News*, 24 February 1900.

with each other'.[72] A 'Young Women's Guild' came to serve a similar end at Devonshire Street Congregational.[73]

Thus, in the context of so much presumed and exacted personal, individual commitment, the prevailing moral ethos of many contemporary religious organisations actually made good, specific, institutional as well as a certain wider, social sense. To be sure, it was often very strict. And many of its injunctions, especially those against drinking, dancing and gambling, reflected a more general abstinence 'from all appearance of evil'.[74] But others, such as Keighley Baptists' 'official' discouragement of members and affiliates, 'by teaching and example', from 'attendance at theatres and music halls' had another, more pragmatic, dimension.[75] For they also preserved the possibility of total dedication, that is, of avoiding all (frivolous) distractions, thereby enabling an individual to devote the whole of his or her time to the requirements of associational effort. By the same token, 'temperance' was also a form of 'self-denial' which, in addition to its pretended parallels with 'his high and holy examples', potentially released a substantial additional sum of money for missionary activity.[76]

Naturally, this interpretation of the puritan ethic has its proper limits. Certainly, it is far from exhaustive. But it does point, in a specific context, to at least one of its purposes. And it also suggests why it was so strong in later nineteenth-century religious organisations. Put simply, they needed it, for in its almost fanatical emphasis upon personal denial, it squared perfectly with their concomitant demand for public commitment. To be sure, such a demand was not, in itself, new. But it was especially strident during the latter years of Victoria's reign. This was because it was so clearly tied to the organisational fortunes of Victorian Britain's evolving religious institutions. Through its agency – the ideal of the committed individual – they hoped to realise their associational goal – the end of a Christianised people. And they trusted, ultimately, that ordinary individuals, extraordinarily motivated, would suffice in this task; put another way, that a good deacon, or even deaconess, properly motivated, could actually 'increase their congregations'.[77]

---

72 CDA, uncat. MSS, Northgate End Unitarian Chapel, Minutes of the Sewing Society, 29 July 1890.
73 Pringle, 'Minister's Address', *Keighley Congregational Church Manual, 1886*, p. 8.
74 Anon., *A Class Book: Containing Directions for Class-Leaders, Ruled Forms for Leaders' Weekly Accounts and the Rules of the Methodist Societies* (London, n.d.), p. 14.
75 Rhodes, *Keighley Baptist History*, p. 73.
76 The Rev. Francis Pigou, 'Intemperance: What Is the Duty of the Christian in Relation to It?', in Pigou, *Sermons and Addresses*, p. 15.
77 CDA, 152/3, St John's, Wesleyan Methodist Chapel, Halifax, Leaders' Meeting, Minute Book, 26 June 1906.

The effect (2): the reality of a diffuse worshipping constituency

In the real world of many competing and evangelising religious organisations, the myth of the committed individual inevitably confronted the reality of a dispersed constituency; that is, of a large, heterogeneous and variously devout population. What that, in turn, pointed to was the unquestionable existence of a very large number of people who were religious, at least by some generally acceptable definition of the term; who were attached to a religious society, albeit to varying degrees and in many different ways; and who were, at least potentially, the committed individuals of the future. In this sense, the true task of contemporary religious mission was as much the problem of the management of a complex dynamic between (relatively rare) dedication and (relatively common) participation as it was the selfless crusade of the saved on behalf of the damned, in the way that contemporaries often depicted it; or, for that matter, the hopeless campaign of the righteous amongst the alienated in the manner portrayed by so many subsequent historians.

None of which is to say that the churches met no hostility in their efforts to Christianise the population in later Victorian West Yorkshire. They did. And, on occasion, they commented upon the fact. Some lamented those seemingly modern traits of 'scientific ... hostility ... worldly ... commercialism ... and [heathen] drinking customs' which hindered the 'Christian enterprise of ... [their] times'.[78] A few, rather more self-consciously progressive, souls noted and castigated a certain institutional 'exclusiveness' which kept the masses, and especially the 'poor[er] ... masses away from the ... churches'.[79] Perhaps the most prescient of all pondered upon the growing distance, as they saw it, between 'the young people' and 'the church'.[80] Yet the overwhelming impression, at least before 1900, was of ecclesiastical organisations relatively confident, because seemingly well-regarded, in their task. Certainly, the anecdotal evidence does not suggest a sense of *pervasive* antagonism between 'church and people' at that time. Stiff challenges, within the culture, amongst the classes, from the young, there were and in abundance. But there was little or no hint, in religious sources anyway, of outright rejection.

Again, this does not mean that the message of the churches reached

---

[78]   Anon., 'Pastor's Address', *Hanover Street, Church Manual, 1877*, p. 9.
[79]   Bailey, *Progressive Congregationalism*, p. 14.
[80]   CDA, CUR 1:13, Harrison Road Congregational Church, Halifax, Church and Deacons' Book, 29 July 1896.

out to all parts of the community equally; still less that every section of society responded to its call in the same degree. They did not. The churches knew that well enough. Questions of class, sex and age mattered. They mattered because they made a difference to the proportions of such persons, so categorised, who actually were members of, affiliates to, or simply participants in, religious organisations. And they mattered because that difference troubled religious organisations continuously throughout this period. For they pointed to a socially differentiated religious body; that is, to an organised religion distinguished by its social differentiation. That was contrary to the Christian message. And, doggedly persisting as they tended to do, they underlined the essential dispersion of the continuing religious body. That threatened the ultimate success of the associational ideal. Accordingly, religious organisations were incessant in their efforts to blur their extent, and even to eliminate their causes. Certainly, it was in that spirit, organisationally driven as well as doctrinally inspired, that contemporary sacred societies set about realising the theological ends of the comprehensive method.

The question of class

Religious commitment – total, partial, negligible – was not a function of social class.[81] During the nineteenth century, the divinely dedicated, whether by organisation, through participation, or in belief, were drawn from all classes. So too were the intermittent; and, for that matter, the indifferent. Nor was their characteristic expression of that religious commitment, in so far as they acknowledged it, a simple, undifferentiated reflection of their collective social consciousness. Established and dissenting (even Roman Catholic), high and low, formal and informal types of religious experience cut across class barriers in late Victorian Britain. On the other hand, no contemporary doubted that religious 'regulars' (of whatever type) came disproportionately from the middle class. Similarly, no one questioned the general assumption that the labouring classes furnished most of the religiously indifferent; even, perhaps, that most of the labouring classes were, or seemed to be, religiously indifferent. Professional observers in contemporary Halifax, Keighley and Denholme were no different in this respect. It was in that vein that some of them referred to 'Darkest England'.[82] Equally, that others lamented the 'unlighted masses' beyond their doors.[83]

---

[81] I am using the word 'function' in its technical sense here; thus, if x then y.

[82] J. Ingram Brooke, 'Parish Notes', *HPCM*, vol. 13, no. 10, October 1890 (no page number).

[83] Anon., *A Brief History of Holy Trinity, Lawkholme, Keighley*, p. 13.

Such concern expressed a simple evangelical imperative; often as not, in fact, an imperative optimistically expressed, as in the example of the Reverend Francis Pigou's 'Underground Mission' to a surprisingly 'quiet [and] intelligent', and even 'willing' group of Lancashire miners.[84] More prosaically, it reflected the unalterable realities of urban industrial society. After all, most of the population were 'of the masses', either by occupation or dependency; and both, increasingly, by geographical location.[85] More progressive churchmen and ministers of the time were even prepared to believe that 'the age' might yet 'belong' to them. To the extent that this was true, cultivation of 'their power' made good organisational sense.[86] Even to the degree that it was false, any body of societies claiming comprehensive concern for the welfare of the community as a whole could scarcely ignore them. For whatever reason, no local organisation ever consciously neglected them. And most went to considerable lengths to ensure that they suffered no unconsciously inspired lack of attention.

Certainly, any notion that religion was essentially a middle-class preserve is false to the experience of late nineteenth-century West Yorkshire.[87] Similarly, the modern assumption of a universal bourgeois piety remains, at best, unproved in this case.[88] Too much credence has been given for too long to Horace Mann's reading of the 1851 religious census in this respect.[89] This is equally true of the selective elegiacs of High Churchmen, especially metropolitan High Churchmen, in their ignorant extrapolations of dimly perceived social change.[90] Through it all, one fact remains. No one, certainly no one in contemporary Halifax, Keighley and Denholme, actually knew what the social distribution of religious regularity actually was; not across their respective urban societies as a whole, and not even within their particular

---

[84] The Rev. Francis Pigou, 'Tales of an Underground Mission', HPCM, vol. 1, no. 3, March 1878.

[85] I have developed this argument at length in S.J.D. Green, 'The Church of England and the Working-Classes of Late-Victorian and Edwardian Halifax', THAS, NS, 1 (1993), 106–20.

[86] Anon., 'Editorial Notes', KWMCM, no. 9, February 1910 (no page number).

[87] Cf. Morris, Religion and Urban Change, pp. 12–13. Such an analysis does not preclude the possibility of regional variation. But it cannot be insignificant that the dynamic invoked here – that urban change made the churches more reliant on the middle classes than before – seems actually to have been inverted in Yorkshire; similarly, that the assumption employed, that material dependency was synonymous with spiritual concern, is unwarranted.

[88] Joyce, Work, Society and Politics, p. 252; this author, for instance, just assumes that the whole of the middle classes attended church every Sunday, and calculates working-class 'religious observance', similarly defined, on that basis. Yet he cites no evidence to sustain that assumption; nor to substantiate its corollary.

[89] Brown, 'Did Urbanization Secularize Britain?', pp. 7–10.

[90] Winnington-Ingram, Work in Great Cities, p. 22.

denominational organisations either. What is more, it cannot be reliably calculated now. And for the simplest of reasons: no one thought at the time to keep the relevant records. They did not seem to be sufficiently important.[91]

For that reason, no observation about comparative class involvement in West Yorkshire's late Victorian religious organisations can be anything more than tentative, and qualified. Post-1851 church and chapel Sunday attendance figures are almost impossible to quantify, *tout court*.[92] The evidence is too patchy, and where it is plentiful it is usually unreliable. If that is true generally, it is especially true of these towns; even, paradoxically, in those associations in these towns where individual society records survive.[93] Only for Keighley, in fact, can even an educated guess be made. For what it is worth, it points to a figure of around 40 per cent of the population attending church or chapel on a normal Sunday.[94] Even allowing for the most generous interpretation of 'middle-class' standing, this suggests that the majority of worshippers must have been drawn from the working classes. Conversely, it also proves that the greater part of the local proletariat was at that time elsewhere engaged.[95]

So much is not surprising. It accords, fairly accurately, with most recent interpretations of the nationwide 1851 Census and its wider implications.[96] It is also consistent with later, and more detailed,

[91]   By this, I mean occupational records of numbers, affiliates and attenders. I have found no evidence of any society keeping such records except for trustees (see below, p. 203), and *parents* of Sunday school scholars (see below, ch. 5).

[92]   For varying perspectives on these matters, see McLeod, *Religion and the Working Classes, passim*; Brown, 'Did Urbanization Secularize Britain?', *passim*; and, finally, J. Obelkevich, 'Religion', in F.M.L. Thompson (ed.), *The Cambridge Social History of Britain, 1750–1850*, vol. III (Cambridge, 1990), pp. 339ff.

[93]   Too rarely do these constitute sequences of information capable of period analysis, let alone worthy of intra- and inter-denominational comparison. And even where they do, they must be treated with caution. In many cases, annual returns by stations to circuits, etc., etc. presented deliberately inflated figures, depicted to further, or protect, individual reputations. This was especially true of attendance figures.

[94]   *Keighley Yearbook, 1878*, pp. 144–5; *1879*, pp. 149–151; *1880*, pp. 77–9; *1882*, p. 57; using the impartial *Keighley Yearbook*, taking the year 1881 as a base, and drawing on statistics submitted within three years of that date, we can say that (a) Roman Catholic 'congregations' were around 2,500; let us say that three-quarters of these were locals; (b) Wesleyan Methodist Circuit membership was around 1,000; probably three times that number attended; (c) non-Wesleyan Methodist, non-Anglican membership was also around 1,000; similarly around three times that number attended; (d) multiplying the resulting figure by 150 per cent, to account for the absence of any figures for the remaining seven (mainly Anglican) societies, we arrive at a figure of 12,000. This represents about 36 per cent of Keighley's population in 1881. Allowing for inadvertent non-attenders – the aged, infirm and sick – on the lines of Mann's contemporary model, we may *guess at* an attendance of around two-fifths of the local population.

[95]   See ch. 1, above, esp. pp. 56–65.

[96]   See J. Roach, *Social Reform in England, 1780–1880* (London, 1978), p. 211; and for a

studies of popular religious involvement elsewhere in Victorian Britain.[97] What was significant, locally, was that plebeian involvement in the churches was active as well as frequent. Contemporary 'trust lists' prove this. More than twenty of these have survived, covering the whole period and representing all the major nonconformist groups. Uniquely amongst contemporary records, these accounts of associational responsibility also listed individual occupations. They reveal a frequent, almost a constant, working-class presence. This is remarkable. Pointing as they did to the especially active and particularly responsible within any organisation, they might have been thought to have obscured a passive proletarian presence. But they do not. There seem to have been two reasons for this. First, and rather obviously, working-class churches invariably elected working-class trustees to preside over them. Generally, this was a matter of simple necessity. There just was no one else available to do the job. This certainly seems to have been the case at Denholme Primitive Methodist Church, where an overwhelmingly plebeian officiate presided over the early twentieth-century chapel.[98] Second, and more remarkably, socially mixed churches and chapels often chose socially mixed representatives to carry out these responsibilities. Hence West Lane Primitive Methodist Trust Board, twenty men strong in 1911, included a gentleman, a mill-owner and a bedding manufacturer, but also a labourer, a gardener and a hospital porter.[99]

Two other aspects of these lists are noticeable. First, the emergence of a female presence: almost exclusively male in composition at the outset, they feature women in increasing numbers by the end of the period. Exley Head Primitive Methodist Church, Keighley, for instance, had no female trustees in 1883. Yet by 1926, its board boasted no fewer than eight, very nearly one-third of a total strength of twenty-six.[100] Secondly, the suggestion of increasing social differentiation of churches *within* denominations. This certainly seems to have been true of Keighley's First Primitive Methodist Circuit. There, the typical social standing of Alice Street and South Street trustees seems to have risen markedly over the years 1892 to 1925 and 1874 to 1925 respectively, whereas those of

recent summary, Richard H. Trainor, *Black Country Elites: The Exercise of Authority in an Industrialised Area, 1830–1900* (Oxford, 1993), pp. 175–7.
[97] See esp. Hillis, 'Presbyterians and Social Class', *passim*.
[98] CDA, Misc. 475/2/1, Denholme Clough, Primitive Methodist Church, Trustees' Meeting, Minute Book, 1 October 1905.
[99] KPL, 105D77/1/1/8/a, Keighley Primitive Methodist, no. 2 Circuit Station Reports, Appendix, West Lane Trust Board, 2 September 1911.
[100] Anon., *Centenary Handbook and Brief History of Exley Head Methodist Church, Keighley, 1854–1954* (Keighley, 1954), p. 11.

Worth Village and Park Lane remained very static.[101] Together they point to the possibility, to put it no more strongly, that the greater social comprehensiveness of the Edwardian Church increased social distinction within Edwardian churches.

Be that as it may, the sheer numerical force of working-class church attendance, taken together with the considerable evidence of working-class associational influence, explains one of the more curious, and certainly one of the least explored, aspects of later Victorian ecclesiastical life: the strong, even the prevailing, sense that West Yorkshire's contemporary sacred institutions provided for the working classes, and were supported in return by them to a very notable extent. Sometimes this was true by origin. Hence South Gate Baptist Church, Denholme, traced its very existence to 'two or three working men of the Baptist persuasion'.[102] Elsewhere, it was a product of particular change, or of specific actions which brought about a greater popular involvement in the churches: for instance, Northgate End's much vaunted free seating policy which sought a 'union of classes ... as real as the means taken to secure it'.[103] And on occasion, it seemingly did just that. Certainly, the trustees of Illingworth Church of England were delighted to celebrate 'a beautiful window', erected there in 1869, 'by subscription amongst the working classes of [the parish]'.[104]

This is not to suggest that such a feeling precluded better-known anxieties about proletarian indifference. It did not. Everyone understood that particular blight. Some denounced it, almost to the extent of condemning the people for their own failings in this respect, such as the Reverend Joseph Wood, who, speaking to the annual meeting of the Yorkshire Unitarian Union in Halifax in 1886, lamented popular failure to respond to a 'simple faith ... most suited to the wants of the masses'.[105] Others, however, excused it, preferring to place the greatest blame on the churches' own weaknesses, whether in charging pew-rents or in maintaining Sunday clothes.[106] A few genuinely tried to understand it, pointing either to the peculiar conditions of 'large cities' as places 'fatal to simplicity of life and mind', to the 'tavern' as the centre of modern 'amusement', to 'indecent ... housing', even to 'poor educa-

[101] KPL, 105D77/1/1/3a, Keighley Primitive Methodist (First) Circuit, Lists of Trustees, 1925.
[102] Private Collection of Mr A. Vine, uncat. MSS, Southgate Baptist Church, Denholme, Church Meeting, Minute Book, 2 October 1894.
[103] Millson, *Two Hundred Years of Northgate End*, p. 33.
[104] Cited in William Henry Sacker, *Illingworth Church: A Brief Account of Illingworth Church and the Particulars of Its Restoration and Reopening* (Halifax, 1873), p. 4.
[105] *Halifax Courier*, 12 June 1886.
[106] Bailey, *Progressive Congregationalism*, p. 14; Cremer, 'Vicar's Notes', HSPKCMP, December 1896.

tion' as causes of plebeian irreligiousness.[107] More simply still, one local authority, the Reverend F.D. Millson, insisted that the overwhelming force of brutal 'poverty', coupled with continued 'tiredness', was the principal cause of the people's failures 'to attend stated services'.[108] But few, if any – and certainly not Millson himself – took such factors to be insurmountable. Hence, if 'the great need of our time' really was 'to elevate popular Christianity', then the most important contemporary instrument for the fulfilment of that task was, paradoxically, the reality of its continuing existence.[109] And not as nebulous cultural resource; but as real and tangible social experience. It was there, ready and waiting to be tapped. To some extent, it had already been drawn out and developed. The most principled goal of associational life remained to exhaust it.

The question of sex

There was another complicating factor in all of this. This was because the life of organised religion in later nineteenth-century West Yorkshire was marked not simply by distinctions of class, but also by differences of sex. Put bluntly, it was consistently a more attractive activity for women than for men. To be sure, the evidence for this proposition is quite limited in its extent. But it is quite unambiguous in its direction. For Halifax, two societies, Northgate End Unitarian Chapel and Harrison Road Congregational Church, have bequeathed statistical materials worthy of computation; two, likewise, in Keighley, Albert Street Baptist Chapel and Devonshire Street Congregational Church. Unfortunately, no comparable records from local Church of England or Roman Catholic societies have survived. There is no reason, however, to believe that nonconformist associations differed markedly from Anglican or Papist associations in this respect. And the nonconformist experience points to marked female domination of membership rolls; also, seemingly, of average weekly attendance figures.

The divergence reported at Harrison Road, Halifax, was so great as perhaps to constitute an exceptional example. There, females made up 211, or 77.3 per cent of 273 listed members in 1870. Yet, if this was a remarkable case it was not an extraordinary year. The corresponding figures for 1880 were 231, or 78.8 per cent, of 333; for 1890, 277, or 77.7

---

[107] Anon., 'Christianity in the Nineteenth Century', *HDCM*, vol. 1, no. 8, November 1883, p. 235.
[108] Millson, *Millson's Address to the A.C.M., 29th January 1894*, p. 19.
[109] J.R. Birtwhistle, *History and Reminiscences of Harrison Road Sunday School* (Halifax, 1894), p. 6.

per cent, of 357; for 1900, 218, or 76 per cent, of 287; for 1910, 198, or 74.5 per cent, of 264; and for 1920, 167, or 75 per cent, of 220.[110] Differences at Northgate were much smaller, so much so that this case may have been an example of the opposite extreme. No figures are available for 1870. But in 1883, the first year for which they do survive, they suggest that men actually outnumbered women at this society, 128 to 95, amongst the 223 registered members. If so, this balance had been reversed by 1893; then women constituted 159 of 307 members. Female numerical dominance continued thereafter. In 1900, it amounted to 155, or 54 per cent of 285. By 1911, it had risen to 144, or nearly 58 per cent of 249. And in 1920, it reached 149, or just under 60 per cent of 251.[111]

The respective variations in Keighley were not quite so great. Women accounted for 71.5 per cent of membership, 181 of 252, at Albert Street Baptist Chapel, in 1894, the first year for which reliable figures have survived. Ten years later, this proportion had fallen very slightly, to 68.7 per cent or 179 of 275, and by 1910 it then diminished just a little further, to 67.9 per cent, that is, 252 of 371. Curiously, it then *increased* during the following decade. In 1920, it stood at 72.7 per cent, 211 of 290.[112] These figures were roughly matched by Devonshire Street Congregational Church during the latter years of the nineteenth century. Some 132, or 68.7 per cent of the 192 members, were female in 1880. Fifteen years later, 165, or 67.3 per cent, of 245 were women. However, this predominance declined, at least to some degree, during the early years of the twentieth century. By 1905, it stood at 59.5 per cent, or 212 of 361. Ten years later it remained at exactly the same proportion, accounting for 228 of 383 members of the society.[113]

In neither town was any significant pattern of associational difference discernible. So female predominance in church membership does not appear to have been particularly associated with any one denomination. Three – Congregationalist, Baptists and Unitarians – are represented in this small sample alone, and their results converge. Nor does it appear to have had a more general institutional history. Respective proportions increased at Northgate End, but decreased at Devonshire Street. On the other hand, they remained remarkably stable, over long periods of time, at both Harrison Road and Albert Street. Common across denomina-

---

[110] CDA, CUR 1:3–7, Harrison Road Congregational Chapel, Halifax, Members' Attendance Roll Books, 1869–1925 (no page number).

[111] CDA, NEC 11, Northgate End Unitarian Chapel, Halifax, List of Registered Members, 1872–1950 (no page number).

[112] *Albert Street Baptist Church, Manual, 1894*, pp. 23–9; *1904*, pp. 20–7; *1910*, pp. 32–40; *1920*, pp. 28–37.

[113] *Keighley Congregational Church, Manual, 1880*, pp. 23–8; *1895*, pp. 15–20; *1905*, pp. 13–23; *1915*, pp. 10–19.

tions, it was also constant over time, rarely at proportions of less than 6 to 4, sometimes at an extent of more than 3 to 1. An average taken across all four societies, calculated to fall within a decade of a nominal fixed base year of 1885, suggests, for what it is worth, an average of 67.8 per cent.[114]

No comparable figures for comparative ratios of male/female attendance survive. And for the simplest of reasons; none were compiled. However, the anecdotal evidence suggests that female predominance amongst membership lists (or their equivalent) was regularly reflected in the normal worshipping congregations, and this across denominations too. Certainly, there was a continued complaint amongst churchmen of 'husbands' not coming to 'communion', even though their 'wives' dutifully did.[115] Similarly, nonconformist ministers lamented the failure of 'men', categorised as such regardless of class, to attend 'services in the same proportions, and with similar enthusiasm as "women"'.[116] At the same time, it seemed that no one, whether Anglican or dissenter, priest, minister or laymen, could offer the slightest explanation as to why this was so. So, for most, it remained a matter of continuous 'disappointment'.[117]

This does not mean that no attempt was made to do anything about the problem. On the contrary. So serious was it understood to be that continual efforts to rectify the seeming imbalance between the sexes in holy worship were undertaken. One such scheme was the practice of specific, occasional 'men's services'. The aim of these periodic events was to attract men to church, and to worship, in an environment where they would not be outnumbered by women, and through which their particular needs and aspirations would be fulfilled. Thus it was hoped they would subsequently be attracted to regular and common congregation. Keighley Parish church ran such a service every second and fourth Sunday of the month, from 1905 onwards.[118] Some societies went further still, organising 'Men's Societies', and seeking in 'organisation ... of some sort' a familiarity and a commitment that would induce the consistency of attendance at worship which they so craved.[119] There is no evidence, however, to suggest that it did.

[114] That is, 672 of 990, adding together the 1880 figures at Harrison Road, the 1883 figures at Northgate End, the 1894 figures at Albert Street, and the 1886 figures at Devonshire Street.

[115] Francis Pigou, 'The Kiss of Charity: A Sermon Preached at the Parish Church, Halifax, 24th July 1887', in Pigou, *Sermons and Addresses*, p. 20.

[116] Anon., 'Mission and Its Effects', *KPCM*, vol. 13, no. 12, December 1890 (no page number).

[117] *Ibid.*

[118] *Keighley Yearbook, 1906*, p. 101.

[119] Anon., 'St Paul's Men's Society', *SPKCPCM* , vol. 16, no. 3, March 1907 (no page number).

Ecclesiastical organisations sought the patronage of males because the Christian message extended as much to men as to women. Hence a shortfall in male membership and attendance represented nothing less than a failing of evangelical purpose. As voluntary organisations, however, they sought the support of men still more fervently than women. This was because men were the more powerful, possibly the more significant, and undoubtedly the richer of the two sexes. And societies that sought to be correspondingly influential therefore needed their commitment – and needed it more than women's otherwise freely given and more easily won dedication. Nevertheless, female dedication, *per se* was far from derided. Indeed, in its supposed simplicity and indubitable constancy it was often especially extolled. True, such praise was occasionally rendered somewhat ambiguous by contemporary notions of a natural feminine dutifulness. In this understanding, the qualities of '[h]umility and love', taken to be 'chief characteristics of Christianity', came 'sweetly and easily' to women whilst they were 'attained [only] laboriously by men'.[120] It may also have been affected by contemporary knowledge that, for instance, of Northgate's women, rarely less than a quarter and sometimes up to a third were spinsters.[121] All of which suggested that respectable sociability might have had something to do with it too.

Whatever the case, the sheer numerical predominance of women in contemporary ecclesiastical organisations is amenable to more than one interpretation. Contemporaries usually emphasised the difficulties it entailed. Certainly, it does suggest that the question of 'masculine' religious commitment may have been a greater problem for Victorian and Edwardian religious societies even than the aggregated evidence of working-class disaffiliation reveals. Yet, by the same token, the very imbalance of the sexes in West Yorkshire's sacred institutions must lead subsequent historians to doubt, to a greater degree still, the image of simple, undifferentiated popular indifference that has so frequently come down to us. In its disaggregated form, the surviving evidence at least allows for the possibility – to put the matter no more strongly – that more than half of all households locally had some significant personal connection – one adult member of the family – with a mainstream denominational church. Certainly, such a supposition is not directly contradicted by any part of the available records. And, to the extent that

---

[120]   The Rev. I.R. Vernon, 'The Love of Women', *HPCM*, vol. 1, no. 7, July 1878, p. 23.
[121]   Northgate End Unitarian Chapel, Halifax, List of Registered Members, 1870–1950 (no page number). In 1893, 43 of 159; in 1900, 49 of 155; in 1911, 53 of 144; in 1920, 43 of 145.

it is true, it effectively puts paid to any plausible notion of an 'alienated' general population.

The question of age

There was one final peculiarity: this was that of age. Watchful contemporaries noted a distinct generational profile in their congregations, particularly in their 'Sunday morning congregations'. These seemed to be made up, disproportionately, of 'large numbers ... of young children ... elder boys and girls [and] old folk'.[122] The middle-aged, and especially the married middle-aged, whether male or female, proletarian or bourgeois, seemed to be underrepresented on these occasions. No figures can be offered to confirm this impression. None was calculated at the time, and no reasonable estimate can be made now. But an understanding, if not of its implications then at least of the existence of such a discrepancy, was commonplace. Some, perhaps rather naive, souls took that fact as an opportunity to applaud the 'striking ... number ... of young people who regularly me[t] for worship'.[123] Other, rather more sceptical, observers lamented the way in which the sacrament of marriage thus impinged upon church life; frequently disruptive in itself and, all too often, the occasion for subsequent inconstancy.[124]

Whatever the case, all agreed that such an apparent discrepancy proved the peculiar importance – thus proved in the breach – of young, male, church life. Above all, it underlined the need to nurture and to preserve it, in order to secure its subsequent (and seemingly vulnerable) continuity. Some local commentators waxed positively lyrical on this theme. One anonymous account in Halifax's *Congregational Magazine*, whilst acknowledging that '[C]hildhood, manhood and old age each ha[d] a claim' none the less insisted that 'young men stand out as peculiar objects of interest and sympathy' in every sacred 'society'. This was, so it argued, on account of their particular ecclesiastical 'importance'. They were the 'next generation' of the 'faithful'; or, if things went wrong, of the potentially 'infidel'. More subtly, they were the most important single subgroup of that future population. For that reason especially, no church could 'afford to lose them'.[125]

It was also on account of their rather more general social significance,

---

122 *Millson Address, 29 January 1894*, p. 19.
123 F. Robinson, *History of the Congregational School and Church, Highroad Well, Halifax* (Halifax, 1915), p. 40.
124 Pigou, *Phases in My Life*, pp. 307–9.
125 D.M., 'Our Young Men', *HDCM*, vol. 3, no. 10, October 1885, pp. 222–4.

for they were, as this account put it, 'common property', eagerly sought after not only by the churches, but also by 'Trade ... Science ... Philosophy ... Agriculture ... Education' and, finally, by 'Religion' itself. As such, they were open not merely to tempting offers, but to temptation itself, still worse to 'those ... temptations to which young men are peculiarly liable'. These included 'Atheism ... and ... [v]ice'; and, seemingly worst of all, 'scepticism'. For those reasons, no church (or churchmen) could be 'too careful' about what it said 'to young men', nor 'too solicitous for their welfare'. It could not do 'too much' to 'guard them from temptation' and 'save them from sin'. To that end 'Books written for them ought to be circulated everywhere. Sermons preached to them should be reported in all directions. Prayers offered for them should be earnest and importunate'.[126]

And they were. Northgate End Unitarian self-consciously remodelled the style of its Sunday morning sermons during the 1890s, pursuing 'moral instruction' rather than 'theological disputation', with the explicit end of 'preparing the young for church life'.[127] Others went further still, appointing 'certain deacons as spiritual supervisors to certain senior classes'. This was done in order to maximise 'the welfare of young people' and more specifically, to 'forge a bridge' which might more effectively 'join senior scholars with the church'.[128] Yet, all the while, they also acknowledged that this and other gestures like it were not enough; that in fact such gestures merely patched up a leak that threatened to widen into a torrent, for they essentially bypassed the one institution which already existed for the nurture of young religious life and which, if properly redirected, might yet educate that life, generally and unfailingly, into the régime of dedicated, mature, adult worship. This was the Sunday school.

---

[126] *Ibid.*, pp. 222–3.
[127] *Millson's Address, 29 January 1894*, p. 19.
[128] CDA, CUR 1:13, Harrison Road, Congregational Chapel, Halifax, Church and Deacons' Book, 2 March 1898.

5 Learning advanced: the Sunday school movement, pedagogical innovation and the theory of juvenile religious development

Introduction: Sunday schools and the mission to the people

To provide the means of worship – materials and money – demanded difficult choices and exacted uneasy compromises in the religious organisations of later Victorian and Edwardian West Yorkshire. But to bear witness to the truth, to teach the word and to inspire others to the faith, was generally understood to be, if not easy, then at least straightforward: at once a spiritual duty and a social obligation. Yet this was rarely the case. Certainly, the worldly frustrations of sacred societies as teacher and proselytiser were no less important than those they endured as trustee and pastor. Committed to teaching the word, they saw only too well how often it was repudiated. Bound to preach the right, they knew how frequently it was traduced; and if not rudely ignored, then acknowledged only with that polite tolerance which foreshadowed subsequent indifference.

Nowhere did that indifference seem more striking to intelligent churchmen and ministers than in the mid-Victorian Sunday school. Here lay a paradox. At one level, no religious institution reached more people in the nineteenth-century town; very few of those born, bred and living in these West Riding towns during the years of their industrial and demographic expansion can have passed through life without some exposure to the ways and word of Christian witness.[1] Yet, at another level, no religious institution more graphically highlighted the problem of popular inconstancy, for, despite being so long exposed to the true way, and at a seemingly impressionable age, the people did not properly respond to it. Only a small fraction of those given such opportunities – in mid-Victorian West Yorkshire as elsewhere – became committed, regular, worshipping, church and chapel

---

[1] And in this respect, they were not peculiar. For the example of Reading, in the south of England, see Yeo, *Religion and Voluntary Organisations in Crisis*, p. 137; and for Glasgow, see Brown, 'Did Urbanization Secularize Britain?', p. 11.

Christians as a result. Most remained – from the point of view of the men of religion – 'irreligious'.[2]

Contemporary churchmen and ministers interpreted this evidence of popular 'irreligion' in many ways: as a form of ignorance to be corrected; as a social evil to be confounded; and, finally, as a spiritual challenge to be confronted. But how? Increasingly after 1870, one solution suggested itself above all others. This was to reform the Sunday school. Thus the very place of failure was to become the new home of success. So inspired, churchmen, ministers and teachers resolved to complete the education of the people in the reformed Sunday school; that is, in a renewed sacred society, more socially comprehensive, better integrated into ecclesiastical life, and shorn of its erstwhile secular pedagogical purposes.[3] To do all that, they had to change the popular habits of a century, and then to shift the institutional prejudices of the age. The history of the later Victorian and Edwardian Sunday school is the story of their attempt at that transformation.

Affiliation, attendance and purpose in the mid-Victorian Sunday school

'It is well known that you must go to Yorkshire or Lancashire if you would [sic] realise the hold which the Sunday school has and retains over its scholars.' So observed the Rev. Francis Pigou, sometime Vicar of St John the Baptist Church of England, Halifax, and President of its adjunct Sunday school, in 1898.[4] Certainly, no religious institution was more popular in this part of Victorian West Yorkshire. For instance, Keighley's thirty Sunday schools boasted a membership of some 7,000 persons in 1877, a total which represented more than one-fifth of the population of the town. And that was not a nominal figure. Of those formally enrolled, about 5,500 actually attended school at least once on an average Sunday.[5] Similarly reliable evidence has not survived for Halifax.[6] And virtually no data remain for Denholme. But such information as exists for these places broadly corroborates the view from Keighley. In 1877, there were probably sixty schools in Halifax.[7] The

---

[2]   A point made forcibly in Clyde Binfield, 'Freedom through Discipline: The Concept of a Celtic Church', in W.J. Sheils (ed.), *Monks, Hermits and Ascetic Tradition,* Studies in Church History, 22 (Oxford, 1985), pp. 403–40.

[3]   For a modern account of these, see Joyce, *Work, Society and Politics,* pp. 246–50; for a general history of the Sunday school in early nineteenth-century England, see Thomas Walter Laqueur, *Religion and Respectability: Sunday Schools and Working Class Culture, 1780–1850* (New Haven, 1976), *passim.*

[4]   Pigou, *Phases in My Life,* p. 343.   [5]   *Keighley Yearbook,* 1877, pp. 109–22.

[6]   But see Harwood, *Centenary Story,* pp. 33–9, for a general account.

[7]   Author's estimate; the difficulties of calculating the exact number of Sunday schools

records of eight have been examined. They reveal an average enrolment of about 200 scholars.[8] Extrapolating from that figure, it may reasonably be guessed that there were about 12,000 scholars enrolled in Halifax at that time. Whatever the precise number, contemporaries certainly remembered Sunday schools as being busy places. 'In the seventies and eighties [i.e. the 1870s and 1880s] the Sunday schools in most instances were crowded,' recalled Alderman Waddington, in 1937. He must have known. He was there at the time.[9]

Who were they? The young, certainly. But not only the young, not at least in this part of late Victorian England. Pigou again: 'We [i.e. St John the Baptist Church of England Sunday School] had a large class of adults ... This is a great contrast to what you see in the south, where children think themselves much too old at 15 or 16 to go to Sunday school.'[10] This was true of local dissenting schools too. In 1891, for instance, Queen's Road Primitive Methodist Church, Halifax, formed a 'Young Men's Class' specifically for its 'scholars above seventeen years of age'.[11] And other schools established their own variations on the theme at much the same time. However, the vast majority of scholars, whether at St John the Baptist Church of England or Queen's Road Primitive Methodist, seem to have left Sunday school before their twenty-first birthdays. To be sure, there were cases of grandfathers and grandsons enrolled at local schools,[12] but these were rare. In other words, a figure of 7,000 scholars, whilst representing a 'mere' one-fifth of the total population in Keighley in 1877, very probably constituted about one-half of the population in the town aged under twenty-one; and, more importantly, about three-quarters of those aged between five and twenty at that time.[13] The proportions for Halifax were probably very similar. So too were those for Denholme.[14] In other words,

are the same as those of calculating the exact number of places of worship in a town at any time: exactly what constituted a school was rarely wholly clear; this estimate, therefore, is based upon an estimate of the number of independent religious associations thriving in Halifax at that time, and an assumption that each society would have maintained a school of some sort.

8   Author's calculations; the exact figure was 207.3, but it cannot be presumed to be more than an estimate.

9   Waddington, 'Changes, 1866–1937', pp. 33–4.

10   Pigou, *Phases in My Life*, pp. 343–4.

11   CDA, Misc. 287:5–10, Queen's Road Primitive Methodist Church, Halifax, Sunday School Minute Book, 22 February 1891.

12   Joyce, *Work, Society and Politics*, p. 247.

13   Author's estimate; i.e. 7,000 of *c.* 15,000 aged under 21; and *c.* 7,000 of *c.* 9,750 aged between five and twenty; these figures have been extrapolated from the 1871 and 1881 Census returns; they are estimates only.

14   Author's estimate, employing the same principle as above; i.e. 5,500 of 7,000 in Keighley; see *Keighley Yearbook, 1877*, pp. 109–22. Moreover, this figure is almost certainly an *underestimate* of that proportion of the juvenile population receiving regular

attendance at Sunday school was a *norm* of life, more especially of juvenile life and, as the figures make inescapably clear, a norm of working-class juvenile life in the late Victorian manufacturing town.

Why did they go? Not just to learn the faith anyway. Even contemporary clergymen were aware, often painfully aware, that the general popularity of Sunday schools was not merely, or even primarily, a function of the religious fervour of the population; or indeed simply of their aspirations for a religious education for their children. It was, after all, a clergyman (albeit a London clergyman) who confided to Charles Booth that, in his view, Sunday afternoon school provided little more than an opportunity for working-class adults to enjoy their conjugal rights in peace, whilst someone else looked after their children.[15] That may have been a rather soured view. Yet it was certainly true that, prior to 1870 at least, it was the demand for cheap secular rather than religious education which ensured the popularity of Sunday schools amongst the working classes. Early nineteenth-century Sunday schools taught literacy and numeracy as well as morality. At least, they did if they wished to be successful; those that failed to do so, and shifted the emphasis too firmly towards things sacred, usually paid a stiff price in diminished enrolment lists.[16] Local clergymen fully recognised this fact. So '[s]ome measure' of the 'remarkable attachment' of Halifax's juvenile population to Sunday schools in the nineteenth century was attributable, as even the Reverend Francis Pigou conceded, 'to the fact that, before the Factory Acts were passed ... children had but little chance [elsewhere] of learning their letters'.[17]

To that degree, early Victorian schools were indeed thwarted in their ostensible religious purpose. Did they instead exercise a mysterious, mundane power over their working-class charges? Some historians have argued as much, suggesting that the secular teaching and moral discipline inculcated thus by the schools constituted a form of 'unadorned social control'. This curious force was, so it is contended, born of the intrusion of bourgeois values, and especially of the ethos of respectability, together with the doctrines of individual restraint and

Sunday instruction in these towns at this time, since it takes no account of the local Roman Catholic population for which, lamentably, no figures and little evidence are available. This assertion is corroborated for the case of Glasgow in Brown, 'Did Urbanization Secularize Britain?', p. 11. For the argument that the Sunday school population was overwhelmingly working-class, *to the virtual exclusion of the middle classes* at this time, see Binfield, 'Big Church, Little Church', pp. 407–10.

[15]   Interview with R.S. Rearney, Vicar of Christ Church, East Greenwich, in the Booth Collection in the Library of London School of Economics, B287, pp. 49–51; cited in Laqueur, *Religion and Respectability*, pp. 147–8.

[16]   Lacqueur, *Religion and Respectability*, pp. 148–51.

[17]   Pigou, *Phases in My Life*, p. 344.

collective orderliness, into an (otherwise) spontaneous, rebellious and unselfconscious working-class culture.[18] Whatever else it is, this is a peculiarly modern understanding of their purpose. And it precludes even the possibility that contemporary Sunday schools were popular with working-class parents precisely because they sought to instil that ethos and those virtues into their charges.[19] It also ignores the large body of evidence which proves that contemporaries found in Sunday schools not a vehicle for the repression of their natural sensibilities, but 'a golden opportunity for the fuller development of their talents which were denied expression elsewhere'.[20] Sunday schools invariably offered their pupils something more than just a cut-price initiation into literacy and numeracy. And they always furnished something more than a miserable lesson in social subordination for the children of the working classes.

Even at their most sombre, Sunday schools were valuable social, recreational and cultural outlets for the people and for their offspring. Through their sick societies, clothing clubs and savings banks they sustained a mentality of self-help.[21] Through their recreational associations, they furnished an outlet for serious and improving leisure activities. And, on the occasion of the annual treat, they afforded the young (and not so young) an opportunity to travel out of town, either to the seaside or to some other local attraction, and to broaden what might otherwise have been sadly straitened personal horizons.[22] Naturally, they also taught religion: bible-readings and the various catechisms, hymns and prayers. Of course, it was rarely sophisticated teaching. But neither its purpose nor its effect was always entirely negligible, for in transmitting not simply the bare message but also some of the rhetoric, even indeed some of the aesthetics of Christianity, Sunday schools performed a vital, if nebulous, function in spreading at least the flavour of Christian witness to the masses of the population in the industrial towns. Moreover, though Sunday schools were scarcely stomping grounds for evangelical enthusiasm, they were not wholly immune to its deeper spiritual impulses either. Some early and mid-nineteenth-century children were converted to Christ there in their early youth. The Reverend Arthur Myers, of the Keighley Wesleyan Circuit, 'first

[18] This phrase is drawn from Joyce, *Work, Society and Politics*, p. 247. See also Laqueur, *Religion and Respectability*, ch. 7; also Robert Moore, *Pit-Men, Preachers and Politics: The Effects of Methodism in a Durham Mining Community* (Cambridge, 1974), pp. 109–11.

[19] I owe this point to Gertrude Himmelfarb, 'Victorian Values/Jewish Values', *Commentary*, 87 (1989), 24–5.

[20] Waddington, 'More Changes', p. 52.

[21] See Laqueur, *Religion and Respectability*, pp. 172–5; also Wickham, *Church and People*, p. 155.

[22] Laqueur, *Religion and Respectability*, pp. 177–8.

confessed Christ [in school] when eleven years of age', he recalled many years later.[23] The 'light entered the soul' of J.T.L. Maggs, bastion of the same connexion, 'as a lad', in the same place.[24]

It should go without saying that theirs was not a common experience. Nor, very probably, was it a common pursuit. There were, after all, many reasons to go to Sunday school. Some children did indeed go to learn skills they might otherwise never have acquired. Others, of course, went under parental coercion. A few probably attended simply by force of habit. The very variety of their motives, and of the purposes of others in keeping them there, should alert subsequent investigators against any facile interpretation of Sunday schools as monolithic instruments of 'social control'.[25] After all, just because Sunday schools demanded strict discipline, they did not necessarily achieve it.[26] Indeed, in some cases, they were rather more like convenient channels for general social disruption. That sense of imminent – and concentrated – anarchy was exquisitely caught in a notice of resignation submitted by one George Fearn to the teachers' meeting of Hanover Street Methodist New Connexion School, Halifax, in which he complained, inter alia, 'that many of the class are, to all appearances, determined to disregard all law or authority in the school and seem to come only to interrupt and disturb those in the class who are well disposed'.[27]

Perhaps. But then much contemporary 'scholarly authority' was not, in truth, very authoritative. It was indeed the teachers, and not their pupils, who were accused of being 'systematically absent from their classes' at Keighley Parish Church School in 1878.[28] A memo from the Superintendent of Queen's Road Primitive Methodist School in Halifax requested, in 1883, that '[b]oth Teachers and Scholars' should 'refrain in future [from] bring[ing] spice [i.e. sweets or other confectionery], or any other article that will interfere with the order of the school'.[29] And a directive from the teachers' meeting of the same school, in the same year, insisted that 'every teacher in this school is expected to take books

[23]   Rev. Arthur Myers, 'Sunday-School Evangelism', *KWMCM*, no. 29, October 1911 (no page number).

[24]   Henry Firth, 'The Late Dr. Maggs and the Child's Religion', *KWMCM*, no. 70, March 1915 (no page number).

[25]   For some illuminating remarks on the imperfection of the tools of social control in Victorian educational institutions, see Thompson, 'Social Control in Victorian Britain', pp. 191–5.

[26]   On Sunday school discipline in general, see Laqueur, *Religion and Respectability*, ch. 7; and Joyce, *Work, Society and Politics*, pp. 247–8.

[27]   CDA, Misc. 57/2, Hanover Street Methodist Sunday School, Halifax, Teachers' Meeting Minute Book, 7 November 1871.

[28]   Anon., 'Teachers' Attendance', *KPCM*, vol. 1, no. 6, June 1878 (no page number).

[29]   CDA, Misc. 287:5–10, Queen's Road Primitive Methodist Sunday School, Halifax, Sunday School Minute Book, 5 June 1883.

out of the Library and [to] encourage their scholars to do the same'.[30] Clearly, many were doing neither. And their failure to do so was apparently mirrored in the region's Congregational Sunday schools, whose contemporary 'failure' was attributed by contemporaries above all – 'the chief and most important reason' – to the 'inferior quality of teaching power in our schools'.[31]

The principal reason for that was widely believed to be the *absence* of middle-class social and pedagogical influence in the Sunday schools. Certainly, the local 'middle classes' did not generally send their children to them. They preferred, for the most part, to do their own 'teaching in the home'. More importantly still, they all too often 'refused to allow their respectable ... daughters to teach' there. In so doing, they condemned future generations to 'messenger[s] ... of Christ ... quite unfitted for the post'.[32] These were often ex-scholars, and sometimes even pupils from the senior classes.[33] Moreover, even those who 'volunteered' from amongst their respective 'congregations' were not necessarily individuals deeply committed to the cause.[34] Temple Street Wesleyan Methodists, for instance, required no more of their teachers, in 1865, than that they be 'of at least unexceptionable moral character'.[35] St Paul's Church of England School, Halifax, demanded in 1892 that its teachers be of 'the highest character'. But apparently so exacting a qualification did not in fact require even that they be 'regular communicants of the church'.[36]

Yet a solution lay at hand, or at least 'within a few hundred yards'. It lay amongst the many 'able-bodied, healthy men and women', more particularly amongst the 'members of the church to which [each] school [was] attached'. Confined to 'sitting dozing and nodding behind the *Christian World* or the *Sunday Magazine* or some other convenient aid to slumber', they might be recruited to 'help in teaching'. They might also be persuaded to send their children to Sunday school 'at least once a Sunday'.[37] But how? Individual attention, clearly, had failed. The

---

30 *Ibid.*, 9 January 1883.

31 Walter H. Scales, 'Reasons for Failure', *HDCM*, vol. 6, no. 5, May 1888, p. 98.

32 *Ibid.*, pp. 98–9; for a corroboration of this view, see Binfield, 'Freedom through Discipline', pp. 407–11.

33 CDA, Misc. 287/40, Queen's Road, Methodist New Connexion Sunday School, Halifax, Sunday School Minutes, 24 August 1878.

34 CDA, Misc. 287:5–10, Queen's Road Primitive Methodist Sunday School Halifax, Sunday School, Minute Book, 9 January 1883.

35 Anon., *Rules and Regulations for the Wesleyan Methodist Sunday School, Temple Street, Keighley* (Keighley, 1865), p. 3.

36 Anon., 'Sunday School Teachers and Choirs', *SPCKCPM*, vol. 1, no. 1, January 1892 (no page number).

37 Scales, 'Reasons for Failure', pp. 98–9.

answer, so contemporaries believed, lay in the 'closer [institutional] integration' of chapel and school.[38] Its pursuit formed the basis of 'the great era of the Sunday school' during the last third of the nineteenth century.[39]

Institutional integration, pedagogical reform and the growth of the proselytising ethos

In 1870, the Wesleyan Methodist Conference 'affectionately recommended' to the committees of 'our Sunday Schools throughout the Connexion' a scheme for the 'formation of Wesleyan Methodist Sunday School Circuit Unions'. The stated objects of the proposed Union were:

1 To establish mutual intercourse amongst the officers and teachers of the schools in town and country.
2 To promote the opening of new, and the extension and improvement of existing, schools.
3 To circulate information relative to the organization and discipline of schools, as well as the best methods of notification.
4 To collect statistics, and report interesting particulars and instances of usefulness.
5 To stimulate and encourage those who are engaged in the religious education of the young in the Circuit to seek greater spiritual results of their labours.

Tentative rules for this projected plan envisaged that 'all officers, teachers and members of committees in connection with the Wesleyan Methodist Sunday Schools shall be considered members of this union'. Accordingly, an executive committee was established in each circuit, constituted of 'the ministers of the circuit, the circuit stewards, a treasurer, two secretaries, the school superintendents and the secretaries of committees'. The stated duty of this body was to appoint an official deputation, itself charged with the responsibility of visiting each school twice a year,

to ascertain from the secretary of each school the number of teachers and scholars with the average number of both; the number of teachers and scholars who are members of the society, and the number of scholars in Select Classes; whether the school regularly attends Divine worship on the Sabbath; to what extent the Conference Catechisms and scripture lessons are used[; and] to present a Report as to the books used in the schools, the modes of instruction employed, and the general order and efficiency of the schools.

Finally, it was hoped that an 'Aggregate [*sic*] Meeting of Members and Friends of the Union shall be held at least once a year for mutual

[38]   Reid Marchbank, *One Hundred Years of Progress*, p. 45.
[39]   *Ibid.*, p. 28.

encouragement and improvement, at which a general report of the state of the schools be presented, and instances of usefulness shall be delivered suited to the occasion'.[40]

At first sight, this might have seemed like an innocent plan for the general improvement of the nation's Wesleyan Methodist Sunday schools. If so, the illusion cannot have lasted for long. Just four years later, the same conference made the real purposes of a 'General Plan' for the 'Connexional Sunday School Union' altogether clearer. They were:

1 To promote the development of the Sunday School system with the special design of securing greater spiritual results, and the gathering of Sunday Scholars into the Wesleyan Methodist Society.
2 To promote a closer sympathy and relationship between the School, the Society and the Ministry.
3 To promote the co-operation among Wesleyan Methodist Society Schools in the several Circuits and to encourage the Connexional Element in the character and working of such schools.[41]

This was, or was to be, an unambiguous departure from past norms. The homely pursuit of spiritual fruit had been translated into the altogether more significant institutional imperative of associational recruitment. That obligation, in turn, had been linked, first, to the properly conceived (i.e. readjusted) relationship of school to church; secondly, and more importantly, to an appropriately redirected (i.e. wholly recast) relationship of school to both church and connexion.

Perhaps because they realised just how much was at stake, the response of local schools to these plans, both in 1870 and in 1874, was cautious. Hainworth Sunday School, Keighley, discussed the issue of 'joining the Methodist Sunday School Union', in 1873, but made no decision on that occasion.[42] Two years later, it debated the matter again and, on this occasion, actually voted not to join the Union, until the General and Connexional Unions 'get more matured'.[43] On the other hand, Exley Head Wesleyan Methodist Sunday School, also in Keighley, 'resolved that we join the Connexional Sunday School Union' at much the same time.[44] The following year, Temple Street, mother church to the circuit and the leading school in the town, openly pondered 'the question ... whether this school joins the Wesleyan Methodist Connexional Sunday School Union through [sic] the provincial centre at

40 Anon., *Principles on Which Wesleyan Methodist Sunday Schools Should Be Conducted* (London, *c.* 1880), p. 7.
41 *Ibid.*, pp. 9–10.
42 KPL, 105D77/2/7/7/9, Hainworth Sunday School Minute Book, 28 January 1873.
43 *Ibid.*, 20 February 1875.
44 KPL, uncat. MS, Exley Head Wesleyan Methodist Sunday School Minute Book, 4 January 1875.

Bradford'. At this stage, its uncertainty about the merits of the case was matched by its irresolution about what to do about it. Accordingly, its management committee voted to 'refer ... the question ... to the next half-yearly meeting'.[45] Just five months later, however, they acceded to the forces of change, voting 'to join the Connexional Union'.[46] With that, the other local schools fell relatively quickly into line. One of the last seems to have been Devonshire Park, which in 1880 voted to 'join Temple Street and the other Wesleyan Schools in the town in forming a "Circuit Sunday School Union"'.[47] Four years later, Keighley Circuit Sunday School Union acquired its own premises in North Street. Drawing $1\frac{1}{2}$d per scholar per annum from each of the schools in the circuit, it soon became a self-supporting institution providing open access to 'useful and choice works and various religious periodicals', for the use and benefit of teachers and pupils alike.[48]

The Connexional Union was and remained, for fairly obvious reasons, a peculiarly Methodist institution. But the idea which informed it, and the organisational impetus which directed its subsequent development, were, as Keighley's Congregational historian knew well, common to all the major denominations at the time. Certainly, administrative centralisation and educational denominalisation (or differentiation) became the norm in most local Sunday schools after 1870. Why? There were, of course, many reasons. To some degree, the simple imperative of demographic change demanded a greater degree of co-ordination in the activities of Sunday schools. So many more children meant, inevitably, many more pupils and led inexorably to much more organisation. To a certain extent, it also represented something of a shift, common across the denominational spectrum, in contemporary evangelical effort, that is, a shift away from mature but incorrigible adulthood and towards impressionable but promising youth. But neither of these factors explains its profoundly significant and increasingly characteristic partisanship. More than any other single cause, it was a direct, explicit and contingent response, as the non-established churches saw it especially, to the denominational and doctrinal implications of the 1870 Education Act.

That non-established religious opinion was outraged by the Act has long been well known. That it understood its voluntary, denominational schools to be particularly threatened by the Act's compulsory provisions

---

[45]   KPL, 105D77/2/21/13/6, Temple Street Wesleyan Sunday School, Committee Minute Book, 28 April 1876.

[46]   *Ibid.*, 18 September 1876.

[47]   KPL, 105077/2/4/2/a, Devonshire Park Wesleyan Methodist Sunday School Minute Book, 8 October 1880.

[48]   *Ibid.*, 24 June 1884.

has been similarly well documented.[49] The challenge to dissenting
Sunday schools which it presented has been less widely acknowledged.
Yet it was immediately identified. And not just by far-sighted central
authorities either. In that very year, Pastor Townsend of Hanover
Street Methodist New Connexion Chapel argued at a teachers' meeting
in the attached school that, more than anything else, 'the future of
Sunday Schools is a question that must engage the most anxious
thought of those concerned in their management'. This was because
the hated 'education bill [had] devolved ... the religious training of the
young ... purely on the Christian Churches'. Consequently, it was
'now doubly important to make our Sunday Schools the medium of
impressing spiritual knowledge on the young, so that increased
intelligence may be fully sanctified by religion'.[50] Nor was his a lone
voice. Speaking on the occasion of the laying of the foundation stone of
the new Harrison Road Congregational Sunday School, in August
1872, the Reverend J.C. Gray, first observing, caustically, that 'the
general trend of recent measures of education ... has ... been to
secularise, to a very considerable extent, our day school instruction',
then concluded that its implications would be 'to throw the onus of
religious education of the masses of the people more than before on the
Sunday schools'.[51]

If so, then a threat was also an opportunity, for as the state assumed
such compulsory, universal and elementary powers so voluntary
authorities were permitted a rather particular indulgence. Specifically,
it relieved them, first in theory and then increasingly in practice, of
their erstwhile obligation to provide for the secular education of the
people. It was not very long before they realised this. Hence the rather
different observations of an (anonymous) observer at the Halifax
Sunday School Union, during the centenary celebrations of 1880. '[A]n
instruction ... which until a few years ago comprehended the
elementary lessons of learning to read', was now, he argued, 'free' from
that 'drawback to religious education ... with the spread of compulsory
secular education'. Consequently, if only the churches could 'impose
their will' more powerfully on the schools, then, he insisted, 'it may be

---

[49] For a modern account of nonconformist reactions to the 1870 Education Act, see
      D.W. Bebbington, *The Nonconformist Conscience: Chapel and Politics, 1870–1914*
      (London, 1982), esp. pp. 127–31, and for the Roman Catholic Church, with special
      reference to Yorkshire, see J.F. Supple-Green, *The Catholic Revival in Yorkshire, 1850–
      1900* (Leeds, 1990), pp. 37–48.
[50] CDA, Misc. 57/2, Hanover Street Methodist New Connexion Chapel, Halifax,
      Teachers' Meeting Minute Book, 1 November 1870.
[51] CDA, CUR 1:188, Harrison Road Congregational Church, Halifax, Sunday School
      Minutes, 14 August 1872.

safely predicted that a further and still more fruitful field [would] lie before [them]'.[52]

Whatever the case, the field still had to be ploughed. No amount of connexional co-ordination, however stridently partisan, did that work or reaped the harvest of itself. National organisation of formal activity was one thing. Local influence over the concrete religious life – and denominational destination – of the scholars was quite another. One way of directing that life was to extend the logic of church extension to school building; quite simply to build church and school *together*. Contemporary officialdom, especially Methodist officialdom, urged this course of action on its associated societies. One Methodist manifesto of the time, for instance, 'earnestly entreat[ed] our friends . . . concerned in the future erection of chapels . . . to include in their plans provision . . . for their children'.[53] And, increasingly, they responded. So too did their competitors; so much so, in fact, that scarcely a church or a chapel was constructed in Halifax, Keighley or Denholme during the post-1870 boom without a contiguous, and associated, Sunday school. And sometimes that meant literally contiguous. Fairfield Methodist Chapel in Halifax began life as a 'New School-Chapel' on Gibbet Road on 14 January 1873.[54] Marlborough Street Congregational Chapel in Keighley was opened on 13 February 1874 as 'a school-chapel . . . consisting of an upper-room for public worship, with a schoolroom and two class-rooms underneath'.[55] Alice Street Primitive Methodist Chapel, also in Keighley, was 'projected [as] New Chapel and Schools' in 1891.[56]

The simple physical contiguity of church and school was not, of itself, entirely novel to the last third of the nineteenth century. What was new was its frequency: it became the commonplace rather than the exception. Also its intensity: it became the literal part of the great project for the 'extension of the Sunday schools'.[57] This project was designed, in the words of one (Anglican) contemporary, to transform mere 'assembl[ies] of the young' into 'societ[ies] for preserving youth . . . in the doctrine and love of Divine Scripture'. More specifically, it was intended to make 'our Sunday school work [more] effectual'. This was to be achieved partly through proximity; more still through the agency of a 'definite

---

[52] *Halifax Guardian*, 22 May 1880; unfortunately, neither the name of the speaker nor his denominational affiliation is revealed in this source.

[53] Anon., *Principles on Which Methodist Schools Should Be Conducted*, p. 5.

[54] Anon., *Church Records from 'Lincoln Academy' to Fairfield Methodist Church, 1872–1934* (Halifax, 1934), p. 3.

[55] Sugden, *Brief History of Knowle Park*, p. 9.

[56] KPL, 105D77/2/1/3/a, Alice Street Primitive Methodist Chapel, Trustees' Meeting Minute Book, 10 September 1891.

[57] *Rhodes Street, Jubilee Celebrations*, p. 17.

programme' of instruction which would make the children 'feel ... that they are present not only at school but at service'.[58] By the means of that 'programme' contemporary churchmen and ministers hoped to end the 'separate' standing of 'church and school'.[59] And in this way, they trusted that Sunday school would 'take its proper place'[60] as a nursery for the church; correspondingly, that 'the Church [would] accept as a most sacred trust the injunction of our Lord: "Suffer little children, come unto me"'.[61]

To transform these assemblies of the young into places where youth might be preserved in a love of the Lord required a subtle, but none the less a very significant, reinterpretation of the proper ends of scholarly life and school discipline. Specifically, it demanded that Sunday school teachers be able to impose upon their pupils an attitude of devout reverence. Those traditional behavioural skills which schools had cultivated in their pupils – respectability, restraint and orderliness – were no guarantees of reverence, whether or not they were bulwarks of the social order. So, to a hitherto unprecedented extent, Sunday schools after 1870 taught the arts of reverent behaviour to their young (and not so young) charges. To be sure, they did not repudiate the old virtues; rather they infused them with a novel, or an intensified, sacred content. In this way, they subtly reinterpreted respectability as a divine duty, restraint as an aspect of ritual submission, and orderliness as a part of reverential behaviour, faithfully conducted.

Precisely what constituted reverential behaviour was by no means universally agreed upon. But there were some areas of consensus. To some extent, it was a question of attitudes. It was widely believed that scholars should 'behave with seriousness [when] singing the praises of God', and that they should be required to 'keep [their bodies] in a position of devotion [during] prayer'.[62] But what was seriousness? Increasingly, seriousness meant co-ordinated participation. And what was devotion? Increasingly devotion meant ritual submission. Schools were 'opened and closed with singing and prayer'.[63] To improve the singing, scholars were invited to join 'singing class[es]'.[64] To improve

[58] H.M.C., 'All Saints', *KPCM*, vol. 18, no. 8, August 1895 (no page number).
[59] CDA, CUR 1:188, Harrison Road Congregational Church, Halifax, Sunday School Minutes, 30 September 1903; a speech by A.E. Hutton, at Yorkshire Congregational Conference held in Leeds, September 1903, recorded by Mr Hooson.
[60] *Rhodes Street, Jubilee Celebrations*, p. 17.
[61] Francis Pigou, *Odds and Ends* (London, 1903), p. 75.
[62] CDA, Misc. 57/2, Hanover Street Methodist New Connexion Sunday School, Teachers' Meeting Minute Book, 1 October 1872.
[63] Anon., *Principles on Which Methodist Sunday Schools Should Be Conducted*, p. 5.
[64] CDA, CUR 1:188, Harrison Road Congregational Church, Halifax, Sunday School Minutes, Teachers' Meeting, 11 December 1884.

the prayers, they were required to kneel: at Hanover Street Methodist New Chapel in Halifax as early as 1870;[65] at Victoria Park Wesleyan Methodist School in Keighley, as late as 1903.[66] More typical perhaps, at least chronologically, was the example of Park Lane Primitive Methodist School, whose teachers resolved that 'the scholars kneel during prayer ... commenc[ing] ... next Sunday', on 18 March 1894.[67]

In this way, through a combination of exhortation and commendation, Sunday school teachers sought to impose definite standards of reverential behaviour upon their scholars. But the pursuit of these standards was rarely slavish. Nor was it usually blinkered, for though it was an end in itself, it was also a means to a greater end. This was rooted in the idea that only through reverence, that is, through the ritual submission of the self to the forms of divine service, was true – religious – learning possible. Only a reverent child, so the argument went, would be amenable to a 'definite programme of instruction'. And what *that* meant, more and more, was an efficient grounding in doctrinal integrity. To take one example: Temple Street's rule book for 1865 declared in its 'General Regulations' that:

As the religious improvement of the scholars forms the leading object of the school, all the scholars shall be regularly taught the First and Second Wesleyan Catechisms, and religious instruction shall be communicated every Sabbath afternoon by addresses from the Superintendent ... The Scriptures shall be used as a reading book, the teachers explaining the lesson, and supplementing them by religious instruction and information as they may think proper.[68]

Fifteen years later, a new rule significantly tightened that definition: 'Its main object [i.e. the object of school] shall be to instruct and train scholars in the doctrines, privileges, and duties of the Christian religion. The Holy Scriptures and the catechisms of the Wesleyan Methodists shall be used as a means of such instruction and training'.[69] But strict instruction did not preclude a high quality of teaching. For instance, 'the elementary books employed in teaching even the younger children shall be such as to contain the largest portion of Scriptural instruction, and the Holy Scriptures shall be regularly used by all who are sufficiently advanced'.[70] So long as it remained orthodox: 'Catechetical exercises all

---

[65] CDA, Misc. 287/26, Hanover Street Methodist New Connexion Chapel, Halifax, Leaders' Meeting Minute Book, 6 September 1870.

[66] KPL, 105D77/2/22/15/c, Victoria Park Sunday School, Keighley, Teachers' (and Officers') Meeting Minute Book, 16 March 1903.

[67] KPL, 105D77/2/15/1/a, Park Lane Primitive Methodist Sunday School Minute Book, 18 March 1894.

[68] *Temple Street, Rules*, p. 6.

[69] *Principles on Which Wesleyan Sunday Schools Should Be Conducted*, p. 1.

[70] *Ibid.*, p. 5.

form a constant part of the system of the school, and the catechisms used shall be those published under the sanction of the Wesleyan Methodist Conference'.[71] Finally, and pointedly, it was ruled that 'neither the art of writing, nor any branch of merely secular knowledge, shall be taught on the Lord's Day'.[72]

Concern for systematic scriptural and catechetical teaching was increasingly common in Sunday schools of all denominations throughout the 1870s. The ubiquitous Pigou, for instance, introduced 'public catechising' at St John the Baptist Church of England Sunday School, in 1876.[73] A year later, the teachers of Devonshire Park Wesleyan Methodist School 'agreed to provide the children with a catechism that they learn at home'.[74] Two years after that, Heber Street decided 'that the Catechism be taught every Sunday morning'.[75] In 1880, Harrison Road Congregational Church teachers' meeting resolved, unanimously, to 'adopt ... the use of [the] catechism in the school'.[76] Then Temple Street Wesleyan Methodists voted to distribute a 'Tablet' with the catechism written on it to all scholars; all for the purpose of regular 'repetition'.[77] At much the same time, Queen's Road Primitive Methodists distributed 'Catechism Cards ... to all scholars under twelve years of age', imploring 'the teachers of those classes above twelve ... to impress the matter contained on the card to their scholars ... [and] to get them to receive the card and become catechism members'.[78] For some schools, especially for some Methodist schools, the intensification of religious instruction was accompanied at this time by a number of small but significant innovations in the religious content of their scholarly instruction. Systematic use of the Lord's Prayer made its way into the curricula. Queen's Road Methodist New Connexion School in Halifax introduced it into their school services in 1879;[79] some nine years later, the Primitive Methodist Chapel on the same road, and of the same name, resolved that it be 'repeat[ed] ... by classes ... in

71 *Ibid.*, p. 4.
72 *Ibid.*, p. 5.
73 Pigou, 'A Pastoral Letter to His Parishioners', p. 6.
74 KPL, 105D77/2/4/2/a, Devonshire Park Wesleyan Methodist Sunday School Minute Book, 24 October 1877.
75 KPL, 105D77, Heber Street Wesleyan Methodist Sunday School Minute Book of the Committee, 18 August 1879.
76 CDA, CUR 1:188, Harrison Road Congregational Sunday School Minute Book, 22 February 1880.
77 KPL, 105D77/2/12/11/a, Temple Street Wesleyan Methodist Sunday School Committee Minute Book, 20 November 1882.
78 CDA, Misc. 287:5–10, Gibbet Road, Queen's Road, Fairfield Primitive Methodist Sunday School Minute Book, 5 August 1884.
79 CDA, Misc. 287/40, Queen's Road Methodist New Connexion Sunday School Minutes, 3 June 1879.

school'.[80] Finally, in an interesting twist to the tale, Victoria Park Wesleyan Methodist School resolved that it 'be sung' in all their departments, in 1903.[81] Other departures along these lines included the 'repetit[ion] of the Ten Commandments after the Superintendents'' by all scholars, a practice adopted 'once a month' by Queen's Road Primitives in 1886.[82]

A new or a newly intensified régime of reverent behaviour and dedicated learning together added up, in most Sunday schools by the mid-1880s, to something like 'a definite programme of instruction'. Gradually, too, that programme solidified into a standardised curriculum. The example of Heber Street Wesleyan Methodist School was probably typical in this respect. Proceedings began there with 'Teacher's Roll' at 9.30 a.m. Singing and prayer followed at 9.35 a.m., lasting for twenty-five minutes. Catechism and scripture lessons occupied the next half-hour. After an interval of five minutes for singing, there was a twenty-minute address, followed by more singing, more prayer and a benediction, before dismissal of the scholars from morning school at 11.00 a.m. Afternoon school began at 1.30 p.m., with a second roll. Singing and prayer followed for ten minutes, then scripture lessons for thirty-five minutes. A break of five minutes was then permitted before service, and five minutes' more singing attuned the scholars (perhaps literally as well as metaphorically) to their entry into chapel.[83]

What were the tests for the success of this new venture? The simplest, of course, was numerical attendance. Continuing high levels of attendance indicated at least a minimal level of popular support. Previously, successful Sunday schools had tended to presume the regular attendance of their scholars. The rule book of Temple Street School in 1865, for instance, simply trusted that '[e]very scholar shall be present at the appointed hour at which the School opens'.[84] But the 'connexional schools' of the following generation actively attempted to make this ideal a reality. Fairly typical in this respect, ironically, was Temple Street itself. In 1876, the Sunday school committee there resolved to 'register ... the attendance of scholars in future [as] present, late or absent, and not the position of the scholar in class as heretofore'.[85] Six years later,

80   CDA, Misc. 287:5–10, Queen's Road Primitive Methodist Sunday School Minute Book, 24 January 1888.
81   KPL, 105D77/2/22/15/c, Victoria Park Wesleyan Methodist Sunday School, Keighley, Teachers' (and Officers') Meetings Minute Book, 2 February 1903.
82   CDA, Misc. 287:5–10, Queen's Road Primitive Methodist Sunday School Minute Book, 6 April 1886.
83   *Heber Street, Rules*, p. 8.
84   *Rules and Regulations for the Wesleyan Methodist Sunday School*, p. 7.
85   KPL, 105D77/2/21/13/b/i, Temple Street Wesleyan Sunday School, Committee Meeting Minute Book, 18 September 1876.

the same body empowered 'teachers ... and if they are not able ... two scholars [to be] ... appointed' to 'visit' irregular attenders.[86] Then, just a little later that same year, they established the mechanism which gradually became common throughout the Keighley Wesleyan Methodist Circuit, and far beyond, around this time: the 'Star-System' of registration and rewards.[87]

The 'Star-System' was exactly what its name suggests: a method of registering attendance, and of encouraging pupils to attend school, by issuing its pupils with a card onto which was stamped a 'star' each morning and afternoon, subject to prompt, continuous attendance. The number of such stars awarded to each pupil was calculated annually and these claiming the highest number of stars were awarded a cash prize. The value of those prizes was not negligible. For instance, Victoria Wesleyan Sunday School, Keighley, awarded first prizes of up to 3s, second prizes of up to 2s and third prizes of about 1s, in 1885.[88] Nor was the number given necessarily small. Northgate End Unitarian Sunday School, Halifax, distributed 49 such prizes amongst a total of 255 pupils in 1885.[89] And the school was more generous still, awarding 55 'good attendance' awards to its 250 pupils the following year. Clearly, the system was working.[90]

The notion of rewards for regular, prompt attendance was not new in 1870. What was new was the regularity and comprehensiveness which it assumed under the 'Star-System'. What was perhaps more significant still was the speed with which the principle was extended beyond the simplicities of physical presence to the complexities of intellectual comprehension. Nor that the two were easily separable; Devonshire Park School in Keighley actually began its 'rewards system' in 1878 by specifically linking 'attendance ... good behaviour' and a capacity (or willingness) 'correctly ... to repeat ... The [Catechism] Tablet'.[91] Temple Street similarly insisted that 'repetition of the Catechism on the Tablet be included with the attendance [sic] in the reward scheme'.[92] Gradually, however, the two were separated, both in the minds of the teachers and in the practices of the schools. And with that distinction arose an altogether more sophisticated notion of testing: the principle of examination.

[86]   Ibid., 3 July 1882.   [87]   Ibid., 20 November 1882.
[88]   KPL, 105D77/2/22/15/a, Victoria Park Sunday School Minutes, 16 March 1885.
[89]   CDA, NEC 179, Northgate End Chapel, Reports of Sunday School Committees, Report for Year Ending September 1885.
[90]   Ibid., September 1886.
[91]   105D77/2/4/2/a, Devonshire Park Wesleyan Methodist Church, Sunday School Minute Book, 31 December 1878.
[92]   KPL, 105D77/2/21/13/b/i, Temple Street Wesleyan Sunday School Committee Meeting, Minute Book, 20 November 1882.

To a modern sensibility, this may seem an obvious development. For the later nineteenth-century Sunday school, it was a revolutionary innovation. To be sure, it could only have arisen subsequent to the establishment of a Union system. But that was sufficient grounds, not a cause. This was rooted in the desire of the schools to impart religious knowledge to their charges, and to find out just how successful they had been in that pursuit. Salem Methodist New Connexion was probably the first circuit in Halifax to adopt this practice, 'recommend[ing] all our schools to enter heartily into the examinations that are going to be held under the auspices of the Sunday School Union' as early as 1880.[93] The following year, Queen's Road New Connexion Methodists, also in Halifax, resolved to empower 'our representatives to the Sunday School Union ... to vote for the scripture examination'.[94] The Halifax 'Congregational Union' began its own version of a 'circuit' scripture examination around 1885. Harrison Road's teachers were implored 'to urge upon their scholars the desirability of going in for the ... examination' during the same year.[95] Keighley seems to have been a bit slower on the uptake. Teachers at Temple Street Methodist School, Keighley, for instance, 'recommended that a competitive examination of the scholars on the catechism and scripture lessons for each quarter be instituted and that the same be confined to written papers' in 1882.[96] Whatever the case, the practice soon became common through West Yorkshire. Indeed, it was almost obligatory by the time Queen's Road Primitive Methodists voted to 'enter competitive examination for the scholars' in 1898.[97]

Organisational diversification, social comprehensiveness and the pursuit of impressionable youth

Yet even so sophisticated a practice as examining taught courses did not address the critical question of institutional transfer. It did not address the fundamental test of Sunday school defined as a 'nursery for the church'. Put another way, it might have ensured – it probably did ensure – an altogether better (religiously) informed population. But that did not

[93] CDA, MR 77, Halifax, Methodist New Connexion, Salem Circuit, Quarterly Meeting Minute Book, 25 October 1880.
[94] CDA, Misc. 287/40, Queen's Road, Methodist New Connexion Sunday School Minute Book, 24 July 1881.
[95] CDA, CUR 1:188, Harrison Road Congregational Church, Halifax, Sunday School Minute Book, 5 November 1884.
[96] KPL, 105D77/2/21/13/b/ii, Temple Street Wesleyan Methodist Sunday School Minute Book, 8 December 1892.
[97] CDA, Misc. 287:5–10, Gibbet Road, Queen's Road, Fairfield Primitive Methodist Sunday School Minute Book, 29 August 1898.

guarantee a truly worshipping people. Contemporaries were aware of this. Indeed, it was precisely their concern about Sunday school as an intermediate *ecclesiastical* institution which made them aware of it. This induced the more sophisticated amongst them actually to attempt to calculate its extent. A caustic notice in Halifax's *Congregational Magazine* as early as 1888 lamented that of '80 per cent of . . . children . . . who at some time . . . pass through Sunday schools . . . about one in ten . . . reach our churches'.[98] Evaluating the 'reasons for failure', this authority paid full tribute to contemporary developments in Sunday school organisation, association and ethos which had recently ensured that 'an irresistible message of God's love and Christ's life and death' had come to form the 'practical' basis of its 'teaching'. Yet he noted that the supposedly 'irresistible message' had not in fact 'taught' a large number to 'live the Christlike life'.[99] Why not? He suggested three possibilities: the quality of the teaching; the attitude of the ministry; and the nature of senior classes.

At first sight, these may appear to be quite disparate – almost unconnected – causes of failure. Yet they all raised the question of integration, albeit in rather different ways, for the problem of teaching, or of 'teaching power', after 1870, was less a matter of content than of context. In the Congregational Church especially, it was often little more than a euphemism for middle-class detachment, or non-integration. Put more bluntly, as expressed in Mr Scales's own words, this was the scandal of those 'gentlemen . . . who would probably be much offended if . . . told . . . they . . . were not Christian[s]' yet who 'refused to allow [their] daughters to teach at Sunday School because fever might be contracted there'.[100] More widely, it was the absence from Sunday school of 'our middle class children' both as scholars and as teachers, for they were the 'boys . . . and girls' who could provide the 'good moral influence of modest . . . educated . . . habit' to their peers in class. And some of them at least might grow up into 'men and women' able to impart the fruits of 'well furnished minds' to 'brisk and lively youngsters'.[101]

Even in so far as this was an accusation which was generally true, it was not a fault of institutional existence which was easily put right. Moreover, for many churches and chapels – including at least some Congregational churches and chapels locally – the problem never arose. This was for the simple reason that there were no members of the redundant middle classes amongst their social constituencies. However, the question of the 'position taken by our ministers' was rather different. Here, the problem was partly the unattractiveness of the service, viewed

[98] Walter H. Scales, 'Reasons for Failure', *HDCM*, vol. 6, no. 5, May 1888, p. 97.
[99] *Ibid.*, p. 98.   [100] *Ibid.*   [101] *Ibid.*, p. 99.

from the child's standpoint; and partly the ministers' 'fear' of 'intruding in the business of the school', seen from the teacher's angle.[102] And for this, some potential solutions were within the grasp of the authorities. Traditional practice had assumed the obligation of scholars to attend chapel. Temple Street's rule book of 1865 said as much.[103] But it could not, in reality, force the issue. Subtle inducement could make it a more attractive proposition. In 1888, a teachers' meeting there voted 'to give a mark [of] some value attached for attendance at chapel on Sunday mornings' and (more blatantly still) to provide 'a free tea to the parents and the scholars so that attendance at Chapel on Sunday mornings ... may be laid before them [sic]'.[104] On the other side, ministers who could not be forced to teach in school might nevertheless be persuaded to provide 'children's services', with 'sermons, hymns and lessons adapted to children's capacity and needs' in church itself.[105] Increasingly they did exactly that.[106]

But the critical question, judged from the viewpoint of the Sunday schools themselves, was actually less a matter of institutional integration, or even of ministerial co-operation, than of the simple fact that 'our senior classes are often too small'.[107] They were too small for the simplest of reasons. Most scholars usually left school before they joined such classes, or soon after joining them. That was very important. Indeed, no aspect of the general reappraisal of Sunday schools after 1870 was more important than the fate of the 'senior classes',[108] for it was in these classes, above all, that the schools hoped to encourage 'real study of the doctrines of the Bible'. Channelling older, more mature, students into 'separate classrooms', whether 'towards the close of Sunday afternoon, or on some convenient weeknight' they thereby sought, through 'Christian experience', to stimulate the development of 'Christian sensibility ... and ... character' amongst their charges. And by that, they meant a sensibility and character to be *learned* in school, but *transferable* to church.[109]

To this end, the number of such classes ballooned after 1870, so much so that it was rare for a school to be without one, or more, less than a generation later. But their development did not, in itself, solve the essential problem of Sunday schools. That problem, as contemporaries increasingly realised, was only partially rooted in the pedagogical

---

[102] *Ibid.*, p. 100.   [103] *Temple Street, Rules*, p. 5.
[104] KPL, 105D77/2/21/13/b/ii, Temple Street Wesleyan Methodist Sunday School Minute Book, 6 November 1885.
[105] Scales, 'Reasons for Failure', p. 100.
[106] See below, ch. 7, pp. 309–10.   [107] Scales, 'Reasons for Failure', p. 99.
[108] *Methodist New Connexion Chapel, Hanover Street, Yearly Handbook, 1877*, p. 48.
[109] *Principles on Which Methodist Sunday Schools Should Be Conducted*, pp. 5, 14.

difficulties of inadequate Christian training. It was also grounded in the sociological paradox of Sunday school, as perceived by contemporary youth. This was the paradox of sufficiency. Put simply, what ecclesiastical authority regarded as preparation, too many adolescents took for completion of the religious life. To overcome that conundrum, contemporary ecclesiastical authority envisaged a fundamental re-evaluation of the whole relationship between school and church as traditionally understood. To do that, it had to forge an institution which was sufficiently *unlike* church to induce a continuing (and preferably rising) number of young persons to remain in voluntary association with it. Yet it had to sustain a society which would convince those same students of the attractions of – indeed train them in their proper duties towards – regular, adult worship.

This, after 1870, it increasingly tried to do. The solution which it hit upon was the mechanism of institutional diversity. In short, auxiliaries for the Sunday schools; or, as one local authority put it, sports clubs, recreation rooms, reading societies and the rest, all 'centred ... on ... local Sunday schools'.[110] The result was nothing less than a 'revolution ... in the whole conception' of the proper relationship of 'young folks to the church'. This was true in two senses. First, in their more religiously elevated, or strictly speaking more denominationally defined, role schools achieved a new 'realiz[ation] ... of ... the value of work amongst the young' at this time. Secondly, in their pursuit of a more socially dynamic, associational profile, they shed much of that 'erstwhile puritan ... confusion ... of innocent amusement with vice' by which they had once been marked.[111] Suddenly, it seemed, 'plays, dances and pantomimes became regular features of Sunday school activity'.[112]

Sunday school auxiliaries paralleled and duplicated church auxiliaries. Indeed, it is important not to exaggerate the degree of institutional distinction involved. After all, Sunday schools themselves were increasingly defined as associational auxiliary political organisations aftter 1870. And many of the auxiliaries of church organisation were very closely replicated in school. At Northgate End, for instance, the two societies effectively shared the Band of Hope and the Penny Savings Bank. But there were some auxiliaries which were peculiar to Sunday school. Again at Northgate End, these included a Mutual Improvement Society, established no later than 1868.[113] Shortly afterwards, the school, on its

[110] Harwood, *Centenary Story, 1848–1948*, p. 35.
[111] *Rhodes Street Jubilee Celebrations*, pp. 17–18.
[112] Harwood, *Centenary Story, 1848–1948*, p. 35.
[113] CDA, NEC 175, Northgate End Chapel, Halifax, Sunday School Administration, 1868 (Report for 1867).

own initiative, seems to have set up a Young Men's Reading Class; and then, for a similar purpose, a Girls' Evening Group.[114] A Violin Class followed in 1886 (probably attached to the Orchestral Society),[115] then a Football Club in 1891.[116]

It is impossible to be certain whether or not this was a complete list. What is clear is that by the early 1890s, Northgate End Sunday School was maintaining at least half a dozen, and possibly ten or even more, associated auxiliary societies. It is also clear that they, in their turn, increasingly sustained the school. Some were large in number. The Football Club certainly seems to have been very popular. And those which were smaller, such as the Mutual Improvement Society, frequently compensated for their paucity of numbers by sustaining the largest number of older members. In that way, they succeeded together in maintaining a great number of persons in the school, and a larger proportion of mature individuals especially, for a longer period of time than had previously proved possible. As such, they were of immediate practical use. Hence the 'Young Men's Class' at Northgate End was almost immediately required 'to assist in keeping order in the school at the close'.[117] But how could mere school assistants be turned into church regulars? At Northgate End, as elsewhere, one auxiliary especially was charged with that task. This was the Mutual Improvement Society.

Mutual improvement and the bridge between church and school

In a talk given to the Sowerby Division of the Conference of Youth in January 1911, the Reverend John Naylor of St John the Baptist Parish Church, Halifax, attempted to delineate what he called 'Some Factors in the Making of the Soul in Halifax Parish'.[118] He identified three groups of factors: religious, educational and artistic. Amongst the educational factors he listed: day schools, Sunday schools, newspapers, libraries, scientific societies, mechanics institutes, public lectures and mutual improvement societies.[119] His description of 'mutuals' was by no means

---

[114] CDA, NEC 175, Northgate End Chapel, Halifax, Sunday School Administration, 1869 (Report for 1868).

[115] CDA, NEC 179, Northgate End Chapel, Halifax, Reports of the Sunday School Committees, Report for the Year Ending September 1886.

[116] CDA, NEC 175, Northgate End Chapel, Halifax, Sunday School Administration, 3 November 1891.

[117] CDA, NEC 175, Northgate End Chapel, Halifax, Sunday School Administration, 12 September 1899.

[118] CDA (HTC), John Naylor, *Some Factors in the Making of the Soul in Halifax Parish* (Halifax, 1911).

[119] *Ibid.*, p. 13. Despite the importance of mutual improvement societies in working-class

uncritical. '[I]t is easy', he noted, 'to smile at the rhetoric, faulty logic, shallow knowledge and stubborn cocksureness which have often marred the essays and speeches of those mutuals.' But, he insisted, 'they have done invaluable service in educing the latent powers of speech and reason of many of our ablest men during the last sixty years. They have been the training schools of our municipal statesmen. They have discovered many a preacher.'[120] So they had. Arthur Henderson, the great socialist statesmen of the inter-war years, served his elocutionary and political apprenticeship in the mutuals of Keighley.[121] Other, lesser lights followed from the mutuals of Halifax and Denholme, and all in a remarkably short period of time.

The first mutual certainly known in Halifax was connected with Square Congregational Church. It opened in 1845.[122] The first in Keighley, or at least the first associated with a church, was probably established at Keighley Baptist Chapel in Slack Lane, established around 1859.[123] The first religious mutual in Denholme may have emerged as late as 1875, founded after a teachers' meeting of Southgate General Baptist Church Sabbath School, which determined on 29 November to 'attempt to form a M[utual] I[mprovement] S[ociety] for all our young men'.[124] Whatever the facts of its origin, institutional proliferation followed quickly in all three towns. Naylor recorded that '[m]any churches soon followed the example of Square', Halifax, noting that 'the most fruitful decade of their genesis seems to have been the sixties'.[125] A case might, in fact, be made for the 1870s. In any case, by 1880 at the latest, mutuals were attached to almost every local church and school. Membership of these societies varied from place to place, even from time to time. But an absolute minimum of twenty persons per society seems a reasonable estimate. If so, there were probably about 2,000 young men in Halifax, nearly 1,000 in Keighley and perhaps 150 in Denholme actively engaged in the task of self-improvement at the turn of the twentieth century.[126]

These mutuals came into the world not only for the mental and moral

culture, relatively little has been written about them. For instance, a recent study of popular co-operative ideas and institutions, Stephen Yeo (ed.), *New Views of Co-operation* (London, 1988), makes no mention of them.

[120] Naylor, *Some Factors*, p. 14.
[121] McKibbin, 'Why Was There No Marxism in Great Britain?', p. 308.
[122] Naylor, *Some Factors*, p. 14.
[123] Rhodes, *Keighley Baptist History*, p. 117.
[124] Southgate Baptist Chapel, Denholme, Sabbath School Minute Book, 29 November 1875; unpub. MS in the private possession of Mr A. Vine.
[125] Naylor, *Some Factors*, p. 14.
[126] Author's estimate; based upon a representative sample of Sunday school and mutual improvement society records.

improvement of their members but also, as their founders openly and candidly acknowledged, 'to keep the Young Men more closely allied to the Sunday School'.[127] Through this device, local church authorities explicitly sought 'to provide a connecting link between the school and the church', and to seek a 'spiritual remedy', and not merely a 'social and recreative expedient', in order to stem the flow of 'so many scholars ... out of the school' and 'the church'.[128] How? Early discussions at Southgate Baptist Church, Denholme, Mutual Improvement Society, are suggestive in this respect. Having determined to form a mutual for the 'religious and mental improvement of its members', the committee presented a syllabus of '[d]evotion[al] Biblical study and literary improvement'.[129] The method of study was distinctive: a written paper, or talk, was presented by one member to the whole group. Subsequently, each member of the group, in turn, discussed the issues it raised, observing strict time limits in order to do so. Southgate Committee determined that the 'lecturer or reader be allowed to talk or read only for one hour', and that subsequently 'each member, after the lecture has finished, be allowed 5 minutes in which to speak or ask the lecturer questions and the lecturer be allowed 10 minutes to reply'.[130] One hour was a long time. Few other societies were quite so demanding. St Peter's Church of England, Keighley, on establishing a mutual in 1878, resolved that 'papers or introductory addresses shall not exceed twenty minutes in length'. There too, 'subsequent speakers' were 'limited to five minutes, with the exception of allowing ten minutes for final reply'.[131]

The emphasis placed upon reading out loud, and upon ex tempore critical response from an engaged audience, evident in those extracts, was crucial. Indeed, it was the defining characteristic of a mutual, for though they pursued other activities, and though they encouraged other skills, they valued and taught the arts of reading aloud and speaking up above all. Everything, at least ostensibly, was directed to that end. As Francis Millson, Pastor of Northgate Unitarian Chapel, Halifax, observed, even 'our entertainments were not got up simply for the enjoyment of those who came to listen, but to show the people what they

---

[127] CDA, CUR 1:199, Harrison Road Congregational Chapel, Halifax, Young Men's Christian Association, Annual Report; Report of the Secretary of the Mutual Improvement Society (no page number).

[128] CDA, CUR 1:150, *Harrison Road Congregational Chapel, Halifax, Church Manual, 1897* (Halifax, 1897), p. 6.

[129] Southgate Baptist Chapel, Denholme, Mutual Improvement Society, Minute Book, 13 December 1875; unpub. MS in the private possession of Mr A. Vine.

[130] *Ibid.*, 21 January 1876.

[131] BDA, 74D83/1/11, Anon., *KPCM*, vol. 1, no. 3, March 1878 (no page number).

[i.e. the class] had learnt'.[132] In the Reverend Naylor's words, they had learned 'to utilise discussion [or drama, or entertainment] as a means of self-expression'. And not as any means of self-expression; but rather as that form which flourished in 'the art of public speaking ... as attained only by constant and persevering practice'.[133]

They did not only learn to speak in public. To a pedagogical end was attached an explicit social purpose: mutuality. The proper end of a mutual improvement society was mutual improvement; that is, for each to seek to teach the others for the mutual advantage of all. J. Blatchford, Secretary of the Harrison Road Congregational Church, Halifax, Mutual Improvement Society, remarked that 'we want [our members] to try to improve one another, to try to make others as good as themselves and not to try to make themselves better than others ... [O]ur aim must be not to be first, but last, not to excel others, but to excel ourselves.'[134] It was in the spirit of mutual improvement that the ideal of mutual criticism found its proper definition. That definition was expressed, with an exquisite insensitivity to human foibles, in the rule book of Temple Street Wesleyan Methodist Chapel, Keighley, Mutual Improvement Society, which decreed, as a matter of policy, that 'no member shall consider any criticism, however severe, which the Chairman may deem honourable, as a cause for offence'.[135]

In this way, the egalitarianism of mutual improvement did not indulge any of the woollier forms of the ideal of fraternity. Instead, it embraced a principle, equally acknowledged by all participants, that 'the discipline which is administered in criticism is not often painful, and it is always wholesome'.[136] So much brutal openness may have had a sociological dimension. With one exception, significantly perhaps Northgate End Unitarian, mutuals were exclusively adolescent male institutions. Lower age limits, usually in the early teens, were firmly set. Upper age limits were adhered to more by convention.[137] But mutual improvement did not pander to the culture of the adolescent. On the contrary, it projected a moral purpose, as well as a procedural method, for his improvement. 'Mutuality' stood, full square, against purposeless

---

[132] CDA, NEC 179, Northgate End Unitarian Chapel, Halifax, Sunday School Elocution Society Minute Book, 11 January 1892.

[133] Naylor, *Some Factors*, p. 13.

[134] CDA, CUR 1:199, Harrison Road Congregational Chapel, Halifax, Young Men's Christian Association Annual Report, 1870; Report of the Secretary of the Mutual Improvement Society (no page number).

[135] KPL, 105D77/2/21/3/b, Temple Street Church Guild (and Mutual Improvement Society) Minute Book, 4 November 1910.

[136] Naylor, *Some Factors*, p. 13.

[137] CDA, NEC 179, Northgate End Unitarian Chapel, Halifax, Mutual Improvement Society Minute Book, 15 October 1893.

'killing of time'.[138] It also discouraged modern vices, especially individual weaknesses such as gambling and smoking. Indeed, specific prohibition of those abuses was actually written into the rule book of Northgate End Young Men's Club.[139]

To further the ethical ideal of egalitarian improvement, mutuals employed the methods of collective discipline and individual participation. They demanded a style of individual behaviour best characterised as serious, perhaps even as reverential. They encouraged members attending society meetings to behave as if they were not in pursuit of amusement; in other words, to be practical, to be quiet and dignified on arrival, and above all to respect the priority of collective activity by remaining in their places until the end of the evening.[140] Once in place, and under collective discipline, mutuals demanded the active participation of every person present in their proceedings, for just as the ideal of mutuality did not tolerate an unwarranted exhibition of the unrestrained ego, so it also discouraged, indeed prohibited, any of the more slothful expressions of personal liberty. Hence the Secretary of Harrison Road Society demanded, in 1870, with apparent success, that members be 'more orderly', that they refrain from 'behav[ing] ... so rudely ... as to compel him [i.e. the secretary] to resign'. But he also demanded, with similar success, that they abstain from 'sleep[ing] ... during meetings', or (still worse), from 'reading their library books while the essayist is reading his paper'.[141] Collective orderliness was, according to this understanding, the best context for individual response, and the sum of individual responses was the means of mutual improvement. He who did not respond, or did not participate, thereby denied the possibility of improvement to others, a heinous sin.

At least, that was true in theory, for it was much easier to impose collective orderliness than to elicit spontaneous individual response. Hence the peculiar concern in mutuals about the infirmities of what were known as 'sleeping members'.[142] Whether or not literally asleep,

---

[138] CDA, CUR 1:199, Harrison Road Congregational Chapel, Halifax, Young Men's Christian Association Annual Report, 1870; Report of the Secretary of the Mutual Improvement Society (no page number).

[139] CDA, NEC 179, Northgate End Unitarian Chapel, Halifax, Young Men's Club (and Mutual Improvement Society) Minute Book, 18 January 1892.

[140] CDA, CUR 1:199, Harrison Road Congregational Chapel, Halifax, Young Men's Christian Association Annual Report, 1868; Report of the Secretary of the Mutual Improvement Society (no page number).

[141] CDA, CUR 1:199, Harrison Road Congregational Chapel, Halifax, Young Men's Christian Association Annual Report 1870; Report of the Secretary of the Mutual Improvement Society (no page number).

[142] CDA, CUR 1:199, Harrison Road Congregational Chapel, Halifax, Young Men's Christian Association Annual Report, 1872; Report of the Secretary of the Mutual Improvement Society (no page number).

this particular form of reprobate attracted especial opprobrium precisely because he did not contribute to the mutual good. On occasion, therefore, the rules of procedure were altered to force his hand. Shortly after its foundation, Northgate End Young Men's Club adopted the debating device of so-called 'Sharp Practice'. Scraps of paper were put into a hat, '[e]ach piece of paper having a name of some subject on it, the hat was passed round ... [E]ach member in turn took a paper out, they having only to speak for five minutes each ... the following being the subjects, viz. "Education", "Socialism", "Invention", "Temperance", "Tobacco", "Music", "Sleeping", "Riding", "Home Rule", "Debates", and "Social Equality".'[143] Evidently, it was not a new idea. Nearly twenty years earlier, Harrison Road Mutual had introduced a similar practice in its society, known there as 'Disclosure of the Hat'. In this game, three subjects for discussion were written on cards and then placed in a hat, along with an appropriate number of blank cards up to the number of members present. The man who drew a card with a subject written upon it was obliged to speak about that topic for five minutes. Discussion followed. This practice was repeated at regular intervals.[144]

Artificial devices of this sort were designed to promote the art of speaking itself. They were concerned only secondarily with the content of that speech. The Secretary of Northgate End Young Men's Club acknowledged this hierarchy of priorities quite candidly. Commenting on the salutary effect of 'Sharp Practice', he remarked that 'he felt certain that a great amount of good [was] done' in this way 'for not only ... did [members] ... learn ... to speak better ... but they also ... derive[d] a certain amount of information which would perhaps help them in different ways'.[145] Yet it would be a travesty of the truth to conclude that those who organised reading and debate amongst young men under the auspices of mutual improvement societies were only concerned about form, and oblivious to the content of group discussion. Even to acquire 'the art of being able to give a comprehensible and graceful expression of one's sentiments in public'[146] presumed a reasonable understanding of the content of those sentiments. Nor was the

---

[143] CDA, NEC 179, Northgate End Unitarian Chapel, Halifax, Young Men's Club (and Mutual Improvement Society) Minute Book, 1 February 1892.

[144] CDA, CUR 1:199, Harrison Road Congregational Chapel, Halifax, Young Men's Christian Association Annual Report, 1874; Report of the Secretary of the Mutual Improvement Society (no page number).

[145] CDA, NEC 179, Northgate End Unitarian Chapel, Young Men's Club (and Mutual Improvement Society) Minute Book, 1 February 1892.

[146] CDA, CUR 1:199, Harrison Road Congregational Chapel, Halifax, Young Men's Christian Association Annual Report, 1881; Report of the Secretary of the Mutual Improvement Society (no page number).

syllabus limited solely to ethereal matters. If the intellectual ideal of improvement embraced something closer to a liberal theory of culture than a practical concept of knowledge, the complementary ethical ideal of seriousness, equally crucial to the goal of mutuality, allowed at least for the possibility of, and a more general openness to, the virtues of usefulness. Certainly the Harrison Road Society believed so. Its discussions for 1876 included subjects such as 'Iron', 'Wrought Iron' and 'Dyeing', on the grounds that 'such subjects we believe are calculated to teach and instruct those who come and listen to them that it is essential in these days that young men should know something of the various branches of industry other than those in which they may immediately be connected'.[147]

Yet what was taught and what was learned in mutuals were not always synonymous. Indeed, a certain level of pedagogic indeterminacy was implied, both in the ends and in the means of the ideal of mutual improvement. This was true of formal organisation and of informal arrangements, for whilst the incumbent minister of the mother church was, invariably, nominal president of the society, mutuals habitually ran themselves. Moreover, the membership, especially the active membership, was, by its very nature, largely adolescent and necessarily transient. Hence, what may have seemed to its progenitors a well-defined intermediary institution, a place where organised discussion furnished a reliable means for the acquisition of certain skills and values, subsequently crucial in church-work, appeared in an altogether more ambiguous light to those who passed through its offices. In reality, the question of purpose was continually contested. And the rules of mutual improvement, especially the conventions of mutuality and the cult of equality, made the questioning of purposes remarkably easy, and the imposition of authority difficult.

Consider the case of the Northgate Mutual. It was a fairly large society, of about forty members,[148] and it served a genuinely popular church. This was because Northgate End was, partly from necessity, partly from choice, a chapel which projected 'a simple faith ... most suited to the wants of the masses'.[149] It was also noted for a social ethos 'actively sympathetic and helpful to the interests of ... working people'.[150] And, in

---

[147] CDA, CUR 1:199, Harrison Road Congregational Chapel, Halifax, Young Men's Christian Association Annual Report, 1877; Report of the Secretary of the Mutual Improvement Society (no page number).

[148] CDA, NEC 19, *Northgate End Unitarian Chapel, Halifax, Chapel Manual, 1893* (Halifax, 1893), pp. 5–7.

[149] *Halifax Courier*, 12 June 1886.

[150] CDA, NEC 19, Northgate End Unitarian Chapel, Halifax, Chapel Meeting Minute Book, 29 January 1894.

the eyes of its incumbent minister at least, that implied an associated political doctrine specifically committed to 'a union of the classes'.[151] But, in 1893, discussion at Northgate End Mutual Improvement Society turned to an altogether more radical hue. This was not altogether surprising. It was a momentous year in Halifax. It witnessed the establishment both of the Independent Labour Party and of the Labour Church in the town.[152] Those events, occurring in the midst of an acute trade depression, signalled the demise, at least in Halifax, of what Patrick Joyce has called the 'attenuated paternalism' of West Riding factory culture.[153] The impact of politicisation and radicalisation amongst the masses was felt in many places. One such place was Northgate End Unitarian Chapel Mutual Improvement Society. Long used to a diet of popular history and English literature, with the occasional whiff of comparative religion, its members suddenly began to talk the language of political theory; specifically, they began to discuss the philosophical principles of ethical and practical socialism.

Matters came to a head around the end of the year. On 5 December 1893, one Mr Swales read a paper entitled 'Individualism and Collectivism'. In it, he condemned the prevailing 'ethic of society today', which he identified as 'competition or individualism', and which he excoriated as no more than the rationalisation of expropriation. Then he elucidated his own position. First, drawing on the work of Henry George, he compared the modern 'ownership of land' with the erstwhile 'ownership of black slaves', describing each as 'equally immoral'. Secondly, with due deference to the influence of Karl Marx, he denounced a 'system of industrial production' in which 'the producer' received 'only one-third of the fruits of his labour'. Finally, he proposed a remedy for both, based upon his own analogies and conclusions. This lay in the principle of collectivism, a 'scientific scheme [for] national government' which combined the efficient 'superiority' of social over 'individual' effort with the moral 'virtue' of 'ideal and practical socialism'.[154]

If Swales's contribution was rather long on the ethical deficiencies of capitalism and a little short on the positive moral virtues of socialism, these lacunae were quickly filled in a paper read to the same society just a fortnight later. On this occasion, a certain Mr Dyche outlined a 'Moral Basis for Socialism'. That, he argued, lay in a careful consideration first of 'why some actions come to be considered moral and others immoral',

---

[151] CDA, NEC 144, F.E. Millson, *Two Hundred Years of Northgate End Chapel: A Sketch* (Halifax, 1896), p. 33.

[152] Howell, *British Workers*, pp. 185–9.

[153] Joyce, *Work, Society and Politics*, see ch. 4 especially.

[154] CDA, NEC 179, Northgate End Unitarian Chapel, Halifax, Mutual Improvement Society Minute Book, 5 December 1893.

conceived in the abstract. And the answer to that question, he insisted, was that the 'most ... immoral tend ultimately to harm that society'. Translated into the context of a 'community of producers' that meant it would be to the permanent benefit of this kind of society (i.e. their society) that 'all should be industrious, honest, truthful, temperate and thrifty'. Correspondingly, it would be to its ineradicable harm if individuals did not uphold these virtues in their common life. And 'socialism' was 'based on the desire to give all men opportunities to exercise *these* virtues'. It was, in other words, the system of social organisation which best extended the possibility of virtuous, thereby efficacious behaviour to the greatest number for the greatest good. Hence it was the most virtuous system of social organisation that could be.[155]

This was all very well in theory. But how could this kind of socialism be brought about? Society members now concentrated on what they saw as three practical steps forward: the cure of unemployment, the diminution of poverty and, as a corollary and a contribution to both, the wholesale reform of the existing Poor Law. On 27 February 1894, a Mr J. Taylor delivered a paper on 'Poverty and the State, or Work for the Unemployed'. There he asserted that:

1 There is much preventable poverty.
2 That the Poor Law is no remedy to poverty and that its administration is shameful.
3 That there is no reason why men should not use their skill for their mutual benefit, rather than sell it in a competitive market.[156]

Each of these propositions achieved general consent. The society, however, did nothing to further their implementation. More pointedly, there was no subsequent discussion on the matter. No associated organisation was established. No ties were forged with outside bodies. Indeed, on 24 April 1894, the society voted to make more provision 'for the physical recreation of its members'.[157]

Curiously, the hiatus in political debate at Northgate End was caused not by expulsions of members, nor even by official gagging of its activities, but by the voluntary exile of the debators itself; a departure much lamented, indeed much resented, by the officiating pastor, the Reverend Francis Millson. Observing, in 1894, that so many of the young men had gone, 'drawn elsewhere by a service of duty to their class', he identified the new Labour Church in Halifax as the place and the cause of his troubles. Its appearance more than anything else had, he

[155] *Ibid.*, 19 December 1893.   [156] *Ibid.*, 27 February 1894.
[157] *Ibid.*, 24 April 1894.

believed, caused the loss of 'so ... many' who should, he thought, 'have felt some ... loyalty ... to the old place'. And the irony of this situation was not lost upon him. 'There is – one cannot but feel', Millson mused, 'a certain hardship in the fact that the Congregation which has been [most] actively sympathetic ... to ... working people, and democratic in its constitution should suffer more than any other by the formation of a new church of the workers, based on the principles of democracy'. But there was another point. The new church which, 'at once', had a 'congregation five times as numerous as ours' had also 'among its promoters and helpers peoples whose religious [and political] opinions our School and Chapel have formed'.[158] And that suggested the intriguing, if rather sobering, possibility that the church's concern for the moral development of its young had produced exactly the opposite outcome of its intended purpose.

That certain forms of church and chapel work actually prepared many of the subsequent leaders of labour, both in trades unions, and in the Labour and Liberal Parties, for their secular-political careers, has long been appreciated.[159] Mutual improvement, given its pedagogic and ethical emphases, especially those of public speaking, collective discipline and individual seriousness, may indeed have served this unanticipated social and political function. After all, it requires no great flight of the imagination to appreciate how individuals, versed in the art of speaking, debate and disciplined organisation, might have been well prepared for an official career in an early twentieth-century trades union. But there is another possibility which few late nineteenth-century divines anticipated, and which fewer modern historians have acknowledged, but which the Reverend Millson took very seriously in 1894: that the doctrines and ethos of mutual improvement actually prepared the ground for so many of the young, especially young men, to pass not from the nurture of mutual societies into the work of the Church, but rather to leave the Church altogether. As he put it, 'our ... democratic constitution ... our ... anxiety ... for social improvement ... our provision for ... instruction of the younger people in certain ... secular things' may even have been 'a cause' of the flight of the young to other places, dedicated to other purposes.[160] Much more than Sunday school, much more, perhaps, than any other aspect of late nineteenth-century church-work, mutual improvement equipped so many – through the

---

[158] CDA, NEC 19, Northgate End Unitarian Chapel, Church Meeting Minute Book, 29 January 1894.

[159] For a classic example, see the story told in David Marquand, *Ramsay Macdonald* (London, 1977), pp. 13ff.

[160] CDA, NEC 19, Northgate End Unitarian Chapel, Halifax, Church Meeting Minute Book, 29 January 1894.

churches – with the cultural, social and political resources they needed to leave the churches.

Disillusionment, crisis and reappraisal: the origins of the modern Sunday school

Whatever the case, a sense of general disappointment, specifically that institutional integration and organisational extension had not produced the desired associational goods, became fairly common around the turn of the century. As the Society Report in Harrison Road Church Yearbook for 1900 put it, 'Sunday schools ... [i]n a sense ... are as popular as they ever were ... but they [have] not accomplish[ed] what we [had] in view'.[161] This was because, in the contemporaneous words of the Reverend Francis Pigou, Sunday schools had proved to be less of a 'gathering' between the nebulous world of childish enthusiasms and the disciplined life of adult worship, and more of a 'mesh', whose 'net [was] too large'.[162] What was chronically disquieting degenerated into something more acutely disturbing when it was accompanied by an overall decline in the number of scholars registered in local schools. That occurred, locally, during the first decade of the twentieth century. For some schools, this was initially a matter of embarrassment, indeed of such embarrassment that it was considered best not discussed. For instance, Harrison Road teachers' meeting resolved, in 1907, following 'some discussion ... [as] to whether the decreasing numbers of the scholars should be reported' in the year's work usually read from the pulpit at the anniversary services, 'that it was best that no mention be made of the fact'.[163] But for others, it was the occasion for a major re-examination of the proper function and workings of Sunday schools, a reappraisal of their ends and means which ultimately led not only to a critical reformation of the characteristic methods by which scholars were taught the faith, but also to a sustained revaluation of the processes by which any particular scholar actually learned it.

In 1908, the Synod of the Halifax and Bradford District Wesleyan Methodist Church conducted an inquiry into the state of local Sunday schools. In order to do this, it circulated a questionnaire to all ministers, superintendents and secretaries. Subsequently, the Education Committee of the Synod reported a decrease of 1,110 scholars and 210

---

[161] CDA, CUR:150, *Harrison Road Congregational Church, Yearbook 1900* (Halifax, 1900), p. 4.

[162] Pigou, *Odds and Ends*, p. 93.

[163] CDA, CUR 1:188, Harrison Road Congregational Church, Halifax, Sunday School Minutes, 6 March 1907.

teachers, compared with the figures for years earlier. In this way, local churches were made aware of the possibility of an absolute diminution in their influence. The schedule sent by the Committee to every school in the district, including, specifically, to all those in Halifax and Keighley, also listed the following questions to be answered at special teachers' meetings in every school:

1 Are any steps being taken in your school to train teachers for their work? if so, what?
2 What proportion of the income is spent upon Bibles and Teaching Appliances such as Helps, Blackboards, Diagrams, etc.
3 (a) Have you School Visitors to look after sick or absent scholars?
   (b) Is any special and organized effort made to secure New Scholars? If so, what is your system?
4 Has your School progressed during the last five years? If so, in which Department – Junior or Senior? If there has been a decline, how do you account for it?
5 Are there any special features in your schoolwork which call for notice?
6 Have you any suggestions to make as to the best way of reviving the Sunday school work in the district?[164]

Of the 252 Wesleyan Methodist Sunday schools in the district, 181 replied.[165] Their answers are worthy of careful consideration. To the first question, 114 declared that they made no provision in this area. (A further 28 offered no answer at all.) Only 11 declared that they held schools' preparation classes more or less regularly. Seven were considering the matter. Three sent teachers to attend the Sunday School Union Class in Halifax; two to the corresponding class in Keighley; and four to Bradford. Twenty-seven supplied their staff with Sunday school magazines, or with some similar help. Five made reference to a library. It proved impossible to tabulate the replies given to the second question on the proportion of income spent on bibles and teaching appliances. The Committee, nevertheless, estimated that the average amount spent was 6 per cent of the total society revenue, but noted that very few possessed any 'aids' to study at all, beyond bibles; and only three even mentioned that they used blackboards. Answers to the third question have not survived. But responses to the fourth were highly revealing. Thirty schools reported an increase in juniors; six a decrease. Fourteen suggested an improvement in the number of

---

[164] CDA, Misc. 191/84, Stafford Square Wesleyan Methodist Sunday School Minute Book, Appendix 1; J. Leonard Webber (ed.), *Wesleyan Methodist Church* (Halifax and Bradford District), *Sunday Schools: Enquiry into the State of Sunday Schools in the District* (Halifax, 1908) (no page number).
[165] There were probably twenty-five Wesleyan Methodist Sunday schools in Halifax at this time; thirteen in the Keighley Circuit; and one in Denholme (author's estimate).

seniors; 24 a decline. In general, only 22 schools (fewer than 10 per cent of the total) thought their overall position had improved. Thirty-six felt that it had deteriorated.

When asked to consider the reasons for their difficulties, only one-third blamed what might be called external causes, that is, reasons beyond their control; and of these, very few pointed either to the particularly low birth-rate in the area or to the more general ageing of the population. To some extent, that was probably a product of ignorance. But it was also a matter of temperament. Self-blame always made more sense to contemporary religious enthusiasts than demographic limitation. And what of those difficulties which were of their own making? Parental and scholarly indifference were thought to be important, but not especially so. Few considered the want of ministerial visitation of schools and houses to be vital; fewer still, a lack of spirituality. Alternative Sunday amusements were regarded as of little significance. In fact, most schools still considered that the quality of their own efforts, and the response of their own pupils to them, were the critical, and therefore also the corrigible, causes of their decline. Accordingly, they regarded their reform as potential agents of their revival. Hence the impetus for the renewed organisation and for new methods of teaching, in the hope of rejuvenating both staff and scholars, seemed plausible to those who were to be charged with implementing them.

However, when directly questioned about how to go about reversing this situation (question 6), nearly half of those who replied offered no suggestions at all. Twenty-seven urged that the minister should take an interest in the school; sixteen suggested central preparation classes should be started; and at least fourteen acknowledged the possible significance of regular visitation. To enhance the participation of the scholars, systematic grading of subjects and pupils was advocated by fourteen. Invited to call to notice any 'special features' in their own schools which produced advantageous results (question 5), several schools made reference to improved order and discipline since the formation of Boys' Brigades and the like in their societies; and nine recounted the vast benefit, to the senior school in particular, of institutes, gymnasiums and cricket clubs, most of very recent foundation. Both in their description of existing arrangements and in their suggestions for the future, the bulk of school responses emphasised the importance of training to those who were to teach; of more careful organisation of those who were to be taught; and of widespread adherence to the theory and practice of variety in educational techniques.

In short, grassroots opinion knew that much was wrong, considered its own failings as principally to blame, but could not think of precisely what to do about it. That ambivalence, uncertainty even, was reflected in the Synodal Report and its recommendations. In essence, the Committee urged more of the same: the newly developed cradle roll to help with recruitment, preparatory classes to aid teaching, more visitation to prevent backsliding.[166] It did not, however, get more of the same. Temple Street Sunday School appointed a subcommittee immediately after the circular, 'to consider an improved way of working and managing the junior school'. And it reported in favour of thoroughgoing reorganisation: proposing, first, that the 'Infants' School' be altered to a 'Primary Department', catering for children from the ages of three to seven; thereafter, that they were to be sent to a newly formed 'Junior Department', to remain there until the age of twelve, and then transferred to a newly conceived 'Intermediate Department'. Primary pupils were to be divided into small classes of not more than five scholars, and to receive appropriate exercises there. The Junior Department was to work 'on similar lines to the Primary Department but with programmes and lessons suitable for scholars of the above age'.[167]

These proposals were quickly complemented in another report, brought out by the Halifax Rhodes Street Circuit Committee, to consider the Sunday school question.[168] That document began with the, by now standard, criticism of the inadequacies of existing work: 'we think that everyone will admit that [the] Sunday school has been too long looked upon as a building behind the church, or even simply as a useful piece of work in connection with it. Our view is that it is one of the most important, if not the most important features of Church work'.[169] Paradoxically, the proof of that importance lay not in its dramatic successes, but in its relative failure. For, despite daunting empirical evidence to the contrary, the Committee insisted that 'it is the essential aim of the Sunday school to retain its scholars for the church'. To realise this ambition, its investigators judged that the work done in 'modernising our day schools' could stand as a model for 'our Sunday schools [since] when it is remembered that a child has spent five days

[166] CDA, Misc. 191/84, Stafford Square Wesleyan Methodist Sunday School Minute Book, Appendix 1; J. Leonard Webber (ed.), *Wesleyan Methodist Church (Halifax and Bradford District), Sunday Schools: Enquiry into the State of Sunday Schools in the District* (Halifax, 1908) (no page number).
[167] KPL, 105D77/2/21/13/b/iii, Temple Street Wesleyan Methodist Sunday School Minute Book, 5 February 1909.
[168] CDA, MR 69, Rhodes Street Wesleyan Methodist Circuit, Halifax, Quarterly Meeting Minute Book, Appendix II, *Report of the Committee Appointed by the Quarterly Meeting on the Sunday School Question* (Halifax, 1910).
[169] *Ibid.*, pp. 2–3.

out of seven in an elementary day school ... we should realise that it is necessary for our Sunday schools to be equally attractive and our methods of teaching equally interesting'.[170]

First, they recommended 'School Grading'; that is, the division of each school into Primary, Intermediate and Senior Departments. Secondly, they suggested that the first department itself should be split into three subdepartments: 'Cradle', for the simple enrolling of names; 'Beginners' for the beginning of proper membership, and then full 'Primary'. Then, in an unprecedented departure, the Committee urged that this section of school 'should meet entirely by itself from the opening to the closing'. Finally, they envisaged that the new 'Intermediate Department' would be taught quite separately from the Juniors; and that the 'Senior Department', similarly, would meet separately from the Intermediates.[171] The principle of the 'graded school', of separating scholars and teaching them 'according to age', had been established.[172]

The uses of developmental psychology, a new theory of religious growth and the emergence of the religion of the child

What was really significant about these changes was not so much the physical segregation of departments which they entailed. Rather it was the psychological theory which underpinned the pedagogical reforms which that segregation demanded. This theory was adapted from contemporary educational psychology. It may be called the theory of the religion of the child. It was a developmental theory, based upon the notion of natural human growth. What it presumed was a natural capacity of human beings to grow into a full religious consciousness *provided* that they had been properly educated into that sensibility. And a proper education, in this sense, increasingly came to be understood by local (and other) authorities as a segregated, graded and developmental education.

The notion of a natural development of juvenile sensibilities – and therefore of an education continually adjusted in order appropriately to develop those sensibilities – was not exactly new to the Sunday schools of Edwardian England. As an educational idea *per se*, it can be traced back at least as far as Rousseau.[173] In a more specifically institutional context, it certainly dates to the Central Society for Education, and its

---

[170] *Ibid.*, p. 4.   [171] *Ibid.*, pp. 4–5.
[172] Harwood, *Centenary Story*, p. 35.
[173] Jean Jacques Rousseau, *Emile: or On Education*, trans. by Allan Bloom (New York, 1979), esp. pp. 117, 146, 151, 180–1, 255ff. and 380–1.

advocacy of Fellenbergian developmentalism, from 1836.[174] Such views, albeit in primitive form, seem to have found their way into local ecclesiastical circles by the later 1880s. Hence Walter Scales's denunciation of those teachers who 'forget that a child thinks as a child', and who fail to use the 'imaginative faculty' of 'pictorial representation' necessary in a 'teacher of children'.[175] But the Edwardian schools did rather more than this. They adapted a full-fledged educational doctrine to their own purposes. They seized upon modern educational psychology, extracted its major premises, and made them serve their own purposes.[176] Precisely why they did so is unclear. Perhaps they believed that they had found a saviour in science. The exact degree to which they understood what it was they were expropriating is also uncertain.[177] Many Edwardian Methodist Church ministers had, however, received a thorough training in theological college. They were scarcely uneducated men. What is significant was the effect that this knowledge, and their faith in it, had on Sunday school teaching and on contemporary ecclesiastical interpretations of the religious development of the child. Its essence was outlined in the report of the committee at Rhodes Street: '[T]he varying faculties and attainments of the children must always be considered. What appeals to a child at one age makes no appeal at another age ... The young child is very imaginative ... and active ... [B]oys of ten to twelve are ... hero-worshippers ... later still [i.e. at around fifteen], the gay spirit is very strong'.[178] That demanded a revolution in what was taught, and to whom it was taught, and especially about when they were taught it. For the very young, the Committee recommended a 'curriculum [in which] music, action and expression [should] play a large part'. It also highlighted the crucial role of diversity.

---

[174] On Fellenberg, see W.A.C. Stewart and W.D. McCann, *The Educational Innovators*, vol. 1 (London, 1971), pp. 141–6; for the debates about education in England during the 1830s, see D.G. Paz, *The Politics of Working-Class Education in Britain, 1830–1850* (Manchester, 1980), ch. 1; and for comments on both, see Brent, *Liberal Anglican Politics*, ch. 6.

[175] Scales, 'Reasons for Failure', *HDCM*, vol. 6, no. 5, May 1888, p. 99.

[176] The Editor, 'The School and the Church', *KWMCM*, no. 54, November 1919 (no page number): 'The importance of grading teaching, according to age and mental development, has been duly emphasised by Geo. H. Archibald, Antoinette A. Lamoreaux and others.' On Edwardian educational psychology, see Adrian Wooldridge, *Measuring the Mind: Psychological Theory and Educational Controversy, c. 1860–1990* (Cambridge, 1994), ch. 3; and on Edwardian views of childhood, see the remarks in Jonathan Rose, *The Edwardian Temperament* (Athens, Ohio, 1988), pp. 178–89; or, more generally, James Walvin, *A Child's World: A Social History of English Childhood, 1800–1914* (Harmondsworth, 1982), *passim*.

[177] Anon., 'The School and the Church'. There is no evidence that this 'Editor' had actually consulted any of these authorities, or that local institutional reforms were really based upon their findings.

[178] Rhodes Street, *Report of the Committee on the Sunday School Question*, p. 10.

'[V]ariety', it argued, 'is necessary to hold children's interests, therefore different items should be changed [*sic*] from week to week.'[179] Others suggested that 'small picture cards ... illustrating the lesson for the day' should be distributed amongst junior scholars 'for presentation weekly to each scholar present'. These, it was suggested, would be a 'tangible token' which would form 'a powerful incentive to the young child' to attend school, and would act 'as a permanent reminder of the stories they represent'.[180] For boys of ten to twelve, those hero-worshippers, the Committee noted that '[b]iblical characters, and especially the bare ... fighters ... appeal most strongly at this age'. So a diet of bloodthirsty stories from the Old Testament would satisfy them.[181] Serious problems – and the most important possibilities – began with 12-year-old children. On that matter, everyone was agreed. One local authority went so far as to call the years from twelve to fifteen an age 'differing so fundamentally from the preceding and succeeding ages ... that it makes ... a special call'. Its peculiar significance was identified through the 'consciousness of ... dawning powers and responsibilities'. Whereas, 'previous to the commencement of this period, children usually accept what is taught to them without doubt or question [this] is a time of great questionings, when doubts as to previously accepted sanctions arise and must be fought, and the personal influence of the comprehending teacher is of incalculable value'.[182] But if it was a time when the teacher must 'if he would influence take a personal interest in each [scholar]', it was also a time when '[l]essons coldly delivered from ... duty ... are hopeless'.[183]

And that meant a departure in teaching practices. The 'new teaching' relied, at least to a degree, on the development of technical aids. Foremost amongst these was the 'new form of Star-Card', introduced unilaterally by Temple Street Methodists in 1905. It contained responsive exercises, catechisms, a list of lessons, the Ten Commandments, and a pledge for scholars.[184] The whole circuit adopted this card shortly after the district review and report on school performance. The ostensible purpose of the new card was to extend the idea behind the old attendance ticket to include the performance of scholarly work. But behind it lay also the idea of different needs:

[179] *Ibid.*, p. 7.
[180] W.S. Dinsdale, 'Aims and Methods of the Sunday School', *KWMCM*, no. 122, July 1919 (no page number).
[181] Rhodes Street, *Report of the Committee on the Sunday School Question*, p. 10.
[182] W.S. Dinsdale, 'The Intermediate Department of the Sunday School', *KWMCM*, no. 120, May 1919 (no page number).
[183] E.T. Smith, 'Boys of Ten to Fifteen', *KWMCM*, no. 122, July 1919 (no page number).
[184] KPL, 105D77/2/21/13/b/iii, Temple Street Wesleyan Methodist Sunday School Minute Book, 7 December 1905.

Adult methods are as unsuitable for child worship as primary methods are for adult worship. Our Senior School has in the past followed too closely on the adult form of service, and although the primary method would be equally unsuitable to this age we need some additional interest to the hymn, prayer and lesson of the average Sunday school session.

Considerable faith was placed in the efficiency of the new method:

the new star-card will contribute to that end. Our prayers and lessons provide little or no opportunity for active cooperation of the scholar. In scores of cases the child will join in the exercises because it is his part, when otherwise he would be indifferent in attitude and mind. It also provides a way of teaching Christian faith in a manner which education[al] authorities consider suitable to the child [and] it [affords] an opportunity for the Superintendent to explain truths which the scholar has in print in his possession.

It also suggested the possibilities of variety in teaching, whilst retaining a discernible core of true belief:

The order has not been arranged to give preference to any part. Some may prefer to use what others omit. The creed, of course is optional, but a creed is not ... We follow on with the exercises of worship and praise. Three out of the four exercises are taken from the Bible, the last being the Beatitudes, and the one who objects to their being repeated by the school together should also object to their being read in the class. The Catechism is selected from our own ... its repetition is an acceptable way of supplementing the truths for which the school exists and affords another opportunity of desk teaching ... The Commandments need no comment ... [T]he contents of the Star-Card will be found as ... helpful as the officials wish to make it.[185]

And it suggested something else too. For the new 'science' seemed to have established that the moment of religious questioning was also the catalyst of adolescent sociability, a time for the realisation of 'the claims of the social group in which they [i.e. the 12- to 15-year-olds] find themselves, and the community at large', and a time in which 'sacrifice for others is of the highest significance'.[186] That meant that education, for this particular group, should be directed as much towards the development of the social, as of the individual, personality. And this, in turn, suggested new youth organisations, especially the Boys' Brigades and Girl Guides.[187] 'Much more interest', the Rhodes Street Committee argued, 'will be displayed in the Sunday School by boys and girls if they are given something to occupy their minds during the week ...

---

[185] Henry Firth, 'The Scholar and the Church', *KWMCM*, no. 22, March 1911 (no page number).

[186] Dinsdale, 'The Intermediate Department of the Sunday School'.

[187] Rhodes Street, *Report of the Committee on the Sunday School Question*, p. 10.

[I]nstitutions of this kind can be the mainstay of the Intermediate Department'. Accordingly,

We have no hesitation in recommending to our ... schools ... the advisability of forming a Boy's Brigade and a Girl's Guild ... [T]he secret of the successes in the Boys Brigade lies in the fact that the lads work together as a company in the Sunday School, the Drill Room, Gymnasium and football field and as a result an 'esprit de corps' ... is established.[188]

These were, of course, not entirely new arguments. Rather, they were psychologically redirected versions of older organisational imperatives. Nor were they confined to the illuminati of the Wesleyan Methodist Circuit. As early as 1903, Harrison Road Congregationalists reported the recommendations of a District Conference arguing that 'influence should be brought to bear on scholars during the week, by having in the school a gymnasium, ambulance classes, [sic] camping out, etc. etc.'.[189]

Two months later, the boys of Harrison Road built a gymnasium, and the girls formed a guild.[190] Queen's Road New Connexion Methodists formed a Boy Scout troop in 1912.[191] The Girl Guides followed the next year.[192] Fairfield Methodists first formed a band in 1913, and then established a separate class for it in their school.[193] The girls were catered for in Guides and Brownies by 1919.[194] What was different about this pattern of growth, when compared to earlier developments in Sunday school activity, was the characteristic justification employed in its use. And that difference was common across Edwardian schools. Hence, in a manner reminiscent of the Rhodes Street Committee, *Keighley Wesleyan Methodist Circuit Magazine* suggested that 'schools ought to have a cricket or rambling club in the summer, while a physical culture class is indispensable in the winter months. The Boy Scout movement is rich in opportunity if properly led. Really it is anti-military, and seeks to develop personality rather than to exert external discipline. Cannot every school have a company of its own?'[195] Within a few years virtually every local school did.[196]

Finally, this new 'science' demonstrated that a real, or a true,

[188] *Ibid.*, p. 11.
[189] CDA, CUR 1:188, Harrison Road Congregational Church, Halifax, Sunday School Minute Book, 30 September 1903.
[190] *Ibid.*, 9 December 1903.
[191] CDA, Misc. 287/40, Queen's Road Methodist New Connexion Sunday School Minute Book, 21 October 1912.
[192] *Ibid.*, 13 September 1913.
[193] CDA, Misc. 287:5-10, Fairfield Primitive Methodist Sunday School Minute Book, 2 November 1913.
[194] *Ibid.*, 6 October 1919.
[195] Rhodes Street Circuit, *Report of the Committee on the Sunday School Question*, p. 12.
[196] Harwood, *Centenary Story*, pp. 98–9.

Christian awakening occurred only after the age of questioning, even after the era of sociability, in the mature adolescent student. It therefore dictated that scholars be subjected to serious study of the Bible only in the 'Senior Department'. There, and only there, so it maintained, would they benefit from the opportunities for 'character-building' which it afforded.[197] That character was, of course, still a 'Christian character.'[198] It was nurtured in order to train church workers, especially Sunday school teachers; also 'to offer opportunities to aspirant local preachers', and other church workers, just as it always had been. But now it was deemed pre-eminently to be the virtuous product of learning, and of a learning which included not only the study of sacred texts, but also the study of 'the history, laws and customs of their association'.[199] That learning found expression through 'activity' too, in 'choirs', or 'string-bands', even in 'cricket clubs, physical culture classes' and the like, each designed in its own way to persuade 'young life' to 'endeavour [to] realise [its] responsibility for the extension of Christ's kingdom on earth'.[200] Or so the theory went.

But the division of academic departments so-defined reflected something more than contemporary wisdom, locally interpreted, about the psychological development of the child. It also reflected contemporary academic wisdom, locally acknowledged, about the propensity of the individual to religious arousal, experience and commitment. The Reverend Henry Firth, writing in the Keighley Wesleyan journal at about that time noted, almost casually, that:

A man seems to lose his susceptibility to the influence which produces conversion or religious awakening almost altogether after he has passed twenty years of age ... [Moreover,] there are three points of maximum sensibility to religious influences, the first appearing between twelve and thirteen years, the second about the sixteenth year, and the third between eighteen and twenty. These are the points at which conversion usually seems to take place.

Thus, if the works of 'contemporary psychologists and anthropologists' really were to be believed, and Firth showed every sign of believing them, the years of susceptibility were few, barely seven.[201] After that, a man (or a woman) was lost to the Church. If that was true, then the state of grace was a vulnerable stage of human development. And, self-evidently, it was also a complex process, so complex indeed that it was

[197] Rhodes Street Circuit, *Report of the Committee on the Sunday School Question*, p. 12.
[198] Anon., 'Our Young Men and Women', *KWMCM*, no. 122, July 1919 (no page number).
[199] Rhodes Street Circuit, *Report of the Committee on the Sunday School Question*, p. 12.
[200] Anon., 'Our Young Men and Women'.
[201] Henry Firth, 'The Scholar and the Church', *KWMCM*, no. 50, July 1913 (no page number).

no longer fully comprehended by the simple notion of conversion; not, at least, in children. Writing in the same magazine just a little earlier, the Reverend J. Williams Butcher accordingly argued that '[o]ur grand old word conversion needs defining, when we use it in regard to children. We are so apt to import into it all that conditions the adult.' And this, he insisted, was wrong, because 'the mental and spiritual processes that are normal to adult life are not normal to child life'. With that observation, he highlighted a relatively novel conceptual distinction in contemporary (Methodist) thinking about the process of conversion in the adolescent soul: that it was both an aspect of individual development and an aspect of the person which itself developed or grew. And, given this under-standing of the idea, what was expected of those young adolescents who (usually between the ages of twelve and fifteen) had displayed the first awakening of an independent religious life was 'Decision, Redefinition [and] concentration rather than ... conversion as the majority will interpret the word'.[202]

This was because 'conversion', now so understood, was also a slow process.[203] Hence the work of awakening a religious sensibility in the child was a gradual labour: 'The harvest for which we look [sic] will be reaped not immediately but in years to come.'[204] And, accordingly, the task of Sunday schools was to secure 'an intelligent ... decision for Christ'.[205] No more and no less. In pursuit of that goal, churchmen and ministers were admonished, quite specifically, 'to avoid ... the pitfall' of seeking 'conversions' amongst youth.[206] Similarly, they were to prevent the efflorescence of 'fictitious excitement' amongst their charges at the moment of decision.[207] Thus they were to seek a 'definite ... decision for Christ and his Church', but as a reasoned and contingent judgement, one which reflected the growth of a mind towards maturity and eschewed all such 'superficial feeling' as might be summoned up by a 'hasty resolve soon revoked', or a 'shallow experience too soon lost'.[208]

But how? The method was the reform of 'Children's Day'. This was a traditional Sunday school institution, particularly prominent in the Methodist Connexion, but not exclusive to it. By convention, it was

---

[202] J. Williams Butcher, 'Children's Day', *KWMCM*, no. 17, October 1910 (no page number).
[203] For a further elaboration of this argument, see ch. 6 below, pp. 275–84.
[204] Anon., 'Missionary Education in the Sunday School', *KWMCM*, no. 25, June 1911 (no page number).
[205] Butcher, 'Children's Day'.
[206] J. Binns, 'The School and the Church', *KWMCM*, no. 54, November 1913 (no page number).
[207] Butcher, 'Children's Day'.
[208] J.T.L. Maggs, 'Sunday School Column', *KWMCM*, vol. 41, October 1912 (no page number).

staged on the third Sunday in October. Its purpose was to exhort the scholars to make a fixed and permanent submission of the self to the Lord: to convert, and to join. In the pre-reformed school, tradition dictated that the plea was made to all scholars, almost arbitrarily. In the graded school the new doctrine demanded that it be made only to those mature enough to decide in a way which they were capable of understanding. So 'Children's Day' became 'Decision Day'.[209] The real point was to change an occasion for 'joyful commemoration' into a specific moment of 'reasoned ... decision'.[210] That could only be done by preparation. An annual event was thus transformed into a continuous institution, 'a class of children' subjected 'to a course of lessons' extending over a period of twelve months.[211] And careful planning meant intensive teaching. So no pupils were admitted before the age of twelve; each was accorded 'personal attention' designed to discover the point at which they are 'most open to influence'.[212] Finally, every 'influenced' scholar was guided towards a 'reasoned ... and ... open conviction' which, by eschewing 'a mass movement of young life', also banished 'transient emotion' to ensure an 'unforced process' of consecration to the Lord.[213]

Such was the ideal. Increasingly, it was also what actually happened. Hence a report of a teachers' meeting at Temple Street Wesleyan Methodist Sunday School, Keighley, in 1922, recorded a 'striking feature' of its 'Decision Day' when 'compared with those ... ingatherings ... of other years [was] the absence of emotionalism'. As a result, many 'trained scholars' had made an 'individual attachment to Christ' on the basis of a 'reasoned ... decision'.[214] But what of those who had not? A Miss Emily Hunter of the local Primitive Methodist Connexion had at least part of the answer. So long as they had not been permitted to 'slip away' at the intermediate age (twelve to fifteen years) but found 'satisfaction in the integration they were receiving of Christ's call', then the churches need 'not feel any pain' at their late loss. For they would not easily 'lose their love of God'.[215] In this way, the Victorian gateway to the Church almost imperceptibly became the Edwardian vehicle for the religious development of the child. And in that subtle transposition

---

[209] KPL, 105D77/1/3/2/c, Keighley Wesleyan Methodist Circuit, Quarterly Meeting Minute Book, 22 September 1913.

[210] Maggs, 'Sunday School Column'.

[211] KPL, 105D77/1/3/2/c, Keighley Wesleyan Methodist Circuit, Quarterly Meeting Minute Book, 22 September 1913.

[212] Maggs, 'Sunday School Column'.   [213] Ibid.

[214] KPL, 105D77/1/3/2/c, Keighley Wesleyan Methodist Circuit, Quarterly Meeting Minute Book, 22 September 1913.

[215] Norman Robson, 'The Intermediate Age', KWMCM, no. 118, March 1919 (no page number).

of institutional priorities ecclesiastical orthodoxy was, if not supplanted, then at least supplemented by the new secular science of educational psychology. Religious indoctrination made way for professional nurture; sacred duty passed harmlessly into personal growth and, perhaps, institutional obligation evolved into associational rites of passage.

Perhaps for those very reasons, not everyone loudly approved of the changes. Some actively opposed them. One of the die-hards was Dr J.T.L. Maggs himself. In later years, he found himself 'at variance with many modern methods for improvement in church and school life'. And one of his 'differences with modern developments' was 'with regard to a child's religion'. This was because he believed 'in the preaching and teaching of the gospel pure and simple, holding that a child's mind was capable of being its own interpreter without outside helps'. As such, he had become an anachronism by 1915. To be sure, his obituarist wrote, he had 'served his day magnificently'. But his day was gone. The 'new way' incorporated the 'machinery' of scientific pedagogy with the 'old ... light', of the true faith, not so much to lead the child (unwillingly) from school to church, but to develop the child (naturally) from juvenile to adult consciousness.[216]

Yet there was more to Maggs's critique of the 'new ways' than his obituarist – actually Firth – appreciated. First, by so differentiating the ontological basis of the religion of the child from the religion of the adult, religious organisations were unconsciously distinguishing – all the more effectively – the experiences and obligations of childhood from those properly appropriate to adulthood; organisationally, nothing could have been further removed from their purposes. Secondly, by grounding Sunday school instruction in the theories and methods of secular elementary education they were unwittingly subordinating the imperatives of sacred to profane learning. Hence a profound paradox. Post-1870 Sunday schools taught more religion than ever before. Post-1914 schools probably taught it better. But the body of knowledge which they passed on cannot but have impressed many of their pupils that, just as their secular education (though incomplete) was now sufficient, so was their religious education (though imperfect) now at an end. In other words, it cannot but have reinforced within their pupils precisely that popular prejudice which the churches had striven to transcend since 1870: that Sunday school was not an initiation into the life of religious association but rather a vehicle for transient religious experience.

Certainly, the surviving evidence supports that view, for it confirms that the immediate impact of Edwardian reform – of reorganisation,

[216] Firth, 'The Late Dr. Maggs and the Child's Religion'.

reappraisal and redirection – was negligible. Consider the experience of Keighley Wesleyan Methodist Circuit. The record reveals that membership of the Junior Society Class – the intermediary body between church and school – declined steadily between 1914 and 1922, rallying briefly in 1923, but by 1925 it had declined to a figure barely more than one-third of its pre-war level.[217] Moreover, if scholars were increasingly failing to convert juvenile into adult society membership, it was unclear that reform had made them any more dutiful at school itself. Hence the Reverend William Dinsdale complained about 'irregular attendance' of scholars in the district in 1919.[218] Yet ironically one of the reasons he advanced as a cause of this sad state of contemporary affairs was the 'tendency ... of ... the young child to look down on that which is intended exclusively for him'.[219] Child-centred education was not, in other words, without its own problems. Early experience had proved that. It had also established that the elixir of juvenile socialisation was nothing more than an ecclesiastical utopia. Nothing, not institutional integration, not organisational extension, nor even pedagogic revolution had prevented or seemingly could prevent, the exodus of 'eight of ten' from Sunday school into spiritual oblivion.[220] The battle to 'draw the people in' thus remained. And it remained, despite so much contemporary theory to the contrary, a battle for the souls of wayward adults.

[217] KPL, 105D77/1/3/2/c, Keighley Wesleyan Circuit, Quarterly Meeting Minute Book, 21 December 1914; 11 December 1922; 10 December 1923; 14 December 1925; the comparative figures were 186 and 441. Interestingly enough, total circuit membership held relatively steady in this period (the comparative figures were 1,110 and 1,342) which suggests particular difficulties at the junior end.

[218] The Rev. William S. Dinsdale, 'Irregular Attendance', *KWMC*, no. 122, July 1919 (n.p.).

[219] J.W.R., 'Parental Responsibility in Relation to the Sunday School', *KWMC*, no. 122, July 1919 (n.p.).

[220] A.W., 'Our Young Men and Women', *KWMC*, no. 122, July 1919 (n.p.).

6 Salvation extended: conversion, revivals and the unending mission to the people

Introduction: submission, consecration and the promise of salvation

Though Victorian churchmen and ministers often accused each other of bearing false witness, whether of preaching unsound doctrine or of practising unholy rites, their wrath, directed so vehemently against those who they presumed were condemning the innocent to eternal damnation, not only presumed the existence of one true and righteous path to salvation, but also presumed their own certain knowledge of how to follow it. And though they condemned each other's heretical deviation from its singular and pristine grace, Victorian and Edwardian churchmen believed implicitly that the road to personal salvation began and ended (at least in this world) in the bosom of the Christian Church. In this sense, they understood that to acknowledge Christ, to submit to Christ and to consecrate one's life to Christ was to be converted to Christ, and only in conversion to Christ *in His Church* was there a way to personal salvation. This view, albeit antagonistically expressed and exclusively interpreted, was true across denominations, for most ministers and amongst the majority of laymen. Even those who truly believed in dual-predestination rarely encouraged their flock to leave so great a matter entirely to God's deliberation. And even those who really upheld the priesthood of all believers seldom sought justification by isolated faith alone. Righteousness, generally conceived, was a common path. It was trodden by those who walked with Christ in the ways of His Church.

That those ways varied from church to church is no more than a banal commonplace of religious history, whether during the nineteenth century or at any other time, whether in West Yorkshire or anywhere else in Christendom. Some churches set more store by the faith of believers; others, by the works of the faithful. Some recognised the spirit of the Lord moving through the soul of the righteous only in the extremities of personal experience; others emphasised the role of reflective decision in that recognition. Some asserted that conversion was an instantaneous event; others insisted that it was a slow process. These varieties of belief and of practice, from Catholic to Protestant, Anglican to nonconformist, Trinitarian to Unitarian, were almost endless. What were less banal, and much less timeless, were the dynamics and the significance of those changes which befell common ecclesiastical understanding in late Victorian and Edwardian West Yorkshire of how best to bring the means of salvation to the mass of the people, that is, of how voluntary religious organisations might – and should – reach out and offer the means of grace to all who would willingly – and capably – receive them.

Common, in this context, means cross-denominational. And in that intepretation, it implies not so much doctrinal agreement as institutional convergence. In one sense, of course, a common interpretation of that challenge never varied at all. Christian dogma, across denominations, had always taught Christians that it was their duty to bear witness to Christ, to spread His word, and to pray that others might find His grace. And if some, of an avowedly evangelical inclination, took up that duty more enthusiastically than others, it was only because they appreciated its call more fervently. But if a common interpretation of the formal requirements of that challenge barely altered over time, commonplace understanding of the pressing necessity for, and of the practical possibilities of a successful implementation of this fundamental Christian duty did change, and at this time. To be sure, no mainstream denomination suddenly came to believe that the task of converting the whole nation to Christian worship was either forlorn or supererogatory. But many, if not all – certainly most – of the leading Protestant organisations in late nineteenth- and early twentieth-century Halifax, Keighley and Denholme gradually revised their perceptions about how this great task might best be fulfilled. And as their hitherto notably distinct views about this matter developed, so they also converged. That is, they came to see the problem as something like a common problem and even as a common task, finally as a common mission for organised faiths to the lives of the people. In that change of perception, this task lost much of its earlier glamour. It became a matter less of instantaneous experience, and more of slow instruction; less a question of mass enthusiasm, and more of individual accretion; less an issue of competitive struggle, and more of collective purpose. In those changes of organised perception and practice may plausibly be seen the roots of modern ecumenicalism. Whether its fruit was the flowering of modern co-operation or modern indifference is another matter.

The significance of conversion: personal experience and institutional commitment

All Christian history bears witness that when a man becomes utterly consecrated to God he is no longer ignorant. One of the marked gifts of God is a quickening and enhancement of the mental powers. The personality too is no longer divided and torn but integrated. The uneducated ploughboy becomes a great scholar and preacher, the mill lass a missionary, the pit lad a brilliant statesman. The consecration of all the powers of the personality to the service of God means also the concentration of those powers. They are canalized, focused to a narrow point.[1]

The author of those words is not a famous figure in English Protestant history. Nor was he a man of notorious memory. His remarks anticipated no great religious revival, whether local or national. And they celebrated no famous event. In fact, they began an official history of Temple Street Wesleyan Methodist Chapel, Keighley, and they were written by one Thomas Metcalf, a local lay preacher, in 1946. Sophisticated Methodists by then probably balked at so explicit a declaration of the transformative possibilities of faith. But it would have occasioned no great surprise, not even amongst the most respectable of Anglican divines, in late Victorian West Yorkshire. So Francis Pigou, Vicar of St John the Baptist, Halifax, addressing the question of the 'inward feeling' that accompanied 'conversion' in the righteous soul, insisted that 'by the Grace of [God]' extended to the faithful, 'apparently feeble efforts will be blessed ... poverty will become riches ... [and] spirit-quickened mind[s] will speak a new tongue'.[2] And its significance for contemporary religious culture was acknowledged even by those actually suspicious of the authenticity, even doubtful of the necessity, of inner experience and outer transformation as the proper basis of Christian soteriology. Hence Francis Millson, Pastor of Northgate Unitarian Chapel, in Halifax, a vocal opponent of 'enthusiastic' religion noted, somewhat ruefully in 1885 that, 'the ordinary Evangelical definition of a Christian is – one who has undergone a "change of heart", who has been converted. This method holds good in judging men and women ... are they born again? That is the test which governs church membership'.[3] Millson chose his words carefully. Conversion, then as now, was an experience particularly (though not exclusively)

---

[1]   Thomas Metcalf, *The Centenary of Wesley Chapel, Temple Street, Keighley, 1840–1940* (Keighley, 1946), p. 6.

[2]   Francis Pigou, 'The Great Motive', in Pigou, *Addresses to District Visitors and Sunday School Teachers* (London, 1880), p. 15.

[3]   Rev. F.E. Millson, *Are We Christian? A Sermon Preached in the Northgate End Chapel, Halifax, 11th October 1885* (Halifax, 1885), p. 6.

associated with those of an 'evangelical' frame of mind.[4] But in the later nineteenth century, this was a very 'ordinary' form of religious consciousness. Obituaries of local Wesleyan Methodist laymen and women, compiled by the Rhodes Street Circuit in Halifax between 1895 and 1909, reveal something of the centrality of such a transformative experience in the lives of many of the committed lay faithful. Naturally, as Methodist obituaries they betray many Methodist preoccupations. But they also demonstrate the sheer variety of experiences which counted for individual transformation amongst those persons. Thus Edwin Smith was 'converted whilst in a field ... as if a light shone round him and he felt such joy in his heart that he praised God for his saving power and deliverance from the Bond of Sin'.[5] Others, however, came to the Lord at a more leisurely pace and in a more conventional way. Sister Anne Robinson 'attended Luddenden Church [for many years] but she did not ... realise a change of heart'. Then she transferred to Illingworth Wesleyan Chapel, and '[t]here she was converted and joined a class'.[6] Similarly, Sister Greenwood of Trinity Chapel in Rhodes Street Circuit was associated with that society for three years before 'she made a still more definite decision for Christ'.[7]

The interval between participation in religious worship and a specific act of personal consecration, so frequently noted in these obituaries, sometimes assumed a more striking institutional significance, at least in its retelling. This was especially true in Methodism, where the organisational, as well as the chronological, gap between full members and 'adherents' was so noticeable. But it held true for other nonconformist associations and even, in a slightly different way, in some Established societies too, for that gap was at once crucial and seemingly bridgeable. It was the moment when evangelical technique was at a premium. Certainly, it explains why so many mid-nineteenth-century evangelical sermons took on the characteristics of what James Obelkevich has called 'performance utterances'.[8]

---

4   The sociological and psychological literature on the phenomenon of 'conversion' and its explanation is vast; it is impossible to provide even a guide to its riches here, but this author gained most from: James A. Beckford, 'Accounting for Conversion', *British Journal of Sociology*, 29 (1978), 249–62; Max Heirich, 'Change of Heart: A Test of Some Widely Held Theories about Religious Conversion', *American Journal of Sociology*, 83 (1977), 653–80; John Lofland and Norman Skonoud, 'Conversion Motifs', *Journal for the Scientific Study of Religion*, 20 (1981), 373–85; James T. Richardson, 'The Active *v.* Passive Convert: Paradigm Conflict in Conversion Research', *Journal for the Scientific Study of Religion*, 24 (1985), 165–74; and Bryan R. Wilson, *Magic and the Millennium*, pp. 22–3.

5   CDA, MR/73, Rhodes Street Wesleyan Circuit, Halifax, Circuit Obituaries, 1895–1909, 4 June 1907.

6   *Ibid.*, 8 July 1903.   7   *Ibid.*, 14 March 1904.

8   Obelkevich, *Religion and Rural Society*, p. 189.

On these occasions, the text of a sermon became a sort of script. By appending to purposive rhetoric the arts of gesture and tone, a good preacher hoped to sway the emotions of his audience. The result was something of a 'performance' in which the congregation became as much participants as onlookers, actively and fervently responding to their minister's provocation. Amongst those 'utterers' (as the minister knew well) were members of the congregation, often long-standing members of the congregation, whose hearts and minds were in the process of conversion. Some were so 'wounded' by a particularly emotional, or stressful, sermon that they would declare their wounds and walk forward to a penitent's form, or pew, especially reserved for them in the chapel. There they were attended to by another minister, preacher or special prayer leader. Then after the service, they were taken to a special meeting, commonly set aside for the final stages of the process. Those who were 'converted' were invited (in a Methodist society) to join a class, and to attend its weekly meetings. There, amongst the other duties and privileges of membership, they would be encouraged to relive the primary religious experience of their lives: the experience of conversion. Other denominations maintained their own variations on this theme.[9]

Rhodes Street obituaries record one, almost perfect, example of this conversion type. A certain Mrs Garsforth was overcome 'in a week-night service which was held in the chapel, while Mr Morton was delivering his sermon. She rose in her pew and declared before the whole congregation that she could stand the strain no longer.' Her actions neither surprised nor disturbed the presiding minister. He 'at once closed his sermon and turned the service into a prayer meeting, and before the close she found peace'. Consequently, '[s]he began to meet in class and remained a consistent member to the end of her life'.[10] The disparity between Mrs Garsforth's apparent lack of control immediately prior to her conversion, and the sure-footedness of the minister's response strongly suggests not merely a general understanding but also a general anticipation of this sort of behaviour within the religious community. It also suggests a form of behaviour which was more studied than spontaneous. And finally, more social than individual; for if these 'changes of heart' were rarely so immediate as appearances implied, neither were they always so peculiarly personal. Conversion was often in effect a family affair. This was scarcely remarkable. The immediate duty of the born-again was to lead others to the way of righteousness. Others naturally included kin. Several obituaries in the

---

[9] *Ibid.*, pp. 191–2.
[10] CDA, MR/73, Rhodes Street Wesleyan Circuit, Halifax, Circuit Obituaries, 1895–1909, 7 May 1899.

Rhodes Street compilation point to the success with which converts persuaded members of their own immediate families to follow the true path. Sister Ann Lyon was 'brought to Christ' in this way. First,

> one of her sons got converted at the Old South Parade [Wesleyan Methodist] Chapel, and ... went home and told ... what great things they had done for him. He asked permission to have family prayer [and] this ... produced good fruits. It made a [great] impression on his father who went to chapel at Skircoat Green Road, and sought and found the Saviour.

The same night as his 'transformation', Brother Lyon (as he became), 'came from service and requested that none [of his family] should retire to rest until he had told them the good news. [Shortly afterwards,] the mother [i.e. Anne Lyon] was invited to go and she got converted [along] with several [other] members of [her] family.'[11] However, just as there was no typical conversion, so there was no clear pattern to the chronology, still less to the genealogy, of conversion experiences. Examination papers set for prospective lay preachers in Keighley's Primitive Methodist Connexion between 1877 and 1900[12] reveal a number of cases of delayed, or gradual, transformation. Charles Tidswell recalled that he had been a Primitive Methodist 'for over twelve years', in fact, 'ever since I was a boy'. But his conversion, he insisted was very recent, having happened a mere 'seventeen months ago'. He dated the event precisely. It occurred on 'November 12th 1880'.[13] Answering the same question, Benjamin Booth was terser still. He joined the connexion on 30 September 1879, and he was converted on 7 October of the same year.[14] However, nearly half the candidates examined claimed to have undergone a significant conversion experience before becoming either members or affiliates of the connexion. In most cases, institutional association with a Primitive Methodist chapel followed soon after their 'change of heart', as a logical, but not necessarily as an instantaneous, response to their transformation.[15] But this was not so in every case. Nor, in every instance, was the Primitive Methodist Connexion the first beneficiary of their institutional commitment to a religious association. Others, briefly patronised, included both the Wesleyan and the New Connexion Methodists.[16]

---

11 *Ibid.*, 27 January 1908.
12 KPL, uncat. MS, Keighley Primitive Methodist Connexion, 'Questions to be Answered by Candidates on the Preacher's Plan, *c.* 1877–1900' (no date).
13 *Ibid.* (no date, no page number).
14 *Ibid.* (no date, no page number).
15 *Ibid.*; 37 scripts have survived and been deciphered; of those, some 17 of 37 candidates claimed a conversion experience prior to their membership of the connexion.
16 *Ibid.* (no page number, no date); one case of Wesleyan Methodism, and two of New Connexion Methodism.

It is important not to read too much into these, necessarily stylised and carefully censored, accounts of personal spiritual transformation. What survives in official records, by definition, reveals little or nothing about those who chose not to 'make a more definite decision for Christ', especially about whether or not they had experienced the necessary, and prior, 'change of heart'. This is significant. After all, they were always in the majority. Similarly, it says nothing about intra-familial strife, or about inter-generational tensions, caused as a result of religious conversion within, but not across, extended kin groups. Yet it is inconceivable that such strife or tension was entirely absent. And it is coy about the real significance of those varying chronologies of personal commitment, for they were often indicative of official uncertainty and popular ambiguity. Finally, it hides much more than it reveals about the chronic, and the acute, conflicts between personal and institutional interpretations of conversion experience which inevitably arose in a society where the boundaries of religious life were never coterminous with the extent of organised religion. However, whatever their weaknesses and limitations, these various, and cross-denominational, accounts do point to something significant in mid-Victorian religious experience. They point to the widespread – and popular – significance of conversion; something significant in its genesis, and significant in its consequences.

It was significant in two distinct senses. First, because it was so widely believed that only through the experience of conversion could each individual come to a 'true, vivid apprehension of our state and condition by nature ... destitute of righteousness, abiding ... under the wrath of God'.[17] Secondly because, as most churchmen and ministers knew, the experience of conversion was more likely to be followed by 'Christian activity, earnest prayer and fuller concentration [of the self] to the service of the master'.[18] This was because 'the grace of God' characteristically stimulated the most strenuous forms of self-improvement in the saved soul. Often quite explicitly so: hence the examination paper for candidates in the Preachers' Plan of Keighley Primitive Methodist Connexion asked, as its third question, 'What books have you read since your conversion?' (The most popular choices were: the Bible, *Pilgrim's Progress* and Wesley's *Sermons*, followed by various nonconformist histories.)[19] And the impetus towards an improvement of the self

[17]   Pigou, 'The Great Motive', in Pigou, *Addresses to District Visitors*, pp. 10–11.
[18]   CDA, CUR 1:13, Harrison Road Congregational Chapel, Halifax, Deacons' Meeting, Minute Book, 30 May 1882.
[19]   KPL, uncat. MS, 'Questions to be Answered' (no page number, no date); of the 37 examples which have survived, 29 cited the Bible, 10 mentioned *Pilgrim's Progress* and 5 instanced works by Wesley.

naturally led to the 'fuller concentration' of the individual to the wider obligations of church membership: missionary work, tract distribution and Sunday school teaching. Hence the institutional drive towards mass conversion – the consecration of the whole population to the true state and the gracious way – was both a doctrinal imperative and an organisational necessity.

Urban society, revivalism and the rise of mission-hall evangelism

But how could it be achieved? Not surprisingly, the most favoured approach to this task varied from church to church, sect to class, and person to person. Sometimes, it constituted no more than an example in righteous living. 'The best way of making others religious is to be religious ourselves,' began the Pastor's Address in the *Keighley Congregational Church Manual* for 1873. This did not mean that good Christians should not be fired by a '[z]eal for the extension of Christianity', but 'in the first instance, let it be zeal for extending it through our own mind and life'. That way was biblically ordained: 'the ... way ... of ... example [is] a method of working enforced by Jesus'. However, Pastor Morris was wise enough to concede that, in the question of evangelisation of the unregenerate, '[e]ach must select his own method'.[20] For, in this matter, his views found little local favour, even amongst his co-denominationalists, and particularly during the 1870s. Certainly, they found no favour with the Reverend B. Wilkinson, Pastor of Holywell Green Congregational Church, Halifax, whose ministry there, between 1871 and 1882, was committed 'not ... to [that] vapid evangelization that has only one message – the salvation of the individual soul – [but] ... rather which, starting from his own gratitude to God, work[ed] for a redeemed society'.[21] Such a distinction, between a 'society of redeemed individuals' and a 'redeemed society', was not entirely pedantic. This was partly because, as 'Mr Wilkinson insisted', the latter and not the former was 'the ultimate aim of the gospels'.[22] It was also partly a question of evangelical sensibilities and their practical possibilities. And this was a matter whose significance extended far beyond the relatively trivial issue of petty disagreements amongst Congregational ministers. Above all, it was a concern which pierced the consciences, as much as it

---

[20] Rev. A.B. Morris, 'Minister's Address', *Keighley Congregational Church Manual*, 1873, p. 16.

[21] Rev. John G. McKenzie, *A History of Holywell Green Congregational Church, 1867–1917* (Stainland, 1917), p. 14.

[22] *Ibid.*, pp. 14–15.

excited the ambitions, of evangelically committed churchmen and ministers in the new industrial towns of later-Victorian England. It pierced their consciences because they were not blind. They could see the difference between the new middle classes in suburban 'villadom' amongst whom they had built successful and 'prosperous churches', and '[t]he mass of the people', huddled together in 'the crowded centres', who seemingly never, or anyway relatively rarely, came to church.[23] They could see, in other words, that it was not sufficient for the saved to be righteous in their isolated ghettos. The religious, especially the committed religious, had to go out and stage a 'mission to the great multitudes outside her [i.e. the church's] fold'.[24] Otherwise, they would never properly come into its fold.

To be sure, the doctrinal imperative behind that mission was scarcely novel. After all, 'Christ's sympathy ever went out [to] the many' who were not yet of His Church.[25] But it acquired a force and a direction, even an urgency, in the later nineteenth-century industrial town which it had never had before. This is because it was directed at mass urban society, addressed to it through the institutions of mass urban society, and concentrated (literally) in the space which mass urban society had created to make that task possible. There, it sought to kindle 'the power of the masses', by 'group[ing] men [together] and appeal[ing] to them in large gatherings deal[ing] with them in organized masses'. The specific technique employed became known as 'meeting hall evangelism'.[26] It was triggered by a change in the law. Until 1855, a long-standing statute forbade the assembly of more than twenty persons for religious worship in any building, except in a church or in a licensed dissenting chapel. The modification of that regulation furnished a new dimension to the theoretical possibilities of public proselytisation and religious evangelism.[27] And the transformation of the new industrial towns, especially of these West Yorkshire industrial towns, through so many civic building projects during the 1850s and 1860s, transformed those theoretical possibilities into a practical proposition.[28]

Town halls, mechanics' institutes and drill rooms, ostensibly the expression of the secular development of their respective towns, were admirable sites for revival meetings and mission services. First, they

23   Rev. A. Westrope, 'Aggressive Work in Large Towns', HDCM, vol. 7, no. 6, June 1889, p. 121.
24   Ibid., p. 123.   25   Ibid., p. 121.
26   J.T.L. Maggs, 'Rector's Address', KWMCM, no. 14, February 1910 (no page number).
27   G. Kitson Clark, The Making of Victorian England (London, 1962), p. 187.
28   Linstrum, West Yorkshire, esp. ch. 12, provides a full account of municipal building projects in this part of England during the nineteenth century.

established a hitherto unknown bridge between sacred and profane public space. This won for the men of God a hearing in places where they might otherwise have been ignored; at the same time, they furnished denominationally neutral ground into which the curious might roam without – unambiguously – crossing the threshold of sacred space. Secondly, as denominationally neutral ground, they permitted erstwhile ecclesiastical opponents to talk with and to help each other and, in effect, to co-operate as well as to compete in the mission of the Church to the people. In that sense, they not only increased the potential audience for the message of God, but they also permitted its messengers an apparent unity of purpose which they might not otherwise have allowed for themselves. Thirdly, the 'large hall with its elaborate ... arrangements and numerous staff' afforded a number of obvious advantages to the professional missionary over the traditional 'open-air' mass meeting.[29] It was not subject to the vagaries of the elements. Nor was it so obviously vulnerable to the interference of passing recalcitrants, seeking to disturb the proceedings. Above all, it enabled a good preacher to concentrate the psychological force of his missionary and evangelical effort in an environment which bore a much closer physical resemblance to a church or a chapel than any 'open-air' venue, and before an audience which was, in all probability, relatively unused to so much exposure of the psyche to the powers of proselytisation; and all in an enclosed, but apparently friendly, public space. In short, it made the business of mass conversion a little easier. Or so it seemed. And whatever its real impact, it made the phenomenon of urban revivalism at once different, exciting, and, for some, even disturbing.[30]

Some of the significance of these 'new dimensions' in the urban religious mission was made clear during the religious revival in Halifax, in 1875. This was, so contemporaries believed, a 'gigantic ... revival', the like of which had 'not been witnessed in the town of Halifax within the recollection of any living person'. It was also protracted, lasting several weeks during February and March of that year, and culminating in a series of 'evangelistic services ... held daily in the town' in early March. Moreover, it was effectively ecumenical, at least amongst Protestant denominations. 'All denominations have united,' recorded one local divine, 'Episcopal and dissent ... clergy, nonconformists and laymen.' Finally, it succeeded in linking the work of these religious organisations to the secular facilities of the town. 'Prayer meetings' were held 'in the Mechanics' Hall', and 'Revival services' in the 'Drill Hall'.

29 Maggs, 'Rector's Address'.
30 The definitive study is John Kent, *Holding the Fort: Studies in Victorian Revivalism* (London, 1978), see esp. chs. 2, 3 and 8.

They were popular. '[Some] 4,000 to 5,000 were present at the ... service ... held in the Drill Hall ... on Thursday, 4th March ... and more than 1,000 had to go to South Parade Chapel, not being able to gain admission to the Hall.' And this popularity was sustained: 'The Drill Hall was again filled to overflowing on the 11th [of March].' So there was 'every encouragement to go on', so much so indeed as to persuade even relatively sober-minded judges that, 'the whole population of the town seemed to be permeated with the spirit of God'.[31] It was, perhaps, less in surprise than in gratitude that a church meeting of Harrison Road Congregational Chapel was able to report in June of that year that, as a direct consequence of the events of February and March, it had 'admit[ted] a larger number of members' to its summer meeting 'than has ever been admitted at any one time since the commencement of the church's interest'.[32]

Events such as the Halifax revival of February and March 1875 inevitably aroused the expectation of some, such as the Pastor of Harrison Road, that there really were 'many outside ... the church ... who seemed to be impressed by the necessity of salvation'.[33] Nor were such hopes entirely without foundation. Harrison Road Chapel gained 51 new members in 1875, an increase of more than one-fifth in its total membership during one year. That increase was matched again only in 1882, when it secured 61 new members, during the second major interdenominational revival staged in the town in the latter half of the nineteenth century.[34] And these successes were not confined to the Congregational Church. In that same year (1882), in the same town, the quarterly meeting of Salem Methodist New Connexion was able to report not only 'a general awakening all through the Circuit' but also, more concretely, 'the addition of 63 members on trial' to the Connexion.[35] Such crude figures should nevertheless be treated with some caution. First, they reveal – at best – only half of the story, for recruitment to religious organisations, even during the dramatic moments of an urban religious revival, was only one side of the institutional coin. Recidivism – the loss of erstwhile members – was the other. Just how great that problem was, and how much its impact varied from denomination to denomination, society to society and year to year,

---

[31] CDA, CUR 1:13, Harrison Road Congregational Chapel, Halifax, Church and Deacons' Book, 15 March 1875.

[32] Ibid., 3 June 1875. Harrison Road was founded in 1836.

[33] Ibid., 16 November 1876.

[34] CDA, CUR 1:3–7, Harrison Road Congregational Chapel, Halifax, Members' Attendance Roll Books, 1869–1925 (no page numbers).

[35] CDA, MR/77, Halifax Methodist New Connexion, Salem Circuit (Halifax North Circuit), Quarterly Meeting Minute Book, 24 April 1882.

is, unfortunately, almost impossible to calculate. Even amongst those societies which kept them at all, membership rolls were poorly maintained, often listing 'members' who were either dead or lapsed. And even amongst those societies which did revise their rolls regularly, such lists rarely revealed the full extent of intake and drop-out for any particular association, at any particular time. Consequently, estimates based upon them are almost certainly at best educated guesses, and at worst positively misleading.[36] In this context, there is much to be said for the value of impressionistic evidence. And that suggests that recidivism was a problem that contemporary ministers, society officials and other concerned laymen were acutely aware of.

It should go without saying that the problem of recidivism was not new in the life of voluntary religious organisations in 1870. Recalling the early days at Harrison Road Congregational Church, Thomas Keyworth noted that, during the ministry of one Mr Obery, which had lasted from June 1838 to November 1849, '176 members had joined the Church, at an average of 16 each year [but] during his ministry 29 had died, 27 had been transferred, [and] 35 had withdrawn, left or been expelled [leaving] a membership ... of ... about 120 when he left'. All this was proof, so Keyworth remarked, that 'there were too many cases of backsliding, and too many members lapsed', and that, '[i]n these respects old times were not better than the new.'[37] Keyworth was not the only person of this era to be concerned with the problem of turnover. The question was debated at a quarterly meeting of Keighley Wesleyan Circuit on 14 June 1897, when its causes were isolated and its effects within the circuit were, at least provisionally, calculated. The meeting concluded that the principal contributory factors to the problem of circuit-member 'turnover' were: 'ceasing to meet, remov[al] to other circuits [and] death'; and that, whilst removals and death could scarcely be averted by any actions which the meeting could prescribe, the overall impact of those leakages was considerable. Of about '1350+ members [in the whole circuit]', the quarterly meeting estimated that 'it requires one hundred and thirty new members every year to provide for the loss from those causes'.[38] In other words, the circuit lost about 10 per cent of its

---

[36] For some extremely important remarks upon the uses, and limitations, of statistical evidence as a means of tracing the path of growth and decline in religious organisations, see Nigel Yates, 'Urban Church Attendance and the Use of Statistical Evidence, 1850–1900', in Derek Baker (ed.), *The Church in Town and Countryside*, Studies in Church History, 16 (Oxford, 1979), pp. 389–400.

[37] Keyworth, *Old Harrison Road*, p. 57.

[38] KPL, 105D77/1/3/2/b, Keighley Wesleyan Circuit, Quarterly Meeting Minute Book, 14 June 1897.

members every year through various forms of wastage. Hence the necessity of periodic revivals to sustain its membership.

But there was a problem. That stimulus was often all too passing, appealing rather more to transient emotion than permanent conviction. This was an unavoidable hazard of mission-hall evangelism. It was only exacerbated by the importation of new techniques, specifically designed for the purpose, and particularly associated with the contemporary American evangelists, Moody and Sankey.[39] Their methods attracted widespread – and more especially educated – opprobrium at the time. Francis Millson, Pastor of Northgate End Unitarian Chapel in Halifax, made a point of denouncing, throughout the 1870s, what he called the 'sensational religion' associated with those two ministers.[40] But in truth, their efforts only highlighted what was a long-standing problem, and one exquisitely defined by local Congregationalists, of admitting to membership of their various societies only those 'person[s] [who] gave evidence of being truly converted'.[41]

In practice, this meant distinguishing, during the revival itself – even, on occasion, at the moment of submission – between those who really were no more than 'fresh enthusiasts', and those who were adherents or members of a congregation, long exposed to the ways of religious commitment if only recently convinced of its necessity. Hence the following example. Celebrating 'a season of spiritual refreshing unparalleled in the past history of the Church', shortly after the revival of 1882, the Deacons' Meeting at Harrison Road Congregational Chapel noted a 'hunger and thirsting for light and salvation', which had marked the special services and lectures in and around the church over the previous two weeks, and had 'awakened' many in 'the church and congregation ... anxious for salvation', but also 'others not previously connected with the chapel'. As a result, 'more than ninety of those enquirers' had 'given their names as anxious to become disciples of Jesus', and of these '43 ... were deemed eligible to be recommended to the Church as suitable for membership', whilst the 'remainder' were 'formed into a "Christian Band", under the superintendence of our Pastor to be trained for and admitted to the Church, when their riper experience and fuller development in Christian life shall warrant their recommendation'.[42]

39   For the best modern study of Moody and Sankey, see Kent, *Holding the Fort*, chs. 4, 5 and 6.
40   *Halifax Courier*, 5 March 1910; obituary of F.E. Millson, sometime Pastor of Northgate End Unitarian Chapel, Halifax.
41   CDA, CUR 1:13, Harrison Road Congregational Chapel, Halifax, Church and Deacon's Book, 1 January 1876.
42   *Ibid.*, 30 May 1882.

So much for instantaneous conversion. But even 'riper experience' did not necessarily suffice. The evidence suggests that the Harrison Road intake of 1882, just like that of 1875, was more than usually transient, even after experiencing these exercises in 'fuller development' prior to full membership of the society. The recruits of 1875 seem to have been especially fickle. For instance, church records show that more than four in every ten (117 out of 288) of those in fellowship at Harrison Road on 1 January 1876 were no longer members of the society on 1 January 1881. The comparable figure for the period from 1 January 1875 to 1 January 1880 was less than one in three (70 of 240). By comparison, the difference between the membership of 1882 and that of the previous year was less dramatic (perhaps church authorities had learned their lesson), but it was very noticeable. More than one-third of those persons in membership at Harrison Road on 1 January 1883 had ceased or lapsed by 1 January 1888 (139 of 388). The comparable figure for the period from 1 January 1882 to 1 January 1887 was just over one-quarter (90 of 331). Looked at another way, nearly one-sixth of those in membership at Harrison Road in 1875 remained in fellowship in 1899 (37 of 240), but scarcely more than one-tenth of the society in 1876 (34 of 288). The proportions for the 1882 and 1883 fellowship were very similar. Forty-two of 331 remained from 1882; 44 of 388 from 1883.[43] Such evidence, so calculated, is far from decisive as a proof of 'revivalist recidivism'. But it does suggest that contemporary fears about the phenomenon may have been justified. And it also points to the possible limitations of contemporary efforts to minimise its impact. However well trained, recruits gained during revivals may have been less reliable, in the long and medium term, than members attracted individually, whether through personal experience, or merely through institutional promotion, into the norms of associational life.

The faithful, the lapsed and the unbaptised: or, the need for and the trials of permanent mission

One thing is clear. Neither the spiritual nor the social functions of revivals were exhausted by the appeal made on those occasions to the masses beyond the churches to come forward and accept a life of Christian commitment. This was because revivals were activities almost as much directed towards the relatively uncommitted within religious societies as to the supposedly unattached beyond them. They were, in this sense, periodic extensions, or institutional exaggerations, of the

---

[43] CDA CUR 1:3–7, Harrison Road Congregational Chapel, Halifax, Members' Attendance Roll Books, 1869–1925 (author's calculations).

permanent duty of evangelical mission.[44] Indeed, they often sprang from missions. Or rather, they sprang from one sort of mission, that is, from the mission which derived its purpose, and drew its strength, from an appeal to all – committed, wavering and ignorant – to come into the Church, and to sample, often over a week or more of peculiarly intense services, prayer meetings and group singings, just what the Church had to offer. As the Vicar of St Paul's, King Cross, Halifax, put it in an address to his parish prior to the mission there in 1896, the event was directed at 'three classes of men': at '(1) the *unbaptized*, that life may be communicated; (2) the *careless*, that life may be recovered and (3) the *faithful*, that life may be promoted'.[45]

This was to distinguish between the different social constituencies for a mission. Others went further still, differentiating between the potential audiences of a mission. The Reverend Frederic Damstini Cremer, announcing the November mission at Keighley parish church in November 1890, insisted that the 'three essentials for success' were: '(1) Careful arrangements; (2) a spirit of sober expectation and (3) a true message from God.' Then he made a number of revealing, additional, 'suggestions'. These included:

1 Come to as many of the Services as you can. Avoid all occasion of distraction 'continuing constant in prayer'.
2 Make attendance at the Services as easy as possible for your family, your household, and your work people. Invite them individually.
3 Avoid criticism. When you hear us say anything with which you do not agree, keep it to yourself; pray about it, and if having done so you are still perplexed, kindly bring the matter to our notice. We wish to give you individual help.
4 Try to help others who receive impressions without intruding yourself. 'Be as wise as serpents, and harmless as doves.'
5 Let all (especially workers) endeavour to maintain a grave, reverent, and yet cheerful demeanour, avoiding gossip and inquisitioners, yet on the alert 'to catch men'. In the case of difficulty apply at once to one of the Parochial Staff, or the Missioners.
6 While interesting yourself in, and praying for the work in the adjoining parishes, abstain from going from church to church. By going about from place to place you are not likely to get nearly so much good.
7 Be careful to honour God in your secular calling. 'Be ye doers of the word, and not hearers only.'

Finally, and remarkably so in a parish magazine, the Rector proffered 'a word or two for the sake of those who do not care about religion, or may happen to have no belief in the Mission'. He asked that they:

---

[44] For this argument, see esp. Currie, *Methodism Divided*, pp. 129–30.
[45] Frederic W. Cooper, 'But What Is a Mission For?', *SPCKCPM*, vol. 5, no. 1, January 1896 (no page number).

1 Do not make light of it. It may be useful to others if not you. It is a solemn opportunity.
2 Give the services an honest trial. Seek to get good and you will not be disappointed.
3 Whatever line you take about the Mission, do not resist the Holy Ghost, do not despise the death of Christ, do not reject the Father's great love.[46]

Why? Because if the 'faithful' generally approved of the – seemingly uncontroversial – end of recapturing the 'careless' and winning the 'unbaptized', it did not follow that they always appreciated the means of achieving so noble a dream. Indeed, experience suggested that frequently they did not. So much so that, continuing his rather curiously defensive missive, the Rector of St Andrew's felt obliged to warn his congregation that 'if our Mission attracts crowds' (and he hoped it would), then, in the natural course of events, 'crowding ... will' necessarily 'cause ... inconvenience [to] our regular worshippers'. He appealed to his regulars nevertheless to 'throw themselves heartily and prayerfully into the spirit of the Mission', in such a way that 'their own comfort may seem a small thing to them.'[47] Clearly, he was not sure that they would.

Nor was this a problem entirely confined to unenlightened outposts of the Established Church. Nonconformists suffered from it too. When, in 1901, the quarterly meeting of Keighley Wesleyan Methodist Circuit voted to recommend 'to each Leaders' Meeting the holding of a mission service on one Sunday evening in each month in the various chapels [of the circuit]', it also stipulated that, for the duration of this mission and its service,

1 All Seats to be Free.
2 The Hymn Books used to be 'Hymns and Songs for Mission Services and Convention'.
3 Any collection which may be planned must be made before the Sermon.
4 Such services to be marked 'Mission Services' in the Circuit Plan.

Then, finally, it requested of all stations that they

5 Make a special effort to ensure the success of the services.[48]

In other words, the quarterly meeting was not convinced that every station in the circuit would make every effort to ensure the success of the services. Items (1) to (3) suggest why this might have been the case.

---

[46] BDA, 74D83/1/11, Frederic Damstini Cremer, 'The November Mission', *KPCM*, vol. 13, no. 10, October 1890 (no page number).
[47] BDA, 74D83/1/11, Frederic Damstini Cremer, 'Crowded Churches', *KPCM*, vol. 13, no. 11, November 1890 (no page number).
[48] KPL, 105D77/1/3/2/c, Keighley Wesleyan Circuit, Quarterly Minute Book, 17 June 1901.

Mission services disturbed the normal patterns of society life. They disrupted the habitual organisation of associational worship. And they threatened the niceties of communal devotion. Consequently, not everyone welcomed their prospect.

Then there was the question of who precisely the 'faithful', the 'careless' and the 'unbaptized', in this context, really were; or rather, who from amongst such people the churches were most keen to reach, to restore and to revitalise. Why? Because, put crudely, the missions were more interested in men than women. This was true across denominations. It reflected the long-standing numerical imbalance between the sexes, common to almost all associations. But it was exacerbated by a belief, equally typical amongst contemporary churchmen and ministers, that such an imbalance was actually worsened by the general run of evangelical and missionary activity. That prejudice makes sense of the following remarks. Commenting on the success of the mission in Keighley in November 1890, the Rector of St Andrew's noted triumphantly that at the close of the mission those remaining at the final service were invited 'to come ... up ... in the face of the congregation ... and sign ... mission cards', proclaiming 'that they had ... given their hearts to the lord [and] received a blessing in their spiritual life during the Mission'. This was an 'open ... and ... [un]ashamed ... acknowledgement' which, he recognised, must have cost them 'a great effort'. Hence he was initially delighted to record that some 'eighty persons came forward'. But then his mood changed. 'Unfortunately', he recalled, 'the vast majority' of them were women. '[H]ardly a dozen ... were ... men.'[49]

There is at least some corroborative evidence to suggest that he might have been pointing to a genuinely common phenomenon. Of elections to membership in the Congregational Society at Harrison Road in 1875, the year of its first great revival, only 11 of 63 were men; in 1882, the year of its second, only 19 of 69. In 1875, males made up approximately one-quarter, and females three-quarters, of the society's membership (69 and 228 respectively). No comparable figure can be calculated for 1882, but it is unlikely that the proportions differed markedly.[50] The more revivals they staged, therefore, the greater the numerical predominance of females in their society. And few contemporary churchmen or ministers, it seems, wanted that.

But the fundamental problem of mission was none of these things. It

[49]   Frederic Damstini Cremer, 'The Mission and Its Effects', *KPCM*, vol. 13, no. 12, December 1890 (no page number).
[50]   CDA CUR 1:3–7, Harrison Road Congregational Chapel, Halifax, Members' Attendance Roll Books, 1869–1925 (author's calculations).

was a question of dynamics. Conceived institutionally, every religious association was a coalition not simply of the young and the adult, nor merely of women and men, but also of the partially committed and the wholly devoted. Each component part of that institution was valued in its own way but just as mature worshippers were valued more than junior scholars, and just as the masculine faithful were treasured more than the feminine devout, so too (and more significantly) committed society members were prized more than affiliated associational adherents. This was, of course, particularly true for nonconformist societies of every hue. But it was also true, if to a lesser extent and if through much less distinct means of institutional differentiation, of the Church of England, and even, for that matter, of the Roman Catholic Church.

In that sense, every religious society, in Victorian West Yorkshire as elsewhere, was essentially an organic being, a body which conceived of itself as an organic whole: that is, which understood itself as being subject to natural laws of growth (and decay), not merely as a whole but also in its component parts. Accordingly, though each part – society members (male and female), associational adherents, worshipping congregation, and junior scholars – was valued, both in itself and as part of the whole, each was not *equally* valued. More important still, the generally acknowledged unequal value of each component part of an organic whole placed the greatest premium on those policies which ensured, or which seemed to ensure, the greatest possible development of each component part towards a higher, or better, form of itself; and thus of the whole being towards its higher teleological end: in other words, towards growth and away from decay.

To be sure, official doctrine, Anglican and nonconformist, Protestant and Catholic, always urged the value of full commitment for all: that is, the best form of development of all. And official practitioners saw in revivals and missions one way of inducing, through periodic reminder and emotional persuasion, the erstwhile outsider to come inside, and the institutionally half-hearted to assume the full responsibilities of their growing convictions. But neither official doctrine nor official practice ever entirely hid the fact that these essentially unequal relationships remained continuously fluid and constantly uncertain. Nor did they always try to do so. In a curious sense the apparent imperfection of any given society's development was often perceived to be the proper measure of its potential for real growth. So, for instance, Illingworth Moor Wesleyan Methodist Chapel counted 121 'members' and 99 regular 'hearers' at its services in 1875.[51] And then Salem Methodist

---

[51] Horace Moore, 'The Story of Illingworth Moor Methodist Church', *THAS*, 69 (1969), pp. 29ff.

New Connexion, Halifax, boasted '500 members and 1,000 adherents' in the five stations of its circuit, at a quarterly meeting in 1902.[52] Finally, Keighley Wesleyan Methodist Circuit claimed 'to represent about 6,000 adherents' in addition to its tabulated '1,289 members' in '16 churches' scattered around the district, in 1918.[53]

At the same time these figures and others like them seem to suggest that the ratio of members to adherents in local nonconformist churches of the region may actually have increased over the period. Put another way, the dynamic of institutional perfection may have stalled, and even reversed, during the early years of the twentieth century. That fascinating possibility cannot be rigorously established. Too little of the relevant record has survived and what remains is inconclusive.[54] But it should not be discounted. What little anecdotal evidence survives appears to support it. At the very least, it does seem to suggest that the problem got worse. Naturally, such difficulties were not unknown in 1870. Hence in that year the Pastor of Hanover Street Methodist New Connexion Chapel, Halifax, lamented that 'in spite of repeated invitations many of the esteemed members of our congregation withhold themselves from church membership'.[55] But such complaints unquestionably became more frequent and more furious later. So, in 1898, Harrison Road Congregational Church complained of the 'foolish cry' that it 'does not matter whether people are members or not'.[56] Eleven years later, Brunswick United Methodist Church lambasted a general 'refusal ... to undertake the burdens of ... responsible ... membership' which it noted amongst its congregation.[57] And, by 1920, Keighley

[52]   CDA, MR/77, Halifax Methodist New Connexion, Salem Circuit, Quarterly Meeting, Minute Book, 6 October 1902.

[53]   KPL, 105D77/1/3/2/c, Keighley Wesleyan Circuit, Quarterly Minute Book, 18 March 1918.

[54]   It is also, very probably, inherently unreliable. Contemporary estimates of the number of adherents in a society were, of necessity, little more than informed guesswork, based upon congregational attendance (itself often an unreliable figure), and affiliation with other society institutions. Moreover, the motives for proffering such a vague calculation in the first place were often tendentious. For instance, the figure calculated at Illingworth Moor in 1875 was established on the occasion of an application made by the chapel to the Wesleyan Chapel Committee in Manchester for permission to erect a new chapel; authorities at Illingworth Moor would have had every reason to exaggerate that figure. Similarly, the number of adherents boasted by the Salem Circuit in 1902 may have been related to the 'emphatic protest' which the meeting, at which it was calculated, 'enter[ed] ... against the Education Bill now before the House of Commons'.

[55]   'Pastor's Address', *Methodist New Connexion Chapel, Hanover Street, Yearly Handbook for 1870* (Halifax, 1870), p. 22.

[56]   Anon., *Harrison Road, Congregational Church, Halifax, Yearbook, 1898* (Halifax, 1898), p. 6.

[57]   CDA, Misc. 57/11, Brunswick United Methodist Church, Church Meeting Minute Book, 31 January 1910.

Wesleyan Methodist Circuit was forced to acknowledge, for the first time, that the 'overwhelming majority' of 'our congregations' were 'not members of the society'.[58]

Theirs seems to have been a common experience. Local churches generally appear to have experienced great and increasing difficulties in persuading regular participants to become full working members of their societies. Why? One possibility is that the costs of membership had risen in line with the increasing complexity of religious associations. Put simply, more sophisticated organisations exacted more, in time and money, from their associated participants. Hence fewer and fewer individuals were willing to commit themselves to full participatory membership. Another, very different, explanation is that this organisational sophistication actually made marginal participation easier; that is, it made religious associations in effect more bureaucratic and religious people more instrumental, in effect more able and more willing to take no more than what they wanted from sacred societies. Finally, the institution of the revival itself may have ceased to do the work expected of it. That, at least, was what contemporaries believed, viewing the failure of revival as symbolic of the wider failure of the churches to reproduce and regenerate themselves in the ways in which contemporary churchmen and ministers thought they ought to have been able to succeed.

The rise of spiritual science, the transformation of religious mission and the end of revivalism

In this respect, the changing attitudes of those who actually undertook church and chapel missions during the early years of the twentieth century may be more revealing. Those changes naturally varied from denomination to denomination; more still, perhaps, from individual to individual. Yet certain constants were increasingly apparent. These repay careful scrutiny. In the Church of England, this shift of collective sensibilities tended to assume the form of an increasing concentration of missionary effort upon the converted and the committed, based upon the presupposition that only through the prosperity of a solid centre of faith could the word of God hope to spread outwards. Amongst dissenting denominations the transformation of missionary ideas was, if anything, still more profound: it demonstrated itself first in a virtual repudiation of mass evangelism; and then through a rejection of the very prospect of 'revival' itself, as traditionally understood; finally, by the

[58] Mr W. Clough, 'The Quarterly Meeting', *KWMCM*, no. 128, January 1920 (no page number).

development of an ecumenical approach to the challenge of the conversion of the people.

In July 1906, *Keighley Parish Church Magazine* announced 'a short mission to the parish', to last from 22 September to 1 October. But, the magazine went on, it was to be an event designed 'primarily for those already trying to serve and follow the Master ... i.e. ... communicants ... clergy ... Sunday school teachers ... [and] ... Christian workers.' In this way, it was 'hoped that through them a larger circle will be touched'.[59] Some of the rationale behind this attitude was developed in an anonymous article published in *St Paul's Church, King Cross, Parish Magazine* at much the same time. Emphasising that missionary work, from biblical times onwards, was designed 'to work outwards from a given centre', it insisted that this 'must be the way', particularly 'in large parishes'. Only from a 'central body of communicants', it continued, could the 'saving grace of the Church's life go forth bringing souls to the faith and knowledge of God.' And only, it suggested, if each person in 'the whole body of the faithful' properly regarded himself or herself as 'a centre to others', and if, 'from this centre' of his or her 'surroundings of friends, acquaintances [and] neighbours', each brought 'to bear, where it is needed, the influence and help of a Christian brother or sister' could the seemingly 'impossible ... task of telling those without ... how we long that they should join us in Christian fellowship' be accomplished.[60]

If this sounded perilously close to quietism it shared much in common with emerging nonconformist suspicions about the efficacy of mass evangelical activity. Some of the force of these doubts was vividly expressed in an article written in the Keighley Wesleyan magazine, at much the same time (1910), by the Reverend Arthur Myers. There, Myers drew a tendentious parallel between General and Mrs Booth's *How to Reach the Masses with the Gospel*, published in 1870, and Henry Drummond's lesser known *The New Evangelism*, published in 1873. The first, Myers argued, had taught the churches the value of mass organisation. This message, he noted, they had taken heed of only too well during the years which had followed. But the second, he insisted, would have taught them, if only they had listened to it, that 'the great need of the Church [now] was not to reach the masses but to deal with units'. Put another way, it was not 'to bring the mob about us, [not] how to clash and storm in passion, [not] how to work in the appeal in the right moment ... but [how] to draw souls one by one ... [T]his is the spiritual science which is so difficult to acquire and so hard to practice

59   Anon., Unmarked Article, *KPCM*, vol. 29, no. 7, July 1906 (no page number).
60   Anon., 'From the Centre Outwards', *SPCKCPM*, vol. 16, no. 9, September 1907 (no page number).

[*sic*].'[61] This, seemingly novel argument – or at least its new emphasis – found immediate local corroboration. Just one month later, the Reverend J.T.L. Maggs, writing in the same Keighley Wesleyan magazine, denounced what he called an unhealthy contemporary obsession with the 'masses', the 'large gathering', and the 'mission hall', and urged upon his co-denominationalists and fellow church workers '[t]he value of the unit'. His reasoning was strikingly similar: 'The unit is but the centre from which lines of influence stream forth.' For the 'Church', that unit was the 'individual worker ... discharg[ing] ... his responsibility by exercising his own power – a contribution to the work of the Church which he alone can give – to the full'. And the 'unit' of his work was the individual soul; the ignorant, confused or wavering person. Everything started from that basic fact.[62]

Much of this apparent change in local evangelical sensibilities may have been purely rhetorical. But not all. Much of it was also probably little more than a nebulous rationalisation of institutional disappointment. But not all. This was because at one level it offered an explanation to intelligent churchmen and ministers of exactly why the churches had proved less successful than they had hoped in retaining the young and recruiting the adult for their agencies and to their work. Moreover, at another level it furnished them with the theoretical basis for a revised plan of urban evangelical effort, and one which would not, so they believed, be tied to those traditional expectations of success (that is, instantaneous success) associated with an uninformed and unbalanced religious enthusiasm. Finally, it enabled church and chapel authorities to justify the integration of periodical parish-circuit, and district-mission events into the more nebulous, but equally important, task of ongoing mission work: in effect, to unlearn a great deal of what they had so recently been taught about the peculiar demands of urban-industrial society for the dynamics of contemporary religious organisations.

These changes, both of outlook and in method, were neither immediately nor wholly effected. The Reverend Myers put this matter blandly, but accurately enough, when he argued that '[b]oth methods', that is, both 'mass appeal' and '[p]ersonal appeal' would be necessary if 'God's house is to be filled and saved'. And so both continued to be employed. However, following fashion he also insisted that the greater emphasis must now be shifted towards the latter method. And to do that, he suggested, the churches should immediately exploit two forms

[61] Rev. Arthur Myers, 'Button-Hole Evangelism', *KWMCM*, no. 8, January 1910 (no page number).
[62] Rev. J.T.L. Maggs, 'The Value of the Unit', *KWMCM*, no. 9, February 1910 (no page number).

of 'personal appeal'. The first was, simply enough, a 'personal appeal in the open-air'. That was of ancient pedigree: 'It was the method adopted by the great Master Himself, whose disciples were, for the most part, won singly.' The second was more complex and of more recent vintage, but 'equally necessary' and, paradoxically, 'much easier of accomplishment'. It was 'work in companies', often known as 'Button-Hole Brigades', and other similar organisations, each consisting of perhaps 'twenty men pray[ing] and work[ing] together', often stopping 'near the largest public-houses to hold meetings', and 'attacking the strongholds of sin', but 'attacking it' one man at a time. The line between these two forms of 'personal appeal' was not easy to draw. Nor was it always worth drawing. As Myers observed, 'our workers would all agree that but for the personal work of quiet men who never enter the ring to speak, yet who get in touch with some man on the outskirts of the crowd, many of our best converts would never have been won'. The real point of his remarks was contained in his final observation, drawn from 'experience', that 'the outsider ... does not come ... even to attractive [Mission] Halls ... unless he is brought'.[63] What this suggested was that a church could not rely upon people coming to it, no matter how attractive and no matter how publicly accessible, it was. It had to go to the people. And in order to go to the people it had to be sufficiently patient and careful to go to them one by one.

Naturally enough, the appeal of one man to another, whether in the open air or anywhere else, was scarcely an invention of Edwardian Methodism. Nor were missionary – even button-hole – brigades strictly a discovery of the first decade of the twentieth century. At the very latest, they dated back (locally) to the mid-1880s. More significantly still, they were, at least initially, associated with the rise of a very specific form of urban evangelism, and one which long preceded the rise of 'spiritual service'. This was called 'aggressive work'. It was based upon the assumption that, especially in 'large towns', the Church could not rely upon the emotional and psychological impact of revival within its own institutions to animate the religious sensibilities of the people. The Church had to go out to the people – literally to go to them – in order to wage a 'true mission to the great mass of the people'.[64] This could be done, so the theory went, in two ways: by creating bodies (usually mission bands) specifically designed for the purpose of mounting a continuous missionary campaign amongst the people; or by staging periodic or continual missionary visitations by the whole Church (specifically by the district church) amongst the people. What was really

63   Myers, 'Button-Hole Evangelism'.
64   Westrope, 'Aggressive Work', pp. 121–3.

significant and novel about Edwardian 'aggressive work' was how it attempted to blend a crude and received institutional policy with a more subtle and innovative psychological theory about human – religious – sensibilities. And that was a product of the failure of its Victorian predecessor; more particularly, of official understanding of the reasons for its failure, and how it might be avoided.

'Mission Band' and 'Visitation' evangelism, whether as established institution on the one hand, or as periodic event on the other, were common features of urban religious effort in this part of West Yorkshire during the 1890s especially. Some bands quite self-consciously drew their inspiration and their justification from the success of similar, co-ordinated, 'aggressive work[s]' in other towns during the same period. Arguing for the necessity of 'carry[ing] on and extend[ing] our aggressive work' to Halifax and its district, in 1889, Harrison Road Congregationalists made particular reference to the success of work begun 'five years ago' in 'Middlesborough and Hull'.[65] Others did not bother with such comparisons. They simply argued for the pressing necessity of forming '[m]ission bands for revival work',[66] or 'mission band[s] ... for conducting open-air services ... cottage and prayer meetings and other aggressive work'.[67] And, by and large, they got their way. Yet it would be naive in the extreme to assume that what came into being so quickly thereby gained success with equal speed. Consider the case of Miall Street Wesleyan Mission Band, established in Halifax in 1889 with the purpose of fostering 'the good of the Chapel and the conversion of sinners'.[68] It aimed to pursue that end by means of periodical 'mission services', weekly 'open-air meetings' (during the summer months), and Sunday evening 'singings'.[69] This was a common enough justification for its existence. But there remained the small matter of resources. Like most other local mission bands, Miall Street was quite small. At least, its active membership was quite small. Myers, for instance, had evoked an image of the wonders which twenty men praying and working together might do. But that was a happy, even an optimistic, number to have lighted upon. The average attendance at general (Saturday) meetings of the Miall Street Band during the ten

[65] CDA, uncat. MS, Harrison Road Congregational Church, Halifax, Letter to the Trustees' Meeting from Mr J.A. Smith, 14 April 1889.

[66] KPL, uncat. MS, 105D77/1/1/1/9, Keighley (First) Primitive Methodist Circuit, Quarterly Meeting, Minute Book, 4 September 1889.

[67] CDA, uncat. MS, Halifax Primitive Methodist Connexion, 2nd Circuit, Circuit Committee, Quarterly Meeting, Minute Book, 1 September 1892.

[68] CDA, Misc. 57/16, Miall Street Wesleyan Mission Band, Halifax, Committee Meeting Minute Book, 19 August 1889.

[69] Ibid., 29 April 1889.

years of its active existence was scarcely half that figure, at between eleven and twelve, though annual general meetings might elicit an audience ten times that number.[70] Less than a year after its formation, Miall Street Band was obliged to hold an 'incentive meeting', in order to 'incite and encourage each other [sic] to duty and diligence, particularly in the open-air department'.[71] And, just a few months after that rather shamefaced institutional innovation, the Band was obliged to 'give up' its (erstwhile) regular Sunday evening prayer meeting on the grounds of 'poor attendance'.[72]

The ambitions, and the strict limitations, of late Victorian missionary brigade work were painfully acknowledged in the first annual report of the band. Its managing committee acknowledged that, despite the encouraging fact that '19 souls [are] recorded to have been saved during the past year', nevertheless, taken overall, '[t]his past year has not been one of great progress.' Indeed, somewhat ruefully, it reported that, whilst '[s]ome of you may remember that last year we had not sufficient tracts. But this year it is quite the reverse.' So much so, in fact, that the committee urged members of the Band at that meeting to 'come forward and volunteer to do a little work for Jesus by carrying the glad tidings of the Gospel of peace to the perishing masses around us.'[73] It was a plea to no avail. True, the first annual tea party, a few weeks later, was attended by 105 people.[74] And the first annual meeting, held a few weeks after that, attracted 150 members, supporters and hangers-on.[75] But over the next year, whilst the number of committee members rose from 13 to 18, the number of Band members fell from 59 to 41, and the average attendance of society meetings fell again, from 11 to 9. Finally, despite the distribution of 2,000 tracts in twenty districts, only 'eight converts [were] recorded for the year.'[76] A bitter lesson had been learned. It was simply this. It was easy to set up a band dedicated to save perishing souls. It was much more difficult to convince a sufficient number of people to do its work. And it was more difficult still to persuade the mass of the population that their souls were really in quite so much danger as these itinerant enthusiasts insisted.

Some of the reasons why that was so can be traced to experiences of

[70] Author's calculations; based on attendance figures recorded in the seven annual reports of the Miall Street Band, 1890–1897 (there was no annual report in 1896).

[71] CDA, Misc. 57/16, Miall Street Wesleyan Mission Band, Halifax, Committee Meeting Minute Book, 11 April 1889.

[72] *Ibid.*, 18 August 1890.

[73] *Ibid.*, 25 August 1890.

[74] *Ibid.*, 13 September 1890.

[75] *Ibid.*, 24 September 1890.

[76] *Ibid.*, 12 September 1891.

those who actually engaged in house-to-house visitation work in these towns during the last years of the nineteenth century. This form of urban evangelism, in itself scarcely an institutional novelty to the late Victorian era, none the less acquired a new sophistication and a new urgency at that time. This was partly the result of developing organisational technique; that is, of the increasing ability of more complex organisations to comprehend the environments they ostensibly served. It was also partly the product of the changing demands of a more strictly segregated urban society. But its real significance lay less in the progress of suburban evolution which it more accurately traced than in the profound intransigence of popular culture to personal evangelical exhortation which it so mercilessly revealed, perhaps for the first time. Consider the following extraordinary example. In 1891, the 'Evangelical Free Churches' of Halifax succeeded in organising an 'experiment[al] ... house-to-house visitation' of the whole town. This self-consciously ecumenical, project was 'undertaken' at the time by all of them (i.e. all of the Protestant nonconformist churches) 'in the special interest of none of them', and 'only in the hope of bringing our ... non-church going fellow townsmen face-to-face with Christ and His Gospel'.[77] Or so they said. But whatever the true motive, it was an extremely well-organised effort, and a tribute not only to their co-operative sentiments but also to the organisational flexibility of their missionary institutions. It was comprehensive in its geographical coverage. Each church or chapel was assigned a precise area of the town to visit, usually in the neighbourhood of the society itself. These districts were small, generally covering an area equivalent to no more than about 500 households. And it was intensive in its spiritual purpose. Every home was visited, some more than once. Work was sustained over several days. Effort was co-ordinated and results tabulated.

And what of the outcome? Some considered it a great success. The Pastor of Park Congregational Church reported that the 'visitation ... was so well-received, as to encourage the ministers [sic] to ask their churches to find a place for regular repetition of it in their plan of work'.[78] Others, however, were more cautious in their judgement. And the reasoning behind such doubts repays the most careful consideration. Reviewing the results of 'visits paid by members of Brunswick Church' to an area in the West Ward of Halifax Borough surrounding the (United Free Methodist) church, the Leaders' Meeting of the society reported that, of some 550 houses which had been visited, a surprisingly

77 Bailey, *Progressive Congregationalism*, p. 21.
78 CDA (HTC), Rev. J.R. Bailey, 'Pastor's Address', *Park Congregational Church, Manual for 1892* (Halifax, 1892), p. 5.

high number – 421 – were recorded as 'attend[ing] places of worship', and only 123 as 'non-attenders'. The remaining houses were empty. Of the 123 non-attenders, 29 were designated as 'special cases' worthy of being 'visited by ministers' at some point in the future.[79] Some of those visitations may have been successful. But it is most unlikely.[80] More to the point, no informed source particularly expected them to be so. Hence, the Leaders' Meeting, though insisting that the 'visiting was efficiently carried out so far as the district allotted to our church was concerned', nevertheless 'feared' that the strikingly high ratio of 'household' attendance at places of worship in the West Ward had less to do with the especially diligent religious commitment of the local population and rather more with the willingness of interviewees to 'report ... themselves as connected with a place of worship when only some of their children attend'. Indeed, 'in only one case have visitors reported that neither parents nor children attended school or any other place of worship'.[81]

In short, the figures were too good to be true. It was not that they were false; rather, that they were true but misleading. And the real message which they conveyed to missionary evangelicals was not the good news of a religiously affiliated people. It was rather the melancholy tale of a population which had, in its own estimation, adequately fulfilled its religious associational needs. Again, it was not that 'the people' were particularly antagonistic to religion, or even towards religious organisations. Rather, it was that their understanding of what organised religion might reasonably expect from them remained at variance with a missionary (or even an associational) interpretation of true personal commitment and its proper requirements. So much so that, for instance, the very same Halifax Primitive Methodist Circuit which had so determinedly established new mission bands, specifically for the purpose of regular visitations in 1892 had resolved, by 1903, that 'in our opinion' they were 'not of service to Town Circuits', and not 'at all commensurate with their cost'.[82] Not only could the people not be relied upon to come to church *en masse*, they could not be relied upon to respond to its subsequent organised entreaties to do so; not, at least, in the way in which the churches actually wanted them to come into their care.

It is only in the context of that discrepancy – or divergence – between

---

[79] CDA, MR/121, Brunswick United Free Methodist Church, Halifax, Leaders' Meeting Minute Book, 1 April 1891.
[80] *Ibid.*, 27 September 1891. This meeting reported no increase in members during the previous quarter.
[81] *Ibid.*, 1 April 1891.
[82] CDA, uncat. MS, Halifax Primitive Methodist Connexion, 2nd Circuit, Circuit Committee, Quarterly Meeting, Minute Book, 3 September 1903.

official and popular understandings about exactly what constituted appropriate religious observance – and the contemporary failure of existing means to bridge the gap between the two – that the organisational obsession with 'button-holing', so common in local early Edwardian evangelical writings, becomes fully comprehensible. Certainly, 'button-holing', or the 'personal appeal' from one man to another in the 'open air', was only rhetorically understood as a noble clarion call to assault the fabled 'strongholds of sin'. In Halifax, Keighley and Denholme anyway, it was directed towards a population for the most part long exposed to Sunday school training. Hence, it was realistically conceived as an institutional mechanism to break down solid walls of spiritual self-sufficiency. Put another way, it was designed to bring a religiously satisfied people into a state of dissatisfaction, thereby to a greater degree of participation. But those walls of contentment proved remarkably strong and continually resistant to changing missionary techniques. Hence the curious debates and regular institutional upheavals at Miall Street Band. At one moment in 1896, the Committee there was embroiled in a debate about whether 'we should go onto the streets singing, or button-hole people who are walking about, or at street corners, and deliver the leaflets with an invitation to the services'.[83] At another moment, in 1897, the same committee was able to report that it had held a large number of 'cottage ... services' in recent months, and that, 'as far as possible' these had been 'held in the homes of people who do not regularly attend any place of worship'. Their hope, and 'trust', was that 'the good seed sown [there] has taken root and will spring up and grow and bring forth much fruit'. In sum, 'button-holing' was about the man in the street, and it was also about people in their homes. But, above all, it was about drawing the people in, one by one.

If this really was a recognition of the essential limitations of traditional missionary work, there was much further contemporary evidence that it was justified. In the same year as the Miall Street Committee extolled the virtues of cottage services, it noted that 'our young people seem to have lost interest in Tract [Distribution] work'.[84] Yet this was not a mark of despair. Rather, as another local source noticed, it was formal recognition that there were many '[m]en and women who [could] be reached' but who would not, as yet, 'consent to enter our church doors'.[85] And, as the Reverend Myers sang the praises of a personal appeal in which the 'presence' even of a 'third person', let alone a huge

[83] CDA, Misc. 57/16, Miall Street Wesleyan Mission Band, Halifax, Committee Meeting, 20 July 1896.
[84] *Ibid.*, 31 August 1897.
[85] Anon., 'Open–Air Work', *KWMCM*, no. 13, June 1910 (no page number).

crowd, would prove 'fatal', so an anonymous contributor to the Keighley Wesleyan magazine in October 1912 denounced those 'sensational, transient and often disastrous phenomena ... falsely called "revival[s]" '. Nor was that an expression of dissent. On the contrary, it was, by the outbreak of the First World War, something of a Methodist orthodoxy. And it heralded a 'winter ... campaign' which sought 'the best and most lasting spiritual results' through 'services extended over several weeks ... instead of one week', a concentration on 'the local chapel ... as the fulcrum ... to the whole', and 'careful preparation' from each believer 'that each may be ready to receive his own blessing and become a means through which blessing may come to others'.[86]

Compromise and synthesis: the Mission of Grace, 1923

In these various ways, the Edwardian churches groped towards a more subtle recognition of the spiritual, devotional and psychological needs – and aspirations – of their variegated social constituencies. They had come to realise that not all those who flocked to their revival services were actually sincere converts; similarly, that not all those who refused to enter their doors each week (or even at all) were actually infidels or atheists. More significantly still, they increasingly appreciated that the official and the popular conceptions of religious experience varied, and that in that variation lay both the possibilities and some of the limitations of the mission of the Church to the people. Hence an ironic juxtaposition: as the social comprehension of church and chapel life extended outwards – through schools, mutuals and socials – so the outward social extent of organised religion became more readily apparent to those most committed to its further extension. Hence too, the division between the saved and the perishing was increasingly blurred: not in all places, not for all persons and not at all times, but blurred, at least, for many, in many places, at much of the time; and blurred not so much as a formal distinction but rather as an effective means of distinguishing between those who were, and those who were not, amenable to God's grace. This is not to argue that churchmen and ministers whose forefathers and predecessors had been so aware of the real and painful existence of so many outside the churches in 1870 were suddenly rendered unaware of their numbers and state by 1920. On the contrary. If anything, men and women of particular evangelical commitment were still more aware of that melancholy divide in the years after the cessation of the First World War than they had been during the mid-Victorian era. It is only to

---

[86]   Anon., 'The Quarterly Meeting', *KWMCM*, no. 41, October 1912 (no page number).

suggest that God's servants of that later generation had formed (or so they believed) a more complex and sophisticated understanding of why this was so; of how much (and how little) could be done about it, and of what should be done (and what should not be done) in the immediate present, to set it right.

Some of the complexity and some of the sophistication of that new understanding was illustrated in the expectations, and through the responses, of churchmen and ministers in Keighley to the so-called 'Mission of Grace' which was extended throughout the town, during the autumn and winter of 1923. This was an ecumenical or 'United Mission', a 'great Evangelistic campaign in which the Anglicans and Free Churches ... join[ed] ... together'.[87] It was also a very carefully planned effort. Preparations for it began as early as the previous winter, with representatives being sent from each of the major Protestant societies in the town to a meeting in the Mayor's parlour on 15 December 1922, 'to further arrange matters'.[88] The Wesleyan Methodist Circuit, much the biggest and most important religious organisation in the town, finally adopted the scheme and resolved to make 'arrangements for its success' in March 1923.[89] That was crucial. Their agreement meant formal plans could be adopted more generally in June of that year. At this time, the Wesleyan Circuit split itself into four groups, each of which was charged with making the necessary arrangements together with other Free Churches, and eventually with the Church of England, in their respective districts. So Temple Street, in conjunction with Wesley Place and Lund Park, arranged to hold common mission services with Devonshire Street Congregational Church, West Lane Primitive Methodist Church, Albert Street Baptist Church and St Andrew's Parish Church.[90] And Victoria Park, in the north-western district of the town, 'join[ed] hands' with two Anglican parishes, Holy Trinity and St Mary's, in addition to Worth (Baptist) Chapel, and a number of Methodist chapels from its own connexion in 'united ... work and prayer'.[91]

After four preliminary conferences, mainly designed to sort out remaining administrative problems, and following after the traditional

---

[87] BDA, 74D83/1/11, Rev. E.T.G. Hunter, 'The Rector's Letter', *KPCM*, vol. 46, no. 1, January 1923 (no page number).

[88] KPL, 105D77/2/21/7/c, Temple Street Wesleyan Society, Leaders' Minute Book, 7 December 1922.

[89] KPL, 105D77/1/3/2/c, Keighley Wesleyan Methodist Circuit, Quarterly Meeting Minute Book, 13 March 1923.

[90] KPL, 105D77/2/21/7/c, Temple Street Wesleyan Society, Leaders' Minute Book, 7 June 1923.

[91] Rev. F.J. Harvey, 'Pastoral', *KWMCM*, no. 169, June 1923 (no page number).

summer holidays, the mission proper began in September. It was an eclectic affair. It blended 'special services' and 'revival preachers'.[92] It mixed 'open-air meetings'[93] with personal appeals. It directed attention both to 'young people' and to their seniors.[94] It proudly proclaimed that its 'final objective' was 'to bring into God's kingdom those who are at present outside it', but it fully acknowledged that, to do this, '[w]e ourselves need to be fitted for the work of winning men and women into God's kingdom', and for that task, the mission would be as much 'for those within our congregation[s]', as those beyond.[95] In short, it was directed at the widest possible social constituency. But it was also motivated by the most comprehensive spiritual goals. As such, it was, so one of its most spirited apologists argued, no ordinary mission, but rather a 'Deep Sea Mission' designed to 'plumb the depths of human nature'. And in order to do that it assumed the concrete expression of what was, in reality, a '[p]ermanent mission', seeking 'permanent results in the religious and moral life of our town'. To that end, it did not seek, and it would not recognise or encourage 'anything, however well-organized', that was 'simply spectacular and evanescent'. Rather, it sought 'a movement which shall permanently lift us up into a severe faith', a movement which may 'come ... to some [of] us ... very slowly', but at whatever pace it came would 'lift us [up] towards the best and the highest'.[96]

The point was striking and simple. Slow progress to a righteous state was no fault. It was a point taken up by Canon Hunter, the Anglican Rector of St Andrew's, Keighley, in the same (Methodist) journal, at much the same time. There, he compared the 'religious and moral development of mankind' with 'the incoming tide'. And he continued: 'Slowly the waves creep up the sand and go back ... [L]ittle progress seemed to be made, but all the time the tide advances ... W]hat is needed [in this context] is not emotion, not passions, not talkativeness, but a quiet surrender of ourselves to God.'[97] Thus, on the question of emotionalism, Hunter (an Anglican) struck a chord with local Methodists. Like them, he sought a mission that 'would save us all from the known weakness and exaggeration of a sentimental Evangelism'. To that

---

[92] *Ibid.*
[93] S.G. Dimond, 'The United Autumn Mission', *KWMCM*, no. 173, October 1923 (no page number).
[94] KPL, uncat. MS, Upper Green Congregational Chapel, Keighley, Deacons' Meeting, Minute Book, 13 October 1923.
[95] Hunter, 'Rector's Letter'.
[96] Rev. F.J. Harvey, 'The Evangelical Mission', *KWMCM*, no. 171, August 1923 (no page number).
[97] E.T.G. Hunter, 'United Mission of Grace', *KWMCM*, no. 173, October 1923 (no page number).

end, he and they particularly sought to spare missioners from 'more than
a certain amount' of that 'intense spiritual emotion' of which 'we are not
capable'. This was because mere 'earthern vessels soon get filled', and
though '[t]here is promised to us an experience [of] Glory ... that is not
ours yet ... [T]his experience of Christ in us while it is perfectly real and
beautiful ... is as yet only the Hope of Glory.'[98] Underneath all the
verbiage something very important was being suggested. For those who
had long since acknowledged the limitation of missions, *per se*, were
beginning to suggest certain limitations to men, and to men's religious
capabilities, which, in turn, suggested certain possibilities and certain
boundaries to the proper forms of man's religion. As the Reverend
Perkins of the Keighley Methodist Circuit put it, whilst '[i]t is indeed
gloriously true that the way into the kingdom [of God] is not dependent
on intellectual knowledge[,] ... that does not mean that we are to
remain babes'. Indeed, 'again and again the apostles [had] to rebuke the
Churches because when they ought to have developed into men they
remained children'. Therefore, '[i]t is of the last [*sic*] importance that we
should go forward in mental and spiritual progress'. And to do that,
'[w]e [should] love the Lord our God with all our heart and with our
soul and with all our mind.'[99]

That rather novel emphasis on the religion of the mind, and the same
concern for growth and progress – rather than inspiration or illumination
– in the life of the soul, was if anything still more marked in subsequent
evaluations of the effects and the benefits of the mission by concerned
churchmen and ministers. Asked to record his impressions of the
mission, the Reverend R.E. Davies, noted first that '[n]o-one' could
have failed to be impressed 'by the successful measure of united purpose
and action achieved by the Anglicans and Free Churchmen' in the
mission. Certainly not the author himself: he was impressed by the mere
fact 'that we were crusading at all', in an environment in which 'the
forward work of the Christian Church has largely halted'. Had the
mission put that effort back on the right tracks? In one sense, no. For it
had failed to 'win the outsider'. About this, Davies was brutally frank.
'Probably 9 out of 10 persons in Keighley are outside the Christian
Church,' he observed. 'A great united effort' had been made 'to bring in
the other 9' and that effort 'had failed'. Yet that was 'far from saying that
the Mission [had been] a failure'. Indeed, '[i]n some respects, it [had
been] splendidly successful'. How? Davies rejoiced in the knowledge
that '[p]ractically every house in the town was visited, in some cases

---

[98] Harvey, 'Pastoral'.
[99] Rev. Harold W. Perkins, 'Progress is Knowledge', *KWMCM*, no. 175, December 1923
      (no page number).

visited twice'. He noted too, and with evident satisfaction, that many 'open-air meetings and demonstrations were held'. Similarly, he was impressed by the number of 'bills and posters and newspaper advertisements distributed too'. And, just because the ' "outsider" has not been won', it must not therefore be concluded that 'he has not been touched'. Most important of all, 'The life of the Churches has been quickened. The permanent mission of the Church has been more fully appreciated. Many, especially of our young people, have joined the discipleship of Jesus, and many more have given themselves anew to Him'.[100] This was not, at first glance, a very impressive list of 'successes'. But if Davies was merely putting a brave face on things, he was in good company. Many others, including the editor of the magazine to which he had been invited to contribute, did just the same.[101] And many more, including those who attended the Deacons' Meeting of Keighley's Congregational Church at Upper Green, were particularly impressed by the numbers of 'young people who came out [for Christ] at the last Mission of Grace',[102] and were determined that the churches do all they could 'to get and keep in touch with [them]'.[103]

But what of the 'permanent mission' of the Church? It is easy to see in these words no more than empty rhetoric, a vague self-commendation by men and women who had committed themselves to so much that they were unable to believe that their efforts could have come to so little. It is easier still to interpret Reverend Davies's words as a blueprint for retrenchment, as an admission that if the wider mission of the Church to the people had failed by 1923, then the narrower mission of the Church to the faithful might, perversely, be more successful in the future. These explanations carry some force. Yet to balance Davies's subsequent observations with the unromantic expectations of his colleagues before the mission, and to weigh his measured approval of much of what had gone on with their anxious anticipation of what might have happened had the mission become 'too emotional', is to appreciate that, by 1923, not only the evangelical expectations, but also the evangelical purpose, of missionary work had subtly changed within the mainstream of Protestant churches. The change may be described as the shift from the evangelism of experience to the mission for worship.

One way of recognising that change is to appreciate the difference

---

[100] Rev. R.E. Davies, 'Impressions of the Mission', *KWMCM*, no. 176, January 1924 (no page number).

[101] Rev. V. Taylor, 'The Mission of Grace', *KWMCM*, no. 176, January 1924 (no page number).

[102] KPL, uncat. MS, Upper Green Congregational Chapel, Keighley, Deacons' Meeting Minute Book, 16 April 1924.

[103] *Ibid.*, 12 December 1923.

which a developmental theory of salvation, a theory formulated in the
Sunday schools in the first and second decade of the century, and
transposed onto evangelical work at much the same time, made for
contemporary Protestant understanding of religious consecration. As
the sociologist David Martin has noted, sacred illumination comes in
various kinds. 'One kind', he observes, 'is the condition of being lit up.
To be lit up is to be stoned out of your mind. When rhythm is
transformed into an insistent hypnotic beat, the rational faculty is
overwhelmed.' Another variety of illumination 'is enlightenment. To be
enlightened is to achieve integrated wisdom. A man recovers ancient
simplicities altered and transformed by experience and discipline. Very
simple sayings are reappropriated in a new sense.' And a third variety of
illumination 'is union with the ground of being: the beatific vision'.[104]
Yet, as he remarks, none of these forms of enlightenment accurately
describes what it is to commit oneself to public worship: 'The first lies
too close to fixation and the "fix". The second and third imply the
existence of levels of wisdom and being which are ... rarely achieved ...
The illumination of ... public worship' entails no more (or less), he
argues, than 'the kind of interior quiet which assists attention. Prayer
and praise are forms of attention.'[105] And it was prayer and praise which
quickened the 'life of post-war Church'. They marked its 'permanent
mission'. They expressed what it held dearest in 1923, for just as the
expectations of the people, held by the Church, had changed by 1923, so
had its expectations of itself. Some of those changes became apparent in
the response of churches and chapels to periodic revivals, and to
occasional mission work. Others were concealed behind the day-to-day
life of public worship. But that had changed just as much as the mission
to the people.

[104] David Martin, *Breaking the Image: A Sociology of Christian Theory and Practice* (Oxford,
1980), pp. 88–9.
[105] *Ibid.*, p. 89.

Part III

The trials of the religious life

7 Worship exalted and experience eclipsed: liturgical orderliness, dutiful observance and the making of a modern Christian witness

Introduction: notes towards a converging system of faiths

Addressing the annual church meeting of Northgate End Unitarian Chapel, Halifax, in 1893, the Reverend F.E. Millson, long-time Pastor of that Society, made the following observation: '[T]here is less need for us to build new chapels because we, in our teaching, are getting close to yours [i.e. to other denominations] and ... the principles ... which we have taught are now accepted as true by most, if not all, of the religious leaders of Halifax.' This had certainly not always been the case: 'When I came here [in 1870],' he recalled, 'I found this congregation professing a belief that all men are the children of God, and [in] no sense children of the devil, and relying on ᵣ ᵣasonable enquiry and common experience as the tests to which all religious teaching should submit itself'. And 'these principles [were] fiercely attacked in the interest of the doctrines of the fallen nature of man, the need of an atoning sacrifice, and the final authority of the Bible as a divine revelation'. However, such 'doctrines', though '[still] enshrined in the Trust Deeds of Halifax churches', he assured his listeners, 'are seldom preached from their pulpits now'. As a result, 'we [i.e. Unitarians] can go into Independent and Baptist and Wesleyan chapels without much risk of hearing a word about doctrines from which we would dissent'.[1]

Writing just five years later, in his autobiography *Phases in My Life*, the then Dean of Bristol and sometime Rector of St John the Baptist Parish Church, Halifax, the Reverend Francis Pigou, made a number of rather different observations about the progress and fortunes of West Riding nonconformity over the same period. He began with a curious generalisation: 'Nonconformity is a vigilant ... and ... active ... beast ... not slow to imitate and utilise anything that the Church of England from time to time introduces into its churches and parishes.' He then supported it with a number of historical examples. 'I introduced at

---

[1] F.E. Millson, *Address to the Annual Church Meeting, 26th January 1893* (Halifax, 1893), pp. 15–16.

Halifax: Choral Festivals, Harvest Festivals, Flower Services and a Choral Union. I lived to see every one of these adopted in every [nonconformist] chapel.' And he concluded, triumphantly, that '[i]n many cases our liturgy [i.e. the liturgy of the Church of England] is largely used, especially at funerals'.[2]

Both men were, of course, boasting. Specifically they were boasting about the extent of their respective inter-denominational influences. But the surviving evidence does not entirely contradict at least some of their claims. In 1883, John Brigg, of the Keighley Congregationalist Church, identified 'the past twelve years' as a 'time of great and important changes in the theological views of many of us'. He referred to 'the great work of the day'. This was 'the emancipation of religion from mere superstition'. That had been the product of 'the most advanced discoveries of science', which had 'made it possible to find out and make plain the connection between the work done and the divine hand which has done it'.[3] Less sophisticated, but equally revealing, were the remarks of the Reverend Ogden Taylor, delivered to Temple Street Wesleyan Chapel, some fourteen years after Millson's address. There, he observed that 'questions relating to God and immortality ... have ... not the fascination for the mind today as the questions which relate ... to man and his happiness'. This was because 'their age' was 'intensely practical'. Hence it followed that church work, even Methodist Church work, must become 'more humanitarian than theological'.[4]

This must have been music to Millson's ears. But things at Northgate End had changed too, and in a way that Pigou – no rational empiricist – would have found very agreeable. In particular, religious services there had undergone a considerable degree of liturgical accumulation and adaptation. So much so that at a presentation at Northgate End Chapel on 7 March 1901 in honour of Pastor Millson, special reference was made to the fact that '[d]uring more than a quarter of a century ... the religious services, improved and elevated by your discrimination and devoted feeling have been conducted in the most reverent spirit and unfailing regularity. As the years have passed, the services of Easter and Christmas have gathered new associations around them which will be cherished in many hearts.'[5] In other words, there were two sides to Millson's triumphant story of 1893. Predestinarian doctrine and experi-

---

[2]   Pigou, *Phases in My Life*, p. 346.
[3]   John Brigg, 'Presentation to Mr Morris', *Keighley Congregational Church Manual, 1883* (Keighley, 1883), p. 65.
[4]   Rev. Ogden Taylor, 'Christianity and Social Progress', *Keighley News*, 17 February 1907.
[5]   CDA, NEC 149, R.E. Nicholson, 'Presentation to F.E. Millson', March 1901, Minute Book of the Presentation (no page number).

ential religion may indeed have been less in evidence there as elsewhere in 1893, by comparison with 1870, but something of the beautiful forms and the holy practices of a devotional faith were more evident in the common worship of Northgate End Chapel at the end of the century than in the early years of his incumbency. Put another way, Millson's boast was no less, but no more, true than Pigou's. Hence a paradox. The preoccupations of the two men could scarcely have been at greater variance. Yet what is most striking about their recollections, judged in retrospect, is not the differences of faith – of its fundamental basis, its proper expression, even its ultimate purpose – which they ostensibly proclaimed, but rather the concurrence of practice which they actually implied. And what remains striking, seen from the point of view of contemporary doctrinal and liturgical developments, was not so much their tendentious purposes in describing these changing worlds as they did, but on the contrary their prescience in observing the way in which their wider horizon was moving as it was. For, willingly or not, these two very different divines thereby succeeded in directing critical attention to what was one of the most important aspects of later Victorian religious history. This was the path and progress of doctrinal and liturgical convergence. More specifically, it was the triumph of *worship* as the characteristic conception of organised religious experience.

It is important to be clear what is meant by this. It is not to suggest that all forms of organised religion became alike in the latter years of the nineteenth century. Nor, necessarily, is it to imply that the spirit which animated them necessarily assumed a more accommodating tone. Outstanding differences endured. Common understanding of what constituted a proper religious life at Denholme Clough Primitive Methodist Chapel where in the mid-nineteenth century, 'the ... zealous ... people' thrived in 'prayer meetings, love feasts and singings', remained a far cry from that of Harrison Road Congregational Chapel, Halifax, where, by the end of Victoria's reign, religion was 'undemonstrative ... something which we do not confess, or proclaim'.[6] Both, in turn, differed markedly from a contemporary High Anglicanism which valued that 'care for ceremonial, ... [that] sense of dignity in worship, and ... [that] approximation of the continuity of the Church' which it felt it was the duty of the Establishment to uphold.[7] Furthermore, such mutual differentiation was, throughout this period, altogether more commonly acknowledged than self-conscious imitation or purposive

---

[6] Anon., unmarked article, *Harrison Road Congregational Church, Halifax, Yearbook, 1892* (Halifax, 1892), p. 5.

[7] Anon., 'A Great Opportunity', *SPCKCPM*, vol. 15, no. 9, September 1906 (no page number).

emulation. Accordingly, the records of late nineteenth-century local religious societies continued to reveal carefully constructed essays in doctrinal or liturgical demarcation. These invariably claimed the 'middle-ground' for their own preferred denomination, and identified the extremities with their opponents. For instance, during its bicentenary celebrations in 1896, Northgate End Unitarian Chapel described itself as 'the religious home of people who cannot conscientiously profess the creeds of the Church of England and who do not believe some of the doctrines of the Evangelical Nonconformist Churches'.[8] And some thirteen years earlier, Mr W.E. Glyde, Chairman of the Yorkshire Congregational Union, described 'the Manner' in which his own denomination 'conduct[ed] ... public worship ... as occupy[ing] a ... middle place between the advance to Popery by the Ritualists in the Church of England and the somewhat wild licence of the Salvation Army'.[9] Subjective differentiation was not, however, quite the same thing as objective difference. Indeed, the narrower these differences actually became, the greater was the temptation for competitively-minded clerics to play them up in a mutually antagonistic institutional environment. Similarly, mutual convergence in doctrine and liturgy neither entailed nor implied open agreement, still less formal co-operation between different denominations. Both were, in fact, perfectly compatible with mutual denunciation and continuing patterns of inter-associational strife. Rather, they defined only that degree of institutional concurrence in the range of devotional demands characteristically made by religious organisations of religious persons, and in the associational means typically afforded to religious persons in their pursuit of a mature devotional life during the latter years of the nineteenth century. That concurrence was rarely the product of explicit inter-denominational consensus, nor even of cross-associational negotiation about matters of doctrine or liturgy. But equally rarely did it come about entirely by accident. Instead, through dispute and by reappraisal, as much within denominations as between them, the priorities of at least Protestant, and especially of dissenting Protestant, life were first re-evaluated and then slowly transformed in this part of later Victorian England.

In that re-evaluation and transformation, many if not most of the erstwhile 'expressive' imperatives in institutional life – the class meeting, the impromptu sermon and free prayer – were discernibly, if incalculably, downgraded as a part of a generally acknowledged religious

---

[8]   Anon., *Northgate End Unitarian Church, Bicentenary 1896* (Halifax, 1896), Appendix (no page number).

[9]   W.E. Glyde, 'Yorkshire Congregational Union', *HDCM*, vol. I, no. 3, May 1883, p. 71.

commitment. At the same time, many if not most of the former 'devotional' imperatives of the institutional life, including Holy Communion and the order of worship, were noticeably upgraded as part of a subtly changing understanding of the proper forms of an organised religious life. This alteration of common perspective was anything but final or complete. And it was wrought almost as much unselfconsciously as deliberately. But it was of critical importance to both official and popular views of what religion was about – and of its fate – in the Edwardian town. It may be summed up in the words of the seemingly omnipresent Francis Millson. Lecturing his flock, on another occasion, about 'The Point of Sunday Services', he contended that 'I don't believe any one of you can afford to neglect the Sunday opportunity of religious culture. There is *nothing else* that I see which at all takes the place of joining in an act of common worship.'[10] The real force of Millson's observation lay in its emphasis; specifically in its assertion that 'nothing else' was quite as important as the 'act of common worship'. That would have been – indeed it was – a controversial Anglican opinion in 1870. It had become an ecumenical commonplace by 1920. Why?

Common concerns: the discovery of beauty and the pursuit of reverence

To some extent, it was the result of a changing physical environment. Religion, in the age of the churches, became something of a religion of the building. Contemporaries noticed this. And not all of them approved; at least, unequivocally. So, when James Miall celebrated (in 1868) some thirty years of nonconformist local building, bringing it 'boldly out of the corners into which [it] had [once] crept for security' and 'plac[ing] its [churches] in commanding positions', he also lamented that '[p]osterity ... has ... yet ... to invent a[n] architectural style ... adapted to preaching ... as its main object'. In this respect at least, neo-Gothic revivalist style left Miall unimpressed 'in [its] taste', and 'in the conveniences [*sic*] for which' the churches so inspired had been 'designed'. For it had, so he argued, given birth to a generation of ecclesiastical buildings with 'arches which no processions are intended to traverse; with huge pillars which serve only to obstruct the hearer's view; with high roofs which defy every principle of acoustics [and] with guiltless [sic] of bells which alone justified their erection'. Still worse, it had threatened dissenting chapels with the prospect of 'ecclesiastical adornments which present windows in the form of mitres, brackets

---

[10]   Rev. F.E. Millson, 'The Point of Sunday Services', *Northgate End Unitarian Chapel, Halifax, Calendar for 1892*, September 1892 (no page number).

suggestive of the Trinity in unity [and] colours ... traditionally Romanistic demons which fly from the face of the consecrated host [and] which can never find in nonconformity a congenial home'.[11] Here, Miall's observations were both true and untrue. He was right to observe a trend to neo-Gothicism, especially amongst wealthier nonconformist congregations, in the 1840s and 1850s.[12] But he was wrong to imply that it was a universal trend. Not at that time, anyway; it was, and remained, a feasible proposition for relatively few nonconformist societies, at least until the turn of the century. However, he was also correct to note a profound sense of unease amongst mid-Victorian nonconformists about what the 'proper' style and true purpose of ecclesiastical building should be: about exactly what it was for, about how best it should be designed, and finally about how it should be laid out. And he was justified in insisting that these were questions which for most dissenting chapels of most denominational affiliations, in most of the towns and cities of Britain in 1868, were as yet quite undecided.[13]

During the three decades after 1870, the years during which the majority of nonconformist chapels were actually built in Halifax, Keighley and Denholme, 'posterity' actually forged an aesthetic and practical compromise between the grand architectural possibilities of the neo-Gothic style, and the mundane associational purposes of church extension and popular evangelism. In so doing, it created, slowly and almost imperceptibly, a style of building appropriate for both preaching and worship, a style which remained both in the Protestant tradition and according to the needs of growing urban communities. That style was generally adopted, across denominational boundaries. Contemporaries called it, for want of a better word, 'beautiful'.[14] By that nondescript term, they sought to contrast the physical attractiveness of late Victorian Protestant churches with the 'utilitarian'[15] emphasis of the past, and also with the 'luxurious'[16] heresies of contemporary pseudo-Romanism. But the implied contrast was not merely physical. It was also pedagogical and spiritual. It combined a rejection of papist aesthetics with a gradual accommodation of the elongated church at the expense of the square preaching-house. It maintained the significance of the pulpit but

---

11   Miall, *Congregationalism in Yorkshire*, pp. 199–200.
12   See Linstrum, *West Yorkshire*, pp. 224–5; also Dixon and Muthesius, *Victorian Architecture*, pp. 229–33; and ch. 2 above.
13   See Binfield, *So Down to Prayers*, ch. 7, esp. pp. 145–9; also Dixon and Muthesius, *Victorian Architecture*, p. 232.
14   The use of this word in contemporary sources is too frequent to document here.
15   Willie Clegg, *A Short History of Hanover Church, Halifax* (Halifax, 1915), p. 1.
16   CDA NEC 179, E.B. Stott, 'Religious Services', Northgate End Unitarian Chapel, Halifax, Mutual Improvement Society, Minute Book, 3 October 1904.

compromised the centrality of the 'speaking box' through a widespread dissemination of the pipe-organ into the body of dissenting chapels. It reaffirmed the significance of the congregation, but slowly acknowledged the additional, and complementary, importance of a choir. It asserted the virtues of devotional simplicity, but it allowed for comfort and homeliness in the physical aspects of internal design. This was the reality, and also the true significance of 'dissenting Gothic'.

Examples abound. Lund Park Wesleyan Methodist Church (the successor to Heber Street Wesleyan Methodist Chapel) was opened in Keighley in 1895, 'at a time when the large, rectangular, galleried-all round [*sic*] preaching houses were going out of fashion. Methodists were beginning to think new thoughts about their buildings and the result, at Lund Park, was a house of prayer [and worship] both homely and beautiful, and appropriate for the friendly ... society which was henceforth to make its spiritual home there.'[17] But the Wesleyans were not the only society to have had new thoughts along those lines. Nor were they the first. The trends of fashion did not escape local Unitarians, particularly those at Northgate End Chapel, Halifax. This society was home to one of the earliest of the 'older congregations to follow the popular architectural trend in rebuilding their chapels (now called "churches" in some instances, as befitted their "churchy" ornamentation and layout)'. That was in 1872.[18] Keighley Baptists were not left too far behind. In 1874, Albert Street Chapel was 'chang[ed] ... from the old place to the present commodious, comfortable and beautiful chapel'.[19]

There was a purpose to these indulgences. Or so their progenitors and apologists believed. For beauty but not luxury was, as E.B. Stott of Northgate End Church believed, 'conducive to a true worshipful spirit ... and frequency of attendance'; and it 'greatly assist[ed] in the receptivity of our minds'.[20] This was a view which quickly found favour elsewhere, and not only amongst the rich. Welcoming the reopening of Upper Green Congregational Church in Keighley in 1874, John Brigg, long-time patron of the cause of Independency in that town, remarked upon its 'interior arrangements of comfort and convenience, and even beauty, which are so important an element in the success of a mission room'.[21] Such fine buildings, in other words, made for institutional

[17] Anon., *Let the Trumpet Sound: Jubilee Handbook of Lund Park Methodist Church, Keighley, 1895–1945* (Keighley, 1945), p. 7.

[18] Frank Walker and John F. Goodchild, *Unitarianism in Yorkshire: A Short History* (n.p., n.d.), p. 22.

[19] Rhodes, *Keighley Baptist History*, p. 78.

[20] CDA, NEC 179, E.B. Stott, 'Religious Services', Northgate End Unitarian Chapel, Halifax, Mutual Improvement Society Minute Book, 3 October 1904.

[21] *Keighley Church Manual, 1883*, pp. 65–6.

popularity. And the right *kind* of popularity too: that is, awe-inspired popularity. That view was exquisitely expressed by one Archdeacon Norris, speaking at the reopening of St Thomas's Church of England, Halifax. Addressing himself rhetorically to the question which 'People Asked: Why won't a very much plainer building do? Why spend so much on your churches? Why all this reverence and order?' he suggested two reasons: 'One, that surely the House of God should be the best'; and 'Two ... as a matter of experience men had found that external things had a strange and abiding influence upon their lives'. Together they created a 'certain subtle ... and uplifting influence'.

How? He offered the following example. 'Vulgar would be the man who could keep his hat on or whistle or misbehave himself in York Minster.' That 'subtle influence arose', so Archdeacon Norris insisted, 'not from the ancientness of this church', for 'they [sic] could find it in a perfectly modern church'. Rather, there was something about 'the spirit of the design itself'. And St Thomas's 'was building in [such] a spirit of reverance [sic] and care ... a subtle spirit [which] was a real influence in their spiritual life'.[22] Some of this was waffle. But not all of it. Some of it betrayed its particular High Church origin. But, again, not all of it. Indeed, much of its force was derived not merely from its widespread inter-denominational acceptability but more widely still from its natural congruity with emerging social and cultural norms. 'Beautiful' churches were, in this sense, part of the beautification of the nineteenth-century city. To be sure, the new churches and chapels of the late Victorian manufacturing town were never *merely* public amenities, but they *were* social resources all the same. And, as such, their nature and purposes reflected at least some of those changes in common sensibilities which affected contemporary collective provision.

These changes expressed the triumph of the 'civilising principle' in later nineteenth-century public life. That principle presumed that free public association constituted in itself the possibility of a civilising, or moralising, influence on the 'public'. But, so the argument went, it could achieve that goal only if its agencies of enlightenment and edification succeeded in encouraging a 'reverential' approach to public space. To this end, self-elected custodians of public culture increasingly sought to exact a more strict public, carefully imposed deference to their social function. That carefully imposed deference became something of a feature, for instance, of contemporary musical and artistic associations. Hence by the 1870s, the theatre- and concert-going public had widely acknowledged the ideal of audience restraint as the very

22   WHQ, D33/27, incom. arch. ref., St Thomas's Church, Charleston, Halifax, Parochial Church Council Minute Book, 14 September 1912.

mark of public respectability. Interruption was discouraged. Talking during the performance was frowned upon. Applause was concentrated at the end of the evening, and only after previously dimmed lights had been raised.[23]

This sense of the general desirability of collective restraint; that taboo – the word is not out of place – against individual violations of an integrated social performance; and, finally, the general emphasis placed upon a limited and predictable participation by the audience were paralleled, even reproduced, in late nineteenth-century clerical and ministerial injunctions against 'irreverent' congregational behaviour in the churches and chapels of Halifax, Keighley and Denholme. Religious worship, of course, was not merely a theatrical performance, and a congregation was something more than an audience. But if 'orderly and seemly behaviour in church' really was 'an essential feature of worship',[24] then the pursuit of that ethereal ideal often necessarily followed a mundane path to its proper fulfilment. One way to plot the course of this change in public sensibilities, and especially in the way in which that change was mediated through religious institutions, is to trace the specific and changing emphasis placed upon a quite distinct concept of 'reverence' by contemporary churchmen, ministers and laymen.

Let it be clear. Reverence was not an invention of late Victorian Christianity. The idea of reverence was, after all, born of the timeless Christian sense of dependence upon an omnipotent deity. But it certainly was an especially critical feature of its later nineteenth-century version. Hence Pigou: 'One essential feature of religion is reverence ... if you are to gain from the Church the blessing which God has to give ... you must, above all things, feel His presence there, and the greatest help to this will be reverence.'[25] Or Millson: 'No external element of public worship is more important than the personal demeanour of the worshippers ... [o]nly through ... a ... reverential [demeanour] might a worshipper ... remember ... that [he is] over here for a definite purpose [and] find and feel Him who is always with us, and yet so seldom

---

[23] This is a vast subject which cannot be pursued in detail here. A start may be made in Richard Sennett, *The Fall of Public Man* (Cambridge, 1972), pp. 206–18; note also the very suggestive remarks, especially about the role of voluntary associations in the progress of this form of cultural change, in David Blackbourn and Geoff Eley, *The Peculiarities of German History: Bourgeois Society and Politics in Nineteenth-Century Germany* (Oxford, 1984), pp. 195–202.

[24] CDA, NEC 179, E.B. Stott, 'Some Points of Church Life and Management', Northgate End Unitarian Chapel, Halifax, Mutual Improvement Society Minute Book, 28 March 1898.

[25] Francis Pigou, 'Sermons Preached in the Parish Church, Halifax, at the Closing Services', in Pigou, *Sermons and Addresses*, p. 27.

perceived.'[26] Moreover, in the mainstream Protestant institutions of late Victorian West Yorkshire, something like a coherent and common understanding of 'reverence', now identified and delineated to a greater degree than ever before, emerged from the daily life and casual disputes of organisational life. It may be described as the definition of those forms of behaviour which were increasingly demanded of each adult member, adherent, or even occasional worshipper as individual demonstrations of the peculiar respect of each for the collective possession by all of the physical reality of sacred space and the figurative significance of sacred time.

Lax observation of sacred time particularly irked contemporary churchmen and ministers. 'You would be greatly amazed', wrote a local Congregationalist minister,

if Sunday after Sunday your minister came into the pulpit five or ten minutes after the time for the service to commence; but it is just as much your duty to be present to worship as it is his duty to be here to lead the worship. Be here on time. A chill falls on the minister, and on the congregation too, if a third of the congregation is absent when the service begins. If all are present there is a glow in the service from beginning to end.[27]

That note struck a distinct local chord. So Millson, in a circular to his congregation, 'A Kindly Word – To Be Kindly Taken', begged, 'Can we ... be more punctual in coming to service at the Chapel ... [S]ometimes one-third of it [i.e. the congregation] come in late, much to the disquieting of the Minister ... and much to the marring of the sense of quiet which is so helpful to the mood of worship.'[28] Subsequently, as part of a set of 'elementary rules' of behaviour in church, presented for the edification of his flock, he stipulated, simply, '[Do] not be late.'[29] And the Pastor of Hanover Street Methodist New Connexion Chapel enjoined his congregation with the same message, a year earlier. 'Do come in time,' he pleaded.[30]

To arrive late was bad enough. To disturb the integrity of collective spiritual activity was worse. Injunctions against uninvited interruptions of collective activity became particularly strict for prayer meetings, or for prayers during service. To prevent these interruptions, several societies took specific action. Queen's Road New Connexion Methodists, Halifax, determined in 1876 that 'one dozen cards be got at once and

26   Rev. F.E. Millson, 'Rules for Public Worship', *Northgate End Unitarian Chapel, Halifax, Calendar for 1896*, July 1896.
27   R.W. Dale, *The Duties of Church Members* (London, n.d.), p. 12.
28   Millson, 'A Kindly Word – To Be Kindly Taken', *Northgate End Unitarian Chapel, Halifax, Calendar for 1892* (Halifax, 1892) (no page number).
29   *Ibid.*
30   Townsend, 'Pastor's Address', *Hanover Street Handbook 1871*, p. 29.

placed at each door requesting persons not to enter [chapel] during prayer'.[31] The idea caught on. One year later, a church meeting of Brunswick United Free Methodist Church, also in Halifax, adopted a resolution 'that a card be printed and suspended in the corridors requesting people not to enter chapel during prayers'.[32] Four years after that, South Parade Wesleyan Methodist Chapel, Halifax, adopted a similar ploy, deciding 'that notices be put in the entrance lobbies of the chapel requesting the congregation not to enter the Chapel during prayer'.[33]

Almost as bad as physical incursion was the invasion of unwanted noise, for once within sacred walls the first duty incumbent upon the faithful was, increasingly, strict silence. So Millson again: '[Do] not whisper or talk.'[34] Or Pigou: 'As soon as [you] enter Church ... be silent ... [You] ... are not hear [sic] to talk to each other, but to God.'[35] Finally, the Vicar of St Paul's Church of England, King Cross, Halifax: 'Our wish and endeavour', he wrote, 'should be to make St Paul's Church a model of quiet reverence and order.' And this 'great duty of reverence' should be applied 'both *before* and *after* ... the service'. He 'notice[d] with regret that there is a great deal of talking in the Church on Sundays before service begins', but he felt sure that he had only 'to remind our people [that i]f our church is ... "none other than the house of God" ... [and] if the Awful Presence, is truly there ... [then] *not one single word* should be spoken within its walls unless absolutely necessary, [for] ... those who enter its courts to worship should remember in who [sic] presence they are'. His faith was justified. Six months later, the same writer, in the same journal, noted, 'with great satisfaction and deep thankfulness ... an increasing reverence on the part of the worshippers in our church'. They were being quiet.[36]

Not a single word, unless necessary; not a single gesture, unless appropriate; that, increasingly, was the ideal. Millson once again: '[Do] not move needlessly. [Do] not look around to see who is coming in. [Do] not estimate the number present.'[37] Pigou concurred: '[You] are not going to see friends ... after you enter the church ... [T]ake [your]

[31] CDA, Misc. 287:37, Queen's Road Methodist New Connexion Chapel, Halifax, Leaders' Meeting Minute Book, 17 September 1876.

[32] CDA, Misc. 57/10, Brunswick United Methodist Free Church, Halifax, Church Meeting Minute Book, 10 December 1877.

[33] CDA, Misc., 481/18, South Parade Wesleyan Methodist Chapel, Halifax, Trustees' Meetings Minute Book, 3 June 1881.

[34] Millson, 'Rules for Public Worship'.

[35] Rev. Francis Pigou, 'Hints to Worshippers', *HPCM*, vol. 1, no. 7, July 1878, pp. 87–8.

[36] Frederic W. Cooper, 'Vicar's Notes', *SPCKCPM*, vol. 1, no. 9, October 1892 (no page number).

[37] Millson, 'Rules for Public Worship'.

place ... and ... at once kneel down and pray.' In this respect, social gestures were frowned upon no less than physical exertions. 'I cannot understand', proclaimed Pigou, 'those who put on their gayest clothing when they go to the House of God [when] surely if at any time we might forget the fashion of the world it would be there.'[38] Others were more damning still. Lamenting the very existence of those 'Sunday clothes' which had probably 'lost more souls than they have saved', the Vicar of St Paul's, King Cross, longed for the day when his church was filled 'with clogs ... and shawls and mill skirts'.[39]

Those who came to church as good Christians were also expected to leave it similarly so. On this matter Pigou was quite blunt: 'Do not leave the church before the clergy have returned to vestry.'[40] That, of course, was clerical authority (or pretension) speaking. The Rector of St Andrew's Church of England, Keighley, put the case more subtly:

While I am speaking of orderly habits of body in outward and visible signs of health and strength in mind and muscle ... let me add a word to those whose instincts and bringing up ... make it impossible for them ... to keep their seats ... as the process of Clergy and Choir ... make official ... exit. The respect shown by clergy, choir and congregation alike is not to men but to God.[41]

And even those who were much less certain of the proper forms of respect owed to clergy and choir were usually prepared to obey the instructions of the Vicar of Halifax that, at the very least, they '[g]o home quietly', leaving sacred premises in obedient and attentive silence.[42]

Anglican innovations: order, unity and communion

But beautiful buildings did not, in themselves, inspire awe. Similarly, improving public norms did not, unaided, exact reverence. Naturally, they helped. But they could not do their work alone. To be truly effective, they had to be supplemented by significant ecclesiastical directives. Above all, they had to be complemented by a reformed, and common, liturgical understanding. And that, by general consent, was precisely what was lacking in late nineteenth-century West Yorkshire. Indeed, conventional historiography, whether for this region or any other part of Victorian Britain, points not to increasing liturgical

---

38 Pigou, 'Hints to Worshippers', p. 87.
39 Frederic W. Cooper, 'Vicar's Notes', *SPCKCPM*, vol. 4, no. 4, April 1895 (no page number).
40 Pigou, 'Hints to Worshippers', p. 88.
41 Frederic Damstini Cremer, 'Order in Church', *KPCM*, vol. 19, no. 8, August 1896 (no page number).
42 Pigou, 'Hints to Worshippers', p. 88.

consensus but rather to bitter division; and not so much to general reappraisal as to partisan innovation and particular reaction. Moreover, this was so not merely between the churches, but within them too. And for no church was that seemingly more true than for the Church of England. The ecclesiological movement transformed the order of many, if not most, Anglican churches around mid-century.[43] Not everyone, certainly not every Anglican, approved, everywhere or every time. The Ritualist campaign did the same for the liturgy a little later. It was similarly opposed, even in Parliament.[44] Other sacramentalists pursuing particular projects, whether for the more regular performance of communion services or for the introduction of a musical Eucharist, performed a similarly innovative and divisive (if somewhat less explosive) function towards the end of Queen Victoria's reign.[45]

These national controversies are well known. They need not be recounted here. Each also furnished a local story of strife. They, too, have been related frequently enough.[46] What is more significant here is to understand the legacy of real change which they left. Consider the following example. The restoration of Halifax parish church, controversial as it was in its day, enabled its Tractarian Vicar to pass off much of his ecclesiological pretension for simple liturgical efficiency. Thus its new minister, motivated supposedly by no other intention than to 'increase the accommodation in the body of the church', to 'allow the service to be more efficiently performed' and (rather more to the point) 'to render the interior worthy of the parish to which it belonged' in fact

levell[ed] the floor ... re-arrang[ed] the pews in order that the occupiers might all look in the direction of the new site for the pulpit ... displac[ed] the organ and demolish[ed] the galleries, open[ed] out and occupied with pews the western part of the church ... and replac[ed] the present screen, now composed of painted wood and plaster ... by one of a more substantial kind, carved in oak to correspond and harmonise with that already in the chancel.[47]

The key to his success was to 're-arrange the interior to make it more adapted to divine worship' in a way that incorporated his particular understanding of 'reverence' and yet which also 'ventilated ... lighted ... and ... used' a building which had previously languished in a state of

---

43 See, above all, Yates, *Buildings, Faith and Worship*, ch. 8, esp. pp. 151–65.

44 James Bentley, *Ritualism and Politics in Victorian Britain: The Attempt to Legislate for Belief* (Oxford, 1970); see esp. ch. 3.

45 Chadwick, *The Victorian Church, Part II*, pp. 308–25.

46 For a concise summary, bringing out much of the local dimension, see Nigel Yates, *The Oxford Movement and Anglican Ritualism* (London, 1983), *passim*; and, for a particular local case, see Yates, *The Oxford Movement and Parish Life: St Saviour's, Leeds, 1839–1929*, Borthwick Papers, no. 48 (York, 1975), *passim*.

47 Anon., *The Restoration of Halifax Parish Church*, p. 8.

'vandalis[ed] and unemployed' neglect.[48] To this end, Pigou compared his improvements to 'the toward [*sic*] condition of the Church' with each member of his congregation's 'refinements for their own homes'. Yet at the same time, he arranged to reorder the pews out of their 'present state ... in which people sat facing each other during divine service' into one more 'conducive to devotion'; specifically one in which, 'if they tried', they might successfully 'kne[el] during prayer'.[49]

This was a common enough concern amongst contemporary Anglican clergymen. Pigou showed that it could be put right by physical restoration. And if the outward order of reverence could be so successfully established, why not the inward? Such sentiments were expressed with a rare eloquence by the Rector of St Andrew's Church of England, Keighley, when in a short article, published in the parish magazine for 1896, he asked:

Would you not enter into the reverent spirit of common worship in God's sanctuary still more thoroughly if you not only made yourselves one with those who lead the service by *standing while they stand* but also by *kneeling with them*? You have already sought God's Blessing on your devotions singly as individuals when you came into Church. Now kneel when we kneel, and join with us in asking Him to bless our United Act of Worship, the sacrifice of praise and thanksgiving, which we are about to offer Him Together ... [I]t is nothing less than a 'means whereby we may receive' ... the inward and spiritual grace of humble and heartfelt devotion.

Together they established that degree of congregational unity which made common worship not merely possible but also beautiful. To this end, he continued:

let me add the wish that the congregation would rise all together and with more promptness when the chapter and verse of the Gospel for the day are given out, and they may be ready to say all together ... the words of thanks and praise 'GLORY BE TO THEE, O GOD' at the commencement as they do the similar 'THANKS BE UNTO THEE, O LORD!' at the close.

'Those little things', he concluded, 'give a sense of unity and strength to public worship in the congregation, rendering it at once more elevating and more dignified.'[50]

More still did one big thing: congregational singing and response. Hence the observation of the Vicar of St Paul, King Cross, Halifax, that

it has long been my conviction that our church has never realised how glorious her worship might be if any person contributed his very best, in the way of singing and response. We shall still need choirs to lead and keep us steady but

[48]   *Ibid.*, p. 4.
[49]   *Ibid.*
[50]   Cremer, 'Order in Church'.

the singing would be of such a kind as the best choir in the world could not make it.

So he proposed 'a plan ... to join together into a union or guild, all those who would help to make our worship ... more congregational. We will have practices', he suggested, specifically 'congregational practices – after Evensong ... and also on Sundays. Those who join such a guild, will not be asked to sit together, but in their own places in Church to sing and respond conscientiously throughout the service, not merely in the more popular hymns, but also in those parts of the service which seem less attractive and more difficult.'[51]

Order permitted unity. And unity, in turn, paved the way for devotion. The highest form of devotion was the sacrament of the Eucharist, or Holy Communion. That, at least, was the view of those of a more ceremonial inclination. 'We have a number of different services in our Church', boomed the Rector of Keighley in the parish magazine for June 1922,

but only two have been given to us by our Lord Jesus Christ. One is used but once on the life of each Christian, because it is the service of Christian Fellowship. The other undoubtedly was meant to be ... the focus of Christian Life and the central act of Christian worship. The Lord's Supper [is] the great service of Thanksgiving (Eucharist) and the great bond of Fellowship (Holy Communion) among Christ's people. To give it pre-eminence over the man-appointed services, the altar-table was raised up, placed at the far end of the Church, and given special prominence, the clergy wore special robes ... and everything was done to give dignity and beauty to this service.[52]

Creeping papism perhaps. Yet the role and significance of Holy Communion within Anglican worship was amenable to a more subtle interpretation, and a more astute appreciation. Nearly thirty years earlier, the Vicar of St Paul's, King Cross, Halifax, expressed his devotion to this rite more delicately. 'The Service for the Holy Communion stands, in dignity and value, above every other service of the church,' he argued, 'and this for many reasons, e.g.,'

1 It is the only service which Christ himself ordained. He did not ordain Matins, or Evensong, or Litany. It has a claim on us, as His direct command and institution, which no other service possesses.
2 It was absolutely *the only Service* of the early church. The disciples came together 'upon the first day of the week *to break bread*' (Acts xx, 7).
3 It is, unlike the rest of our Services, essentially, *dramatic*. It is a Passion-Play.

[51] Frederic W. Cooper, 'The Vicar's Letter', *SPCKCPM*, vol. 7, no. 1, January 1898 (no page number).
[52] E.T.G. Hunter, 'Holy Communion', *KPCM*, vol. 31, no. 6, June 1922 (no page number).

It appeals to the eye, as well as the ear ... And [that] which we *see*, we remember always better than what we hear. Common Sense, as well as religious instinct, bids us to come and worship.

4 It reminds the careless of a forgotten duty. 'Out of sight, out of mind.' All the baptized have a right to be present to worship, and the driving away of all save the actual communicants from our Churches, is the cause of a deplorable neglect of a Sacred ordinance which millions of professing Churchpeople have never even seen!

5 It is the only service which is, throughout, a preparation for the worship of the Saints in light. In it, we actually join with angels and archangels and the company of heaven. If we are not fit to worship *Christ veiled* in these solemn mysteries, how shall we be fitted to worship Him *unveiled* hereafter in the glory of the open vision?[53]

These were rousing words, but they were tinged with melancholy, for what was so fit for men of good faith, so many had never done or even seen. They did not come to Holy Communion. And even if they did, they did not actually take communion. This was not an experience unique to St Paul's, King Cross. The old parish church of Halifax offered communion services twice on Sundays (every Sunday before and after Matins) and every Saint's Day, but a mournful Reverend Francis Pigou recorded in the parish magazine for January 1878 that 'many of our congregation never or very rarely communicate'.[54] Yet Pigou was nothing if not optimistic. He was convinced that 'Holy Communion ought to be celebrated weekly in every Parish Church like ours'. He was certain that 'weekly celebration' offered 'more frequent opportunities' for its observation.[55] And he advanced some persuasive figures. In 1875, there had been only 1,480 communicants at St John the Baptist. This figure had risen to 2,872 in 1876, and to 3,683 in 1877. These were new riches indeed, 'and a more reliable test of increasing spirituality than a full attendance [at service]'.[56]

There was, of course, much partisan special pleading in those remarks. Few local Anglican churches in the district celebrated Holy Communion every week in 1878. Indeed, the Vicar of All Souls', Haley Hill, discontinued the weekly 'Early Communion' in 1884 on the grounds that it was 'so poorly attended'. If, however, he was at that time more sceptical of the real extent of public piety than Pigou, he was also, perhaps, more resourceful. In the same year he proposed to

alter the role for the administration of the Holy Communion ... Since I find that

53 Frederic W. Cooper, 'Vicar's Letter', *SPCKCPM*, vol. 5, no. 1, January 1896 (no page number).
54 Rev. Francis Pigou, 'The Vicar's Pastoral', *HPCM*, vol. 1, no. 1, January 1878, p. 5.
55 Pigou, 'A Pastoral Letter to His Parishioners', in Pigou, *Sermons and Addresses*, p. 5.
56 Pigou, 'Vicar's Pastoral', p. 5.

the Sunday Evening congregation is our largest and I have reason to believe that there are many (women especially) who can *only* come out in the evening, I have ... arrange[d] for an Evening Communion once a month, which I hope will enable many to come to the Lord's Table who are otherwise prevented.

Then he went further. For, in his judgement, merely altering the timetable was not sufficient. 'I propose also', he added, 'at an early date to form a "Communicants' Union", which I trust will serve the double purpose of binding all our Communicants more closely together, and of providing occasional instruction for our younger Communicants. I feel sure that a Quarterly Communicants' Meeting of a devotional character would be helpful to all of us.'[57]

Others followed suit. In April 1893, the Vicar of St Paul's, King Cross, announced the formation of a Communicants' Guild at that church which 'we trust that the bulk of the newly confirmed, and all our regular communicants, will join'. The idea was to form a 'nucleus of faithful Churchmen and Churchwomen [to] encourage others to persevere in a regular use of the means of grace', and 'to hold monthly meetings which [will] serve, not only for instruction and mutual help, but also to bind the members all together in the Name of our Common Lord'.[58] Six years later, following an address by the Rector of Keighley to 'a large congregation ... on ... the [question] of the Holy Communion', it 'was proposed to form a Communicants' Guild, and about 50 names ... of persons wishing to become members' were recorded. The purpose of this society was explicitly stated:

The following are the obligations of membership:
Guild of Communicants and Church Workers
For the better realising of our blessings and duties, or
Communicant of the Church of Christ
OBJECTS
1 To help in uniting us more closely to one another in Jesus Christ
2 To encourage us to work for God
3 To enable us to make some preparation for regularly partaking of the Holy Communion
As a member of the Guild I will endeavour by His grace –
1 To pray daily – Morning and Evening
2 To read the Bible every day
3 To receive Holy Communion *regularly*
4 To pray each Sunday Morning for the other Members of the Guild and for the Clergy of the Parish
5 To do some work of God
6 To attend the Service of the Guild

[57] Rev. Henry Askwith, 'The Vicar's Monthly Letter', *ASHHPM*, p. 3.
[58] Frederic W. Cooper, 'Vicar's Letter', *SPCKCPM*, vol. 2, no. 4, April 1893 (no page number).

'It is hoped', the circular concluded, 'that by attention to the above simple obligations the number of our Communicants may be increased, and that the Guild may be the means of deepening the spiritual life of the Parish'.[59] Whether borne of realistic intent or galvanised by mere wishful thinking, the formation of communicants' guilds in Anglican churches throughout the district during the last quarter of the nineteenth century was inspired by one overriding purpose: to revive the centrality of Holy Communion in the worship of the Church of England, thereby 'to restore to its rightful place [His] Master's own service and to give it its ancient dynasty and beauty, much of which is lost when it is not taken as a complete service'. Whether there had ever been a golden age of the Eucharist in Anglican life was not, and is not, the point. The idea of restoration was almost universal at this time amongst local Anglican clergymen. And to that end, they pursued three strategies, in which the guilds offered vital institutional support: liturgical separation, ritual elaboration, and ceremonial intensification.

For many late Victorian clergymen nothing so demeaned the ceremony of the Holy Communion as its unfortunate timing. And in the Church of England at least, that was, so they understood, the product of eighteenth-century decadence, the inglorious legacy of '[an] age that ... to a large extent dissociated beauty from religion, and was spiritually slack, careless and irreverent'. In this way, argued the Rector of Keighley, 'the Holy Communion lost its unique place in the life and worship of the Anglican Church'. Specifically, 'music and ceremonial were transferred [to] Matins and Evensong ... and for many these services took the chief place, while the Lord's own service was relegated to the inferior position of being tacked on to Matins or attended by a few at 8.00 a.m.' Thus, 'bereft of much that ... had been associated with it, it became the practice for congregations to walk out in the middle of the service, and to leave behind just a few faithful people to receive the sacrament and obey the Lord's command'.[60]

The first task, accordingly, was to re-establish the liturgical distinction, or separation, of Holy Communion. Mid-nineteenth-century custom had permitted, even encouraged, the amalgamation of Matins and Holy Communion as one, three-hour service on the day (usually the first Sunday of the month) of the celebration of the Eucharist. In January 1896, the Vicar of St Paul's, King Cross, announced to his parishioners that '[h]enceforth ... the Late (Choral) Celebration with Sermon will

---

[59]   Frederic Damstini Cremer, 'Communicants' Guild', *KPCM*, vol. 22, no. 7, July 1899 (no page number).
[60]   Hunter, 'Holy Communion'.

begin at 10.30 a.m., and form a *separate service in itself* . . . on the First Sunday of the month and at great Festivals'. He continued,

on those Sundays, Morning Prayer will be said [plain] at 9.30[,] we shall by this mean [*sic*] avoid a function of wearisome length, lasting from 10.30 to 12.45 or even later, trying alike to Priest, Choir and the people, and no service in our Church (except the 'Three Hours' Service' on Good Friday) will ever last more than an hour-and-a-half.

Strict separation had two advantages: first, it enabled 'those who [were] unable to come to Church [before] 10.30 [to] come in quietly then, and take their seats for the second (i.e. the Communion) service';[61] secondly, the shortening of the overall length of the two (near distinct services) permitted officious Anglican clergymen an additional justification for their pleas to 'our people to *remain in church* and reverently worship during the Celebration, instead of leaving the Church after the Prayer of the Church Militant'.[62] As one divine observed, 'there is no authority in our prayer book' for such exits. They were 'the result of a lax and unspiritual age'.[63] Hence the communicants' guilds: 'We know that old abuses die hard . . . and . . . no change – even for the better – is ever very popular at first . . . but if more instructed Church people (e.g. the Guild members) will show the example, others will not be slow to follow it.'[64]

Proper celebration of so distinguished a service called for strict adherence to its appropriate liturgical forms. Or so an increasing number of contemporaries believed. 'Most of you will agree', began another editorial in St Paul's parish magazine, that 'the Holy Eucharist is the Church's highest act of worship and that as such it ought . . . to . . . be [made] clear that we do really think it the most important service of the day. It ought to be choral and to be accompanied with reverent and dignified ritual.'[65] The then Rector of Keighley certainly did agree. 'Occasionally, at least' (in fact, the third Sunday of the month at St Andrew's) the service should, so he judged, be afforded 'the added beauty and dignity of a simple musical setting'.[66] This was a problem, since 'a great many of us – an increasing number – make it a point to communicate before breakfast, and it is usually thought impossible to have a choral so early in the day.' But he proposed to do exactly that.

[61] Cooper, 'Vicar's Letter', January 1896.
[62] WHQ, D72/134, incom. arch. ref., Frederic W. Cooper, 'Vicar's Letter', *SPCKCM*, vol. 3, no. 9, October 1894.
[63] Hunter, 'Holy Communion'.
[64] Cooper, 'Vicar's Letter', October 1894.
[65] WHQ, D72/134, Frederic W. Cooper, 'Vicar's Letter', *SPCKCPM*, vol. 7, no. 1, January 1898 (no page number).
[66] Hunter, 'Holy Communion'.

The Eucharist, he insisted, was 'both a Feast and an offering, or act of worship ... [T]he two cannot rightly be divided ... I]t is important to count upon the unity of this our highest act of worship.' This being so, he confessed

that ... I do not set much store ... by ... the fact ... that ... there will be so few people ... at the early service ... Ten people with enough faith and love to bring them to Church at eight o'clock will offer a better act of worship than a hundred who are attracted to Church only by beautiful music at a late and convenient hour. So let us make a great deal of our early Eucharist. Let us make it both the most beautiful and the most devotional service of the day.[67]

Institutional intensification was as much a state of mind as a guide to worship. It placed the sacrament of Holy Communion above all other expressions of religious witness. It argued for weekly observance of the rite. And it insisted upon the centrality of the rite in the celebrations of the Lord's Day. This view found perhaps its finest expression, and certainly its highest (in every sense of the word) evaluation, in the remarks of Canon Winter, Vicar of nearby Elland, made at the ceremonies to mark the opening of a newly rebuilt and enlarged St Paul's, King Cross, in 1912. 'A churchman', he argued,

is one ... who depends ... on sacramental grace from the cradle to the grave ... Churchmanship does not mean ... going to churches one likes ... listening to one's favourite preacher, in one's favourite chair ... It means ... sacramental union with Christ. The altar, not the pulpit, not the organ [is] the focus of a true Churchman's worth ... I rejoice ... to know the place of honour [is] given to the festival of the Eucharist ... and ... I trust and believe ... that St Paul's is going to set an example of making that service the general service for [the] Lord's Day.[68]

Dissenting adjustment: variety, integrity and devotion

No self-respecting nonconformist could go that far: not in 1870, and not in 1920 either. Yet what is really striking about the ecclesiastical history, more specifically about the liturgical history of this period, is not so much the intra-Anglican debates which such avowedly Tractarian innovations invariably inspired – important though those no doubt were – but the inter-denominational convergence which so much contemporary aesthetic, devotional and organisational change expressed – largely neglected though this has subsequently been.[69] For the High

---

67   Cooper, 'Vicar's Letter', January 1898.
68   WHQ, D72/105, St Paul's Church, King Cross, Halifax, New Church Building Committee Minute Book, 2 November 1912.
69   Though for a hint, see Binfield, *So Down To Prayers*, esp. pp. 149ff.; also Chadwick, *The Victorian Church, Part II*, pp. 325–7.

church movement in West Yorkshire's Establishment was complemented by a parallel quest for a renewed vigour, and a significantly altered understanding, in the style, form and even in the content of public worship in the mainstream dissenting Protestant organisations. That change was so considerable, and so closely did it follow contemporary changes in Anglican thinking and practice, that it might reasonably be described as a form of liturgical convergence.

The notion of 'convergence' is employed advisedly here. It is understood to mean a growing similarity, not an actual sameness. And it is taken to imply a practical concurrence rather than a theoretical consensus. This underlines the fact that what united contemporary churchmen and ministers was not really ecclesiology, still less the theory of the priesthood, but the search for a certain liturgical orderliness. Each in their own way actively sought a more ordered and thus a more reverent service. To this end, each attempted to ally the advantages of beautiful buildings and polite culture to the goal of a more generally satisfying, but also more carefully controlled, form of public worship. In that pursuit, three concepts governed prevailing notions of progress: the ideal of liturgical variety, especially in the use of music; the virtue of congregational integrity, specifically of a congregation acting and being as one; and finally the quality of individual devotion, or the duty of each member of the congregation to believe as emerging norms of worship dictated.

Such progress was invariably the product of much internal soul-searching, even wrangling. Hence the earlier observations of James Miall, lamenting yet another aspect of recent change in his beloved Congregationalist society: 'I am exceedingly sorry', he wrote, 'that any attempt should have been made amongst us to introduce a liturgy, either in place of, or even as a supplement to, Free Prayer'. In so doing, he argued, 'we [i.e. Congregationalists] should [sic] be sacrificing life, freedom and power to the mere form and beauty of words'. In this vein, he continued: 'No doubt there ought to be decency and order – but that subjection is conformity to inward personal law of propriety and good sense, not bondage to any outward antiquated form.' Yet he concluded: 'At the same time I am very ready to admit that, without giving up our freedom, we ought to seek after more beauty, more variety and more solemnity in our devotions.'[70]

Beauty, variety and solemnity had to come from somewhere. And sometimes they came from elsewhere. The Chairman of the Yorkshire Congregational Mission, Mr W.E. Glyde, writing some ten years later

<hr />

[70]   Miall, *Congregationalism in Yorkshire*, pp. 219–20.

than Miall, suggested one possibility. '[T]here [is] much to be said in favour of the Ritualistic Movement', he argued,

as to worship, though not as to doctrine ... appealing as it [does] to the eye and the ear, and through them to the imagination ... [Indeed] owing to change of circumstances [we] need not consider it imperative to adhere closely to the studied plainness of worship adopted by [our] fathers, and might introduce the luxury of the organ and its frequent accompaniment, the chant and the anthem.

'But', he added cautiously, 'too much importance must not be attached to this attention, or desire to proceed too quickly in this direction.' And his final words uncannily echoed those of the anxious historian: 'They [i.e. these changes] must not, at least without very careful consideration, proceed to substitute a liturgical form for the Free Prayers which had been so long the practice of their fathers and themselves; but rather direct attention to the ordering of their service that it should be ... intelligent ... and ... devout.'[71]

However, what was an anathema, at least to some, as late as the 1880s, became the object of more generally sympathetic consideration for others, barely a decade later. Writing in 1892, the Reverend J.R. Bailey of Park Congregational Church, Halifax, proposed a major 'reform in the expression of the spirit of devotion'. 'First', he argued, 'we have ... underrated the importance of beauty and variety in the externals of our worship ... Secondly, the time has come [to] make it imperative upon us to revise our forms of service.' In the past, he noted, Congregationalists had determined that the 'Commandments should have no place in our worship on Sundays ... They had also ... objected to choirs singing anthems ... [and] insisted that one voice alone, that of the minister, shall be heard offering up the prayer of the congregation.' 'But', he observed, both mournfully and presciently, '[p]raise [can] not take the form of a solo.'

Congregational worship, so the Reverend Bailey contended, was not actually 'in error in making so much of the sermon'. But he insisted, 'we have been wrong in regarding the devotional parts of our services as altogether subsidising [sic] to the preaching function'. Thus he proposed a compromise. In future, he suggested, services should 'combin[e] free prayer ... with responsive supplications, confessions and thanksgivings ... so arranged that the whole congregation may join in them'. To this end, they might 'draw ... freely on the rich stores of devotional expression at our command in the litanies, collects and orders of the Book of Common Prayer'. And they must shorten ... the length [of the service] while adding to the number and variety of individual items in

[71]   W.E. Glyde, 'Yorkshire Congregational Union', pp. 71–2.

our services ... call ... in the aid of so-styled laymen in the reading of the lessons ... and mak[e] ... larger use of the best music'. By doing all this they would 'remove the reproach of irreverence in our outward demeanour as worshippers'.[72]

These were not lame words. On the contrary. They spoke to a powerful movement for liturgical and devotional change within local Congregationalism. In fact, as early as 1872, Harrison Road Congregationalists began a 'conversation ... on desirability of altering our form of service'. The deacons of this society recommended, on that occasion, 'that certain enquiries be made as to the order at various places, to aid us in coming to ... a decision ... as to the form we should adopt'.[73] Six years later, the same body resolved 'that the order of services be rearranged on the first Sunday in January 1879'. And this time, the priorities of reform were laid bare: 'The objects sought in the alteration [are: f]irst, more variety in the service; [s]econd, improvement in the choral portion; third, more attention to the devotional portion in all our services.'

Specifically, that meant more hymns, more chants and (new) anthems in the Sunday service at Harrison Road in the 1880s and 1890s; in short, more variety and an 'improvement' in the devotional portion of the service. The liturgical impact of these changes was complex and ambiguous. Hence too the ambiguousness of contemporary reactions to it and the cautious progress of innovation, there as elsewhere. But contemporaries definitely noticed *a* change, a subtle shift in the fundamentals of chapel liturgy, away from the 'exhortatory' and towards the 'devotional', in the means and ends of public worship. And something of that sea-change in devotional sensibilities found its way into the hearts and minds of their brethren in Keighley too. As a result, John Brigg, the great Congregationalist layman, noted 'eventful changes' during 'the past twelve years' (i.e. 1871–83) in the 'forms of worship' practised at Keighley, especially an 'alteration in the forms of ritual' and the intruding 'novelty of ceremony'.[74] Over the next ten or fifteen years those changes became more 'eventful' still: 'In 1885, the practice of singing "Amen" after the prayers were [*sic*] introduced ... In 1893 a trial period of singing or chanting the Lord's Prayer was [agreed] and in 1902 ... a new Hymn book – "The Congregational Church Hymnal and Worship" was ... distributed amongst local societies.'[75]

---

[72] Bailey, *Progressive Congregationalism*, pp. 6–8.
[73] CDA, CUR 1:13, Harrison Road Congregational Chapel, Halifax, Church and Deacons' Book, 2 April 1872.
[74] *Keighley Congregational Church Manual, 1883*, p. 65.
[75] Reid Marchbank, *One Hundred Years of Progress*, p. 43.

The same concern for more variety in the service and greater attention to the devotional aspects of worship characterised contemporary
liturgical manoeuvres amongst most branches of local Methodism. On
26 July 1872, the trustees of South Parade Wesleyan Methodist Chapel,
Halifax, determined at their quarterly meeting to introduce a number of
changes in the forms of public worship at their church. These included:

1   The Psalms as Chants be introduced into public service.
2   A second lesson from the scriptures to be read at Evening Service.
3   Hymns to be sung through; the Preacher 'giving out' the first verse only.
4   The Sunday morning sacrament to be celebrated not by Chants, but with the
    Ten Commandments read from the pulpit and responses sung by the choir
    and congregation.[76]

Then on 18 November 1878, a special church meeting of Hanover
Street Methodist New Connexion Chapel, Halifax, resolved, 'that we
accept the order of service recommended by the October Quarterly
Meeting as tending to the improvement of the mode of worship and the
spiritual profit of the congregation'.

The order, so reformed, was as follows:[77]

1   Hymn
2   Prayer
3   Chant or Anthem
4   First Lesson
5   Hymn
6   Second Lesson
7   Notices
8   Hymn
9   Prayer
10 Sermon
11 Hymn
12 Prayer

Similar, reformed, versions quickly spread across the various Methodist Connexions in late nineteenth-century Halifax. As they spread, self-
conscious novelties were intruded into the traditional forms of public
worship in many local societies. On 25 July 1890, a trustees' meeting
considered 'suggestions for improvement of Sunday Service'. They
included: '(1) Repeating of the Lord's Prayer led by the Choir and (2)
Reading of the Ten Commandments on the First Sunday of the month.'

---

[76] CDA, Misc. 481/18, South Parade Wesleyan Chapel, Halifax, Trustees' Meetings
Minute Book, 8 July 1872.
[77] CDA, Misc. 287/26, Hanover Street, Methodist New Connexion Chapel, Halifax,
Leaders' Meeting Minute Book, 18 November 1878.

These suggestions bore immediate fruit. The order of public service determined for chapel worship the following year was:

1 Hymn
2 Prayer (with Lord's Prayer repeated)
3 Chant
4 First Lesson
5 Hymn
6 Second Lesson
7 Notices
8 Hymn
9 Sermon
10 Hymn
11 Prayer

In addition, the minister was empowered to read the twentieth chapter of Exodus on the first Sunday of the month. There were to be 'no responses' from the choir.[78]

Compare this with the order of worship established at Brunswick United Methodist Free Church, one year later:

1 Start Hymn or Sanctus
2 Short Prayer and Lord's Prayer repeated
3 Hymn
4 First Lesson
5 Chant
6 Second Lesson
7 Notices
8 Hymn
9 Prayer
10 Hymn
11 Sermon
12 Hymn
13 Benediction with Amen Intoned[79]

The bug spread to Keighley at much the same time. Here, resistance to such change proved at least a little tougher. A trustees' meeting of Temple Street Methodist Chapel, 'mother church' to the local Wesleyan Methodist Circuit, noted widespread 'dissatisfaction with the choral portion of the service' in April 1872. So it resolved to recommend changes in the near future with 'a view to its improvement'.[80] So far so good. However, the Leaders' Meeting of the society 'suggest[ed] to the

78 CDA, Misc. MR/151, Rhodes Street Wesleyan Methodist Chapel, Halifax, Trustees' Meetings Minute Book, 16 July 1891.
79 CDA, MR/121, Brunswick United Methodist Free Church, Halifax, Leaders' Meeting, Minute Book, 11 May 1892.
80 KPL, 105D77/2/21/15/b, Temple Street Methodist Church, Keighley, Trust Minute Book, 13 April 1872.

Trustees the desirability of arranging with the choir not to introduce anthems into the service except on Anniversary occasions and when specially requested by the officiating minister'.[81]

Debate on the issue was protracted and not a little heated. But the self-consciously progressive forces eventually won at least a partial victory. One month later, the trustees decreed that 'the Choir be allowed to sing an anthem at either service on the first Sunday of the month and at the Sunday school anniversary services'.[82]

A similar pattern was observable amongst Keighley's Baptists. On 27 January 1868, a special church meeting of Albert Street Chapel debated 'the delicate subject' of 'chanting' during services.[83] It came to no decision. The matter was raised again five years later, with the same indecisive conclusion.[84] Five years after that, the church determined to introduce 'experimentally for two months' a 'chant time' at each service.[85] But the forces of conservatism were still not vanquished. This first experiment lasted just the stipulated two months. The matter was finally resolved in 1881. Then at a church meeting it was moved

that we adopt the Chanting of Psalms as suggested by the choir but the choir be requested to hold congregational practice on evenings each week for a month before it be introduced into the Lord's Day Service ... in order that members of the Congregation may have an opportunity of becoming acquainted with the mode of chanting. It was strongly felt that praises to Almighty God should be such as could be entered into freely by all and a good Congregational sing is desired.

This motion was duly passed.[86]

It is, of course, important to be clear about the limits of liturgical change. The notion of a musical service, long familiar to the Roman tradition, and increasingly popular in the (High Anglican) Church of England, remained alien to local dissenting custom. Reform in the mainstream of Protestant nonconformity envisaged at this time the ideal of music in a service; no more.[87] Such 'musical intrusion' into dissenting worship assumed three basic forms: as anthems, which became a regular

---

81 KPL, 105D77/2/21/7/4, Temple Street Methodist Society, Keighley, Leaders' Meeting Minute Book, 15 January 1885.
82 KPL, 105D77/2/21/15/b, Temple Street Methodist Church, Keighley, Trust Minute Book, 27 February 1885.
83 Rhodes, *Keighley Baptist History*, p. 63.
84 *Ibid.*, p. 68.
85 *Ibid.*, p. 72.
86 KPL, uncat. MS, Albert Street Baptist Chapel, Keighley, Church Meeting Minute Book, 28 March 1881.
87 For a fuller discussion of some of these differences, see Jim Obelkevich, 'Music and Religion in the Nineteenth Century', in Obelkevich et al., *Disciplines of Faith*, pp. 550–65.

part of almost every nonconformist service; as hymns, something of an excuse for a virtuoso performance by the chapel organist, but which also permitted the congregation to join in proceedings more freely and fully; and finally, if more rarely, as cantata, seldom performed at ordinary services but usually reserved for the great festivals. For the most part, these were piecemeal incursions into the life of its churches which did not threaten their essentially Protestant tone. But that did not mean that they were insignificant. Nor that they passed off unnoticed. Rather the contrary.

At a ceremony in February 1900, to mark the opening of the new organ at Lund Park Wesleyan Methodist Chapel, Keighley, the Reverend S. Whitehead, Chairman of the Bradford and Halifax District Wesleyan Methodist Connexion, delivered, with suitable corroboration from Ephesians v. 18–20, an 'eloquent plea and justification for the ministry of sacred song'. His argument and reasoning bear careful scrutiny. 'It is admitted', he declared, 'that to hear God's word [is] a duty, and that it [is] a duty to pray, but', he continued, 'the duty of Christian song [is] not always felt to be so obvious. And yet that it legitimately enters ... into public worship would appear [sic] from various considerations.' Specifically, 'The mere possession of this unrivalled power [to] join speech with music [to] inform while [it] delighted [and to] charm the ear but fill the mind with lofty sentiments ... was of itself proof that we were not only to sing, but to employ the power in divine service.' More binding proof still could be found in the Bible: '[W]e might gather the duty from examples in Holy Writ, and especially from our Lord and his apostles [also] ... In Genesis we had the first mention of a choir [of] psalm and prophecy [in] the triumphant hallelujas [sic] of Revolution.' Finally, Christian custom, carefully interpreted in a nonconformist mentality, suggested the virtues not only of music in general, but of particular varieties of music: '[T]hat is ... in worship we are to sing not in one form, but various[:] solo, response, chorus; not in one kind of composition only, but in different kinds – psalms, chants, anthems, hymns. Then this duty of sacred song might be inferred from what was the worship of Heaven.' The duty of sacred song also imposed a dutiful manner. 'We should sing', Whitehead insisted, 'with understanding ... [I]t should be a rational exercise ... [T]he more the psalmody was understood, the more it would be loved.' That it was a collective exercise in religious understanding and not an opportunity for the performance of particular human abilities ensured that 'those to whom tune [is] denied [may] accompany with the melody of the heart ... We should sing with the spirit ... [T]he inward mind ... [is] ... the accompaniment of the outward manifestation ... This melody of the heart [is] altogether a different thing from musical taste or musical gift.'[88]

Indeed. But the 'melody of the heart' was also different from the power of the word, traditionally understood, for it appealed to a liturgical order which elevated the significance of the devotional service over the witness of the preacher. 'Vanity' and 'devotion' made the institution of worship something more than the sum of the inspired word, fervent prayer, and obedient response. They made it an integrated event in itself: a means to attention and to reflection and submission certainly, but also a sacred occasion in and of itself. Nothing so clearly highlighted the sacred character of the entire performance – conceived as an entire performance – than the continual intrusion of music in its presentation and unfolding: music and musical intrusion into the service not only diminished the liturgical significance of the preacher's words in the prevailing system of Protestant worship; they also disciplined his audience. They regulated its participation in the service, and they defined its role in its proper execution. They made it an ordered, a reverent and, above all, a unified congregation.

Speaking before Representatives of the Halifax District of the Yorkshire Congregational Union in September 1888, the Reverend M. Perry, Chairman of the District, observed, somewhat blandly, that 'the manner of our worship and the spirit we throw into it has much to do with the prosperity or otherwise of the church', but then referred, in this context, to 'The Service of Song in our Churches', which he insisted 'ought to be *attractive* and *helpful*'. Much of his reasoning was unremarkable. 'Most men have a love of music, and are attracted by it ... [T]he power of harmony to elevate the spirit ... is quite proverbial.' Some of his subsidiary justifications were, however, more interesting:

Good singing may sometimes make up for poor preaching, and what may be lacking in the sermon may be supplied by the hymn. Many of our hymns are well fitted to inspire thought and awaken conviction ... and to sing some of those beautiful sentiments, often so full of prayer and praise to the Great Creator and Redeemer is no small part of our worship. The effects are good and we frequently hear references made to the singing by persons who have even forgotten the text on which the minister based his discourse.

But not everyone sang. And this was unfortunate. Or so Perry insisted: 'I want to emphasise the term "Congregational Singing"', he intoned. And he continued,

---

[88] KPL, uncat. pub., Rev. S. Whitehead, 'The Duty of Christian Song', *Keighley News*, 24 February 1900.

[a]s this is almost the only part of worship in which the congregation is expected to take part, we ought to attach great importance to it ... But all singing in our churches is *not Congregational*, it is often confined to an elect people ... and the rest of the congregation are mute admirers or otherwise of the performances of their brethren constituting the choir. This ought not to be so.

Sure enough, Perry acknowledged that 'during the last twenty years wonderful improvements have been made in our hymnology, and in our choral music ... But', he added, 'this is a hindrance more than a help in worship when the singing is uncongregational, and rendered by a few persons only.' Thus he concluded: 'Let us have ... the *best hymns* and the *most elegant music* and the *most accomplished singers*, we need ... in our worship ... but let us have our CONGREGATIONS trained to sing, to sing with the heart and with the understanding, I would add, *and with the lips* also.'[89] This argument, in rather a different form, spilled over into the affairs of Keighley's Baptists. No sooner had they agreed on the 'chanting of psalms' during the service than the question of how and by whom they should be chanted arose.[90] On 28 January 1884, 'the sitting and standing of the congregation during the chanting of the psalms' was 'a subject of comment'.[91] On 27 February 1888, 'Brother William Rhodes, having drawn attention to the attitude of the congregation during the singing of the chant ... suggested that an invitation to stand during that portion of the service be given from the pulpit'.[92] The motion was vigorously debated and withdrawn under duress. It was raised again five years later when 'Brother Thomas Day moved that inasmuch as we had been unable to secure uniformity of position during Chanting, in place of Chant [*sic*], one of Sankey's hymns be sung, or an occasional anthem'.[93] Again, the case was forcefully argued on both sides, and again the question left unresolved. Finally, on 26 December 1894, it was agreed that there be a chant (or an anthem) at each service, 'during the singing of which the congregation be requested to remain seated'.[94]

This was, on the face of things, a different solution. Yet, paradoxically, it also pointed to a profound similarity of liturgical purpose, for the various questions about singing – who did it, when, and how – raging in

---

[89]   Rev. M. Perry, 'Conditions of Success in Our Congregational Churches', *HDCM*, vol. 6, no. 11, November 1888, p. 249.

[90]   KPL, uncat. MS, Albert Street Baptist Chapel, Keighley, Church Meeting Minute Book, 28 March 1881.

[91]   Rhodes, *Keighley Baptist History*, p. 75.

[92]   KPL, uncat. MS, Albert Street Baptist Chapel, Keighley, Church Meeting Minute Book, 27 February 1888.

[93]   *Ibid.*, 26 December 1893.

[94]   Rhodes, *Keighley Baptist History*, p. 89.

the various nonconformist societies of this time – all addressed a wider liturgical issue. This may be called the question of congregational integrity. And that was a question not merely about congregational participation, but also about congregational obedience; that is, about collective reverence and its proper forms. Less than one year after Brunswick Methodists revised their service order, a Leaders' Meeting of the society determined that 'an announcement be made from the pulpit to the effect that the congregation be requested ... to bow the head with eyes closed during prayer'. Afterwards, '[a] conversation arose as to the want of reverence on the part of many in the congregation by sitting upright with eyes opened during prayer'.[95]

Moreover, that 'want' of congregational reverence, at least in this respect, was not confined to Halifax's Methodists. A 'Compendium of Later Regulations', in a copy of *Rules of the Society of the People Called Methodists*, filed amongst the papers of Heber Street Wesleyan Methodist Chapel, Keighley, contained the following observations 'Of Public Worship and the Sacraments':

1 We strongly recommend it to all our people to *kneel* at prayer; and we desire that all our pews may, as far as possible, be so formed as to admit of this in the easiest manner ... We request that all our chapels be furnished with hassocks, or with kneeling boards; so that every excuse may be taken away from those who persist in the irreverent and unscriptural custom of sitting while at prayer.
2 We strongly urge on the congregations the propriety and importance of *standing* while singing the praises of God.[96]

The manner of genuflexion here mattered less than the fact (or the presumption) of individual submission to collective forms. The fact of individual submission to collective forms mattered more because it constituted a ritual expression of the essential unity between the submission of each man to God and of all men, of whatever worldly standing, to that same God; a submission which might be expressed, nevertheless, with such collective dignity and individual integrity that it would also, at the same time, elevate each man in the eyes of God.

Liturgical order gave a sense of unity to public worship. Music gave it dignity. Ritual genuflexion elevated its form. But nothing gave greater unity, dignity and elevation to the institution of the public religious service – nothing, in effect, made it more an occasion of devotion – than the sacrament of Holy Communion. Or so many even of the nonconfor-

95 CDA, MR/121, Brunswick United Methodist Free Church, Leaders' Meeting Minute Book, 16 August 1893.
96 KPL, 105D77/2/9/1/f, Anon., *Rules of the Society of the People Called Methodists* (London, n.d.), p. 13.

mists increasingly came to believe. So much so that participation in the Holy Communion became the essential test for membership in many local dissenting societies during the latter years of the nineteenth century. And even amongst those of traditional dissenting bent, the Lord's Supper became a much more regular part of Sunday services. Naturally, it never became so frequent, or so significant, as to enable the altar to supplant the pulpit for the literal (as well as the symbolic) focus of devotional life in any nonconformist chapel. That remained the prerogative of the Roman Catholic Church, and (to a lesser extent), the purpose of High Anglican polemics. But it did become sufficiently frequent and significant to adjust the balance, if not the form, of a common, dissenting religious life.

To be sure, the road to institutional frequency and significance often began from a very low plateau indeed. Only after much discussion was 'provision' made at Northgate End Unitarian Chapel, Halifax, 'for a Communion Service to be held [there] three times a year', in 1873.[97] On the other hand, Devonshire Street Congregational Church in Keighley held a communion service 'monthly, on the first Sunday in the month', at much the same time.[98] Most later Victorian societies aimed for the higher level of frequency. For instance, the Leaders' Meeting of Temple Street Wesleyan Methodist Church, also in Keighley, drew 'the attention of the Superintendent Minister to the irregularity of the appointments of the Sacrament' at that place in 1884, and 'requested' that he 'appoint one each month' in subsequent years.[99] But the frequency of such 'appointments' was not the only issue at stake. More pointed, in many societies, was the frequency of individual attendance on these occasions. As early as 1872, the officers of Hanover Street Methodist New Connexion Chapel, Halifax, responding to a resolution at their own circuit conference held at Elland on 28 September of that year, determined to find 'means' to 'increase the attendance' of their members and adherents at the 'ordinance of the Lord's Supper'.[100] Ten years later, a Deacons' Meeting, at Harrison Road Congregational Church, in the same town, 'called attention to the irregularity of attendance at the Lord's Supper, and the importance of acquainting ... members with [that] fact

[97] CDA, NEC 2, Northgate End Unitarian Chapel, Halifax, Chapel Meeting Minute Book, 22 February 1873.
[98] *Keighley Congregational Church Manual, 1873*, p. 6.
[99] KPL, 105D77/2/21/7/a, Temple Street (Keighley), Wesleyan Methodist Society, Leaders' Meeting, Minute Book, 12 June 1884.
[100] CDA, Misc. 57/2, Hanover Street Methodist New Connexion Chapel, Halifax, Sunday School Teachers' Meetings, 1 October 1872.

periodically to ... prevent, if possible, coldness and indifference, and the tendency to lapsing'.[101]

Here, polite admonition gradually turned to strict ultimatum. Six years later, the church noted that '[s]ome members [of the church] do not attend the Lord's Supper', and warned those recalcitrants that 'those who are able to attend, and do not, will [in future] be understood as expressing a desire to withdraw from membership', adding, as a somewhat contemptuous and officious rider, that '[i]t is important that the names of the Members' Roll should be those of real members'.[102] Nor was this a change of custom (or emphasis) peculiar to the Congregationalists. The previous year, Lower Skircoat Green United Methodist Free Church, also in Halifax, passed a motion that 'the sacrament should be the test of membership'.[103] Their reasoning was highly significant. This was, they concluded, the best 'criterion' for 'religious activity' which they knew.[104] Over the next two decades, that 'knowledge', if such it was, gradually became a commonplace. So, when the Annual Church Meeting at Brunswick United Methodist Church, Halifax, 'learn[ed] with regret', in January 1917, 'that some members of our churches connected with the circuit do not attend the sacramental services', it instructed the incumbent minister of Brunswick to remind the faithful that 'this ordinance is a recognised condition of membership of our and almost every other Christian church[, and] to look upon [their] attendance at such occasions as a duty binding upon all professed disciples of Christ'.[105]

[101] CDA, CUR 1:13 Harrison Road Congregational Chapel, Halifax, Church and Deacons' Book, 22 May 1883.
[102] CDA, CUR 1:100, *Harrison Road Congregational Church, Halifax Yearbook, 1889* (Halifax, 1889), p. 16.
[103] CDA, MR/227, Lower Skircoat Green United Methodist Free Church, Society Minute Book, 1 February 1888.
[104] *Ibid.*, 2 April 1888.
[105] CDA, Misc. 57/11, Brunswick United Methodist Church, Church Meeting Minute Book, 31 January 1917.

8 Christianity within and beyond the churches: the pattern of the devotion and the authenticity of expression

Introduction: from ordered witness to common practice

A public religious sensibility which was now more self-consciously 'devotional' than 'experiential' was not necessarily any less intense. But it was, so to speak, more obviously regulated. Put another way, it observed the chronological divisions of life more closely: the week, the year, the seasons, and even of the generations. To be sure, this moral concentration upon the sacred dimensions of chronological order was rather more a matter of shifting than of wholly altering characteristic ecclesiastical and communal emphases. This was true, if for no other reason, because sacred division of life was scarcely new to the later nineteenth century. Nor was its more profound cultivation in Victorian West Yorkshire entirely planned. But, just as the contemporary beautification of religious space had, seemingly by a super-denominational logic of its own, surreptitiously intruded an enhanced sacralisation of particular religious events into a converging devotional life, so the elaboration of religious worship, again apparently almost with a momentum of its own, gradually created a more settled order of religious observance in a common spiritual experience. This, increasingly, made religious worship not only the characteristic form of local religious life, but actually gave new, that is, newly characteristic, forms to that life, forging an appropriate type of worship for each part of an ever more appreciably *consecutive* individual and collective religious existence. And that change had significant consequences: for the churches, and beyond them too. They began in the increasing formalisation of the religious week.

Liturgical change and the formalisation of the religious week

In this scheme of things, the pivotal unit of liturgical organisation was the religious week. And the most important day of the religious week was Sunday. This, of course, to a considerable extent, had always been so. Certainly, it was not a nineteenth-century invention. Indeed, in its most extreme form, as the doctrine and practice of Sabbatarianism, it had a long-standing place in the English Protestant tradition.[1] But it enjoyed something of a mid-nineteenth-century heyday. The evangelical revival and the cult of civilised improvement together made the early Victorian Sunday special.[2] They made it, in fact, the 'English Sunday'; a phenomenon carefully differentiated, both at the time and subsequently, from the corrupt 'continental' form. Its observance was 'almost universally considered . . . right and proper'. This was true even amongst those – perhaps particularly amongst those – who were not especially 'religious themselves'. Even amongst the indifferent, 'conventions of respectability' could, if outraged, exact severe penalties of 'caste' forfeiture for indulgent or scandalous behaviour.[3]

However, its later Victorian, associational form was arguably something rather different again, for it operated in an environment which, however minimally, was now less amenable to the conventions of social restraint. And it acted within institutions which had, in their very ambition, themselves blurred the distinction between religious life and Sunday observance. It was therefore motivated by two subtly different concerns: first, a desire to prevent the growth of secular intrusion – hence the tirade from Keighley Wesleyan Circuit against 'Sunday trad[ers]' seeking what they called 'unfair advantage' for 'one section of the public' against another;[4] and secondly, a determination to restrict the range of proper religious activity permitted on that day to what they themselves considered appropriate – thus the Reverend F. Chapman's complaint against 'so-called sacred concerts' put on by a 'Sunday Band', and attended by so many of his 'young people' in that town during 1892.[5] This is why it was an uphill struggle to preserve that 'divine . . . merciful provision of a day of rest' from those trends in local society which 'tend[ed] alternatively to secularise it', or to 'render it valueless', or both.[6]

[1]   The fullest pre-Victorian account is now found in B.W. Ball, *The Seventh-Day Men: Sabbatarians and Sabbatarianism in England and Wales, 1600–1800* (Oxford, 1994), *passim*.
[2]   John Wigley, *The Rise and Fall of the Victorian Sunday* (Manchester, 1980); see esp. chs. 2 and 3.
[3]   George H. McNeal, 'The Modern Sunday and Its Influence on National Life', *KWMCM*, no. 74, July 1915 (no page number).
[4]   KPL, 105D77/1/3/2/c, Keighley Wesleyan Circuit, Quarterly Meeting Minute Book, 23 March 1903.
[5]   KPL, 105D77/1/3/2/b, Keighley Wesleyan Circuit, Quarterly Meeting Minute Book, 18 September 1892.
[6]   KPL, 105D77/1/3/2/c, Keighley Wesleyan Circuit, Quarterly Meeting Minute Book, 23 September 1912.

Bad enough in itself, the insidious diminution of the sabbath was potentially disastrous for a religion of dutiful observance. This point was made quite explicitly by the Reverend J.W. Laycock in a paper highlighting the 'Two Things Absolutely Necessary to the Success of Our Ministry', which he delivered to the Keighley Wesleyan Methodist Quarterly Circuit Meeting in February 1894. These he identified as the 'Authoritative Book' and 'The Sacred Day'. The first was obvious. It was 'evidence of the truth ... of ... all our distinctive doctrines'.[7] The second was more complex. At one level, it was self-evidently vital, a condition of Methodist membership, in accordance with 'the ... directions of conference and, above all, with the abiding precept of God's word'.[8] But at another level, more especially at the level which was Laycock's particular concern, it was vital for 'the continuance of public worship'. More specifically still, it was crucial for the future 'attendance of the unconverted' at church, for he believed that their subsequent attachment to the institutions of organised religion would 'depend ... absolutely' upon 'general recognition of the sanctity of the day of rest'.[9] That being so, it was essential to preserve its integrity; even, if possible, to extend its influence. Most contemporaries agreed. To this end, vigilant authorities employed three strategies: first, they resisted creeping secularisation wherever they could; second, they sought to enhance the religious significance of the occasion itself, incorporating mission, worship and prayer into one holy day; and finally, they attempted to educate the public into a proper appreciation of its significance, even if necessary through the paradoxical ploy of a partial sacralisation of the other days of the week.

Resisting secularisation meant embracing puritan politics, or opposing social and cultural innovation – however mild and inoffensive – wherever it occurred. In general, the more Protestant a society or a minister, the more willing they were to do this. It was, for instance, only amongst local nonconformists that strident opposition to 'Sunday military exercises' was maintained prior to the First World War.[10] But such a reactionary courage also varied within denominations and amongst individuals. For instance, self-consciously progressive opinion in the Church of England, represented by a Joint Committee of both Houses

[7]   KPL, 105D77/1/3/7/b, Keighley Wesleyan Circuit, Local Preachers' Minute Book, 9 February 1894.
[8]   Anon., *Rules of the Wesleyan Methodist Sunday School, Heber Street, Keighley* (Keighley, 1880), p. 14.
[9]   KPL, 105D77/1/3/7/b, Keighley Wesleyan Circuit, Local Preachers' Minute Book, 9 February 1894.
[10]   KPL, 105D77/1/3/2/c, Keighley Wesleyan Circuit, Quarterly Meeting Minute Book, 23 September 1912.

of Convocation, saw no threat to the 'cause of true religion' in the 'Sunday opening' of 'libraries, picture-galleries and museums'. But the lower clergy and common laity did. A supportive motion, put to conference in 1896, had to be withdrawn 'without ... a resolution' following widespread 'opposition' from the floor. This was a national dichotomy which reflected local realities in the parish of Keighley. There, its Rector, Frederic Damstini Cremer, was generally in favour. But his church, as he knew well, was not. Accordingly, nothing was done.[11]

But the real problem on which both informed élites and general opinion, whether Established or nonconformist, could happily agree was the general 'tendency' of society in the 'direction ... of ... Sunday pleasure', which in turn provoked the spectre of 'Sunday trading', and all of which added up to the 'modern drift' towards a 'Continental Sunday'. Against that powerful force, mere verbal objection, even 'strenuous ... protest' was clearly never going to be enough.[12] So the churches increasingly determined, often by separate resolve but with an increasingly converging effect, to elevate the significance – by increasing the attraction – of Sunday itself. That meant appealing to different types of persons in Sunday worship. Hence Brunswick United Methodist Church's self-conscious 'Popular Services' – shorter, more vigorous, less cerebral – held on the third Sunday of each month during 1909.[13] It also meant engaging in different kinds of appeal on Sunday, at worship. This explains Keighley Wesleyan Methodist's 'Mission Service[s]', held on one Sunday evening in each month during 1901.[14]

Finally, as these examples implicitly suggest, it meant the enhanced differentiation of religious time, within the Holy Day itself – that is, it meant not simply extending its purposes into different forms of activity, but also emphasising the peculiar significance, and thus proper timing, of reverent worship. That, in turn, meant Sunday morning. So the Reverend Millson's 'Sunday ... Lectures', designed to spread a 'reasonable religion ... founded on the best and latest knowledge', were reasonably confined to the 'evening'.[15] And the Reverend Bright's strident advocacy of a 'morning Eucharist', if it did not rule out evening

[11]   Frederic Damstini Cremer, 'Sunday Opening of Museums etc.', *KPCM*, vol. 19, no. 11, November 1896 (no page number).
[12]   The Rev. Arthur Myers, 'Are We to Have a Continental Sunday?', *KWMCM*, no. 20, January 1911 (no page number).
[13]   CDA, Misc. 57/11, Brunswick United Methodist Church, Church Meeting Minute Book, 31 January 1910.
[14]   KPL, 105D77/1/3/2/c, Keighley Wesleyan Circuit, Quarterly Meeting Minute Book, 17 June 1901.
[15]   CDA, NEC 2, Northgate End Unitarian Chapel, Halifax, Chapel Minutes, 7 February 1884.

worship – since it was 'better to come to worship God on Sunday evening than not to worship Him at all on His Holy Day' – nevertheless insisted that 'nothing else' but an early witness constituted the proper 'fulfilment of the duty of worship in the forefront of the day'.[16]

More: if the point of all this rhetoric (and labour) was to emphasise the significance of Sunday, it also pointed to the different, but considerably enhanced, importance of 'religious' Saturday. Why? Because, as Bright shrewdly observed, Sunday morning worship was the principal victim of the generally widespread 'need for a long rest on Sunday morning'. That need was widely believed to be the product of 'late hours kept on Saturday nights'. This therefore needed to be changed. Christian tradition pointed to 'the custom of beginning [its] festivals at the Evensong of the preceding day'. And modern necessity suggested that those 'people who ... [had] ... at their disposal "religious" Saturday afternoon and evenings' (this was the majority) should make it a 'practice to come to the Church's Evensong on Saturday and thus make it a preparation for the Sunday Festival'. Even a 'half-an-hour or so spent in Church on Saturday evening would have an incalculable effect in preparing us for a fuller and better use of Sunday services'.[17]

To be sure, early nineteenth-century Christian teaching had not ignored the religious significance of Saturday. After all, the evangelical understanding of its message had presumed the (potential) relevance of each and any day. And from another, pre-Victorian perspective, ecclesiastical involvement in the weekend was often as much a function of institutional sophistication as it was a result of sacred pretension. More complex organisations had to provide new services for their expectant clients. This they did. Similarly, improving associations were expected to furnish their subscribers with wholesome activities to maximise the whole of their time. They consequently did that too. And yet the 'sacralisation of "religious" Saturday' answered one final call: it served, in its specific differentiation of the religious purposes of this (and thereby of each) day, putatively to prepare the people for Sunday, and even to educate them into its special purposes.

The local history of 'religious' Saturday followed this understanding unerringly. It began, often enough, with an explicit evangelical intent. Hanover Methodist New Connexion, Halifax, inaugurated 'Saturday Evening Meetings for Working People' in 1870, specifically designed to 'bring into ... the congregation ... some of those [unchurched] living

---

[16]   H. Bright, 'Saturday Evening – a Suggestion', *SPCKPCM*, vol. 17, no. 9, September
		1892 (no page number).
[17]   *Ibid.*

on the South side [of the church]'. In the event, this effort proved rather more successful in securing 'the attendance ... principally ... of our own friends'.[18] Perhaps that was one reason why the tone slowly changed, for change it surely did. The early twentieth-century version usually went under the title of 'Pleasant Saturday Evening'. It took the form more of 'music, singing and recitations' rather than prayer services. And if it was staged partially to 'counter' the attraction of '[other] entertainments' held 'on undesirable premises [i.e. public houses]', it also had the effect – like Bright's more formal Evensong – of preparing people, through agreeable 'social intercourse', to pass on 'to the Sunday services of our church'.[19]

Much the same was increasingly true of week-night services and prayer meetings. Again, these were events of long standing in local churches and chapels. In earlier times, they even had specific functions. Mid-Victorian class meetings, for instance, were invariably held during the evening in the middle of the week. But more and more, mid-week events became preparatory occasions for Sunday's worship. In case after case, attendances fell at traditional 'prayer meetings'.[20] Then, partly to boost the numbers and partly as an acknowledgement of their changing function, 'younger scholars' were invited 'to attend week-night classes'.[21] Finally, in a symbolical gesture, the physical location of services was shifted from 'the preaching room' to 'the chapel'.[22] Differences did not entirely diminish. Week-night worship remained less formal and more relaxed. But such variation as survived served essentially to emphasise Sunday's significance, and to prepare the flock for it.

The progress of the seasons and the evolution of the ecclesiastical year

The formalisation of the religious week, and especially the concentration of spiritual attention upon the sacred day of worship, was largely engineered by ecclesiastical authority. It was not, for the most part, an expression of popular values. But neither did it arise in a cultural vacuum. Indeed, in many ways it reflected the harsher realities of

---

[18] Anon., 'Hanover Street District Mission', *Hanover Street Wesleyan Methodist Church, Halifax, Handbook for 1871* (Halifax, 1871), p. 35.

[19] Anon., 'Pleasant Saturday Evening', *KWMCM*, no. 9, February 1910 (no page number).

[20] Anon., 'Minister's Address', *Devonshire Street Church Manual, 1886*, p. 7.

[21] CDA, Misc. 37/3, Methodist New Connexion Chapel, Hanover Street, Halifax, Minutes of Teachers' Meetings, 2 May 1877.

[22] CDA, Misc. 152/3, St John's Wesleyan Methodist Chapel, Prescott Street, Leaders' Meeting Minute Book, 30 October 1893.

contemporary life. Sunday was, after all, the only day of rest for the majority of West Yorkshire's industrial population. And religion was, by definition, a form of leisure activity for most people. A system of organised worship which sought to maximise its appeal therefore concentrated its efforts accordingly. Its success or failure in this direction was, of course, quite another matter, the product rather more of common custom than of organisational offensive. But that it should have been attempted at all was testimony to the degree to which formal institutions paid deep, if largely unacknowledged, respect to nebulous norms.

If this was true of the emergence of the later Victorian religious week, it was still more so for the evolution of the contemporary ecclesiastical year. For that was nothing if not a complex compromise, painstakingly negotiated between public authority and a disparate public. The result was a curious amalgam of those specifically Christian celebrations which made devotional sense to informed opinion, and the many, less obviously authentic commemorations which stuck in the heart of common sensibilities. That meant an ecclesiastical calendar which, apart from anything else, recognised few denominational boundaries. Certainly, the faithful, even some of the most devout, moved quite unashamedly amongst different creeds and customs in search of the most fulfilling celebrations. It also meant a religious year which observed something more than just a purely Christian understanding of the passing of the seasons; naturalism and even paganism had a stake here too. And finally, perhaps most paradoxically of all, it meant a sacred year which not only continued to acknowledge the traditional rites of rural passage but which even added a few more of its own creation; almost as if to divide the industrial year by conscious artifice as once nature had differentiated the different phases of agricultural production.

In all this, the fundamental division of the ecclesiastical year was between celebratory occasions and customary seasons. Celebratory occasions were defined by the traditional (or biblical) and also by the modern (or organisational) Christian calendar. Customary seasons were marked by the ancient understandings, and also by the emerging aspirations, of urban society more generally. Naturally, the churches at least pretended to lay greater formal emphasis upon their own, doctrinally substantiated, celebrations. The greatest of these, by informed consent, were the four 'Great Festivals', all historically connected with the life and after-life of Christ, 'viz., Christmas, Easter, Epiphany and Ascension Day'.[23] But informed consent was never quite

---

[23] Anon., 'The Patronal Festival', *SPCKPCM*, vol. 14, no. 2, February 1905 (no page number).

the same thing as popular observance. Even the most minimal exposure to common life soon revealed that the public valued the last of these biblical celebrations least. And, on occasion, they had to be cajoled into acknowledging it at all.[24] More strikingly still, the brutal realities of social existence demonstrated that, official thinking notwithstanding, all four were, in fact, 'relegated to a secondary [social] place compared with that given to the two modern and popular feasts connected with the Harvest and Sunday Schools'.[25]

This did not mean that Christmas and Easter were somehow mysteriously unimportant in the ecclesiastical calendar of later Victorian and Edwardian West Yorkshire. On the contrary. They were very important. Only the most extreme Protestants repudiated Christmas. And everyone acknowledged the various festivals of Easter. Proof of their social significance is easily established by the sheer array of essentially customary, or quasi-secular, celebrations which surrounded them. Christmas, for instance, would scarcely have been Christmas without a customary as well as an official Christmas Eve. So the very 'first Congregational Tea and Entertainment' held in connection with St George's Church of England, Ovenden, near Halifax, was staged on Christmas Eve 1877.[26] Similarly, the Holy Days of Good Friday and Easter Sunday were, from 1900 onwards, accompanied by an 'annual Saturday Tea' at Victoria Park Methodist Chapel, Keighley.[27] And, of course, Whitsuntide – sometimes piously described as 'The Birthday of the Church' – was in reality a good excuse to decorate the buildings and, for the Monday treat, to take teachers, scholars and parents on an outing out of town where all might stretch their legs, breathe in some fresh air and consume a hearty tea.[28] This was as true for nonconformists as for Anglicans. Methodists openly celebrated 'Parish Feast Monday'.[29] More pointedly still, it was the occasion for the Roman Catholic Whitsuntide Procession in Halifax, a defiant act of annual witness by 'Catholic schools, and Catholic teachers for Catholic children' which 'astonished the town'.[30]

At these times of year, then as now, people who otherwise rarely crossed the sacred threshold came to church. Often, they brought their

---

[24] Anon., 'Ascension Day', *SPCKPCM*, vol. 13, no. 5, May 1904 (no page number).
[25] Anon., *Origins of the Baptist Churches in the Halifax and Calder Valley District* (Halifax, n.d.), p. 63.
[26] Anon., *Early Reminiscences of St. George's Church, Ovenden* (Halifax, 1923), p. 18.
[27] 105D77/2/22/15/c, Victoria Park Sunday School Teachers' Meeting, 1 March 1900.
[28] E.H.R., 'Whitsuntide', *SPCKCPM*, vol. 33, no. 6, June 1924 (no page number).
[29] KPL, 105D77/2/12/11/a, Heber Street Wesleyan Sunday School, Minute Book of the Committee, 20 May 1878.
[30] J.J. Mulroy, *Upon This Rock: The Story of the Church in Halifax* (Halifax, 1952), p. 103.

families. Usually, they gave some money. This was especially true of Easter Sunday, and especially in the Church of England.[31] At St Thomas's Church of England, Halifax, for instance, more than twice the number of the faithful took communion than on any other ceremonial day.[32] This is unlikely to have been an atypical example. Moreover, the phenomenon was not unknown elsewhere, even in dissenting chapels. And yet, both in terms of general popularity and as a means of raising society funds, the modern festivals of Harvest Thanksgiving and the Sunday School Anniversary were, if anything, more important still. As such, and as celebrations which tended to be staged towards the end of the summer, they came to form something of a distinctive, or a second, 'Festival Season' in the churches' calendar. The first, the official season, largely based around Easter and its aftermath, lasted from around late March to the end of May.[33] Then, through July, August and September, the unofficial celebrations, or, as one caustic observer put it, the 'sensuous services' took over.[34]

Of these, probably the most important of all was the Sunday School Anniversary. Its timing varied, though it was rarely before July and seldom after the end of August. The event itself, usually graced with a sermon preached by the attached minister or a visiting dignitary, was of no great consequence. What mattered was that it was an 'occasion ... esteemed of interest' and 'enthused with kind feelings'.[35] So much so that, for many, it was quite simply 'the chief event of the Church's year'.[36] This was partly because it served as an excuse for a general reunion. Sunday school was, after all, the one religious institution with which almost everyone was, or had been, associated. And for many, the Sunday School Anniversary was the 'only time ... on which they attend[ed] ... God's house'.[37] But it was mainly because it channelled its general popularity into critical fund-raising activity; it was, in fact, the critical fund-raising institution for Sunday schools.

It is difficult to put a precise figure on this. One thing, however, seems clear. More money was raised on the Sunday School Anniversary

---

[31] Gilbert, *Religion and Society in Industrial England*, p. 28; Chadwick, *The Victorian Church*, vol. II, p. 169.

[32] WHQ, D33/22, St Thomas's Church, Charleston, Halifax, Records of Communions and Collections, 1899–1919; these records give details of communions at St Thomas's on the Sunday School Anniversary, the Harvest Festival and Easter Day.

[33] J.B. Rowsell, 'Vicar's Letter', *SPCKPCM*, vol. 32, no. 7, July 1923 (no page number).

[34] Anon., *The Church of St. Paul, Denholme Gate, 1846–1946* (Denholme, 1946), p. 5.

[35] Anon., 'On Sunday Schools', *St. Augustine, Church of England, Halifax, Church Handbook for 1873* (Halifax, 1873), p. 5.

[36] Anon., *Origins of the Baptist Churches in the Halifax and Calder Valley District* (Halifax, n.d.), p. 63.

[37] Anon., 'On Sunday Schools', *St. Augustine*, p. 5.

than on any other day in the typical church calendar. The records of St Thomas's, Halifax, reveal that the Anniversary was the single most lucrative event in the ecclesiastical year for fifteen of the twenty years between 1900 and 1919. This was true even though the Anniversary was, in general, less well attended than, for instance, Easter Day Communion. Indeed, Easter revenues were never more than one-half of those raised at the Anniversary.[38] And this seems to have been true of virtually every other Sunday school in the region. To take another example: Sunday School Anniversary collections amounted to £92 1s 1d, or something like 78 per cent of a total income of £118 1s 10d raised for Devonshire Street Congregational Sunday School, at Keighley, in 1902.[39]

The rise of the Sunday School Anniversary after 1870 directly reflected the increased significance of Sunday school in church and chapel life after that time. And it substantially contributed to the emergence of another, highly popular event, during the 1880s and 1890s. This was the so-called 'Flower Service', an occasion on which, typically, children brought flowers to decorate the church prior to an afternoon address and followed by the distribution of the flora to local infirmaries or other deserving causes. Sometimes the Flower Service was explicitly linked to the Anniversary. This was the case at St Paul's, King Cross, Halifax, where the event was inaugurated in 1892, in the hope that it would become an 'annual institution' and 'always form a part of the Sunday School Anniversary'.[40] Elsewhere the link was merely implicit, but clear enough. Halifax Primitive Methodists made space for a Flower Service in their circuit at 'the request of the Young Women's Class' in June 1895.[41] And Queen's Road Methodist New Connexion in the same town determined in 1900 to hold a 'Flower Service on the last Sunday in July' and asked its youthful 'Christian Endeavour [Society] to provide "a service of song" in the chapel on that occasion'.[42]

The growth of an autumn Harvest Festival, and the rise of its accompanying 'Fruit Banquet', followed much the same chronological pattern locally. If Pigou's boast about his pioneering work at St John the Baptist is true, then the Harvest Festival must have been introduced

[38]   WHQ, D33/22, St Thomas's Church, Charlestown, Halifax, Records of Communions and Collections, 1899–1919; these records gave details for financial collections at St Thomas's on the Sunday School Anniversary, the Harvest Festival and Easter Day.

[39]   *Devonshire Street Church Manual, 1903*, p. 25.

[40]   Anon., 'Flower Service', *SPCKPCM*, vol. 1, no. 7, July 1892 (no page number).

[41]   CDA, uncat. MSS, Halifax, Primitive Methodist Connexion, 2nd Circuit, Minutes of the Quarterly Meetings at Circuit Committees, 6 June 1895.

[42]   CDA, Misc. 278/40, Queen's Road Methodist New Connexion Chapel, Sunday School Minutes, 11 June 1900.

there some time after 1875.[43] Even if the specific claim is false, a date around that time seems plausible. The nearby church of St Paul, Denholme Gate, for instance, appears to have 'decorated [itself] for Harvest Thanksgiving for the first time ... in 1874'.[44] Similarly persuasive, if unprovable, was his assertion that this was an Anglican innovation which begat nonconformist imitations. Certainly there is no record of a dissenting Harvest Festival before 1880. But there were plenty of local examples shortly afterwards. The First Primitive Methodist Circuit in Keighley seems to have introduced the practice, at its Queen's Street Station, in 1885.[45] The Second Circuit apparently copied the gesture the very next year.[46] A 'request' for a thanksgiving service was 'accepted' by Queen's Road Methodist New Connexion Chapel, Halifax, also in 1886.[47] Four years after that, Keighley's Baptists followed suit.[48]

Fruit Banquets tended to follow as a matter of course. Sometimes they were directly, and precisely, linked to the Harvest Festival. So Keighley's First Primitive Methodist Circuit inaugurated a 'Fruit Banquet ... at each place ... the following day ... after the Harvest Festival', in 1891.[49] Others, such as Halifax's Second Primitive Connexion, merely arranged to have such a festival, sometime in September; this from 1886 onwards.[50] And a few, like Long Lee Wesleyan Methodists in Keighley, grandly joined Flower and Fruit Services together at the end of August and September 1890, subtly differentiating them from, but of course linking them to, the Harvest Festival which they had staged for the first time the previous year.[51]

In all this, these West Riding churches – Established or nonconformist – were no great innovators. Indeed, they were probably slightly behind the times in these matters. Harvest Festival, Flower Services, Fruit Banquets and the like were, of course, largely Victorian inventions; if not quite *ex nihilo* then certainly in their later nature and repetitive form. As such, they were fairly common in many parts of the country by mid-

---

[43] See p. 294, n. 2; Pigou became Vicar of Halifax in 1875.

[44] Anon., *St. Paul's, Denholme, 1846–1946*, p. 5.

[45] KPL, 105D77/1/1/1/f, Keighley, First Circuit (Primitive Methodist), Quarterly Meeting Minute Book, 8 June 1885.

[46] KPL, 105D77/1/1/4/b, Keighley Primitive Methodist Second Circuit, Minute Book, 5 June 1886.

[47] CDA, Misc. 287/40, Queens Road Methodist New Connexion, Sunday School Minutes, 30 August 1886.

[48] Rhodes, *Keighley Baptist History*, p. 111.

[49] KPL, 105D77/1/1/1/f, Keighley, First Circuit (Primitive Methodist), Quarterly Meeting Minute Book, 8 June 1891.

[50] CDA, uncat. MSS, Halifax, Primitive Methodist Connexion, Second Circuit, Minutes of the Quarterly Meeting and Circuit Committee, 15 September 1886.

[51] KPL, 105D77/2/11/3/c, Long Lee, Sunday School Minute Book, 21 July 1890.

century at the latest.[52] What is perhaps more remarkable is that they should have come to the industrial, urban West Riding at all. For if the first – Easter season – of church festivals celebrated God's timeless gift of His own Son, then the second – summer season – seemed rather more to commemorate His passing benevolence for traditional good things. Contemporaries acknowledged the apparent incongruity of so considerable a conglomeration of 'agricultural ... celebrations' in 'manufacturing districts such as ours', where the ancient joy of 'a harvest safely gathered in' was 'not [of] immediate and direct interest'.[53] But for the most part, they reacted only by emphasising the 'greater need', thus indirectly established, of bringing 'before the minds of the people God's goodness in seeding time and harvest'.[54] And, in emphasising the 'true humility' that might be gained from 'modern' man's renewed awareness of 'that glorious dependence', it was perhaps indicative that they characteristically misdated this, 'the oldest of the festivals' in celebrating its 'conventional relics'.[55]

Whatever the case, the real purpose of the Harvest Festival, like the Sunday School Anniversary, was to raise money. And to that end, it was uncommonly successful. At St Thomas's, Halifax, for instance, it accounted for the five occasions denied to the Anniversary as the most successful fund-raising event of the year.[56] This was partly because it was a widely acknowledged 'social gathering ... visited from all parts of the town'.[57] It was also partly because, first in the local Methodist Circuit and then quite commonly, it was characteristically something like a multiple celebration, staged on different days in each of the different stations, or other associated churches and chapels, most usually over the month of September.[58] And finally, it was because it was a magnificent spectacle. True, some chapels planned for 'special preachers and special sermons'.[59] But most were content to ride the wave of a church 'beautifully decorated', with 'an abundance of Fruit and Flowers' specially 'sent for the purpose'.[60]

Initially so, at least; in time a small, but significant, number of

[52] Obelkevich, *Religion and Rural Society*, pp. 58 and 158–61.
[53] Anon., 'The Harvest Festivals', *KWMCM*, no. 185, October 1924 (no page number).
[54] Anon., *St. Paul's, Denholme, 1846–1946*, p. 5.
[55] Anon., 'The Harvest Festivals'.
[56] WHQ, D33/22, St Thomas's Church, Charlestown, Halifax, Records of Communions and Collection, 1899–1919.
[57] *Keighley Yearbook, 1898*, p. 213.
[58] KPL 105D77/1/1/1/g, Keighley First Circuit (Primitive Methodist) Quarterly Meeting Minute Book, 4 June 1888.
[59] CDA, MR/151, Rhodes Street Wesleyan Methodist Chapel, Halifax, Trustees' Meetings Minute Book, 7 June 1893.
[60] Anon., 'Harvest Festival', *SPCKCPM*, vol. 9, no. 10, October 1900 (no page number).

churchmen and ministers, particularly those of a more rigorous theological bent, came to resent the Harvest Festival generally, and more especially those 'spread throughout September and October'. This was because, by contrast with those celebrations staged on 'one day ... set apart' in the year, it appealed more and more to 'people who ... at other times do not attend public worship', and who merely 'went round ... churches' at that time simply 'in order to see the decorations and hear the music'. In such circumstances, so the argument went, it was scarcely surprising that the 'spiritual' results of these efforts were 'increasingly ... disappointing'. Still more damningly, the liturgical effects were often, so these critics concluded, positively 'harmful'. This was because they debased the act of church attendance – 'enter[ing] the house of God' – making a 'mockery' of its 'true spirit'.[61]

This was, however, an unusually caustic view. Generally, a balance between very necessary money for 'the Chapel ... Renovation Fund' and a slightly indulgent popular interest was acknowledged and accepted.[62] Nor were the putative benefits always purely material, for Harvest Festival funds were as often placed at the disposal of evangelical as of building work. And that was something more than a purely contingent fact. This was because the passing of the Harvest Festival and of the Fruit Banquet symbolically concluded the summer festival season. And, in so doing, albeit rather more by implicit detachment than through conscious ritual action, it also inaugurated the autumn missionary effort. It was not that no missionary work was done during the summer. Those 'long warm evenings', after all, provided an excellent 'opportunity ... for open-air work'.[63] Rather it was the case that '[s]ave in the matter of open-air mission work', there was a general 'sapping of [evangelical] energy during the long bright days'.[64]

This was especially true for the various Methodist connexions. But it was not unique to them. Others too reported the festival season to be a time when, paradoxically, 'congregations [were] apt to be low'.[65] Certainly it seemed, to Methodists in particular, to be an especially burdensome time in their ecclesiastical calendar. To some extent, this was a simple product of the circuit system and the tradition of switching ministers between stations during the months of August and

---

61   Anon., 'Harvest Festivals', *KPCM*, no. 28, no. 11, November 1905 (no page number).
62   CDA, Misc. 207/14, Wesleyan Methodist Chapel, Northowram, Trustees' Minute Book, 1 September 1896.
63   Anon., 'Open Air Work', *KWMCM*, no. 13, June 1910 (no page number).
64   Anon., 'The Dark Evenings', *KWMCM*, no. 16, September 1910 (no page number).
65   CDA, NEC 16, Northgate End Unitarian Chapel, Halifax, Calendar for July 1893 (no page number).

September.[66] Partly it was the inevitable concomitant of Methodism's 'complex organisation for edification and aggression'.[67] No doubt, it was also because so many erstwhile supporters had other things to do in warm weather and good light. Whatever the case, it led to a curious mentality which viewed 'August ... as a period of transition and September ... as a time of beginnings', a time when 'church machinery was overhaul[ed]' and 'new programmes [were] carefully prepared'; the Methodist New Year, in fact.[68]

No other church was quite so explicit about the matter. Some churchmen, after all, affected to date everything from Whitsuntide. And Northgate End Unitarian Chapel in Halifax 'began ... the Church Year with ... the first Sunday in Advent'.[69] But the sense of a new start in the autumn was really cross-denominational and appropriately strong. Hence the Vicar of St Paul's, King Cross, looked forward to 'our general parochial organisations ... getting somewhat into working order again ... with September'.[70] Others just hoped for better congregations after what they, no doubt paradoxically but quite seriously, described as 'the coldness ... that seems ... to prevail in the church during the summer months'.[71] A few made their greatest efforts at that time 'to win those homes from which Christ has hitherto been excluded', by door-to-door visitation, evangelical mission and revival services.[72]

This last imperative became, if anything, more pressing still as autumn passed into winter. So much so that one K. Jackson, in a circular passed around the Halifax New Connexion Circuit, referred to 'Winter' as the 'harvest-time of Methodism'. Then, he argued, 'in the long, dark evenings, when the attractions of the country have ceased to rival those of the sanctuary ... the people are more easily reached by the operations of the church'. Then too, the people came to the church, 'multitudes of the young ... family circles ... members of our congregations', all 'inspired' towards 'a decision for God'.[73] Many more, perhaps, came to the church in the strictly literal sense. For it was in the 'winter months', above all, that most societies were

[66]   Anon., 'The Methodist New Year', *KWMCM*, no. 4, September 1909 (no page number).
[67]   Anon., 'The Dark Evenings'.   [68]   Anon., 'The Methodist New Year'.
[69]   CDA, NEC 16, Northgate End Unitarian Chapel, Halifax, Calendar for November 1891 (no page number).
[70]   The Rev. Hugh Bright, 'Vicar's Letter', *SPCKPCM*, vol. 19, no. 9, September 1892 (no page number).
[71]   Anon., 'Pastor's Address', *Hanover Street, Manual for 1873*, p. 9.
[72]   Anon., 'Harvest Prospects', *KWMCM*, no. 5, October 1909 (no page number).
[73]   CDA, MR77, Halifax Methodist New Connexion, Salem Circuit, Quarterly Meetings, 17 October 1887.

able to 'use their premises ... nearly every night of the week', so better exploiting 'the opportunities ... for carrying out [our] great purposes'.[74]

In that way, Christmas, the last major festival of the year, descended upon religious associations which were, in some ways, already feverish; certainly at their most lively, and probably at their most influential. It followed late October Decision Day, or Children's Day, in many Methodist Sunday schools. And it ran soon after the (virtually annual) November Mission in many more, Established and dissenting, societies. It was, accordingly, not just a season of goodwill for all men. It was a moment of consolidation for the churches. Not necessarily of formal consolidation: actual recruiting, meticulous direction or specific exhortation; rather of that type of consolidation which more firmly grounded the churches in the affections of the people, whether affiliated or loosely attached. To this extent, what was notable about Christmas celebrations in many places was just how informal they were. The 'Christmas Eve Tea' at Hainworth Road Wesleyan Methodist Sunday School, Keighley, was followed, in 1874, by an 'entertainment', of 'speeches, recitations and readings' for 'teachers, scholars and friends'.[75] A generation later, it had turned into (another) Fruit Banquet, adorned with 'coffee and buns'.[76] At much the same time, Heber Street School, in the same circuit, organised its 'Christmas Festivals' around a 'musical' celebration.[77] This became increasingly common towards the end of the century, adding fuel to the general, and growing, sense of an essential unity between chapel and communal existence, celebrated around the end of the year.

This sense was confirmed by the gradual generalisation of the New Year's Eve 'Watchnight Service' and celebration. The precise origins of this service are unclear. Certainly, they derived more from popular custom than religious doctrine. 'Letting in the New Year' had a long and cherished local history.[78] So it seems likely that churches, wishing to tap that popular sensibility for their own purposes, slowly introduced an appropriate ecclesiastical celebration of their own. No record of the event appears locally before 1875. Then, Brunswick Methodists 're-

---

[74] Anon., *Harrison Road Congregational Church, Halifax, Yearbook for 1906* (Halifax, 1906), p. 5.

[75] KPL, 105D77/2/7/7/a, Hainworth Road Sunday School Minute Book, 30 November 1874.

[76] *Ibid.*, 2 November 1896.

[77] KPL, 105D77/2/12/11/a, Heber Street Wesleyan Sunday School, Minute Book of the Committee, 4 November 1878.

[78] On which, from a contemporary perspective, see Tattersall Wilkinson, 'Local Folk Lore', *THAS*, 4 (1904–5), 3–12.

solv[ed] to have a Watchnight'.[79] Not every church, not even every Methodist church, followed suit immediately. Harrison Road Congregational Chapel seems to have decided to initiate the trend in 1884.[80] But Temple Street Methodists, in Keighley, often the harbingers of innovation there, apparently did nothing in this respect before 1894.[81] A few places, such as Northgate End Unitarian, may have held out for as long as 1908. Then, Millson's successor there, the Reverend Schroeder, finally won the 'cordial ... acceptance' of the whole chapel that there be 'a Watchnight Service on New Year's Eve'.[82]

There is little reason to doubt that by the turn of the century the practice was pretty well universal. Sometimes, it was specifically linked with other, rather more formally religious services. Hence Victoria Park Methodists' decision to attach a Watchnight Service to a 'Covenant Service' in their church, from 1907.[83] More usually, it became a very well-recognised occasion for the raising of funds. So St John's Wesleyan Methodists, in Halifax, made a point of 'plac[ing] collection boxes at the doors of the chapel at the Watch Night Service'.[84] Most commonly of all, it served as an ecclesiastical excuse for a good, popular celebration on New Year's Eve. And that was of no small importance for the churches. For it served to remind the people, at the very beginning of the year, that they were attached to their churches; still more, that they were glad to be so. Whether they remained so closely attached for the rest of the year was of course quite another matter – for both churches and people.

The rites of passage and the limits of popular loyalty

The formalisation of the religious week represented an intelligent institutional response to contemporary cultural norms. The evolution of the ecclesiastical year expressed a more delicate social bargain between associational imperatives and popular expectations. But the periodic recognition through the churches of the central rites of human passage – birth, marriage and death – constituted little more than an ungracious

[79]   CDA, Misc. 57/10, Brunswick United Methodist Free Church, Church Meeting Minute Book, 13 December 1875.
[80]   CDA, CLR 1:13, Harrison Road, Congregational Chapel, Halifax, Church and Deacon's Book, 25 November 1884.
[81]   KPL, 105D77/2/21/7/b, Temple Street (Wesleyan), Leaders' Minute Book, 22 December 1894.
[82]   CDA, NEC 4, Northgate End Unitarian Chapel, Halifax, Chapel Minutes, 11 December 1908.
[83]   KPL, 105D77/2/22/2/a, Victoria Park, Leaders' Meeting Minute Book, 7 January 1907.
[84]   CDA, St John's Wesleyan Methodist Chapel, Prescott Street, Leaders' Meeting, Minute Book, 7 December 1896.

capitulation of organisational aspiration in the face of the overwhelming force of common custom. True, the churches willingly celebrated the people's journey through life's major symbolic passages. And, to be sure, they had good – Christian – reasons for doing so. However, to a greater degree and to an increasing extent, they did so because the people wanted them to, indeed expected them to do so, and expected them to do so rather more on popular terms – that is, according to popular mores – than by their own, specifically religious understanding of these symbolically significant – and potentially institutionally important – events.

Of course, the churches were always willing to bury the people's dead. And, generally, the people sought and obtained a Christian funeral for their deceased loved ones. The living presented slightly more of a problem. This was true even of the newborn; at least in so far as their births were properly celebrated through the Christian rite of baptism. Churches performed this rite, and the attendant 'churching' (or ritual purification of the mother) ceremonies eagerly enough; and usually free of charge.[85] But, with the best will in the world, popular demand in this respect still interfered with official preferences in the matter. So much, or rather so frequently was this so, that, on occasion, the authorities attempted to circumscribe the regularity of the rite. So Keighley's (Second) Primitive Methodist Circuit resolved, in 1882, 'that a note be put to the plan limiting the time of baptisms to morning and afternoon services and stating that they must not take place on Special Occasions or at Sunday Evening service except under specially urgent circumstances'.

Even so carefully staged an event did not necessarily train ignorant parents to interpret infant baptism in a properly Christian – and an appropriately denominational – manner. Hence a second resolution, passed at the same meeting: 'that a slip be printed at the expense of the Circuit Fund requesting parents who bring their children to our places of worship to be baptized to send them to our Sunday Schools when they shall have become old enough to appreciate Sunday School tradition; and that a slip be given to the parents at the time of baptism'.[86]

If this was the case for baptisms, it was even more so for weddings. This was partly because marriage for so many represented the end, or at least the severe curtailing, of a religious life. The ubiquitous and world-weary Millson put it thus: 'My experience of many years is that as soon as young people get themselves married they give up attending the

---

85 Anon., 'Baptisms', *KPCM*, vol. 19, no. 11, November 1878 (no page number).
86 KPL, 105D77/1/1/4/b, Keighley Primitive Methodist (Second) Circuit, Local Preachers' and Circuit Committee, Quarterly Meetings Minute Book, 2 September 1882.

services with the same old regularity [and] some I see in the chapel for the last time when I shake hands with them when the marriage service is at an end'.[87] Moreover, it was not as if it was done with very much dignity. So Pigou, noting that 'I and my staff feel' that this 'marrying and giving in marriage' was 'the least agreeable of our offices', specifically resented 'the unseemingly behaviour' of many working-class couples at Anglican marriage services of the time, additionally criticising 'the speedily ... read ... banns', and the generally 'undevout' nature of the whole occasion.[88]

Progress and decline

The assault on popular superstition

Even on occasions such as weddings, where church revenue was not at stake, the ecclesiastical blind eye only turned so far. In this way, churches that had adapted to the principle of exchange in order to sustain their associational finances, schools which had assimilated the notion of pleasure so as to maintain their institutional significance, and even individuals who had accepted the ideas of science that they might widen their common appeal, drew the line at what they defined as popular superstition. And, paradoxically, the more socially comprehensive they became, whether in economic understanding, social toleration or psychological insight, the less indulgent they were towards remnants of pagan belief in their midst. For so extensive an ecclesiastical outlook and such a sophisticated doctrinal teaching also implied, indeed demanded, the repudiation of surviving unchristian practices. Where the churches could exact this price, they invariably did. And even where they could not, they made their attitude all too well known.

This is not to suggest that the late Victorian churches ruthlessly attacked all those popular customs which they came across in their missionary work. They did not. Certainly, they would have been unwise to have done so. For the evolving ecclesiastical year was, to a large degree, itself imposed upon, and yet also in constant cultural negotiation with, a long-surviving customary calendar. This began with Letting in the New Year and then passed on (variously) to: St Valentine's Day (14 February), Collop Monday (February/March), Shrove Tuesday (just before Lent), Pace-Egg (Good Friday), May Day (1 May), Rush-Bearing (first Thursday in August), Gunpowder Plot (5 November),

[87]   CDA, NEC 16, Northgate End Unitarian Chapel, Halifax, Calendar for February 1892 (no page number).
[88]   Pigou, *Phases in My Life*, pp. 308–9.

Letting Christmas In (Christmas Eve), Boxing Day and Sweeping Out the Old Year. All these festivals were accompanied by widely acknowledged customs: singing, games, dressing up; and by their accompanying superstitions.[89] The churches happily acknowledged, even partially inveigled, *some* of these customs into their own festivals and other activities. This was particularly true around Easter time. One local authority, indeed, spoke quite warmly about 'several such customs'. These included the 'custom of buying and eating buns with only the sign marked upon them [i.e. hot cross buns]', a practice 'acquiesce[d] ... in ... by ... even ... the stiffest puritanism', even though it took 'us back to the time of our heathen forefathers' and might perhaps have 'been offered by an idolatrous people to the goddess ... queen of heaven (Jer. vii. 18)'. Similarly amongst their number was the custom 'of lads going around ... on Good Friday ... dressed in dominoes ... perform[ing] some mutilated fragments of one of the old ... medieval ... Miracle Plays'. They were 'called ... Paste Eggers ... the name obviously enough suggesting the true derivation *Pasch-Eggers* from its association with the Passover, and from the symbol of life bursting forth from the tomb.' They lasted until 'quite recent years'.[90]

But some they resisted. Letting in the New Year, for instance, was often associated with the custom of boys grouping together as so-called mummers, blackening their faces, and going round houses spreading good (or alternatively bad) luck. This practice was condemned amongst Halifax's Methodists around the turn of the century.[91] By default, it may well have been the basis for their enthusiasm for the Watchnight Service. Similarly, local churchmen, though happily promoting Christmas Eve Teas, vigorously attacked 'the custom of having a party on the evening before (which as a matter of fact is appointed by the Church to be observed as a Fast) and keeping it up late, even into the small hours of the morning'. And if there was an acceptable compromise between these two views, they affected not to notice it; perhaps because their real concern was that the faithful should, whatever else, 'join ... together in the great act of Communion and Thanksgiving in the early hours of Christmas morning'.[92]

Nor were the communal rites of passage immune from such criticism. In fairness, this was sometimes because the relevant ministers doubted

---

[89] H.W. Harwood and F.H. Marsden, *Pace-Egg: The Midgely Version* (Halifax, 2nd edn, 1977), pp. 5–6.

[90] Anon., 'Some Old Customs', *SPKCPM*, vol. 19, no. 4, April 1910 (no page number); for further details on the paste-eggers, Harwood and Marsden, *Pace-Egg*, refers to 'the dawn of this century' (p. 5).

[91] Anon., *The Halifax Methodist Circuit, 1785–1985*, p. 22.

[92] Anon., 'Christmas', *SPKCPM*, vol. 23, no. 12, December 1904.

their antiquity. The Vicar of St Andrew's, Keighley, derided the 'heathenish and semi-barbarous practice' of 'rice throwing at weddings', claiming that was 'lately imported from India', had 'no English antiquity' and was 'a waste of good food'.[93] But they were not always consistent in the matter. Thus the Vicar of St Paul's, King Cross, Halifax, later lamenting the passing of the custom of 'throwing ... rice' which 'at all events was emblematic of the prosperity which their friends hoped would be the lot of the newly-married pair', made a particular point of castigating the novel practice of 'throwing coloured paper' at newly-married couples as they leave the church 'as a thoroughly meaningless ... foolish and stupid' habit, coming as it did 'directly as a young man or woman' had 'risen from their knees at the most solemn moment of their lives', and deriving as it so clearly had from 'foreign importation'; hence its 'designation by an un-English term "confetti"'.[94]

That particular campaign self-evidently failed. Others, however, succeeded. The same Rector of Keighley positively encouraged the gradual demise of 'the custom of handing round wine ... at ... funerals'. Anyone thereby 'called mean' he advised to 'tell your guest that you are forwarding a certain sum to the Hospital'. The point was to preserve 'the rigid simplicity of your funeral and mourning arrangements'.[95] More strikingly still, the fabled Reverend Millson, from Northgate End Unitarian, mounted something of a personal crusade during the 1890s against 'heathen customs' associated with 'popular funerals' which exhibited what he called 'a sad lack of faith in God'. The worst of these, he argued, was the 'false view of death ... symbolized by barring out the blessed sunlight from the chamber in which we lay the body and by hanging crepe from the door'. The 'teachings of our Lord' and 'early Christian practice' suggested to him that a 'bunch of flowers be suspended from the door' and 'the windows thrown open to the common day'. Gradually, they were.[96]

This, at least ostensibly, was a matter of doctrine. Other objections, however, seem to have been more a matter of aesthetics. The authorities at St Paul's, King Cross, Halifax seem to have taken issue, and quite strongly, with 'tall, oblong, tombstones' which 'disfigure[d] the church-yard' there; and still more to 'wreaths of artificial flowers or bell glasses, containing such wreaths or funeral cards'. For the first, they proposed

---

[93] Frederic Damstini Cremer, 'Rice Throwing at Weddings', *KPCM*, vol. 17, no. 10, October 1894 (no page number).

[94] Hugh Bright, 'Confetti', *SPKCPM*, vol. 16, no. 5, May 1907 (no page number).

[95] Frederic Damstini Cremer, 'Wine at Funerals', *KPCM*, vol. 17, no. 5, May 1894 (no page number).

[96] CDA, NEC 16, Northgate End Unitarian Chapel, Halifax, Calendar for August 1891 (no page number).

'tombstones not exceeding 3 ft. 6 in. or 4 ft. at most in height'; also the additional proviso that 'crooked' specimens be 'put straight', or 'perhaps laid level'. Of the second, they suggested the alternative of 'real flowers ... neatly ... kept ... and thrown away when dead'. Finally, 'paths should be properly cleaned and edged' (the work of those who had custody of the graveyards) and lastly, and most importantly, 'children should be taught that the churchyard is not a playground' (the responsibility of all).[97]

If that was a bit precious, a campaign against 'a certain abomination called a "Chain Prayer"' urged by Keighley Methodists was deadly serious. This 'prayer' was 'sent to members of our Congregation', anonymously, in the summer of 1910, 'asking them to fetter themselves with it'. This they were to do first by validating that it was 'an exact copy of an ancient prayer', and then passing it on to others. The uncertainty of the text, and still worse the anonymity of the author, drove Keighley's Wesleyans to denounce the whole charade as a veritable 'crime against sincerity'. Worse still, the demand that it be circulated, based on the unexplained authority, as what 'is said in Jerusalem' was accompanied by the threat 'that he who will not copy this prayer will meet with misfortune'. This was decried by local officialdom as something little 'short of blasphemy'. They concluded:

The God to whom we pray is not the God referred to ... in this circular. A God who deals in a vindictive spirit with people who do not at the bidding and threatening of some anonymous scribe copy prayers and circulate them anonymously is not the God in whom we believe ... The vicar of a mechanical deity who counts the nine days the prayer is written and anonymously circulated, and blesses on the ninth day, reeks of superstition ... we urge our readers to leave this matter severely alone.[98]

Clearly, they were uncertain about how well their charges would bear up under the strain. In this, they were not atypical. Certainly, for ministers and churchmen alike, it remained a sad but simple truth, even up to the outbreak of the First World War, even after reformed Sunday school training, even after reinvigorated public worship, even within their own societies that the 'mind of the masses' remained 'essentially ... unlighted'; or at least always vulnerable.[99] For them accordingly, the price of religious righteousness, even into the twentieth century, was eternal ecclesiastical vigilance. Nothing else would be sufficient. For beneath the thin veneer of Christian civilisation, albeit of late more generously imparted, the dark undergrowth of pagan superstition,

[97] W.W.W., 'Tombstones', *SPKCPM*, vol. 1, no. 8, August 1892 (no page number).
[98] Anon., 'Chain Prayer', *KWMCM*, no. 15, August 1910 (no page number).
[99] Anon., *A Brief History of Holy Trinity, Keighley*, p. 13.

ignorance and malice remained, ever present, ever threatening, always a challenge.

The trials of the church meeting, the demise of class and the end of the love feast

This vigilance was required because the veneer of Edwardian Christian civilisation was itself a significantly altered religious surface. It had assumed an overwhelmingly devotional aspect, where once it had also displayed a consciously experiential front. Contemporaries noticed this change. And some lamented it, blaming it for the diminishing quality (as they saw it) of modern religious life. Consider the following remarks: 'Even if you grant that neglect of the [Communion] Service denotes neglect of spiritual privileges, it does not follow', insisted Arthur Furner, of the Congregational Union of England and Wales, 'that attendance at the service denotes the culture of the spiritual life; it may arise from the desire to retain a position from which it would be unpleasant for many reasons to be removed'. This being so, it followed that mere 'participation in [this] ordinance' should 'not be regarded as . . . due discharge of the responsibilities of church membership'. That would be an 'inadequate conception of its duties' and would 'misrepresent', even diminish, a true understanding of the proper obligations, and the real possibilities, of 'church fellowship'.[100]

Accordingly, this self-styled authority proposed a 'new' test. Regular attendance and participation in 'the church meeting' should now be 'the suitable test of witness for church membership'.[101] This was all well and good. The only problem, as Furner knew all too well, was that by 1900 'the Church Meeting' no longer 'occupied' what he believed to be its 'rightful place' in church life; indeed, in reality, it 'counted for nothing in [the] question of [church] membership'.[102] Why not? A subsequent chapel history provides a clue. The mid-nineteenth-century Congregational church meeting, this account suggests, had been a vibrant affair, 'with prayer, scripture, reading and hymn singing . . . complete with an address by the minister . . . and . . . usually the exposition of a biblical text'. By contrast, its early twentieth-century successor was 'little more than an official institution, obsessed with trivial items of business and procedure'.[103]

---

[100] KPL, uncat. pub., Arthur Furner, *The Place of the Church Meeting in the Life and Work of Our Churches* (London, 1990), p. 10.

[101] *Ibid.*, p. 11.   [102] *Ibid.*, p. 10.

[103] J.W. Franks, *On the Edge of the Moor: The Story of the Congregational Cause at Highroad Well, Halifax* (Halifax, 1965), p. 15.

The trials of the Congregational church meeting found a curious complement in the virtual demise of the Methodist class meeting at much the same time. The passing of this institution can, to a remarkable degree, be dated locally. In 1900, the Keighley Wesleyan Methodist Circuit adopted a 'memorial' for presentation to its National Conference that argued for 'a modification of our present test of membership'. Specifically, it suggested that the test be '(a) An open confession of faith in Christ, (b) Regular Attendance at the Lord's Table and (c) work for the church and/or financial help' to the church. Most importantly, it proposed that membership of a class, and regular attendance at a class-meeting *cease* to be requirements of church membership. This was because, of late, many members 'had not found the class meeting a suitable or profitable means of grace', whilst 'some persons' who show 'clear [evidence] of their conversion and of their sympathy with our church ... are totally averse to joining any class-meeting'.[104] In fact, antagonism towards this institution, which the Keighley Wesleyan Circuit reported to Conference in 1900, was of long standing, and was not confined to Keighley. As early as 1886, the quarterly meeting of Halifax (Second) Primitive Methodist Circuit was warned of 'strong feelings against attending class' amongst 'members of the congregation[s]', in the various stations of the circuit.[105] And in 1888, the quarterly meeting of the Salem Methodist New Connexion, in the same town, recommended that its own conference 'modify the rules relating to the tests of church membership so as to give the Leaders' Meeting discretionary power to accept as well as to retain persons who for various reasons do not find the class meetings a helpful means of grace'.[106]

Contemporaries were tantalisingly discreet, not to say uninformative, about just what those 'various reasons' for popular disenchantment with the spiritual and institutional efficacy of the class meeting actually were. Indeed, not one single piece of explanatory evidence has survived from local records: no memo, no letter, no account of a debate in a church or chapel meeting. Why this is so can only be a matter for speculation. But one thing is clear: the class meeting went into an irreversible decline in the Methodist societies of this part of West Yorkshire during the latter years of the nineteenth century.[107] A historical record of Fell Lane

---

[104] KPL, 105D77/1/3/2/c, Keighley Wesleyan Circuit, Quarterly Meeting Minute Book, 18 June 1900.

[105] CDA, uncat. MSS, Halifax, Primitive Methodist Connexion, 2nd Circuit, Quarterly Meeting Minute Book, 15 December 1886.

[106] CDA, MR/77, Halifax, Methodist New Connexion, Salem Circuit, Quarterly Meeting Minute Book, 16 January 1888.

[107] For national evidence, see Currie, *Methodism Divided*, pp. 125–9; for evidence of the

Wesleyan Methodist Church in Keighley put the matter succinctly. 'As in some other churches', it recounted, 'the number attending ... the society class ... fell away considerably' during this period.[108] Moreover, in most places its religious significance was gradually diminished. Even when and where, at least before the First World War, it was preserved 'as a condition of membership', it nevertheless 'ceased to be a means of grace'. Increasingly bereft of 'experience, consecration, prayer and regular attendance', the institution became 'bankrupt'.[109] Finally, in some places, it was effectively, though of course not officially, abolished. At Pye Nest Primitive Methodist Church, Halifax, founded in 1902, 'a class meeting was held every Monday night [from foundation] for a few years until the Christian Endeavour [Society] was formed', a society dedicated principally to guide laymen and adolescents into the art of devotional worship.[110]

The demise of the class meeting inevitably prefigured the degeneration of the Leaders' Meeting in many local Methodist societies. One local history put it thus. At the 'turn of the twentieth century ... Leaders' Meetings' dealt 'with pastoral affairs only, with the shepherding of the flock', since the '[p]rimary duty of the Meeting was the pastoral oversight of its members'. Then, 'each leader in turn [was] called upon by the minister to go through the names of his class paper [to find out] what progress he [i.e. the member] was making in his Christian life ... and whether any member [had] fallen from grace, and ... if so ... what discipline [might] be imposed' to restore him to favour. The 'second concern of the meeting' was with 'evangelism'; primarily to find out 'where new classes were required, and where they might be established'. The third was to find 'new leaders'; and the fourth was to 'care for the widow and the fatherless and the poor'. In this way 'membership of the Body of Christ ... was more carefully guarded ... than in the whole [i.e. previous and subsequent] history of the church'. And through the 'utter consecration of these Class Leaders', West Riding Methodism found 'the secret of [its] steady growth and power'. Now, 'Leaders' Meetings' [are] no more than ... management committees ... dealing with all sorts of matters'. It followed as a matter of course, and (inevitably) as a matter for the

unpopularity of the class meeting in another district of England, see Obelkevich, *Religion and Rural Society*, p. 192.

[108] KPL, 105D77/2/6/8/9, Anon., *Historical Record of the Fell Lane Wesleyan Sunday School and Chapel* (Keighley, n.d.), p. 11.

[109] KPL, uncat. pub., Anon., 'The Class Meeting', *KWMCM*, no. 25, June 1911 (no page number).

[110] CDA (HTC), John Brearley, *A History of Pye Nest Primitive Methodist Church, Halifax, 1902–1932* (Halifax, 1932), p. 6.

profoundest regret, that the 'decline of our church began when the class meeting fell into disrepute'.[111]

If this was an extreme statement, it was by no means a wholly atypical view. Nor was it confined to the Wesleyan Methodist Connexion. A history of Denholme Clough Primitive Methodist Chapel, written to celebrate that society's centenary in 1934, elegiacally compared the mid-nineteenth-century church with its inter-war successor, noting that whilst the zealots of early Victorian Primitive Methodism very 'nearly lived in the chapel' their modern successors were 'occasional' men (and women). Then it contrasted an erstwhile 'religious life' of 'prayer meetings, love feasts, and singings' with a contemporary régime of unvaried 'worship' and 'preaching'. Finally, it juxtaposed a creative liturgical anarchy in which '[t]he hymns were given out two lines at a time and were selected not by the minister but by "Old Rusher" according to what tunes he knew and could play', with the stultifying modern ethos of 'order' and 'decorum' in service.

These developments were traced to technological and institutional changes in the society. The 'musical part of Church developed' as the 'fiddle' gave way to 'a little harmonium'; then this 'great achievement' gave way 'to the present beautiful memorial organ'. Chapel preaching and proper reverence were nurtured by 'improvements' to the chapel, first in 'the straight-backed pews' (as opposed to the old square pews), and then through a 'considerable advancement in the character of the heating arrangements', which induced more of the congregation to stay, and to be quiet while they stayed, at service. Order and harmony in worship were established and encouraged by the 'attractive ... interior decoration' of the latter-day chapel.[112]

In this way, the architectural, liturgical and spiritual history of Denholme Clough Primitive Methodist Chapel reflected the history and development of organised religion, writ large, in the whole region, during this period. The means of religious observance became comfortable. The forms of religious observance became more dignified. The demonstration of religious observance became more restrained. Such changes, of resources, of institutions, and of sensibilities, varied between denominations, even between societies of the same denomination. They varied owing to doctrinal differences, also according to associational foibles, even as a result of prevailing social customs. The altar was the centre of worship only in Roman Catholic and (High) Anglican churches. The musical service never triumphed amongst the dissenting churches. Otherwise, the boundaries of change, both of organisational

[111] *Ibid.*, pp. 4–5.
[112] Davis, *Denholme Clough Centenary* (no page numbers).

change, and of change in collective sensibilities, were determined more by the means available to each society, and through the influence of dominant personalities within it, than by the rigid imperatives of denominational doctrine and practice. More important, however, the drift of change was the same everywhere, at least amongst the mainstream Protestant denominations. As such, it marked a slow but steady progress away from 'experience' and towards 'worship' in the characteristic understanding and practice of collective religious observance. Whether that progress, in turn, truly represented a spiritual loss or an organisational gain, is another matter.

The forward march of the Christian churches halted? Organisational stasis and the crisis of the associational ideal in early twentieth-century religious institutions

Introduction: an emerging sense of failure

When it considered the vital questions of organisational advance and decline – or of spiritual gain and loss – in the years leading up to the outbreak of the First World War, informed local opinion invariably arrived at depressing conclusions. Pastors and priests, whether Anglican, Roman Catholic or dissenter, counted more churches than ever. But Catholics aside, they saw fewer people in them. Churchmen, ministers and laymen presided over more complex religious institutions. Yet these organisations attracted fewer regular members than they had hoped for. Teachers and volunteers dedicated themselves to more sophisticated Sunday schools. However, they induced fewer of the young into the life of religion than their best efforts warranted. Edwardian churches and chapels organised more frequent religious missions and visitations than their mid-Victorian counterparts. Nevertheless, these efforts won fewer conversionary gains than expected. New and revived liturgies forged a quality of religious witness in public worship which was more solemn, more dignified and more reverential than that of old. Still, most informed locals doubted the evidence of real spiritual progress amongst their fellow worshippers. Uncertain of the commitment of those amongst their number, and fearing the worst of those beyond their walls, they began to envisage, with a barely concealed dread, the real possibility of a halt, that is, a permanent halt, to the forward march of the Christian churches.

In this way, they also began to contemplate the possible decline of religion; first in contemporary West Yorkshire, then more generally in modern Britain as a whole. By that, they meant nothing less than the gradual, and sometimes the precipitate, abandonment of God by man. They viewed this prospect not only with alarm but in terms of degeneration, for the diminution of God's role in human life, and by implication of the significance of organised religion in human society, meant inevitably the reduction of man, in effect the creation of a lesser human being. Contemporaries did not balk at this conclusion. Indeed, they asserted it vigorously. Men of faith amongst them could scarcely do otherwise. This was because, as they witnessed what they took to be a tragedy, they saw the possibility of other, still more tragic, consequences entwined in its unfolding. And the course of human affairs up to the outbreak of the First World War did little to convince them that such a possibility might easily be averted.

Institutional decline and the question of numbers

That possibility was generally defined during the early years of the twentieth century – and has generally been so defined ever since – in the harsh light of ecclesiastical numbers. Declining numbers: the declining numbers of mainstream church members; the declining regularity in popular attendance at Sunday worship, even at Sunday school; and, finally, the declining financial liquidity of denominational and other religious organisations. To be sure, the strength of such institutions and the significance of sacred beliefs in society was then, and is now, rather poorly measured by the use of such statistical evidence. These figures, even as the product of the most sophisticated techniques and the most accurate empirical data, measure indices only. Exactly what such indices really represent is a matter that can rarely be reduced to the precision of a single metric. Membership of a religious organisation is at once a religious duty and a social custom; similarly, attendance at a service of worship and witness before a sacred rite. Hence the relationship between duty and custom within any given act of membership, attendance, or even witness, is seldom something which can be satisfactorily measured. Furthermore, whilst statistics may describe the dynamics of social processes, and especially correlations between those processes, they do not reveal the causes of change, or even the importance (or otherwise) of continuing tensions and ambiguities, within existing institutions.[1]

If anything, this unsatisfactory ambiguity, true generally, was actually truer still of those changes, tensions and ambiguities within late Victorian and Edwardian Established and voluntary religious organisations. The task of collecting and interpreting statistical data in local churches and chapels at this time was never reducible to the application of competent technique. It was an inherently complex matter, at once complicated by questions of denominational rivalry and the (no small) matter of public face; complicated also by central and regional tensions

[1] For some helpful remarks on this problem, see Wilson, *Contemporary Transformations of Religion*, pp. 13–14, 23–5 and 27–8.

and the problem of associational authority; and complicated finally by those cultural and social ambivalences surrounding changing attitudes towards different forms of religious experience and liturgical obligation. Put bluntly, no national denomination was keen to publish figures, whether national, regional or even purely local, which proved it was falling behind its rivals. Conversely, few local societies happily reported particular numerical regressions to censorious central officials. And every religious authority was confronted by the considerable problem of balancing the particular, and changing, significance of certain forms of evidence (such as communication at the Lord's Supper) against other forms of information (such as class attendance).

In this way, denominational rivalry, institutional defensiveness and attitudinal change together rendered even the possibility of statistical precision in the question of organisational dynamics fairly remote at this time. And the sheer variety of the available evidence, whether of membership figures, estimates of adherence, service registers, sacramental tickets or auxiliary affiliations, generally transformed a remote chance into a certain impossibility. Still more: if this was true within denominational boundaries, it was doubly so across them. This was not merely because one denominational authority was often less than fully willing to disclose some of its most intimate associational secrets to another. Even had the spirit been willing, the ambiguities of that evidence would have ensured that each authority would have spoken to the other in a (statistical) language which, though it sounded remarkably similar, was not quite the same as that of its rival.[2]

Neither the possibilities of, nor the strict limitations to, the value of statistical evidence, and the legitimacy of inter-denominational comparisons of that evidence, were lost upon contemporaries. On the contrary. They were fully understood. And they were frequently, and often shamelessly, exploited as such. Yet, in a curious way, what contemporaries exploited they also respected, for the associational ideal demanded that they respect not only a nebulous sense of spiritual advance and regression, but also that they command a very practical understanding of numerical strength and weakness in their various societies. So, in a questionnaire prepared by Fairfield Primitive Methodist Circuit, and sent to Queen's Road station, question 15 asked simply: 'If the station be prosperous, say in what respect; if not prosperous, state the cause or causes of its non-prosperity.' Prospective answers, or the space necessary for them, were divided under three

---

[2]   On the question of the interpretation of nineteenth-century statistical evidence from ecclesiastical sources the reader is, once again, referred to Yates, 'Urban Church Attendance', esp. pp. 389–90 and 396–9.

subheadings: 'financial', 'numerical' and 'spiritual'. Only the first two parts of the answer were couched in terms of an exact, and purely statistical, response.[3]

Again, neither numerical nor financial concerns of this kind were especially new to Primitive or, indeed, any other form of Methodism, in the 1870s. Methodists had always counted their people and their money carefully. What was, perhaps, if not strictly speaking new, then of novel significance in the later nineteenth century was the importance accredited to statistical records and statistical method by churchmen, ministers and lay officials more generally. 'I alluded in my charge two years ago [i.e. in 1897] to the importance of statistics,' observed the Archdeacon of Halifax in 1895. '[A]nd', he continued, 'the value of ... statistics increases year by year.' As if to prove his point, he noted, to his own satisfaction, that 'since my last charge, two years ago, five churches had been "recommended", eight missions had been "planned" and "there are ten additional clergy at work", as a result of which, the proportion of the population to each clergyman ... in the Deanery of Halifax ... which was estimated at 1:3600 is now about 1:2800'.[4]

Whatever the intrinsic merits of the Archdeacon's observations, there can be little doubt that they caught the drift of a general mood. And one reason why, so the Archdeacon thought, was that by 1895 ecclesiastical statistics were so much 'more complete' than in the past.[5] If so, they quickly became still more complete. For instance, church statistics collected and collated in the *Keighley Parish Church Magazine*, in February 1900, provided no more than overall totals for the number of communicants at Easter services, and at the offertory, and of the number of baptisms, funerals and marriages held, under parish auspices, during the year.[6] But a much more sophisticated 'Statistical Record of Parochial Work', compiled at Holy Trinity Church, Halifax, from 1909 onwards, included detailed analysis of: population movements; baptisms (both infant and adult); confirmations; communicants (both on the roll and at Easter); church accommodation and church services; church day school enrolment and attendance; Sunday school enrolment and attendance. Just for good measure, it also included complete records of lay participation in the church, with exhaustive numerical records of the numbers of churchwardens and sidesmen, Sunday school teachers,

---

3   Queen's Road Primitive Methodist Chapel, Annual Reports, 1877–1925 (no page numbers).

4   *A Charge by the Venerable Joshua Ingram Brooke, Archdeacon of Halifax, Read in the Parish Church of Halifax, on 1st May, 1895* (Halifax, 1895), pp. 5–6.

5   *Ibid.*, p. 6.

6   Anon., 'Church Statistics', *KPCM*, vol. 23, no. 2, February 1900 (no page number).

organists, choir, bell-ringers, licensed readers and district visitors who had served the church during the year.[7]

More important, however, was the interpretation of that evidence. Again, contemporaries were anything but naive in this respect. They did not assume that columns of figures revealed the whole truth about an aspect of human life so alien to the possibilities of calculation. Indeed, concerned officials occasionally pointed out that raw statistical data, crudely interpreted, were often positively misleading. Noting a decline in absolute numbers of members of the circuit in October 1881, the quarterly meeting of Salem Methodist New Connexion in Halifax actually 'persuaded' itself, on the basis of 'ministerial reports', that 'the decline is more apparent than real'. Why? Because it merely reflected the 'determination on the part of the Leaders' Meetings' at each station this year 'to give a more faithful return of the state of our churches'.[8] And theirs was not even a particularly unusual rigour. In 1899, St John's Wesleyan Methodist Circuit in Halifax suffered a loss of some 52 members, as enrolment in the circuit dropped from 766 to 694. But at the quarterly meeting in December of that year, the Reverend Henry Oyston explained to circuit members that 'the large decrease ... was for the most part accounted for by a revision of the Class Books, whereby several names had been crossed off of those who had long since ceased to meet'.[9] Just two years earlier, the circuit had endured a loss of 67 members. This time, the Reverend W.B. Daly assured the quarterly meeting of December 1897 that, '[a]lthough a decrease of members was shown ... the spiritual state of the circuit [was] most encouraging ... with ... a healthy tone existing throughout it'.[10] And sure enough, by 1902, membership levels in the St John's Circuit, at 771 full-timers, plus another 17 on trial, were restored to pre-1897 levels, a development which enabled the Reverend Oyston to remark upon the evidence of 'spiritual growth in the circuit'.[11] Numbers, for once it seems, spoke the truth.

Yet, in prosperity as in adversity – numerically speaking – all was not quite what it seemed. For the soothing words of the Reverends Daly and Oyston were intended not only for the comfort of their own society members. In the latter case especially, they were also guarded responses to a public concern, publicly expressed, at 'the recent synod ... [about]

[7] WHQ, D109/36, incom. arch. ref., Holy Trinity Church, Halifax, Statistical Return of Parochial Work, 1909–19.

[8] CDA MR/77, Halifax Methodist New Connexion, Salem Circuit, Quarterly Meeting Minute Book, 23 October 1881.

[9] CDA, uncat. MS, Halifax, St John's Wesleyan Methodist Circuit, Quarterly Meeting Minute Book, 18 December 1899.

[10] Ibid., 20 December 1897.   [11] Ibid., 17 March 1902.

the decreased membership in the district', which had requested that all local 'quarterly meetings ... give special consideration to [this] question'.[12] And not every numerical reverse could be explained away quite so easily as the statistical blip in St John's Circuit. Elsewhere, and especially in the years immediately after the death of Queen Victoria, these blips became patterns. More: they became consistent patterns. As such, they suggested the possibility of a long-term decline in the numbers of members, adherents, worshippers, scholars and even of those informally affiliated with religious organisations. For anyone committed to the associational ideal as an expression of the health of religious life, that decline was ominous.

Even then, some affected not to care. After all, the equation of personal salvation with individual affiliation had always had a vulgar air. So in good times, it was easy to deny, even to repudiate, that equation. At the annual meeting of the Harrison Road Evangelising Society in 1868, members of the auxiliary organisations were assured 'that we have somewhat improved', but they were warned that, 'since it is impossible to gauge religious life or the amount of spiritual growth by any numerical process, we therefore deem it impractical to employ figures either in illustration, comparison or proof of [these] positive results'.[13]

In fact, the number of members enrolled on society books in January 1869 was 338, a figure considerably higher than for the previous year, and one not to be exceeded in the history of the church until after the 'great revival' of 1882.[14] Forty years later, this contempt for a numerical calculus of the state of contemporary religious life remained. But the reasoning behind it was more defensive. Forced to concede that 'we do not seem to be able to accomplish much to increase our quantity', the annual church record for 1907 nevertheless insisted that 'quality matters more than quantity'.[15] Perhaps. But the number of registered members on the roll at Harrison Road in that year was 267, ten fewer than in the previous year. Over the next twenty years it gradually declined further, falling to a figure below 200 in 1925.[16]

Harrison Road was unusual in the degree to which official opinion was prepared to pull the wool over its own eyes. Most officials, in most

[12]   *Ibid.*, 20 March 1899.
[13]   CDA CUR 1:200, Harrison Road Congregational Church, Halifax, Evangelising Society Minute Book, 5 December 1868.
[14]   CDA CUR 1:3–7, Harrison Road Congregational Church, Halifax, Members' Attendance Roll Book, 1869–1925 (no page numbers); the figure for 1882 was 385.
[15]   CDA, CUR 1:100, *Harrison Road Congregational Church, Yearbook 1907* (Halifax, 1907), p. 5.
[16]   CDA, CUR 1:3–7, Harrison Road Congregational Church, Halifax Members' Attendance Roll Book, 1869–1925 (no page numbers); the figure for 1925 was 194.

societies, actually kept their eyes wide open. And the trend they observed in the associational dynamics of religious organisations around the turn of the twentieth century did not fill them with much hope. One aspect of this depressing trend may be called the decline of associational density. That decline was caused by the fact that membership of religious organisations failed to keep pace with the rise in population in this part of England during the latter years of the nineteenth century. Absolute numbers of persons affiliated with religious associations continued to grow, but relative numbers declined. Contemporaries became aware of this phenomenon in the very last years of the nineteenth century. Speaking to the quarterly meeting of the Keighley Wesleyan Methodist Local Preachers' Association, the Reverend Almond noted that careful inspection of 'the comparative number of persons in the circuit in 1871 and 1896 showed that the increase was only 215, whereas the population [of the town] had nearly doubled'.[17]

These figures cannot quite be taken at face value. True, an increase of 215 persons in a circuit which, in 1896, boasted about 1,400 members, represented an increase in membership of barely 20 per cent, taken over a period of 25 years. But the population of Keighley had not, in fact, doubled over that period. It had actually risen from around 28,000 to about 41,000. And part of that increase had been occasioned by a boundary extension in 1895 which had brought Ingrow, Hainworth, Exley Head and Utley into the new Municipal Borough of Keighley.[18] Moreover, each of these hamlets already boasted a chapel in the Wesleyan Methodist Circuit at that date. The decline in associational density in the Keighley Circuit between 1877 and 1896 must therefore have been much less than the Reverend Almond assumed. Yet that it had occurred at all was significant enough. More important, to those concerned it was both a baffling and a disturbing development.

More disturbing still – for being more obviously degenerative – was the absolute stagnation of, and then the slow decline in, the numbers of persons formally associated with local religious organisations. People became aware of this problem during the first decade of the twentieth century. In March 1904, the quarterly meeting of the same Keighley Wesleyan Methodist Circuit was blithely informed that, 'for the last ten to twelve years ... we [have] not ma[de] much progress in numbers'.[19] This was true. Indeed it was something of an understatement. The

[17] KPL, 105D77/1/3/7/c, Wesleyan Methodist Church, Keighley Circuit, Local Preachers' Meeting Minute Book, 21 February 1896.
[18] Dewhirst, *History of Keighley*, p. 108.
[19] KPL, 105D77/1/3/2/c, Keighley Wesleyan Circuit, Quarterly Meeting Minute Book, 21 March 1904.

annual circuit meeting, in December 1903, recorded a membership of 1,354, with a further 82 on trial, and some 445 young persons enrolled in junior classes.[20] In December 1892, the corresponding meeting had reported a circuit membership of 1,371, plus 72 on trial and 414 in junior classes.[21] In fact, the circuit had enjoyed no substantial increase in its membership since the mid-1880s. Total membership in December 1885 was 1,220.[22] Two years later it rose to 1,352.[23] But it never rose above 1,400.[24] On the other hand, it did not fall very quickly either. It held its own, at around 1,300, falling in some years but recovering in others, until 1917. In that year, it fell to 1,287.[25] In 1918, it fell again, very slightly, to 1,280.[26] From there, it began a slow decline, falling each year, minimally but significantly, to reach a figure of 1,100 in 1925.[27]

This pattern – of diminishing densities after about 1890 and an absolute decline in membership figures from the turn of the century – was probably quite typical. Certainly, it was not atypical. It was reflected, for instance, in the associational fortunes of the highly influential, and socially significant, Northgate End Unitarian Chapel in Halifax. The society enjoyed a dramatic rise in its membership between 1875 and 1885. Crude numbers at that time more than doubled, from 122 to 258. However calculated, this was a gain much faster than the growth in local population. Thereafter, they rose much more slowly until the débâcle of 1893–4, peaking at a figure of around 300. But permanent decline did not set in there until the turn of the twentieth century. Even then, it was very slow. The fall in the members' roll between 1900 and about 1916 was barely faster than the decline of local population, and never falling below 200. Only after the end of the First World War did a permanent institutional rot set in.[28]

Naturally the chronology and gradient of change varied from case to case. In this way, Congregationalism in Halifax may have fallen into decline a little earlier than either Methodism or Unitarianism. The evidence, for instance, from Harrison Road at least suggests that the popularity of this society peaked shortly after the 'great revival' of 1882. Following a very substantial reduction in membership between 1869 and 1870, from 338 to 273 (caused almost entirely by the foundation of Park Congregational Church at that time), the numbers at Harrison Road

[20] *Ibid.*, 21 December 1903.   [21] *Ibid.*, 19 December 1892.
[22] *Ibid.*, 21 December 1885.   [23] *Ibid.*, 27 December 1887.
[24] The highest figure recorded in the Quarterly Meeting Minute Books up to 1925 was 1,388 on 20 December 1898.
[25] *Ibid.*, 17 December 1917.   [26] *Ibid.*, 16 December 1918.
[27] *Ibid.*, 14 December 1925.
[28] CDA, NEC 11, Northgate End Unitarian Chapel, Halifax, List of Registered Members, 1872–1950 (no page numbers).

increased from 248 in 1874, to 398 in 1886: a rate of growth of about 60 per cent, or about three times the growth of population in the town during those years.[29] But that progress was not sustained. Indeed, decline set in fairly steadily from the mid-1890s onwards. Membership at Harrison Road fell to about 300 in 1894, and down to 287 in 1900, thence to 257 in 1911, rallying around the 230 mark during the early part of the war, only to fall below 200 shortly afterwards.[30] Some of that decline, however, may be accounted for by the progress of Park Church, at least during the period before the turn of the twentieth century. The membership roll at Park increased steadily throughout the 1880s, and though it fell back in the mid-1890s (in conjunction with Harrison Road), it rose again in the early 1900s, to reach an all-time peak of 447 in 1901. Thereafter it declined very slowly for a decade, falling to a low of 398 in 1912, but rallied again in 1914, rising to 431. No figures survive for subsequent years. And no data at all remain for Square Church.[31]

However, the fortunes of the church in Keighley may have been more favourable. Certainly, the surviving evidence for Devonshire Street suggests so. True, its faithful historian woefully compared the fruitful years of the early Victorian era with the frustrations of later decades: 'While the population of the town increased two and a half times between 1831 and 1871,' he observed, 'the congregation and membership of the church more than quadrupled.'[32] However, 'from the turn of the century ... its influence waned with falling attendances'. And 'the impact of the First World War gave added impetus to the drift from the church'.[33] Be that as it may, the progress of the church was not, in fact, wholly unimpressive during these years. Indeed, it continued to rise, in absolute terms, throughout the period 1880–1920, starting at 195[34] and reaching a figure of 282 in 1920.[35] The growth of the church in the period 1880–1900, of about 25 per cent (195 to 248), was parallel with the demographic expansion of the town. And in the years after 1911, at a time when net emigration actually reduced the population of Keighley, the church held steady. That was no mean achievement.

What of the Baptists? Unfortunately, no reliable evidence is available

---

[29] CDA, CUR 1:3–7, Harrison Road Congregational Chapel, Halifax, Members' Attendance Books, 1869–1925.
[30] Ibid.
[31] CDA (HTC), Anon., Park Congregational Church, Manual for 1915 (Halifax, 1915), p. 13.
[32] Reid Marchbank, One Hundred Years of Progress, p. 25.
[33] Ibid., p. 38.
[34] KPL, uncat. pub., Keighley Congregational Church Manual, 1880 (Keighley, 1880), pp. 23–8.
[35] KPL, uncat. pub., Devonshire Street Congregational Church Manual, 1920 (Keighley, 1920), pp. 12–24.

for Halifax.[36] And no figures have survived from Denholme. But extensive data exist for Albert Street Chapel in Keighley. Moreover, the pattern of associational change they reveal seems to have been fairly typical of the town. Opened in 1865, Albert Street boasted 226 members in 1879.[37] That figure rose very slowly over the next decade, to 257, in 1889, a rate of growth probably a little slower than that of local demographic increase.[38] The church, however, did surprisingly well in the next decade, acquiring very nearly another 50 members at a time when the population of the town was barely growing at all. But the figure of 301, established in 1896, probably represented something of a peak.[39] Certainly, that number declined dramatically during the next ten years, falling to a low of 229 in 1906.[40] Effective amalgamation with Worth Village artificially 'raised' the levels of membership at Albert Street, so much so that the figure recorded for 1907, at 374, was 147 up on the previous year.[41] And the church rallied in the next four years. Total membership actually stood at 472 in 1912.[42] But thereafter it declined steadily, falling to 334 in 1920.[43]

Even less can be said, with certainty, about the pattern of associational 'membership' for the Church of England, whether in Halifax, Keighley or Denholme. At one level, the reason for this is very simple. The Church of England did not keep formal records of its 'membership'. This was partly a result of political dogma. The Church conceived of the whole nation as its members. It was also partly a product of ecclesiastical doctrine. The Church did not lay down strict regulations for membership in its society, either in terms of imperatives or taboos. Finally, it was a matter of convenience. Membership rolls were always difficult to maintain. Furthermore, they were often hopelessly inaccurate as a basis for calculating the number of active workers and participants in any given society. The Church, however, recognised the significance of personal participation in the sacrament of the Lord's Supper as a mark of committed 'membership' in its society. And most contemporary Anglican churches counted the number of communicants in their congregations. St Thomas's Church in Charlestown, Halifax, counted the separate number of communicants at each service during the day on

---

36 It may or may not survive; repeated requests by the author for access to local records and papers met with no response.
37 *Keighley Yearbook, 1879* (Keighley, 1879), p. 151.
38 *Keighley Yearbook, 1889* (Keighley, 1889), p. 77.
39 *Keighley Yearbook, 1896* (Keighley, 1896), p. 191.
40 *Keighley Yearbook, 1906* (Keighley, 1906), p. 150.
41 *Keighley Yearbook, 1907* (Keighley, 1907), p. 143.
42 *Keighley Yearbook, 1912* (Keighley, 1912), p. 147.
43 KPL, uncat. pub., *Keighley Baptist Church, Yearbook, 1920* (Keighley, 1920), pp. 32–41.

Ash Wednesday, Easter Day, Ascension Day, Whitsun Day, Sunday School Anniversary Day, and Harvest Festival Day. And they made an overall calculation for the total number of communicants of the Lord's Supper in the church over the whole year.[44] Keighley parish church calculated totals for the number of communicants, both at the parish church itself, and also in all its associated chapels-of-ease. But they refrained from an elaborate breakdown of the evidence undertaken at St Thomas's.[45]

The difficulties associated with the interpretation of those figures are legion. First, such methods invariably involved counting many people twice. Hence they cannot but be overestimates of the number of individuals who actually partook of the Lord's Supper during the year in any given place. Secondly, they were often restricted to a particular day – Easter Day – when counting was especially carefully undertaken. In this way, they allow for the possibility of 'institutional occasionalism' being mistaken for devoted commitment. Moreover, by equating spirituality with communion they beg the question of what commitment truly was rather than illuminate the problem of how membership was properly judged. To the general difficulties of interpretation must be added the problem of the evidence itself. Put simply, the surviving evidence of communicants' rolls, and communicant attendances, at the churches of this region, whether on a single day (Easter Sunday), or during the whole of the year, is insufficient to plot a reliable statistical map for the course of the changing popularity of, and of affiliation to, the Church of England in this part of late Victorian and Edwardian Britain. The gaps in that evidence are too great to establish reliable chronological patterns. And the range of data is too narrow to permit legitimate generalisation about it. What remains is of anecdotal value only. That value lies primarily in the fact that what it points to is at least compatible with other evidence, from other denominations, collected in different ways.

The records of St Thomas's Church, Charlestown, Halifax, complete for the years 1900–19, are both instructive and inconclusive in this respect. They show that the number of communicants at church on Easter Sunday hovered around a figure between 140 and 160 during this period. No clear pattern of change, still less of unambiguous decline, emerges from the evidence of these years. Similarly, the total number of communicants recorded each year in the church varied between 1,605 in the year 1 April 1900 to 31 March 1901, and 756 in the year 1910–11.

[44] WHQ, D33/22, incom. arch. ref., St Thomas's Church, Charlestown, Halifax, Records of Commissions and Collections, 1899–1919 (no page numbers).
[45] 'Church Statistics', *KPCM*, vol. 23, no. 2, February 1900 (no page number).

There was a major decline in the number of communicants at its services during the first decade of the twentieth century, but the levels of attendance seem to have picked up in subsequent years, especially during the First World War, reaching another peak of 1,588 in 1917–18.[46] On the other hand, the records of All Soul's, Haley Hill, which survive for the years 1888 to 1908, describe, for the most part, a chronicle of decline. The number of communicants in that church reached a peak of 1,109 in 1889. Thereafter, it fell steadily throughout the 1890s to reach a low of 665 in 1898. The church then rallied briefly around the turn of the century, so much so that the number of communicants rose above 1,000 in 1900. But this revival (if such it was) did not last long. By 1907–8, the total figure was once again down to around 600.[47] Whether or not this tale of decline was of general significance, or merely another lamentable aspect of the unfortunate history of All Soul's Church in the twentieth century, cannot now be established. Most unfortunately, no comparable evidence has survived for the parish church of St John the Baptist.

The statistical records of Keighley parish church are only marginally more revealing. Numerical data survive only for the period from 1897 to 1907. They show a slight increase in the number of communicants at church services (both in the parish church and throughout the parish in the various chapels-of-ease), rising from a figure of 2,530 acts of communion in 1898.[48] This reached a high of 3,804 in January 1903.[49] Then it fell back slightly to 3,519 in 1907.[50] The record for public attendance at the Easter services there was, if anything, more encouraging still, at least in so far as may be judged from so limited a time-period and from such exiguous evidence. The number of acts of communion recorded at the parish church, and in the various chapels-of-ease associated with it, stood at 356 in 1899.[51] It rose to 669 in 1907.[52] This agreeable change was widely noted. When, in 1902, the figure topped 600 for the first time, the Rector of Keighley cited that fact

[46] WHQ D33/22, St Thomas's Church, Charlestown, Halifax, Record of Communion and Collections, 1899–1919 (no page number).
[47] WHQ, D/78, incom. arch. ref., All Soul's Church, Haley Hill, Halifax, Communicants' List, 1888–1908 (no page numbers).
[48] 'Church Statistics', KPCM, vol. 23, no. 2, February 1900 (no page number).
[49] BDA, 74D83/1/11, Anon., unmarked article, KPCM, vol. 26, no. 2, February 1903 (no page number).
[50] BDA, 74D83/1/11, Anon., unmarked article, KPCM, vol. 30, no. 2, February 1907 (no page number).
[51] BDA, 74D83/1/11, Anon., 'Easter Statistics', KPCM, vol. 26, no. 5, May 1903 (no page number).
[52] BDA, 74D83/1/11, Frederic Damstini Cremer, 'Communicants at Easter', KPCM, vol. 30, no. 5, May 1907 (no page number).

as proof 'of the growth of a definite religion on the part of a large number of our church people'.[53] If so, it continued to grow, at least in the short term. The 1907 figure represented 'the greatest number of communicants ... that so far has been recorded in the history of the parish'.[54] Unfortunately, insufficient evidence survives to plot its subsequent course with any degree of certainty.

Taken together, these figures point to three conclusions. First, that even the 'more complete' statistical records of later nineteenth-century religious organisations furnish information that, a century later, remains remarkably incomplete. Second, that in so far as any general pattern towards lower associational densities is observable locally during the last decade of the nineteenth century, that trend does not in itself establish a proof for the decline of local religious organisations. It points only to a change in the characteristic form of the preferred local mode of appropriate affiliation. Indeed, there is at least some local evidence that this new, and newly preferred, type actually proved *more* popular in the early twentieth century.[55] Third, that in no instance amongst the mainstream churches was the subsequent decline in absolute membership figures significantly greater, conceived as a proportion, than the concomitant decline in the real levels of local population, at least until 1920. Put another way, there appears to have been no particular decline in religious association or affiliation locally until well after the end of the First World War. That, at least, is what the numbers tell us.[56]

None of which is to say that all was well to 1920, still less that anyone locally thought it was. On the contrary: most observers in the mainstream religious organisations of late nineteenth- and early twentieth-century West Yorkshire were neither so sectarian as to condemn – in their judgement – the majority of the population to eternal damnation, nor were they so ecumenically latitudinarian as to remain indifferent to the numerical fate of their own societies. Similarly, they were neither so pluralistic nor so pessimistic as to concede that a good religious life either might be, or indeed could be, wholly fulfilled beyond the reaches of organised societies and authoritative doctrine. Hence their ambitions for organised religion generally, and for their own organisations

---

[53] BDA, 74D83/1/11, Frederic Damstini Cremer, 'Definite Religion', *KPCM*, vol. 25, no. 4, April 1902 (no page number).

[54] BDA, 74D83/1/11, Anon., 'Communicants at Easter', *KPCM*, vol. 30, no. 5, May 1907 (no page number).

[55] See ch.6, pp. 273–5.

[56] I have not, in this context, considered the question of 'new religious movements', and whether they were replacing the mainstream Protestant denominations as the principal vehicles of evangelical Christianity in those towns by 1920. The reason for this neglect is simple. In 1920, they were few in number, and the numbers of persons associated with them were negligible.

particularly. Hence too, their commitment to the associational ideal as a means of making those organisations stronger, more comprehensive and more successful generally and particularly. Hence, finally, their disappointment at their limited success, dubious comprehensiveness and shaky fortunes, in 1920. In that context, the real significance of all the various statistical data was that they served at this time to confirm the impression gained from other evidence about the doubtful progress of Christian organisations in early twentieth-century English urban society. There were, in fact, many reasons for a concerned churchman, minister or lay official in any West Riding religious association to be pessimistic in 1920.

Poor attendances and empty churches

Not the least of these concerns was the increasingly poor level of attendances at so many churches at their services of public worship. It seemed, according to the Reverend Walter Norton of Keighley's Methodist Circuit, as if 'the gathering of people together for united worship' had become a religious duty 'increasingly neglected'.[57] And he was not alone in that view. A lugubrious report by Halifax's Northgate End Chapel Committee, published just a few months later, acknowledged that 'we too are suffering' from the widely 'recognised falling off of ... interest [in] religious worship'.[58] What was generally, if uncertainly, observed before the war was understood, quite unambiguously to have spread to 'nearly all ... local ... churches' after it.[59] The sole exception appears to have been the Roman Catholic Church. St Mary's, Halifax, for instance, continued to hold five services every Sunday, each accommodating up to 900 people in what was, boastfully but truthfully, described as 'one of the best attended churches in Halifax and District' to mid-century and beyond.[60]

This diminution in public enthusiasm for worship may have made no more than logical sense of the concurrent stagnation in church membership. But few local churchmen or ministers actually saw it that way. Hence the Reverend John Edwards, also of Keighley's Methodist Circuit, seemingly ignoring the dismal matter of declining association, quite unselfconsciously described '[t]he question of the non-attendance

57   The Rev. Walter Norton, 'The Modern Neglect of Public Worship', *KWMCM*, no. 51, August 1913 (no page number).
58   Anon., *Northgate End Unitarian Chapel, Halifax, Church Manual for 1914* (Halifax, 1914), p. 9.
59   WHQ, D33/27, St Thomas's, Charlestown, Church of England, Parochial Church Council Minutes, ? March 1921.
60   Mulroy, *Upon This Rock*, p. 39.

of so many persons at the public services of the church' as 'one of the most perplexing problems of the moment'.[61] Yet he was not a fool: it really was difficult for such a man to explain, or even to understand, the increasing evidence that even church members themselves were more and more rarely attending. Nor was he alone in this failure. It was accompanied by Northgate End Chapel Committee's unrestrained irritation at discovering its now lower 'proportion of worshipping members'.[62] Similarly grieved was Brunswick Methodists' expression of concern, just over a year later, that 'members ... do not attend', followed by the forlorn hope that 'they will ... do so in future'.[63]

Moreover, those who came were not even being especially active when they got there. Thus Brunswick Methodists also complained, at much the same time, about a society membership which was increasingly unwilling to 'take on ... the business ... of office', or to give the church the benefit of 'its practical advice'.[64] And this was not such an abnormal complaint. The Vicar of St Paul's, King Cross, lamenting the 'shortage of staff' to which he was subject in 1920, also remarked upon the lack of 'voluntary enthusiasm' amongst his flock.[65] Some of these complaints specifically boiled down to a lack of money. But not all. The Superintendent of Keighley's Wesleyan Methodist Circuit, berating the lackadaisical atmosphere of post-war churches, claimed that 'the financial resources of the circuit as a whole' were, at that time, 'the equal [of] the utmost support of such an organisation'. This, given the right sort of 'spiritual consecration', would, he claimed, 'bring back all and more of the former influence of the church'. It was just that no one seemed to want to do anything about it.[66]

Up to 1914, outbursts of this kind tended to be cast in tones of fear: this spirit was admirably caught by Brunswick Methodists again who admonished themselves in 1907 that '[i]f some effort is not made now ... the attendance will be very small ... in ... six or seven years ... time'.[67] After the end of the war, the characteristic style of criticism (at Brunswick as elsewhere) gradually changed more to one of embarrass-

---

61   The Rev. John Edwards, 'Why People Do Not Come to Church', *KWMCM*, no. 33, February 1912.
62   Anon., *Northgate End Chapel, Manual for 1914*, p. 9.
63   CDA, Misc. 57/11, Brunswick United Methodist Church, Halifax, Church Meeting Minute Book, 17 February 1915.
64   *Ibid.*, 31 January 1910.
65   The Rev. J.B. Rowsell, 'Vicar's Letter', *SPCKPCM*, vol. 29, no. 5, May 1920 (no page number).
66   J. Sutcliffe Allen, 'Superintendent's Letter', *KWMCM*, no. 133, June 1920 (no page number).
67   CDA, Misc. 57/11, Brunswick United Methodist Church, Halifax, Church Meeting Minute Book, 21 January 1907.

ment: of a sense that so depleted was the level of public support for religious institutions that their historical inheritance – above all their Victorian and Edwardian churches – had come to seem curiously inappropriate, even somewhat profligate. Hence, for instance, Sutcliffe Allen's description of contemporary Wesleyan congregations as being 'pathetically out of proportion with the size of our Chapels'.[68] Similar, if still worse, was the laconic and biting observation by the Reverend G.H. East that the entire congregations of all the six 'Free' (i.e. nonconformist) societies located in the centre of post-war Keighley could easily be 'accommodated' on any given Sunday 'in just one of the churches'.[69]

Suddenly, it seemed as if no one wanted to go into a church. The most accessible of all public institutions had mysteriously become the most distrusted. Sutcliffe Allen quoted a 'demobilised soldier', who spoke to him with this effect:

I have no quarrel with the professed creed of the Churches, their members reckon to be following Christ and doing His work and to believe what He taught, but you know as well as I do, sir, that they don't really believe anything of the sort, they don't look upon people outside as He did, they aren't really concerned about anybody but themselves, they aren't in earnest about the people they call lost. Oh! I know there are some people in the Churches who are Christians, but I mean the Churches as bodies. They are mostly just religious clubs for respectable people.[70]

Some people did have a quarrel with the churches and a pretty basic one too. An anonymous article published in the *Keighley Parish Church Magazine* in September 1906 noted that, recently, 'a good deal of unbelief has been spreading ... among intelligent and thoughtful working-men'. So much so that an earlier 'attitude of indifference seems to be giving way to ... an awakening of real hostility to the Christian faith'.[71] Sixteen years later, that suspicious development had become something like a melancholy commonplace. In this vein, Keighley's *Wesleyan Methodist Circuit Magazine* lamented the existence of 'a widespread and definitely anti-Christian spirit' abroad. It pointed to how indifference had passed into absence and absence into opposition, both locally and nationally. Then it blithely announced that an age of 'fatuous optimism' – otherwise understood as one of the greatest eras of ecclesiastical expansion – was 'at an end'.[72] Why?

68 J. Sutcliffe Allen, 'Superintendent's Letter', *KWMCM*, no. 133, June 1920 (no page number).
69 The Rev. G.H. East, *Keighley News*, 26 February 1927.
70 Sutcliffe Allen, 'Superintendent's Letter'.
71 Anon., 'Unbelief', *KPCM*, vol. 28, no. 9, September 1906 (no page number).
72 KPL, uncat. pub., Anon., unmarked article, *KWMCM*, no. 163, December 1922 (no page number).

The rise of popular socialism and the radical critique of institutional religion, c. 1900–14

A report of the Chapel Committee, published in the *Northgate End Church Manual* for 1906, noted with sadness upon the retirement of Mr Millson that this legendary incumbent had 'not had the satisfaction of counting a large congregation' in the church towards the end of his tenure. This was because too many of its members had, in recent years, 'been lured away by various outside influences'. One of these malignant influences, which the Committee specifically named, was the local Labour Church.[73] This was, of course, not the first time that the fortunes of Northgate End Church had been adversely connected with the emergence of socialist organisations in Halifax. The formation of the Labour Church in 1893 had caused an initial 'falling off in numbers' there.[74] But thirteen years later, these complaints assumed a wider significance locally. By 1906, the Independent Labour Party was well established in Halifax.[75] So too in Keighley.[76] Its success made the socialist challenge to the old order clear, both at the critical level of formal political organisation, as well as in the more nebulous field of existing ecclesiastical institutions. That it was so constituted and so motivated – a very real challenge to the tradition of popularity (hence social significance) of the churches – few contemporaries questioned. Certainly, few local churchmen or ministers ever entertained any doubts about the matter. That may have been paranoia. But if so, it was a symptom mirrored in the antagonistic optimism of West Yorkshire's socialists. And this was for the simplest reasons. Even the smallest leakage of adult male involvement was more than the early twentieth-century churches could bear. Their opponents knew as much.[77]

Desperate straits induced dramatic measures. In October 1905, the Rector of Keighley was moved to arrange a public debate, staged between himself and a 'socialist leader in the town'. Its subject was: 'Why Socialists Oppose the Church'. That was how they (the socialists) described it anyway. Damstini more tactfully interpreted it to his flock as a 'Discussion on Unbelief'. Whatever the title, both sides clearly understood what was at stake. Exactly what transpired in that discussion is unknown. Damstini, at least, believed that 'by the end of the meeting' the antagonists 'probably

---

[73] *Northgate End Unitarian Church, Annual Report for 1906* (Halifax, 1906), p. 11.
[74] Millson's Address to the Annual Church Meeting, January 1894, p. 17.
[75] Howell, *British Workers*, pp. 198–200.   [76] Dewhirst, *History of Keighley*, p. 105.
[77] For a general view, see Hobsbawm, 'Religion and the Rise of Socialism', in his *Worlds of Labour*; also Susan Budd, *Varieties of Unbelief: Atheists and Agnostics in English Society, 1850–1960* (London, 1977); and Edward Royle, *Radicals, Secularists, and Republicans: Popular Free Thought in Britain, 1866–1915* (Manchester, 1980).

understood each other better than at the beginning'. This may have been because of his acknowledgement that 'the church has not been as active in the matter of social reform as her gospel ought to have made her'. It was probably less because of his forceful reminder, directed towards all those socialists present, that they 'must not forget their debt to the Church', nor 'neglect their duty to worship ... Him' since it remained 'more important to fulfil our duties than claim our rights'.[78]

Certainly, it did not put an end to informed clerical concerns. Still less did it diminish the ideological chasm which increasingly divided their anxieties from contemporary socialist thinking. Indeed, if anything, the divide became progressively more difficult to bridge. This was not for want of trying. Nor, curiously, was it because the gap was all that great. On the contrary. In some ways, there seemed to be little gap at all. As one ingenuous local worthy put it: 'Those who [are] forming Labour Churches, and who [are] trying to influence considerable numbers of the labouring population to adopt their views, [are] beginning to see that Christianity [is] really on their side'.[79] Similarly, in the words of one, altogether more worldly, local cleric: 'Christianity ... wherever it had spread [had] brought great ... blessings to the masses of the people ... creat[ing] new and loftier conceptions of the dignity of manhood'.[80] So might the two now progress harmoniously together? No. As Millson knew, and as the Rector of Keighley understood, Labour Churches, and then the Labour Party, meant 'Public Worship on separatist lines'.[81]

Why? Because doctrinal differences, though small, mattered. No one put this more bluntly than the Reverend Ogden Taylor. In his words: 'Socialists assumed that all that was needed for regeneration of society was a change in the outward conditions of life. Change man's environment and thereby they [sic] would change man himself; that was the gospel of socialism'.[82] Many agreed. Socialists, the Reverend Norris insisted, simply mistook 'thy kingdom come' for a 'material kingdom'.[83] In that way, they arrived at the fallacious belief that 'the establishment [of] a commonwealth founded upon justice and love' could effect the 'realization of universal well-being'.[84]

---

78 Frederic Damstini Cremer, 'Public Discussion on Unbelief', *KPCM*, vol. 28, no. 11, November 1905 (no page number).

79 KPL, uncat. pub., Sir Henry Mitchell, 'Grand Wesleyan Bazaar at Keighley', *Keighley News*, no date (unmarked clipping in the uncatalogued papers of Temple Street Wesleyan Methodist Chapel, Keighley).

80 Rev. Ogden Taylor, 'Christianity and Social Progress', *Keighley News*, 17 February 1907.

81 Cremer, 'Public Discussion on Unbelief'.

82 Taylor, 'Christianity and Social Progress'.

83 Norris, *Sermon Preached at the Consecration of St. Paul's Church*, p. 35.

84 'Statement of Principles', *Labour Church Hymn Book* (Bradford, 1908), p. 1.

No churchman could believe that. No minister either. Not the Reverend Norris. And certainly not the Reverend Taylor. Whilst they knew well enough that 'the condition of at least one-tenth of the population was deplorable', it remained axiomatic to them, as Christians, that 'man is not wholly swayed by the inspirational god of circumstances'. True, he was 'sometimes degraded by his circumstances'. On the other hand, he 'not infrequently degraded his circumstances'. Thus 'it was ... very often ... found that the greatest happiness and the most impressive moral purity was in the midst of degrading circumstances, while on the other hand they [i.e. fortunate circumstances] were met with misery'. Hence it simply followed that 'the socialist assumption ... does violence to the facts of experience ... and ... [t]o remedy [human misery] one must begin where the malady existed. The healing must be inward ... [As] the kingdom of heaven made man anew in Jesus and endowed him with a power to create for himself a new and better set of circumstances'.[85]

This was, in its own way, a heroically sustained doctrine. But it was a view maintained at a price. That price was paid by the churches in the 'industrial towns' especially just before the war, where a 'strong artisan element' that was now not simply '[o]utside the church' became also 'sceptical of, or [even] hostile [towards] religious influence' altogether.[86] And this, in its turn, did further damage to the churches. It exacerbated a fault within them that Millson, for one, had noticed as early as 1894. Not only did it – marginally – reduce their congregations. It also – and more importantly – changed their 'character ... somewhat', for it further reduced the numbers of men in them. And that necessarily increased still more the predominance of women. This brought, often literally, '[t]he bonnets ... more into prominence'.[87] It made more figurative sense still, albeit a rather cruel sense, of the demobilised soldier's gibe: the churches were – had increasingly become – just another of those all too numerous and monumentally ineffectual clubs for respectable people; still worse, respectable ladies.

The decline of holy Sunday, the demise of family faith and the end of the social solidarity of religion, c. 1900–14

The elegiac report of Northgate End's Chapel Committee identified one other 'outside influence' which had caused the Reverend Millson's diminished latter-day congregation. This was the 'Sunday Lecture

85 Taylor, 'Christianity and Social Progress'.
86 Dr Maggs, 'Keighley Baptist Minister's Welcome', *Keighley News*, 1 April 1911.
87 *Millson's Address to the Annual Church Meeting, 29th January 1894*, p. 17.

Society'.[88] In retrospect, such a benign organisation must seem a curious candidate for the title of second great corrupter of public morals. Yet many contemporaries would not have been surprised by the accusation. Indeed, they would have well understood its motive. Moreover, they would have heartily concurred with its sentiment, for it reflected the conviction, shared by almost every late Victorian and Edwardian churchman and minister, that the task of evangelising the nation was conceivable only in the context of a specially sanctified Sunday. Further, that this condition, so far from being some curious relic of a puritan past was, in fact, all the more critical in the framework of a modern urban society. And finally, that this trust had not been sustained. Instead, it had been abandoned under fire – and with disastrous results.

To be sure, this was probably as much a matter about perception as of reality. Certainly, that view was critically linked to the additional emphasis which so many churches had placed upon the properly distinctive observances of Sunday during the previous generation. But one thing is clear. However slowly and however imperceptibly, the character of Sunday really did change in these towns around the turn of the century. One anonymous contributor to St Paul's parish magazine, writing in 1907, put it this way: 'Nobody, who is even on the sunny side of Middle Life, can fail to have seen a great change within his own experience with regard to the way in which Sunday is regarded'. This was not, in itself, altogether a bad thing: 'It is ... hardly to be wondered at, that the present generation should have broken away from a narrow, Puritanical conception of Sunday'. But it had led to a bad thing; specifically, to 'a reaction, and a widespread one', in which 'all sense of restriction has gone, and people have in a number of cases begun to use the day as their own, and not as the Lord's, as a day for pleasure and amusement and not for the worship of God'.[89]

This 'reaction', so called, quite accurately described the rise of modern leisure patterns in early twentieth-century Britain. It also increasingly defined Sabbatarianism in opposition to the people's pleasure; increasingly, that is, as a form of sententiousness which struck at, rather than conformed with, a popular sense of decency and appropriateness. In this way, it rendered organised religion itself more unpalatable to many who might otherwise have found political radicalism quite unattractive. Certainly, it induced more public antagonism to religion than in the past. Contemporary churchmen and ministers

[88]   *Northgate End, Report for 1906*, p. 11.
[89]   Anon., 'Sunday Observance', *SPCKCPM*, vol. 16, no. 4, April 1907 (no page number).

were acutely aware of this difficulty. Yet they were also, for the most part, staunchly committed to Sunday's peculiarity. They therefore apologised for its dullness, but they highlighted the virtues of its maintenance. Hence Edward Pringle, Pastor of Keighley Congregational Church, in 1912: 'The old way of Sabbath-keeping might be strict but at least it secured [sic] quiet, and rest and companionship, and [at least] Sunday was the holy day, not the day for excursions, not the holiday'.[90] Then they argued that, once tolerated, 'innocent amusements' soon became 'pernicious' diversions. They 'encroached' upon the 'religious observance of Sunday'. They discouraged family attendance at church. And they split members of the family from each other, depriving them of those 'brief hours' set aside for the 'interchange of affection ... quiet thought and worship, and the ministries of the truth'. This was, of course, a romantic view. Even its author was fully aware that 'people [in 1912] may smile at all that [i.e. at that romanticism]'. But he was also certain that it was true. Or at least that it had once been true; and that 'in the simple joys of paterfamilias in his family' there had been, and not so long ago, a general 'recognition of divine authority'. Consequently, whilst such a commitment, and the life it implied, might have been 'dull and uninteresting', it had also represented, so Pringle believed, at least 'an attempt to order it [i.e. life] aright', and to acknowledge 'the solemn claims of religion' rather than 'thrust [them] aside in the interests of pleasure'.[91]

What Pringle lamented in terms of severed family union, local Methodists denounced on the grounds of diminished social solidarity. 'The growing secularization of ... Sunday' was, so the Reverend Arthur Myers argued in the *Keighley Wesleyan Methodist Circuit Magazine*, nothing less than a callous repudiation of 'one of the historical evidences of the love of God to the "common people"'. He explained: 'long before working men had either the right or the desire to combine in fighting for their own interests ... they had at least one day a week on which they could call their souls their own, and when the peasant could lift up his head and say "I too am a man"'. It followed that '[t]he man who breaks the Sabbath law as interpreted by Jesus is an enemy to mankind, and especially to the poor', because, put simply (and truthfully), 'you cannot have Sunday pleasure without Sunday work', and it is 'the weak who go to the wall'. Nor was the Sabbath-breaker a friend of liberty. 'We pride ourselves', he noted, 'on civic and religious liberty, but', he insisted, 'the Sunday pleasure-seeker leads us back into bondage. Perhaps he says, "You shall not compel me to keep the

---

[90] Anon., *Rhodes Street Wesleyan Church, Jubilee Celebrations*, p. 17.
[91] Pringle, 'The Influence of Family Religion', p. 7.

Sabbath on puritanical lines." We heartily reply, "Agreed"; but we also answer, "At any rate, we must see to it that you do not compel another man to lose his Sabbath for your selfish enjoyment." ' He concluded:

We have no desire to be narrow and intolerant but in the interests of the community . . . we must offer a firm opposition to the present tendency . . . In the social interests of the poor, particularly of the children; in the interests of the sacredness of home life, which is largely dependent on a quiet Sunday; and, above all, in the spiritual interests of all men, it is high time we entered on a holy crusade in defence of the Christian Sunday.[92]

These were fine words. They were also forlorn gestures. The secularisation of Sunday, so defined, continued locally apace. Neither elegiac recollection nor aggressive protest made much difference to its progress. Perhaps a 'holy crusade' might have done. But it never materialised. Or, at least in so far as it did, it had remarkably little effect. In part, this was because of the disunity of the modern churches themselves. Strong though the Sabbatarian impulse remained across Protestant denominations (and also in the Roman Catholic Church), the exact forms which it took, and the degree to which it was upheld, varied across those denominations and varied, to some extent, between individual societies. In part, it was because the forces of anti-Sabbatarianism proved to be surprisingly powerful. This was a result, above all, of their sheer variety. 'Sunday Band Performances in the Parks of Halifax' remained vulnerable to the expression of organised public opinion.[93] But Sunday golf did not. Nor did bicycle clubs. And still less did those forms of outdoor activity and indoor recreation tacitly acknowledged by at least some of the churches – parks and museums and the like. Finally, strict Edwardian Sabbatarianism was confronted by a direct challenge which not only probed its reasonableness, but also sapped its spirit. This was the First World War.

War, work and social change c. 1914–20

For the vast majority of the *civilian* population of Britain, male and female, young and old, upper-class, bourgeois and proletarian, the war years were good years. General levels of mortality – for infants, mothers, even the middle-aged (especially amongst the working classes) declined.[94] This was partly because health care

---

92   KPL, uncat. pub., Rev. Arthur Myers, 'Are We to Have a Continental Sunday?', *KWMCM*, no. 20, January 1911 (no page number).
93   CDA, uncat. MS, Halifax, St John's Wesleyan Methodist Circuit, Quarterly Meeting Minute Book, 17 December 1923.
94   See J.M. Winter, *The Great War and the British People* (London, 1985), ch. 4, esp. pp. 107–8, 117–40 and 144–53.

improved.[95] It was also partly because the standard of living, particularly for the more low-paid workers, rose.[96] If this was true generally, it was particularly true of towns like Halifax, Keighley and Denholme, for the 'Great War' brought about drastic alterations in the structure and functioning of local industry. From 1915 onwards, engineering factories were diverted to munitions, and textile manufactures to the production of khaki and flannel. In this way, a chronically declining local economy suddenly boomed. Regular work, captive markets and general prosperity pushed wages (and prices) up. In Keighley, for instance, a turner or fitter's weekly wage of about 41s in 1914 soared to 88s by 1920. A builder's hourly rate rose from 10d to 2s 4d. in the same period. Prices rose too: bacon from about $11\frac{1}{2}$d per pound in 1914, to 2s 3d in 1918; jam from $4\frac{1}{2}$d per pot to 1s; a bar of soap from 2d to 10d.[97] But consumer durables remained fairly steady. And many people were at last able to afford them.

War also brought about significant changes in local working customs. The shortage of men, particularly of young skilled men, caused first by voluntary recruitment and then by conscription, enabled working women slowly but steadily to move into trades which had been traditionally barred to them, notably 'overlooking' in the textile mills.[98] Then, following explicit appeals to do so, 'women who [did] not usually do paid work' were persuaded to take employment in munitions factories, on farms, in shops and offices, hospitals, banks and public transport.[99] The long-term effects of those changes in the economic structure and upon social mores in what remained a fairly traditional region of industrial Britain, can easily be overestimated. To a remarkable extent, things in these respects returned to normal after the war.[100] But the deleterious effects of this particular upheaval of war upon the churches lasted for some while afterwards, for wartime women's work, skilled and unskilled, new and old, above all meant *Sunday* work. And that meant more trouble for the apologists of traditional religious life. As George McNeal, writing in the *Keighley Wesleyan Methodist Circuit Magazine*, put it: 'Since August last [i.e. August 1914] the advocates of the old-fashioned Sunday have been in a most difficult position.' 'In order to cope with the demand for munitions of war, there has been an enormous increase in Sunday Labour.' Hence 'there is ... probably ... more Sunday work in England ... today [1915] than there has ever been before'.

The effect was striking and immediate. The Pastor of Northgate End

---

95   *Ibid.*, ch. 5, esp. pp. 155–67.   96   *Ibid.*, ch. 7, esp. pp. 213–40.
97   Dewhirst, *History of Keighley*, p. 115.   98   *Ibid.*, p. 115.
99   *Ibid.*, p. 114.   100   *Ibid.*, pp. 123ff.

Church, in the Manual for 1916, noting that '[t]he attendances at Chapel have been somewhat affected by the war', instanced the obvious effects of 'death', 'illness' and 'perhaps, in some cases ... a lessening of interest', as possible causes of this lamentable phenomenon.[101] The Chapel Committee, reporting in the same manual for the same year, took these observations a good deal further. They insisted that '[t]he year 1915 will be remembered as one that has made great inroads in our customs', particularly since 'the better attendance at public worship that [had been] recorded in the early months of the war does not appear to have been kept up'.[102] What they were pointing to, however hesitantly, was the seemingly novel and potentially catastrophic decline of *female* attendance at church on Sundays. It was that which, implicitly, McNeal was referring to when he asserted that 'this [i.e. Sunday work] is a ... sin'. Yet some insisted that it was patriotic. This, he argued, was 'a mistake', which caused 'overstrain' and actually diminished the number of munitions produced.[103] It can have come as little surprise that no one believed him or that no one acted on what he said. Sunday work, including female Sunday work, continued. And, in the words of Keighley's redoubtable Congregationalist historian, in this way the 'impact of the First World War gave added impetus to the drift from the churches, modern or not'.[104]

The spectre of modernity and the impetus to modernisation c. 1920–5

As associational membership declined, attendances dropped and finances wilted. As the most articulate men moved into socialist organisations, so the best women began Sunday work. As Sunday became like any other day, families ceased to worship, or even to pray, together. As one contemporary put it: 'Public worship is neither a duty or a delight to the majority of the people ... the Bible does not hold the place in our homes which it once did ... domestic religion is not kept up as it used to be ... Sunday is not observed in the good old-fashioned quiet and reverent way'.[105] For him, and for others like him, these fateful developments threatened all the 'pieties of family life' and the 'moral welfare of society'. They also expressed a sea-change in the 'tone

---

[101] CDA, NEC 18, *Northgate End Unitarian Chapel, Halifax, Manual for 1916* (Halifax, 1916), p. 4.
[102] *Ibid.*, p. 5.
[103] KPL, uncat. pub., George H. McNeal, 'The Modern Sunday and Its Influence on National Life', *KWMCM*, no. 74, July 1915 (no page number).
[104] Reid Marchbank, *One Hundred Years of Progress*, p. 38.
[105] Pringle, 'The Influence of Family Religion', p. 4.

of public opinion', one which now defined all the great questions in 'materialist' terms, while judging them by criteria no more profound than 'the pursuit of pleasure' and the 'desire to possess'.[106] And finally, they reflected a human sensibility, a view of man characterised by 'a certain lightness of mind ... a loss of seriousness, a failure to realise responsibility', and 'a devotion to amusement and sport'.[107]

But what had caused this contemporary catastrophe? To answer that question, self-consciously 'thoughtful minds' turned their attention away from Labour churches, Sunday bands and wartime working hours. They found their answers 'in the stress of modern life'.[108] Still worse, the root of these stresses they discovered in the 'general characteristic[s]' of the 'modern world itself'.[109] These were the qualities of 'abstracted' sacred feelings and 'reified' mundane thoughts. Abstracted feelings 'forced' the 'spiritual life' into the 'outer realms of living'. Reified thoughts put the 'opinion of men' at the 'centre of [human] existence'. But replacement of God by man left most men 'harassed by uncertainty'. So belittled, so uncertain, they plunged into a 'practical' world, judged only by 'utilitarian standards'. What remained of their religion became 'a vague, impracticable something ... concerned with a certain part of one's life ... but quite unrelated to the everyday tasks of life'.[110]

Here was a crisis of faith, observed by intelligent contemporaries, experienced by everyone. No account of religion in the West Riding at the end of the First World War is true to the record unless it comes to terms with that crisis. But churchmen and ministers, around 1920, made little of the possibilities contained in ambiguous evidence on numbers. Still less were they willing to view the challenges to their social and moral standing from a detached academic perspective. Their trials, as they saw them, were for real. And they were quite unprecedented. To be sure, it was not as if religion had not been in trouble before. Methodists especially knew that. The lull in eighteenth-century English spiritual life had brought them into existence.[111] Nor was the evidence lacking that there were men and women at large still 'reaching out for self-improvement'.[112] This was a true crisis because the modern churches seemingly could no longer reach them. Still more: they no longer wanted to be reached by the churches.

---

[106] Edwards, 'Why People Do Not Come to Church'.
[107] Pringle, 'The Influence of Family Religion', p. 4.
[108] Rev. W.L. Shroeder, 'A Continuing Change of Emphasis', *Northgate End Unitarian Chapel, Halifax, Annual Report, 1912* (Halifax, 1912), pp. 5–6.
[109] The Critic, 'Life and Religion', *KDCM*, vol. 5, no. 8, August 1906, p. 7.
[110] *Ibid.*   [111] Norton, 'The Modern Neglect of Religion'.
[112] Frederic Damstini Cremer, 'Mission Rooms', *KPCM*, vol. 19, no. 8, August 1896 (no page number).

That sense of urgency, even of a certain enormity, passed far beyond the local chattering classes. Indeed, it became something of a surrogate article of faith in local organisational life. Hence, quite typically, a 'Special Meeting' was convened in July 1920 by the Keighley Wesleyan Methodist Circuit to discuss what was openly described as the current 'crisis of spiritual confidence'. This crisis, so the first circular informed all those concerned, had been 'building up' in the circuit (and elsewhere) 'since the end of the war'. In response, the meeting determined that a letter be sent in its name to all members and adherents (figures estimated at 1,400 and 7,000 respectively) of the circuit 'inviting them' to 'direct their thought and prayer to the following matters':

1 A reverent sense of the duty, privilege and joy of public worship.
2 A realization of the value and necessity of Fellowship.
3 A more definite concentration of effort upon the evangelistic mission of the church.
4 The avoidance of unnecessary diffusion of our limited spiritual resources.
5 That the ministers be requested to arrange for meetings of our people in every place in order to emphasise the importance of sincere and concentrated effort to maintain our Sunday congregations, and weekday devotional meetings, and to do our best to win the outsider for Christ.[113]

But, significantly, to nothing else. And, self-evidently, to nothing new. Yet it would be inappropriate to accuse such men (and women) of institutional complacency. Indeed, the contrary, or something like collective hysteria, would be closer to the truth. Similarly, it would be plainly false to assert that they presumed all their woes to be externally caused. They did not. The same men (and women) who so berated the emerging culture of modernity, with its materialism, secularism and indifference, also lamented the 'divided state of Christendom' in their time. Pointedly, they also denounced those 'class interests' which had 'obscured the brotherhood of Christ's people', 'divid[ing] congregations' and standing in the way of truth and progress'. Finally, presciently perhaps, they condemned that 'lack of leadership in the churches ... and of Christian character in professors of religion' which, together, had induced an institutional 'complacency and self-satisfaction' disastrous, amongst other things, for the churches' potential 'influence on the outsider'.[114]

Nevertheless, so chastened, they still sought their salvation in more of the same: more fellowship, more worship, more reverence, and much more on Sundays. And that reaffirmation of, indeed that rededication

[113] KPL, 105D77/1/3/2/c, Keighley Wesleyan Circuit, Quarterly Minute Book, 19 July 1920.
[114] Norton, 'The Modern Neglect of Public Worship'.

to, the basic organisational principles of a lifetime was actually enhanced, not compromised, by the one significant institutional innovation of the era. Denominational ecumenicalism, whatever else it stood and stands for, represented at the time the logical extension of the associational principle.[115] With its emphasis on the putative benefits of co-operative organisation rather than upon the dogmatic niceties of strict doctrine, it constituted the intelligent culmination of so much of that towards which so many of the contemporary apologists of association had been working for so long. It underpinned common Christian virtues – reverence, worship and obedience – whilst elevating novel religious goals – toleration, understanding and forbearance. And it did so within an organisational culture which demanded that, for the sake of simple survival, seemingly soluble internal divisions be approached before – perhaps even at the expense of – possibly intractable external limitations.

Contemporaries were aware of this. They knew that the great amalgamation of Methodist organisations, beginning in 1907 and culminating in 1932, together with the less dramatic inter-denominational discussions of the same period, had deep roots in their organisational pasts.[116] It also had obvious institutional forebears. Halifax's nonconformists specifically formed a 'Nonconformist Society', designed to co-ordinate Protestant missionary activity in the town, probably in 1892.[117] Denholme seems to have gained a 'Free Church Council' in 1901, for much the same purpose.[118] It is unlikely that Keighley went without something similar, and at much the same time. Co-operation between Church and dissent remained informal at this time, yet even in as divided a town as Keighley locals could celebrate the United Meetings of Churchmen and Nonconformist Leaders at the Church Congress of 1898, a full generation before the famous joint session in the United Mission of Grace.[119]

Clearly, there were many types, both of informal and of embryonic ecumenicalism. Yet one dynamic characteristic stands out. This began with a particular emphasis upon the special claims of the evangelical imperative in the specific context of an industrial urban environment.

---

[115] Currie, *Methodism Divided*, chs. 3 and 9; Wilson, *Religion in Secular Society*, ch. 10.
[116] Currie, *Methodism Divided*, ch. 7; John Kent, *The Age of Disunity* (London, 1966), ch. 1.
[117] CDA, Misc. 152/3, St John's Wesleyan Methodist Chapel, Prescott Street, Halifax, 13 June 1892.
[118] Uncat. MS, Southgate Baptist Church, Regular Church Meeting Minute Book, 3 April 1901.
[119] Frederic Damstini Cremer, 'The Church Congress', *KPCM*, vol. 21, no. 10, October 1898 (no page number).

Hence the Reverend Bailey's exhortation in 1892, to all 'nonconformist evangelical churches', that they consider the 'possibility of a much closer approximation to each other', and a 'much more extended cooperation with each other', in the task of undertaking the 'spiritual necessities of the population of large towns'.[120] But it ended with an altogether more general appreciation of the previously unacknowledged benefits of denominational diversity in the now almost universal context of an indifferent, modern mass society. Thus the Bishop of Lichfield's curiously warm appreciation of the 'work of other religious bodies' in the 'working-class district' of St Hilda's, Halifax, prior to the Church's establishment there (in 1911) and as a bulwark against that 'state of heathenism which might [otherwise] have ... prospered' in the interim.[121]

Formal amalgamation incorporated the tone of the later rather than of the earlier years. That is, behind the rational tone, it packed a fairly emotional, not to say a dispirited, punch. Sometimes indeed, it was fatalistic in its expression. Hence Brunswick Methodists celebrated the first great reunion, between their own United Methodists, the New Connexion and the Bible Christians with the vague 'hope' that this decision might prove to be a 'blessing', adding to 'the numbers of all concerned', but without the slightest explanation about how this might prove to be so.[122] Later, something like an invisible revival mechanism was invoked, so that the very ordinariness of the gains anticipated – size, rationality and convenience – was curiously linked to the possibility, indeed the probability, of a 'new ... and a real ... spiritual awakening' which would surely result from benevolent motive and beneficent action placed together.[123]

That, unintentionally perhaps but strikingly, still said a very great deal about the nature of the 'crisis of faith' facing churchmen and ministers around 1920, for this was a crisis of the associational ideal, strictly defined. It is only in the light of that ideal, and of the institutional imperatives which it entailed for growth, comprehensiveness and the promise of eventual triumph that the severe expression of ecclesiastical disappointment in the years immediately after the First World War becomes fully intelligible. And it is only through that perspective that the reassertion of the same goal, albeit now through its logical – ecumenical – extension, makes any sense at all. Yet it was also only within the

---

[120] Bailey, *Progressive Congregationalism*, p. 21.
[121] *Halifax Guardian*, 29 April 1911.
[122] CDA, Misc. 57/11, Brunswick United Methodist Church, Church Meeting Minute Book, 21 January 1907.
[123] The Rev. J.T. Wadding, 'Methodist Re-Union', *KWMCM*, no. 133, June 1920 (no page number).

context of the associational ideal, so interpreted, that the fundamental dilemma of the churches in modern society became so apparent. Through its auspices, they had staked their claim to institutional centrality. Yet by tying the fortunes of religion to the vicissitudes of association in an increasingly unsympathetic urban environment, they had also risked the survival of God's Word on earth. That risk has only become more acute in the years which have followed.

Conclusion: The strange death of religious Britain

Some time during the 1920s the local religious classes lost heart. They ceased to believe in their mission to evangelise the nation. Not, of course, in its necessity; only its practicality. It no longer seemed possible. And it had become a burden. In that pessimism, they were in good company. It was widely shared by their superiors, in Canterbury, London and abroad. A new, and a disturbing sense that *society as a whole* had ceased to be, or was gradually ceasing to be, in any meaningful sense, religious, and was therefore now strictly speaking beyond even the very best efforts of a committed Christian minority to save it, became something of an official commonplace at that time.[1] Certainly, it has been well reported, and widely corroborated, ever since.[2] And it generally forms the empirical basis, the fundamental evidence, for that widely identified shift in social mores and of cultural expression which marks the secularisation of society.[3]

As such, it was an attitude which stood in stark contrast to the characteristic sensibilities of dedicated churchmen and ministers, in West

---

[1]   E.g., Anon., 'Editorial Notes', *KWMCM*, no. 163, December 1922, n.p., 'only a fatuous optimism can deny the existence of a widespread ... anti-Christian Spirit'. Cf. *Report of Archbishops' Committee on the Supply of Candidates for Holy Orders* (London, 1926), p. 28, 'The problem [of diminished supply] is owing ... to the secularization of our modern life generally.' Cited in Anon., 'Preface', *Crockford's Clerical Dictionary, 1926* (Oxford, 1926), p. xv. On the wider background, see Hastings, *A History of English Christianity*, ch. 11.

[2]   E.g. Hugh Brogan, *The English People* (London, 1943), p. 121: 'in the generation ... that passed [from] the great Liberal landslide of 1906 [there] was ... a ... general weakening of the hold of Christianity on the English people'. Or A.J.P. Taylor, *English History, 1914–1945* (Oxford, 1965), p. 259: 'By the time of ... [t]he great parliamentary stir of 1927 and 1928 [i.e. the Prayer Book controversy] England had ceased to be, in any real sense, a Christian nation.' Even Hastings, *A History of English Christianity*, p. 193, suggests that 'in the 1920s ... [t]he institution of the ... Church was crumbling on many a side'.

[3]   See, e.g., Wilson, *Religion in Secular Society*, esp. ch. 1; or Martin, *A General Theory of Secularization*, ch. 3. This is not to say that a *theory* of secularisation needs such evidence; one of the most famous of such theories was based on no evidence at all, viz. Harvey Cox, *The Secular City: Secularization and Urbanization in Theological Perspective* (London, 1965), see esp. 'Introduction'.

Yorkshire as elsewhere in the United Kingdom, around 1870. In almost every case, what these people emphasised were not the burdens but the possibilities of mission. Local and national ecclesiastical history during the late part of the nineteenth century makes no sense in any other light. So many churches would not have been built, so many new societies formed, so much proselytising done by organisations and individuals with no belief in themselves or in what they were doing. That contemporary confidence, and the activity which it inspired, have (belatedly) impressed a new generation of religious historians. Certainly it was the impetus to growth in mid-Victorian religious systems which now most interests them.[4] Equally, it was the sheer ubiquity, the real popularity and the undoubted social significance of religion which they highlight in the cultural order of the early twentieth-century town.[5] A few, emboldened by the evidence of organisational expansion and experiential vigour within the context of modern industrial society, have gone further, to challenge the causal principles of secularisation theory, *tout court*.[6]

Hence the existence of two, by now pretty well mutually exclusive, intellectual parties in modern British religious historiography. Callum Brown has usefully classified them as 'pessimists' and 'optimists' respectively.[7] In this division of interpretative judgement, the so-called pessimists emphasise the long-term downward trends in religious

---

[4]   Brown, 'Did Urbanization Secularize Britain?', pp. 10–12; Brown, 'A Revisionist Approach to Religious Change', pp. 40–9; also his 'The Mechanism of Religious Growth in Urban Societies', esp. pp. 248–54; Gill, 'Secularization and Census Data', pp. 108–13; and Smith, *Religion in Industrial Society*, esp. ch. 7; an exceptionally careful consideration of this question, conceived in a wider, comparative context, can be found in Hugh McLeod, 'Secular Cities? Berlin, London and New York in the Later-Nineteenth and Early-Twentieth Centuries', in Bruce (ed.), *Religion and Modernization*, pp. 59–89.

[5]   Brown, 'Did Urbanization Secularize Britain?', pp. 11–12; and for comparative corroboration, see Carl Strikwerda, 'A Resurgent Religion: The Rise of Catholic Social Movements in Nineteenth-Century Belgian Cities'; also Hans Otte, ' "More Churches – More Churchgoers": The Lutheran Church in Hanover between 1850 and 1914', both in McLeod (ed.), *European Religion in the Great Cities*, respectively, pp. 61–89 and 90–118.

[6]   Especially Brown, 'Revisionist Approach to Religious Change', p. 55: 'secularization theory is logically deficient as a theory of historical change and is insufficiently "bedded down" in the empirical evidence of growth and decline in the social significance of religion in the world's ... industrial nations'. In fairness, it might be added that the most far-reaching of contemporary anti-secularisation theories, viz. the Stark–Bainbridge model, was dismissed in Wallis and Bruce, *Sociological Theory, Religion and Collective Action*, p. 73, for *exactly* the same fault: 'some of the main problems of the Stark–Bainbridge theory came from an excessive distance from their subject matter'. So it seems that no theory, for or against secularisation, is consistent with all, or even most, of the evidence.

[7]   Brown, 'Did Urbanization Secularize Britain?', p. 1; he, in turn, pays homage to Cox, *The English Churches in a Secular Society*, ch. 1, for the original use of the word 'pessimist'. Dr Brown is, by common consent, our first, and leading, 'optimist'. But see also Smith, *Religion in Industrial Society*, 'Introduction' and 'Afterword'.

membership, affiliation and attendance, and point to wider changes in society – industrialisation, urbanisation and rationalisation – as the critical background for their explanation: in short, for the continuity of decline and the causality of exogenous forces.[8] In this scheme of thinking the mentality of the 1920s represents nothing more (nor less) than the belated recognition of reality by ecclesiastical authority. The optimists, on the other hand, emphasise the strength of the nineteenth-century response and point to the health of later Victorian religious institutions: put another way, to the discontinuity of decline and the causality of endogenous factors.[9]

Both of these general views have real merits. They also have real difficulties associated with them. Many of these have been recounted above.[10] They may be reduced to a simple proposition: neither argument refutes the other. Pessimists, so drawn to general theories for a general phenomenon, fail to account for the remarkable buoyancy of religious organisation and experience during the very period, the second half of the nineteenth century, when the presumed factors of their demise were actually at their strongest.[11] On the other hand, optimists have vigor-ously demonstrated the extraordinary success of ecclesiastical response to social change during the era of its most rapid impact, only limply to explain why it endured such miserable fortunes at a time when the industrial and urban bases of modern British life were, if anything, rather more stable.[12] It is as if exogenous forces proved least effective in

---

[8]   Currie et al., Churches and Churchgoers, pp. 96ff.; Gilbert, Religion and Society, ch. 2; Yeo, Religion and Voluntary Organisations in Crisis, pp. 2–4, maps out the argument in formal, if complex, terms.

[9]   Brown, 'A Revisionist Approach to Religious Change', see esp. pp. 49–56; Cox, The English Churches in a Secular Society, ch. 8; also K.D.M. Snell, Church and Chapel in the North Midlands: Religious Observance in the Nineteenth Century (Leicester, 1991), pp. 25ff.; and, for the earlier period, Smith, Religion in Industrial Society, passim.

[10]   'Introduction', above, pp. 5–16; see also the thoughtful and wide-ranging 'Introduction' to Hugh McLeod (ed.), European Religion in the Age of the Great Cities, pp. 1–39.

[11]   Some of the necessary interpretative contortions which result can be found in, inter alia, Gilbert, Religion and Society, pp. 113ff.; also A.D. Gilbert, The Making of Post-Christian Britain (London, 1980), pp. 74 and 78–9; or Harold Perkin, The Origins of Modern English Society, 1780–1880 (London, 1969), p. 196; they are excoriated in Brown, 'Did Urbanization Secularize Britain?', pp. 3–5. One seemingly coherent account is found in Wickham, Church and People, ch. 4. But just how untypical the case of Sheffield was, and how illegitimate were Wickham's conclusions from it, is brought home by Gill, 'Secularization and Census Data', pp. 100–1.

[12]   See, e.g., Brown, 'Did Urbanization Secularize Britain?', p. 12; also Brown, 'The Mechanism of Religious Growth in Urban Societies', pp. 254–7; for something like bafflement, note the observations in Nigel Yates, Robert Hume and Paul Hastings, Religion and Society in Kent, 1640–1914 (Woodbridge, 1994), pp. 89–90; and, for the beginnings of a post-revisionist critique in this matter, note the particularly interesting remarks of McLeod, in his 'Introduction' to European Religion in the Age of the Great Cities, esp. pp. 23–31.

the age of their greatest demands, yet endogenous factors were unworthy of the challenge during the years of their freest manoeuvre.

To be sure, the hopes of 1870 were probably less than fully justified. By the same token, so were the fears of 1920. True, much of the expansion of the nineteenth-century churches may be put down, at least in retrospect, to the growth of the contemporary population. Similarly, the real decline – the demographically discounted decline – of their early twentieth-century counterparts was something less than dramatic. But neither the cheer of 1870 nor the melancholy of 1920 should be gainsaid. Instead, they should be understood. And the beginnings of such an understanding may be found less in denying them, less even in taking them for the unambiguous opposites which their respective proponents, optimists and pessimists in the debate over modern British religious history, take them to be but rather in appreciating the altogether more subtle, more ambivalent, and ultimately more persuasive *link* between the two seemingly mutually exclusive sensibilities.

To be blunt: they are not only true; they are also *related*. This is so not only in the obvious fact that most of the great ecclesiastical goals of 1870 had not been entirely fulfilled by 1920. It is the case in the rather more significant sense that many of these projects had, in fact, largely succeeded; but that, in their success, they had so changed the very nature of the institutions which they sought to sustain as to render them peculiarly vulnerable, and subject to unprecedented failure, just a generation later. The impetus to growth, in other words, succeeded all too well. But it was bought at the price of real change, essentially unintended or at least unplanned change, in the characteristic purposes of organised religious life. Not that such change was necessarily or wholly bad. A strong case can be made out to suggest that much of it was largely to the good. But it was real change all the same, especially in and through the mechanism of the associational ideal, which particularly emphasised the weaknesses – and which thus prepared the decline – of religious organisations – in the years immediately following the end of the First World War.

In this sense, there is no contradiction in arguing for the impetus to growth as being part of the pattern of decline: they were mirror-images of each other. And this was especially true during the critical years of *change*, running from about 1870 to 1920. To understand that is to appreciate that the great hopes of those years were always tinged with real fears. At their worst, those fears were reducible to a single proposition: that the churches must grow or die. Population increase, the emergence of class society, and the spatial evolution of the urban order simply demanded more churches, more wide-ranging institutions and more comprehensive social concern. The churches chose to live. The price of living was institutional change. The mechanism was the associational ideal, in all its ramifications. Because an attachment to that ideal, and a willingness to live with the ramifications of its wider deployment were common across denominations, it makes sense to speak of a change in the general nature of organised religion, even in the quintessence of religious experience, in the industrial towns of later Victorian Britain, or at least of later Victorian West Yorkshire, more generally.

Under this scheme of things, organised religion changed in three ways: it became more responsive; it became more inclusive; and finally, it became more complex. Characteristic religious experience changed too: it became more ordered; also more devotional; and lastly more learned. To be sure, these were new emphases, not novel departures. It was not that organised religion had never been responsive to popular concerns, to wider social developments, and to the more general cultural climate before. Of course it had. It was that it became more positively, explicitly and, above all, more self-consciously so at this time; as never before and, arguably, as never since. The same followed and follows, *mutatis mutandis* for the characteristic changes of contemporary organisation and experience. The point is that these were indeed new emphases; that they were understood as such; and that they had profound consequences.

Responsive here means the enhanced responsiveness of contemporary religious institutions to prevailing social change. As such, it is contrasted with what is understood as the historical norm of Christian mission, or the notion of a reaction against social reality which it implied. To an unprecedented degree, anyway, the mainstream churches of nineteenth-century industrial Britain worked with the grain of social change. They became, in that sense, modern industrial churches. They followed its movements; they went literally where industrial society went. They used its materials, incorporating the latest technology, even the latest fashion, in their designs. They even imitated its wisdom, becoming more businesslike, and certainly more efficient, producers and distributors of religious goods.

This was because they wished to become more inclusive societies. Inclusive here is taken to mean the increasingly exhaustive effort made by the churches to include all of the people in their available associations. Again, it is not presumed that pre-industrial churches entertained no such idea.[13] But it is suggested that the religious

---

[13]   At the same time, it is important not to exaggerate the extent to which they fulfilled it; on this under-researched question, see the remarks of McLeod, *Religion and the People*

organisations of nineteenth-century Britain virtually predicated themselves on their special responsibility, and enhanced capacity, to do just this. That is, in the spirit of the times, they took the spiritual and moral socialisation of the people to be their especial, organisational task.[14] And, to an increasing degree, they judged their success or failure as organisations by their proven ability – or inability – to achieve that end. Becoming self-consciously inclusive churches, they went to inordinate lengths to find out precisely who in the community was not largely or regularly of their number. Then they undertook sustained and sacrificial efforts to make them so.

The result of all these commitments was to make later Victorian religious organisations altogether more complex institutions than they had ever been before. Complexity here is understood to reflect both the formal dimensions, and the cultural pretensions, of sacred societies. Formal complexity was marked out, figuratively speaking, in the plethora of auxiliaries which religious organisations acquired at this time. Cultural complexity was the result of their many purposes and various, by no means always intended, possibilities. That the two forms of complexity were linked is obvious enough. The precise nature of the connexion is less clear. Suffice to say here that, whilst it was something less than functional, it was something more than frequent.

This complexity in turn had a profound effect upon the characteristic forms of common religious life in later Victorian and Edwardian West Yorkshire. Such characteristic forms, and the common life, are defined here in terms of typical practice and normal experience. It should go without saying that neither such practice nor experience was exhaustively described in contemporary religious organisations. And if that is true within denominations, it is especially so between conflicting and competing Christian orders. Nevertheless, they depict a reality which later nineteenth- and early twentieth-century churchmen and ministers understood. They include most of what went on in these churches and chapels; more still of what it was believed should, properly, be going on. As such, although they relate necessarily to (generally divergent) doctrine and liturgy, they were, above all, concerned with (an increasingly uniform) manner and tone of, organised religious life.

of *Western Europe*, pp. 54–67; and McLeod, 'The De-Christianization of the Working-Class in Western Europe, 1850–1900', *Social Compass* (2/3), 1980, 191–204, esp. pp. 197–8. On the curious case of nineteenth-century rural Ireland, see Emmet Larkin, 'The Devotional Revolution in Ireland, 1850–1875', *American Historical Review*, 77 (1972), 636ff., and, for an earlier period still, note the remarks of Keith Thomas, *Religion and the Decline of Magic: Studies in Popular Beliefs in Sixteenth- and Seventeenth-Century England* (Harmondsworth, 1973), pp. 178–93.

[14] See above, ch. 5, pp. 213–32.

That became increasingly more ordered. This was true in the sense that it became a more carefully controlled, even a less exciting and a more procedural, form of religion. It is also true in that it became a more rationally planned, that is, a less spontaneous, but a more continuous expression of Christian witness. In the first instance, that meant above all a qualitative shift away from an experiential and towards a devotional understanding of common Christian practice. The latter implied the demise of so many impromptu expressions and the rise of a so much more developmental interpretation of what that common Christianity truly was.

These were profound changes, institutionally wrought and institutionally represented, both in religious organisations and of religious experience. They also had profound effects. They made religion part of a more general civilising process; perhaps too, part of an insidious modernising commitment in the emerging industrial towns of West Yorkshire. They also did a lot of good in, and for, local religious institutions. They made them socially comprehensive, more culturally respectable and more morally influential. But they were enacted at a considerable cost – by those institutions and for the fortunes of modern religion. These may be summarised as: the burden of institutional proliferation; the paradox of institutional formalisation; and the significance of institutional decline.

At one level, institutional proliferation was no more than a banal physical commonplace. That is, it was the simple fact of more churches, chapels, mission halls, Sunday schools, and even of more reading rooms and gymnasia; often built at a rate faster than the growth of population, and seemingly always built faster than the growth of effective demand. However, at another level, institutional proliferation was a profound state of mind: more specifically, it was an idea, or an understanding of the religious life, which reacted first to demographic growth and urban evolution, and then particularly to suburbanisation and social segregation, with an almost compulsive urge towards ecclesiastical comprehensiveness. This represented a desire to go out, literally, to the physical extremities of growing towns, and to go out, metaphorically, to the sociological peripheries of expanding societies. In that sense, institutional proliferation reflected a widespread contemporary assumption that popular, and especially plebeian, loyalties should, and would, naturally follow institutional outreach. To build, in this analysis, was to provide. But it was also to impose a heavy burden on those who bore it: an organisational burden, an economic burden, and a psychological burden. In that way, it demonstrated not only the dedication of the churches to the people, but also their vulnerability in relation to them.

Hence, too, the paradox of institutional formalisation. At one level, nothing more vividly highlighted the sophistication of Edwardian religious organisations, by comparison with their mid-Victorian counterparts, than the extent of their institutional formalisation. Thus, the Edwardian churches marked the urban landscape not only by their physical proliferation or merely by their social extension – the simple fact that there were so *many* churches and chapels spread so far out across the early twentieth-century town – but also by the more subtle significance of their institutional tentacles, reaching into much of urban life, specific institutions serving specific needs and purposes at specific times for specific people. Yet at the same time, nothing so facilitated the growth of instrumental participation by the people in voluntary religious organisations. This form of participation would have been impractical, if not inconceivable, only a generation earlier. The distinction which it implied – between what churchmen, ministers and committed laymen believed they were doing, as they extended the boundaries of their organisations to bring in the people, and how the population actually responded to such organisational development and institutional change – determined much of the dynamics, and described a good deal of the tragedy, of religious organisations in the early years of the twentieth century.

For it was in this growing distinction that the real significance of contemporary decline lay. Certainly, it was through this distinction that churchmen and ministers at the time came to see that the process of decline upon which they were now reluctantly embarked was not simply unprecedented but also permanent. This was because it now showed itself to be the product as much of an internal deficiency within modern religious organisations as of the external pressures which had been brought to bear upon them during the past fifty years and more. This endogenous, institutional fault-line may be called the deficiency of structural similarity. Its origins may be traced to the impetus for growth in the mid-Victorian religious system. Its effects constituted the basis of modern decline. Its legacy remains to this day.

As the churches developed in these towns, first by proliferation, and then through formalisation, so they created, seemingly willingly and usually self-consciously, a panoply of extended ecclesiastical institutions which were indeed more open to public involvement and participation than they had ever been before. But those same ecclesiastical institutions themselves also developed, sometimes by self-conscious decision, more often by unreflective action, into characteristic forms of social organisation altogether more like those of, and thus more vulnerable to, other contemporary secular and voluntary societies. This is why the much-heralded 'threat' of the Labour Party, or of the Sunday Lecture Society, or even of various bicycle clubs, mattered so much in 1920, in a way that they would not have mattered, or at least nothing like as much, in 1870. It was simply that a newly informed public could now make increasingly effective decisions about which organisations to devote its loyalty (and its time and money) to. It was also that, in making these individual decisions, each member of the public increasingly now had less to choose from between his or her affiliation to a religious or a non-irreligious association. And for ecclesiastical institutions still committed to a comprehensive understanding of the associational ideal, this was a fatal development, embodying as it did an all too effective mechanism for decline within an ideal which had, for so long, presumed only an unproblematic dynamic of growth.[15]

Hence the associational ideal *itself* became part of the crisis of post-First World War religious organisations. That, in turn, highlighted the degree to which those institutions now seemed to be subject to forces beyond their control, to the exogenous processes of contemporary social change. This mutually reinforcing bond – of crisis allied to helplessness – all too painfully defined the paradox of early twentieth-century British religion: that is, of a body of faith subject to an enervating sickness seemingly without a diagnosis of disease, and of a system of institutions plunged into decline apparently without even the comforting tradition of a history of prior growth. Yet, at the same time, the searcher after sea-change in popular urban religion at this time will continue to explore curiously unrewarded. There really was no such sea-change, post-Edwardian ecclesiastical concerns aside. Similarly, the seeker for a magic moment of decline during this era will remain uninformed. There was no such single, ascertainable, relevant event. Contemporary religious organisations simply found the job of recruiting and retaining comparable numbers of persons in specifically directed sacred communities more difficult than they once had. Naturally, many different exogenous and endogenous developments contributed, in different degrees, to that problem. So much is well known and generally accepted.[16] What the evidence described above suggests is that, ironically, some of those endogenous factors were themselves a product of the very ambition of contemporary societies to achieve a hitherto unimagined degree of comprehensiveness and accessibility. And, perversely, it also suggests that they wrought much of their insidious

[15] For a not entirely dissimilar argument, but of wider *theoretical* application, see Steve Bruce, *A House Divided: Protestantism, Schism and Secularization* (London, 1990), ch. 9, esp. p. 232.

[16] Cf. the related conclusions in McLeod, 'Secular Cities?', pp. 84–6.

damage in the very act of achieving those ostensibly unobjectionable goals.

This contemporary process of institutional degeneration was important. Certainly, it cannot be dismissed by glib notions of recurrent institutional renewal, for what went into decline, sometime around the end of the First World War, was not just a small group of corrupt, elitist or politicised institutions but the full panoply of committed, popular, sacred societies. That *their* decline has not been paralleled by the growth of a swathe of new, revivalist religious associations since should not therefore surprise us. Rather, it should direct our attention to the real significance of what has happened during the intervening years.[17] Nor can the significance of that decline be diminished by vague suggestions of the social divergence it necessarily obscures. Later Victorian religious organisations drew freely from all classes. Their modern counterparts secure the loyalty of none.[18] Finally, its impact is scarcely undermined by panglossian notions of divine relocation. If the sacred really did relocate itself in twentieth-century British society, it did not do so in a recognisably Christian form.[19]

More: by mid-century at the latest, the British people had not simply ceased to go to church. They had ceased to *respect* the Christian churches: institutions, personnel and dogma.[20] And, as they ceased to respect them, so they ceased also significantly to learn from them. To be sure, they retained their religion. But their religion ceased to be meaningfully Christian.[21] It was not simply that they continued to believe in the Church whilst no longer belonging to it. They came to believe something different, something altogether more mystical, even more pagan.[22] There lies an intriguing possibility. Conventional wisdom and common sense suggest that the people stopped going to church

[17] Stark and Bainbridge, *The Future of Religion*; also see 'Introduction', above, pp. 14–16.
[18] Glock and Stark, *Religion and Society in Tension*; also see 'Introduction', above, pp. 12–14.
[19] Bellah, *Beyond Belief*; also see 'Introduction', above, pp. 10–12.
[20] The Findings of B. Seebohm Rowntree and G.R. Lavers, *English Life and Leisure: A Social Study* (London, 1951), see esp. pp. 345–53: 'In the lives of a large majority of the people ... the Church is no longer relevant'; or, 'we have found so widespread a dislike of ministers of religion ... that it can only be described as anti-clericalism'; and finally, 'a fundamental belief in the resurrection of the body ... is partly or wholly rejected by a large proportion of people today'.
[21] *Ibid.*, pp. 312–14; corroborated and extended in Geoffrey Gorer, *Exploring English Character* (London, 1955), see esp. pp. 252–69. Gorer estimated that only 6 per cent of the population at that time believed in 'the full Christian dogma' (p. 255); conversely, about one-quarter of the same sample subscribed to a completely 'magical' view of the world (p. 269).
[22] For a number of observations on this theme, see Davie, *Believing without Belonging*, ch. 6; note especially the 'typology' of contemporary beliefs, and their geographical and social variations, on p. 105.

because they no longer believed what the churches taught them. Perhaps the causal mechanism was really closer to the opposite: they stopped believing because they stopped going. If so, the decline of the churches in early twentieth-century Britain turns out to have been very significant, after all.[23]

[23]   Cf. Cox, *The English Churches in a Secular Society*, ch. 9.

Bibliography

PRIMARY SOURCES

MANUSCRIPT SOURCES

Public Record Office
Census of England and Wales, 1871; unpublished enumerator manuscripts for the township of Halifax; township and Local Board District of Keighley; and Local Board District of Denholme

Calderdale District Archive
Financial accounts, minute books and miscellaneous papers of:
Rhodes Street Circuit Wesleyan Methodist Connexion, Halifax
St John's (South) Wesleyan Methodist Circuit, Halifax
Salem Methodist New Connexion Circuit, Halifax
Ebenezer First Primitive Methodist Circuit, Halifax
Second Primitive Methodist Circuit, Halifax
United Methodist Church, Brunswick Circuit, Halifax
United Methodist Church, Hanover Circuit, Halifax
United Methodist Church, North Circuit, Halifax
United Methodist Church, West Circuit, Halifax
Broad Street Wesleyan Methodist Chapel, Halifax
Caddy Field Wesleyan Methodist Chapel, Southowram
Illingworth Wesleyan Methodist Chapel, Ovenden
King Cross Wesleyan Methodist Chapel, Halifax
Miall Street,Wesleyan Methodist Mission, Halifax
Northowram Wesleyan Methodist Chapel, Northowram
Pellon Lane Wesleyan Methodist Chapel, Halifax
Providence Wesleyan Methodist Chapel, Halifax
Rhodes Street Wesleyan Methodist Chapel, Halifax
St John's Wesleyan Methodist Chapel, Halifax
Siddal Wesleyan Methodist Chapel, Skircoat
Skircoat Green Wesleyan Methodist Chapel, Halifax
South Parade Wesleyan Methodist Chapel, Halifax
Ambler Thorn Methodist New Connexion Chapel, Halifax
Hanover Street Methodist New Connexion Chapel, Halifax
King Cross Methodist New Connexion Chapel, Halifax
Queen's Road Methodist New Connexion Chapel, Halifax
Denholme Clough Primitive Methodist Chapel, Denholme

Queen's Road Primitive Methodist Chapel, Halifax
St Thomas's Primitive Methodist Chapel, Claremount
Brunswick United Methodist Free Church, Halifax
King Cross United Methodist Free Church, Halifax
Lower Skircoat Green United Methodist Free Church, Halifax
Salterhebble United Methodist Free Church, Salterhebble
Harrison Road Congregational Chapel, Halifax
Highroad Well Congregational Chapel, Halifax
Providence Congregational Chapel, Halifax
Sion Congregational Chapel, Halifax
Northgate End Unitarian Chapel, Halifax
Rhodes Street Wesleyan Methodist Sunday School, Halifax
Stafford Square Wesleyan Methodist Sunday School, Halifax
Ambler Thorn Methodist New Connexion Sunday School, Halifax
Hanover Street Methodist New Connexion Sunday School, Halifax
King Cross Methodist New Connexion Sunday School, Halifax
Queen's Road Methodist New Connexion Sunday School, Halifax
Harrison Road Congregational Sunday School, Halifax
Northgate End Unitarian Sunday School, Halifax

Keighley Public Library
Financial accounts, minute books and miscellaneous papers of:
Keighley Wesleyan Methodist Circuit, Keighley
Keighley Primitive Methodist Connexion (First Circuit), Keighley
Keighley Primitive Methodist Connexion (Second Circuit), Keighley
Cavendish Street Wesleyan Methodist Chapel, Keighley
Devonshire Park Wesleyan Methodist Chapel, Keighley
Exley Head Wesleyan Methodist Chapel, Keighley
Fell Lane Wesleyan Methodist Chapel, Keighley
Hainworth Wesleyan Methodist Chapel, Keighley
Heber Street Wesleyan Methodist Chapel, Keighley
Hermit Hole Wesleyan Methodist Chapel, Keighley
Laycock Wesleyan Methodist Chapel, Keighley
Long Lee Wesleyan Methodist Chapel, Keighley
Lund Park Wesleyan Methodist Chapel, Keighley
Sun Street Wesleyan Methodist Church, Keighley
Temple Street Wesleyan Methodist Church, Keighley
Victoria Park Wesleyan Methodist Church, Keighley
Alice Street Primitive Methodist Chapel, Keighley
Oakworth Road, Primitive Methodist Chapel, Keighley
Park Lane, Primitive Methodist Chapel, Keighley
South Street Primitive Methodist Chapel, Keighley
Devonshire Street, Congregational Church, Keighley
Ingrow Congregational Mission, Keighley
Upper Green, Congregational Chapel, Keighley
Utley, Congregational Chapel, Keighley
Albert Street, Baptist Chapel, Keighley
Cavendish Street Wesleyan Methodist Sunday School, Keighley

Devonshire Park Wesleyan Methodist Sunday School, Keighley papers
Fell Lane Wesleyan Methodist Sunday School, Keighley
Hainworth Wesleyan Methodist Sunday School, Keighley
Heber Street Wesleyan Methodist Sunday School, Keighley
Hermit Hole Wesleyan Methodist Sunday School, Keighley
Long Lee Wesleyan Methodist Sunday School, Keighley
Lund Park Wesleyan Methodist Sunday School, Keighley
Temple Street Wesleyan Methodist Sunday School, Keighley
Victoria Park Wesleyan Methodist Sunday School, Keighley
Park Lane Primitive Methodist Sunday School, Keighley
Devonshire Street, Congregational Sunday School, Keighley
Utley, Congregational Sunday School, Keighley
Albert Street Baptist Sunday School, Keighley

West Yorkshire Archive Service, Wakefield
Financial accounts, minute books and miscellaneous papers of:
All Souls' Church of England, Haley Hill, Halifax
Christ Church Church of England, Mount Pellon, Halifax
Holy Trinity Church of England, Halifax
St John the Baptist Church of England, Halifax
St Paul's Church of England, King Cross, Halifax
St Thomas's Church of England, Charlestown, Halifax

West Yorkshire Archive Service, Bradford
Financial accounts, minute books and miscellaneous papers of:
 St Andrew's Church of England, Keighley
Holy Trinity Church of England, Lawkholme, Keighley
St Peter's Church of England, Keighley

West Yorkshire Archive Service, Leeds
Financial accounts, minute books and miscellaneous papers of:
Halifax and District Association of Congregational Churches
Yorkshire Congregational Union

Roman Catholic Diocesan Curia, Leeds
Financial accounts, minute books and miscellaneous papers of:
Roman Catholic Church of St Mary, Gibbet Street, Halifax

St Paul's Vicarage, Denholme
Financial accounts, minute books and miscellaneous papers of:
St Paul's Church of England, Denholme

Private collection of Mr A. Vine
Financial accounts, minute books and miscellaneous papers of:
Southgate Baptist Chapel, Denholme

PRINTED SOURCES

Official publications

Census of England and Wales, 1871: Population Tables Area, Houses and Inhabitants, vol. II, *Registration of Union Counties* (London, HMSO, 1872).

Census of England and Wales, 1871: Population Abstracts; Ages, Civil Condition, Occupations and Birth-Places of the People, vol. III (London, HMSO, 1872).

Census of England and Wales, 1921: Yorkshire (London, HMSO, 1923).

PP, 1889, LXX, *Return of the Rates of Wages in the Principal Textile Trades of the United Kingdom, with Report Thereon.*

PP, 1893–4, LXXXIII, pt 2, *Report on the Wages of the Manual Labour Classes in the United Kingdom with Table of the Average Rates of Wages and Hours of Labour and Persons Employed in Several of the Principal Trades in 1886 and 1891.*

PP, 1909, LXXX, *Report of an Inquiry by the Board of Trade into the Earnings and Hours of Labour of Work-People of the United Kingdom, I. Textile Trades in 1906.*

Newspapers and periodicals

All Souls', Haley Hill, Parish Magazine
Halifax Courier
Halifax Parish Church Magazine
Halifax Guardian
Halifax Parish Church Magazine
Keighley Chronicle
Keighley and District Congregational Magazine
Keighley News
Keighley Parish Church Magazine
Keighley Wesleyan Methodist Circuit Magazine
St Paul's Church, King Cross, Halifax, Parish Magazine

Printed primary works

Church and chapel histories

Anon., *Centenary Handbook and Brief History of Exley Head Methodist Church, Keighley, 1854–1954* (Keighley, 1954).

Church of St Hilda, Halifax: Jubilee, 1911–1936 (Halifax, 1936).

Church of St John the Evangelist, Warley: Centenary (Todmorden, 1978).

The Church of St Paul in Denholme Gate, 1846–1946 (Denholme, 1946).

Church Records from Lincoln Academy to Fairfield Methodist Church, 1872–1934 (Halifax, 1934).

Denholme Clough, Primitive Methodist Chapel: Centenary Celebrations, 1834–1934 (Denholme, 1934).

Denholme Independent Chapel: Jubilee Celebrations (Denholme, 1894).

Early Reminiscences of St George's Church, Ovenden, Halifax (Halifax, 1923).

Ebenezer Primitive Methodist Church, Halifax: Centenary, Souvenir Handbook, 1822–1922 (Halifax, 1922).

Fairfield Methodist Church, Queen's Road, Halifax: Jubilee Celebrations, 1891–1941, Souvenir Handbook (Halifax, 1941).

Historical Record of the Fell Lane Wesleyan Sunday School and Chapel (Keighley, n.d.).

Historical Record of the Park Congregational Church Down to the Close of the Year 1869 (Halifax, 1869).

Historical Sketch of Mount Tabor Wesleyan Methodist Church, Halifax, 1820–1920 (Halifax, 1920).

Independent Chapel, Denholme: Centenary Celebrations, 1844–1944 (Denholme, 1944).

Ingrow Congregational Mission, Souvenir (Keighley, 1911).

Let the Trumpet Sound: Jubilee Handbook of Lund Park Methodist Church Keighley, 1895–1945 (Keighley, 1945).

Northgate End Unitarian Chapel, Halifax: Bicentenary, 1896 (Halifax, 1896).

Oakworth Road Methodist Mission Hall, Keighley Circuit: Jubilee Souvenir Handbook, 1893–1943 (Keighley, 1943).

The Restoration of Halifax Parish Church (Halifax, 1877).

Rhodes Street Wesleyan Church, Halifax: Jubilee Celebrations, 1867–1917 (Halifax, 1917).

St Andrew's Methodist Church, Queen's Road, Halifax: Diamond Jubilee Souvenir, 1877–1937 (Halifax, 1937).

St Jude's Church, Halifax, 1890–1940: Jubilee Souvenir (Halifax, 1940).

St Paul's Church, Denholme Gate: An Account of the Consecration, Jubilee and Diamond Jubilee of This Church (Denholme, 1906).

The Salvation Army: Keighley Corps, Jubilee Souvenir Handbook (Keighley, 1931).

Wesleyan Chapel, Hermit Hole: A Short History of the Society from its Beginning (Keighley, 1917).

Baker, Rev. Frank, *Sidelights on Sixty Years: Being Contributions to the History of West Lane Primitive Methodist Church, Keighley* (Keighley, 1940).

Barnes, W.R., *The Story of Halifax Parish Church* (Halifax, 1985).

Berry, P., *Keighley Catholic Church: One Hundred and Fifty Years: Anniversary Celebrations, 1835–1985* (Keighley, 1985).

Brearley, John, *History of Pye Nest Primitive Methodist Church, Halifax, 1902–1932* (Halifax, 1932).

Bright, Hugh, *St Paul's, King Cross, 1847–1913: Being Some Account of the Formation of the Parish and the Building of the Old and New Churches* (Halifax, 1913).

Carr, H.J. and Arthur Wilson, *Jubilee and Memorial: Lee Mount Baptist; A History of the Church and Sunday School, 1872–1922* (Halifax, 1922).

Chapman, E.V., *King Cross Methodist Church and School, 1808–1958: A Historical Survey Compiled on Behalf of the Re-Union Committee* (Halifax, 1958).

Clegg, Lillie, *A Short History of Hanover Church, Halifax* (Halifax, 1915).

Coulson, John, J.H. Farrington, and H. Feather, *Centenary of the Methodist Cause at Wesley Place, Keighley, 1840–1940* (Keighley, 1946).

Cox, J. Thornton, *A Brief History of the Church and Parish of Holy Trinity, Lawkholme, Keighley* (Keighley, 1932).

Eccles, Clarissa, Robert Eccles and A. Elliott Peaston, *The History of Northgate End Chapel, 1696–1946* (Halifax, 1946).

Feather, W., *Sidelights on Sixty Years: Being Contributions to the History of West Lane Primitive Methodist Church, Keighley* (Keighley, 1940).

Franks, Rev. J.W., *On the Edge of the Moor: The Story of the Congregational Cause at Highroad Well, Halifax* (Halifax, 1965).

Goodwin, A., 'How the Ancient Parish of Halifax was Divided', *Transactions of the Halifax Antiquarian Society*, 61 (1961), 23–36.

Handley, Thomas, *Church of St Peter, Keighley: Jubilee Handbook, 1882–1932* (Keighley, 1932).

Hood, Rev. Canon J.C.F., *The Story of Keighley Parish Church* (Keighley, n.d.).

Jones, David, *Centenary Memorial of the Church and Congregational Assembling for Christian Worship at Booth Chapel, Halifax* (Halifax, 1861).

Keighley, J.H., *Wesley Church, Broad Street, Halifax: Centenary, 1829–1929* (Halifax, 1929).

Keyworth, Thomas, *Old Harrison Road: A Study in Origins* (Halifax, 1894).

Lewis, D. Rhys, *Those Fifty Years, 1863–1913: West Vale Baptist Church, Jubilee Celebrations* (Elland, 1915).

Mackay, Archibald, *All Saints Parish, Salterhebble, Halifax, 1846–1946* (Halifax, 1946).

McKenzie, Rev. John G., *History of Holywell Green Congregational Church, 1867–1917* (Stainland, 1917).

Metcalf, Thomas, *The Centenary of Wesley Chapel, Temple Street: Methodism in Keighley, 1742–1846* (Keighley, 1946).

Michael, Rev. T., *Pellon Lane Baptist Church, Halifax: A Historical Account* (Halifax, 1890).

Millson, Rev. F.E., *Two Hundred Years of Northgate End Chapel: A Sketch* (Halifax, 1896).

Moore, Horace, 'The Story of Illingworth Moor Methodist Church', *Transactions of the Halifax Antiquarian Society*, 69 (1969), 29–54.

Petty, G.H., *A Short History of King Cross, Compiled on the Occasion of the Centenary of the Parish* (Halifax, 1947).

Robinson, F., *History of the Congregational School and Church at Highroad Well, Halifax, 1829–1915* (Halifax, 1915).

Secker, William Henry, *Illingworth Church: A Brief Account of the Illingworth Church and the Particulars of its Restoration and Reopening* (Halifax, 1873).

Smith, David, *'What Has God Wrought?': Being An Account of What God Has Done for the Strict Baptists at Siddal during the Last Thirty Years, together with the First Sermon Preached in the New Chapel* (London, 1887).

Sugden, John, *A Brief History of Knowle Park, Congregational Church, 1893–1919: With Notes on the Development of Congregationalism in Keighley* (Keighley, 1950).

Taylor, D., 'Annals of the Parish of Halifax', *Transactions of the Halifax Antiquarian Society*, 72 (1972), 107–30.

Teasdale, Christopher, *Historical Sketch of Booth Congregational Chapel, Halifax* (Halifax, 1919).

Thorpe, A.J., *A Brief History of Pellon Wesleyan Chapel and Sunday School* (Halifax, 1905).

Tiffany, Thomas, *Jubilee History of Trinity Road Baptist Church, Halifax* (Halifax, 1901).

Trigg, Charles A., *Providence Congregational Church, Ovenden: A Short History, 1837–1907* (Halifax, 1907).

Trigg, W.B., *A History of Providence Congregational Church, Halifax* (Halifax, 1937).

Wadsworth, George Priestly, *Square Sunday School: A Short History* (Halifax, 1903).

Denominational histories

Anon., *Origins of Baptist Churches in the Halifax and Calder Valley District* (Halifax, n.d.).

Biggs, (?), 'Congregationalism: Its Growth and Development in Halifax' (unpublished typescript, n.d.).

Chapman, Eve, *The Halifax Methodist Circuit, 1785–1985* (Halifax, 1985).

Miall, James G., *Congregationalism in Yorkshire* (London, 1868).

Mulroy, J.J., *Upon This Rock: The Story of the Church in Halifax* (Halifax, 1952).

Naylor, Rev. John, *Some Factors in the Making of the Soul in Halifax Parish* (Halifax, 1911).

Reid Marchbank, W., *One Hundred Years of Progress: An Account of the Expansion of Congregationalism in Keighley* (Keighley, 1956).

Rhodes, Joseph, *A Centenary of Keighley Baptist History, 1810–1910* (Keighley, 1910).

Sunderland, Edward, 'A Brief History of Methodism in Keighley From the Year 1742' (unpub. MS, n.d.).

Walker, Frank and John F. Goodchild, *Unitarianism in Yorkshire: A Short History* (n.p., n.d.).

Wilson, Rev. W.B. and Rev. W.S. Davies, *A History of the Halifax and Calder District Baptist Churches* (Halifax, 1968).

Church and chapel manuals and rule-books

Albert Street Baptist Church, Keighley, Yearbooks, 1894–1920 (Keighley, 1894–1920).

Anon., *A Class Book; Containing Directions for Class-Leaders, Ruled Forms for Leaders' Weekly Accounts and the Rules of the Methodist Societies* (London, n.d.).

Principles on Which the Wesleyan Methodist Sunday Schools Should Be Conducted (London, n.d.).

Rules of the Society of People Called Methodists (London, n.d.).

Rules for the Wesleyan Methodist Sunday School, Heber Street, Keighley (Keighley, 1880).

Rules for the Wesleyan Methodist Sunday School, Lund Park, Keighley (Keighley, 1895).

Rules for the Wesleyan Methodist Sunday School, Temple Street, Keighley (Keighley, 1865).

Dale, R.W., *The Duties of Church Members* (London, n.d.).

Furner, Arthur, *The Place of the Church Meeting in the Life and Work of our Churches* (London, 1900).

Harrison Road Congregational Church Halifax, Yearbooks, 1895–1914 (Halifax, 1895–1914).

Keighley (later Devonshire Street), Congregational Church, Manuals, 1873–1926 (Keighley, 1873–1926).

King Cross, St Paul's, Church of England, Halifax, Handbook, 1917 (Halifax, 1917).

Northgate End Unitarian Chapel, Halifax, Annual Reports, 1911–1925 (Halifax, 1911–25).

Northgate End Unitarian Chapel, Halifax, Calendar, 1868–1906 (Halifax, 1868–1906).

Northgate End Unitarian Chapel, Halifax, Chapel Manuals, 1890–1930 (Halifax, 1890–1930).

Park Congregational Church, Halifax, Manual, 1892 (Halifax, 1892).

Park Congregational Church, Halifax, Manual, 1915 (Halifax, 1915).

Providence Congregational Chapel, Ovenden, Manual, 1880 (Ovendon, 1880).

Workman, Rev. Edward, *Duties of Wesleyan Stewards, With Other Information concerning Their Office* (London, 1892).

Wrigley, Rev. Francis, *Church Membership: Its Basis, Its Claims, Its Obligations* (London, n.d.).

Yearbook for the Use of the Church and Congregation Worshipping in Hanover Street Methodist New Connexion Chapel, Halifax, 1870–1874 (Halifax, 1870–74).

Sermons, addresses and charges

Bailey, Rev. J.R., *Progressive Congregationalism: An Address Delivered at the Annual Meeting of the Yorkshire Congregational Union and Home Missionary Society, Held at Keighley, 5th April 1892* (Halifax, 1892).

Brooke, Rev. Joshua Ingham, *A Charge Delivered by the Ven. Joshua Ingham Brooke (Archdeacon of Halifax), Read in the Parish Church of Halifax, on 1st May 1895* (Halifax, 1895).

A Charge Delivered on Wednesday 22nd April 1896, by the Venerable Archdeacon of Halifax (Halifax, 1896).

A Charge Delivered at Halifax by the Archdeacon of Halifax, May 1902 (Halifax, 1902).

A Charge Delivered at Halifax by the Archdeacon of Halifax, 6th May 1903 (Halifax, 1903).

Millson, Rev. F.E., *Address to the Annual Church Meeting, 26th January 1893* (Halifax, 1893).

Address to the Annual Church Meeting, 29th January 1894 (Halifax, 1894).

Are We Christians? A Sermon Preached in the Northgate End Chapel, Halifax, 11th October 1885 (Halifax, 1885).

Tenderness and Trust: A Christmas Day Sermon Preached in Northgate End Chapel by Rev. F.E. Millson, on 25th December 1881 (Halifax, 1881).

Pigou, Rev. Francis, *Addresses to District Visitors and Sunday School Teachers* (Halifax, 1880).

Discouragements and Encouragements in Connection with the Christian Ministry (Halifax, 1883).

Intemperance: What Is the Duty of the Christian in relation to It? A Sermon Preached in the Parish Church, Halifax, in connection with the Halifax Union Temperance Mission, on Sunday, 16th November 1879 (Halifax, 1879).

The Kiss of Charity: A Sermon Preached at the Parish Church, Halifax, on Sunday, 24th July 1887.

A Palace Not for Man but for God: A Sermon Preached in the Parish Church,

Halifax on Sunday 12th December 1879, on the Occasion of Its Reopening after Restoration (Halifax, 1879).

A Pastoral Letter To His Parishioners, 1st January 1877 (Halifax, 1877).

The Powers That Be: A Sermon Preached in the Parish Church, Halifax, on the Occasion of the 49th Anniversary of Her Majesty's Accession, 20th June 1886 (Halifax, 1886).

A Sermon to Friendly and Trades Societies, 20th May 1877 (Halifax, 1877).

Sermons and Addresses (Halifax, n.d.).

Two Sermons Preached in the Parish Church, Halifax, at the Closing Services, 18th May 1878 (Halifax, 1878).

Unity: An Address Delivered to the Clergy of the Deanery of Halifax, on 20th March 1876 (Halifax, 1876).

Local and other histories; miscellaneous works

Akroyd, E., *The Yorkshire Penny Bank* (Leeds, 1872).

Almond, A., *Biography of James Ickringhall, Esq., Balcony House, Keighley and Sunset House, Heysham, Morecombe* (Keighley, 1919).

Anon., *History of the Firm of James Akroyd and Sons* (Leeds, 1874).

Industrial Advantages of Denholme (London, n.d.).

Baines, Edward, *Edward Baines' Directory for 1823* (Keighley, 1823).

Bancroft, Harry, Asa Briggs and Eric Treacy, *One Hundred Years: The Parish of Keighley, 1848–1948* (Keighley, 1948).

Brendan, J.M., 'Evolution of the Machine-Tool Trade' in J.J. Mulroy (ed.), *Story of the Town That Bred Us* (Halifax, 1948).

'John Mackintosh', in Mulroy (ed.), *Story of the Town That Bred Us*.

Bretton, R., 'Crossleys of Dean Clough', *Transactions of the Halifax Antiquarian Society*, 47 (1950), 1–9; 48 (1950), 71–83; 49 (1952), 49–58; 50 (1953), 1–20; 87–102; 51 (1954), 11–28.

'Colonel Edward Akroyd', *Transactions of the Halifax Antiquarian Society*, 45 (1948), 61–100.

Brogan, Hugh, *The English People* (London, 1943).

Builder, vols. 15–21 (London, 1857–63).

Cole, G.D.H. and W. Mellor, 'Sectionalism and Craft Prejudice: Yorkshire's Need for Greater Unionism', *Daily Herald*, 14 April 1914.

Craven, A., *Commercial and General Directory of Keighley, Bingley, Skipton and Surrounding Districts, 1884* (Keighley, 1884).

Crutchley, George W. *John Mackintosh: A Biography* (London, 1921).

Davis, W.A., 'Local Educational History' in J.J. Mulroy (ed.), *Story of the Town That Bred Us* (Halifax, 1948).

Dewhirst, Ian, *A History of Keighley* (Keighley, 1974).

Fletcher, J.S., *The Story of English Towns: Halifax* (London, 1923).

Fortunes Made in Business, vol. III (London, 1887).

Hanson, T.W., *In Search of Halifax, No. 1, Halifax Street Lore* (Halifax, 1932).

In Search of Old Halifax, 2nd rev. edn. (Halifax, 1968).

Harwood, H.W., *Centenary Story, 1848–1948* (Halifax, 1948).

'The Making of Our Municipality' in J.J. Mulroy (ed.), *Story of the Town That Bred Us* (Halifax, 1948).

Hodgson, John, *Textile Manufacture and Other Industries in Keighley* (Keighley, 1879).

Industries of Yorkshire, 2 vols. (London, 1890).

Keighley, William, *Keighley, Past and Present, or an Historical, Topographical and Statistical Sketch of the Town, Parish and Environs of Keighley* (Keighley, 1879).

Keighley Yearbook, 1877–1917 (Keighley, 1877–1917).

Mulroy, J.J. (ed.), *Story of the Town That Bred Us* (Halifax, 1948).

Parker, James, 'Looking Back a Century' in J.J. Mulroy (ed.), *Story of the Town That Bred Us* (Halifax, 1948).

Pigou, Francis, *Phases in My Life* (London, 1898).

Odds and Ends (London, 1903).

Robinson, E., *Commercial and General Directory of Halifax, 1906* (Halifax, 1906).

Roth, H. King, *The Genesis of Banking in Halifax* (Halifax, 1914).

Scott, G.G., *Personal and Professional Recollections* (London, 1879).

Snowdon, Keighley, *The Master Spinner: A Life of Sir Swire Smith, LL.D., M.P.* (London, 1921).

Spence Hardy, R., *Memorials of Joseph Sugden* (London, 1858).

Waddington, J.H., *Essays and Addresses* (Halifax, 1938). (This volume contains the essays, 'Changes, 1866–1937'; 'More Changes, 1838–1938'; and 'Shops and Shopkeepers'.)

Winnington–Ingram, A.F., *Work in Great Cities* (London, 1896).

SECONDARY SOURCES

PUBLISHED WORKS

Absalom, F., 'The Anglo-Catholic Priest: Aspects of Role Conflict', *A Sociological Yearbook of Religion*, 4 (1971), 46–61.

Acquaviva, S.S., *The Decline of the Sacred in Industrial Society*, trans. by Patricia Lipscomb (Oxford, 1979).

'Some Reflections on the Parallel Decline of Religious Experience and Religious Practice', in Barker, Beckford and Dobbelaere (eds.), *Secularization, Rationalism and Sectarianism* (1993).

Anderson, Olive, 'Gladstone's Abolition of Compulsory Church Rates: A Minor Political Myth and Its Historiographical Career', *Journal of Ecclesiastical History*, 25 (1974), 185–98.

Baker, Derek, *Renaissance and Renewal in Christian History*, Studies in Church History, 14 (Oxford, 1977).

Religious Motivation: Biographical and Sociological Problems for the Church Historian, Studies in Church History, 15 (Oxford, 1978).

(ed.), *The Church in Town and Countryside*, Studies in Church History, 16 (Oxford, 1979).

Ball, B.W., *The Seventh-Day Men: Sabbatarians and Sabbatarianism in England and Wales, 1600–1800* (Oxford, 1994).

Banks, J.A., 'Population Change and the Victorian City', *Victorian Studies*, 11 (1968), 277–89.

Barker, Eileen, James A. Beckford and Karel Dobbelaere (eds.), *Secularization,*

Rationalisation and Sectarianism: Essays in Honour of Bryan R. Wilson (Oxford, 1993).

Barrow, Logie, *Independent Spirits: Spiritualism and English Plebeians, 1850–1910* (London, 1986).

Bebbington, D.W., 'The City, the Countryside, and the Social Gospel in Late Victorian Nonconformity', in Derek Baker (ed.), *The Church in Town and Countryside*, Studies in Church History, 16 (Oxford, 1979).

The Nonconformist Conscience: Chapel and Politics, 1870–1914 (London, 1982).

Evangelicalism in Modern Britain: A History from the 1730s to the 1980s (London, 1989).

Becker, Gary S., *The Economic Approach to Human Behaviour* (Chicago, 1976).

Beckford, James A., 'Accounting for Conversion', *British Journal of Sociology*, 29 (1978), 249–62.

Religion and Advanced Industrial Society (London, 1990).

Bell, Daniel, 'The Return of the Sacred? The Argument on the Future of Religion', *British Journal of Sociology*, 28 (1977), 418–49.

Bellah, Robert N., *Beyond Belief: Essays on Religion in a Post-Traditional World* (New York, 1970).

Bentley, James, *Ritualism and Politics in Victorian England: The Attempt to Legislate for Belief* (Oxford, 1970).

Berger, Peter L., *The Sacred Canopy: Elements of a Sociological Theory of Religion* (New York, 1967).

A Rumour of Angels: Modern Society and the Rediscovery of the Supernatural (New York, 1969).

Facing Up to Modernity: Excursions in Society, Politics and Religion (New York, 1977).

Best, G.F.A., *Temporal Pillars: Queen Anne's Bounty, the Ecclesiastical Commissioners and the Church of England* (Cambridge, 1964).

'Popular Protestantism in Victorian Britain', in R. Robson (ed.), *Ideas and Institutions in Victorian Britain* (London, 1967).

Binfield, Clyde, 'Temperance and the Cause of God', *History*, 57 (1972), 403–10.

So Down to Prayers: Studies in English Nonconformity, 1780–1920 (London, 1977).

'Freedom through Discipline: The Concept of a Little Church', in W.J. Sheils (ed.), *Monks, Hermits and the Ascetic Tradition*, Studies in Church History, 22 (Oxford, 1985).

Blackbourn, David and Geoff Eley, *The Peculiarities of German History: Bourgeois Society and Politics in Nineteenth-Century Germany* (Oxford, 1984).

Bradley, Ian, *The Call to Seriousness: The Evangelical Impact on the Victorians* (London, 1976).

Brent, Richard, *Liberal Anglican Politics: Whiggery, Religion and Reform, 1830–1841* (Oxford, 1987).

Brierley, P. 'Religion', in A.H. Halsey (ed.), *Social Trends in Britain since 1900* (London, 1988).

Briggs, Asa, *Victorian Cities* (London, 1963).

Images, Problems, Standpoints, Forecasts: The Collected Essays of Asa Briggs, vol. II (Brighton 1985).

Serious Pursuits: Communication and Education: The Collected Essays of Asa Briggs, vol. III (Brighton, 1990).

Brothers, J., 'Social Change and the Role of the Priest', *Social Compass*, 10 (1963), 477–89.

Brown, Callum G., 'The Costs of Pew-Renting: Church-Management, Church-Going and Social Class in Nineteenth-Century Glasgow', *Journal of Ecclesiastical History*, 38 (1987), 347–61.

The Social History of Religion in Scotland since 1730 (Cambridge, 1987).

'Did Urbanization Secularize Britain?', *Urban History Yearbook, 1988* (London, 1988).

'A Revisionist Approach to Religious Change', in Bruce (ed.), *Religion and Modernization* (1992).

'The Mechanism of Religious Growth in Urban Societies', in McLeod (ed.), *European Religion in the Great Cities* (1995).

Bruce, Steve, *God Save Ulster! The Religion and Politics of Paisleyism* (Oxford, 1986).

The Rise and Fall of the New Christian Right: Conservative Protestant Politics in America (Oxford, 1988).

A House Divided: Protestantism, Schism and Secularization (London, 1990).

(ed.), *Religion and Modernization* (Oxford, 1992).

Budd, Susan, *Varieties of Unbelief: Atheists and Agnostics in English Society, 1850–1960* (London, 1977).

Busfield, Deidre, 'Skill and the Sexual Division of Labour in the West Riding Textile Industry, 1850–1914', in Jowett and McIvor (eds.), *Employers and Labour* (1988).

Butterfield, Herbert, *The Whig Interpretation of History* (London, 1931).

Cannadine, David, 'Residential Differentiation in the Nineteenth Century English Town: From Shapes on the Ground to Shapes in Society', in J.H. Johnson and C.G. Pooley (eds.), *The Structure of Nineteenth Century Cities* (London, 1982).

Chadwick, Owen, *The Victorian Church*, vol. II (London, 1970).

The Secularization of the European Mind in the Nineteenth Century (Cambridge, 1975).

Chamberlayne, John H., 'From Sect to Church in British Methodism', *British Journal of Sociology*, 16 (1974), 139–49.

Christiano, Kevin J., *Religious Diversity and Social Change: American Cities, 1890–1906* (Cambridge, 1988).

Clark, David, *Between Pulpit and Pew: Folk Religion in a North Yorkshire Fishing Village* (Cambridge, 1982).

Clifton-Taylor, Alec, *English Parish Churches as Works of Art*, 2nd rev. edn. (London, 1985).

Collinson, Patrick, 'What Is Religious History?', in Juliet Gardner (ed.), *What Is History Today?* (London, 1988).

Corsi, Pietro, *Science and Culture in Victorian Britain* (Bloomington, Ind., 1989).

Cowling, Maurice, *Religion and Public Doctrine in Modern England*, vol. II: *Assaults* (Cambridge, 1985).

Cox, Harvey, *The Secular City: Secularization and Urbanization in Theological Perspective* (London, 1965).

Cox, Jeffrey, *The English Churches in a Secular Society: Lambeth, 1870–1930* (New York, 1982).

'Reviews of Books', *American Historical Review*, 93 (1988), 702.

'On the Limits of Social History: Nineteenth-Century Evangelicalism', *Journal of British Studies*, 31 (1992), 198–203.

'A Reply to Albion Urbank', *Journal of British Studies*, 32 (1993), 282–4.

Coxon, A.P.M., 'Patterns of Occupational Recruitment: The Anglican Ministry', *Sociology*, 1 (1967), 73–80.

Crossick, Geoffrey (ed.), *The Lower-Middle Class in Britain, 1870–1914* (London, 1976).

Cumming, G.J. and Derek Baker (eds.), *Popular Belief and Practice*; Studies in Church History, 8 (Cambridge, 1972).

Currie, Robert, *Methodism Divided: A Study in the Sociology of Ecumenicalism* (London, 1968).

Currie, Robert, Alan Gilbert and Lee Horsley, *Churches and Churchgoers: Patterns of Church Growth in the British Isles since 1700* (Oxford, 1977).

Davie, Grace, *Religion in Britain since 1945: Believing without Belonging* (London, 1994).

Davies, E.T., *Religion in the Industrial Revolution in South Wales* (Cardiff, 1965).

Davies, R.E. and E.G. Rupp, *A History of the Methodist Church in Great Britain*, vol. I (London, 1965).

Davies, R.E., A.R. George and E.G. Rupp, *A History of the Methodist Church in Great Britain*, vol. II (London, 1978).

A History of the Methodist Church in Great Britain, vol. III (London, 1983).

Dennis, Richard, *English Industrial Cities in the Nineteenth Century: A Social Geography* (Cambridge, 1984).

Dixon, Keith, *The Sociology of Belief: Fallacy and Foundation* (London, 1980).

Dixon, Roger and Stefan Muthesius, *Victorian Architecture* (London, 1985).

Dobbelaere, Karel, 'Church Involvement and Secularization: Making Sense of the European Case', in Barker, Beckford and Dobbelaere (eds.), *Secularization, Rationalism and Sectarianism* (1993).

Donohue, John J. and John L. Esposito (eds.), *Islam in Transition* (Oxford, 1982).

Durkheim, Emile, *The Division of Labour in Society*, trans. by W.D. Halls (London, 1984).

The Evolution of Educational Thought: Lectures on the Formation and Development of Secondary Education in France, trans. by Peter Collins (London, 1977).

Dyos, H.J. (ed.), *The Study of Urban History* (London, 1968).

Dyos, H.J. and Michael Wolff (eds.), *The Victorian City: Images and Realities* (2 vols.) (London, 1973).

Field, Clive D., 'The Social Structure of English Methodism: Eighteenth–Twentieth Centuries', *British Journal of Sociology*, 28 (1977), 199–225.

Flinn, M.W. and T.C. Smout (eds.), *Essays in Social History* (London, 1974).

Foster, John, *Class Struggle and the Industrial Revolution: Early Industrial Capitalism in Three English Towns* (London, 1974).

Fraser, Derek, *Cities, Class and Communication: Essays in Honour of Asa Briggs* (Hemel Hempstead, 1990).

Gardner, Juliet, *What is History Today?* (London, 1988).

Garnett, Jane, ' "Gold and the Gospel": Systematic Beneficence in Mid-

Nineteenth-Century England', in W.J. Sheils and Diana Wood (eds.), *The Church and Wealth*, Studies in Church History, 24 (Oxford, 1987).

Gilbert, Alan D., *Religion and Society in Industrial England: Church, Chapel and Social Change, 1740–1914* (London, 1976).

'Methodism, Dissent and Political Stability in Early Industrial England', *Journal of Religious History*, 10 (1979), 381–99.

The Making of Post-Christian Britain: A History of the Secularisation of Modern Society (London, 1980).

Gill, Robin, *Competing Convictions* (London, 1989).

'Secularization and Census Data', in Bruce (ed.), *Religion and Modernization* (1992).

Gilley, Sheridan, 'The Catholic Faith of the Irish Slum', in H.J. Dyos and Michael Wolff (eds.), *The Victorian City: Images and Realities*, vol. II (London, 1973).

Glock, Charles, 'The Religious Revival in America?', in Jane Zahn (ed.), *Religion and the Face of America* (Berkeley, 1959).

Glock, Charles Y. and Rodney Stark, *Religion and Society in Tension* (Chicago, 1965).

Goodridge, R.M., 'Nineteenth-Century Urbanisation and Religion: Bristol and Marseille, 1830–1880', in D. Martin (ed.), *Sociological Yearbook of Religion in Britain*, vol. I (London, 1968).

Gorer, Geoffrey, *Exploring English Character* (London, 1955).

Gould, Julius (ed.), *Penguin Survey of the Social Sciences* (Harmondsworth, 1965).

Gowland, D.A., *Methodist Secessions. The Origins of Free Methodism in Three Lancashire Towns: Manchester, Rochdale and Liverpool* (Manchester, 1979).

Gray, R.Q., 'Religion and Culture in Late Nineteenth-Century and Early Twentieth-Century Edinburgh', in Geoffrey Crossick (ed.), *The Lower-Middle Class in Britain, 1870–1914* (London, 1976).

Greeley, A.M., *The Sociology of the Paranormal: A Reconnaissance* (Beverley Hills, 1975).

Green, S.J.D., 'Religion and the Rise of the Common Man: Mutual Improvement Societies, Religious Associations and Popular Education in Three Industrial Towns in the West Riding, c. 1850–1900', in Derek Fraser (ed.), *Cities, Class and Communication: Essays in Honour of Asa Briggs* (Brighton, 1990).

'Secularization by Default? Urbanization, Suburbanization and the Strains of Voluntary Religious Organization in Victorian and Edwardian England', *Hispania Sacra*, separata del volumen, 42 (1990), 423–33.

'The Religion of the Child in Edwardian Methodism: Institutional Reform and Pedagogical Reappraisal in the West Riding of Yorkshire', *Journal of British Studies*, 30 (1991), 377–98.

'The Death of Pew-Rents, the Rise of Bazaars, and the End of the Traditional Political Economy of Voluntary Religious Organisations: The Case of West Yorkshire, c. 1870–1914', *Northern History*, 27 (1991), 198–235.

' "Spiritual Science" and Conversion Experience in Edwardian Methodism: The Example of West Yorkshire', *Journal of Ecclesiastical History*, 43 (1992), 428–46.

'In Search of Bourgeois Civilisation: Institutions and Ideals in Nineteenth-Century Britain', *Northern History*, 28 (1992), 228–47.

'The Church of England and the Working Classes in Later Victorian and Edwardian Halifax', *Transactions of the Halifax Antiquarian Society*, new series, 1 (1993), 106–20.

'Review of Books', *Journal of Modern History*, 65 (1993), 398–402.

'Unestablished Versions: Voluntary Religion in theVictorian North', *Northern History*, 30 (1994), 193–207.

'Christian Manliness and the Nonconformist Tradition: The West Riding of Yorkshire, c. 1880–1920', *Northern History*, 31 (1995), 267–80.

'Religion in the Twilight Zone: Britain, 1920–1960', in Hugh McLeod and Stuart Mews (eds.), *A Religious History of Great Britain, 1789–1992* (Paris, forthcoming).

'Religion in Industrial Societies: The North of England since 1750', *Northern History*, 33 (forthcoming).

Hall, Basil, 'The Welsh Revival of 1904–5: A Critique', in G.J. Cumming and Derek Baker (eds.), *Popular Belief and Practice*, Studies in Church History, 8 (Cambridge, 1972).

Hammond, Phillip E. (ed.), *The Sacred in a Secular Age: Toward Revision in the Scientific Study of Religion* (Berkeley and Los Angeles, 1985).

Hammond, Phillip E. and Mark A. Shibley, 'When the Sacred Returns: An Empirical Test', in Barker, Beckford and Dobbelaere (eds.), *Secularization, Rationalism and Sectarianism* (1993).

Harris, Christopher, Graham Martin and Anson Scharf (eds), *Industrialisation and Culture, 1830–1914* (London, 1970).

Harrison, Brian, 'Religion and Recreation in Nineteenth-Century England', *Past and Present*, 38 (1967), 98–127.

Hastings, Adrian, *A History of English Christianity, 1920–1985* (London, 1986).

Hay, D., 'Religious Experience amongst a Group of Postgraduate Students: A Qualitative Study', *Journal for the Scientific Study of Religion*, 18 (1979), 164–82.

Heaton, H., *The Yorkshire Woollen and Worsted Industries* (Oxford, 1965).

Heeney, Brian, *A Different Kind of Gentleman: Parish Clergy and Professional Men in Early- and Mid-Victorian England* (Hamden, Conn., 1976).

Heirich, Max, 'Change of Heart: A Test of Some Widely Held Theories about Religious Conversion', *American Journal of Sociology*, 83 (1977), 653–80.

Hill, Michael (ed.), *The Sociological Yearbook of Religion*, 6 (London, 1973).

Hillis, Peter, 'Presbyterians and Social Class in Mid-Nineteenth-Century Glasgow: A Study of Nine Churches', *Journal of Ecclesiastical History*, 32 (1981), 47–64.

Himmelfarb, Gertrude, 'Victorian Values/Jewish Values', *Commentary*, 87 (1989), 23–31.

Hirsch, Fred, *Social Limits to Growth* (Cambridge, Mass., 1981).

Hobsbawm, Eric, *Worlds of Labour: Further Studies in the History of Labour* (London, 1984).

Hoggart, Richard, *The Uses of Literacy* (London, 1957).

Howell, David, *British Workers and the Independent Labour Party, 1888–1906* (Manchester, 1983).

Hudson, Pat, 'Proto–Industrialisation: The Case of the West Riding Wool Textile Industry in the Eighteenth and Early Nineteenth Centuries', *History Workshop*, 12 (1981), 34–61.

The Genesis of Industrial Capital: A Study of the West Riding Wool Textile Manufacture, c. 1750–1850 (Cambridge, 1986).

(ed.), *Regions and Industries* (Cambridge, 1989).

Hunter, James Davison, *Evangelicalism: The Coming Generation* (Chicago, 1987).

Inglis, K.S., *Churches and the Working Classes in Victorian England* (London, 1963).

Jackson, John Archer, *The Irish in Britain* (London, 1963).

James, D., 'Paternalism in Keighley', in Jowett (ed.), *Model Industrial Communities* (1986).

Jeremy, David J. (ed.), *Business and Religion in Britain* (London, 1988).

'Chapel in a Business Career: The Case of John Mackintosh, 1868–1920', in David J. Jeremy (ed.), *Business and Religion in Britain* (London, 1988).

Johnson, J.H. and C.G. Pooley (eds.), *The Structure of Nineteenth Century Cities* (London, 1982).

Jowett, J.A. (ed.), *Model Industrial Communities in Mid-Nineteenth-Century Yorkshire* (Bradford, 1986).

'Religion and the Independent Labour Party', in Keith Laybourn and David James (eds.), *'The Rising Sun of Socialism': The Independent Labour Party in the Textile District of the West Riding of Yorkshire between 1890 and 1914* (Wakefield, 1991).

Jowett, J.A. and A.J. McIvor (eds.), *Employers and Labour in the English Textile Industries, 1850–1939* (London, 1988).

Joyce, Patrick, *Work, Society and Politics: The Culture of the Factory in Later Victorian England* (Brighton, 1980).

Kellett, J.R., *The Impact of Railways on Victorian Cities* (London, 1969).

Kent, John, 'Feelings and Festivals: An Interpretation of Some Working-Class Religious Attitudes', in H.J. Dyos and Michael Wolff (eds.), *The Victorian City: Images and Realities*, vol. 2 (London, 1973).

'The Role of Religion in the Cultural Structure of the Later Victorian City', *Transactions of the Royal Historical Society*, 5th series, 23 (1973), 153–73.

'A Late Nineteenth-Century Nonconformist Renaissance', in Derek Baker (ed.), *Renaissance and Renewal in Christian History*, Studies in Church History, 14 (Oxford, 1977).

Holding the Fort: Studies in Victorian Revivalism (London, 1978).

Kitson Clark, G.S.R., *The Making of Victorian England* (London, 1962).

Churchmen and the Condition of England, 1832–1885 (London, 1973).

Koditschek, Theodore, *Class Formation and Urban Industrial Society: Bradford, 1750–1850* (Cambridge, 1990).

Koss, Stephen, *Nonconformity in Modern British Politics* (London, 1975).

Lacquer, Thomas Walter, *Religion and Respectability: Sunday Schools and Working-Class Culture, 1780–1850* (New Haven, 1976).

Larkin, Emmet, 'The Devotional Revolution in Ireland, 1850–1875', *American Historical Review*, 77 (1972), 625–52.

Law, C.M., 'The Growth of Urban Population in England and Wales, 1801–1911', *Transactions of the Institute of British Geography*, 41 (1967), 125–43.

Le Bras, Gabriel, *Etudes de sociologie religieuse* (2 vols.) (Paris, 1955 and 1956).

Lewis, Donald M., *Lighten Their Darkness: The Evangelical Mission in Working-Class London, 1828–1860* (Westport, Conn., 1986).

Linstrum, Derek, *West Yorkshire: Architects and Architecture* (London, 1978).

Lofland, John and Norman Skonoud, 'Conversion Motifs', *Journal for the Scientific Study of Religion*, 20 (1981), 373–85.

Luker, David, 'Revivalism in Theory and Practice: The Case of Cornish Methodism', *Journal of Ecclesiastical History*, 37 (1986), 603–19.

Machin, G.I.T., *Politics and the Churches in Great Britain, 1869–1921* (Oxford, 1987).

McKay, J.P., *Tramways and Trolleys: The Rise of Urban Mass Transport in Europe* (Princeton, N.J., 1976).

McKibbin, Ross, 'Why Was There No Marxism in Great Britain?', *English Historical Review*, 99 (1984), 297–331.

Maclaren, A.A., 'Presbyterianism and the Working-Class in a Mid-Nineteenth-Century City', *Scottish Historical Review*, 46 (1967–8), 115–39.

Religion and Social Class: The Disruption Years in Aberdeen, 1830–1860 (London, 1974).

McLeod, Hugh, *Class and Religion in the Late Victorian City* (London, 1974).

'Recent Studies in Victorian Religious History', *Victorian Studies*, 21 (1978), 245–55.

'Religion in the City', *Urban History Yearbook, 1978* (London, 1978).

'The De-Christianization of the Working-Class in Western Europe, 1850–1900', *Social Compass*, 2/3 (1980), 191–214.

Religion and the People of Western Europe, 1789–1970 (Oxford, 1981).

Religion and the Working-Class in Nineteenth-Century England (London, 1984).

'New Perspectives on Victorian Class Religion: The Oral Evidence', *Oral History*, 14 (1986), 31–49.

'Secular Cities? Berlin, London and New York during the Later-Nineteenth and Early-Twentieth Centuries', in Bruce (ed.) *Religion and Modernization* (1992).

'Varieties of Victorian Belief', *Journal of Modern History*, 64 (1992), 321–37.

(ed.), *European Religion in the Great Cities, 1830–1930* (London, 1995).

Marquand, David, *Ramsey Macdonald* (London, 1977).

Marshall, Gordon, *In Search of the Spirit of Capitalism: An Essay on Max Weber's Protestant Ethic Thesis* (London, 1982).

Marshall, J.D., 'Colonialism as a Factor in the Planning of Towns in North-West England', in H.J. Dyos (ed.), *The Study of Urban History* (London, 1968).

Martin, David, 'Towards Eliminating the Concept of Secularization', in Julius Gould (ed.), *Penguin Survey of the Social Sciences* (Harmondsworth, 1965).

Sociology of English Religion (London, 1967).

(ed.), *The Sociological Yearbook of Religion in Britain*, vol. 1 (London, 1968).

The Religious and the Secular (London, 1969).

A General Theory of Secularization (Oxford, 1978).

The Breaking of the Image: A Sociology of Christian Theory and Practice (Oxford, 1980).

'The Land of the Free to Believe', *Times Literary Supplement* (12–18 February 1988), 170.

Tongues of Fire: The Explosion of Protestantism in Latin America (Oxford, 1990).

Matthew, H.C.G., *Gladstone, 1809–1874* (Oxford, 1986).

Meachan, Standish, 'The Church in the Victorian City', *Victorian Studies*, 11 (1968), 359–78.

Mews, Stuart, 'The Revival of Spiritual Healing in the Church of England, 1920–1926', in W.J. Sheils (ed.), *The Church and Healing*, Studies in Church History, 19 (Oxford, 1982).

Mole, David E.H., 'The Victorian Town Parish: Rural Vision and Urban Mission', in Derek Baker (ed.), *The Church in Town and Countryside*, Studies in Church History, 16 (Oxford, 1979).

Moore, Robert, 'The Political Effects of Village Methodism', in Michael Hill (ed.), *The Sociological Yearbook of Religion*, vol. VI (London, 1973).

Pit-Men, Preachers and Politics: The Effects of Methodism in a Durham Mining Community (Cambridge, 1974).

Morris, J.N., *Religion and Urban Change: Croydon, 1840–1914* (Woodbridge, 1992).

Morris, R.J., *Class, Sect and Party: The Making of the British Middle Class: Leeds, 1820–1850* (Manchester, 1990).

'Clubs, Societies and Associations', in F.M.L. Thompson (ed.), *The Cambridge Social History of Britain*, vol. III (Cambridge, 1990).

Morris, R.J. and Richard Rogers (eds.), *The Victorian City, 1820–1914* (London, 1993).

Nelson, Geoffrey K., *Cults, New Religions and Religious Controversy* (London, 1987).

Nisbet, Robert, *History of the Idea of Progress* (New York, 1980).

Norman, E.R., *Church and Society in England, 1770–1970: A Historical Study* (Oxford, 1976).

The Victorian Christian Socialists (Cambridge, 1987).

Obelkevich, James, *Religion and Rural Society: South Lindsay, 1825–1875* (Oxford, 1976).

'Music and Religion in the Nineteenth Century', in Jim Obelkevich, Lyndal Roper and Raphael Samuel (eds.), *Disciplines of Faith: Studies in Religion, Politics and Patriarchy* (London, 1987).

'Religion', in Thompson (ed.), *The Cambridge Social History of Britain*, vol. III (1990).

Oppenheim, Janet, *The Other World: Spiritualism and Psychic Research in England, 1850–1914* (Cambridge, 1985).

Otte, Hans, ' "More Churches – More Churchgoers": The Lutheran Church in Hanover between 1850 and 1914', in McLeod (ed.), *European Religion in the Great Cities* (1995).

Park, R.E., E.W. Burgess and R.O. McKenzie, *The City* (Chicago, 1925).

Parry, J.P., *Democracy and Religion: Gladstone and the Liberal Party, 1867–1875* (Cambridge, 1986).

Paul, L., *The Development and Payment of the Clergy* (London, 1964).

Paz, D.G., *The Politics of Working-Class Education in Britain, 1830–1850* (Manchester, 1980).

Pelling, Henry, 'Religion and the Nineteenth-Century British Working Class', *Past and Present*, 27 (1964), 128–33.

Popular Politics and Society in Late Victorian Britain (London, 1968).

Perkin, Harold, *The Origins of Modern English Society, 1780–1880* (London, 1969).
The *Structured Crowd: Essays in English Social History* (Brighton, 1981).
Phillips, D.Z., *Through a Darkening Glass: Philosophy, Literature and Cultural Change* (Oxford, 1982).
Phillips, Paul T., *The Sectarian Spirit: Sectarianism, Society and Politics in Victorian Cotton Towns* (Toronto, 1982).
Pickering, W.S.F. (ed.), *A Social History of the Diocese of Newcastle* (London, 1981).
Pollard, Sidney, *The Genesis of Modern Management: A Study of the Industrial Revolution in Great Britain* (London, 1965).
Pope, Liston, *Mill-Hands and Preachers: A Study of Gastonia*, 2nd edn. (New Haven, 1965).
Ranson, S., A. Bryman and B. Hinings, *Clergy, Ministers and Priests* (London, 1977).
Reynolds, Jack, *The Great Paternalist: Titus Salt and the Growth of Nineteenth-Century Bradford* (London, 1983).
Richardson, James T., 'The Active v. Passive Convert: Paradigm Conflict in Conversion Research', *Journal for the Scientific Study of Religion*, 24 (1985), 165–74.
Rieff, Philip, *The Triumph of the Therapeutic: Uses of Faith after Freud* (New York, 1966).
Roach, J., *Social Reform in England, 1780–1880* (London, 1978).
Roberts, Elizabeth, *Working-Class Barrow and Lancaster, 1890–1930* (Lancaster, 1976).
A Woman's Place: An Oral History of Working-Class Women, 1890–1940 (Oxford, 1984).
Robson, R. (ed.), *Ideas and Institutions in Victorian Britain* (London, 1967).
Rogers, A., 'When City Speaks for Country: The Emergence of the Town as a Focus for Religious Activity in the Nineteenth Century', in Derek Baker (ed.), *The Church in Town and Countryside*, Studies in Church History, 16 (Oxford, 1979).
Roof, Wade Clark and William McKinney, *American Mainline Religion: Its Changing Shape and Fortune* (New Brunswick, N.J., 1987).
Rose, Jonathan, *The Edwardian Temperament* (Athens, Ohio, 1988).
Rousseau, Jean Jacques, *Emile; or on Education*, trans. by Allan Bloom (New York, 1979).
Rowell, G., *Hell and the Victorians* (Oxford, 1974).
Rowntree, Seebohm and G.R. Lavers, *English Life and Leisure: A Social Study* (London, 1951).
Royle, Edward, *Radicals, Secularists, and Republicans: Popular Free Thought in Britain, 1866–1915* (Manchester, 1980).
Russell, Anthony, *The Clerical Profession* (London, 1980).
Scargill, D.I., 'The Factors Affecting the Location of Industry: The Example of Halifax', *Geography*, 48 (1963), 166–74.
Sennett, Richard, *The Fall of Public Man* (Cambridge, 1972).
Sheils, W.J., *The Church and Healing*, Studies in Church History, 19 (Oxford, 1982).
The Church and War, Studies in Church History, 20 (Oxford, 1983).

Monks, Hermits and the Ascetic Tradition, Studies in Church History, 22 (Oxford, 1985).

Voluntary Religion, Studies in Church History, 23 (Oxford, 1986).

Shiels, W.J. and Diana Wood, *The Church and Wealth*, Studies in Church History, 24 (Oxford, 1987).

Shils, Edward, *Center and Periphery: Essays in Macro-Sociology* (Chicago, 1975).

'Center and Periphery', in Edward Shils, *Center and Periphery: Essays in Macro-Sociology* (Chicago, 1975).

Sigsworth, E.M., *Black Dyke Mills: A History* (Liverpool, 1958).

Smelser, N.J., 'Sociological History: The Industrial Revolution and the British Working-Class Family', in M.W. Flinn and T.C. Smout (eds.), *Essays in Social History* (London, 1974).

Smith, M.A., *Religion in Industrial Society: Oldham and Saddleworth, 1740–1865* (Oxford, 1994).

Snell, K.D.M., *Church and Chapel in the North Midlands: Religious Observance in the Nineteenth Century* (Leicester, 1991).

Stark, Rodney, 'Class, Radicalism and Religious Involvement in Great Britain', *American Sociological Review*, 29 (1964), 698–706.

'Towards a Theory of Religion: Religious Commitment', *Journal for the Scientific Study of Religion*, 19 (1980), 114–28.

Stark, Rodney and William Sims Bainbridge, *The Future of Religion: Secularization, Revival and Cult Formation* (Berkeley and Los Angeles, 1985).

Stark, Rodney and Charles Y. Glock, *American Piety: The Nature of Religious Commitment* (Berkeley and Los Angeles, 1986).

Stedman Jones, Gareth, *Outcast London: A Study in the Relationship between Classes* (Oxford, 1971).

Steele, E.D., 'Class, Religion and Politics', *Northern History*, 21 (1985), 309–19.

Stewart, W.A.C. and W.O. McCann, *The Educational Innovators*, vol. 1 (London, 1971).

Stone, Norman, *Europe Transformed, 1878–1919* (London, 1983).

Strikwerda, Carl, 'A Resurgent Religion: The Rise of Catholic Social Movements in Nineteenth-Century Belgian Cities', in McLeod (ed.), *European Religion in the Great Cities* (1995).

Supple-Green, J.F., *The Catholic Revival in Yorkshire, 1850–1900* (Leeds, 1990).

Sutcliffe, A., 'The Growth of Public Intervention in the British Urban Environment during the Nineteenth Century: A Structural Approach', in J.H. Johnson and C.G. Pooley (eds.), *The Structure of Nineteenth Century Cities* (London, 1982).

Taylor, A.J.P., *English History, 1914–1945* (Oxford, 1965).

Thomas, Keith, *Religion and the Decline of Magic: Studies in Popular Beliefs in Sixteenth and Seventeenth Century England* (Harmondsworth, 1973).

Thompson, David M., 'War, the Nation and the Kingdom of God: The Origins of the National Mission of Repentance and Hope, 1915–1916', in Baker (ed.), *Religious Motivation* (1978).

'Theological and Sociological Approaches to the Motivation of the Ecumenical Movement', in Baker (ed.), *Religious Motivation* (1978).

'Church Extension in Town and Countryside in Later Nineteenth-Century

Leicestershire', in Derek Baker (ed.), *The Church in Town and Countryside* (1979).

'The Making of the English Religious Classes', *Historical Journal*, 22 (1979), 477–91.

Thompson, F.M.L., 'Social Control in Victorian Britain', *Economic History Review*, 2nd series, 34 (1981), 189–208.

Thompson, Kenneth, 'Religion: The British Contribution', *The British Journal of Sociology*, 41 (1990), 531–5.

Towler, R., 'The Social Status of an Anglican Minister', in R. Robertson (ed.), *Sociology of Religion* (Harmondsworth, 1969).

Trainer, Richard H., *Black Country Elites: The Exercise of Authority in an Industrialised Area* (Oxford, 1993).

Troeltsch, Ernst, *The Social Teaching of the Christian Churches*, trans. by O. Wynn (New York, 1931).

Walker, R.B., 'The Growth of Wesleyan Methodism in Victorian England and Wales', *Journal of Ecclesiastical History*, 24 (1973), 267–84.

'Religious Changes in Nineteenth-Century Liverpool', *Journal of Ecclesiastical History*, 19 (1968), 195–211.

Waller, P.J., *Town, City and Nation: England 1850–1914* (Oxford, 1983).

Wallis, Roy and Steve Bruce, *Sociological Theory, Religion and Collective Action* (Belfast, 1986).

'Religion: The British Contribution', *The British Journal of Sociology*, 40 (1989), 493–520.

Walvin, James, *A Child's World: A Social History of English Childhood, 1800–1914* (Harmondsworth, 1982).

Ward, Keith, *The Turn of the Tide: Christian Belief in Britain Today* (London, 1986).

Watkin, David, *A History of Western Architecture* (London, 1986).

Wearmouth, R.F., *Methodism and the Struggle of the Working Classes* (London, 1954).

The Social and Political Influence of Methodism in the Twentieth Century (London, 1957).

Weber, Max, *The Protestant Ethic and the Spirit of Capitalism*, trans. by Talcott Parsons (London, 1976).

Economy and Society: An Outline of Interpretive Sociology, ed. by Guenther Roth and Claus Wittich (2 vols.) (Berkeley and Los Angeles, 1978).

General Economic History, ed. by Ira J. Cohen (New Brunswick, N.J., 1981).

From Max Weber: Essays in Sociology, trans. and ed. by H.H. Gerth and C. Wright Mills (London, 1984).

Wickham, E.R., *Church and People in an Industrial City* (London, 1957).

Wigley, John, *The Rise and Fall of the Victorian Sunday* (Manchester, 1980).

Williams, Sarah, 'Urban Popular Religion and the Rites of Passage', in H. McLeod (ed.), *European Religion in the Great Cities, 1830–1930* (London, 1995).

Wilson, Bryan R., 'Pentecostal Ministers: Role Conflicts and Status Contradictions', *American Journal of Sociology*, 64 (1959), 494–504.

Religion in Secular Society: A Sociological Comment (London, 1966).

Magic and the Millennium: A Sociological Study of Religious Movements of Protest among Tribal and Third World Peoples (London, 1973).

'The Debate over "Secularisation"', *Encounter*, 45 (1975), 5–10.
Contemporary Transformations of Religion (Oxford, 1976).
'The Return of the Sacred', *Journal for the Scientific Study of Religion*, 18 (1979) 268–80.
Religion in Sociological Perspective (Oxford, 1982).
Winter, J.M., *The Great War and the British People* (London, 1985).
Wirth, L., 'Urbanism as a Way of Life', *American Journal of Sociology*, 44 (1938–9), 1–24.
'Urban Society and Civilization', *American Journal of Sociology*, 45 (1939–40), 743–55.
'Urban Communities', *American Journal of Sociology*, 47 (1941–2), 829–40.
Wooldridge, Adrian, *Measuring the Mind: Psychological Theory and Educational Controversy in England, c. 1860–1990* (Cambridge, 1994).
Yates, Nigel, *The Oxford Movement and Parish Life: St Saviour's, Leeds, 1839–1929* (York, 1975).
'Urban Church Attendance and the Use of Statistical Evidence, 1850–1900', in Derek Baker (ed.), *The Church in Town and Countryside*, Studies in Church History, 16 (Oxford, 1979).
The Oxford Movement and Anglican Ritualism (London, 1983).
Buildings, Faith and Worship: Liturgical Arrangement of Anglican Churches, 1600–1900 (Oxford, 1991).
Yates, Nigel, Robert Hume and Paul Hastings, *Religion and Society in Kent, 1640–1914* (Woodbridge, 1994).
Yeo, Stephen (ed.), *New Views of Co-operation* (London, 1988).
Religion and Voluntary Organisations in Crisis (London, 1976).
Zahn, Jane (ed.), *Religion and the Face of America* (Berkeley, 1959).

UNPUBLISHED THESES

Bartlett, Alan, 'The Churches in Bermondsey, 1880–1939' (University of Birmingham, Ph.D. thesis, 1987).
Chadwick, R.E., 'Church and People in Bradford and District, 1880–1914: The Protestant Churches in an Urban Industrial Environment' (University of Oxford, D.Phil. thesis, 1986).
Connolly, Gerard, 'Catholicism in Manchester and Salford' (University of Manchester, Ph.D. thesis, 1980).
Daniels, S.J., 'Moral Order and the Industrial Environment in the Woollen Textile District of West Yorkshire, 1780–1880' (University of London, Ph.D. thesis, 1980).
Dingsdale, Alan, 'Yorkshire Mill Town: A Study of the Spatial Patterns and Processes of Urban Industrial Growth and the Evolution of Spatial Structure in Halifax, 1801–1901' (University of Leeds, Ph.D. thesis, 1974).
Garnett, E.J., 'Aspects of the Relationship between Protestant Ethics and Economic Activity in Mid-Victorian England (University of Oxford, D.Phil. thesis, 1986).
Gaskell, S.M., 'Housing Estate Development, 1848–1919, with Particular Reference to the Pennier Towns' (University of Sheffield, Ph.D. thesis, 1974).
Jennings, Elizabeth, 'Sir Isaac Holden, 1807–97; The First Comber in Europe: A

Critical Appraisal of a Victorian Entrepreneur, with Special Reference to Textiles, Politics and Religion and Their Interdependence' (University of Bradford, Ph.D. thesis, 1982).

Johnson, C. 'The Standard of Living of the Worsted Workers of Keighley during the Nineteenth Century' (York University, D.Phil. thesis, 1978).

Laybourn, K., 'The Attitudes of Yorkshire Trade Unions to the Economic and Social Problems of the Great Depression' (University of Lancaster, Ph.D. thesis, 1972).

Luker, D.H., 'Cornish Methodism, Revivalism and Popular Belief, c. 1780–1870' (University of Oxford, D.Phil. thesis, 1987).

Smith, M., 'Robert Clough Ltd., Grove Mill, Keighley: A Study in Technological Redundancy' (University of Leeds, MA thesis, 1982).

Index